Aristotle

Generation of Animals
&
History of Animals I,
Parts of Animals I

Aristotle

Generation of Animals

&

History of Animals I, Parts of Animals I

Translated
With an Introduction and Notes
By

C. D. C. Reeve

Hackett Publishing Company, Inc.
Indianapolis/Cambridge

22 21 20 19   1 2 3 4 5 6 7

For further information, please address
  Hackett Publishing Company, Inc.
  P.O. Box 44937
  Indianapolis, Indiana 46244-0937

  www.hackettpublishing.com

Cover design by Deborah Wilkes
Interior design by E. L. Wilson
Composition by Aptara, Inc.

Library of Congress Cataloging-in-Publication Data

Names: Aristotle. | Reeve, C. D. C., 1948– translator, editor. | Aristotle.
  De generatione animalium. English. | Aristotle. De partibus animalium.
  English. | Aristotle. Historia animalium. English.
Title: Aristotle Generation of animals & History of animals I, Parts of animals I /
  translated with an introduction and notes by C.D.C. Reeve.
Description: Indianapolis : Hackett Publishing Company, Inc., [2019] | Includes
  bibliographical references and index.
Identifiers: LCCN 2019018970 | ISBN 9781624668272 (paperback) |
  ISBN 9781624668289 (cloth)
Subjects: LCSH: Zoology—Pre-Linnean works.
Classification: LCC QL41 .A725413 2019 | DDC 590—dc23
LC record available at https://lccn.loc.gov/2019018970

The paper used in this publication meets the minimum requirements of
American National Standard for Information Sciences—Permanence of Paper
for Printed Library Materials, ANSI Z39.48–1984.

∞

For

Mark Bedau & Kate O'Brien

Contents

History of Animals

Book I

Parts of Animals

Book I

Generation of Animals

Book I

Book II

Book III

Book IV

Book V

Preface

A reliable translation of any treatise of Aristotle's needs to be accurate and consistent. No surprise there. It also needs to be accompanied by sufficient annotation to make it intelligible. Some of this can take the form, as it does here, of texts selected from other works by Aristotle himself, so that, while traveling through the region of the Aristotelian world the present treatises describe, the reader can also travel through other regions of it, acquiring an ever widening and deepening grasp of the whole picture—something that is crucial, in my view, to understanding any part of it adequately or, perhaps, at all. But much commentary must simply be explanatory, clarificatory, and interpretive.

To make the journey as convenient as possible, footnotes and glossary entries are replaced by sequentially numbered endnotes, so that the information most needed at each juncture is available in a single place. The non-sequential reader, interested in a particular passage, will find in the detailed Index a guide to places where focused discussion of a term or notion occurs. The Introduction describes the book that lies ahead, explaining what it is about, what it is trying to do, how it goes about doing it, and what sort of audience it presupposes. It is not a comprehensive discussion of every aspect of *Generation of Animals* and its companions, nor is it, I should add, an expression of scholarly consensus on the issues it does discuss—insofar as such a thing exists—but my own take on them. The same goes for many of the more interpretative notes. They are a place to start, not a place to finish—a first step in the vast dialectical enterprise of coming to understand Aristotle for oneself.

Some readers will, I have assumed, be somewhat new to Aristotle, so I have tried to keep their needs in mind. But it is the resolute reader that Aristotle most repays, and it is such a reader, of whatever level of knowledge or sophistication, that I have tried to serve. Many different sorts of interests, moreover, converge on these extraordinary treatises, and I have tried to cater to more of them than editors and translators typically do. This is especially true of the rich trove of evidence they provide about Aristotle's metaphysics (for example, his hylomorphism), his conception of a science, and his epistemology more generally.

I have benefited greatly from the work of previous translators and commentators, especially (in the case of *GA*) that of David Balme, David Lefebvre, Pierre Louis, A. L. Peck, and Arthur Platt; (in the case of *HA* I) that of Pierre Louis, A. L. Peck, D'Arcy Thompson, and Pierre Pellegrin; and (in the case of *PA* I) that of James Lennox, Pierre Louis, William Ogle, and A. L. Peck.

I thank Adam Woodcox for his careful reading of the typescript and for discussion of *GA* II 8; Abraham Bos for his corrections and for the stimulus provided by his work and correspondence; David Murphy for his very careful reading of the typescript and his expert advice on points of translation and doctrine; and Philip Bold for help correcting the page proofs.

I renew my thanks to ΔΚΕ, the first fraternity in the United States to endow a professorial chair, and to the University of North Carolina for awarding it to me. The generous research funds, among other things, that the endowment makes available each year have allowed me to travel to conferences and to acquire books, computers, and other research materials and assistance, without which my work would have been much more difficult.

Lastly, I again very warmly thank Deborah Wilkes for her enthusiastic support of my work and of the New Hackett Aristotle Series.

Abbreviations

Aristotle

Citations of Aristotle's works are made to Immanuel Bekker, *Aristotelis Opera* (Berlin: 1831 [1970]), in the canonical form of abbreviated title (omitted when unneeded), book number (when the work is divided into books), chapter number, page number, column letter, and line number. An * indicates a work whose authenticity has been seriously questioned, ** indicates a work attributed to Aristotle but generally agreed not to be by him (similarly in the case of Plato). The abbreviations used are as follows:

APo.	*Posterior Analytics*
APr.	*Prior Analytics*
Cael.	*De Caelo (On the Heavens)*
Cat.	*Categories*
Color.	*On Colors***
DA	*De Anima (On the Soul)*
Div. Somn.	*On Divination in Sleep* (Ross)
EE	*Eudemian Ethics*
Fr.	*Fragments* (Rose)
GA	*Generation of Animals*
GC	*On Coming to Be and Passing Away (De Generatione et Corruptione)*
HA	*History of Animals*
IA	*Progression of Animals (De Incessu Animalium)*
Insomn.	*On Dreams* (Ross)
Int.	*De Interpretatione*
Juv.	*On Youth and Old Age, Life and Death, and Respiration* (Ross)
LI	*On Indivisible Lines***

Long.	*On Length and Shortness of Life* (Ross)
MA	*Movement of Animals* (Nussbaum)
MM	*Magna Moralia** (Susemihl)
Mem.	*On Memory* (Ross)
Met.	*Metaphysics*
Mete.	*Meteorology* (Louis)
Mu.	*De Mundo** (On the Cosmos)*
NE	*Nicomachean Ethics*
Oec.	*Economics**
PA	*Parts of Animals*
Peri Id.	*Peri Ideôn* (Fine)
Ph.	*Physics*
Phgn.	*Physiognomics***
Plant.	*On Plants***
Po.	*Poetics*
Pol.	*Politics*
Pr.	*Problems**
Protr.	*Protrepticus* (Düring)
Rh.	*Rhetoric*
Rh. Al.	*Rhetoric to Alexander***
SE	*Sophistical Refutations*
Sens.	*De Sensu (On Sense and Sensibilia)* (Ross)
Somn.	*On Sleep* (Ross)
Spir.	*De Spiritu (On Breath)*
Top.	*Topics*
Xen.	*On Melissus, Xenophanes, and Gorgias***

I cite and translate the *Oxford Classical Texts* (OCT) editions of these works, where available, otherwise Bekker or the editions noted here or under Other Abbreviations:

Düring, I. *Aristotle's Protrepticus: An Attempt at Reconstruction* (Göteborg, 1961).

Mayhew, R. *Aristotle: Problems* (Cambridge, Mass., 2011).

Nussbaum, M. *Aristotle's De Motu Animalium: Text with Translation, Commentary, and Interpretative Essays* (Princeton, 1978).

Rose, V. *Aristotelis Fragmenta,* 3rd ed. (Leipzig, 1886).

Ross, D. *Aristotle Parva Naturalia* (Oxford, 1955).

Susemihl, F., *Aristotelis Magna Moralia* (Leipzig, 1883).

Plato

Ap.	*Apology*
Chrm.	*Charmides*
Crat.	*Cratylus*
Cri.	*Crito*
Def.	*Definitions***
Epin.	*Epinomis*
Euthphr.	*Euthyphro*
Grg.	*Gorgias*
Hp. Ma.	*Hippias Major*
La.	*Laches*
Lg.	*Laws*
Ly.	*Lysis*
Men.	*Meno*
Phd.	*Phaedo*
Phdr.	*Phaedrus*
Prt.	*Protagoras*
Rep.	*Republic*
Smp.	*Symposium*
Sph.	*Sophist*
Tht.	*Theaetetus*
Ti.	*Timaeus*

Other Abbreviations and Symbols

Alex. = Alexander of Aphrodisias, *in Aristotelis Meteorologicorum Libros Commentaria* (Berlin, 1899).

Aubert & Wimmer = H. Aubert and F. Wimmer, *Aristoteles Tierkunde: Kritisch Berigichter Text mit Deutscher Übersetzung* (Leipzig, 1868).

Balme-1 = Balme, D. *Aristotle: Historia Animalium* (Cambridge, 2002).

Balme-2 = D. Balme, *Aristotle's De Partibus Animalium and De Generatione Animalium I* (with passages from II.1–3) (Oxford, 1972).

Barker = A. Barker, *Greek Musical Writings II* (Cambridge, 1989).

Barnes = J. Barnes, *The Complete Works of Aristotle: The Revised Oxford Translation* (Princeton, 1984).

Bos-1 = A. Bos, Review of Thom. *Acta Classica* 58 (2015): 232–237.

Bos-2 = A. Bos, *Aristotle on God's Life-Generating Power and on Pneuma as Its Vehicle* (Albany, 2018).

Connell = S. Connell, *Aristotle on Female Animals* (Cambridge, 2016).

Crowley = T. Crowley, "Aristotle's 'So-Called Elements.'" *Phronesis* 53 (2008): 223–242.

DK = H. Diels and W. Kranz, eds., *Die Fragmente der Vorsokratiker*, 6th ed. (Berlin, 1951).

DL = Diogenes Laertius, *Lives of Eminent Philosophers*, ed. T. Dorandi (Cambridge, 2013).

Dittmeyer = L. Dittmeyer, *Aristotelis: De Animalibus Historia* (Leipzig, 1907).

Düring = I. Düring, *Aristotle's De Partibus Animalium: Critical and Literary Commentaries* (Göteborg, 1943).

Falcon & Lefebvre = A. Falcon and D. Lefebvre, eds., *Aristotle's Generation of Animals: A Critical Guide* (Cambridge, 2018).

Furth = M. Furth, *Substance, Form, and Psyche: An Aristotelian Metaphysics* (Cambridge, 1988).

Gotthelf = A. Gotthelf, *Teleology, First Principles, and Scientific Method in Aristotle's Biology* (Oxford, 2012).

Gotthelf & Lennox = A. Gotthelf and J. Lennox, eds., *Philosophical Issues in Aristotle's Biology* (Cambridge, 1987).

Gregoric = P. Gregoric, "The Heraclitus Anecdote: *De Partibus Animalium* i 5. 645ª17–23." *Ancient Philosophy* 21 (2001): 73–86.

Heath = T. Heath, *A History of Greek Mathematics*, vols. I and II (Oxford, 1921).

Henderson = J. Henderson, *The Maculate Muse: Obscene Language in Attic Comedy* (New Haven, 1975).

Herodotus = Herodotus, *Histories.*

Jacoby = F. Jacoby, *Die Fragmente der Griechischen Historiker* (Berlin, 1923).

Kupreeva = I. Kupreeva, *Philoponus: On Aristotle's On Coming-to-be and Perishing I.6–2.4* (Ithaca, 2005).

Langkavel, B., *Aristotelis De Partibus Animalium* (Leipzig, 1868).

Lefebvre = D. Lefebvre, *Génération des Animaux.* In P. Pellegrin, ed., *Aristote: Oeuvres Complètes* (Paris, 2014).

Lennox-1 = J. Lennox, *Aristotle: On the Parts of Animals I–IV* (Oxford, 2001).

Lennox-2 = J. Lennox, *Aristotle's Philosophy of Biology: Studies in the Origins of Life Science* (Cambridge, 2001).

Lewis = E. Lewis, *Alexander of Aphrodisias: On Aristotle's Meteorology 4* (Ithaca, 1996).

Littré = E. Littré, *Oeuvres Complètes d'Hippocrate* I–X (Paris, 1839–1861).

Lonie = I. M. Lonie, *The Hippocratic Treatises "On Generation," "On the Nature of the Child," "Diseases IV"* (Berlin, 1981).

Louis-1 = P. Louis, *Histoire des Animaux* (Paris, 1964–1969).

Louis-2 = P. Louis, *Les Parties des Animaux* (Paris, 1956).

Louis-3 = P. Louis, *Aristote: De la Génération des Animaux* (Paris, 1961).

Ogle = W. Ogle, *De Partibus Animalium.* In J. Smith and D. Ross, eds., *The Works of Aristotle*, vol. V (Oxford, 1912).

Peck-1 = A. Peck, *Aristotle: History of Animals I–III* (Cambridge, Mass., 1965).

Peck-2 = A. Peck, *Aristotle: Parts of Animals* (Cambridge, Mass., 1937).

Peck-3 = A. Peck, *Aristotle: Generation of Animals* (Cambridge, Mass., 1953).

Pellegrin = P. Pellegrin, *Aristote: Histoire des Animaux* (Paris, 2017).

Platt = A. Platt, *De Generatione Animalium.* In J. Smith and D. Ross, eds., *The Works of Aristotle*, vol. V (Oxford, 1912).

Ross = D. Ross, *Aristotle's Physics: A Revised Text with Introduction and Commentary* (Oxford, 1936).

Schiefsky = M. Schiefsky, *Hippocrates on Ancient Medicine: Translated with an Introduction and Commentary* (Leiden, 2005).

TEGP = D. W. Graham, *The Texts of Early Greek Philosophy: The Complete Fragments and Selected Testimonies of the Major Presocratics* (Cambridge, 2010).

Thom = J. Thom (ed.), *Cosmic Order and Divine Power: Pseudo-Aristotle, On the Cosmos* (Tübingen, 2014).

Van Praagh = R. Van Praagh and S. Van Praagh, "Aristotle's 'Triventricular Heart' and the Relevant Early History of the Cardiovascular System." *Chest* 84 (1963): 462–468.

von Staden = H. von Staden, "The Discovery of the Body: Human Dissection and Its Cultural Contexts in Ancient Greece." *The Yale Journal of Biology and Medicine* 65 (1992): 223–241.

Wellmann = M. Wellmann, *Die Fragmente der Sikelischen Ärzte Akron, Philistion, und des Diokles von Karystos* (Berlin, 1901).

Wilson = M. Wilson, *Structure and Method in Aristotle's Meteorologica* (Cambridge, 2013).

A = B = A is identical to (equivalent to) B.

A ≈ B = A is roughly the same as or roughly equivalent or analogous to B.

A ⊃ B = If A then B, or A implies B.

Introduction

Life and Works

Aristotle was born in 384 BC to a well-off family living in the small town of Stagira in northern Greece. His father, Nicomachus, who died while Aristotle was still quite young, was allegedly doctor to King Amyntas of Macedon. His mother, Phaestis, was wealthy in her own right. When Aristotle was seventeen his guardian, Proxenus, sent him to study at Plato's Academy in Athens. He remained there for twenty years, initially as a student, eventually as a researcher and teacher.

When Plato died in 347, leaving the Academy in the hands of his nephew Speusippus, Aristotle left Athens for Assos in Asia Minor, where the ruler, Hermias, was a patron of philosophy. He married Hermias' niece (or ward) Pythias, and had a daughter by her, also named Pythias. Three years later, in 345, after Hermias had been killed by the Persians, Aristotle moved to Mytilene on the island of Lesbos, where he met Theophrastus, who was to become his best student and closest colleague.

In 343 Aristotle seems to have been invited by Philip of Macedon to be tutor to the latter's thirteen-year-old son, Alexander, later called "the Great." In 335 Aristotle returned to Athens and founded his own institute, the Lyceum. While he was there his wife died and he established a relationship with Herpyllis, also a native of Stagira. Their son Nicomachus was named for Aristotle's father, and the *Nicomachean Ethics* may, in turn, have been named for him or transcribed by him. In 323 Alexander the Great died, with the result that anti-Macedonian feeling in Athens grew stronger. Perhaps threatened with a formal charge of impiety (*NE* X 7 1177^{b}33), Aristotle left for Chalcis in Euboea, where he died twelve months later, in 322, at the age of sixty-two.

Legend has it that Aristotle had slender calves, small eyes, spoke with a lisp, and was "conspicuous by his attire, his rings, and the cut of his hair." His will reveals that he had a sizable estate, a domestic partner, two children, a considerable library, and a large circle of friends. In it Aristotle asks his executors to take special care of Herpyllis. He directs that his slaves be freed "when they come of age" and that the bones of his wife, Pythias, be mixed with his "as she instructed."

Although the surviving writings of Aristotle occupy almost 2,500 tightly printed pages in English, most of them are not works polished for publication but sometimes incomplete lecture notes and working papers. This accounts for some, though not all, of their legendary difficulty. It is unfair to complain, as a Platonist opponent did, that Aristotle "escapes refutation by clothing a perplexing subject in obscure language, using darkness like a squid to make himself hard to catch," but there is darkness and obscurity enough for anyone, even if none of it is intentional. There is also a staggering breadth and depth of intellect. Aristotle made fundamental contributions to a vast range of disciplines, including logic, metaphysics, epistemology, psychology, ethics, politics, rhetoric, aesthetics, zoology, biology, physics, and philosophical and political history. When Dante called him "the master of those who know," he was scarcely exaggerating.

The Place of HA, PA, and GA in Aristotle's Thought

One thing we might mean by *GA* is what we now find inscribed on the pages that make up H. J. Drossaart Lulofs' OCT (Oxford Classical Texts) edition of the Greek text (available in the *Thesaurus Linguae Graecae*), first published in 1965, which is the basis of the present translation. This is the descendant of texts derived—via manuscripts copied in the Byzantine period (from the tenth to the fifteenth centuries AD)—from manuscripts that derive from the edition of Aristotle's works produced by Andronicus of Rhodes in the first century BC. Its more precise transmission is discussed in the OCT Introduction, pp. v–xxx. This edition, like most other modern editions, records in the textual apparatus at the bottom of the page various manuscript readings alternative to the one printed in the body of the text. In some cases, I have preferred one of these readings and have (where necessary) indicated so in the notes. Divisions of the text into books and chapters are the work of editors, not of Aristotle himself. Also present in the OCT edition are the page numbers of Bekker, *Aristotelis Opera*. These appear here in the margins of the printed version and enclosed in vertical lines ($|789^b15|$) in the electronic one at the end of the line to which they apply. Occasional material in square brackets in the text is my addition.

The second thing we might mean, and are perhaps more likely to mean, is the work itself—that more abstract thing that is embodied in good Greek texts and (ideally) in any translation of them. But it is best approached by exploring the place of *GA* in Aristotle's thought more generally. In this edition, therefore, *GA* is prefaced by the opening books of *History of Animals* (*HA*) and *Parts of Animals* (*PA*), the treatises that immediately proceed it, and about which we shall have more to say later on. The Greek text of these (again available in the *Thesaurus Linguae Graecae*) is that of Pierre Louis. However, these treatises too are best approached as parts of a larger picture.

The opening sentence of *On Coming to Be and Passing Away* (*GC*) tells us that it deals with the causes and accounts of "the coming to be and passing away of the things that by nature come to be and pass away, alike with regard to all of them (*homoiôs kata pantôn*)," and with growth and withering (increase and decrease) and alteration and how these differ, if they do, from coming to be (generation) and passing away (I 1 314ª1–6). A little later we learn that the focus includes "unconditional coming to be and passing away *in general* (*holôs*)" (I 2 315ª26), and this is the one assigned to *GC* in the *Meteorology* (*Mete.*):

> Now [1] the primary causes of nature, [2] all natural movement, [3] the stars arranged in the upper spatial movement, and [4] the elements of bodies, how many they are and of what sorts, their change into each other, and coming to be and passing away *in general* (*tês koinês*), have been spoken about previously. It remains to get a theoretical grasp on a part of this methodical inquiry, which all our predecessors have called meteorology. It is concerned with whatever things happen in accord with nature, but are more disorderly, certainly, than the primary element of the bodies, and which occur in the place nearest to the spatial movement of the stars—for example, the Milky Way, comets, shooting stars, and meteors. It is also concerned with whatever affections may be regarded as common to air and water, and further the parts and forms (*eidos*) of earth and the affections of the parts, on the basis of which we may get a theoretical grasp on the causes of winds, earthquakes, and all the consequences that are in accord with their movements. Some of these we puzzle over, while others in a certain way we grasp. Further, it is concerned with the fall of thunderbolts, with whirlwinds, fire-winds, and whatever other recurrent affections of these same bodies as are due to solidification. [5] After we have discussed these things, let us then get a theoretical grasp on whether we can give some account, in the way we have laid down, of animals and plants, both universally and separately. For when we have stated it, all of what we deliberately chose for ourselves at the start would pretty much have achieved its end. (I 1 338ª20–339ª10)

[1] refers to *Physics* I–II, [2] to *Physics* III, V–VIII, [3] to *De Caelo* I–II, [4] to *De Caelo* III–IV and *GC*, but with a difference we shall be returning to, and [5] to (among other things) *HA*, *PA*, and *GA*. Our first task is to determine what the generalizing (italicized) phrases mean here.

At the risk of trying to illuminate a difficulty by means of a yet greater difficulty, let us look at a parallel issue raised as a puzzle in the *Metaphysics*:

> We might raise a puzzle indeed as to whether the primary philosophy is universal or concerned with a particular genus and one particular nature. For it is not the same way even in the mathematical sciences, but rather geometry and astronomy are concerned with a particular nature, whereas universal mathematics is common to all. If, then, there is no other substance beyond those composed by nature, natural science will be the primary science. But if there is some immovable substance, this [that is, theological philosophy] will be prior and will be primary philosophy, and it will be universal in this way, namely, because it is primary. And it will belong to it to get a theoretical grasp on being qua being, both what it is and the things that belong to it qua being. (*Met.* VI 1 1026^{a}23–32)

The thought is that primary philosophy is the universal science of being qua being not because it deals with every sort of being, but because it deals with the primary being, namely, god, who as the immovable mover is the cause of all the others. Thus when we discover that discussion in *GC* focuses chiefly on the elements and their coming to be from and passing away into each other, affecting and being affected by each other, and mixing, we should see this as being general in the same way—not now in terms of top-down causation (theology), but of bottom-up. Thus we find *GC* I 7 referred to as "our universal accounts concerning affecting and being affected," and indeed we find evidence of its generality in the remark that "it is natural for a body to be affected by a body, flavor by flavor, color by color, and, in general, what is the same in genus by what is the same in genus" (324^{a}33–324^{a}1). By the same token along with the transformation of water into air, and vice versa, we find a reference to blood coming "from semen [changing] as a whole" (I 4 319^{b}16), as well as references to flesh and bone and their coming to be from the elements (II 7 334^{b}25–30).

What *GC* is, then, is a universal investigation of unconditional coming to be and passing away, and the rest, which is universal because—as focused on elemental transformation—bottom up. That is why, indeed, to read it in conjunction with *Mete.* IV, which also focuses on the transformation of the elements, deepens our understanding of them. Thus, Alexander of Aphrodisias in his commentary writes:

> The book entitled "the fourth" of Aristotle's *Meteorology* does belong to Aristotle, but not to the work on meteorology. For the things spoken about in it are not proper to meteorology. Rather, as far as the things spoken about are concerned, it would follow *On Coming to Be and Passing Away*. (179.3–6 = Lewis, p. 65)

So our next task must be to discover what sort of universal investigation we are talking about.

It is clear from the beginning that the distinctive focus of *De Caelo*, to begin with *GC*'s own immediate predecessor, is not primarily or exclusively on the world of sublunary nature (*phusis*), which consists canonically of matter-form compounds, whose material component involves the elements (earth, water, air, and fire), but on the superlunary or *super*-natural realm, *ho ouranos* ("the heaven"), as Aristotle calls it, consisting of celestial spheres, composed of primary body or ether (*Cael.* I 3 270^{b}21), as well as the stars and planets affixed to them. Nonetheless, if its scope is more catholic than a strictly natural science, much of what it discusses, for example, the sublunary elements, heaviness and lightness, up and down, has obvious application in the sublunary realm. Some topics belonging to the superlunary one (to super-nature), indeed, are included in natural science's purview:

> The next thing to get a theoretical grasp on [is] . . . whether astronomy is distinct from natural science or a part of it. For if it belongs to the natural scientist to know what the sun or the moon is, for him not to know their intrinsic coincidents would be absurd—especially since it is evident that those who speak about nature discuss the shapes of the sun and the moon, and in particular whether the earth and the cosmos are spherical or not. (*Ph.* II 2 193^{b}22–30)

Finally, and perhaps most tellingly, the evidentiary basis of the *De Caelo* science is that of natural science:

> The result [of making natural bodies be composed of planes] is that people speaking about the things that appear to be so say things that are not in agreement with the things that appear to be so. And the cause of this is not correctly grasping the primary starting-points, but instead wishing to lead everything back to

certain definite beliefs. For presumably the starting-points of perceptible things must be perceptible, of eternal ones eternal, of things capable of passing away things capable of passing away, and, in general, each must be of the same genus (*homogenês*) as what falls under it. But out of love for these beliefs of theirs they seem to do the same thing as those defending their theses in [dialectical] arguments. For they accept a consequence on the supposition of its having true starting-points, as if starting-points must not sometimes be judged on the basis of what follows from them, and most of all on the basis of their ends. And the end in the case of productive science is the work, and in that of natural science what appears to be so to perception has the controlling vote in every case. (*Cael.* III 7 306ᵃ5–17)

That is why it is "experience in astronomy" that must provide the starting-points of astronomical science (*APr.* I 30 46ᵃ19–20). Even very high-level principles, such as that "nature neither omits any of the things possible in each case nor produces any pointlessly," are assumed based on observation (*GA* V 8 788ᵇ20–22).

It could hardly be clearer that however we are to conceive of the super-natural it cannot be as a realm entirely different in kind from the natural one. Super-nature, to put it this way, is a sort of nature, not a sort of something else. Similarly, in *GC* we are reminded that the discussion must be conducted *phusikôs*—in a way appropriate to natural science (see I 2 316ᵃ11, II 9 335ᵇ25) and that perception is not something reason (theory) should overstep or disregard (I 8 325ᵃ13–14), but should be in agreement with our arguments (II 10 336ᵇ15–17). Indeed, if it fails in this regard, it is reason that must go:

On the basis of reason (*logos*), then, and on the basis of what seem to be the facts about them, matters having to do with generation of bees appear to be this way. The facts, though, have certainly not been sufficiently grasped, but if at some time they are, one should take perception rather than reasonings to be what must carry conviction, and reasonings [only] if what they show agrees with what appears to be the case. (*GA* III 10 760ᵇ27–33)

Conviction even on such fundamental matters as the four causal factors distinguished for the elements in *GC* II 1–6 is "based on induction" (*Mete.* IV 1 378ᵇ10–14). The lab, to be anachronistic, not the armchair, has pride of place, even if there is also much that can be done in that more cozy place: "We consider that we have adequately demonstrated in accord with reason (*logos*) things unapparent to perception if we have led things back to what is possible" (*Mete.* I 7 344ᵃ5–7). This has obvious application not just to astronomical objects inaccessible in the absence of telescopes, but to cellular structure and the like that are similarly inaccessible in the absence of microscopes.

Now if the various bodies, natural and super-natural, were the only substances, the only primary beings, the science of them would be the science that the *Metaphysics* proposes to investigate, and refers to as theoretical wisdom (*sophia*), the science of being qua being, primary science or primary philosophy, and identifies with theological philosophy (*Met.* VI 1 1026ᵃ19) or theological science (XI 7 1064ᵇ1–3). That there is a substance that is eternal and immovable is argued in *Physics* VIII, and presupposed in *GC* II 10, and that the gods, including in particular *the* god (the primary god), are among them is presupposed from quite early on in the *Metaphysics*. Thus in *Met.* I 2 we hear that theoretical wisdom is the science of this god, both in having him as its subject matter and in being the science that is in some sense *his* science. When it is argued in XII 9 that he must be "the active understanding [that] is active understanding of active understanding" (1074ᵇ34–35), we see how much his it is, since actively understanding itself—contemplating itself in an exercise of theoretical wisdom—is just what Aristotle's primary god *is*.

With just this much on the table there is already a puzzle whose difficulty is increased by special doctrine. Aristotle usually divides the bodies of knowledge he refers to as *epistêmai* ("sciences") into three types: theoretical, practical, and productive (crafts). When he is being especially careful, he also distinguishes within the theoretical sciences between the *strictly theoretical* ones (astronomy, theology), as we may call them, and the *natural* ones, which are like the strictly theoretical ones in being neither practical nor productive but unlike them in consisting of propositions that—though necessary and universal in some sense—hold for the most part rather than without exception:

> If all thought is either practical or productive or theoretical, natural science would have to be some sort of theoretical science—but a theoretical science that is concerned with such being as is capable of being moved and with the substance that in accord with its account holds for the most part only, because it is not separable. (*Met.* VI 1 1025ᵇ25–28; compare *Ph.* II 9 200ᵃ30–ᵇ9)

Psychology, as a result, has an interestingly mixed status, part strictly theoretical (because it deals with understanding, which is something divine), part natural (because it deals with perception and memory and other capacities that require a body):

> It is clear that the affections of the soul are enmattered accounts. So their definitions will be of this sort, for example: "Being angry is a sort of movement of such-and-such a sort of body, or of a part or a capacity, as a result of something for the sake of something." And that is why it already belongs to the natural scientist to get a theoretical grasp on the soul, either all soul or this sort of soul. But a natural scientist and a dialectician would define each of these differently—for example, what anger is. For a dialectician it is a desire for retaliation or something like that, whereas for a natural scientist it is a boiling of the blood and hot stuff around the heart. Of these, the scientist gives the matter, whereas the dialectician gives the form and the account. For this is the account of the thing, although it must be in matter of such-and-such a sort if it is to exist. And so of a house the account is this, that it is a shelter to prevent destruction by winds, rain, and heat. But one person will say that it is stones, bricks, and timbers, and another that it is the form in them for the sake of these other things. Which of these people, then, is the natural scientist? Is it the one concerned with the matter but ignorant of the account, or the one concerned with the account alone? Or is it rather the one concerned with what is composed of both? Who, then, is each of the others? Or isn't it that there is no one who is concerned with the attributes of the matter that are not separable and insofar as they are not separable? And isn't it, rather, the natural scientist who is concerned with everything that is a function or attribute of this sort of body and this sort of matter? And isn't anything not of this sort the concern of someone else, in some cases a craftsman, if there happens to be one, such as a builder or a doctor? And aren't those things that are not actually separable, but are considered insofar as they are not attributes of this sort of body and in abstraction from it, the concern of the mathematician? And insofar as they are actually separable, that of the primary philosopher? (*DA* I 1 403ᵃ25–ᵇ16)*

Psychology has a theological dimension, then, as well as a more naturalistic biological or psychological one. Indeed, biology, at any rate when dealing

---

* See *PA* I 1 641ᵃ32–ᵇ4 and notes (this vol.).

with embryology, and so with the transmission of understanding from progenitor to offspring, itself has a foot, so to speak, in the super-natural (see *GA* II 3 736ᵇ15–29, discussed below).

With all this before us, we are in a position to say something further about the science of *De Caelo*. That it is not a work of strictly natural science, but rather of super-natural science, we know. That it is theoretical rather than productive or practical is plain. But what sort of theoretical science is it exactly? Insofar as it is a work of astronomy (or what we would probably call cosmology), we know at least where Aristotle himself puts it, since he refers to astronomy as "the mathematical science that is most akin to philosophy" (*Met.* XII 8 1073ᵇ4–5). Yet it is not a branch of pure mathematics but rather something closer to what we would call applied mathematics:

> Odd and even, straight and curved, and furthermore number, line, and figure will be without movement, whereas flesh, bone, and human will not, but rather all of them are said of things just as snub nose is and not as curved is. This is also clear from the more natural-science-like parts of mathematics, such as optics, harmonics, and astronomy. For these are in a way the reverse of geometry. For whereas geometry investigates natural lines, but not insofar as they are natural, optics investigates mathematical lines, but not insofar as they are mathematical. (*Ph.* II 2 194ᵃ3–12)*

A mathematical science, then, but a more natural-scientific one than one pure or abstract.

At the same time, Aristotle tells us too that while we think about "the stars as bodies only, that is, as units having a certain order, altogether inanimate," we should in fact "conceive of them as participating in action and life" (*Cael.* II 12 292ᵃ18–21) and of their action as being "like that of animals and plants" (292ᵇ1–2). And the complexity does not end there. For he also includes the primary heaven, the sphere of the fixed stars, as among things divine:

> The activity of a god is immortality, and this is eternal living. So it is necessary that eternal movement belong to the god. And since the heaven is such (for it is a certain divine body), because

---

* Also, "Mathematical beings are without movement, except for those with which astronomy is concerned" (*Met.* I 8 989ᵇ32–33).

> of this it has a circular body, which by nature always moves in a
> circle. (*Cael.* II 3 286ᵃ9–12)

Thus the science to which *De Caelo* contributes is apparently at once a natural-scientific branch of mathematics, a biological science, and a theological one.

When science receives its focused discussion in the *Nicomachean Ethics*, however, Aristotle is explicit that if we are "to speak in an exact way and not be guided by mere similarities" (VI 3 1139ᵇ19), we should not call anything a science unless it deals with eternal, entirely exception-less facts about universals that are wholly necessary and do not at all admit of being otherwise (1139ᵇ20–21). Since he is here explicitly epitomizing his more detailed discussion of science in the *Posterior Analytics* (as 1139ᵇ27 tells us), we should take the latter too as primarily a discussion of science in the exact sense, which it calls *epistêmê haplôs*—unconditional scientific knowledge. It follows that only the strictly theoretical sciences are sciences in this sense. It is on these that the others should be modeled to the extent that they can: "it is the things that are always in the same state and never undergo change that we must make our basis when pursuing the truth, and this is the sort of thing that the heavenly bodies are" (*Met.* XI 6 1063ᵃ13–15).

Having made the acknowledgment, though, we must also register the fact that Aristotle himself mostly does not speak in the exact way but instead persistently refers to bodies of knowledge other than the strictly theoretical sciences as *epistêmai*. His division of the *epistêmai* into theoretical, practical, and productive is a dramatic case in point. But so too is his use of the term *epistêmê*, which we first encounter in the *Metaphysics* as a near synonym of *technê* or craft knowledge, which is productive, not theoretical (I 1 981ᵃ3), and in *GC* as concerned with coming to be and alteration and whether or not they are distinct (I 2 315ᵇ15–19).

An Aristotelian science, although a state of the soul rather than a set of propositions in a textbook, nonetheless does involve an affirmational grasp of a set of true propositions (*NE* VI 3 1139ᵇ14–16). Some of these propositions are indemonstrable starting-points or first principles (*archai*), which are, or are expressed in, definitions, and others are theorems demonstrable from these starting-points. We can have scientific knowledge only of the theorems, since—exactly speaking—only what is demonstrable can be scientifically known (VI 6). Yet—in what is clearly another lapse from exact speaking—Aristotle characterizes "the most exact of the sciences," which is theoretical wisdom, as also involving a grasp by understanding (*nous*) of the truth where the starting-points themselves are concerned (VI 7 1141ᵃ16–18). He does the same thing in the *Metaphysics,* where theoretical wisdom is the *epistêmê* that provides "a theoretical grasp of the primary starting-points and causes"—among which are included "the good or the for-the-sake-of-which" (*Met.* I 2 982^{b}7–10). It is for this reason that the god's grasp of himself through understanding is an exercise of scientific knowledge.

Now each of these sciences, regardless of what group it falls into, must—for reasons having to do with the nature of definition and demonstration—be restricted in scope to a single genus of beings (see *PA* I 1 649^{a}3n(4)). Since being is not itself a genus (*APo.* II 7 92^{b}14), as Aristotle goes out of his way not just to acknowledge but to prove (*Met.* IV 2), it apparently follows that there should be no such science as the science of being qua being—as theoretical wisdom. To show that there is one thus takes some work. By the same token, there should be no such science as natural science, but only a collection of distinct sciences, each focused exclusively on its own distinct genus of natural beings.

It is a cliché of the history of philosophy that Aristotle is an empiricist and Plato a rationalist, and like all clichés there is some truth in it. In fact, Aristotle is not just an empiricist at the level of the sciences we call empirical, he is an empiricist at all levels. To see what I mean, think of each of the special, genus-specific sciences—the *first-order* sciences—as giving us a picture of a piece of the universe, a region of being. Then ask, what is the universe like that these sciences collectively portray? What is the nature of reality as a whole—of being as a whole? If there is no answer besides the collection of special answers, the universe is, as Aristotle puts it, episodic—like a bad tragedy (*Met.* XII 10 1076^{a}1, XIV 3 1090^{b}20). But if there is an answer, it should emerge from a meta-level empirical investigation of the first-order sciences themselves. As each of these looks for universals (natural kinds) that stand in demonstrative causal relations to each other, so this meta-level investigation looks for higher-level universals that reveal the presence of common structures of explanation in diverse sciences:

> The causes and starting-points of distinct things are distinct in a way, but in a way—if we are to speak universally and analogically—they are the same for all. . . . For example, the elements of perceptible bodies are presumably: as *form*, the hot and, in another way, the cold, which is the *lack* [of form]; and, as *matter*, what is potentially these directly and intrinsically. And both these and the things composed of them are substances, of which these are the starting-points (that is, anything that comes to be from the hot and the cold that is one [something-or-other], such as flesh or bone), since what comes to be from these must be distinct from them. These things, then, have the same elements and starting-points (although distinct things have distinct ones).

> But that all things have the same ones is not something we can
> say just like that, although *by analogy* they do. That is, we might
> say that there are three starting-points—the form and the lack
> [of form] and the matter. But each of these is distinct for each
> category (*genos*)—for example, in colors they are white, black,
> and surface, or light, darkness, and air, out of which day and
> night come to be. (*Met.* XII 4 1070ª31–ᵇ21)

The first-order sciences show the presence in the universe of a variety of
different explanatory structures. The trans-generic sciences, by finding
commonalities between these structures, show the equally robust presence
there of the *same* explanatory structure: form, lack of form, matter.

The science to which form, lack of form, and matter belong is, in the
first instance, trans-generic or universal natural science, which is the one
of which biology—the science in *HA, PA,* and *GA,*—is a part. Natural science is the one that would be the primary science, as we saw, were there no
eternal immovable substances separable from the natural ones. But there is
also a trans-generic—or universal—mathematical science:

> We might raise a puzzle indeed as to whether the primary phi-
> losophy is universal or concerned with a particular genus and
> one particular nature. For it is not the same way even in the
> mathematical sciences, but rather geometry and astronomy are
> concerned with a particular nature, whereas universal math-
> ematics is common to all. (*Met.* VI 1 1026ª23–27)*

---

* Many theorems in mathematics are special to some branch of it, such as arithmetic or geometry, but there are also "certain mathematical theorems of a universal
character" (*Met.* XIII 2 1077ª9–10). Here is an example: "That proportionals alternate might be thought to apply to numbers qua numbers, lines qua lines, solids
qua solids, and times qua times, as used to be demonstrated of these separately,
although it is possible to show it of all cases by a single demonstration. But because
all these things—numbers, lengths, times, solids—do not constitute a single
named [kind] and differ in form from one another, they were treated separately.
But now it is demonstrated universally: for what is supposed to hold of them universally does not hold of them qua lines or qua numbers but qua this [unnamed
kind]" (*APo.* I 5 74ª17–25). Nonetheless, the universality of the demonstration is
open to challenge on the grounds that lines and numbers differ in genus. For "it is
necessary for the extreme and middle terms in a demonstration to come from the
same genus" (I 7 75ᵇ10–11), so that trans-generic demonstrations are ruled out:
"it is impossible that what is shown should cross from one genus to another" (I 23
84ᵇ17–18). Hence "the why [that is, why the theorem about proportionals holds
in the case of lines and of numbers] is different" (II 17 99ª8–9), and so separate

The introduction of intelligible matter (*Met.* VII 10 1036ª11–12), as the matter of abstract mathematical objects, allows us to see a commonality in explanatory structure between the mathematical sciences and the natural ones. Between these two trans-generic sciences and the theological one (VI 1 1026ª19), on the other hand, the point of commonality lies not in matter, since the objects of theological science have no matter (XII 6 1071ᵇ20–21), but rather in form. For what the objects of theology, namely, divine substances (which include human understanding or *nous*), have in common with those of mathematics and natural science is that they are forms, though—and this is the crucial point of difference—not forms in any sort of matter whatsoever. That form should be a focal topic of investigation for the science of being qua being is thus the result of an inductive or empirical investigation of the various first-order sciences, and then of the various trans-generic ones, which shows form to be the explanatory feature common to all their objects—to all beings.

It is a nice question, but one now within reach of an answer, as to how the science of *De Caelo* is to be incorporated into this uniform explanatory structure. But it is perhaps enough to notice that its objects of study are matter-form compounds, like those of natural science, but with this one difference: their matter is primary body (ether) rather than earth, water, fire, and air in some combination or other. And because the difference this makes is that astronomical objects, though in many cases biological, are amenable to being studied by an applied mathematical science, it must be that primary body is relevantly similar to intelligible matter. It must be like it in not deforming geometrical shapes, unlike it in being concrete rather than abstract: a sphere made of earth (say) cannot be a perfect sphere; a sphere made of primary body can. Result: the heavenly bodies are perfect or exact models of geometrical theorems, while sublunary bodies are no

---

demonstrations seem to be needed in the case of each. Nonetheless, "qua such-and-such an increase in quantity" (99ª9–10) the demonstration is the same, so that the theorem "holds in common of all *quantities*" (*Met.* XI 4 1061ᵇ19–21). For "while the genera of the beings are different, some attributes belong to quantities and others to qualities alone, with the help of which we can show things" (*APo.* II 32 88ᵇ1–3). But though the universal theorem holds of all quantities, it does so *by analogy*: "Of the items used in the demonstrative sciences some are special to each science and others common—but common by analogy, since they are only useful insofar as they bear on the genus falling under the science. Proper—for example, that a line is such-and-such, and straight so-and-so. Common—for example, that if equals are taken from equals, the remainders are equal" (*APo.* I 10 76ª37–41). Thus the kind to which lines, numbers, and so on belong, which is the ontological correlate of a theorem of universal mathematics, is not a first-order genus, but an analogical unity—a quantity.

better than imperfect ones. Hence the need to take account of the margin of error. Thus super-natural science of the *De Caelo* variety enters the uniform explanatory structure required for the existence of the science of being qua being by doors already opened by natural and mathematical science.

It is all this that provides the science of being qua being with a genuine trans-generic object of study, thereby legitimating it as every bit as much a science as any first-order or universal one. The science of being qua being is accordingly a science of form. The question now is how can that science at the same time be theology, the science of divine substance? And to it Aristotle gives the succinct answer that we have already noticed:

> If there is some immovable substance, this [that is, theological philosophy] will be prior and will be primary philosophy, and it will be universal in this way, namely, because it is primary. And it will belong to it to get a theoretical grasp on being qua being, both what it is and the things that belong to it qua being. (*Met.* VI 1 1026ᵃ23–32)

So the primacy of theology, which is based on the fact that theology deals with substance that is eternal, immovable, and separable, is supposedly what justifies us in treating it as the universal science of being qua being.

To get a handle on what this primacy is, we need to turn to being and its structure. The first thing to grasp is that beings are divided into categories: substance, quality, quantity, relation, and so on (*PA* I 1 649ᵃ3n). But of these, only beings in the category of substance are separable, so that they alone enjoy a sort of ontological priority that is both existential and explanatory.* Other beings are attributes or affections of different sorts,

---

* Thus walking and being healthy are characterized as "incapable of being separated," on the grounds that there is some particular substantial underlying subject of which they are predicated (*Met.* VII 1 1028ᵃ20–31). Often, separability is associated with being such a subject: "The underlying subject is prior, which is why the substance is prior" (V 11 1019ᵃ5–6); "If we do not posit substances to be separated, and in the way in which particular things are said to be separated, we will do away with the sort of substance we wish to maintain" (XIII 10 1086ᵇ16–19). Similarly, not being separable is associated with being predicated of such a subject. Being predicated of a substance—being an attribute—seems, then, to be a sufficient condition of not being separable. Moreover, not being separable seems itself to be a sufficient condition of being ontologically dependent: "All the other things are either said of the primary substances as subjects or in them as subjects. So if the primary substances were not, it would be impossible for any of the other things to be" (*Cat.* 5 2ᵇ3–6).

which exist only by belonging to some substance. So if we want to explain what a quality is, for example, we have to say what sort of attribute it is, and ultimately what in a substance is receptive of it. It is this fact that gives one sort of unity to beings: they are all either substances or attributes of substances. Hence the famous claim:

> Indeed, the question that was asked long ago, is now, and always will be asked, and is always raising puzzles—namely, What is being?—is just the question, What is substance? . . . And that is why we too must most of all, primarily, and (one might almost say) exclusively get a theoretical grasp on what it is that is a being in this [substantial] way. (*Met.* VII 1 1028ᵇ2–7)

The starting-points and causes of the beings qua beings, then, must be substances. Thus while things are said to be in as many ways as there are categories, they are also said "with reference to one thing and one nature" (*Met.* IV 2 1003ᵃ33–34)—substance. It could still be the case, of course, that the universe is episodic like a bad tragedy, made up of lots of separate substances having little ontologically to do with each other, but the number of episodes has at least been systematically reduced.

Before turning to the next phase in being's unification, we need to look more closely at substance itself as it gets investigated and analyzed in *Met.* VII–IX. The analysis begins with a *legomenon*—with something said and accepted quite widely:

> Something is said to be (*legetai*) substance, if not in more ways, at any rate most of all in four. For the essence, the universal, and the genus seem to be the substance of each thing, and fourth of these, the underlying subject. (*Met.* VII 3 1028ᵇ33–36)

Since "the primary underlying subject seems most of all to be substance" (*Met.* VII 3 1029ᵃ1–2), because what is said or predicated of it depends on it, the investigation begins with this subject, quickly isolating three candidates: the matter, the compound of matter and form, and the form itself (1029ᵃ2–3), which is identical to the essence (7 1032ᵇ1–2). Almost as quickly (3 1029ᵃ7–32), the first two candidates are at least provisionally excluded, leaving form alone as the most promising candidate for being substance. But form is "most puzzling" (1029ᵃ33) and requires extraordinary ingenuity and resources to explore.

Aristotle begins the investigation into form with the most familiar and widely recognized case, which is the form or essence present in sublunary matter-form compounds. This investigation is announced in *Met.* VII 3

1029^b3–12, but not begun till some chapters later and not really completed till the end of IX 5. By then the various other candidates for being substance have been eliminated or reconceived, and actuality and potentiality have come to prominence. Hence in IX 6 it is with actuality or activity—*entelecheia* or *energeia* (*GA* I 19 726^b17n)—that form, and so substance, is identified, and matter with potentiality.

Precisely because actuality and potentiality are the ultimate explanatory factors, however, they themselves cannot be given an explanatory definition in yet more basic terms. Instead, we must grasp them by means of an analogy:

> What we wish to say is clear from the particular cases by induction, and we must not look for a definition of everything, but be able to comprehend the analogy, namely, that as what is building is in relation to what is capable of building, and what is awake is in relation to what is asleep, and what is seeing is in relation to what has its eyes closed but has sight, and what has been shaped out of the matter is in relation to the matter, and what has been finished off is to the unfinished. Of the difference exemplified in this analogy let the activity be marked off by the first part, the potentiality by the second. (*Met.* IX 6 1048^a35–$^b6$)

What is common to matter-form compounds, mathematical objects, and divine substances, then, is actuality. In the case of matter-form compounds and numbers, the actuality is accompanied by potentiality—perceptual sublunary matter in the first case, intelligible matter in the second. In the case of divine substances and other such unmoved movers, it is not. They are "pure" activities or actualities, wholly actual at each moment. Matter-form compounds, by contrast, are never wholly actual—they are always in some way potential. You are actually reading this now, not reading *Much Ado About Nothing*, but you could be reading *Much Ado About Nothing*, since you have the presently unactualized capacity (or potential) to read it.

The science of being qua being can legitimately focus on form, or actuality, as the factor common to divine substances, matter-form compounds, and mathematical objects. But unless it can be shown that there is some explanatory connection between the forms in these different beings, the non-episodic nature of being itself will still not have been established, and the pictures given to us by the natural, mathematical, and theological sciences will, so to speak, be separate pictures, and the being they collectively portray, divided. We notice fairly quickly how important actuality and potentiality are in *GC*, since these play a crucial role in explaining each of its focal topics: affecting and being affected (I 9 326^b31), elemental transformation (II 6 334^{b}9), growth (I 5 322^{a}6), mixing (I 10 327^{b}23), and unconditional coming to be and passing away (I 3 317^{b}24). It has an equally fundamental part to play, as we shall soon see, in the generation of animals, since it is crucial to explaining how sexual reproduction traits can be inherited from both male and female progenitors. But, of course, *GA* also takes on board many of the concepts and tools—many of the starting-points—used in sciences that are prior to it. As our biology presupposes our chemistry and our physics, so too does Aristotle's. Indeed *Meteorology* IV is sometimes referred to as Aristotle's "chemical treatise."

The next stage in the unification of being, and the legitimation of the science dealing with it qua being, is effected by an argument that trades, unsurprisingly, on the identification of form with actuality and matter with potentiality. Part of the argument is given in *Met.* IX 8–9, where the various sorts of priority requisite in a substance are argued to belong to actuality rather than potentiality. But it is in XII 6 that the pertinent consequences are most decisively drawn:

> If there is something that is capable of moving things or acting on them, but that is not actively doing so, there will not [necessarily] be movement, since it is possible for what has a capacity not to activate it. There is no benefit, therefore, in positing eternal substances, as those who accept the Forms do, unless there is to be present in them some starting-point that is capable of causing change. Moreover, even this is not enough, and neither is another substance beyond the Forms. For if it will not be active, there will not be movement. Further, even if it will be active, it is not enough, if the substance of it is a capacity. For then there will not be *eternal* movement, since what is potentially may possibly not be. There must, therefore, be such a starting-point, the very substance of which is activity. Further, accordingly, these substances must be without matter. For they must be eternal, if indeed *anything* else is eternal. Therefore they must be activity. (*Met.* XII 6 1071^{b}12–22)

Matter-form compounds are, as such, capable of movement and change. The canonical examples of them—perhaps the only genuine or fully fledged ones—are living metabolizing beings (*Met.* VII 17 1041^{b}29–30). But if these beings are to be actual, there must be substances whose very essence is activity—substances that do not need to be activated by something else.

With matter-form compounds shown to be dependent on substantial activities for their actual being, a further element of vertical unification is introduced into beings, since layer-wise the two sorts of substances belong together.

Laterally, though, disunity continues to threaten. For as yet nothing has been done to exclude the possibility that each compound substance has a distinct substantial activity as its own unique activator. Being, in that case, would be a set of ordered pairs, the first member of which is a substantial activity, the second a matter-form compound, with all its dependent attributes.

In *Met.* XII 8 Aristotle initially takes a step in the direction of such a bipartite picture. He asks how many substantial activities are required to explain astronomical phenomena, such as the movements of the stars and planets, and answers that there must be forty-nine of them (1074ª16). But these forty-nine are coordinated with each other so as to form a system. And what enables them to do so, and constitute a single heaven, is that there is a single prime mover of all of them:

> It is evident that there is but one heaven. For if there are many, as there are many human beings, the starting-point for each will be one in form but in number many. But all things that are many in number have matter, for one and the same account applies to many, for example, human beings, whereas Socrates is one. But the primary essence does not have matter, since it is an actuality. The primary immovable mover, therefore, is one both in account and in number. And so, therefore, is what is moved always and continuously. Therefore, there is only one heaven. (*Met.* XII 8 1074ª31–38; also *Cael.* I 8)

The argument is puzzling, to be sure, since the immateriality that ensures the uniqueness of the prime mover would seem to threaten the multiplicity of the forty-nine movers, since they are also immaterial. Nonetheless the point of it is clear enough: what accounts for the unity of heaven is that the movements in it are traceable back to a single cause—the prime or primary mover.

Leaving aside the question of just how this primary mover moves what it moves directly, which is left unanswered (as not belonging to natural science) in the *Physics*, *De Caelo*, and *GC* but discussed in *Met.* XII 7, the next phase in the unification of beings is the one in which the sublunary world is integrated with the already unified superlunary one studied by astronomy. This takes place in *Met.* XII 10, although elements of it have emerged earlier. One obvious indication of this unification is the dependence of the reproductive cycles of plants and animals on the seasons, and their dependence, in turn, on the movements of the sun and moon:

> The cause of a human is both his elements, fire and earth as matter and the special form [as form], and furthermore some other

external thing, such as the father, and beyond these the sun and its movement in an inclined circle. (*Met.* XII 5 1071ª13–16; also *GC* II 10)

And beyond even this there is the unity of the natural world itself, which is manifested in the ways in which its inhabitants are adapted to each other:

All things are jointly organized in a way, although not in the same way—even swimming creatures, flying creatures, and plants. And the organization is not such that one thing has no relation to another but rather there is a relation. For all things are jointly organized in relation to one thing—but it is as in a household, where the free men least of all do things at random, but all or most of the things they do are organized, while the slaves and beasts can do a little for the common thing, but mostly do things at random. For this is the sort of starting-point that the nature is of each of them. I mean, for example, that all must at least come to be disaggregated [into their elements]; and similarly there are other things which they all share for the whole. (*Met.* XII 10 1075ª16–25)

Just how much unity all this results in—just what it means to speak of "the nature of the whole" (*Met.* XII 10 1075ª11) or of the universe as having "one ruler" (1076ª4)—is a matter of dispute, to which we shall have to return later on. The fact remains, though, that the sublunary realm is sufficiently integrated with the superlunary one that we can speak of them as jointly having a nature and a ruler, and as being analogous not to Heraclitus' "heap of random sweepings" (DK B24), but to an army (1075ª13) and a household (1075ª22). *Mete.* I 1 begins, as we saw, by describing how, at any rate, the natural sciences are integrated into a single body of knowledge.

We may agree, then, that the divine substances in the superlunary realm and the compound substances in the sublunary one have prima facie been vertically integrated into a single explanatory system. When we look at the form of a sublunary matter-form compound, then, we will find in it the mark of a superlunary activator, just as we do in the case of the various heavenly bodies, and, as in the line of its efficient causes, we find "the sun and its movement in an inclined circle" (*Met.* XII 5 1071ª15–16). Still awaiting integration, though, are the mathematical objects, and their next of kin, Platonic Forms.

That there is mathematical structure present in the universe can seem to be especially clear in the case of the superlunary realm, just as mathematics itself, with its rigorous proofs and necessary and certain truths, can seem the very paradigm of scientific knowledge. So it is hardly surprising that some of Aristotle's predecessors, especially Pythagoreans and Platonists, thought that the primary causes and starting-points of beings are to be found in the part of reality that is mathematics friendly, or in some way mathematizable. For example, some Platonists (Plato among them, in Aristotle's much disputed view) held that for each sort of sublunary (or perceptible) thing there was an eternal intelligible Form or Idea to which it owed its being, and which owed its own being, in turn, to "the one," as its substance, and the so-called indefinite dyad of the great and the small, as its matter. So when we ask what makes a man a man, the answer will be, that it participates in the Form or Idea of a man, which owes its being to the way it is constructed or generated from the indefinite dyad and the one (*Ph.* IV 2 209^{b}7–16, 209^{b}33–210^{a}2). And because the Forms are so constructed, Aristotle says (anyway on one reading of the text) that "the Forms are the numbers" (*Met.* I 6 987^{b}20–22). Between these so-called Form (or Ideal) numbers, in addition, are the numbers that are the objects of mathematics: the intermediates. This elaborate system of, as I put it, mathematics-friendly objects, then, are the substances—the ultimate starting-points and causes of beings qua beings.

Against these objects and the ontological role assigned to them, Aristotle launches a host of arguments (thirty-two or so in *Met.* I 9, twenty-four in XIII 8–9, and many others elsewhere), proposing in their place an entirely different account of mathematical objects, which treats them not as substantial starting-points and causes but as abstractions from perceptible sublunary beings—dependent entities, in other words, rather than self-subsistent or intrinsic ones:

> The mathematician too busies himself about these things [planes, solids, lines, and points], although not insofar as each of them is the limit of a natural body, nor does he get a theoretical grasp on the coincidents of natural bodies insofar as they are such. That is why he separates them. For they are separable in the understanding from movement, and so their being separated makes no difference, nor does any falsehood result from it. (*Ph.* II 2 193^{b}31–35)

This completes the vertical and horizontal unification of being: attributes depend on substances, substantial matter-form compounds depend on substantial forms, or activities, numbers depend on matter-form compounds.

Beings are not said to be "in accord with one thing," then, as they would be if they formed a single genus, but "with reference to one thing"—namely, a divine substance that is in essence an activity. And it is this more complex unity, compatible with generic diversity, and a genuine multiplicity of distinct first-order sciences, but just as robust and well grounded as the simpler genus-based sort of unity, that grounds and legitimates the science of being qua being as a single science dealing with a genuine object of study (*Met.* IV 2 1003^{b}11–16). The long argument that leads to this conclusion is thus a sort of existence proof of the science on which the *Metaphysics* focuses.

It is the priority of a divine substance with that science that justifies the description we looked at twice before of what the *Metaphysics* is about:

> If, then, there is no other substance beyond those composed by nature, natural science will be the primary science. But if there is some immovable substance, this [that is, theological philosophy] will be prior and will be primary philosophy, and it will be universal in this way, namely, because it is primary. And it will belong to it to get a theoretical grasp on being qua being, both what it is and the things that belong to it qua being. (*Met.* VI 1 1026^{a}27–32)

The science of being qua being is a sort of theology, as *Met.* II 2 already told us it was, but it is a sort of theology only because of the special role of the primary god among beings.

Is the Investigation in GA and Its Predecessors a Scientific One?

If we think of a science in the exact sense as consisting exclusively of what is demonstrable, as we saw Aristotle himself sometimes does, we will be right to conclude that a treatise without demonstrations cannot be scientific. But if, as he also does, we include knowledge of starting-points as parts of science, we will not be right, since a treatise could contribute to a science not by demonstrating anything but by arguing to the starting-points themselves—an enterprise which could not without circularity consist of demonstrations *from* those starting-points: "For of a starting-point there is another sort of knowledge and not a demonstration" (*GA* II 6 742^{b}32–33). Arguments leading *from* starting-points and arguments leading *to* starting-points are different, we are invited not to forget (*NE* I 4 1095^{a}30–32), just as we are told that because establishing starting-points is "more than half the whole" (I 7 1098^{b}7), we should "make very serious efforts to define them correctly" (1098^{b}5–6). We might reasonably infer, therefore, that *GC*, *Mete.*, and *GA* are a contribution to natural science, *at least in part* by establishing the correct definition of some of its starting-points. And unconditional coming to be (*GC* I 3), and its material, formal, final, and efficient causes (II 9–10), alteration (I 4), growth and withering (I 5), contact (I 6), affecting and being affected (I 7–9), mixing (I 10), the elements, their transformation and capacities (II 1–8), like putrefaction (*Mete.* IV 1) and concoction (IV 2), all certainly seem to be scientific starting-points of some sort. The same goes in *GA* for male, female, and their spermatic residues, semen and menses (*GA* I 2 716ᵃ4–13).

Now in our investigation of starting-points, "we must," Aristotle says, "start from things known *to us*" (*NE* I 4 1095ᵇ3–4). That is why biology starts as it does:

> First, then, we must grasp the parts of a human. For just as each group of people evaluates currency in relation to the one best known to themselves, it is the same way, of course, in other things. But of the animals the human is of necessity the best known to us. (*HA* I 6 491ᵃ19–23)

For the sake of clarity, let us call these *raw starting-points*. These are the ones we start from when we are arguing *explanatory scientific starting-points*. It is important not to confuse the two. In the case of the special sciences the *explanatory starting-points* include, in particular, definitions that specify the genus and differentiae of the real (as opposed to nominal) universal essences of the beings with which the science deals (*APo.* II 10 93ᵇ29–94ᵃ19). Since scientific definitions must be apt starting-points of demonstrations, this implies, Aristotle thinks, that the "extremes and the middle terms must come from the same genus" (I 7 75ᵇ10–11). As a result a single canonical science must deal with a single genus (I 28 87ᵃ38–39).

To reach these definitions from *raw starting-points*, though, we first have to have the raw starting-points at hand. Aristotle is clear about this, as he is indeed about what is supposed to happen next:

> The method (*hodos*) is the same in all cases, in philosophy as well as in the crafts or any sort of learning whatsoever. For one must observe for both terms what belongs to them and what they belong to, and be supplied with as many of these terms as possible, and one must investigate them by means of the three terms [in a syllogism], in one way when refuting, in another way when establishing something. When it is in accord with truth, it must be from the terms that are catalogued (*diagegrammenôn*) as truly belonging, but in dialectical deductions it must be from premises that are in accord with [reputable] belief. . . . Most of

the starting-points, however, are special to each science. That is why experience must provide us with the starting-points where each is concerned—I mean, for example, that experience in astronomy must do so in the case of astronomical science. For when the things that appear to be so had been adequately grasped, the demonstrations in astronomy were found in the way we described. And it is the same way where any other craft or science whatsoever is concerned. Hence if what belongs to each thing has been grasped, at that point we can readily exhibit the demonstrations. For if nothing that truly belongs to the relevant things has been omitted from the collection, then concerning everything, if a demonstration of it exists we will be able to find it and give the demonstration, and if it is by nature indemonstrable, we will be able to make that evident. (*APr.* I 30 46^{a}3–27)

Once we have a catalogue of the *raw starting-points*, then, the demonstrative explanation of them from explanatory scientific starting-points is supposedly fairly routine. (In the case of biology, we might think of *HA* as providing the relevant catalogue.) We should not, however, demand "the cause [or explanation] in all cases alike. Rather, in some it will be adequate if the fact that they are so has been correctly shown (*deiknunai*), as it is indeed where starting-points are concerned" (*NE* I 8 1098^{a}33–^{b}2). But what exactly is it to show a starting-point correctly or adequately?

The science of *GA* and its predecessors *GC* and *Mete.*, as we saw, is a branch of theoretical natural science or natural philosophy, and to the explanatory scientific starting-points of philosophical sciences, Aristotle claims, there is a unique route:

Dialectic is useful in the philosophical sciences because the capacity to go through the puzzles on both sides of a question will make it easier to judge what is true and what is false in each. Furthermore, dialectic is useful in relation to the primary [starting-points] (*ta prôta*) in each science. For it is impossible to say anything about these based on the starting-points properly belonging to the science in question, since these starting-points are, of all of them, the primary ones, and it is through reputable beliefs (*endoxa*) about each that it is necessary to discuss them. This, though, is a task special to, or most characteristic of, dialectic. For because of its ability to stand outside and examine (*exetastikê*), it has a route toward the starting-points of all methods of inquiry. (*Top.* I 2 101^{a}34–^{b}4)

And this is repeated almost word for word in the *Physics* with reference to the concept of place, which is a natural scientific starting-point:

> We must try to make our investigation in such a way that the what-it-is is given an account of, so that the puzzles are resolved, the things that are believed to belong to place will in fact belong to it, and furthermore, so that the cause of the difficulty and of the puzzles concerning it will be evident, since this is the best way of showing each thing. (*Ph.* IV 4 211ᵃ7–11)

Prima facie, then, the three treatises we are looking at should correctly show explanatory starting-points by going through puzzles and solving these by appeal to reputable beliefs and perceptual evidence. But before we rush off to see whether that is what we do find, we need to be clearer about what exactly we should be looking for.

Dialectic is recognizably a descendant of the Socratic elenchus, which famously begins with a question like this: *Ti esti to kalon?* What is the noble? The respondent, sometimes after a bit of nudging, comes up with a universal definition, what is noble is what all the gods love, or whatever it might be (I adapt a well-known answer from Plato's *Euthyphro*). Socrates then puts this definition to the test by drawing attention to some things that seem true to the respondent himself but which conflict with his definition. The puzzle or *aporia* that results from this conflict then remains for the respondent to try to solve, usually by reformulating or rejecting his definition. Aristotle understood this process in terms that show its relationship to his own:

> Socrates, on the other hand, busied himself about the virtues of character, and in connection with them was the first to inquire about universal definition. . . . It was reasonable, though, that Socrates was inquiring about the what-it-is. For he was inquiring in order to deduce, and the what-it-is is a starting-point of deductions. For at that time there was not yet the strength in dialectic that enables people, and separately from the what-it-is, to investigate contraries, and whether the same science is a science of contraries. For there are two things that may be fairly ascribed to Socrates—inductive arguments and universal definition, both of which are concerned with a starting-point of scientific knowledge. (*Met.* XIII 4 1078ᵇ17–30; also I 6 987ᵇ1–4)

In Plato too dialectic is primarily concerned with scientific starting-points, such as those of mathematics, and seems to consist in some sort of elenchus-like process of reformulating definitions in the face of conflicting evidence so as to render them puzzle free (*Rep.* VII 532a–533d). Aristotle can reasonably be seen, then, as continuing a line of thought about dialectic, while contributing greatly to its exploration, systemization, and elaboration in works such as *Topics* and *Sophistical Refutations*.

Consider now the respondent's first answer, his first definition: what is noble is what the gods love. Although it is soon shown to be incorrect, there is something quite remarkable about its very existence. Through experience shaped by acculturation and habituation involving the learning of a natural language, the respondent is confident that he can say what nobility is. He has learned to apply the word "noble" to particular people, actions, and so on correctly enough to pass muster as knowing its meaning, knowing how to use it. From these particular cases he has reached a putative universal, something the particular cases have in common. But when he tries to define that universal in words, he gets it wrong, as Socrates shows. Here is Aristotle registering the significance of this: "The things that are knowable and primary for particular groups of people are often only slightly knowable and have little or nothing of the being in them. Nonetheless, beginning from things that are poorly known but known to ourselves, we must try to know the ones that are wholly knowable, proceeding, as has just been said, through the former" (*Met.* VII 3 1029^{b}8–12).

The route by which the respondent reaches the universal that he is unable to define correctly is what Aristotle calls induction (*epagôgê*). This begins with (1) perception of particulars, which leads to (2) retention of perceptual contents in memory, and, when many such contents have been retained, to (3) an experience, so that for the first time "there is a universal in the soul" (*APo.* II 19 100^{a}3–16). The universal reached at stage (3), which is the one the respondent reaches, is described as "rather confused" and "more knowable by perception" (*Ph.* I 1 184^{a}22–25). It is the sort of universal, often quite complex, that constitutes a nominal essence corresponding to the nominal definition or meaning of a general term. Finally, (4) from experience come craft knowledge and scientific knowledge, when "from many intelligible objects arising from experience one universal supposition about similar objects is produced" (*Met.* I 1 981^{a}5–7).

The *nominal* (or analytic, meaning-based) definition of the general term "thunder," for example, might pick out the universal *loud noise in the clouds*. When science investigates the things that have this nominal essence, it may find that they also have a real essence or nature in terms of which their other features can be scientifically explained:

> Since a definition is said to be an account of what something is,
> it is evident that one sort will be an account of what its name,

or some other name-like account, signifies—for example, what triangle signifies . . . . Another sort of definition is an account that makes clear why it exists. So the former sort signifies something but does not show it, whereas the latter will evidently be like a demonstration of what it is, differing in arrangement from a demonstration. For there is a difference between saying why it thunders and saying what thunder is. In the first case you will say: because fire is being extinguished in the clouds. And what is thunder? The loud noise of fire being extinguished in the clouds. Hence the same account is given in different ways. In one way it is a continuous demonstration, in the other a definition. Further, a definition of thunder is a noise in the clouds, and this is a conclusion of the demonstration of what it is. The definition of an immediate item, though, is an indemonstrable positing (*thesis*) of what it is. (*APo.* II 10 93^{b}29–94^{a}10; compare *DA* II 2 413^{a}13–20)

A real (or synthetic, fact-based) definition, which analyzes this real essence into its "elements and starting-points" (*Ph.* I 1 184^{a}23), which will be definable but indemonstrable within the science, makes intrinsically clear what the nominal definition made clear only by enabling us to recognize instances of thunder in a fairly—but imperfectly—reliable way. As a result, thunder itself, now clearly a natural and not just a conventional kind, becomes better known not just to us but entirely or unconditionally.* These analyzed universals, which are the sort reached at stage (4), are the ones suited to serve as starting-points of the sciences and crafts: "experienced people know the that but do not know the why, whereas craftsmen know the why, that is, the cause" (*Met.* I 1 981^{a}28–30).

Socrates too, we see, wanted definitions that were not just empirically adequate but also explanatory: in telling Euthyphro what he wants in the case of piety, he says that he is seeking "the form itself *in virtue of which* all the pieties are pieties" (*Euthphr.* 6d). That is why he rejects the definition of

---

* Compare: "Unconditionally, what is prior is more knowable than what is posterior—for example, a point than a line, a line than a plane, and a plane than a solid, just as a unit is more so than a number, since it is prior to and a starting-point of all number. Similarly, a letter is more so than a syllable. To us, on the other hand, it sometimes happens that the reverse is the case. For the solid falls most under perception, the plane more than the line, line more than point. For ordinary people know things of the former sort earlier. For to learn them is a task for random thought, whereas to learn the others is a task for exact and extraordinary thought" (*Top.* VI 4 141^{b}5–14).

piety as being what all the gods love. This definition is in one way correct, presumably, in that if something is pious it must be loved by the gods and vice versa, but it is not explanatory, since it does not tell us what it is about pious things that makes all the gods love them, and so does not identify the form in virtue of which they are pious (9e–11b).

Let us go back. We wanted to know what was involved in showing a scientific starting-point. We were told how we could *not* do this, namely, by demonstrating it from scientific starting-points. Next we learned that dialectic had a route to it from reputable beliefs. At the same time, we were told that induction had a route to it as well—something the *Nicomachean Ethics* also tells us: "we get a theoretical grasp of some starting-points through induction, some through perception, some through some sort of habituation, and others through other means" (I 7 1098^{b}3–4). This suggests that induction and dialectic are in some way or other related processes.

What shows a Socratic respondent to be wrong is an example that his definition does not fit. The presentation of the example might be quite indirect, however. It might take quite a bit of stage setting, elicited by the asking of many questions, to bring out a puzzle. But if it does succeed in doing so, it shows that the universal grasped by the respondent and the definition of it produced by him are not entirely or unconditionally knowable and that his state is not one of clear-eyed understanding:

> A puzzle in thought makes manifest a knot in the subject matter. For insofar as thought is puzzled it is like people who are tied up, since in both cases it is impossible to move forward. That is why we must get a theoretical grasp on all the difficulties beforehand, both for these reasons and because those who inquire without first going through the puzzles are like people who do not know where they have to go. And, in addition, a person [who has not already grasped the puzzles] does not even know whether he has found what he is inquiring into. For to someone like that the end is not clear, whereas to a person who has already grasped the puzzles it is clear. (*Met.* II 1 995^{a}30–^{b}2)

But lack of such clear-eyed understanding of a scientific starting-point has serious downstream consequences:

> If we are to have scientific knowledge through demonstration, . . . we must know the starting-points better and be better persuaded of them than of what is being shown, but we must

also not find anything more persuasive or better known among things opposed to the starting-points from which a contrary mistaken conclusion may be deduced, since someone who has unconditional scientific knowledge must be incapable of being persuaded out of it. (*APo.* I 2 72^{a}37–^{b}4)

If dialectical examination brings to light a puzzle in a respondent's thought about a scientific starting-point, then, he cannot have any unconditional scientific knowledge even of what he may well be able to demonstrate correctly from it. Contrariwise, if dialectical examination brings to light no such puzzle, he apparently does have clear-eyed understanding, and his route to what he can demonstrate is free of obstacles.

At the heart of dialectic, as Aristotle understands it, is the dialectical deduction (*dialektikos sullogismos*). This is the argument lying behind the questioner's questions, partly dictating their order and content and partly determining the strategy of his examination. In the following passage it is defined and contrasted with two relevant others:

> Dialectical arguments are those that deduce from reputable beliefs in a way that reaches a contradiction; examinational arguments are those that deduce from those beliefs of the respondent that anyone must know (*eidenai*) who pretends to possess scientific knowledge . . . ; contentious (*eristikos*) arguments are those that deduce or appear to deduce from what appear to be reputable beliefs but are not really such. (*SE* 2 165^{b}3–8)

If we think of dialectical deductions in this way, a dialectician, in contrast to a contender, is an honest questioner, appealing to genuinely reputable beliefs and employing valid deductions. "Contenders and sophists use the same arguments," Aristotle says, "but not to achieve the same goal. . . . If the goal is apparent victory, the argument is contentious; if it is apparent wisdom, sophistic" (*SE* 11 171^{b}27–29). Nonetheless, he does also use the term *dialektikê* as the name for the craft that honest dialecticians and sophists both use: "In dialectic a sophist is so called in virtue of his deliberate choice, and a dialectician is so called not in virtue of his deliberate choice, but in virtue of the capacity he has" (*Rh.* I 1 1355^{b}20–21). If dialectic is understood in this way, a dialectician who deliberately chooses to employ contentious arguments is a sophist (I 1 1355^{a}24–^{b}7).* We need to

---

* Compare: "There are some things that cannot be put in only one genus—for example, the cheat and the slanderer. For neither the one with the deliberate

be careful, therefore, to distinguish *honest dialectic* from what we may call *plain dialectic*, which—like all crafts—can be used for good or ill (*NE* V 1 1129ᵃ13–17).

The canonical occasion for the practice of the Socratic elenchus, obviously, is the examination of someone else. But there is nothing to prevent a person from practicing it on himself: "How could you think," Socrates asks Critias, "that I would refute you for any reason other than the one for which I would refute myself, fearing lest I might inadvertently think I know something when I don't know it?" (*Chrm.* 166c–d). Dialectic is no different in this regard:

> But the philosopher, who is investigating by himself, does not care whether, though the things through which his deduction proceeds are true and knowable, the answerer does not concede them, because they are close to what was proposed at the start, and he foresees what is going to result, but rather is presumably eager for his claims to be as knowable and as close to it as possible. For it is from things of this sort that scientific deductions proceed. (*Top.* VIII 1 155ᵇ10–16; compare *Ph.* VIII 8 263ᵃ15–23)

> An inquiry with another person is carried out by means of words (*logôn*), whereas an inquiry by oneself is carried out no less by means of the things at issue themselves. (*SE* 7 169ᵃ38–40)

What we are to imagine, then, is that the philosopher surveys the raw scientific starting-points, constructing detailed catalogues of these. He then tries to formulate definitions of the various universals involved in them that seem to be candidate scientific starting-points, testing these against the raw scientific starting-points by trying to construct demonstrations from them. But these definitions will often be no more than partial: the philosopher is only on his way to complete definitional starting-points, just as the demonstrations will often be no more than proto or nascent demonstrations. The often rudimentary demonstrations that we find in Aristotle's scientific treatises are surely parts of this process of arguing *to* not *from* starting-points. We argue to these in part by seeing whether or to what extent we could demonstrate from them. There are many such arguments in *GC, Mete.*, and *GA*: but they are typically arguments that show,

---

choice to do it but without the capacity, nor the one with the capacity but not the deliberate choice, is a slanderer or a cheat, but rather the one with both" (*Top.* IV 5 126ᵇ8–11).

not arguments that demonstrate.* But that we must not overwork the distinction is clear:

> It is no less possible to state a deduction or an enthymeme based on it about matters of justice than it is about matters of natural science, or about anything else whatsoever, even though these things differ in species. Special [topics] on the other hand are the ones based on premises concerning a given species and genus. For example, there are premises concerning natural things on which neither an enthymeme nor a deduction can be based concerning ethical things, and about the latter there are others on which none can be based concerning natural ones. And the same holds in all cases. The common ones will not make someone wise about any genus, since they are not concerned with any underlying subject. But as to the special ones, the better someone is at selecting premises,**[the more] he will without noticing it produce a science that is distinct from dialectic and rhetoric. For if he hits upon starting-points, it will no longer be dialectic or rhetoric, but instead will be that science whose starting-points he possesses. (*Rh.* I 2 1358ᵃ14–26)

---

* The verb *apodechesthai* occurs just once in *GC* (at II 6 333ᵇ35), and in *Mete.* (at I 7 344ᵃ6), in neither case referring to something accomplished in the work itself. And when *GA* offers a demonstration of its own (as opposed to criticizing one attributed to Democritus and Empedocles) it is a logico-linguistic one, not one from scientific starting-points (see *GA* II 8 747ᵃ28, ᵇ28 and note). In general, indeed, *GA* speaks in terms of sign (*sêmeion*) (over 25 times) and proof (*tekmêrion*) (6 times), and of something as reasonable (*eulogos*) (around 40 times). These are listed in the Index. For argument bearing on the scientific status of *De Caelo*, which has application to *GA*, see A. Falcon and M. Leunissen, "The Scientific Role of *Eulogos* in Aristotle's *Cael* II 12." In D. Ebrey (ed.), *Theory and Practice in Aristotle's Natural Science* (Cambridge, 2015), pp. 217–240.

** Compare: "Unconditionally, then, it is better to try to make what is posterior known through what is prior. For proceeding in this way is more scientific. Nevertheless, in relation to those who cannot know through things of the latter sort it is presumably necessary to produce the account through things knowable to them. . . . One must not fail to notice, however, that it is not possible for those who define in this way to make clear the essence of the definiendum, *unless it so happens that the same thing is more knowable both to us and also unconditionally more knowable*, if indeed a correct definition must define through the genus and the differentiae, and these are among the things that are unconditionally more knowable than the species and prior to it" (*Top.* VI 4 141ᵇ15–28).

The two instances (and there are only two) in *De Caelo* where Aristotle refers to something he has shown (or takes himself to have shown) as something that has been demonstrated, namely, I 3 269^b18 (*apodedeiktai*) and 6 273^b24 (*apodeixin*), are probably best seen in this light.

So: First, we have the important distinction between dialectic proper, which includes the use of what appear to be deductions from what appear to be reputable beliefs, and honest dialectic, which uses only genuine deductions from genuine reputable beliefs. Second, we have the equally important distinction between the use of dialectic in examining a potentially hostile respondent and its use by the philosopher in a perhaps private pursuit of the truth. Third, we have an important contrast between honest dialectical premises and philosophical ones or scientific ones: honest dialectical premises are reputable beliefs, philosophical and scientific premises must be true and knowable. Fourth, we have two apparently equivalent routes to scientific starting-points, one inductive, which starts from raw starting-points, and the other dialectic, which starts from reputable beliefs.

According to the official definition, reputable beliefs are "things that are believed by everyone, by the majority, or by the wise—either by all of them, or by most, or by the most well known and most reputable" (*Top.* I 1 100^b21–23). Just as the scientist should have a catalogue of scientific (often perception-based) truths at hand from which to select the premises of his demonstrations, so a dialectician ought also to select premises "from arguments that have been written down and produce catalogues (*diagraphas*) of them concerning each kind (*genos*) of subject, putting them under separate headings—for example, 'Concerned with good,' 'Concerned with life'" (14 105^b12–15). But for obvious reasons reputable beliefs in *outré* subjects like natural science (unlike, for example, ethics and politics) are likely to have predominantly expert rather than non-expert sources—although in Aristotle's world, as to some perhaps lesser extent in ours—everyone knows *something* about plants, animals, and so on. Thus the views that are reputable beliefs because they are those of other thinkers loom larger in *GC*, *Mete.*, and *GA* than beliefs reputable because they are held by ordinary people rather than the wise. By the same token, things that appear to be so on the basis of observation should figure along with these beliefs (notice *tôn endoxôn kai tôn phainomenôn* at *Cael.* III 4 303^a22–23), since these, as we saw, have the controlling vote in natural science. Observation of various sorts, more professional and more humdrum, is appealed to around thirty times in *GA*.

Clearly, then, there will be considerable overlap between the scientist's catalogue of raw starting-points and the honest dialectician's catalogue of reputable beliefs. For, first, things that are believed by reputably wise people are themselves reputable beliefs, and, second, any respondent would accept "the beliefs of those who have investigated the subjects in question—for example, on a question of medicine he will agree with a doctor, and on a question of geometry with a geometer" (*Top.* I 10 104ᵃ8–37). The catalogues also differ, however, in that not all reputable beliefs need be true. If a proposition is a reputable belief, if it would be accepted by all or most people, it is everything an honest dialectician could ask for in a premise, since his goal is simply this: to show by honest deductions that a definition offered by any respondent whatsoever conflicts—if it does— with other beliefs the respondent has. That is why having a complete or fairly complete catalogue of reputable beliefs is such an important resource for a dialectician. It is because dialectic deals with things only "in relation to belief," then, and not as philosophy and science do, "in relation to truth" (I 14 105ᵇ30–31), that it needs nothing more than reputable *beliefs*.

Nonetheless, the fact that all or most people believe something leads us "to trust it as something in accord with experience" (*Div. Somn.* 1 462ᵇ14– 16), and—since human beings "are naturally adequate as regards the truth and for the most part happen upon it" (*Rh.* I 1 1355ᵃ15–17)—as containing some truth. That is why having catalogued some of the things that people believe happiness to be, Aristotle writes: "Some of these views are held by many and are of long standing, while others are held by a few reputable men. And it is not reasonable to suppose that either group is entirely wrong, but rather that they are right on one point at least or even on most of them" (*NE* I 8 1098ᵇ27–29). Later he generalizes the claim: "things that seem to be so to everyone, these, we say, are" (X 2 1172ᵇ36–1173ᵃ1). Raw starting-points are just that—raw. But when refined some shred of truth is likely to be found in them. So likely, indeed, that if none is found, this will itself be a surprising fact needing to be explained: "when a reasonable explanation is given of why an untrue view appears true, this makes us more convinced of the true view" (VII 14 1154ᵃ24–25).* It is the grain of truth enclosed in a reputable belief that a philosopher or scientist is interested in, then, not in the general acceptability of the surrounding husk, much of which he may discard.

The process of refinement in the case of a candidate explanatory starting-point is that of testing a definition of it against reputable beliefs and perceptual evidence. This may result in the definition being accepted as it stands or in its being altered or modified: when a definition is non-perspicuous, Aristotle tells us at *Top.* VI 13 151ᵇ7–8, it must be "corrected and reconfigured

---

* Compare: "What we are about to say will also be more convincing to people who have previously heard the pleas of the arguments disputing them" (*Cael.* I 10 279ᵇ7–9); "refutations of those who dispute them are demonstrations of the contrary arguments" (*EE* I 3 1215ᵃ6–7).

(*sundiorthôsanta kai suschêmatisanta*)" until it is made clear. The same process applies to the reputable beliefs and perceptual evidence themselves, since they may conflict not only with the definition but also with each other. Again, this may result in their being modified, often by uncovering ambiguities within them or in the argument supporting them, or by drawing distinctions that uncover complexities in these, or they may be rejected entirely, provided that their appearance of truth is explained away.

The canonical occasion for the use of honest dialectic, as of the Socratic elenchus and plain dialectic, is the examination of a respondent. The relevant premises for the questioner to use, therefore, are the reputable beliefs in his catalogue that his respondent will accept. Just how wide this set of beliefs is in a given case depends naturally on how accessible to untrained respondents the subject matter is on which he is being examined. We may all have some beliefs about thunder, birds' eggs, animal reproduction, and other phenomena readily perceptible to everyone and which are—for that very reason—reputable. But, as we mentioned earlier, about fundamental explanatory notions in an esoteric science we may have none at all.

When a scientist is investigating by himself, the class of premises he will select from is the catalogue of *all* the raw starting-points of his science, despite a natural human inclination to do otherwise:

> [People] seem to inquire up to a certain point, but not as far as it is possible to take the puzzle. For it is customary for all of us to make our inquiry not with an eye to the thing at hand but with an eye to the person who says the contrary. For a person even inquires within himself up to the point at which he is no longer able to argue against himself. That is why a person who is going to inquire well must be capable of objecting by means of objections proper to the relevant genus, and this comes from having a theoretical grasp on all the differentiae. (*Cael.* II 13 294^{b}6–13)

It is a common complaint in *GA* about previous thinkers that they have failed in this regard:

> Democritus made this error [about shedding of teeth], then, in speaking universally without investigating what happens in all cases. But this is what we must do. For it is necessary for the one who speaks universally to say something about all cases. (*GA* V 8 788^{b}17–20)

Hence a scientist will want to err on the side of excess, adding any reputable belief, any perceptual evidence, that appears to have any relevance whatsoever to his catalogue. When he formulates definitions of candidate scientific starting-points from which he thinks he can demonstrate the raw ones, he must then examine himself to see whether he really does have the scientific knowledge of it that he thinks he does. If he is investigating together with fellow scientists, others may examine him: we all do better with the aid of co-workers (*NE* X 7 1177^{a}34). What he is doing is using honest dialectic on himself or having it used on him. But this, we see, is little different from the final stage—stage (4)—of the induction we looked at earlier. Induction, as we might put it, is in its final stage (possibly self-directed) honest dialectic.

In a famous and much debated passage, Aristotle writes:

> We must, as in the other cases, set out the things that appear to be so, and first go through the puzzles, and, in that way, show preferably all the reputable beliefs about these ways of being affected, or, if not all of them, then most of them and the ones with the most authority. For if the objections are refuted and the reputable beliefs are left standing, that would be an adequate showing. (*NE* VII 1 1145^{b}2–7)

The specific topic of the comment is "these ways of being affected," which are self-control and its lack as well as resilience and softness, as in the parallel passage in the *Physics* that we looked at, namely IV 4 211^{a}7–11, about place. Some people think that it applies only to this topic and should not be generalized, even though "as in the other cases" surely suggests a wider scope. And, as we can now see that scope *is* in fact entirely general, since it describes the honest dialectical or inductive route to the starting-points of *all* the sciences and methods of inquiry, with *tithenai ta phainomena* ("setting out the things that appear to be so") describing the initial phase in which the raw starting-points are collected and catalogued.

Now that we know what it means for honest dialectic of the sort employed by the philosopher to provide a route to the explanatory starting-points of the philosophical sciences, we are in a position to see that it is just such a route that *GC*, *Mete.*, and *GA* take to those of natural science (a glance at the Index will show how often puzzles are in focus). Since this route is the sort any science must take to show its explanatory starting-points, the investigation it undertakes is indeed a scientific one. It is not, to be sure, a demonstration from starting-points, but rather a showing of the starting-points themselves, which, if successful, allows us to achieve the sort of puzzle-free grasp on them that comes with genuine understanding.

Prime Matter and the Transformation of the Elements

The *Physics* ends with the following sentence: "the primary mover causes eternal movement for an unlimited time. It is evident, therefore, that it is indivisible and without parts, and has no magnitude" (VIII 10 267^{b}24–26). This mover, as we have seen, is the primary god, the immovable mover, which is "the sort of starting-point on which the heaven and nature depend" (*Met.* XII 7 1072^{b}13–14), and whose location (though not place: the god has no place) is outside the universe. Hence, as no part of the universe, he falls outside the ambit even of a science like astronomy (cosmology) that deals with the superlunary world, and with the sublunary, only as a part, so to speak, of it. It is this double fact that explains the odd structure of the *De Caelo*. For in Books I–II *De Caelo* deals with the universe as a whole, including the superlunary part, which the *Physics*, as natural science, left largely unexplored, although of course, many of the concepts it analyzes, such as movement, place, time, and causation have application there. But then in Book III, as in *Mete.* I 2, *De Caelo* explores the elements from that same general perspective: thus it discusses not just the superlunary element, ether or primary body, which (as such) is absent from the *Physics*, but also the sublunary ones—earth, water, air, fire. For the earth, after all, is as much a part of the universe as the various celestial spheres.

Moreover, the affections on which it focuses have to do with the sorts of movements used to determine the elements in the first place, whether upward (fire), downward (earth), or in a circle (ether). These are the lightness and heaviness discussed in *Cael.* IV, where "the unconditionally heavy is what sinks to the bottom of all things, and the unconditionally light, what rises to the top" (IV 4 311^{a}17–18). It is noteworthy—indeed, Aristotle explicitly notes it—how ill suited these affections are to explain how the elements are transformed into each other:

> Of these, heavy and light are neither capable of affecting nor of being affected. For they are not said of things in virtue of their affecting something else or being affected by something else. The elements, though, must be capable of affecting and being affected by each other, since they mix and change into each other. (*GC* II 2 329^{b}20–24)

Cael. III 6–7 explains why such a transformation must occur, but without explaining how it happens, since the affections of bodies used to explain it in *GC* II 4—hot, cold, wet, dry—lie outside its purview.

Three questions naturally arise at this point. The first concerns the definitions of the elements themselves. The first few chapters of *De Caelo* suggest that earth, water, fire, air, and ether are defined by their natural movements, and these by their proper places. Thus earth naturally moves down because its proper place is down at the center of the universe, while fire naturally moves up because its proper place is up at the universe's periphery. The following text, however, makes it clear that heaviness and lightness derive from the more primitive differentiae used in the explanation of elemental transformation:

> Because there are three compositions (*suntheseôn*), one might put first the one from what some people call the elements—for example, earth, air, water, and fire. And yet perhaps it is better to speak of composition from the capacities, and not from all of them, but as stated previously in other works.* For wet, dry, hot, and cold are matter of the composite bodies, while the other differentiae—for example, heaviness and lightness, density and rarity, roughness and smoothness, and the other corporeal affections of this sort—follow along with these. (*PA* II 1 646ᵃ12–20).

So one problem is to explain just how heaviness and lightness do follow along with these others: is one lot basic and the other derived? A second problem, adverted to in the second sentence of this text, with its suggestion that composition is from capacities, not from what some people call elements (see *GC* II 3 330ᵇ21–25), is that of the status and identity of the elements as the basic building blocks from which "all the works of nature are composed" (*Mete.* IV 12 389ᵇ27–28). The third problem, related to this one, is raised precisely by elemental transformation. For if elements can come to be from each other, so that what was earth is water, then air, then fire, it seems that there must be some underlying material substrate m that persists as one and the same through the change. But m, which obviously cannot be itself an element, now seems to be yet more primitive, more basic, than the supposedly most basic things. Since the traditional name for m is "prime matter," this problem may be put this way: is Aristotle committed to the existence of prime matter?

When Aristotle tells us that by matter he means "that which, intrinsically, is neither said to be a [this] something, nor some quantity, nor anything else by which being is determined" (*Met.* VII 3 1029ᵃ20–21), the matter he is referring to is part of a thought experiment in which the

---

* The reference is to *GC* II 2.

ultimate subject of predication is isolated by a process of stripping away attributes and dispositions from the substance to which they belong—a thought experiment alienated onto thinkers other than Aristotle himself by the phrase "for those who investigate in this way" (1029ª19) and later by the phrase "for those who try to get a theoretical grasp on things in this way" (1029ª26–27). Nonetheless, Aristotle seems to be committed, as we just saw, to an intrinsically featureless matter of this sort—thought, indeed, to be just what the term *prôtê hulê* refers to.

Let us start, then, with his use of that term. At *Ph.* II 1 192ª29 what *prôtê hulê* refers to is a thing's matter-based nature, which is not intrinsically featureless. At *GA* I 20 729ª32 the female menses, again not intrinsically featureless, are said to be like it because they provide the matter for the embryo, not the form. At *Met.* V 4 1015ª7–10, it is once more a thing's matter-based nature, which would be water "if all meltable things are water." At *Met.* 3 1014ᵇ32 it is the matter, again not featureless, from which a thing is first made. At V 6 1017ª5–6, where it is contrasted with ultimate matter, it is "divisible in form," and so must have a form. At VIII 4 1044ª23, it is again contrasted with ultimate matter, and so cannot be featureless prime matter, which must be ultimate if it is to underlie the transformation of the elements. At IX 7 1049ª24–27, fire (again not intrinsically feature-less) would be *prôtê hulê* if other elements were composed of it, but not it of anything else (a similar story is told in greater detail in *Ph.* II 193ª9–28). From this complete survey it is clear that Aristotle does not use *prôtê hulê* to refer to intrinsically featureless prime matter.

Better evidence for a commitment to such matter is provided by the following text, which uses the cognate term *prôton hupokeimenon*:

> In one way too the matter passes away and comes to be, and in another way it does not. For as *that in which*, it does intrinsically pass away, since what passes away—the lack—is present in it; but as what is potentially, it does not intrinsically pass away, but must be incapable of passing away and coming to be. For if it came to be, there must have been some first underlying subject (*prôton hupokeimenon*) from which it came to be and is present in it. This, though, is the [material] nature itself, so that it will be before coming to be [which is impossible]. (For by "matter" I mean the first underlying subject of each thing from which it not coincidentally comes to be and which is present in it.) And if it passes away, it will come to this [material nature] at last, so that it will have passed away before it has passed away [which is also impossible]. (*Ph.* I 9 192ª25–34)

This text, with its focus on change and its conceptual requirements, provides a nice segue into the problem of elemental transformation.

The elements earth, water, air, and fire, which are by definition the most primitive of sublunary bodies, can nonetheless change into one another in a way determined by their ultimate differentiae—hot, cold, wet, dry. If elements are adjacent, so that like earth and water, they share a differentia, transformation occurs when one of the differentia masters its contrary (*GC* II 4 331ª27–30). Suppose, then, that earth (E) is first transformed into water (W), then into air (A), then into fire (F), so that m (the underlying subject requisite for all change) is E at t_1 and W at t_2 and A at t_3 and F at t_4. Since m underlies all elemental transformation, it cannot have any of the ultimate differentiae as an intrinsic attribute: if it did, it would not be able to lose them. But because these differentiae are the ultimate ones, there are no others m can possibly have (II 1 329ª10–13). So it must have these differentiae, but not in the same way as the elements themselves (329ª24–35). Thus while fire is essentially or intrinsically hot, m, while it may in fact be hot, must also be potentially cold, and so must be hot only coincidentally. For matter is "that which, primarily and intrinsically, is *potentially*" hot, cold, and the rest, without being any of them intrinsically or actually (*Met.* XII 4 1070ᵇ12–13). It seems, then, that m must be intrinsically featureless matter.

However, if m is to underlie elemental transformation, a numerically identical portion or quantity of it must persist through the transformation: "The thing (whatever it is) by being which it underlies is the same, but its being is not the same" (*GC* I 3 319ᵇ3–4). But because it seems to possess none of the ultimate contrary differentiae intrinsically, such a portion of intrinsically featureless matter seems to impose no constraints whatsoever on element transformation. So, at the elemental level (and hence on up), anything could come from anything. But this Aristotle rules out:

> Let us first take it, then, that no being whatsoever is by nature such as to do or suffer any random thing due to any random thing, nor does anything come to be from just anything, except if one takes a coincidental case. For how could pale come to be from musical, unless musical were coincident with the not pale or with the dark?* Instead, pale comes from not pale—and not from any not pale but from dark, or something intermediate between the two. And musical comes to be from not musical—except not from any not musical but from unmusical, or

---

* That is, unless musical and pale or dark were coincidental attributes of the same substantial subject.

something intermediate between the two, if there is such. Nor again do things pass away into the first random thing—for example, the pale does not pass away into the musical, except coincidentally, but into the not pale, and not into any random one but into the dark or the intermediate. Similarly too the musical passes away into the not musical, and not into any random one but into the unmusical or into some intermediate, if there is such. (*Ph.* I 5 188^{a}31–^{b}8)

Since elemental transformation is not in fact indiscriminate, then, but is constrained by the causal relations holding between the ultimate differentiae, m's defining potentialities must themselves be constrained by these causal relations. That is why Aristotle can simultaneously think that the elements come to be from *prôtê hulê*, and that they come to be from each other: "Since the elements cannot come to be either from an incorporeal thing or from another body, it remains for them to come to be from each other" (*Cael.* III 6 305^{a}31–32). What an element comes from, then, is another element, but what underlies the transformation of one into the other is *prôtê hulê*, which is not a body separate from the elements, and has no essential or intrinsic attributes besides the potentialities determined by the causal relations between the ultimate differentiae. Thus *Mete.* IV 1 378^{b}34 and 2 379^{b}19–20 actually identify matter with the affectable capacities, namely, dry and wet.

Normally, of course, a thing's potentialities or dispositional properties are based in its actual or categorical properties, as table salt's solubility in water is based in its molecular structure. But when we get down to ultimate components, there may be no base of this sort, as may be true, for example, in the case of mass or gravitational attraction. At that point, what we confront are dispositions or potentialities that are simply brute. All we can say is that m is something that (a) when coincidentally cold and dry (earth) has the potentiality to become cold and wet (water), and (b) when coincidentally cold and wet (water) has the potentiality to become hot and wet (air), and (c) when coincidentally hot and wet (air) has the potentiality to become hot and dry (fire), and (d) when coincidentally hot and dry (fire) has the potentiality to become cold and dry (earth). The higher-order disposition that m possesses to behave in these four ways but not in others shows that it is not a parcel of featureless matter, which is dispositionless as well as in all other ways indefinite. These causal continuities exhibited across the four ways explain why m is the same thing throughout them. After all, causal continuity (perhaps between their successive stages or so-called time-slices) may be what explains the diachronic identity of substances themselves.

Overall, then, there seems to be no compelling reason to think that the intrinsically featureless matter that is part of the thought experiment is something that Aristotle himself needs or uses. In fact, it is something he pretty clearly rejects as incoherent.

> By matter I mean that which, intrinsically, is neither said to be a something, nor a quantity, nor anything else by which being is given definition. For there is something that each of these is predicated of, whose being is distinct from that of each of the things predicated. For while the other things are predicated of the substance, this is predicated of the matter. And so the last thing [in this series] will not be intrinsically a something, or a quantity, or anything else—nor indeed is it the denials of these, since they too will belong to it coincidentally. (*Met.* VII 3 1029ª20–26)

For how could something intrinsically featureless, and so lacking an essence, a what-it-is, or a definition possibly be primary in knowledge, as substance is required to be (*Met.* VII 1 1028ª33)?

What Are the Elements?

The textbook answer to the question of what Aristotle's elements are is, earth, water, air, and fire. The Aristotelian sublunary world, we all learn, is an EWAF one. It can be a bit of a shock, therefore, to come across passages that put the textbook answer in question. Here are some from the treatises we are looking at:

> Fire, however, and air and each of the others that have been mentioned are not simple, but mixed. The simple ones are like these, but not the same as them—for example, if something is like fire, it is fire-form (*puroeides*), not fire, and if like air, it is air-form (*aeroeides*), and likewise in the other cases.* (*GC* II 3 330ᵇ21–25)

> At the center and around the center what is heaviest and coldest is set apart, namely, earth and water. Around these, and continuous with them, are air and what due to custom we call "fire,"

---

* The words *puroeides* and *aeroeides* occur only here in Aristotle, though the latter also occurs in the pseudo-Aristotelian, *Color.* 3 793ᵇ5.

but it is not fire. But we must understand that of what we call "air" the part surrounding the earth is wet and hot because it is vaporous and contains exhalations from the earth, whereas the part above this is actually hot and dry. For vapor's nature is wet and cold, that of exhalation hot and dry. And vapor is potentially like water, exhalation potentially like fire. (*Mete.* I 3 340^{b}19–23)

In addition, we have the text we looked at earlier from *PA*: "perhaps it is better to speak of composition from the capacities" (II 1 646^{a}14–15)—that is, from hot, cold, wet, dry. Notice how much in harmony with our account of the transformation of the elements that thought is. Notice too that in *GA* the elements are always referred to as "the *so-called* elements" (I 1 715^{a}11, II 3 736^{b}31)—not necessarily implying that they are not elements, but leaving open the possibility that they are not.*

Distinguishing, then, the fire-form, which is simple and genuinely elemental, from so-called fire, which is mixed, let us try to find out what it is. In the case of the latter Aristotle gives a fairly explicit answer:

Cases in which the underlying subject is hot in virtue of being affected also make it apparent that cold is not a certain nature but a privation. Maybe even the nature of fire may turn out to be something of this sort. For perhaps the underlying subject is smoke or charcoal, smoke being always hot (for smoke is a vapor**), whereas charcoal, when extinguished, is cold. (*PA* II 2 649^{a}18–22; also *GC* II 5 331^{b}25–26)

What, though, of elemental fire? In its case what is insisted on is that it is hot and dry. But what is also insisted on, as we saw, is that it by nature moves upward to its proper place on the periphery of the universe, just as earth moves downward toward its proper place at the center. But this follows along, as we also saw, with its hotness and dryness:

Wet, dry, hot, and cold are matter of the composite bodies, while the other differentiae—for example, heaviness and lightness, density and rarity, roughness and smoothness, and the other corporeal affections of this sort—follow along with these. (*PA* II 1 646^{a}16–20)

---

* See Crowley for discussion of the meaning of the phrase τὰ καλούμενα στοιχεῖα.

** See *Mete.* I 3 340^{b}2n.

Is it hotness and dryness, then, that hold the key to elemental fire, or is it natural movement?

Let us start with hotness and dryness. About their nature, Aristotle is also explicit:

> The elements must be capable of affecting and being affected by each other, since they mix and change into each other. Hot and cold, by contrast, and wet and dry are said of things, the one lot in virtue of their affecting, the other in virtue of their being affectable. For hot is what aggregates things of the same genus (for the disaggregating, which is just what they say fire does, is the aggregating of things of the same genus, since this results in removing what is alien), and cold is what brings together and aggregates alike things of the same genus and things not of the same genus. Wet is what is not bounded by any defining mark proper to it but easily bounded; dry is what is easily bounded by a defining mark proper to it, but difficult [for other things] to bound. (*GC* II 2 329^{b}22–33)

Moreover, the fact that the hot and the dry go together is itself explained by the "active" member of the pair: "the sort of thing heat accomplishes is to make things more composed, denser, and drier" (*Mete.* IV 2 380^{a}5–6). But though the hot aggregates and composes, so too, we see, does the cold. For "cold solidifies those things consisting of water only, while fire solidifies those things consisting of earth" (*PA* II 2 649^{a}30–31). But since cold is just a lack or deficiency of heat (*GC* I 3 318^{b}17, *Mete.* IV 2 380^{a}8, *GA* II 6 743^{a}36), heat again emerges as the key player: "Drying things is always either heating them or cooling them, and in both cases is due to heat, whether internal heat or external heat" (*Cael.* IV 5 382^{b}16–18).

Focusing on heat, then, we may renew our question: are hotness and dryness the key to what heat is, or is it its natural movement—most manifest in fire—upward?

Pneuma and the Animate

According to Aristotle we find in nature an apparently continuous scale of beings, in which, for example, animate beings—beings with souls—differ only very slightly from inanimate ones in their level of formation:

> Nature proceeds from the inanimate to the animals by such small steps that, because of the continuity, we fail to see to

which the boundary and the middle between them belongs. For the first genus of thing after the inanimate is the plant genus, and, among these, one differs from another in seeming to have a greater share of life; but the whole genus, in comparison with the other inanimate bodies, appears almost as animate, while in comparison with the animal genus it appears inanimate. The change from plants to animals is continuous, as we said before. (*HA* VIII 1 588^{b}4–12)

The sublunary so-called elements aside, the simplest beings on this scale are homoeomerous or uniform stuffs, such as wood, olive oil, flesh, and bone, whose parts have the same account as the whole (*GC* I 1 314^{a}20, 10 328^{a}10–12). These are constituted out of the elements in some ratio, when the active capacities (hot, cold) in the elements master the corresponding passive ones (dry, wet):

> Having determined these things, we must grasp the workings of these, namely, the workings of the ones capable of affecting, and the species of the affectable ones. First off, then, universally [speaking], unconditional coming to be and natural change is the function of these capacities, as is the opposite passing away that is in accord with nature. And these processes occur both in plants and in animals and their parts. Unconditional and natural coming to be is a change due to these capacities—when they stand in the right ratio (*logos*)—in the matter that by nature underlies a given thing, this being the capacities to be affected that we have just mentioned. When the hot and the cold master the matter they cause coming to be. (*Mete.* IV 1 378^{b}26–379^{a}1)

The fundamental form of such mastery is concoction (*pepsis*), which is responsible for producing a uniform stuff, and for preserving its nature thereafter:

> Concoction, then, is a completion due to the natural and proper heat that comes from the underlying affectables, these being the matter proper to the given thing. For when it has been concocted it is completed and has come to be. And the starting-point of the completion comes about due to the proper heat, even if certain external aids helped to accomplish it—for example, nourishment is helped to concoct even due to baths and due to other things of this sort. And the end in some cases is the nature—but nature, we say, as form and substance. . . . Concoction, in fact,

is what everything is affected by when its matter—that is, its liquid—is mastered. For this is what is determined by the heat in its nature. For as long as the ratio (*logos*) is in this, the thing has its nature. (*Mete.* IV 2 379ᵇ18–35)

Natural heat is thus *formative* heat—the thing in nature partly responsible for the coming to be and preservation of matter-form compounds.

Uniform stuffs, as minimally formed, have a low level of such heat. As form is added, so that stuffs come to constitute the structural parts of animals (such as hands and eyes), and these to constitute whole animals of different degrees of complexity, natural heat increases: "the more complete ones are hotter in nature and wetter and not earthy" (*GA* II 1 732ᵇ31–32). Such animals more completely pass on their form to offspring (733ᵃ33–ᵇ2). Since human beings are the most complete or most perfect animals (II 4 737ᵇ26–27), they are also the hottest and most estimable:

> All animals with lungs breathe. . . . Why some have this part, and why those having it need to breathe, is that the more estimable of the animals are hottest. For at the same time their soul must have been made more estimable, since they have a more estimable nature than the cold ones. Hence too . . . that animal in which the blood in the lung is purest and most plentiful is the most upright, namely, man. The cause due to which he alone has his upper part directed to the upper part of the universe is that he possesses such a part. (*Juv.* 13 477ᵃ13–23)

Although male and female human beings both have formative heat, its level is not the same in each. This is revealed by the different roles played by their respective spermatic products—seed (*sperma*) or semen (*gonê*) in the case of males, menses (*katamênia*) in that of females—in reproduction: "the male provides both the form and the starting-point of movement, while the female provides the body, that is, the matter" (*GA* I 20 729ᵃ9–11).

What seed does to menses to form them into a fetus is likened to what a carpenter does to wood to make it into a piece of furniture:

> Nothing comes away from the carpenter to the matter of the pieces of wood he works on, nor is there any part of the craft of carpentry in what is being produced, but the shape—that is, the form—is produced from the carpenter by means of the movement in the matter, that is, his soul, in which the form is present, and his scientific knowledge move his hands or some other part with a certain sort of movement—distinct when what comes

to be from it is distinct, the same when what comes to be from it is the same—and the hands move the instruments, and the instruments move the matter. Similarly, the nature present in the male, in those that emit seed, uses the seed as an instrument and as possessing active movement, just as in craft productions the tools are in movement. For the movement of the craft is in a way in them. (*GA* I 22 730^{b}11–23)

In the way that the movement of the carpenter's hands has its starting-point in the form of the product present in his soul, then, the movement in the seed has its starting-point in a form—namely, that of the male progenitor. Hence the very same formal constituents exemplified as potentialities in his form are exemplified as movements in his seed, guaranteeing that these movements are (at least to begin with) formally identical to the potentialities that transmit them: "when it comes into the uterus it composes and moves the female's residue with just the same movement that it is moving with itself" (*GA* II 3 737^{a}20–22). Were this not so, their transmission to seed could not result in the transmission of the male's form to the offspring.

What enables the transmission of such movements to seed is, first, that they are present in the male's blood—where, encoded in formative heat, they are responsible for the preservation of his form—and, second, that seed itself is a very concentrated or concocted blood product:

That blood is the last stage of the nourishment in blooded animals, and its analogue in bloodless ones, has been said previously. And since semen too is a residue of nourishment, that is, from its last stage, it will be either blood, its analogue, or something composed of these. And since each of the parts is produced from blood as it is being concocted and somehow divided into parts, and since the seed (although quite different from blood when, having been concocted, it is secreted), when non-concocted and when forced out by too frequent indulgence in sexual intercourse, is sometimes still bloodlike when it has come out, it is evident that the seed must be a residue of nourishment, namely, of the blood, the one that is finally distributed to the parts. And because of this it has great capacity (and in fact the discharge of the pure and healthy blood is cause of weakness) and that offspring should be like their parents is reasonable. For what has gone to the parts is like what is left over. So the seed of the hand, of the face, or of the whole animal is in an undifferentiated way a hand, a face, or a whole animal—that

> is, as each of the latter is actually, such the seed is potentially.
> (*GA* I 19 726^{b}1–18)

When the male's formal movements are transmitted by concoction to menses, therefore, they first initiate the formation of the fetal heart. Once the heart is formed, the fetus then grows automatically, drawing its nourishment from its mother through the umbilicus, and in the process transmitting formative movements via the blood to the other developing parts (II 1 735^{a}12–26).

However, menses are also a type of seed—"seed that is not pure but needs working on" (*GA* I 20 728^{a}26–27). For a female's formative heat is cooler than a male's, and so cannot complete the final stage of forming or concocting menses into pure seed (I 20 728^{a}18–21). In species without "separated" males, however, this may not be so:

> If there is any genus of animal that, though the female exists, contains no separated male, it is possible that this generates an animal from itself. Though this has not been observed in a reliable way up to now at least—although a case in the fish genus does make one hesitate. For among the ones called erythrinus no male has so far been seen, whereas females full of embryos have been. But of this we have as yet no reliable experience. (*GA* II 5 741^{a}32–38)

Nonetheless, even in species where males and females are clearly distinguished, a female can concoct her menses (or the spermatic residue in it) to within that last stage of becoming pure seed, so that for each actual movement in seed, there is a corresponding potential movement stemming from the female form (*GA* IV 3 768^{a}11–14). While menses have the potential to move in such a way as to become a fetus, therefore, they cannot do so until they are set moving by seed, since "in the things that come to be by nature or by craft, |734^{a}30| what is potentially comes to be due to what is actually" (II 1 734^{a}29–31). Equally well, of course, without menses to move, no new animal is generated either.

Just which movements will underlie the offspring's form—whether, for example, it will be male or female—depends on the interaction between the movements in the seed and the potential movements in the menses (*GA* IV 3 768^{b}5–12). If a male movement is transmitted successfully to the menses, the offspring will have the corresponding component of the male form. If it fails to be transmitted, it may be wholly resisted, in which case it is replaced by the opposing movement in the menses, or resisted to a lesser degree, with different consequences in each case (768^{a}7–9, 768^{b}7–8).

The difference, then, between male *gonê* (always "semen" in the translation) or *sperma* (always "seed" in the translation) and the seed (or spermatic residue) in female menses is in one way quite small: they both encode more or less the same genetic information, as we would say. But in another way it is quite large: only male semen contains that information as actual movements, making it "the first thing containing a starting-point of generation" (*GA* I 14 724^{b}12–14) (leaving aside possible species in which female seed also contains it). The question is, how does the semen encode this information?

Semen, as we now know, is made up of individual sperms, each viable one of which is in principle capable of fertilizing a female ovum. Aristotle's view is quite different. For him the quantity of semen ejaculated is the fertilizing agent, not its sub-parts, and its viability, to call it that, depends on the level of formative or soul-producing heat in it relative to the quantity of female menses that it must work up:

> In general, then, female and male are set apart from each other in relation to production of males and production of females due to the causes just mentioned. Nonetheless there must also be a proportion in their relation to each other. For all things that come to be either in accord with craft or nature exist in virtue of a certain ratio (*logos*). Now the hot, if it too is mastering, dries up the wet things, whereas if it is very deficient it does not compose them, instead it must stand in the mean ratio (*logos*) in relation to what is being handicrafted. If it does not, just as in cooking where too much fire burns the food, while too little does not cook it, and either way the result is that what is being produced fails to be completed, likewise too in the case of the mixing of what comes from the male and what comes from the female there must be a proportion. (*GA* IV 2 767^{a}13–23)

Nonetheless, if the menses is not to be uniformly concocted, but rather differentially so, in the way requisite for stage-wise embryonic development, in which first the fetal heart is formed, then the parts around the head, and so on, then the semen too, as Aristotle recognizes, must be "somehow divided into parts" (*GA* I 19 726^{b}5–6). Nothing is said explicitly about how this division actually takes place. But since semen is foamy, and foam contains bubbles, it is likely that the surrounding membranes of these are what mark the divisions, and encapsulate the formative heat in them:

> The cause of the whiteness of seed is that the semen is a foam, and foam is white, and most so that composed of the smallest particles, and small in the way that each bubble is invisible,

just as actually happens in the case when water and olive oil are mixed and beaten. (*GA* II 2 736ᵃ13–18)

It seems, then, that we should think of the male semen as somehow divided into bubbles, with different ones embodying the different movements needed to form the different parts of the embryo, and to endow them in turn with the formative heat needed for their growth and preservation.* Thus it is that we hear about "the proper heat present in each part" (*GA* V 4 784ᵃ35–ᵇ1, 6 786ᵃ20–21).

While seed, as a concocted blood product, is a very purified type of nourishment, its natural heat, in which its formative movements are encoded, is of a quite special sort:

> Now the capacity of all souls seems to be associated with a body distinct from and more divine than the so-called elements. And as souls differ from each other in esteem and lack of esteem, so too this sort of nature differs. For within the seed of everything there is present that which makes the seeds be fertile, the so-called hot. This is not fire or that sort of capacity, but the pneuma enclosed within the seed and within the foamy part— that is, the nature in the pneuma, which is an analogue of the element belonging to the stars. (*GA* II 3 736ᵇ29–737ᵃ1)

Characterized as "connate" (*sumphuton*), because it is not drawn in from outside but produced and maintained inside the body (*PA* II 2 648ᵃ36– 649ᵇ8), it is the sort of pneuma that plays a fundamental role in nourishment and reproduction (*GA* II 6 741ᵇ37–742ᵃ16). It is distinguished from air and breath (also *pneuma*) in only one text that may not be by Aristotle**:

> From the dry exhalation, when it is pushed by the cold so that it flows, wind is produced. For this is nothing except much air moving and gathered together. It is at the same time also said to be pneuma. But something is said to be pneuma in another way when it is the ensouled and fertile substance (*empsuchos te kai gonimos ousia*) in plants and animals and which pervades all things. (*Mu.* 4 394ᵇ7–11)

---

* For further discussion, to which my account is indebted, see Marwan Rashed's probing paper, "A Latent Difficulty in Aristotle's Theory of Semen: The Homogeneous Nature of Semen and the Role of the Frothy Bubble" in Falcon & Lefebvre, pp. 108–29.

** On the authorship of *De Mundo*, see Thom, pp. 3–5 and Bos-1.

The reproductive system, indeed, is in many ways simply a means of transmitting the form-preserving digestive system (of which blood and the heart are parts) into new matter, thereby initiating the formation of a new self-maintaining creature. That is why both functions are assigned to the *threptikon* or nutritive part of the soul (*DA* II 4 416ᵃ19–20, 416ᵇ11–12).*

Although many natural beings (for example, ones we think of as inanimate) do not preserve their form by means of nourishment, or transmit it by means of sexual reproduction, pneuma has a fundamental role to play in their existence too:

> Animals and plants come to be on earth and in liquid because in earth there is water present and in water pneuma, and in all pneuma there is soul-involving heat, so that in a certain way all things are full of soul. (*GA* III 11 762ᵃ18–21)

> Democritus, however, omitting to mention the for-the-sake-of-which, reduces to necessity all that nature uses—but though they are such, they are nonetheless for the sake of something and in each case for the sake of what is better. So nothing prevents the teeth from being produced and being shed in the way he says, but it is not because of these things, but rather because of the end—although these are causes as movers, as instruments, and as matter, since it is reasonable, indeed, for nature to make most things using pneuma as instrument. For just as some things have many uses where the crafts are concerned—as in blacksmithing are the hammer and the anvil—so does pneuma in those composed by nature. (*GA* V 8 789ᵇ2–12)

Yet despite its manifest importance, no focused discussion of pneuma occurs in Aristotle's extant works—unless we count *De Spiritu* among them.** This makes it difficult to determine his views with confidence—difficulty exacerbated by the fact that pneuma may be more than one thing (as a glance at the Index will show). But by piecing together what he does say, a reasonably clear picture emerges.

---

* In "What is Aristotle's *Generation of Animals* About?" (Falcon & Lefebvre, pp. 77–88), Pierre Pellegrin argues indeed that *GA* is itself fundamentally a treatise on generation and nutrition.

** A. Bos and R. Ferwerda, *Aristotle on the Life-Bearing Spirit (De Spiritu)* (Leiden, 2008) argues.

From its role in embryology alone, for example, we can see that pneuma transmits movement by being itself in movement. The role accorded to it in animal movement confirms this fact:

> [*Pneuma*] is evidently well disposed by nature to impart movement and supply strength. At all events, the functions of movement are pushing and pulling, so that its instrument (*organon*) must be capable of increasing in size and contracting. And this is just the nature of pneuma, since it increases in size and contracts unforcedly, and is able to pull and push for the same reason. (*MA* 10 703ᵃ18–23)

Moreover, because the movements it imparts are formative, they must be complex and various—able, as geneticists now put it, to *code for* all of an animal's parts. Since movements are "either in a circle or in a straight line or in a combination of the two" (*Ph.* VIII 8 261ᵇ28–29), all the complex movements pneuma can produce must be some such combination. What makes this possible is that by actively expanding and contracting, and so pushing and pulling, it can cause not just rectilinear but also circular movements: "Spinning in a circle is a compound of pushing and pulling, since what causes something to spin must be pushing one part of it and pulling another, for it draws one part away from itself and another part toward itself" (*Ph.* VII 2 244ᵃ2–4). Hence all movements—rectilinear, circular, or a combination of the two—can be caused by pneuma (*DA* III 10 433ᵇ25–26).

Initially pneuma is assigned a role in the transmission of form to noncontroversially animate beings. However, its role gets expanded to explain other phenomena, such as transparency:

> For it is not insofar as something is water or insofar as it is air that it is visible, but because there is a certain nature in it that is the same in both of them and in the [eternal] body above. (*DA* II 7 418ᵇ7–9)

> What we call transparent is not something special to air, or water, or any other of the bodies usually called transparent, but is a common nature or capacity present in these, and in all other bodies in a greater or lesser degree, and does not exist separately. (*Sens.* 3 439ᵃ21–23)

Then, because pneuma is involved in soul transmission, soul is to some extent itself attributed to anything in which pneuma is present. When "the capacity of all soul" is associated with "the nature in the pneuma that is an analogue of the element belonging to the stars," then, the point of analogy is that the nature in question is both transparent and—when combined with other elements, whose movements are rectilinear—an appropriate transmitter of soul, form, and life. For the element that belongs to the stars, which is *ether* (*aithêr*) or primary body (*sôma prôton*), is a body "different from and additional to the elemental ones met with here, more divine than, and prior to, all of them" (*Cael.* I 2 269ª30–32), and is both transparent and in eternal circular movement (I 3 270ª12–ᵇ25). Hence pneuma is a "body more divine than the so-called elements," because it is an analogue of ether, which is in fact more divine than they.

Focusing now on pneuma, let us see how best to understand it. One thing we know is that "it increases in size and contracts unforcedly, and is able to pull and push for the same reason" (*MA* 10 703ª21–22), but another is that it is "hot air" (*GA* II 2 736ª1). Putting the two together we have air increasing in size and contracting due to heat. And this heat, we are within an inch of seeing, is primarily a factor to be understood in terms of its natural upward movement. For pneuma, we see, is not a new element, but rather a construction from old ones introduced to explain the existence in the sublunary world of the circular movements crucial for the transmission and preservation of forms, and so for the coming to be and passing away of the matter-form compounds whose forms they are. But it is equally central to the explanation of animal movement, perception, and thought:

> The movement of animals is like that of automata, which are set moving when a small movement occurs: the strings are released and the pegs strike against one another. . . . For animals have instrumental parts that are of the same sort as these, namely, sinews and bones; when these are relaxed or loosened movement occurs. . . . In an animal, however, [unlike in an automaton] the same part is capable of becoming both larger and smaller and to change its shape, as the parts increase in size because of heat, contract again because of cold, and undergo alteration. Alteration, however, is caused by appearances, perceptions, and intelligible objects. For perceptions are an immediate sort of alteration, and appearances and intelligible objects have the capacity of the things themselves [that gave rise to them]. For in a way the intelligible form of the pleasant or painful is like the thing itself. That is why we shudder and are frightened because of understanding on its own. All these are affections and alterations; and when things in the body are altered, some become larger and some smaller. And it is not

hard to see that a small change occurring in a starting-point produces great and numerous changes at a distance from it— just as by shifting the rudder a hair's breadth you get a large shift at the prow. Besides, when under the influence of heat or cold or some other similar affection, an alteration is produced in the region of the heart, even in an imperceptibly small part of it, it produces a large difference in the body—blushing, for example, or turning white, as well as shuddering, trembling, and their contraries. (*MA* 7 701^{b}1–32)

Form of every variety, one might *almost* say, just is a sort of movement.

Immortal Soul

To the account of soul as "form of a natural body that has life potentially," the understanding (*nous*) is an intriguing exception, since it is unique among the human soul's activities in having no sublunary bodily correlate: "bodily activity is in no way associated with its activity" (*GA* II 3 736^{b}28–29; also *DA* II 1 413^{a}6–7). The puzzle immediately arises of how what is without such a correlate can develop in a fetus as a result of movements in the pneuma contained in male seed:

It is necessary to determine whether what is being composed in the female receives something, or not, from what has entered her, but also, concerning the soul in virtue of which an animal is so called (and it is an animal in virtue of the perceptual part of the soul), whether it is present within the seed and the fetus or not, and where it comes from [if it is]. For one could not regard the fetus as soulless, as in every way lacking in life. For both the seeds and the embryos of animals are no less alive than plants, and are fertile up to a certain point. That they have nutritive soul, then, is evident (and why they must acquire this first is evident from the determinations about the soul made elsewhere), but as they proceed they also have perceptual soul in virtue of which they are animals.* For they do not at the same time become animal and human, or animal and horse, and likewise in the case of the other animals. For the last thing to come to be is the end, and the end of the coming to be of each thing is what is special to it. That is why where understanding is concerned,

---

* Some editors mark a lacuna at this point.

when, how, and from where it is acquired by those that participate in this starting-point, involves a very great puzzle, and we
must try hard to get a grasp on [these things] in accord with our
capacity and to the extent possible. (*GA* II 3 736^{a}27–^{b}8)

The reason it is such a puzzle is that the various psychological functions
can be present as capacities or potentialities in seed or fetus in only a
certain number of ways:

> For [1] either they must all be produced [in the menses or mat-
> ter] without existing beforehand, or they must all preexist, or
> some must, but not others; and [2] they must be produced in
> the matter either without having entered in the male's seed, or
> having come from there; and [3] in the male they must either all
> be produced [in the seed] from outside it, or none from outside,
> or some but not others. Now then that it is impossible for all to
> be present beforehand is evident from the following. For [4] it is
> clear that it is impossible for all starting-points whose activity is
> bodily to be present without body (for example, walking without
> feet). So [5] they cannot enter [the seed] from outside. For they
> can neither enter by themselves, being inseparable, nor enter in a
> body. For the seed is a residue produced by a change in the nutri-
> ment. [6] It remains, then, that the understanding alone enters
> additionally from outside and alone is divine. For bodily activity
> is in no way associated with its activity. (*GA* II 3 736^{b}15–29)

Here [1] concerns the menses and what it contributes to the fetus; [2] concerns the seed and what it contributes; and [3] concerns the male progenitor and what he contributes to the seed. And the line of descent, as we
know, is from formative movements in the pneuma contained in the male
progenitor's blood to his seed, from seed to menses, and so to fetus. [4]
restricts our attention to starting-points of psychological functions whose
active varieties are bodily, in that they require bodily organs, as walking
requires feet and seeing requires eyes. [5] tells us the two conditions under
which these could enter something "from the outside." This signals, as [3]
makes clear, that the something they enter is the male seed. [5] then shows
that the starting-points cannot meet either of the conditions: they cannot
enter by themselves, apart from body, because they are inseparable from
it; they cannot enter as a body, because seed, as a residue produced by
nutriment, does not contain bodily parts. On the other hand, [6] because
bodily activity is in no way associated with the activity of understanding,
understanding does enter the male seed from outside. That is the picture.

Just how understanding manages to enter the seed from outside, however, is left unexplained. All that we are told is that in embryogenesis it is transmitted along with the seed yet separate from it:

> As for the body of the semen, in which comes away part of the seed of the soul-involving starting-point, part of which is separable from the body in all the ones in which a divine something is enclosed (and what is called the understanding is of this sort) and part inseparable—this body of the semen dissolves and evaporates, having a liquid and watery nature. (*GA* II 3 737ª7–12)

As a result of being transmitted in this way, however, the understanding "seems to be born in us as a sort of substance, and not to pass away" (*DA* I 4 408ᵇ18–25) and to be "presumably something more divine" (408ᵇ29). Moreover, it is "in substance an activity," and so is not "sometimes understanding and at other times not," but rather of all the elements in the human soul "it alone is immortal and eternal" (III 5 430ª18–23). These characteristics make it reasonable to suppose that understanding is transmitted along with the male seed as movements in *ether* that code for it. The following description of ether makes the supposition all but certain:

> It is equally reasonable to suppose about this body [= ether] that it is incapable of coming to be and passing away, incapable of increase and decrease, and incapable of alteration, because everything that comes to be comes to be from its contrary and from an underlying subject, and passes away similarly, namely, from an underlying subject, because of a contrary, and to a contrary, as was said in our first accounts [in *Ph.* I 7–9]. Also, contrary spatial movements are of contraries. If, then, this body can have no contrary, because there cannot in fact be a movement contrary to spatial movement in a circle, nature seems to have correctly removed from among the contraries the body that was going to be incapable of coming to be and passing away. For coming to be and passing away belong in the realm of contraries. But then too everything that increases, increases because of something of the same genus (*suggenous*) being added to it and dissolving into its matter. But there is none from which this body has come to be. But if it is not capable of either increase or decrease, the same thinking leads us to suppose that it is not capable of alteration either. For alteration is movement with respect to quality, and qualitative states and dispositions— for example, health and disease—do not come about without

change with respect to the affections. But all natural [sublunary] bodies that change with respect to an affection we see are subject both to increase and decrease—for example, the bodies of animals and plants and their parts, and also those of the elements. So if indeed the body in circular movement does not admit of either increase or decrease, it is reasonable for it to be unalterable as well. (*Cael.* I 3 270ª12–35)

If understanding were coded for by anything other than the circular movements in ether, then, it seems that it could not itself be immortal, eternal, or ever active.

Ether, to be sure, is a bit hard to get a handle on, since it seems, for one thing, to be a sort of perpetual motion machine—something that by its very essence cannot be inactive or run out of steam. At the same time, though, it is fairly clearly something material. Hence the understanding, which is coded for by its movements, while it can come apart from earth, water, air, and fire, cannot ever become wholly disembodied. Its entry into the male seed in embryogenesis, then, is not a case of a ghost entering a machine, but—to continue the metaphor—of one sort of machine entering another. This lessens the mystery that understanding seemed to present us with even if it does not dispel it altogether. (The fact that it raises another problem, namely, of the presence of ether in the sublunary sphere, will be returned to shortly.)

The Hot, the Cold, the Wet, and the Dry

Elemental fire, we saw, is a combination of what we will now, following Aristotle, call the hot (*to thermon*) and the dry (*to xêron*)—with the hot being the active or affecting factor and the dry being the passive, affectable one. By the same token, elemental air is a combination of the hot and the wet (*to hugron*). Rather than seeing these elements as internally static things on a par with Democritean elements, however, we should see them as internally dynamic, as involving a struggle for mastery, as Aristotle calls it, in which victory now goes to one factor, now to another. And this mastery, as our exploration of pneuma makes vivid, depends on internal (natural, formative) heat and on external heat:

> For boiled things do not draw liquid into themselves, since the external heat masters the internal. But if a thing's internal heat did master, it would draw it into itself. (*Mete.* IV 3 380ᵇ22–24)

But the nature of this struggle, precisely because it is dynamic, must be understood in terms of movement—again our exploration of pneuma and its explanatory role shows us why. So within elemental air the internal dynamic struggle for mastery is one between the hot's natural upward and the wet's natural movement in a contrary direction—it is, so to speak, the resultant of those two movements.

The discussion of perceived hotness shows how resourcefully this struggle can be exploited for explanatory purposes:

> It is the differentiae of body, insofar as it is body, that are objects of touch. I mean the differentiae that determine the elements, namely, hot, cold, dry, and wet, of which we have spoken earlier in our account of the elements. The perceptual organ for these, in which the perceptual capacity called "touch" primarily belongs, is the part that is potentially such as they are. For perceiving is a sort of being affected, and so what does the affecting makes that part such as it is actually, the part being such potentially. That is why we do not perceive what is equally as hot, cold, hard, or soft [as the part], but only the excesses, the perceptual capacity being a sort of mean between the pairs of contraries in the perceptible objects. And that is why it discerns the perceptible objects. For the mean is capable of discerning, since in relation to each extreme it becomes the other. And just as what is to perceive white and black must be neither of them actively, although both potentially (and similarly too in the case of the other perceptual capacities), so in the case of touch it must be neither hot nor cold. (*DA* II 11 423^{b}27–424^{a}10)

Thus when the perceptual mean that responds to and to some extent measures hotness is tipped one way, the touched thing feels hot, while if tipped the other way, cold. But this "tipping" is precisely a movement. As we see from the account of what happens when the thing is too hot to have its temperature measured by touch:

> It is evident from this why it is that excesses in perceptible objects destroy the perceptual organs (for if the movement is too strong for the perceptual organ, the ratio is dissolved—and this, as we saw, is the perceptual capacity—just as the consonance and pitch [of a lyre] are if the strings are struck too forcefully). (*DA* II 12 424^{a}28–32)

The answer to the question, then, as to which of elemental fire's capacities should be taken as basic or defining, its tendency to move upward or its hotness and dryness, is clearly that it is the former. The Aristotelian world is in this sense a world of different sorts of movements—which is just what the *Physics* and the *De Caelo* should have led us to suspect.

But they do much more than simply *lead us to suspect* that the primary beings are substances; they tell us so outright. And in this they can hardly be thought to be alone: pretty much every work of Aristotle's from the *Categories* to the *Metaphysics* is at one in telling us that the world of beings is primarily a world of substantial beings—substances. This puts immediate pressure on the idea, which our discussion so far might mistakenly be thought to foster, that the hot, the cold, and the rest have emerged as the primary beings. For while hot exists in combination with the wet in air and with the dry in fire, it does not exist in separation from either of them. Yet being separable—being in some sense ontologically primary—is the very mark of a substance. From a different perspective, in other words, we have re-engaged with the problem of prime matter. As it cannot exist in separation from the hot, the cold, the wet, and the dry, so their active members (hot, cold) always go together with their passive ones (wet, dry). The dynamic tension at the heart of the elements that makes their natural movements their defining features requires as much.

Perhaps at this point no more is needed than a reminder that being for Aristotle is expressed by a verb, and that the god, the most substantial substance of all, the most substantial being, is an activity. For movement is "incomplete activity" (*Met.* XI 9 1066^{a}20–21), and the elements "by being always active," "by having their movement both intrinsically and within themselves," imitate "the things that cannot pass away" (IX 1050^{b}28–30).

Hylomorphism, Females, and Monsters

Astronomy is a strictly theoretical science. And it is one because ether—super-natural matter—is perfectly receptive of the forms of the various heavenly bodies, so that the theorems of astronomy, like those of mathematics, hold not just for the most part, like those of natural science, but always and with unconditional necessity. Put another way, ether does not deform those forms. Now ask yourself this question. What would happen if sublunary matter (including most importantly female menses) were like ether, what if it were perfectly receptive of form?

To get the right feel for the depth of this question we need to consider different sorts of hylomorphism, different sorts of matter-form theories.

Possible worlds are ways things might be: as it might be that you never read this. In the actual world, W_a, let us suppose, nothing could be a saw, nothing could perform the sawing function, unless it is made of iron, since no other sorts of matter in W_a are hard enough to take and keep the requisite sort of edge. In other possible worlds, however, other matter might be available to make saws out of, since in one of them, a sort of matter other than iron might be capable of acquiring and holding the edge necessary to perform the sawing function. So it will apparently not be a theorem—a necessarily true (because form-based or partly form-based) proposition—of the (productive) science of saws that all saws are, for example, magnetizable, or that all are prone to rust. But now suppose that there is a sort of matter, namely, metal, of which iron and other ferrous metals are one variety, and that in all possible worlds well-functioning saws can be made of metal, and in no possible world can they be made of something other than metal. And suppose that all metals are meltable in fire, but that not all are magnetizable. It seems, then, that it will be a theorem of the science of saws that all saws are meltable in fire, even though it is not a theorem that all saws are magnetizable.

Let us turn now to Aristotle's hylomorphism:

> Why is a saw such as it is? So that *this* may be, and for the sake of *this*. But in fact it is impossible that this thing that the saw is for the sake of should come to be unless it is made of iron. It is necessary, therefore, for it to be made of iron, if there is to be a saw with its function. The necessity, then, is hypothetical (*ex hupotheseôs*), but not [necessary] as an end. For the necessity lies in the matter, whereas the for-the-sake-of-which lies in the account. (*Ph.* II 9 200ᵃ10–15)

And in *PA* he repeats the story:

> What is of necessity is not present in all the things that are in accord with nature in the same way … what is unconditionally necessary is present in the eternal things, while what is hypothetically necessary is also present in all generated things, as it is in the products of craft—for example, a house or anything else of this sort. It is necessary, though, that a certain sort of matter be present if there is to be a house or any other sort of end, and this must come to be and be changed first, then that, and so on continuously up to the end and the thing for the sake of which a given thing comes to be and is. And it is the same way too in things that come to be by nature. (*PA* I 1 639ᵇ21–640ᵃ1)

So we might think of a natural being's Aristotelian form as what selects the matter hypothetically necessary to produce or generate a hylomorphic compound with that form. But should we think of the Aristotelian form as doing so only in W_a, or also in other possible worlds? For on this will depend the theorems that the form will support.

Now the primary god is, as we saw, the ultimate teleological cause in W_{ar} (the actual world as Aristotle conceives it).* That is why the following is true:

> It is the most natural function in those living things that are complete and not deformed or spontaneously generated, to produce another like itself—an animal producing an animal, a plant a plant—in order that they may partake in the eternal and divine insofar as they can. For all desire that, and it is for the sake of it that they do whatever they do by nature. . . . Since, then, they cannot share in what is eternal and divine by continuous existence, because nothing that admits of passing away can persist as the same and numerically one, they share in them insofar as each can, some more and some less. And what persists is not the thing itself but something like itself, not one in number but one in form. (*DA* II 4 415^{a}26–^{b}7)

In W_{ar}, then, this teleological structure is, so to speak, written into the forms at least of the living substances. But since "in a certain way all things are full of soul" (*GA* III 11 762^{a}21), the structure extends in one way or another to all the hylomorphic compounds. To have a handy way of referring to worlds that are like W_{ar} in this respect, let us call them *telic worlds*, and the forms in them *telic forms*.

Back, now, to saws. The form of a saw, as we were understanding it, is something that is the ground or truth-maker for a scientific theorem about saws, in some cases because of the nature of the hypothetically necessary matter it selects. Thus it is apparently a theorem that all saws are meltable in fire because the hypothetically necessary matter, selected by the form of

---

* Notice that this seems to be a world-specific and not a trans-world fact about the primary god. He, in essence, is just an understanding actively understanding itself. That he is an unmoved mover seems to be a result of his being in a world in which other living things strive to immortalize themselves to the extent that they can by actualizing his form as fully as he actualizes his (something their hylomorphic nature sets natural limits to). For further discussion, see Michael Bordt, SJ, "Why Aristotle's God Is Not the Unmoved Mover," *Oxford Studies in Ancient Philosophy* 40 (2011): 91–109.

a saw, regardless of what possible world we consider, is meltable in fire. The question is, is this still true if the form of a saw is a telic form? And obviously it is not. For the meltability of saws is not a telic feature of them, since it is entirely irrelevant to the function of saws.

Putting it generally, then, the matter selected by a telic form need not, even considered as so selected, be the basis for any scientific theorems about the kind of things that have that form. That is precisely the point that Aristotle is making about eye color in the following text:

> For none of the things that are not works of the nature, whether common or special to a given genus, either exists or comes to be for the sake of something. For though the eye is for the sake of something, it is not blue for the sake of anything, unless this affection is special to the genus. Nor, in some cases, does the affection lead to the account (*logos*) of the substance [or essence], but rather, as coming of necessity, one must refer to the matter and the moving starting-point as the causes. (*GA* V 1 778ᵃ30–ᵇ1)

It is a theorem of biology, based in the telic form of an animal, that animals have eyes. The color of their eyes, however, is not so based. It is based in the matter, and while it has an efficient and a material cause, it has no final or telic cause. It is not for the sake of anything. Selected by the form, the matter indeed is, but because the form is telic, there need be no telic consequences of that fact, no theorem of biology that explains them.

I say "need be" advisedly, because in one very important case at least, there are such consequences:

> And in fact what is not like its parents is already in a certain way a monster. For nature in these cases has in a certain way deviated from the genus. And a first starting-point is when a female comes to be and not a male—but this is necessary by nature. For the genus that is separated into female and male must be preserved, and since it is possible for the male sometimes not to master, either due to youth or age, or due to some other cause of this sort, it is necessary for production of females to occur among the animals. The monster, by contrast, is not necessary in relation to the for-the-sake-of-which and the final cause, but is necessary coincidentally. (*GA* IV 3 767ᵇ5–15)

Though a female is "like a deformed male" (*GA* II 3 737ᵃ27–28), and is to that extent a monster, femaleness is a "natural deformation" (IV 6 775ᵃ16), not like an animal with extra feet or heads (3 769ᵇ25–27). And the deformation is natural because, unlike that in creatures with birth defects, it is "necessary in relation to the for-the-sake-of-which and the final cause," since, without females, sexually dimorphic species would not be preserved. So the answer to the question we raised earlier as to what would happen if sublunary matter (including most importantly female menses) were like ether, what if it were perfectly receptive of form, is that females would not be generated, and so—or so eventually—neither would males.

If we leave the issue there, however, we are left facing too brute a fact. Because we naturally want to know what exactly is providing the ultimate explanatory basis for what. And here, I think, we are driven back to the very beginning of *GA* and the first definition of male and female given there: "By a male animal we mean what generates in another, by a female what does so within itself" (II 1 716ᵃ13–15).* Thus if we start with the telic form of a male animal, which as such is seeking to eternalize itself in the only way available, namely, sexual reproduction, we will find in it a natural basis for its urge to mate:

> First, then, those who are incapable of existing without each other necessarily form a couple, as female and male do for the sake of procreation (they do not do so from deliberate choice, but, like other animals and plants, because the urge to leave behind something of the same sort as themselves is natural), and as what rules by nature and what is by nature ruled do for the sake of preservation. (*Pol.* I 2 1252ᵃ26–31)

The telic form of the male, then, is what grounds the difference between eye color and sexual dimorphism. But why, one might reasonably ask, is it not the telic form of the female that does this? And the answer to that lies in the (supposed) fact, fundamental to Aristotle's entire account of sexual reproduction, that the female, because of her deficient natural heat, is "incapable of concocting the nourishment in its last stage" (*GA* IV 1 766ᵃ32–33), and so of producing seed that contains active—rather than merely potential—formative movements.

In the final sentence of the text just quoted from the *Politics*, it is worth noting, we hear the normative echo of the view that it is the movements in the male semen that by nature "master" those in the female menses; we can see how readily the biological notion of mastery turns into the political

---

* "Of those in which generation of animals belongs, in one emission [of seed] is within the animal itself, in the other it is within another. The one in which emission is within itself is called the female, within another, the male" (*HA* I 3 489ᵃ10–12).

notion of rule. But we do well to remember that Aristotle had no direct access to the microphysical facts about blood and formative heat—no direct access to what in our current theory are genes and DNA—that are the explanatory starting-points of his embryology. What he had by way of raw starting-points are relatively macroscopic observations of what he took to be the natural domination of females by males that holds for the most part across the animal kingdom, which thus became things to be explained at the microscopic level. It is not so much, then, that facts about domination were derived from (supposed) microphysical facts, as that the microphysical facts were posited to support (supposedly) natural facts about domination.

We can now see why and how the existence of biological females is grounded in male telic forms, and how this differentiates femaleness from eye color, as something grounded in the hypothetically necessary matter that such forms select in a telic world like W_{ar}—the actual world as Aristotle conceives of it. But it is also worth noticing how close Aristotle comes to a different thought, which we could put as a question in this way: might a species, S, that is sexually dimorphic in W_{ar}, be hermaphroditic in another telic world, W_h? Indeed, the following text might lead us to think that S is in an important sense hermaphroditic even in W_{ar} itself:

> Male and female, however, are attributes that do properly belong to the animal, not in virtue of its substance but in the matter— that is, the body. That is why the same seed becomes female or male when it is affected in regard to a certain attribute. (*Met.* X 9 1058^{b}21–24)

Here the sameness of seed might be taken to be what ensures the unity of the heritable form of S, while its being "affected in regard to a certain attribute" is what is responsible for making it male or female.* And this takes us back once again to the issue of what would happen if, not now female menses, but their hermaphroditic analogue, were, like ether, perfectly receptive of form. What would happen, surely, is that S would be a species in which offspring were perfect clones of their hermaphrodite progenitor.

Suppose that S is an internally viviparous species, as the human one is. Would its individual members be more like human males or human females? Surely, they would be more like actual females than like actual males (think of those fish Aristotle mentions that are full of roe, though maybe no males exist). For the members of S would need an analogue of the uterus in which to incubate embryo and fetus and an analogue of breasts to feed the newborns, whereas all they would need of the male starting-point

---

* See *GA* IV 1 764^{b}20–765^{a}2, 765^{b}6–766^{a}30.

is something like a greater degree of the formative heat needed to concoct the analogue of menses without an actual male. Of course, to reach that result we have had to imagine that S needs a uterus and breasts because S is an internally viviparous species. If S were, instead, oviparous, we might rather think that its members would be more like human males.

Back one last time to eye color. Suppose that all progenitors in S do have gray eyes. Well, gray eyes are such due to having an intermediate amount of liquid in their eye-jelly, which because it is in a mean between blue (too little liquid) and dark (too much), results in the best daytime and nighttime vision:

> The one that is intermediate between little and much liquid is the best sight. For it is neither so small that it gets disturbed and hinders the movement of the colors, nor so large in quantity that it is made difficult to move. (*GA* V 1 780ᵃ22–25)

Since nature "makes everything either because it is necessary or because it is better" (*GA* I 4 717ᵃ15–16), it seems that eye color now does trace back to the telic form of members of S in just the way femaleness does in W_{ar}. And that in fact is the right answer: "For though the eye is for the sake of something, it is not blue for the sake of anything, *unless this affection is special to the genus*" (V 1 778ᵃ32–34). For as we have imagined it, of course, being gray-eyed *is* special to S. So it will now be a theorem—a necessarily true (because form-based or partly form-based) proposition—of biology that all members of S are gray-eyed!

What this reveals is that in Aristotle's hylomorphic account the offloading of eye color from form to matter registers not just one fact, but two. The first is that while the quantity of liquid material in the eye-jelly determinative of color is selected as hypothetically necessary by the telic form of the eye, it is not selected as itself telic (or for the sake of something). The second is that eye color varies within the species whose form does the selecting, and so is not special to that species. This raises a question, however, as to why it is the species, and what is special to it, that is so important. I mean, when we look at the details of how form is transmitted sexually in W_{ar}, isn't it the individualized form of the male progenitor, the one that is special to him, that is causally important, not the species form that he shares with his co-specifics?

The Nature of Biological Forms

Suppose that M and F, members of the sexually dimorphic species S, are the male and female progenitors of offspring O, and that |M| is the complex of movements that, because they code for M's form, and are present in his semen, are involved in its transmission to O. And suppose that N_m is the sort of nose that M has (aquiline, say), and |N_m| the sub-movements in |M| that "code for" N_m. If |N_m| masters the corresponding potential movements in F's menses, namely, |N_f|, which are the ones that code for N_f, which is her sort of nose (snub, say). O will then have an aquiline nose of the same sort as N_m, which will be formed and sustained by |N_m|, the movements transmitted undeformed to F's menses. If, on the other hand, |N_f| masters |N_m|, O will have F's snub nose. And the same applies to all the rest of the heritable characteristics of O and O's parts, including those that determine whether O will be male or female. Suppose, then, that O is a male with his mother's nose. Doesn't it follow that M's form and O's form must be different? After all, M's form is transmitted by |M|, of which |N_m| is a part, whereas O's form is transmitted by |O|, the complex of movements that code for it, of which not |N_m| but rather |N_f| is a part. Yet M and O are co-specifics, members of the same species, S. So their species form—the one in virtue of which they are members of S—must be the same. It seems, then, that the forms needed by embryology must be thicker (richer) than the corresponding species forms.

Yet what Aristotle tells us about M and O (Socrates and Coriscus in his example) is that their forms are the same: "it is the ultimate species (*eidos*) that are the substances, and these are undifferentiated with respect to form (*eidos*) (for example, Socrates, Coriscus)" (*PA* I 4 644ᵃ23–25); "And once we have the whole, such-and-such sort of form in this flesh and bones, this is Callias or Socrates. And they are distinct because of their matter (for that is distinct), but the same in form (for the form is indivisible)" (*Met.* VII 8 1034ᵃ5–8). Similarly, if it is evident, as we are told it is, that the ultimate differentia is "the substance [or essence] of the thing and the definition" (*Met.* VII 12 1038ᵃ19–20). Then, once again, M and O, as co-specifics, will have the same essence and definition.

Now the different parts of different kinds of animals can differ from one another in a number of importantly different ways:

> Some of the animals have parts that are the same as each other, others that are distinct. [1] Some parts are identical in form (*eidos*)—for example, one human being's nose and eye and another human being's nose and eye, one's flesh with another's,

one's bone with another's. And it is the same way with the parts of a horse, and whichever other animals we say are the same as each other in species. For as the whole is to the whole, so too each part is to each part. [2] In other cases, though they are the same [in form], they differ by excess and deficiency, namely, whichever ones are the same in genus. By genus I mean, for example, bird and fish. For each of these has a differentia with respect to genus, and there are several species of fishes and of birds. [3] Now pretty much most of the parts in animals differ in the contrarieties of their affections (for example, of colors and shapes), in that some have the same ones to a greater degree, others to a lesser one, and additionally in greater or fewer number, and larger or smaller size, and, in general, in excess or deficiency. Thus some are soft-fleshed, others hard-fleshed; some have a long beak, others a short one; some have many feathers, others few. Nonetheless, even in the cases we are considering, it sometimes happens that different ones have different parts—for example, some have spurs, others do not, some have crests and others do not. [4] But (one might almost say) most of the parts, and those out of which the bulk of the body is composed, are either the same [in form] or differ by way of a contrariety with respect to excess or deficiency. For greater or lesser [degree] may be taken as a sort of excess or deficiency. [5] Some animals, however, have parts that are neither the same in form nor [different] in excess or deficiency, but analogous—for example, bone in relation to fish-spine, nail to hoof, and hand to claw, feather to scale. For what in bird is feather, this in the fish is scale. (*HA* I 1 486ª14–ᵇ22)

Focus first on the parts described in [2]. They differ, but because they differ only in excess or deficiency, they are genuinely the same in form, not, like those in [5], simply analogous. Why so? Why is this sort of difference compatible with sameness, while that between feathers and scales is not?

The answer seems to be that differences in excess and deficiency are due to differences in matter:

Wet, dry, hot, and cold are matter of the composite bodies, while the other differentiae—for example, heaviness and lightness, density and rarity, roughness and smoothness, and the other corporeal affections of this sort—follow along with these. (*PA* II 1 646ª16–20)

(We have seen the text before.) Presumably, then, crane feathers are sufficiently similar in function to sparrow feathers that their forms are the same,
even though, because of differences in their matter, they differ in other
ways. This does not hold, however, of scales and feathers. Their functions,
though analogous, are sufficiently different that their forms are different.

Though *HA* I 1 is not perhaps entirely clear on the question, Aristotle
is explicit elsewhere that the differences described in [3], such as those of
color and shape, are also differences in excess or deficiency. Witness, for
example, the following discussion of nose shape:

> Just as a nose that deviates from the most noble straightness
> toward being hooked or snub can nevertheless still be noble and
> please the eye, if it is "tightened" still more toward the extreme,
> the part will first be thrown out of due proportion, and in the
> end will appear not to be a nose at all, because it has too much
> of one and too little of the other of these contraries. (*Pol.* V 9
> 1309^{b}23–29)

Here the difference between straight, hooked, and snub noses is a matter of
excess or deficiency in contraries. The same is true in the case of colors. For
while many colors are constituted out of white and black in some definite
ratio, others are constituted in "some incommensurable ratio of excess or
deficiency" (*Sens.* 3 439^{b}29–30). Thus, however finely shades of blue are
discriminated, the very same shade may differ in sheen or velvetiness when
exemplified by the same type of feather in different blue jays.

The parts described in [1] have the same form because they are the parts
of animals that belong to the same species. But if things belong to the same
species, they also belong to the same genus. Hence these parts must be a
sub-set of the parts described in [2]. It follows that though O's parts have the
same form as M's, they too may differ in excess or deficiency from his. Take
nosed (which is what something is if it belongs to a species whose members
by nature have noses), for example, and suppose that it is an ultimate differentia of S, the species to which O and M belong. O and M will then both
be nosed. But their noses may, and almost certainly will, differ in size (M's
is larger, O's smaller), in consistency (M's harder, O's softer), in texture (M's
rougher, O's smoother), in shape (M's broader, O's narrower), in color (M's
darker, O's paler), and so on. But these differences are not further differentiae of nosed—by hypothesis, nosed is ultimate, so that nosed has no more
finely divided defining features that give rise to a difference in species.

What holds of nosed, however, also holds of all the other ultimate differentiae of S. Hence it holds of the form as a whole, which is identical to some
combination of these ultimate differentiae. Whatever differences there may

be between M's form and O's form, therefore, must be differences in excess or deficiency that are due to differences in the matter in which they are realized. That is to say, they must be differences between these forms considered as realized in matter. For "as number does not admit of greater or lesser degree, neither does the substance in respect of the form, but if indeed any substance does, it is the one that involves matter" (*Met.* VIII 3 1044^{a}9–11).

For simplicity, then, let us remain focused on nosed, which is just one component of M's and O's species essence, but let us consider it as present in (hypothetically necessary) matter, and, in different individuals, in different parcels of that matter, so that nosed$_m$ is nosed as present in the parcel of matter m of M's nose, while nosed$_o$ is nosed as present in the parcel of matter o of O's nose. In M and O nosed (the form of a nose) is the same. But because sublunary matter, unlike ether, is indeterminate, the parcel of matter m is bound to differ in various ways from the parcel o. The very same form, therefore, that results in M having a large, hard, rough, broad, dark nose results in O having a small, soft, smooth, narrow, pale one. For what explains these differences is not form as such, but form as realized in a particular parcel of hypothetically necessary matter. But it is "the [ultimate] differentia in the matter that is the species" (*PA* I 3 643^{a}24). Hence differences in the matter in which that differentia is realized can explain why it has different effects. Once that is made explicit, however, we can see that thin species forms are all embryology really needs.

Here is a thought experiment to drive the point home, though it is not Aristotelian and will not bear too much scrutiny. Imagine that M is the first member of S, as Adam in the Bible story is the first human being. Imagine that his form is just species form, and that he reproduces hermaphroditically by producing menses of his own. Suppose that different parcels of these menses differ, but only by excess or deficiency. Bear in mind that the natures of offspring are affected by such things as winds, seasons, and the age and general physical condition of their progenitors (*GA* IV 2 766^{b}34). Allow reproduction to begin. If it continues long enough, there will be members of S that differ as much as M and O or even as much as M and F—male and female. Yet only thin species form will have been ultimately involved in their generation.

The Nature of a Species

For reasons we now understand a natural being's form is "more [its] nature than the matter is" (*Ph.* II 2 193^{b}6–7), and so its substance or essence is its form (*Met.* VII 7 1032^{b}1–2). But if something is to be a natural essence—indeed, an essence of any kind—it must have a definition. For essences are the ontological correlates of definitions that are themselves the epistemological starting-points of sciences. The fact that sciences are structures of demonstrations, therefore, must be reflected in these definitions, and so in the essences they define (see *PA* I 1 649^{a}3n). One important form of such reflection is described as follows:

> To proceed from primary things (*prôtôn*) is to proceed from starting-points. For I call the same things primary things and starting-points. A starting-point of a demonstration is an immediate proposition, and a proposition is immediate if there is no other proposition prior to it. A proposition is one part of a contradictory pair—one thing said of one. (*APo.* I 2 72^{a}5–9)

Thus if "F is G" is a definition, both F and G must, in the appropriate way be "one thing"—one intrinsic being. But because a definition is perforce complex, there is a puzzle here:

> I mean this puzzle: why on earth is something one when the account of it is what we call a definition? For example, let the account of the human be the two-footed animal. Why, then, is this one and not instead many—animal *and* two-footed? (*Met.* VII 12 1037^{b}10–14)

Since this puzzle concerns the unity of a genus (animal) and its differentia (two-footed), let us call it *the genus problem*.

The genus puzzle would be solved, Aristotle claims, if genera participated in their differentiae, so that the genus and the differentiated genus were one and the same. For then being two-footed, for example, would be part of being an animal and not some further thing in addition to it. If genera participated in their differentiae, however, "the same thing would participate in contraries at the same time, since the differentiae that divide the genus are contraries" (*Met.* VII 12 1037^{b}19–21). Moreover, such participation would give rise to a second puzzle:

> But even if it did participate, the argument would be the same, if indeed the differentiae are many—for example, footed, two-footed, featherless. Why are these one and not instead many? For it is not because these are present [in one genus], since that way there will be one from all.* But surely the things in the

---

* "These" refers to the differentiae, footed, two-footed, featherless. If what made these three one was simply their presence in one genus, all the differentiae of that

definition must be one. For the definition is a certain account that is one and of substance, so that it must be the account of one something. For the substance signifies one something and a this something, as we say. (*Met.* VII 12 1037^{b}21–27)

This new puzzle concerns the unity of the differentiae themselves and has two quite different components. The first of these is the *vertical puzzle*. It asks why differentiae at different levels in the same divisions—such as footed and two-footed—are one rather than many. The second is the *horizontal puzzle*. It asks why differentiae at the same level in different divisions—such as footed and featherless (supposing these to be at the same level)—are one rather than many.

If the following text is to be our guide, these three problems admit of a single solution:

[1] We should first investigate definitions that are by division. For there is nothing else in the definition except the genus that is mentioned first and the differentiae; the other genera are in fact the first one along with the differentiae combined with it. The first, for example, may be animal, the next two-footed animal, and next again featherless two-footed animal, and similarly if it is said by means of more differentiae. And in general it makes no difference whether it is said by means of many or of few—nor, therefore, whether by means of few or by means of just two. And of the two one is differentia and the other genus—for example, in the two-footed animal, the animal is genus and the other differentia. [2] If, then, the genus is unconditionally nothing beyond the species as species of a genus, or if it is, it is as matter (for the voiced sound is genus and matter, and the differentiae produce the phonetic elements from this), then it is evident that the definition is the account composed of the differentiae. [3] But in addition the division should take the differentia of the differentia—for example, the footed is a differentia of animal, and next again we should know the differentia of the footed animal insofar as it is footed. So we should not say that of the footed there is on the one hand the feathered and on the other the featherless, if indeed we are to speak correctly (on the contrary, it is through lack of ability that we will say this), but rather that there is on the one hand

---

genus would also be one, so that, for example, two-footed and four-footed would be (parts of the same) one.

the cloven-footed and on the other the not cloven-footed. For these are differentiae of foot. For the cloven-footed is a sort of footed. And we should try to proceed always in this way until we reach the undifferentiated [species]. [4] At that point there will be precisely as many species of foot as there are differentiae, and the footed animals will be equal in number to the differentiae. . . . If, then, we take a differentia of a differentia, one differentia—the ultimate one—will be the form and the substance. (*Met.* VII 12 1037^{b}27–1038^{a}26)

It is easy to see how the genus puzzle is solved here. For [1] shows that only one genus is involved in a definition, and [2] that this one genus is nothing besides a set or collection of species taken generically (*DA* I 1 402^{b}5–8). Thus a two-footed animal is not a generic animal plus something else as well. Rather, being two-footed is a way of being an animal, and there is no way of being an animal other than some such specific way.

Similarly, [3] offers an equally intelligible solution to the vertical puzzle. For if the ultimate differentia is a differentia of all its predecessors in the same division, they constitute a sort of determinate-determinable chain. Hence just as there are no generic animals, there are no simply footed ones. Rather, to be a footed animal is to be either a footed$_1$, a footed$_2$, or a footed$_3$ animal—where the subscripts signify the ultimate differentiae of footedness (webbed, toed, and so on). Finally, in [4] it is argued that the (definition of the) species, form, or substance is identical to the (definition of the) ultimate differentia. Hence, if being two-footed is the ultimate differentia of the human species, being a human would be a case of being just one thing, namely, two-footed.

The solution to the horizontal puzzle, on the other hand, is harder to discern. It could be readily solved if each species had only one ultimate differentia, as [4] seems to be assuming, but this is not so:

One must try to grasp the animals by genera, in the way already shown by ordinary people, distinguishing a bird genus and a fish genus. For each of these has been defined by many differentiae, not by dichotomy. For by dichotomy either it is impossible to grasp them at all (for the same one falls into several divisions and contrary ones into the same division), or there will be only one differentia, and this one, whether simply or the result of interweaving, will be the final species. If, on the other hand, one does not take the differentia of a differentia, one will necessarily make the division continuous in the same way that one makes the account (*logos*) one by being bound together. I mean the sort of thing that results in the divisions into the wingless and the winged, and winged into the tame and the wild, or the white and the black. For neither the tame nor the pale is a differentia of winged; instead each is a starting-point of another differentia, whereas here each is coincidental. That is why one must from the outset divide the one [genus] into many [differentiae], as we say. (*PA* I 3 643^{b}10–24)

Species have many ultimate differentiae, then, not just one. Since these are not all differentiae of a differentia, why are they one? Why is being a featherless, two-footed animal being one thing?

What [1] suggests is that differentiae at the same level in different divisions, such as different ultimate differentiae, are united—made into one thing—by being differentiae of the same genus, namely, animal. The problem is that the genus, since it is just the species taken generically, seems poorly suited to play this unifying role. The threat of circularity, indeed, is palpable: the species is one thing because its differentiae are a horizontal unity; its differentiae are such a unity because they are differentiae of one thing, namely, the species taken generically. The following text, however, seems to offer the beginning of an explanation of how such circularity may be avoided:

Now if we wanted to grasp the species (*eidos*) of animals, we would first determine what it is that every animal must have, for example, some of the perceptual-organs, something with which to masticate and absorb food, such as a mouth and a stomach, and in addition to these parts by which each of them moves. If, then, there were only this many parts, but there were differentiae in them (I mean, for example, if there were several genera of mouths, stomachs, and sense-organs, and further also of parts for movement), then the number of ways of combining these will necessarily produce several genera of animals. For the same animal cannot have many differentiae of mouth, nor of ears either. So, when all the possible ways of coupling them have been grasped, they will produce species of animals, and as many species as there are combinations of the necessary parts. (*Pol.* IV 4 1290^{b}25–37)

For what is described here is a way of constructing the various species of animals in terms of the necessary parts of an animal. But what exactly is the mode of construction?

One thought is that it is mereological, that species are defined in terms of their parts (*meros*) in such a way that the latter are prior in definition to the former.* The result would be that the essences of the parts of animals, rather than the essences of whole animals, would be scientific starting-points and, as such, substances. But while we do indeed "*say* that animals and plants and their parts are substances" (*Met.* VII 2 1028^{b}9–10), what we say provides only the starting point for an investigation into the problem of whether what we say is true. Hence it leaves open the possibility that "only some of these things" or "none of them, but only some others" are substances (1028^{b}13–15). The outcome of the investigation, moreover, makes it plain that animal parts are not substances at all:

> It is evident that even of the things that seem to be substances, most are capacities, whether the parts of animals (for none of them exists when it has been separated, and whenever they are separated they all exist only as matter) or earth, fire, and air (for none of them is one, but instead they are like a heap, until they are concocted and some one thing comes to be from them). (*Met.* VII 16 1040^{b}5–10)

It seems to follow that *Pol.* IV 4 is not advocating mereology at all, since on so fundamental an issue as this Aristotle is unlikely to have dithered.

What it is advocating seems on inspection to be a quite different doctrine. To identify the necessary parts of an animal, we must already have a grasp of what a generic whole animal—an animal of any species—needs in the way of such parts. We are able to achieve this, without having already defined the animal species, because our pre-theoretical observation allows us to develop a sufficiently rich conception of what capacities an animal of any species requires in order to live a characteristically animal life: perception, absorption of nourishment, movement, and so on.** If these parts were differentiated (something that biological research would reveal), different combinations of them will give rise to different species. For the ultimate differentiae—which are the ultimate differentiae of the necessary

---

* This is the sort of account embraced by Pierre Pellegrin in his stimulating book, *Aristotle's Classification of Animals* (Berkeley, 1986): "Only rational zoology, the only real zoology . . . can construct a priori, by the combination of the various species of each part, the entire animal world" (p. 156).

** See *PA* I 2 642^{b}13–14, where a pre-theoretically defined genus is referred to as a "similarity class" (explained at I 4 644^{b}1–15) and 3 643^{b}10–12, where we are instructed to "try to grasp the animals by genera, in the way already shown by ordinary people, distinguishing a bird genus and a fish genus."

parts—just are the species, form, or substance (*Met.* VII 12 1038^{a}17). That is why animals of the same species cannot have mouths that have multiple differentiae.

Let us suppose that mouth, stomach, perceptual organ, and locomotive part are the only necessary parts of an animal, that each species of animal has exactly one of each of these parts, and that each of the parts comes in exactly three differentiated types: mouth$_1$, mouth$_2$, mouth$_3$, stomach$_1$, stomach$_2$, stomach$_3$, and so on for the others. How many species of animals will there then be? If *Pol.* IV 4 were proposing a mereological account of species, in which a species is just a logical sum or conjunction of necessary parts, the answer would seem to be eighty-one (3^4). For the general recipe for an animal species would then be:

mouth + stomach + perceptual organ + locomotive part,

and each species of animal can have exactly one of the three different types of each of these four parts.

Look back again now at *Met.* VII 12 [4], which says that the species of footed animal will be equal in number to the ultimate differentiae of foot. In the case we are imagining, therefore, it seems that there will be just *three* species of animal, corresponding to the three types of locomotive part. [1] makes it very likely, however, that Aristotle is assuming for the sake of simplicity that a species has just one necessary part, or one ultimate differentia in just one division, since he claims that the number of differentiae is irrelevant to the argument. For he is explicit elsewhere that an ultimate differentia of this sort is not the one to which the species is identical:

> But that it is impossible for there to be many differentiae of this sort is clear. For by proceeding continuously one arrives at the ultimate differentia (although not at the final one that is the species). For it is either split-footed alone, if one is dividing human or the whole complex—for example, if one were to combine footed, two-footed, and split-footed. On the other hand, if the human were split-footed alone, by proceeding in this way one might arrive at this one differentia. But as things stand, since this is not so, it is necessary for there to be many differentiae that are not under one division. (*PA* I 3 644^{a}1–8)

So presumably the ultimate differentia that is identical to the species is some sort of combination of the ultimate differentiae of the necessary parts that determine the species. But what sort?

The necessary parts of an animal do not constitute a unified species simply "by being bound together, like the *Iliad*" (*Met.* VIII 6 1045^{a}12–14). Rather, they must constitute a telic system. Thus, for example, "the matter for the elements is necessary for the sake of the homoeomerous parts . . . and those for the sake of the non-homoeomerous ones" (*PA* II 1 646^{b}6–13). The parts are not the system they constitute, however; rather they stand to it as matter to form, since "the matter for the animals is their parts" (*GA* I 1 715^{a}9). The ultimate end of this entire telic system, then, is the realization of an animal's distinctive telic form or essence, the achievement of its end—its *telos*.

So species of animals are *not* mere mereological sums of their necessary parts. But they do not live in featureless, abstract environments either. Hence these parts must not just be teleologically organized, they must be so organized as to fit the resulting species for some available natural habitat:

> But then there are indeed many species (*eidos*) of food, because the ways of life of both animals and human beings are also many. For it is impossible to live without food, so that differences in food have produced distinct ways of life among the animals. For some beasts live in herds and others live scattered about, whichever is advantageous for getting their food, because some of them are carnivorous, some herbivorous, and some omnivorous. And so with a view to their convenience and their preference in these matters, nature has made their ways of life different. And since the same things are not naturally pleasant to each, but rather distinct things to distinct ones, among the carnivores and herbivores themselves the ways of life are different. The same is also true of human beings. (*Pol.* I 8 1256^{a}19–29)

Not every type of mouth, stomach, sense-organ, and locomotive part, therefore, will go together to constitute a viable species of animal. A mouth and teeth suitable for grazing, for example, cannot be paired with a stomach that cannot digest grass—and similarly in the cases of the other necessary parts. Hence we ought not to consider "the ways of combining" (*Pol.* IV 4 1290^{b}24) necessary parts as merely logical possibilities, knowable a priori, but as real biological ones, discoverable only by observation. The number of species in the scenario we imagined earlier is not likely to be three, then, since the ultimate differentia of just one of an animal's necessary parts is not the ultimate differentia to which the species is identical. But neither is it likely to be eighty-one, since not all logically possible combinations of types of necessary parts are likely to be real biological possibilities.

Since the unity among the horizontal differentia of a genuine species is unity of a biologically significant sort, it seems reasonable to grant that Aristotle is on intelligible ground in claiming (*Met.* VII 12 1037^{b}29) that the solution he provides to the genus puzzle also solves the horizontal puzzle. For if the form of a human is something like featherless, two-footed animal (if that is its ultimate differentia, substance, and species), its form *is* one thing, and so is sufficiently unified—sufficiently one thing—to be a starting-point of an Aristotelian science.

The very structure of animal essences is reflected, moreover, in the inter-relations of the various sciences that deal with animals:

> For there are four underlying causes: the for-the-sake-of-which as end, the account of the substance (and these must be taken pretty much as one), third and fourth, the matter and where the starting-point of the movement comes from. Well, the others have been spoken about (for the account and the for-the-sake-of-which as end are the same and the matter for the animals is their parts—for the animal as a whole, the non-homoeomer-ous parts, for the non-homoeomerous parts, the homoeomer-ous ones, and for these, the so-called elements of bodies). But it remains to speak about the parts that contribute to the gen-eration of animals, about which nothing was determined pre-viously, and about what sort of starting-point is cause of the movement. And to investigate this latter cause and to investi-gate the generation of each animal is in a way the same. That is why the account has brought them together as one, by put-ting these parts at the end of our accounts of the parts, and the accounts of the starting-point of generation next after them. (*GA* I 1 715^{a}7–18)

This text refers to *De Partibus Animalium* and *De Generatione Animalium*, and explains why the former precedes the latter. It also refers to a discus-sion of the essence or final cause, but does not make explicit in what trea-tise it occurs, or whether that treatise is prior or posterior to *De Partibus*. The following text, however, provides the information we need to fill this gap:

> [1] It is necessary to get a theoretical grasp on [the various spe-cies of animals] by grasping the nature of each of them sepa-rately. What has just been said, then, is by way of an outline sketch, a foretaste of the things and attributes on which we must get a theoretical grasp. But in what follows we shall speak about

them with exactitude, in order to grasp, first, the differentiae and coincidental attributes of all of them. After that, we should try to discover the causes. [2] For this is the way to make the methodical inquiry in accord with nature, once the investigation of each is already in existence. For the things about which and from which there must be a demonstration become evident of the basis of these. [3] So first of all we must grasp the parts from which animals are composed. For it is most of all and primarily with respect to these that the whole [animals] are differentiated, either by having some and not having others, or by their position, or by their order, or by the differentiae mentioned earlier, those of species, excess or deficiency, analogy, and contrariety among the affections. (*HA* I 6 491ᵃ4–19)

Focus first on [2]. It tells us that the investigation described in [1] will result in definitions of each of the species (essences) (for these are the starting-points from which demonstrations that reveal causes proceed) and also in knowledge of their (intrinsic) coincidental attributes, since demonstrations are about these (see *PA* I 1 649ᵃ3n). [3] then tells us how the investigation described in [2] should proceed: it should focus on the parts of animals. This seems to suggest that the investigations detailed in *Historia Animalium* are not investigations into the distinct animal species at all, even though that is what [1] leads us to believe. But, as [3] makes clear, the apparent suggestion to the contrary is apparent only. For the parts of animals are the focus simply because "it is most of all and primarily with respect to these that whole [animals] are differentiated." In other words, an investigation into parts is an investigation into species, because what the latter reveals is that species can be differentiated and defined by appeal to their parts.

Historia Animalium is, then, an investigation of the various species that will in the end lead to definitions of their species essences. Hence it is a treatise on formal and final causes. As such, it must precede *De Partibus Animalium*. For the parts of an animal are its matter (*GA* I 1 715ᵃ9), and matter is posterior to form:

But in coming to be things are a contrary way to the way they are in substance. For things posterior in coming to be are prior in nature, and the final stage (*teleutaion*) in coming to be is primary in nature (for the house is not for the sake of the bricks and stones, but rather these are for the sake of the house—and this holds in the same way of other sorts of matter). (*PA* II 1 646ᵃ24–29)

Just as a whole is prior to its parts, in other words, so the sciences of the whole are prior to the sciences of the parts. Since the sciences collectively must describe a unified universe, it could really be no other way.

Residues and Hylomorphic Extent

Although residues (*perittômata*) are important players in Aristotle's biological thinking, their existence, like that of monsters, can seem like a sort of failure on nature's part (something the notion of "perfect" hermaphroditic reproduction highlights). For a residue is a "leftover (*hupoleimma*) of the nourishment" (*GA* I 18 724^{b}26–27), and, while some parts of it, such as semen and the seed in female menses, are useful, others such as urine and feces are useless, and are therefore excreted as waste products (725^{a}9–12). Yet the role assigned to nature seems in tension with the existence of waste:

> Each of the other parts [besides the eyelids] is produced from the nourishment: the most estimable ones and the ones participating most in the most controlling starting-point, from the nourishment that is concocted, purest, and first*; the ones that are necessary and for the sake of the former ones, from the inferior nourishment, and from the leftovers and residues. For like a good household manager, nature too is not accustomed to throw anything away from which something useful can be made. (*GA* II 6 744^{b}11–17)

For while it may be that nothing useful can be made of urine and feces *within* the animal, something useful can be made from them, as every farmer or gardener knows, in the larger sphere of nature of which animals are a part. Is there, then, a larger nature—a manager of something larger than a household—that does make use of these?

Within the animal too, as this text from *GA* II 6 shows, within the smaller natural sphere of its body envelope, there are things akin to urine and feces that are made use of. These are the inferior nourishment, leftovers, and residues from which the parts that are necessary and for the sake of the most estimable parts (see *PA* I 5 644^{b}24n) are produced by the nature. A case in point is the production of horns. In the viviparous animals, horns are for the sake of protection and the strength needed to overpower another (*PA* III 2 662^{b}27–30):

---

* This is not first-stage nourishment, but rather last-stage, the one from which each of the parts first comes to be (I 18 725^{a}11–21).

But as there is a necessary nature, we must state how the nature that is in accord with the account (*logos*) makes use of things that are present of necessity for the sake of something. First, then, what is corporeal and earthy is present in greater quantities in the larger animals, while we know of no altogether small horn-possessing one. For the smallest known one is a gazelle. And one must get a theoretical grasp on nature with an eye to the many. For it is what happens in every case or for the most part that is in accord with nature. What is bone-like in the bodies of animals is in origins earthy. That is also why, speaking with an eye to what holds for the most part, it is most abundant in the largest animals. For the excess residue of this sort of body, being present in the larger of the animals, is used by nature for protection and advantage, and that part of it that of necessity flows to the upper place, in some cases it distributes to teeth and tusks, in other cases to horns. (*PA* III 2 663^{b}22–36)

The picture is this. The nature that is in accord with the account (in other words, the male form) of, for example, an ox, first selects in W_{ar} (the actual world as Aristotle conceives of it) the hypothetically necessary matter needed to produce oxen: this is the menses of the female. Some of this (namely, the female seed present in them) is mobilized by the male form in transmitting its formative movements, resulting in an embryo that embodies that form (though perhaps in a somewhat deformed way). But other— from this perspective *residual*—parts of the menses, the male form uses to make things like horns. Because such parts are produced in this way, from residues that are left over from the production of the embryo itself, yet contribute to the advantage of the more mature animal, they have been called "luxury parts."*

The question such parts raise is that of how they are related to the formal nature: are the movements that code for them part of the set of movements that code for the form itself, or not? If they are, the telic form is telic in only one way: its aim, to call it that, is simply to transmit itself to new matter. If they are not, the telic form is telic in two ways: one aim—its primary aim—is to transmit itself, but another—secondary—one is to add luxurious advantageous parts to the embryo it has transmitted itself to. Thus the idea emerges of two levels of teleology: a primary one (corresponding to the primary aim) and a secondary one (corresponding to the secondary aim).

---

* See Mariska Leunissen, *Explanation and Teleology in Aristotle's Science of Nature* (Cambridge, 2010), especially pp. 81–99.

If there were two such levels, however, it should be possible for a telic form to accomplish its first aim successfully, producing a normal off-spring, without accomplishing its second aim at all. What we would have in the case of oxen, then, is an offspring that never grows horns, yet is not deformed in this respect. But that is surely impossible. The only thing that could make it impossible, however, is that the telic form's two aims are inseparable. And the only thing that could ensure that, it seems, is that they are in reality just one aim. What is true, though, is that the single-aimed telic form has something like two ways of operating.

When food is concocted in the stomach, some goes to make blood. What is left over at this first stage of residue production is useless—at any rate for any purposes internal to the animal—and is excreted as urine and feces. Then, while some blood goes to the various parts of the animal, for their maintenance and growth, other blood is left over. This is the second stage of residue production. From this residue, at a third stage, spermatic residues are produced in males and females. But within these too there is useful residue (semen, seed) and useless residue, which is again excreted (menstrual fluid, the liquid part of semen):

> But when the seed from the male (in those animals that emit seed) has entered, it composes the purest part of the residue. For the greater part of the menses, being liquid, is useless too, just as the most liquid part of the male semen is, that is, of a single emission. For the earlier part is more infertile than the later in most cases. For it contains less soul-involving heat due to being non-concocted, whereas the concocted part has thickness and is more corporeal. (*GA* II 4 739^{a}6–13)

Present in the useful residue, however, are things that are necessarily there because of its material, as opposed to its formal nature. In animals such as oxen this includes earthy fibers in which their blood is particularly rich. These are residual, not in being something that might be separated off and secreted, but simply in being things that follow along of necessity with the material nature.

Thus the seed of the male ox in working up that of the female operates on its formal nature (the potential movements present in it) and on its earthy material nature. The result—if all goes according to plan, as for the most part it does—is an ox (perhaps male, perhaps female) that will, at the appropriate time, grow horns. If it does not do so, it is in this respect deformed and monstrous. But the formative movements that, given earthy (initially) female ox blood to work up, code for and result in horns are as much a part of the one, unified formal nature of an ox as any other sub-set of such movements. Thus luxury parts need no thicker forms—no more structured forms—to explain them than the thin species ones needed for the rest of embryology, so that one layer of teleology is enough. Where we do encounter a genuine second layer is, for example, in the *Nicomachean Ethics*, with the distinction between a flute-player and a good flute-player—a human being and an excellent or virtuous human being (*NE* I 7 1098ª7–18). For this distinction extends to the animals too: a fine specimen is different from an unhealthy or disabled one. But unlike the ox with missing horns, there need be nothing (in the technical sense) *deformed* about these.

All of which brings us back to urine and feces (and whatever other residues there may be that have no use within the animal and animal generation). Let us suppose, to start with, that they are absolutely useless. Then, though the universe as a whole might not be a heap of random sweepings, it would have parts—excremental parts—that would be such sweepings. That Aristotle's universe is not intended to be like that is especially clear in the following text, part of which we looked at earlier in another context:

> We must also investigate in which way the nature of the whole possesses the good and the best—whether as something separated and intrinsic, or as its order. Or is it rather in both ways, like an army? For the good of an army is in its order, and is also the general—and more so the latter. For he is not due to the order, but it is due to him. All things are jointly ordered in a way, although not in the same way—even swimming creatures, flying creatures, and plants. And the order is not such that one thing has no relation to another but rather there is a relation. For all things are jointly ordered in relation to one thing—but it is as in a household, where the free people least of all do things at random, but all or most of the things they do are ordered, while the slaves and beasts can do a little for the common thing, but mostly do things at random. For this is the sort of starting-point that the nature is of each of them. I mean, for example, that all must at least come to be disaggregated [into their elements]; and similarly there are other things which they all share for [the good of] the whole. (*Met.* XII 10 1075ª11–25)

Thus urine and feces too, if in no other way, contribute to the good of the whole by being disaggregated into their elements, and in that way made available to become the matter of other hylomorphic compounds. But this seems to be so because the universe is like a household with a—albeit cosmic—good household manager of its own, and also (hence the reference to order) with a form of its own.

The universe, on this showing, seems to be a hylomorphic compound: a substance of some sort. But since many other substances are within the universe, some or all of which are its parts, it seems to follow that substances can have substantial parts. Yet that seems to be something that Aristotle explicitly denies: "It is impossible for a substance to be composed of substances that are actually present in it" (*Met.* VII 13 1039ª3–4).* But problematizing the denial, and so making it less stark, is another text: "What is intrinsically intelligible is the one column [of opposites], and in this substance is primary, and in *this* the simple one and an activity" (XII 7 1072ª30–32). For this also tells us quite explicitly that in the category of substance there are substances of different levels of primacy: the one that is simple and an activity is the primary god, as we saw, but, by implication, there are others that are less so. So, while a truly primary substance (like the simple primary god) would indeed have no substantial parts, the same might not be true of the other primary, but less primary, substances. And what could these be if not those hylomorphic substances that though they have a formal nature, also have a material one? Indeed, if things like universes, heavenly bodies, planets, and moons—not to mention cities, households, and so on—are not primary substances of some sort, what sorts of beings are they? They certainly aren't quantities, qualities, or relations. Moreover, how can there be sciences of them?

Residues, then, especially those useless to the animals that produce them, lead quite naturally to the issue of hylomorphic extent, and in that rather different way lead us back to the relatively more cosmic issues with which, in trying to situate *HA, PA,* and *GA* within Aristotle's philosophy more generally, we began.

---

* For discussion of this text, see my *Aristotle: Metaphysics* (Indianapolis, 2016), pp. 439–440.

History of Animals

BOOK I

I 1

486ᵃ5 Of the parts present in animals some are incomposite, namely, those that divide into homoeomerous parts (for example, flesh into flesh), and the others composite, namely, those that divide into non-homoeomerous ones (for example, the hand does not divide into hands, nor the face into faces). Of the latter, some are called not only parts but members. Of this sort are whichever ones, while being wholes, have

10 other parts within them—for example, head, leg, hand, arm as a whole, and trunk. For these are themselves whole parts, and there are other parts belonging to them. All the non-homoeomerous parts, though, are composed of homoeomerous ones—for example, a hand of flesh, sinews, and bones.

15 Some of the animals have parts that are the same as each other, others that are distinct. Some parts are identical in form (*eidos*)—for example, one human being's nose and eye and another human being's nose and eye, one's flesh with another's, one's bone with another's. And it is the same way with the parts of a horse, and whichever other animals we say are the same as each other in species. For as the whole is to

20 the whole, so too each part is to each part. In other cases, though they are the same [in form], they differ by excess and deficiency, namely, whichever ones are the same in genus. By genus I mean, for example, bird and fish. For each of these has a differentia with respect to genus, and there are several species of fishes and of birds.[1]

25
486ᵇ5 Now pretty much most of the parts in animals differ in the contrarieties of their affections (for example, of colors and shapes), in that some have the same ones to a greater degree, others to a lesser one, and additionally in greater or fewer number, and larger or smaller size, and, in general, in excess or deficiency. Thus some are soft-fleshed,

10 others hard-fleshed; some have a long beak, others a short one; some have many feathers, others few. Nonetheless, even in the cases we are considering, it sometimes happens that different ones have different parts—for example, some have spurs, others do not, some have crests and others do not. But (one might almost say) most of the parts, and those out of which the bulk of the body is composed, are either the

15 same [in form] or differ by way of a contrariety with respect to excess or deficiency. For greater or lesser [degree] may be taken as a sort of excess or deficiency.

2

Some animals, however, have parts that are neither the same in form nor [different] in excess or deficiency, but analogous—for example, bone in relation to fish-spine, nail to hoof, hand to claw, and feather to scale. For what in bird is feather, this in the fish is scale.

The parts, then, that the animals possess are each in this way the same or distinct; as, further, is the position of the parts.[2] For many animals have the same parts, but differently positioned—for example, some have breasts on the chest, some near the thighs.

And of the homoeomerous parts some are soft and liquid, others dry and solid, and those that are liquid may be so generally or only while in their natural condition—for example, blood, serum, fat, suet, marrow, semen, bile, milk (in those that have it), flesh, and the analogues of these.[3] And, further, in another way, the residues—for example, phlegm and the excretions of the bowels and the bladder.[4] And examples of dry and hard are: sinew, skin, blood-vessel, hair, bone, cartilage, nail, horn (for it is a homonym related to the part when due to the shape the whole is said to be horn), and, further, those analogous to them.[5]

The differentiae of the animals, though, are in accord with their lives, actions, characters, and parts, about which we speak first in outline, and later speak scientifically about each genus [of animal].

The differentiae with respect to their lives, actions, and characters are of the following sorts: some animals are aquatic, others terrestrial. But the aquatic ones are twofold: some because they live and get their nourishment in a liquid, take in liquid and expel it, and when deprived of it are incapable of living (for example, this happens in the case of many of the fishes); others get their nourishment and pass their time in liquid, yet do not take in liquid, but rather air, and generate offspring outside it. Many of these are also footed (for example, otter, beaver, crocodile); many are winged (for example, puffin and grebe); and many are footless (for example, water-snake).[6] And some animals, though they get their nourishment in a liquid and are not capable of living out of it, are yet not capable of taking in either water or air (for example, sea-anemone and shell-fish).

Of the aquatic animals, some are in the sea, others in rivers, others in lakes, others in marshes (for example, fishing-frog and water-newt).[7]

Of the terrestrial ones, some take in and expel air, which is called inhalation and exhalation (for example, human and all the terrestrial ones that have a lung), others do not take in air, although they live and get their nourishment on land (for example, wasp, bee, and the other insects). (I call insects (*entoma*) those ones that have their body in sections (*entoma*), whether on their undersides only, or both there and on

their backs). And many of the terrestrial animals, as was said, procure
487ᵇ1 their nourishment from liquid, whereas none of the aquatic ones that
takes in sea-water does so from land.[8]

Some animals first live in liquid, then change to another shape and
live out of it—for example, in the case of larvae in rivers. For gnats
5 come to be from them.[9]

Further, some animals are stationary, while others change with
respect to place. The stationary ones are found in liquid; none of the
terrestrial ones is stationary. But in liquid we find many that live by
being attached to something—for example, many genera of shell-fish.
The sponge too seems to have a sort of perception. A sign of this is
10 that it is more difficult to detach, unless the movement is produced
surreptitiously—or so they say. On the other hand, some both attach
and detach themselves—for example, a certain genus of so-called
sea-anemone (for some of these detach themselves at night and for-
age). Many animals, though detached, are un-moving—for example,
shell-fish and so-called sea-cucumbers. But some are swimmers—for
15 example, fishes, cephalopods, crustaceans (for example, crayfish). And
some perambulate—for example, the crab genus. For, though they are
aquatic, their nature is capable of perambulating.

Of the terrestrial animals, some are winged (such as birds and bees,
and these are so in a different way from each other), others footed. And
20 of the footed ones, some perambulate, others creep, and others wiggle.
None though is able only to fly, as a fish is able only to swim. For even
the skin-winged animals can perambulate—even bats have feet (as also
seals have docked-feet).[10]

Of the birds, some have bad feet, because of which they are called
25 footless birds. But this sort of small bird is a good flier. And the ones
that are like it are pretty much good fliers and have bad feet—for
example, swallow and swift.[11] For all birds of this sort have similar ways and similar feathers, and look similar to each other. The
footless is visible in every season, the swift—but when it has been
raining—in summer. For then it is seen and caught, but, in general,
30 this bird is rare. Many animals, though, are capable of perambulating
and capable of flying.

There are also differentiae (*diaphora*) of this sort with respect to lives
and actions. For some animals are gregarious, others solitary, whether
488ᵃ1 they are footed, winged, swimmers, or play a double game.[12] Also, of
the gregarious ones and solitary ones, some are political, whereas others are more dispersed.[13] Examples of gregarious animals are: among
birds, the pigeon genus, crane, and swan (no taloned bird, though, is
5 gregarious); among swimmers, many genera of fishes—for example,

4

those called migrants (tuna, pelamys, and bonito).[14] The human, though, plays a double game.[15]

The political animals are those among whom some one work common to all is produced, which is just what not all gregarious ones produce.[16] Of this sort are: human, bee, wasp, ant, crane. Also, of these some are under a leader, whereas others are without a ruler—for example, crane and the bee genus are under a ruler, ants and innumerable others are not. And of the gregarious ones and of the solitary ones, some stay in one place, while others roam around.

Also, some are carnivorous, others fruit-eating, others omnivorous, while some eat a diet special to them—for example, the bee genus and the spider genus. For bees use honey and a few other sweet stuffs for their nourishment, spiders live by catching flies, and other animals use fish for their nourishment. Again, some catch their food, and some store it up, while others do not.

Also, some have habitations, some are without habitations: having habitations—for example, mole, mouse, bee; without habitations— many insects and quadrupeds. Further, in their places of habitation, some live in holes (for example, lizards and snakes), others above ground (for example, horses and dogs). Also, some are burrowers, others non-burrowers.[17]

Also, some are nocturnal (for example, owl, bat), others live in daylight.

Further, some are tame, others wild. And some are always tame (for example, human, mule), some always wild (like leopard and wolf), others capable of being easily tamed (for example, elephant).[18] Further, there is another way [of dividing them].[19] For every genus of animal that is tame is also wild (for example, horses, oxen, pigs, human beings, sheep, goats, dogs).

Also, some emit sounds, others are mute, and others have a voice, and of these some have speech, whereas others are unable to utter articulate sounds; some are vocal, others silent; some are singers, others song-less.[20] But it is common to all of them to sing or vocalize most of all around the times of mating.

Also, some live in the fields (for example, the ring-dove), others in the mountains (for example, the hoopoe), some alongside humans (for example, the pigeon).

Also, some are overly eager for sexual intercourse—for example, the partridge and the chicken; others are inclined to chastity—for example, the raven-like genus of birds (for these rarely mate).

Also, of marine animals, some live out at sea, others by the shore, others on the rocks.

10

15

20

25

30

488^b1

5

Further, some are aggressive, others defensive. The aggressive ones
are those that set upon others or retaliate when injured, whereas the
defensive ones are those that have some place of shelter within themselves against suffering any injury.[21]

Animals also differ in the following ways with respect to character.
Some are mild-mannered, spiritless, and non-aggressive (for example,
ox); others are spirited, aggressive, and ineducable (for example, wild
pig); others are intelligent and cowardly (for example, deer and hare);
others are servile and cunning (for example, serpent); others free,
courageous, and well-bred (for example, lion); others are well-bred,
wild, and cunning (for example, wolf).[22] For an animal is well-bred if it
comes from good stock; it is true to its stock in not being a degeneration
from its own nature.

Also, some are crafty and mischievous (for example, fox); others are
spirited, affectionate, and fawning (for example, dog); others are mild-
mannered and easily domesticated (for example, elephant); others are
shy and on their guard (for example, goose); others are envious and
vain (for example, peacock). But of the animals only human beings are
capable of deliberation.[23] Also, many animals share in memory and are
capable of being taught, but no other is capable of recollecting except
a human.[24]

About each of the genera of animals, and about their characters and
ways of life, we shall speak with exactitude later on.[25]

I 2

All animals have in common the part with which they take in nourishment and the part they take it into. And these are the same and distinct
in the ways described, namely, with respect to species, with respect to
excess and deficiency, or by analogy, or differing in position.

In addition to these, most animals have other parts in common with
each other as well with which they discharge the residue of the nourishment.[26] For not all animals have it. The part with which they take it
in is called a mouth, the one they take it into, a stomach. The remaining
parts have many names.

Now because the residues are twofold, those animals that have
a part receptive of the wet residue also have one receptive of [that
from] the dry nourishment, but those that have the latter do not all
have the former. That is why the ones that have a bladder also have
a bowel, whereas those that have a bowel do not all have a bladder
(for the part receptive of the wet residue is named bladder, and of the
dry, bowel).

I 3

Many of the remaining animals have these parts and, further, a part by which they emit seed. And of those in which generation of animals belongs, in one emission is within the animal itself, in the other it is within another. The one in which emission is within itself is called the female, within another, the male (in some, though, there is neither male nor female). Also, the parts that are for this handicrafting [of animals] differ in form (*eidos*).[27] For one has a uterus, another its analogue.[28]

These, then, are the parts most necessary to animals: on the one hand, those that belong to all animals, on the other, those that belong to most.

To all animals, though, only one perceptual capacity belongs in common, namely, touch, so that the part in which it naturally comes to be is nameless. For it is the same part in some animals, in others the analogue.[29]

I 4

Every animal also possesses liquid, and if it is deprived of it, either by nature or by force, it passes away. Further, what it is in—this is another [part]. In some, this is in the one case blood and in the other blood-vessel, in others the analogue of these. But the latter are incomplete—for example, fiber and serum.[30]

Now touch is situated in a homoeomerous part (for example, flesh or something of this sort), and, in general, in sanguineous ones, in those that have blood; in the others, it is situated in their analogue, but in all cases in a homoeomerous part. The productive capacities, on the other hand, are situated in the non-homoeomerous parts—for example, the capacity for working on nourishment in the mouth, the one for movement with respect to place in the feet, wings, or their analogue.

In addition to this, some animals are blooded (for example, human, horse, and all those that when complete, are footless, biped, or quadruped), others bloodless (for example, bee, wasp, and, of the marine animals, cuttlefish and crayfish, and all those with more than four feet).

I 5

Also, some animals are viviparous, others oviparous, others larviparous. Examples of the viviparous ones are: human, horse, seal, and all the others that have hairs. And, of aquatic animals, the cetaceans (for example, dolphin), and the so-called selachians.[31] Some of these have a blow-pipe but no gills (for example, dolphin, whale). For the dolphin's blow-pipe is through its back, the whale's is in its forehead).

5 Others have uncovered gills (for example, the selachians, such as the dog-fishes and rays).

Of the embryos that are complete the one that is called an egg is the one from which the animal that is coming to be comes to be, from one part of which comes the starting-point, while the other is nourishment for what comes to be.[32] A larva, on the other hand, is that from the whole of which the whole of the animal comes to be, as the embryo becomes articulated and grows.

10 Some of the viviparous animals are internally oviparous (for example, the selachians), others are internally viviparous (for example, human and horse). What is brought to light when the embryo has reached completion is in some cases a living animal, in others an egg, in others a larva. Of eggs, some are hard-shelled and two-colored (for example, those of

15 birds), other are soft-shelled and single-colored (for example, those of the selachians).[33] And of larvae, some are capable of movement from the outset, others incapable of movement. But these things must be spoken about with exactitude later on in *Generation [of Animals].*[34]

Further, some animals have feet, others are footless. Of those having

20 feet, some have two feet (for example, human being and bird, and these alone), others four feet (lizard and dog), others more (for example, millipede and bee). But all have an even number.[35]

Of the swimmers that are footless, some have fins, like fish. Of these,

25 some have four fins, two above on the back, two below on the belly (for example, gilt-head and sea-bass), others two only, namely, the ones that are very long and smooth (for example, eel and conger), others none at all (for example, muraena and whichever others make use of the sea just as serpents do the earth, in fact, in a liquid they swim in a

30 similar way).[36] Of the selachians, some have no fins (for example, the ones that are flat and long-tailed, like ray and sting-ray), but swim by means of their flat bodies; but the fishing-frog does have fins, as do those whose flatness does not thin out to a sharp edge.[37] The swimmers that seem to have feet, like the cephalopods, swim with these and with their fins, and do so faster in the direction of their cavity (for example,

35 cuttlefish, calamary, and octopus, but neither of the first two walks, as

490^a1 the octopus does).[38]

The crustaceans (for example, crayfish) swim with their tail-parts, but faster in the direction of their tail, with the fins they have on it.[39]

And the water-newt swims with feet and tail-parts alike. The water-newt has tail-parts that resemble those of the sheatfish, as small compared to great.[40]

Of the fliers, some are feather-winged (for example, eagle and hawk), others membrane-winged (for example, bee and cockchafer), others skin-winged (for example, flying-fox and bat).[41] Now those that are feather-winged are blooded, and the skin-winged ones likewise. The bloodless ones are skin-winged (for example, the insects). And the ones that are feather-winged or skin-winged are all two-footed or footless. For there are said to be certain serpents of this sort around Ethiopia. The feather-winged genus of animals is called bird, the two remaining genera are not named by one name [each].

Of the fliers that are bloodless some are coleopterans (for they have their wings in a sheath (*eleutron*))—for example, the cockchafer and the dung-beetle. Others, though, have no sheath. And of these some are two-winged, others four-winged: four-winged are ones that are of large size or have their sting in the rear; two-winged are the ones that are not of large size or have their sting in the front. Of the coleopterans, however, none has a sting. The two-winged ones have their stings in the front (for example, fly, horsefly, and gnat).

All the bloodless animals are smaller in size than the blooded ones, with the exception of a few bloodless ones in the sea that are larger (for example, certain of the cephalopods). And the largest of these genera occur in the hottest places, and in the sea rather than on land or in fresh water.

All animals that move around move with four or more points of movement. The blooded ones do so with four only (for example, a human does so with two hands and two feet, a bird does so with two wings and two feet), whereas quadrupeds use four feet and fishes four fins. Those that have two fins or none at all (for example, serpents) move with four points nonetheless. For their flexions are at four points, or at two plus their fins. The bloodless ones that have many feet, whether they are winged or footed, move with more than four points of movement—for example, the so-called day-fly does so with four feet and four wings. For special to this animal is not only what happens with regard to its lifespan (from which it gets its name), but also that it is winged and quadruped.

All animals—quadruped as well as multiped—move in a similar way. For they move with respect to a diagonal.[42] And whereas the other animals have two feet leading, the crab alone has four.

I 6

The chief genera of animals, into which the various animals are divided, are these: [1] one for the birds; [2] one for the fishes; [3] another for cetaceans.[43] All these are blooded. Another genus is [4] that of the hard-shelled animals, which are called shell-fish. Another, [5] that of the soft-shelled ones, which are not named by one name (for example, crayfish and certain genera of crabs and lobsters); another [6] that of the cephalopods (for example, little calamary, big calamary, and cuttle-fish); [7] another that of the insects. All these are bloodless, and the ones that have feet, are multiped; and some of the insects have wings as well.

Of the remaining animals there are no chief genera. For one species does not encompass many species, but rather in some cases the species is simple and does not have a differentia (for example, human), other times they do have one but the species are nameless.[44] For the wingless quadrupeds are all blooded, but some of them are viviparous, others oviparous. The viviparous ones all have hair, whereas those that are oviparous have horny plates. And a plate has a location similar to that of a fish-scale. Footless by nature, the serpent genus is blooded and terrestrial, and it is horny-plated. And all the other serpents are vivipa-rous, the viper alone being oviparous. For not all viviparous animals have hair. For certain fishes are also viviparous. However, those that do have hair are all viviparous. For we must also consider as a form (*eidos*) of hairs the sorts of spiny hairs that hedgehogs and porcupines have. For these serve the purpose of hairs, not of feet, like those of the sea-urchin.

Of the quadruped and viviparous animal genus there are many spe-cies, but they are without a [common] name, instead each one is spo-ken of in the way we say human, lion, deer, horse, dog, and the others spoken of in this way (although there is one single sort of genus in the case of the so-called "ones with long hairs in their tails"—for example, horse, ass, mule, ginnus, and the ones in Syria called half-asses, which are so called through similarity, but they are not unconditionally the same species (*eidos*)).[45] That is also why it is necessary to get a theoreti-cal grasp on [the various species of animals] by grasping the nature of each of them separately.[46]

What has just been said, then, is by way of an outline sketch, a fore-taste of the things and attributes on which we must get a theoretical grasp. But in what follows we shall speak about them with exactitude, in order to grasp, first, the differentiae and coincidental attributes of all of them.[47] After that, we should try to discover the causes. For this is the way to make the methodical inquiry in accord with nature, once the investigation of each is already in existence.[48] For the things about which and from which there must be a demonstration become evident on the basis of these.

So first of all we must grasp the parts from which animals are composed.[49] For it is most of all and primarily with respect to these that the whole [animals] are differentiated, either by having some and not having others, or by their position, or by their order, or by the differentiae mentioned earlier, those of species, excess or deficiency, analogy, and contrariety among the affections.

First, then, we must grasp the parts of a human. For just as each group of people evaluates currency in relation to the one best known to themselves, it is the same way, of course, in other things. But of the animals the human is of necessity the best known to us.

Now to perception the parts are quite clear. Nonetheless, for the sake of not neglecting the proper order of exposition, and of having reason (*logos*) together with perception, we must speak first of the instrumental parts, then of the homoeomerous ones.[50]

I 7

Now of the parts into which the whole composite body is divided the chief ones are these: head, neck, chest, two arms, two legs (the cavity from the neck to the private parts is called the trunk).[51]

Of the parts of the head, the one covered with hair is called the cranium. Of it, the front part is the bregma, which is late generated (for it is the last of the bones in the body to solidify), the back part is the occiput, and the part between the bregma and the occiput is the crown.[52] Under the bregma is the brain, whereas the occiput is empty. The entire cranium is permeable bone, round-shaped, and encompassed by fleshless skin. That of women has one circular suture, that of men is for the most part in three sutures, joining together at one point, though a male head having no sutures at all has already been observed.[53] The part of the cranium called a crown is the middle line where the hairs part. In some cases this is double. For some people are double-crowned, not in virtue of the bone, but in virtue of the parting of their hairs.

I 8

The part below the cranium, in a human alone among the animals, is named the face. For we do not speak of the face of a fish or of an ox.[54] The part of the face that is below the bregma and between the eyes is the forehead. Those in whom this is large are slower, those in whom it is small, quicker.⁵⁵ Those in whom it is broad are excitable, those with a rounded one, contented.⁵⁶

I 9

Below the forehead are the eyebrows, which are two in nature. Straight ones are a sign of a soft character, those that bend in toward the nose, of a harsh one; those that bend out toward the temples, of a mocking and self-deprecating one; those that are drawn in toward each other, of an envious one.⁵⁷

Below these are the eyes. They, when in accord with nature, are two. Of these, a part of each is an eyelid above and below. The hairs on their extremities are eyelashes. In the interior of the eye, the liquid part, the one with which we see, is the eye-jelly, and around this is the black, and outside it is the white.⁵⁸ The common part of the upper and lower eyelids is a pair of corners, one near the nose, the other near the temples. If these are long, it is a sign of a cynicism; if they have a fleshy part near the nose, resembling scallops, it is a sign of wickedness.⁵⁹

All other genera of animals—except the testaceans and any other incomplete animals—have eyes. And all the viviparous ones do, except the mole.⁶⁰ Though one might suppose that in a way it does have them, but not unconditionally speaking. For unconditionally speaking it neither sees nor has eyes that are clearly apparent. But when the skin is taken away, it has a space for the eyes, and has the black parts of the eyes in the place and in the space that is in accord with nature for the eyes, suggesting that the eyes are deformed in the process of generation and the skin grows over them.

I 10

The white of the eye is for the most part similar in all animals, but the so-called black differs. For in some animals it is black, in others very blue, in others bluish-gray, in others greenish.⁶¹ This last is a sign of the best character, and is best for sharpness of sight.⁶²

The human is the one that alone—or most of all—among the animals has eyes of many colors. The others have one species. Although some horses have blue eyes.⁶³

Some eyes are large, others small, others intermediate in size. The intermediate ones are best. Also, some protrude, others are deep-set, others are intermediate. Of these, the deep-set ones are in all animals the most keen-sighted; the intermediate a sign of the best character.

Also, they may tend to blink, to be staring, or be intermediate. The   10
intermediate are a sign of the best character, and of the others, the second is a sign of shamelessness, the first of instability.[64]

I 11

Further, there is a part of the head, incapable of breathing, through
which an animal hears, namely, the ear. For Alcmaeon is not speaking
the truth in saying that goats breathe with their ears.[65] One part of the
ear is nameless, the other is the lobe. The whole is composed of car-   15
tilage and flesh. The interior has a nature resembling that of trumpet-
shells; the bone that is at the extremity is similar to the ear, and into
this, as into a vessel, the sound at last arrives. There is no duct from
this to the brain, but there is one to the roof of the mouth, and a blood-
vessel from the brain extends to it. (The eyes also reach to the brain,   20
and each is situated on a small blood-vessel.)

Of the animals that have this part, the human alone has an ear that
is immovable. For of animals that have hearing, some have ears, others
do not have them, but that they have the duct is evident—for example,
the ones that are feathered or horny-scaled. But the viviparous ones—
except for seal, dolphin, and the other such cetaceans—have ears. For   25
the selachians too are viviparous. But the human alone does not move
them.[66] The seal, then, has visible ducts by which it hears, whereas the
dolphin, though it hears, has no ears. All the other animals move their
ears.[67]

The ears are situated on the same circumference as the eyes, and not,   30
as in the case of some quadrupeds, higher up. And of the ears, some
are smooth, some hairy, and some intermediate. The last are the best
for hearing, but signify nothing about character. Also, they are large,
small, or intermediate in size, very prominent, not prominent at all, or
intermediate. The intermediate ones are a sign of the best character,   **492**[b]**1**
large, prominent ones, of a tendency to silly talk and babbling.[68] The
part between eye, ear, and crown is called the temple.

Further, the part of the face that is a duct for breathing is the nose.   5
For one both inhales and exhales through it, and sneezing, which is
the expulsion of a gathered mass of pneuma, occurs through the nose.
Of the pneumas, sneezing alone is taken as something prophetic and
sacred.[69] At the same time, inhalation and exhalation occur in the
chest, and it is impossible separately with the nostrils to inhale or
exhale, because it is from the chest, along by the uvula, that inhalation   10
and exhalation come, and not from any part of the head.[70] And it is in
fact possible to live without making use of this part.

Smelling, though, does take place through this part: it is the perception of odor. The nostril is easily moved, unlike the ear, to which being

15 immovable is special. One part of it is a cartilaginous partition, the other an empty passage. For the nostril is cut in half. In elephants the nostril is long and strong, and is used as a hand. For by means of this it draws things toward it, grasps them, and conveys nourishment, both

20 wet and dry, to its mouth, and it alone of the animals does so.

Further, there are two jaws. The front part is the chin, the back part is the cheek. All animals move the lower jaw, except the river crocodile, which moves the upper jaw only.

After the nose are two lips, fleshy and immovable. The mouth is

25 in the interior of the jaws and the lips. Its parts are the palate and the pharynx.

The part that can perceive taste is the tongue. Its perceptual capacity is in its tip. And if something is placed on the flat part, [its flavor is] less.[71] The tongue also perceives all the things that other flesh can (for example, hard, hot, cold) in any part of itself, just as it also perceives

30 flavor.[72] And it is broad, narrow, or intermediate. But the intermediate is the best and most perspicuous [in its discriminations].[73] Also, it is detached or tightly attached, as in those who mumble or lisp.[74] The tongue is composed of flesh that is soft and spongy. The epiglottis is part of it.

Also, the part of the mouth that is divided in two is the tonsil, and

493^a1 the one that is multiply divided is the gum. These parts are fleshy. In the gums are the teeth, which are bony.

In the interior is another part, shaped like a hanging bunch of grapes, a pillar with prominent blood-vessels.[75] If when over-moistened it gets enflamed, it is called a bunch of grapes and causes choking.

I 12

5 The neck is the part between the face and the chest. Of this the front part is the larynx, the back part, the gullet.[76] The cartilaginous and front part of this, through which passes the voice and the breath, is the windpipe. The fleshy part is the gullet. It is in the interior, in front of the spine. The back part of the neck is the *epomis*.

10 These, then, are the parts down to the chest.

Of the parts of the chest, some are at the front, others at the back. First, then, after the neck, in the front parts, is the chest, which is divided into two breasts. On these are two nipples, through which in females the milk filters; and the breast is loose-textured.[77] Milk is

produced in males as well [as females]. But in males their breast is
dense, whereas in women it is spongy and full of ducts.   15

I 13

After the chest, in the front parts, is the abdomen, and its root is the
umbilicus. Below this root, divided in two, is the flank. The undivided
part under the navel is the lower-abdomen (the extreme part of which
is the pubic region). Above the navel is the upper-abdomen. And the   20
part common to the upper-abdomen and the flank is the gut-cavity.

A supporting girdle for the back parts is the loin (*osphus*). From
this indeed its name derives. For it seems to be symmetrical in nature
(*isophuês*). Of the part for evacuation, the one that is a sort of seat is the
buttock, and the one in which the thigh turns is the hip-socket.

A part special to the female is the uterus, while the penis is special
to the male. It is external, situated at the end of the trunk, in two parts.   25
[Of the one,] one part, the tip, is fleshy, always (one might almost say)
of an equal size, and it is called the glans, while the other, the skin
around it is nameless. (If it is cut, it does not grow back together, any
more than does the jaw or the eyelid.[78]) Common to this part and to
the glans is the tip of the foreskin. The remaining part is cartilaginous,
grows large easily, and gets erect and flaccid in contrary ways.[79]   30

Below the penis are two testicles. The surrounding skin is called the
scrotum. The testicles are neither the same as flesh nor that far from flesh.

The way in which all parts of this sort are possessed will be spoken
about with exactitude in universal terms later on.[80]   493^b1

I 14

The private part of a woman is contrary to that of males. For the part
below the pubis is hollow and not, as with that of the male, projecting.
And there is a urethra outside the uterus, which serves as a passage for
the seed of the male, and is an outlet for the wet residue in both [male   5
and female].

The part common to the neck and the chest is the throat; the part
common to the side, arm, and shoulder is the armpit; the part common to the thigh and lower-abdomen is the groin. The part inside the
thigh and the buttocks is the perineum; the part outside the thigh and
the buttocks is the hypoglutis.

The front parts of the back have now been talked about. The part   10
behind the chest is the back.

I 15

The parts of the back are the two shoulder-blades, the spine, and below, on a level with the abdomen, is the loin. Common to the upper and lower part of the trunk are the ribs, eight on each side. (For about the so-called seven-ribbed Ligurians we have not yet heard anything reliable.)

The human has an upper and lower part, front parts and back parts, right ones and left ones. The right sides and the left ones are pretty much similar in their parts, and the same in all respects, except that the left ones are weaker. The back parts, though, are not similar to the front ones, nor the lower ones to the upper ones, except for the following points of resemblance: if the face is well supplied with flesh or poorly supplied with flesh, so are the lower parts of the lower-abdomen; the legs correspond to the arms, and those that have short upper arms for the most part also have short thighs, and those with small feet have small hands too.

Of the limbs, one pair are arms. The parts of the arms are: shoulder, upper-arm, elbow, forearm, and hand. Those of the hand: the palm, five fingers. Those of the finger: the one that bends is the knuckle, the unbendable one, the phalanx. The thumb is single-jointed, the other two-jointed.⁸¹ The bend of both arm and finger is inward in all cases; the arm bends at the elbow. The interior of the hand is the palm, which is fleshy and divided by lines; in long-lived people by one or two going through the whole of it; in short-lived ones, by two, and they do not go through the whole of it.⁸² The joint at the hand and arms is the wrist. The outer part of the hand, which is sinewy, is nameless.

Another pair of limbs is the legs. Of the legs, the double-headed part is the thigh-bone, the sliding part is the kneecap, the double-boned part, the shank. The front part of the shank is the shin, the back part is the calf, which is sinewy and has blood-vessels. In some people (those that have large hips) it is drawn up toward the part behind the knee, in others it is drawn in the contrary direction. At the extremity of the shin is the ankle, which is double in each of the two legs. The many-boned part of the leg is the foot. The back part of the foot is the heel, and the front part is split into five toes; the fleshy underneath part is the ball of the foot; the upper part at the back is sinewy and nameless. Of the toe, one part is the nail, the other the bend [or joint]. In all cases, the nail is at the extremity, and in all the toe is single-jointed. In those people the interior [or sole] of whose foot is thick and not arched, and so walk on the whole of it, are unscrupulous.⁸³ The bend common to thigh and shank is the knee.

These, then, are the parts common to female and male.

The position that the parts have in relation to up and down, front   20
and back, and right and left, might seem to be evident on the basis of
perception as regards the external ones. Nonetheless, it must be spoken
about due to the same cause as the very one due to which we also spoke
about the previous parts: that is, so that the exposition be brought to an
end in proper order, and that, by enumerating them, we are less likely   25
to overlook those that are not had in the same way in the case of the
other animals as in the case of human beings.

It is in a human above all other animals that the upper parts and the
lower parts are determined in relation to the places that are in accord
with nature. For the upper parts and lower parts are positioned in relation to the upper and lower parts of the universe.[84] In the same way too
a human has the front parts and the back parts, the right parts and the
left parts, in accord with nature. Of the other animals, though, some   30
do not have them, while others, while they do have them, have them in
a more confused way. Now in all cases the head is up above in relation
to the animal's own body. But only the human, as was just said, when
completed, has this part up above in relation to the universe.

After the head is the neck, then chest and back, the one in front,   **494ᵇ1**
the other behind. And after these are the abdomen, loin, private part,
and haunch; then thigh, shank, and lastly feet. Toward the front too is
the bend the legs have, which is also the direction of perambulation,   5
as well as of the more movable part of the foot and its bend; the heel
is at the back and each of the two ankles correspond to the ears. On
the sides, right and left, are the arms, which have their bend inward,
so that the convexities of the bent legs and bent arms face each other   10
most of all in a human.

The perceptual capacities and the perceptual organs, eyes, nostrils,
and tongue, all face in the same direction and are had at the front. But
the capacity of hearing and its perceptual organ, the ears, are at the
side, on the same circumference as the eyes. Of the animals, though,
the eyes are least far apart, for his size, in a human. And a human has   15
the most exact perception of touch, and the second most of taste. But
in the others he falls short of many animals.

I 16

The parts visible on the outside surface of the body, then, are arranged
in this way, and, as was said, they are mostly distinguished by name and   20
are known through intimacy with them.[85] The inner parts, however,
are the contrary. For the inner parts of human beings are especially

unknown, so that we must refer our investigation to those of the other animals that have a nature that is about the same.[86]

First, then, situated in the head, and having a position in the front, is the brain. And it is likewise too with whatever other animals have this part. And all the ones that have blood have it, and furthermore so do the cephalopods. But proportional to size it is a human that has the largest and wettest brain. Two membranes encompass it, the one around the bone is stronger, the one around the brain itself less strong than the former.[87] In all animals the brain has two parts.[88] Behind this, at the extremity, is the so-called cerebellum, which has a shape that to both touch and sight is distinct.

The back of the head is empty and hollow in all animals, in keeping with the size that each has.[89] For some have a large head, but the part of the face below is comparatively small (the ones that are round-faced), whereas others have a small head and long jaws (for example, all of the genus with long hairs in their tails).

The brain is bloodless in all animals, that is, it has no blood-vessels in it at all, and is naturally cold to the touch. It has at its center in most animals a very small hollow.[90] The meninx around the brain is full of blood-vessels (the meninx is the skin-like membrane that encompasses the brain). Above the brain is the finest and weakest bone in the head, which is called the bregma.[91]

From the eye three ducts lead to the brain, the largest and the middle one to the cerebellum, the smallest to the brain itself; the smallest is the one nearest the nostril. The largest ones are parallel and do not meet, but the middle ones do meet (this is especially clear in the case of the fishes).[92] For these are also nearer the brain than the large ones are. The smallest ones are farthest apart from each other and do not meet.

In the interior of the neck is what is called the esophagus (it gets its derived name from its length and narrowness), and the windpipe.[93] The windpipe is situated in a position in front of the esophagus, in all animals that have it; and the ones that have it are precisely all the ones that have a lung. The windpipe is cartilaginous in nature and has little blood, but it is encompassed by many fine blood-vessels. It is situated, in its upper part, near the mouth, below the passage from the nostrils to the mouth, where too, when people are drinking and they inhale some of their drink, it advances from the mouth out through the nostrils. Between the two apertures is what is called the epiglottis, which is capable of being folded over the aperture that leads to the mouth.[94] To it the extremity of the tongue is attached. At the other end the windpipe reaches down to the middle of the lungs, then from there it splits, going to each of the two parts of the lung. For the lung tends to have two parts in all the animals that have it.⁹⁵ But in the viviparous animals the division is not evident to the same degree, and is least so in a human. And it is not split into many parts in the human, as in some of the viviparous animals, nor is it smooth, but rather exhibits unevenness. 495ᵇ1

In the oviparous animals (for example, the birds) and in those quadrupeds that are oviparous the two parts are quite split apart from each other, so that they seem to have two lungs.⁹⁶ And from the single windpipe there are two parts, one extending to each of the two parts of the lung. It is also attached to the great blood-vessel and to what is called the aorta. 5

When the windpipe is inflated, the pneuma is distributed to the hollow parts of the lung. These have cartilaginous partitions that meet at an acute angle. And from the partitions there are apertures going through the entirety of the lung, that are always so distributed that from larger ones smaller ones come. 10

The heart too is attached to the windpipe, by fatty, cartilaginous, fibrous ligatures; and at the point of attachment it is hollow. And when the windpipe is inflated, though in some animals this is not made visible, in the larger animals it is clear that the pneuma enters into the heart. 15

The windpipe, then, has this mode of arrangement, and only receives and emits pneuma, but receives nothing else, whether dry or wet, or else produces pain, until one coughs up what has gone down it.

The gullet [or esophagus] is attached at the top to the mouth, contiguous to the windpipe, and conjoined with the spine and the windpipe by membranous ligatures, ending, by way of the diaphragm, in the stomach. Its nature is fleshy and it has an elasticity both in length and in breadth. 20

The stomach of the human is similar to that of the dog. For it is not much larger than the intestine, but rather is like a sort of intestine that has a certain size. Next is the simple intestine, which is twisting; next the intestine having breadth.⁹⁷ The lower part of the bowel is similar to that of the pig.⁹⁸ For it is large, and the part going from it to the fundament is thick and short. The omentum is attached to the middle of the stomach, and has the nature of a fatty membrane, just as also in the other single-stomached animals that have teeth in both jaws.⁹⁹ 25
30

Above the intestines is the mesentery.¹⁰⁰ This too is membranous and large and becomes fatty. It is attached to the great blood-vessel and to the aorta, and throughout it are many blood-vessels densely packed together, which extend to the position of the intestines, starting above and continuing to down below. 496ᵃ1

Things having to do with the gullet [or esophagus] and the wind-pipe, then, stand this way.

I 17

The heart has three cavities, is situated above the lung at the point where the windpipe splits into two, and has a membrane that is fatty and dense where it is attached to the great blood-vessel and the aorta.[101] And it is situated with its pointy end on the aorta. And its pointy end is situated toward the chest, alike in all animals that have a chest. And in all animals, both those that have and those that do not have this part, the heart has its pointy end turned toward the front, though this may escape notice because of its migration during dissection. The rounded end of it is at the top. The pointy end is fleshy in most cases and dense, and there are sinews present in its cavities. While it is situated in the middle of the chest in the other animals (the ones that have a chest), in human beings its position is more in the left, leaning a little away from the division of the breasts toward the right breast.

Also, the heart is not large, and its form (*eidos*) as a whole is not elongated but roundish, except for the extremity where it comes to a point. It has three cavities, as was just said, the largest is on the right, the smallest on the left, and the medium-sized one in the middle.[102] All of them, even the two smaller ones, are connected to the lungs by passages, though quite visibly so [only] with regard to one of the cavities.[103] Below, at the point of attachment, from the largest cavity, there is an entrance to the great blood-vessel, near where the mesentery is, and from the middle one to the aorta.[104]

Ducts also lead to the lung from the heart, and split in two just as the windpipe does, following over all the lung the paths of those from the windpipe. Uppermost are the ones from the heart. There is no common duct, but because of their contact they receive the pneuma and transmit it to the heart. For one of the ducts leads to the right cavity, the other to the left.

About the great blood-vessel and the aorta by themselves we shall speak in common later on.[105]

Of the parts present in the animals that both have a lung and are internally and externally viviparous the lung has the most blood. For the entirety of it is spongy, and alongside the bronchial passages ducts lead to the great blood-vessel. But those who consider the lung to be empty are utterly deceived, because of looking at lungs that have been removed from animals during dissections, from which the blood has immediately all withdrawn at once.

Of the other viscera the heart alone has blood. And the lung has it not within itself but in its blood-vessels, whereas the heart has it within itself. For it has blood in each of its cavities, and the finest-grained is in the middle one.

Below the lung is the thoracic diaphragm, the so-called midriff, which is attached to the ribs, the upper-abdomen, and the spine, and in the middle has something fine and membranous. It has blood-vessels extending through it. The midriff of the human is thick in proportion to its body.

Below the diaphragm on the right side the liver is situated, and on the left the spleen, and likewise in all animals that have these parts in accord with nature and not in a monstrous way.[106] For cases have already been seen in certain quadrupeds in which the position is exchanged.[107] They are connected to the stomach through the omentum.

In appearance the spleen of the human is narrow and long, similar to that of a pig. And the liver for the most part and in most animals has a gallbladder, but in some animals it does not.[108] The liver in the human is roundish, similar to that in the ox. (This absence of the gallbladder is also met with in sacrificial animals—for example, in a certain place in Chalcis, in Euboea, the sheep do not have a gallbladder, whereas in Naxos pretty much all the quadrupeds have one so large that strangers when offering sacrifice get quite a shock, thinking the [large gallbladder] to be a sign special to themselves, not that this is the animal's nature.[109])

The liver is attached to the great blood-vessel, but has no communication with the aorta. For the blood-vessel that is part of the great blood-vessel traverses the liver at a point called the liver's portals. The spleen too is connected to the great blood-vessel alone. For a blood-vessel extends from it to the spleen.

After these are the kidneys, situated near the spine, and similar in nature to those in oxen. The right one is higher up in all the animals that have kidneys. And the right one also has less fat than the left and is drier.[110] And it is this way in all the other animals too. Ducts lead to them from the great blood-vessel and from the aorta, though not into the cavity. For the kidneys have a cavity in the middle, some a larger one, some a smaller one, except for those of the seal. For these are similar to those of oxen, but are most solid of all.

The ducts extending to the kidneys lose themselves in the body of the kidneys. A sign that they do not penetrate [the cavity] is that the kidneys do not have blood, nor does it coagulate in them. For they have a small cavity, as was just said.[111] From the cavity of the kidneys two sturdy ducts lead into the bladder. Others come from the aorta

that are strong and continuous.¹¹² At the middle of each of the two
kidneys is attached a hollow and sinewy blood-vessel that extends
all along the spine through narrow regions, then they disappear into
either haunch, and become clearly visible again in extending to the
haunch. These branches of the small blood-vessels reach down in due
course to the bladder.

For the bladder is situated at the extremity, having an attachment
there via the ducts that extend from the kidneys along the stalk that
extends to the urethra, and pretty much all around it is fastened by
fine sinewy membranes that are in a certain way about the same as the
thoracic diaphragm. In the human the bladder has moderate size.

To the stalk of the bladder is attached the penis, the outermost orifice is a running together [of two] into the same one, the other is a little
lower down. One of the orifices leads to the testicles, the other to the
bladder. [The penis] is sinewy and cartilaginous. To this, in males, the
testicles are attached. The way in which they have these will be determined in the common accounts.¹¹³

In the female too all the parts are naturally possessed in the same
way. For it does not differ in the internal ones, except for the uterus,
whose appearance one must observe on the basis of the diagrams in
the *Dissections*.¹¹⁴ Its position is over the bowels. And over the uterus
is the bladder. But the uterus too in all animals in common must be
spoken about in what follows.¹¹⁵ For it is not similar in all of them nor
is it possessed in a similar way.

The parts, then, of a human, both the internal ones and the external
ones, are these and of these sorts, and it has them in this way.

Parts of Animals

Book I

I 1

Regarding every sort of theoretical knowledge and every methodical inquiry, the more humble and more estimable alike, there appear to be two ways for the state to be, one that may be well described as scientific knowledge of the subject matter, the other a certain sort of educatedness.[116] For it is characteristic of a well-educated person to be able to judge accurately what is well said and what is not.[117] For we consider someone who is well educated about the whole of things to be a person of this sort, and we think that being well educated consists in having the capacity to do what was just stated. But in one case, we consider a single individual to have the capacity to judge about (one might almost say) all things, in the other case, about a definite nature.[118] For there might be another person with the same capacity as the one we have been discussing but about a part. So it is clear in the case of inquiry into nature too that there must be certain defining marks by reference to which we can appraise its way of showing things, separately from the question of what the truth is, whether thus or otherwise.[119]

I mean, for example, must one take each substance singly and, where it is concerned, define it by itself (for example, where the nature of a human is concerned, or of a lion, or in fact of any other sort of animal, discussing it by itself), or must one assume, in accord with something common, the attributes common to all?[120] For many of the same things belong to many distinct genera of animals—for example, sleep, respiration, growth, withering, death, and in addition any remaining affections and dispositions of this sort.[121] For at the moment it is possible [only] to speak unclearly and indefinitely about them. But it is evident, especially in speaking with respect to a part, that we shall repeatedly say the same things about many genera. For even to horses, dogs, and human beings each of the ones just mentioned belongs. So if one speaks of the attributes with respect to a particular [species], it will be necessary to speak repeatedly about the same ones, whenever the same ones belong to different species of animals, while they themselves have no differentia.[122]

But presumably there are other attributes that include the same predicate, but differ due to a difference (*diaphora*) in the form (*eidos*)— for example, the perambulation of animals.[123] For it is evident that it is not one in form. For flying, swimming, walking, and crawling differ. That is why the way one must investigate should not be overlooked—I mean whether one must observe what is common with respect to genus first, and then later the special attributes, or [what is common] with respect to the particular [species] from the outset.[124] For as things stand this has not been determined, nor indeed has what will now be stated, namely, whether just as the mathematicians show the things that astronomy is concerned with, so in that way too the natural scientist, having first observed the things that appear to be so concerning the animals and the parts of each, must then state the why, that is, the cause, or else proceed in some other way.[125]

In addition to this, since we see several causes where natural generation is concerned—for example, both the for-the-sake-of-which and the one from which comes the starting-point of movement, it must be determined also about these, which sort is naturally first, which second.[126] It is evident, though, that first is the one we call a for-the-sake-of-which. For this is an account (*logos*), and the account is a starting-point alike in the things composed in accord with craft and in those composed by nature.[127] For once the doctor has defined health and the builder has defined a house, whether by thought or by perception, they give the accounts and the causes of each of the things they produce, and why they must be produced in this way. Yet the for-the-sake-of-which and the nobly beautiful are present more in the works of nature than in those of craft.[128]

But though what is of necessity is not present in all the things that are in accord with nature in the same way, pretty much everyone tries to bring their accounts back to it, without having distinguished in how many ways things are said to be necessary. For what is unconditionally necessary is present in the eternal things, while what is hypothetically necessary is also present in all generated things, as it is in the products of craft—for example, a house or anything else of this sort.[129] It is necessary, though, that a certain sort of matter be present if there is to be a house or any other sort of end, and this must come to be and be changed first, then that, and so on continuously up to the end and the thing for the sake of which a given thing comes to be and is. And it is the same way too in things that come to be by nature.

But the mode of demonstration and of necessity is distinct in the case of the natural and the theoretical sciences.[130] (These have been spoken about elsewhere.[131]) For the starting-point in the latter is what is, and in the former, what will be. For example, "since health or the human is such-and-such sort of thing, it is necessary for *this* to be or come to be"; but not, "since *this* is or has come to be, *that* of necessity is or will be." Nor is it possible to link eternally the necessity of this sort of demonstration, so as to say, "since *this* is, [it is necessary] that *that* is." (About these things too determinations have been made elsewhere,

and about what sorts of things necessity is present in, what sort converts, and due to what cause.)^{132}

10   But neither must we forget to ask whether it is fitting to state, as those
who earlier produced theoretical knowledge did, in what way each thing
has naturally come to be rather than in what way it is. For the one differs
in no small way from the other. It seems, though, that one must begin
from what we said earlier, namely, that first one must grasp the things
that appear to be so about each genus, then state their causes, even where
15   generation is concerned.^{133} For it is rather the case that these things happen in building too because the form (*eidos*) of a house is such-and-such
sort of thing than that the house is such-and-such sort of thing because
it comes to be in this way. For generation is for the sake of the substance,
not the substance for the sake of generation.

That is why Empedocles did not speak correctly when he said that
20   many things are present in animals because of the way things happened
during the process of generation—for example, that the spine is such as
it is because it happened to be broken when the animal was bent [in the
uterus].^{134} He went wrong, first, because the seed that composes it must
be present having this sort of capacity, and, second, that its producer must
be present prior to it, not only in account (*logos*) but also in time.^{135} For
25   it is the human that generates a human. So it is because of *that* first one's
being such-and-such sort of thing that the generation is of such-and-such
sort for *this* second one. It is likewise in the case of things that seem to
come to be spontaneously as in the case of products of craft.^{136} For in
some cases things that come to be due to craft also do so spontaneously—
for example, health. Now in the case of the former something similar to
them that is capable of producing them pre-exists—for example, the craft
30   of sculpting.^{137} For a statue does not come to be spontaneously. And the
craft is the account of the work without the matter (and likewise with
what is due to luck). For as the craft has it, so it is produced.^{138}

That is why it is best of all to say that since this is the essence of a
human, because of this it has these things.^{139} For it is not possible for it
35   to be without these parts. Otherwise, one must say the closest thing to
it, namely, either in general that it is impossible to be another way or
that it is noble to be this way. And these things follow.^{140} And since it is
640^{b}1   of this sort, it is necessary for its generation to happen in this way and
be of this sort. That is why of the parts *this* one comes to be first, then
that one.^{141} And [one must proceed] in this way, then, likewise in the
case of all the things composed by nature.

Now the ancients who first philosophized about nature investi-
5   gated the material starting-point and this sort of cause, what it is, what
sort of thing it is, how the whole comes to be from it, what moves it

(for example, strife, love, understanding, or chance), and what sort of
nature the underlying matter has of necessity (for example, that of fire
hot, of earth cold, and that of fire light, that of earth heavy).[142] For in
this way too they generate the cosmos. And they speak in a similar way
about the generation both of plants and of animals—for example, saying that as water flowed into the body a stomach and every part that
receives nourishment and residue came to be, and that, as the pneuma
passed through, the nostrils were torn open.[143]

And air and water are matter for the bodies. For it is from these
sorts of things that all of them compose the nature of the bodies. But
if human beings, animals, and their parts exist by nature, one must
speak about flesh, bone, blood, and all of the homoeomerous parts.
Similarly too in the case of the non-homoeomerous parts (for example,
face, hand, foot), one must say in virtue of what each of them is the
sort of thing it is, and with respect to what sort of capacity.[144] For it is
not enough to say what things they are composed of (for example, fire
or earth), [instead,] just as if we were speaking about a bed or anything
else of this sort, we must try to define the form of it rather than the
matter (for example, the bronze or the wood). But if not, then at any
rate the matter of the compound. For a bed is a *this in this* or a *this
such-and-such sort of thing*, so that one must speak of its configuration
as well, and what its visible form (*idea*) is.[145] For nature in accord with
shape [or form] is more controlling than material nature.[146]

Now if it is by its configuration and by its color that each of the
animals and its parts is what it is, Democritus might be speaking correctly.[147] For he appears to suppose this. At any rate, he says that it
is clear to everyone what sort of thing a human is by its shape, on
the supposition that it is known by its configuration and color. And
yet though the configuration of a corpse has the same shape, nonetheless it is not a human. Further, it is impossible for something in
any and every condition (for example, made of bronze or of wood) to
be a hand, except homonymously, like a doctor in a drawing.[148] For
such a hand will not be capable of performing its function, any more
than either stone flutes or a doctor in a drawing.[149] Similarly, none of
the parts of a corpse is any longer the sort of thing it is—I mean, for
example, an eye or a hand.

Democritus, then, has spoken in too simple a way, and in the same
way as a carpenter might speak of a wooden hand.[150] This is also the
way, indeed, that the physicists speak of the processes of generation
and the causes of configuration (for [ask them] from what capacities
things are handicrafted, and perhaps the carpenter says an axe or an
auger, whereas the physicists say air or earth), except that what the

10 carpenter says is better.[151] For it will not be enough for him to say just this much, that when his instrument fell, in one case a hollow was produced, in another a plane surface; instead, by saying why he struck the blow in this way, and for the sake of what (namely, in order that such-and-such sort, or such-and-such other sort, of shape might be produced), he states the cause.

It is clear, therefore, that the physicists do not speak correctly, and
15 that one must state that the animal is of *this* sort, and where each of its parts are concerned, say what it is and what sort of thing it is, just as where the form (*eidos*) of the bed is concerned.[152] If, then, this thing is soul, a part of soul, or not without soul (when the soul has departed, at least, there is no longer an animal, nor do any of the parts remain the same, except in configuration, like the mythologi-
20 cal ones that are turned to stone)—if these things are so, then it will belong to the natural scientist to speak and know [1] about the soul (and if not about all of it, about this part by itself in virtue of which the animal is the sort of thing it is), that is, what the soul (or this part by itself) is, and [2] about the coincidental attributes it has in
25 virtue of the sort of substance it has, especially as a thing's nature is said of it in two ways and *is* in two ways, one as matter, the other as substance.[153] And nature as substance is nature both as the mover and as the end. And this sort of thing in the case of the animal is the soul, either all of it or some part of it. So in this way too the person getting a theoretical grasp on nature must speak about the soul more
30 than about the matter, inasmuch as it is more the case that the matter is nature because of soul than the reverse. For even the wood is a bed or a tripod because it is potentially these things.

Someone might raise a puzzle, though, in view of what was said just now, as to whether it belongs to natural science to speak about all soul, or about a certain part of it. For if it is about all of it, beyond
35 natural science there is no philosophy left.[154] For understanding is of the intelligible objects.[155] So natural science would be knowledge of all
641^{b}1 things.[156] For it belongs to the same science to get a theoretical grasp on understanding and on the intelligible objects, if indeed they are in relation to each other and the theoretical knowledge of things that are in relation to each other is in all cases the same knowledge, just as is also the case with perception and perceptible objects.[157] Not all soul, however, is a starting-point of movement, nor are all its parts, rather
5 of growth it is the very part that is also present in plants, of alteration it is the perceptual part, and of spatial movement some other part, and not the one capable of understanding.[158] For spatial movement is present in other animals too, but thought in none.[159] So it is clear that [the

natural scientist] must not speak about all soul. For not all soul is a nature, although some part of it—whether one part or several—is.[160]

Further, of the results of abstraction none is an object of theoretical natural science, since nature does everything for the sake of something.[161] For it is evident that, just as the craft is present in the products of craft, so in the things themselves there is a certain other starting-point and cause of this sort, which we have, like the hot and the cold, from the universe.[162] That is why it is more likely that the heaven came to be from a cause of this sort, if it came to be, and is due to a cause of this sort, than the mortal animals.[163] At any rate, the ordered and the definite are much more evident in the heavens than around us, while the variable and chance are much more so around what is mortal. Some people say, though, that each of the animals is and came to be by nature, while the heaven, in which no chance or disorder whatsoever is evident, was composed in that way by luck and chance.[164]

We say "this is for the sake of that" wherever there appears to be some end toward which the movement proceeds if nothing impedes it. So it is evident that there is something of this sort that is in particular what we call a nature. For surely it is not some random thing that comes to be from each seed, but rather *this* one from *that* one, or a random seed from a random body. Therefore the seed is a starting-point and is productive of what comes from it. For these things are by nature; certainly, they grow from seed. But surely prior again to it is what the seed is a seed of. For while the seed is becoming, the end is substance.[165] And prior again to both of these is what the seed is from. For the seed is twofold, *from* which and *of* which. For it is a seed both of what it came from (for example, from a horse) and of what will be from it (for example, a mule), although not in the same way, but of each in the way just mentioned. Further, the seed is potentially [something]; and we know how potentiality is related to actuality.[166]

There are, therefore, these two causes, the for-the-sake-of-which and the of-necessity. But perhaps someone might be puzzled as to what sort of necessity those who say things are of necessity are speaking about. For of two of the modes distinguished in the works in philosophy neither can apply. The third, though, does apply, at any rate to the things that have a process of generation.[167] For we say that nourishment is something that is necessary in accord with neither of these two modes, but because it is not possible to exist without it. But this is so as something hypothetically necessary. For just as since the axe must split things, it is necessary for it to be hard, and if hard, then made of bronze or iron, so too since the body is an instrument (for each of the parts is for the sake of something, and similarly the whole is too), it is

therefore necessary for it to be of such-and-such a sort and composed
of things of such-and-such sorts, if that is to be so.

It is clear, then, that there are two modes of cause, and that as far
as possible one must succeed in stating both, but if not, at any rate try
15   to do so, and that all those who do not, state (one might almost say)
nothing about nature.[168] For the nature is more a starting-point than
the matter is. Even Empedocles stumbled onto this, led by the truth
itself, and is compelled to say that the substance and the nature is the
20   ratio (*logos*)—for example, when he says what bone is.[169] For he does
not say that it is some one of the elements, or two, three, or all of them,
but rather that it is the ratio of their mixture. It is clear, therefore, that
flesh too is the same way, as well as each of the other parts of this sort.

A cause of our predecessors not arriving at this mode is that there
25   was then no essence and defining of the substance.[170] But Democritus touched on this first, not as something necessary to the theoretical
knowledge of nature, but because he was carried away by the facts. In
the time of Socrates, however, [interest in] it grew, but inquiry concerning natural things abated, and philosophers turned instead to use-
30   ful virtue and political science.[171]

One should, though, show things in the following way, for example, that respiration is for the sake of *this*, whereas *that* comes to be
of necessity because of *these* things. But necessity sometimes signifies
if *that*—the for-the-sake-of-which—is to be, it is necessary for these
things to hold, whereas at other times it signifies things holding that
way by their very nature. For it is necessary for the hot to go out and
35   come in again on meeting resistance, and for the air to flow in. This is
immediately necessary. And the beating back of the internal heat in the
642^b1   process of the cooling of the external air is inhalation.[172]

This, then, is the mode of the methodical inquiry, and it is concerning these, and things of this sort, that one must grasp the causes.

I 2

Some people [try to] grasp the particular [species] by dividing
5   the genus into two differentiae.[173] But this is in one respect not easy,
and in another, impossible. For of some things there will be only one
differentia, the others being superfluous—for example, footed, two-
footed, split-footed. For this one differentia is a controlling one. Otherwise, it is necessary to say the same thing many times.[174] Further,
it is fitting not to tear each genus asunder—for example, the birds,
10   putting some in one division and some in another, as we have in the
diagrammed divisions.[175] For there the result is that some have been

divided off with the aquatic animals, some in another genus. Now this similarity class has an established name, "bird," and a distinct one, "fish." Other similarity classes are nameless—for example, the blooded and the bloodless (for there is no established name for either of these). If indeed, then, none of the things that are the same in genus (*homogenês*) must be torn asunder, division into two is pointless. For people who divide in this way necessarily separate and tear asunder. For some of the many-footed are among the terrestrial animals, others among the aquatic ones.

15

20

I 3

Further, it is necessary to divide by a lack, and those who dichotomize do divide by it.[176] But there is no differentia of a lack insofar as it is a lack. For it is impossible for there to be forms (*eidos*) of what is not (for example, of footless or wingless), as there are of winged and of footed.[177] But there must be forms of a universal differentia. For if this were not so, why would it be a universal and not a particular [species]?[178] Some differentiae, though, are universal and have forms—for example, winged (for one wing is unsplit, another split). And footed is the same way, one foot has many splits, another two splits (for example, the cloven-hoofed), another has no splits and is undivided (for example, the solid-hoofed animals).[179] It is difficult, then, to distribute the animals even into differentiae of this sort, of which there are forms, so that any animal whatsoever belongs in them and the same animal does not belong in more than one—for example, winged and wingless. For the same animal is both of these—for example, ant, glowworm, and certain others. But most difficult of all, or else impossible, is to distribute them into[, for example,] the bloodless ones.[180] For it is necessary for each of the differentiae to belong to one of the particular [species], so that the opposing one does so too. But it is not possible for some indivisible species that is part of the substance to belong to animals that differ in species; instead it will always have a differentia—for example, bird differs from human being (for their two-footedness is other and different), and even if they are blooded, their blood is different, or blood must be supposed to be no part of their substance. But if this is so, one differentia will belong to two [species of] animals. And if *this* is so, it is clear that it is impossible for a lack to be a differentia.[181]

25

30

643^{a}1

5

The differentiae will be equal in number to the indivisible [species of] animals, on the assumption that both the [species of] animals and the differentiae are indivisible, and there is no common differentia.[182] But if it is possible for one that is in fact common to be present, though

it is indivisible, it is clear that, in accord with the common one at any
rate, animals that are distinct in species, are in the same differentia.[183]
So it is necessary, if the differentiae into which all the indivisible [spe-
cies of] animals fall are special, for none of them to be common.[184]
Otherwise, distinct [species] will go in the same differentia. But the
same indivisible one must not go now into one and now into another
differentia in the divisions, nor must different ones go in the same one,
and all should go into these.

It is evident, therefore, that it is impossible to grasp the indivisible
species by dividing in the way that those people do who divide the
animals, or any other genus, into two. For even according to them it
is necessary for the ultimate differentiae to be equal to all the animals
that are indivisible in species. For if there is a certain genus of which
shades of white are the first differentiae, and of each of these there are
other differentiae, and in this way on down to the indivisible ones,
the final differentiae will be four, or some other quantity obtained by
doubling from one, and the species too will be that many. And the species is the differentia in the matter.[185] For no part of an animal is either
without matter or is matter alone. For a body in any and every condition will not be an animal, nor any of its parts, as has often been said.[186]

Further, one must divide by things in the substance and not in the
intrinsic coincidents—for example, if someone were to divide the [geo-
metrical] figures, so that some have angles equal to two right angles,
others angles equal to more (for having angles equal to two right angles
is a sort of coincidental attribute of the triangle).[187]

Further, one must divide by opposites.[188] For opposites are different
from each other—for example, whiteness and blackness, straightness
and curvature. So if one of the two is a differentia, one should divide by
its opposite and not one by swimming and the other by color.

In addition to these, animate beings at any rate must not be divided
by the common functions of the body and the soul—for example, in
the divisions mentioned just now, walkers and fliers (for there are certain genera to which both differentiae belong and are fliers and wingless, just like the ant genus).[189] Also, [they must not] be divided by
wild and tame. For in the same way this would seem to divide species
that are the same. For (one might almost say that) whatever is tame is
also wild—for example, human beings, horses, oxen, Indian dogs, pigs,
goats, and sheep).[190] For each of these, if homonymous, has not been
divided separately, and if these are one in species, wild and tame cannot be differentiae.[191]

In general, however, this is the necessary result of dividing any
sort of [genus] whatsoever by a single differentia. Instead, one must

try to grasp the animals by genera, in the way already shown by ordi-   10
nary people, distinguishing a bird genus and a fish genus. For each of
these has been defined by many differentiae, not by dichotomy. For by
dichotomy either it is impossible to grasp them at all (for the same one
falls into several divisions and contrary ones into the same division),
or there will be only one differentia, and this one, whether simply or   15
the result of interweaving, will be the final species.[192] If, on the other
hand, one does not take the differentia of a differentia, one will necessarily make the division continuous in the same way that one makes
the account (*logos*) one by being bound together.[193] I mean the sort of
thing that results in the divisions into the wingless and the winged,   20
and winged into the tame and the wild, or the white and the black. For
neither the tame nor the pale is a differentia of winged; instead each is
a starting-point of another differentia, whereas here each is coincidental. That is why one must from the outset divide the one [genus] into
many [differentiae], as we say. For in this way too lacks will produce a
differentia, whereas by dichotomy they will not produce one.[194]   25

   That it is impossible to grasp the particular species by dividing the
genus in two, as some people have thought, is also evident from the following. For it is impossible for just one differentia to belong to the undivided particular [species], whether one takes simple or interwoven ones.
(I say that they are simple if they have no differentia, for example, split-   30
footed, and interwoven if they do have a differentia, for example, the
multi-split-footed in relation to the split-footed.) For what the continuity
of the differentiae that stem from the genus in accord with the division
means is that the totality is one thing, although the mode of express-
ing it makes it seem that the final one alone is the [one] differentia—for   35
example, "multi-split-footed," or "split-footed"—and that "footed" and
"many-footed" are superfluous.

   But that it is impossible for there to be many differentiae of this sort   644^{a}1
is clear. For by proceeding continuously one arrives at the ultimate differentia (although not at the final one that is the species). For it is either
split-footed alone, if one is dividing human or the whole complex—for
example, if one were to combine footed, two-footed, and split-footed.   5
On the other hand, if the human were split-footed alone, by proceeding in this way one might arrive at this one differentia. But as things
stand, since this is not so, it is necessary for there to be many differentiae that are not under one division. Yet there cannot be *many* differentiae of the same thing under one dichotomous division; instead,
one must end with one [differentia] in accord with one [division]. So it
is impossible for those who divide in two to grasp any of the particular
[species] of animals whatsoever.   10

I 4

Someone might be puzzled as to why human beings have not called by one name embracing one genus what encompasses at the same time both the aquatic animals and the fliers. For there are some affections common both to these and to all the other animals. Nonetheless, they are correctly distinguished in this way. For whatever genera differ by excess and by the more and the less have been yoked together under one genus, while those that are analogous, have been separated.[195] I mean, for example, that bird differs from bird by the more or by excess (for one is long-feathered, another short-feathered), whereas fishes differ from birds by analogy (for what is feather in the one is fish-scale in the other).[196] But to do this in all cases is not easy. For most animals have the same affections by analogy.

But since it is the ultimate species (*eidos*) that are the substances, and these are undifferentiated with respect to form (*eidos*) (for example, Socrates, Coriscus), it is necessary either to state the things that belong universally first, or to say the same thing many times.[197] And universals are things that are common. For things that belong to many we say are universal. But there is a puzzle as to which of the two to make our business. For insofar as a substance is what is indivisible in form, it would be best, if one could, to get a theoretical grasp separately on the things that are particular and indivisible in form, just as on human, so too on bird, or rather (for this genus has species) on whichever of the indivisible [species] of birds it is—for example, sparrow, crane, or something of this sort. On the other hand, insofar as it will result in speaking often about the same affection because it belongs in common to more than one [species], in this respect it is somewhat absurd and tedious to speak separately about each one.

Perhaps, then, the correct course is to speak of some affections in common with respect to genera, wherever the genera are said of things by human beings in a well-defined way, and have both a single common nature and species in them that are not too distant—[for example,] bird, fish, and any other there may be that, though nameless, encompasses in a similar way to a genus the species within it. But wherever they are not of this sort, we should speak of the particular [species]—for example, about human being and any other there may be of this sort.

The genera have been defined pretty much by the figures of the parts and of the whole body, when they bear a similarity—for example, as things in the genus of the birds do in relation to each other, as well as those in that of the fishes, cephalopods, and testaceans. For the parts of these differ not by analogous similarity, as bone in human being is related to fish-spine in fish, but rather by bodily affections—for example, large small, soft hard, smooth rough, and such—and, in general, by the more and the less.

How, then, the methodical inquiry into nature must be appraised, and in what way the theoretical knowledge of these things might proceed methodically and most easily, further, where division is concerned, in what way it is possible by means of it to grasp things in a useful way, and why dichotomy is in some respects impossible and in others empty, has been stated.

Having determined these things, let us speak about what comes next, making the following a starting-point.

I 5

Of the substances composed by nature, some are un-generated and incapable of passing away for all eternity, while others participate in coming to be and passing away. But it has happened that where the former are concerned, though they are estimable and divine, our branches of theoretical knowledge are less developed (for both about the things on the basis of which one would investigate them and the things about them we long to know, the things evident to perception are altogether few).[198] But where the plants and animals that are capable of passing away are concerned we are better equipped with a view to knowledge because of living together with them. For many things can be grasped about each genus if one wishes to take sufficient pains. Each of the two has its charms. For even if our contact with the eternal things is small, nonetheless because they are the most estimable ones knowing them is more pleasant than knowing all the things around us, just as a random small glimpse of the ones we love is a greater pleasure than seeing many other great things in exact detail. But because of knowing the others more and in greater number they take pre-eminence in scientific knowledge. Further, because they are nearer to us and more of our own nature, they provide some compensation in comparison to the philosophy concerned with divine things. But since where these are concerned we are through with stating what seems to be so to us, it remains to speak about animal nature, if possible omitting nothing whether less estimable or more estimable.[199]

For even in the theoretical knowledge of animals disagreeable to perception, the nature that handicrafts them likewise provides enormous pleasures to those capable of knowing the causes by nature. For it would in fact be unreasonable, even absurd, if we enjoyed getting

15

20

25

30

35

645^{a}1

5

10

theoretical knowledge of the likenesses of animals because of at the same time getting it of the craft (for example, painting or sculpture) that handicrafted them, while not loving even more the theoretical knowledge of the ones composed by nature, at any rate when we are capable of seeing their causes distinctly. That is why we must not be childishly disgusted at the investigation of the less estimable animals.[200] For in all natural things there is something wondrous present. And as Heraclitus is reported to have said to those strangers who wished to meet him but stopped as they were approaching on seeing him warming himself at the oven. For he told them to enter confidently, "for there are gods even here."[201] In this way too one must approach inquiry concerning each of the animals without disgust, on the supposition that in each one there is something natural and nobly beautiful.[202] For what is not random but rather for the sake of something is present most of all in the works of nature, the end for the sake of which each has been composed or has come to be has taken the place of the nobly beautiful.[203]

But if someone has considered the theoretical knowledge of the other animals to be without esteem, he must think the same thing about himself as well. For it is impossible to look at what the human genus is composed of—for example, blood, flesh, bones, blood-vessels, and other parts of this sort—without considerable disgust. But in the same way as someone discussing the parts or the equipment of anything whatsoever must be considered as doing so not to produce a record concerning the matter, nor for the sake of it, but rather for the sake of the whole shape [or form] (for example, concerning the house in fact, and not bricks, mortar, and timbers), so where nature is concerned too one must consider the discussion to be about the composition and the whole substance, but not about those things that do not occur in separation from their substance.[204]

It is necessary first, though, in relation to each genus to divide off the coincidental attributes that belong intrinsically to all the animals, and after this to try to divide off their causes.[205] Now it has been said previously too that many things belong in common to many animals, some unconditionally (for example, feet, wings, and scales, and affections of course in the same way as these), some by analogy.[206] I mean by analogy that while to some a lung belongs, to others belongs, not a lung, but something else instead of it, which is to them what a lung is to those that have one. And to some blood belongs, to others its analogue does, having the very same capacity that blood has for the blooded ones. To speak separately about each of the particular [species], though, as was also said before, will result in saying the same things many times, whenever we speak about all the things that belong to them.[207] For the same ones belong to many. Let these issues, then, be determined in this way.

But since every instrument is for the sake of something, and each of the parts of the body is for the sake of something, and what they are for the sake of is a sort of action, it is evident that the whole body too has been composed for the sake of a sort of full action.[208] For sawing is not for the sake of the saw, but the saw for that of sawing. For sawing is a certain use. So the body too is in a way for the sake of the soul, and the parts for that of the functions for which each has naturally grown. Therefore one must speak first about the activities—the ones that are common to all, the ones that are so with respect to genus, and the ones that are so with respect to species. I mean by "common" those that belong to all animals, by "with respect to genus," those whose differentiae in relation to each other we see to [differ] by excess—for example, I speak of birds with respect to genus, of human with respect to species, as too of everything that in accord with its universal account has no differentia at all.[209] For what is common some have by analogy, others with respect to genus, others with respect to species.

Wherever [1] actions are for the sake of other actions, then, it is clear that the [parts] they are the actions of are distinguished in the very same way as the actions. Similarly, [2] if some actions are in fact prior to, and the end of, other actions, it will be the same way too with each of the parts, whose actions are of these sorts; and, thirdly, [3] things whose existence necessitates the presence of [other things].[210] By "affections" and "actions" I mean generation, growth, mating, waking, sleep, perambulation, and any other things of this sort that belong to animals. By "parts" I mean nose, eye, and the composite face, each of which is called a "member." And likewise too with the other parts.

And about the mode of our methodical inquiry let this much be said. We must, though, try to state the causes both of the common and of the special attributes, starting, in the way we have determined, first with those that are first.

15

20

25

30

35

646^{a}1

Generation of
Animals

Book I

I 1

715ᵃ1 The other parts present in animals have been spoken about, both generally and with respect to the special attributes of each particular genus
separately, and about what way each part is due to this sort of cause, I
mean, the for-the-sake-of-which as end.[211] For there are four underlying causes: the for-the-sake-of-which as end, the account of the sub-
5 stance (and these must be taken pretty much as one), third and fourth,
the matter and where the starting-point of the movement comes
from.[212] Well, the others have been spoken about (for the account and
the for-the-sake-of-which as end are the same and the matter for the
animals is their parts—for the animal as a whole, the non-homoeomerous parts, for the non-homoeomerous parts, the homoeomerous
10 ones, and for these, the so-called elements of bodies).[213] But it remains
to speak about the parts that contribute to the generation of animals,
about which nothing was determined previously, and about what sort
of starting-point is cause of the movement.[214] And to investigate this
latter cause and to investigate the generation of each animal is in a way
15 the same.[215] That is why the account has brought them together as one,
by putting these parts at the end of our accounts of the parts, and the
accounts of the starting-point of generation next after them.[216]

Of the animals some come to be from the copulation of female and
male, namely, in those genera of animals in which there exist both the
female and the male.[217] For they do not exist in all, but rather in those
20 blooded ones, with few exceptions, in which the male and the female
are completed, and in those bloodless ones in which, though some
have the female and the male, so that they produce offspring of the
same genus as themselves, others, though they do produce offspring,
the offspring are certainly not of the same genus.[218] The ones that come
to be not from animal copulation but from putrefying earth and resi-
25 dues are of this sort.[219]

Generally speaking, however, among all those that are capable of
changing with respect to place, whether they are capable of swimming,
flying, or walking, the female and the male exist—and this applies
not only to the blooded ones, but also to the bloodless.[220] And among
30 the latter, sometimes it applies to the whole genus (for example, the
715ᵇ1 cephalopods and crustaceans), but in the insect genus [only] to the
majority.[221] Of these, the ones that come to be from the copulation

of animals of the same genus also produce in accordance with sameness of genus. On the other hand, those that come to be not from
animals but from putrefying matter produce something of a distinct
genus, and what comes to be is neither female nor male. Some of the
insects are of this sort.^{222} And this happens quite reasonably. For if the
ones that did not come to be from animals, themselves produced animals by copulating, if these were of the same genus as themselves, then
from the start the generation of their procreators should have been the
same way (for this is what we quite reasonably expect, since it is evident that it is so in the case of the other animals). But if they are not of
the same genus but capable of copulating, there should again come to
be from them things of a distinct nature, and again from these something of a distinct nature, and this should go on without limit. Nature,
however, avoids the unlimited.^{223} For the unlimited is without an end,
and nature always seeks an end.

Those that do not perambulate about, like the testaceans, and those
that live by being attached to something, are in substance about the
same as plants, and just as in the latter, so in these, the female and
the male do not exist—although they are immediately said to be
female or male by way of similarity and by analogy.^{224} For the difference (*diaphora*) of this sort that they have is small.^{225} For even in plants
we find in the same genus some trees that are fruit-bearing and others
that, while not bearing fruit themselves, contribute to the concocting
of what is borne by the others, as happens, for example, with the fig
and the caprifig.^{226}

It is the same way in plants too. For some come to be from seeds,
others, as it were, by the spontaneous operations of nature.^{227} For they
come to be when either the earth or certain parts of [other] plants
putrefy. For some of them are not composed separately by themselves
but come to be on other trees—for example, mistletoe.^{228}

Well, plants must be investigated separately by themselves.^{229}

I 2

As for the generation of the various animals, we must speak about it
in accord with the account that falls to each of them, connecting it to
what has just been said. For, as we have said, the starting-point of their
generation one may posit no less than the female and the male; the
male one as containing the starting-point of the movement and the
generation, the female one as containing that of the matter.^{230} One may
be most convinced of this by getting a theoretical grasp on how seed is
produced and from where.^{231} For though the ones composed by nature

come to be from seed, we must not fail to notice how it comes to be
from the female and from the male. For it is because a part of this sort
is secreted from the female and the male, the secretion being in these
and out of these, that the female and the male are starting-points of
the generation.[232] For by a male animal we mean what generates in
another, by a female what does so within itself.[233] That is why even in
the case of the whole universe people consider the nature of the earth
as female and mother, but address heaven, the sun, or anything else of
this sort as progenitor and father.[234]

The male and the female, however, differ with respect to their
account, because each is capable of a distinct thing, and with respect to
certain of their perceptible parts: with respect to their account, because
the male has the capacity to generate in another, as was said previously,
while the female has the capacity to generate within itself, that is, it is
what the thing produced, which was present in the progenitor, comes
to be from.[235] But since they are distinguished by their capacity and by
a certain function, and since instruments are needed for all work, and
since the parts of the body are the instruments of its capacities, it is
necessary for there to be parts for procreation and copulation, and for
these to differ from each other, and with respect to which the male will
differ from the female.[236] For even if the whole animal is said to be on
the one hand the female and on the other the male, it is not in virtue
of the whole of it that it is female or male, but in virtue of a certain
capacity and in virtue of a certain part (just as too with being capable
of seeing and capable of perambulation), namely, just the one that is
evident to perception.[237]

Now in fact in all blooded animals such parts in the female are
called the uterus, and in the male the ones having to do with the testes
and the penis.[238] For some of them have testes and others spermatic
ducts.[239] But there are differences (*diaphora*) belonging to the female
and the male in those bloodless ones that among themselves have
this contrariety, although in the blooded ones the parts for intercourse
differ in their configurations.[240] One must understand, however, that
when a small starting-point changes it is usual for many of the things
that follow the starting-point to change along with it. This is clear in
the case of castrated animals. For though the generative part alone is
destroyed, pretty much the whole shape of the animal changes along
with it to such an extent that it seems to be female or not far short of
it, suggesting that it is not in virtue of some random part or in virtue
of some random capacity that it is female or male.[241] It is evident, then,
that [the difference between] the male and the female appears to be a
sort of starting-point.[242] At any rate, when an animal changes in that

wherein it is female or male, many things change along with it, suggesting that a starting-point is undergoing a change.

I 3

What has to do with testes and uterus—and in the *first* place what has to do with the testes of the males—is not possessed in a similar way in all the blooded animals. For some animals of this sort do not have testes at all (for example, the fish genus and the serpent genus), but only two spermatic ducts.[243] Others do have testes, but have them inside, near the loin, by the region of the kidneys, and from each of them runs a duct (as in the animals that have no testes), and these join together into one (again like those others)—for example, among animals breathing air and having a lung, all birds and oviparous quadrupeds.[244] For all these too have their testes inside, near the loin, with two ducts leading from them in a similar way to the serpents—for example, lizards, tortoises, and all the horny-plated animals. But all the viviparous ones have their testes in the front, though some of them (for example, the dolphin) have them inside, at the end of the abdomen, and have no ducts but rather a private part reaching from them to the outside (for example, the ox-fish).[245] Others, though, have the testes outside, either hanging down (like a human) or near the fundament (like pigs). I have made more exact determinations about these in the *History of Animals*.[246]

Every uterus is bipartite, just as the testes in males are two in every case.[247] Some animals have it near the sexual parts (as do women, all animals that are viviparous not only externally but also internally, and such fish as lay eggs that are visible to the eye), others near the diaphragm (as in all birds and viviparous fishes).[248] The crustaceans and the cephalopods also have a bifurcated uterus. For the membranes encompassing their so-called eggs have a uterus-like quality.[249]

The uterus is most indistinct in the octopuses, so that it appears to be unipartite.[250] The cause of this is that the mass of the octopus's body is similar at every point. It is bifurcated too in the larger insects, while in the smaller ones it is unclear due to the smallness of the body.

This, then, is the way the aforementioned parts of animals are possessed.

I 4

With regard to the difference (*diaphora*) there is in the spermatic instruments in males, if we are going to get a theoretical grasp on the

causes to which it is due, it is first necessary to grasp what the testes
are composed for the sake of. Now if nature makes everything either
because of what is necessary or because of what is better, this part
should exist because of one of these two things.[251] Well, that it is not
necessary for generation is evident. For then every progenitor would
have it. But as things stand neither serpents nor fish have testes. For
they have been seen copulating and with their ducts full of milt.[252] It
remains, then, for it to be for the sake of what is better.

Now the function of most animals is pretty much nothing other than
that of plants, namely, [to produce] seed and fruit.[253] But just as in the
case of nourishment, where animals with straight intestines are greedier
in their appetite for food, so the ones that have no testes but only ducts,
or that do have them, but have them internally, are all quicker in the
activity of copulation.[254] But those that need to be more temperate, in
the one case have non-straight intestines and in the other helices in their
ducts, with a view to their appetite being neither quick nor greedy.[255] It
is with a view to this that the testes have been contrived. For they make
the movement of the spermatic residue more stable: in the viviparous
ones (for example, in horses and others of this sort and also in human
beings), they do this by preserving the doubling-back [of the ducts] (one
should get a theoretical grasp on the way they do this from the *History of
Animals*).[256] For the testes are no part of the ducts, but attached to them,
just like the stone weights that women attach to their looms when weaving.[257] For if these are removed, the ducts are drawn up internally, so that
castrated animals are incapable of generating, since if the ducts were not
drawn up, they would be capable of it. In fact a bull immediately after
castration has been known to mate with and impregnate a cow because
the ducts had not yet been drawn up.

In birds and oviparous quadrupeds the testes receive the spermatic
residue, so that its emission is slower than in fishes. This is evident
in the case of birds. For their testes are much larger around mating
time.[258] And those birds that mate at one season of the year have such
small ones when this time has passed that they are pretty much indis-
cernible, whereas around mating time they are very large.

The ones having the testes internally mate more quickly. For in fact
those having them externally do not discharge seed before the testes
are drawn up.

I 5

Further, the quadrupeds have the instrument for copulation. For it is
possible for them to have it, whereas for birds and footless animals it

is not possible, because the former have their legs under the middle of their abdomen, and the latter have no legs at all, and it is the nature of the private part to hang there and its position lies there.[259] (That is also why in sexual intercourse there is tension of the legs, since the private part is sinewy and the nature of the legs is sinewy too.) So, since it is not possible for them to have this instrument, it is necessary either for them also to have no testes, or else not to have them there. For in those animals that have [both penis and testes] the position of both is the same.

Further, in those animals at any rate that have external testes, because of the movement and heating up of the private part, the seed is gathered together before emission: it is not ready immediately on making contact, as with the fishes.

All the viviparous animals have their testes in front, either inside or outside, except the hedgehog. This one alone has them near the loin. This is due to the very same cause as it is also due to in the birds. For it is necessary for their copulation to take place quickly. For unlike the other quadrupeds they do not mount on the back, but have intercourse standing upright because of their spines.[260]

The cause due to which animals that have testes have them has now been stated, as has the cause due to which some have them outside, others inside.

I 6

The ones that do not have testes do not have this part, as was said, not because of what is good but because of what is necessary, and also because it is necessary for their mating to take place quickly. The nature of fishes is of this sort, as is that of serpents. For fishes mate by placing themselves side to side and ejaculating.[261] For just as in the case of human beings and in all the others of this sort it is necessary to hold in pneuma before emitting the semen, so fishes at such times must not take in sea-water, and they easily pass away if they do not do this.[262] Therefore they must not concoct their seed during copulation, as the viviparous terrestrial animals do, but instead have their seed concocted and gathered together at the proper time, so that they do not concoct it while making contact with each other but emit it already concocted.[263] That is why they have no testes but rather straight and simple ducts, like the small part around the testes that quadrupeds have. For of the part of the duct that is doubled back one part is blooded and another bloodless, and the liquid is already seed when it is received by and travels through this latter part, so that when the seed has arrived there, ejaculation takes place quickly in these animals too.²⁶⁴ In fishes the whole of the duct is like this latter part of it in the case of human beings and other animals of this sort, that is, the other [straight, bloodless] part of what is doubled back.

I 7

Serpents mate by twining around each other, but do not have testes or even a private part, as was said previously (no private part, because they have no legs either; no testes because of their length), but rather ducts just as fish do.²⁶⁵ For because their nature is to be so long, if there were further delay having to do with testes, the semen would get cooled down because of its slow progress. This is just what happens in the case of those with large private parts. For they are less fertile than those who have more moderately sized ones because cold seed is not fertile, and it gets cooled down by traveling too great a distance. What the cause is due to which some animals have testes while others do not have them has now been stated.

Serpents twine around each other because they are not naturally suited for placing themselves side to side. For being so long, and the part by which they attach themselves being so small, they are not easily fitted together. Since, then, they have no parts with which to embrace, instead of this they make use of the suppleness of their bodies, twining around each other. Because of this too they seem to be slower to ejaculate than fish, not only because of the length of the ducts, but also because of the great care taken about these proceedings.²⁶⁶

I 8

In the case of females, one might raise a puzzle about the way the things having to do with the uterus are possessed. For many contrarieties are found in these. For not even all the viviparous ones have them in a similar way, but rather human beings and all the terrestrial animals have the uterus low down near the sexual parts, whereas the viviparous selachians have it higher up near the diaphragm; nor do the oviparous ones, but rather fish have it low down just like the human and the viviparous quadrupeds, whereas birds have it higher up as do the oviparous quadrupeds.²⁶⁷ Yet even these contrarieties are in accord with reason (*logos*).

For first of all the oviparous ones have different ways of laying their eggs. For some eggs are incomplete when emitted—for example, those of fish. For these are completed and do their growing outside the fish.²⁶⁸

The cause is that fish are prolific; in fact, this is their function just as it is of plants.[269] If, then, the eggs are completed inside themselves, it is necessary for them to be few in number. But as things stand they have 10 so many that each uterus seems to be [all] egg, at any rate in the small fishes. For these are the most prolific of all, just as in the case of other things—both among plants and among animals—that have a nature analogous to theirs.[270] For growth in size turns in them to seed.[271]

Birds, however, and quadrupedal oviparous animals lay eggs that 15 are complete, which must, with a view to preservation, be hard-shelled (for they are soft-shelled until they have grown). But their shell comes about due to heat, which evaporates the liquid from the earthy material. It is necessary, then, for the place where this will happen to be hot. 20 And the one around the diaphragm is like this. For it in fact concocts the nourishment.[272] If, then, it is necessary for the eggs to be within the uterus, it is necessary for the uterus to be near the diaphragm in those animals that lay eggs that are complete, but to be low down in those that lay incomplete ones. Also, it is more natural for the uterus to be low down, whenever there is not some other function of nature to 25 prevent it. For the limit of the uterus is low down too, and the uterus is where its function is.[273]

I 9

The viviparous animals too have a difference (*diaphora*) in relation to each other. For some produce their young alive, not only externally, but also internally—for example, human beings, horses, dogs, and all those having hair, and among aquatic animals, dolphins, whales, and 30 cetaceans of this sort.[274]

I 10

Selachians and vipers, though they produce their young alive externally, first lay eggs internally. And the egg they lay is a complete one. For this is the way an animal comes to be from the egg, whereas from incomplete ones nothing comes to be. They do not lay eggs externally because of the coldness of their nature, and not, as some people say, 35 because of its heat.[275]

I 11

At any rate, the eggs they [selachians and vipers] produce are soft-shelled. For, because they have so little heat, their nature does not dry

the extremity [of the egg]. It is because of the cold, then, that they produce soft-shelled ones, and because they are soft-shelled they do not
719ᵃ1   do so externally. For they would have been destroyed.

When the animal comes to be from an egg, the way it comes to be is
mostly just the same as the one in which birds come to be, that is, [the
egg] descends and the animal comes to be near the sexual parts, just as
in those animals too that are viviparous from the outset.[276] That is also
5   why in animals of the sort we are discussing the uterus is dissimilar to
that of the viviparous and the oviparous animals, because they participate in both forms (*eidos*). For in all the selachians it is at once near the
diaphragm and stretching along downward. (But one must get a theoretical grasp on the way this and the other sort of uterus are possessed
10   from the *Dissections* and the *History of Animals*.[277]) So, because they
are oviparous and lay complete eggs, the selachians have their uterus
high up, but because they are viviparous, they [also] have it low down,
participating in both.

Animals that are viviparous from the outset all have the uterus low
down. For no function of nature impedes this nor do they double-
bear.[278] In addition, it is impossible for an animal to come to be near
15   the diaphragm. For fetuses necessarily possess heaviness and movement, and that place, because it is vital for life, would not be capable of
enduring these things.[279] Further, delivery would necessarily be painful because of the length to be traveled, since, even as things stand, in
the case of women, if they draw up the uterus around the time of delivery, by yawning or doing something of this sort, they have a difficult
20   delivery. But even when empty the uterus produces a stifling sensation
if moved upward. And in fact it is necessary, if it is going to contain
an animal, for the uterus to be stronger [than in oviparous animals],
which is why it is fleshy in all the viviparous ones, whereas those that
are near the diaphragm are membranous. And in the case of those that
double-bear it is evident that this is so. For they hold their eggs high
25   up and on the side, but hold the living young in the lower part of the
uterus.

What the cause is due to which what has to do with the uterus is
possessed in contrary ways in some animals, and, in general, why in
some it is low down, in others high up near the diaphragm, has now
been stated.

I 12

30   Why do all animals have the uterus inside, while some have their testes
inside, others outside? The cause of the uterus always being inside is

that what is coming to be is in this, and it needs safeguarding, shelter, and concoction, whereas the place outside the body is easily harmed and cold. The testes, though, are outside in some animals, inside in others.[280] But because they also need shelter and a covering to pre-   35
serve them and with a view to the concoction of the seed (for when   719ᵇ1
chilled and stiffened, it is impossible for them to be drawn up and emit semen), those animals that have their testes visible have a covering of skin over them called the scrotum. Those, on the other hand, the   5
nature of whose skin opposes this arrangement, because it is very hard and is neither capable of enclosing them nor of being softened and like [true] skin, necessarily have them inside—for example, those that have fish-like skin or are horny-plated. That is why the dolphins and those cetaceans that have testes have them inside, as do the horny-plated   10
animals that are oviparous and four-footed. And the skin of birds is also hard, so that it will not conform to the magnitude of anything and enclose it—in fact, this is a cause in all these cases [of their having their testes inside] that is in addition to the others mentioned previously, stemming from facts about the necessities of mating.[281] Due to the same cause the elephant and the hedgehog also have their testes   15
inside. For in their case too the skin is not naturally well-disposed to keeping the protective part separate.[282]

{Contrary positions for the uterus are also found in those animals that are viviparous internally and in those that are externally oviparous, and in the latter again some have it low down, others near the diaphragm—for example, the fishes in comparison to the birds and   20
the oviparous quadrupeds. And [it is different again] in those that pro-
duce in both ways, being oviparous internally and viviparous exter-
nally. For those that are viviparous both internally and externally have their uterus placed on the abdomen—for example, human being, ox,   25
dog, and others of this sort. For it is advantageous for the fetus that no weight be put on the uterus.[283]}

I 13

The duct through which the dry residue and that through which the wet one issues are also distinct in all these animals.[284] That is why all   30
animals of this sort, both male and female, have private parts by which the wet residue is excreted, and in males the seed, and in females the embryo.[285] This duct is above and in front of the duct for [the excre-
tion] of the dry nourishment.[286] {Oviparous animals that lay incom-
plete eggs—for example, the oviparous fishes—have their uterus not   35
under the abdomen but near the loin. For the growth of the egg does   720ª1

not impede this, because what is grown is completed and develops outside.[287]} The duct is the same as that for the solid nourishment in those
animals that have no generative private part, namely, in all the oviparous ones, even in those of them that have a bladder—for example, the
tortoises.[288] For it is for the sake of generation, not for the excretion of
wet residues, that the ducts are twofold. And it is because the nature of
seed is liquid, the wet residue also shares the same duct. This is clear
from the fact that though all animals bear seed, wet residue is not produced in all of them.

Since, then, the spermatic ducts in males must be fixed in position
and not wander about, as must the wombs in females, and it is necessary for this fixing to take place at either the front or the back of the
body, in viviparous animals, because of the fetuses, the wombs are in
the front, in oviparous ones they are at the back near the loin, and
those that are internally oviparous but externally viviparous have them
both ways, because they participate in both, being both viviparous and
oviparous. For the upper part of the uterus, where the eggs are produced, is under the diaphragm near the loin and the back, but its continuation is low down near the abdomen.[289] For it is in this part that it
is actually viviparous. And there is one duct in these animals for the
dry residue and for mating. For none of them has a private part, as was
said previously, hanging down.[290]

The ducts of males, whether they have or do not have testes, are
possessed in a similar way to the wombs of oviparous animals. For in
all of them they are attached near the back over against the place of the
spine. For they must not wander about, but rather be fixed in position,
and the place at the back is of this sort. For it provides continuity and
stability.

In those that have their testes inside, indeed, they are fixed in position from the outset, and similarly in those that have them outside.
Then they meet and unite near the place of the private part.

The ducts are also possessed in a similar way by the dolphins,
although they have their testes hidden under the abdominal cavity.

How the animals have the parts positioned that have to do with contributing to generation, and due to what causes, have now been stated.

I 14

In the case of the other animals, the bloodless ones, the way they have
the parts having to do with contributing to generation is neither the
same as among the blooded ones nor among themselves. We have
four genera remaining: first, the crustaceans; second, the cephalopods;

third, the insects; and fourth, the testaceans (but though it is not clear   5
about all of them, it is evident that most of them do not copulate; in
what way they get composed must be stated later).[291]

The crustaceans copulate like the animals that urinate from behind,
when, with one supine and the other prone, they fit their tails together.   10
For their tails, because they have long flaps attached to them, prevent
them from doing so belly to back. The males have fine spermatic ducts,
while the females have a membranous uterus alongside the intestine,
divided on either side, in which the egg is produced.

I 15

The cephalopods intertwine at the mouth, pushing against each other   15
and twining together their tentacles. This way of twining together is of
necessity. For nature has turned around the end of the duct for residues
and brought it near the mouth, as was said previously.[292] The female   20
in each of these animals, it is evident, has a uterus-like part. For it
contains an egg which at first is indistinct, but then becomes disaggregated into many, each of which is incomplete when it is produced,
as with the oviparous fishes. And the same duct is for the residues and
for the uterus-like part both in the crustaceans and in these. In fact,   25
it is through this duct that the animal releases its ink. And it is on the
under-surface of the body where the mantle is open and the sea-water
enters in.[293]

That is why the copulation of the male with the female takes place
at it. For if indeed the male discharges something, whether seed or   30
a part, or some other capacity, it is necessary for him to intertwine
with her at the uterus-like duct.[294] But in the case of the octopuses, the
insertion of the tentacle of the male through the funnel of the female,
by which tentacle the fishermen say he mates, is for the sake of inter-
twining, not as an instrument useful for generation. For it is outside
the duct [of the male], indeed outside his body.   35

Sometimes too the cephalopods copulate front down; but whether
for the sake of generation or due to some other cause has not been   721ᵃ1
observed.

I 16

Among the insects, some copulate, and the generation of them is from
synonymous animals (just as in the case of the blooded animals)—for
example, locusts, cicadas, spiders, wasps, and ants.[295] Others, although
they copulate and generate, do not produce things of the same genus   5

as themselves but only larvae, nor do these come to be from animals, but rather from putrefying liquids, and some from putrefying dry materials—for example, fleas, flies, cantharides.[296] Others again neither come to be from animals nor do they copulate, like gnats, mosquitoes, and many such genera.[297]

In most of the sorts that copulate, the females are larger than the males; and the males do not appear to have any spermatic ducts.[298] And the male, speaking of what holds in the majority of cases, does not insert any part into the female, but rather the female does so upward from below into the male. This has been observed in many cases, the contrary in few.[299] But we have not yet been able to see how to divide them by genus.

And this is so too in the case of pretty much the majority of the oviparous fishes, also in the case of the quadrupeds that are oviparous. For the females being larger than the males is because of its being advantageous to them due to the mass of eggs produced during gestation. And in the females of these the part analogous to the uterus is divided and alongside the intestine, as in the other animals, and the embryos come to be in it. This is clear in the case of locusts and whatever, having the size of these, naturally copulates. For most insects are too small [for this to be clear].

These, then, are the ways the generative instruments in animals, which were not spoken about previously, are possessed.[300] Of the homoeomerous parts left aside there, namely, semen and milk, about these it is now the opportune time to speak—about semen immediately, about milk in what follows.[301]

I 17

It is evident that some animals emit seed—for example, those whose nature is to be blooded. But whether insects and cephalopods do is unclear. So this is something we must get a theoretical grasp on, namely, whether all male animals emit seed, or not all of them do, and if not all of them do, what the cause is due to which some do while others do not. Also, whether the females too contribute any seed or not, and if not seed, whether nothing else at all, or though they do contribute something, it is not seed. Further, we must also investigate what the ones that do emit seed contribute, by means of their seed, to generation, and, in general, what the nature of seed and of so-called menses is, in the case of those animals that emit these liquids.

It seems that all are come to be from seed, and the seed from the progenitors. That is why it belongs to the same account to ask whether both female and male emit it or only one of the two, and whether it comes from all the body or not from all. For it is reasonable to suppose that if it does not come from all of it, neither does it come from both progenitors. That is precisely why, since some people say that it comes from all the body, we must investigate how things stand on this question first.[302]

There are pretty much four things that someone might use as proofs.[303] [1] First, the intensity of the pleasure involved.[304] For an affection is more pleasant when it is more intense, and what happens to all the parts is more intense than what happens to one or a few. [2] Further, that from docked things docked things come to be.[305] For because the thing is missing the part, no seed, they say, proceeds from there, with the result that the part that would have come from there does not come to be.[306] [3] In addition to these, the similarities to the progenitors. For the young look like them not only as regards the body as a whole but also part for part. If indeed, then, the cause of the similarity of the whole is the seed coming from the whole, then the cause of the similarity of the parts should be its also coming from each of the parts as well. [4] Further, it would seem reasonable to suppose just as there is also some primary thing from which the whole comes to be, it is this way too with each of the parts.[307] So if there is a seed for the whole, there should also be a special seed for each of the parts.

And the following sorts of things are taken as convincing evidence for these beliefs: children come to be who are like their parents not only in congenital characteristics but also in acquired ones. For when the progenitors have had scars, certain of the offspring have been known to have the imprint of the scar in the same places, and there was a case in Chalcedon where the father had a brand on his arm and the letter was marked on the child, though blurred, to be sure, and not clearly articulated.

It is pretty much on the basis of these considerations, then, that some people are convinced that the seed comes from all [of the body].

I 18

On examining the argument, however, the contrary appears more [convincing]. For to refute the things just stated is not difficult, and in addition the argument involves saying other impossible things. First of all, then, similarity is no sign that the seed comes from all the body, because similarities occur in voice, nails, hair, and even in movement, from which nothing comes.[308] And there are some things that people do not yet have when they generate—for example, a beard or gray hair.

Further, children are like their distant ancestors from whom nothing has come. For these likenesses recur after many generations—for
example, the woman in Elis who had intercourse with an Ethiopian.
For it was not her daughter but her daughter's son who became Ethiopian.[309] And the same argument applies to plants. For it is clear that in
their case as well the seed would have to come from all the parts. But
many parts are in some cases not possessed, in others may be removed,
and in others still they grow on afterwards. Further, the seed does not
come from the seed-case either, and yet this too comes to be having the
same shape [as in the parent plant].

Further, does the seed come only from each homoeomerous part (for
example, from flesh, bone, sinew) or also from the non-homoeomerous ones (for example, face and hand)? For if only from the former, [we
object that] they are like their parents more in the latter (namely, the
non-homoeomerous ones, such as face, hands, and feet).[310] If indeed,
then, not even similarity in these is due to the seed's coming from all
the parts, what prevents similarity in the former from not being due to
its coming from all of them either, instead of to some other cause? And
if it comes only from the non-homoeomerous parts—then it does not
come from all the parts. And it is more fitting for it to come from the
homoeomerous ones because they are prior and the non-homoeomerous ones are composed of them, and just as likenesses occur in face and
hands, so they do too in flesh and nails.[311] If, however, it comes from
both, what would be the mode of generation? For the non-homoeomerous parts are composed from the homoeomerous ones, so that to
come from the former would be to come from the latter and from their
composition. It is just like if something came from a written name: if
it came from all of it, it came from each of the syllables, and, if it came
from these, it came from the letters and from their composition. So, if
indeed flesh and bone are composed of fire and things of that sort, the
seed would come rather from the elements.[312] For how could it possibly come from their composition? But without it there would not be
the similarity. If something handicrafts this later, it would be the cause
of the similarity, not the seed's coming from all the parts.[313]

Further, if the parts are torn asunder in the seed, how are they alive?
On the other hand, if they are connected, they would be a tiny animal.

And what about what belongs to the private parts? For what comes
from the male and what comes from the female are not similar.[314]

Further, if the seed comes from all parts of both parents alike, two
animals come to be. For it will have every part of each parent. That is
why, if indeed one must speak in this way, Empedocles seems to speak
most in agreement with this account.[315] For he says that there is a sort

of token in the male and in the female, and that the whole offspring comes from neither one:

> Torn asunder is the nature of the limbs, this part in man's . . .³¹⁶

For otherwise why do the females not generate from themselves, if indeed the seed comes from all the parts and they have a receptacle? But, as it seems, either it does not come from all the body or it does so in the way Empedocles says, namely, not the same thing from each parent—which is why in fact they need to have sexual intercourse with each other. Yet even this is impossible—as impossible, in fact, as it is for the full-grown parts, when torn asunder, to survive and be animate, which is how Empedocles speaks of them as coming to be under the influence of love:

> as many heads sprouted without necks

—and later, in this form, grew together.³¹⁷ But it is evident that this is impossible. For neither having a soul nor being alive they would be incapable of surviving—nor, if they were like several living animals could they grow together so as to be one again.³¹⁸ Yet saying that it is this way follows from saying that seed comes from all the body, and just as it was then in the case of the earth under the influence of love, so, on this view, it is in the case of the body. For it is impossible for the parts to come to be [already] connected, that is, to come from [the bodies of parents] and go off together into one place. Next, how were the upper and lower parts, right and left ones, and front and back ones torn asunder? For all these things are unreasonable (*logos*).

Further, some parts are distinguished by capacity, others by affections: the non-homoeomerous ones (for example, tongue and hand) by their capacity to do something, the homoeomerous ones by hardness and softness and other affections of this sort.³¹⁹ It is not in any and every state, then, that a part is blood or flesh. It is clear, therefore, that what has come from them cannot be synonymous with the parts—for example, blood from blood or flesh from flesh.³²⁰ But then if it is from *something else* that blood is produced, the cause of the similarity would not be—as those who speak this way say—the coming of seed from all the parts. For it is enough that it come from one part, if indeed it is not from blood that blood is produced. For why could not all come to be from one? For their account seems to be the same as that of Anaxagoras, in having none of the homoeomerous things come to be—except that he makes it apply to all things, these thinkers to the generation of animals.³²¹

Next, in what sort of way will these parts—the ones that come from all the body—grow? For Anaxagoras quite reasonably says that [particles of] flesh from the nourishment are added to [particles of] flesh.[322] But if they do not say this, yet say that [seed] comes from all, how, by the addition of something else, will something get bigger, if what is added is not changed? But then if what is added is capable of changing, why from the outset is the seed not such that blood and flesh can come to be from it, although it itself is neither blood nor flesh? For it certainly is not open to them to say that later growth is due to mixing, like wine when water is poured into it. For each part would have been most of all itself when still unmixed. But as things stand it is rather later on that it is flesh, bone, and each of the other parts. And to say that some of the seed is sinew and bone, it is beyond us, as the saying goes.

In addition, if female and male differ during gestation, as Empedocles says:

[Seeds] were poured into pure places; some became women
When they encountered cold.[323]

In any case, it is evident that just as both women and men change from infertile to fertile, so they also change from female-bearing to male-bearing, which suggests that it is not in the coming from all or not from all that the cause lies, but in the proportion or disproportion between what comes from the woman and what comes from the man, or else it is due to some other cause of this sort. It is clear, therefore, if we assume it to be this way, that a female is not due to the seed's coming from a certain thing, with the result that neither is the part specially possessed by the male or the one specially possessed by the female—if indeed the same seed is capable of coming to be either female or male, implying that the part is not present in the seed.[324] What difference is there, then, between saying this of it and saying it of any of the others? For if seed does not come to be even from the uterus, the same argument will apply to the other parts as well.

Further, certain animals come to be neither from those of the same genus nor from those of a different genus—for example, the flies and the genera called fleas.[325] And though animals come to be from these, but no longer ones of a similar nature, but a genus of larvae. It is clear, then, that offspring of a distinct genus do not come to be from every part. For they would be similar to [the parents] if indeed similarity were a sign of coming from every part.

Further, from one act of sexual intercourse even some of the animals produce several offspring (and the plants in fact do so always—for it is

clear that from one movement these bear all their yearly fruit).[326] And
yet how is this possible if the seed were secreted from all the body? For
then it is necessary for one secretion to be produced from one act of
sexual intercourse and one disaggregation [of seed]. It is not possible
for it to get separated up in the uterus.[327] For by then the separation
would be, as it were, from an animal, not from seed.[328]

Further, plant cuttings bear seed from themselves. It is clear, then,
that even before they were cut, they bore the fruit from their own magnitude, and not from seed coming from all of the plant.

But a greater proof than these is one we have adequately observed
in the case of the insects. For if not in all, yet in most cases, during
mating the female extends a part of itself into the male. (That is why
they mate, as we said previously, the way they do.[329] For it is evident
that the ones below insert something into the ones above, not in all
cases, but in most of those observed.) So it is evident, even in those
males that emit semen, that the seed's coming from all the body is
not the cause of generation, but it occurs in some other way that
must be investigated later on.[330] For even if it did indeed happen to
come from all the body, as they say, still they should not claim that it
comes from everything, but only from what does the handicrafting—
from the carpenter, as it were, but not from the matter. But as things
stand they speak as if it even came from shoes. For it is pretty much
the case that a son who is similar to his father wears shoes that are
similar to his.

The cause of pleasure's being very intense during sexual intercourse is
not that the seed comes from all the body but that there is a strong titilla-
tion. That is why if this intercourse happens often, the pleasure is less for
the partners. Further, the pleasure is at the end, but [on the view under
discussion] it should be in each of the parts, and not at the same time,
but earlier in some and later in others.

Docked offspring come to be from docked progenitors due to the
same cause as that due to which they are similar to them. But offspring
that are not mutilated also come to be from mutilated ones, just as
some are not similar to their procreators. We must get a theoretical
grasp on the cause of these things later on.[331] For the problem in these
cases is the same.

Further, if the female does not emit seed, by the same argument it
does not come from all the body. And if it does not come from all, there
would be nothing unreasonable in its not coming from the female, but
for the female to be in some other way a cause of generation. This is the
next thing to be investigated, since it is now evident that the seed is not
secreted from all the parts.

As starting-point both of this investigation, however, and of the ones that follow, the first thing to grasp about the seed is what it is. For in this way it will be easier to get a better theoretical grasp both on its functions and the facts concerning it.

Seed means the sort of thing whose nature is to be that from which the things composed in accord with nature first come to be, not from that thing which is the progenitor—for example, a human (for they come to be from it because the seed belongs to it).[332] But there are many ways in which one thing comes to be *from* another.[333] For there is a distinct way in which we say night comes to be from day and man from boy, namely, because *this* one comes after *this* one. Another is as a statue comes to be from bronze, a bed from wood, and whichever other things come to be as things are said to come to be from matter—from something pre-existing having been given a certain configuration the whole thing exists. Another way is as non-musical comes to be from musical, sick from healthy, and, in general, contrary from contrary.[334] Further, beyond these, there is the way Epicharmus produces his climax, namely, from slander abuse, from abuse a fight.[335] In all these cases the starting-point of the movement is from something. And in some cases of this sort the starting-point of the movement is within the things themselves (for the slander is a part of the entire disturbance), whereas in some it is external—for example, the crafts [are the starting-points of movement] for things handicrafted and the torch for the burning house.[336]

It is evident, however, that the seed is come from in one or other of two ways. For it is either as matter, or as the primary mover, that what comes to be has come to be from it.[337] For it certainly does not do so as *this* comes after *this* (for example, from the Panathenaean festival comes the sea voyage), nor as contrary does from contrary (for it is from the passing away of its contrary that the contrary comes to be, and there must be some other subject underlying and remaining present from which it will first come to be).[338] Of the two, then, it is necessary to grasp in which the seed must be put, whether as matter and affected, as form of a sort and affecter, or indeed as both. For at the same time it will perhaps also be clear how generation from contraries belongs to everything that comes to be from seed. For generation from contraries is natural too. For some things come to be from contraries, namely, from male and female, others from one thing only—for example, plants and certain of the animals in which male and female are not distinct and separate.

Now what comes away from the progenitor in whatever naturally copulates is called semen, namely, the first thing containing a

starting-point of generation, whereas seed is what contains the starting-points from both copulators (like the seeds of plants and of certain animals in which male and female are not separated), as the first   15
mixture that comes from female and male, being as it were a sort of
embryo or an egg (for these already contain what comes from both
parents).[339]

Seed and fruit differ by the prior and the posterior.[340] For fruit [is
posterior] in that it is from another thing, seed [is prior] in that another   20
comes from it, since both are in fact the same thing.

But it must be stated again what the primary nature is of what is
called seed.[341]

Now it is necessary for everything that we find in the body to be
either a part in accord with nature (and it either non-homoeomerous
or homoeomerous) or contrary to nature, like a tumor, a residue,
a colliquescence, or nourishment. (By a residue I mean a leftover of   25
the nourishment, by a colliquescence what has been secreted from a
growth-producer by contrary-to-nature dissolution.[342])

Well, that it could not be a part is evident. For, although it is homoeomerous, nothing is composed of it as of sinew and flesh.[343] Further,   30
neither is it separated, whereas all the other parts are.[344] But then it is
not one of the contrary-to-nature ones either, nor a deformation.[345] For
it is present in all and the nature comes to be from it. Nourishment, on
the other hand, is evidently something brought in from outside. So it is
necessary for seed to be either a colliquescence or a residue.

Now the ancients seem to have thought it to be a colliquescence.
For saying that it comes from all the body because of the heat from   35
the movement [in copulation] has the force of saying it is a colliquescence.[346] But colliquescences are something contrary to nature, and   725^{a}1
from things contrary to nature nothing comes to be that is in accord
with nature. It is necessary, therefore, for it to be a residue. But now
every residue is surely either from useless or from useful nourishment.
Now I call useless that from which nothing further is contributed to
the nature, while much injury is done by using up too much of it, use-   5
ful the contrary.[347] That seed could not be the former sort of residue
is evident. For those in the worst condition, because of time of life or
disease, have the most of this sort of residue present in them, but the
least seed. For either they have none at all or it is not fertile because of
being mixed with useless and morbid residue.   10

The seed, then, is some part of the useful residue. The most useful, though, is the last stage, that is, the one from which each of the
parts comes to be from the outset. For there is some [that is produced]
earlier, some later. The one from the first stage of the nourishment is

phlegm and anything of that sort (for even phlegm is a residue of the
useful nourishment: a sign of which is that when mixed with pure
nourishment it is nourishing and is used up in cases of disease).[348] But
the last stage of the nourishment is smallest in proportion to the quantity of nourishment. One must understand, however, that the quantity
of daily nourishment due to which animals and plants grow is small.
For if a very small quantity of the same material were added the thing's
size would become excessive.

We must, therefore, say the contrary of what the ancients said. For
they said that the seed is what comes from all the body, whereas we
say that it is what naturally goes to all of it, and while they thought
it a colliquescence, it is evident that it is a residue instead.[349] For it is
more reasonable for the last thing going there to be similar to what is
left over from it, as painters often have flesh-colored pigment left over
that is similar to what they used up. But everything that undergoes colliquescence is destroyed and departs from its nature.

A proof that seed is not a colliquescence, but instead a residue, is
that large animals have few young, whereas small ones are prolific. For
it is necessary for there to be more colliquescence in large animals, but
less residue. For the body being large most of the nourishment is used
up so that little residue is produced.

Further, no place is assigned to a colliquescence in accord with nature,
rather it flows wherever there is an easy route in the body, whereas to all
the residues a place in accord with nature is assigned—for example, that
of the dry nourishment is the lower stomach, that of the liquid is the
bladder, that of the useful is the upper stomach, and of the spermatic
residues the places are uterus, private parts, and breasts. For into these it
is gathered and flows together.

The things resulting from it are also evidence that seed is what we
have said it is. These result because the nature of the residue is the
sort it is. The lassitude that occurs from the smallest departure of
seed is obvious, suggesting that bodies are being deprived of the final
thing to come from the nourishment. A few individuals, it is true, for
a short time, in accord with the time of life, obtain relief through its
departure when it is excessive in quantity, just as with the first nourishment if it is excessive in quantity. For on its discharge too the body
thrives more. Further, this results when other residues depart with
it. For what departs is not seed alone, rather other capacities that are
mixed with it also depart along with it in these cases, and these ones
are morbid. That is why in certain cases at least what departs is in fact
infertile through containing little of what is spermatic. But speaking of most cases and for the most part, the result of acts of sexual

intercourse is lassitude and incapacity rather than relief, due to the causes just stated.[350]

Further, no seed is present either in first time of life, old age, or in illnesses—in sickness because of incapacity, in old age because the nature does not concoct enough of it, in childhood because of growing because all is used up beforehand (for in pretty much five years, in the case of human beings at any rate, the body seems to gain half of the total size that it comes to have in all the rest of its lifetime).

In many animals and plants, however, a differentia results in this regard both between one genus in relation to another genus and, within the same genus, between things of the same species (*eidos*) in relation to each other—for example, human being in relation to human being, or vine in relation to vine. For some have abundant seed, some have little seed, and others no seed at all—not because of weakness but, in some cases at any rate, because of the contrary. For it is all used up on the body, as in the case of some human beings. For being in good condition and becoming very fleshy and rather too fat they emit less seed and have less appetite for sexual intercourse.[351] A similar thing is the affection having to do with "goatish" vines, the ones that because of their nourishment become rampant (for goats also mate less when they are fat, which is why in fact they thin them down before [the mating season]; and the vines are called goatish after the affection of the goats). And fat people, women as well as men, appear to be less fertile than those who are not fat, because the residue when concocted in well-fed bodies becomes fat. For fat too is a healthy residue caused by good feeding.

Some, though, bear no seed at all—for example, the willow and the poplar.[352] This affection too has both sorts of cause.[353] For through incapacity they do not concoct [their nourishment] and through capacity they use it up, as was mentioned.[354] Similarly, both prolific [seed] and abundant seed are due in some cases to capacity and in others to incapacity.[355] For much useless residue is mixed together with it, so that some even become ill when there is no easy route for the evacuation of these.[356] And though some regain their health, others actually die of it. For they [the useless residues] get dissolved in it [the seed] as also in urine. For this is also an ailment that has been known to befall some people.

Further, the duct is the same for the residue and for the seed. And in those in which both liquid and dry [residues from] nourishment are produced, the duct for the liquid one is the very same as the one for the secretion of the semen produced (for it is a residue of the liquid nourishment—for the nourishment for all things is more wet), but in

20   those that do not have a wet residue the excretion of the semen is by the way of the dry residue.

Further, a colliquescence is always morbid, whereas the subtraction of a residue is beneficial. But the discharge of seed plays a double game because it takes with it some of the nourishment that is not useful. If it were a colliquescence, however, it would always cause harm. But as 25   things stand it does not do this.[357]

That the seed, then, is a residue of the useful nourishment, that is, the last stage of the nourishment, whether emitted by all or not, is evident from what has been said.

I 19

After these issues we must determine of what sort of nourishment the seed is a residue, and of what sort the menses. For menses are pro- 30   duced in some of the viviparous animals. For through this means it will also be evident whether the female emits seed like the male and what comes to be is a mixture of two seeds, or whether no seed is secreted from the female; and if no seed, whether she contributes nothing else to generation but only provides a place, or does contribute something, 35   and if so how and in what way.

726^{b}1   That blood is the last stage of the nourishment in blooded animals, and its analogue in bloodless ones, has been said previously.[358] And since semen too is a residue of nourishment, that is, from its last stage, it will be either blood, its analogue, or something composed of these. And since each of the parts is produced from blood as it is being con- 5   cocted and somehow divided into parts, and since the seed (although quite different from blood when, having been concocted, it is secreted), when non-concocted and when forced out by too frequent indulgence in sexual intercourse, is sometimes still bloodlike when it has come out, it is evident that the seed must be a residue of nourishment, namely, of 10   the blood, the one that is finally distributed to the parts. And because of this it has great capacity (and in fact the discharge of the pure and healthy blood is cause of weakness) and that offspring should be like their parents is reasonable. For what has gone to the parts is like what 15   is left over. So the seed of the hand, of the face, or of the whole animal is in an undifferentiated way a hand, a face, or a whole animal—that is, as each of the latter is actually, such the seed is potentially, either in virtue of its own mass or in virtue of having a certain capacity within it.[359] (For it is not yet clear from these determinations whether the body 20   of the seed is the cause of generation, or whether it contains a certain state and starting-point of movement that is capable of generation).

For neither the hand nor any other part, without being soul-involving or having a certain other capacity, is a hand or any other part whatsoever except homonymously.[360]

{It is also evident that in cases where a colliquescence is produced that is spermatic, it too is a residue. This happens when it is resolved into what went before, just as when a fresh coat of plaster falls off immediately (for what comes away is the same as what was first applied). Similarly the final residue is the same as the first colliquescence.}[361] And let these things be determined in this way.[362]

Since, however, it is necessary for what is weaker to produce more abundant and less concocted residue, and being of this sort, it is necessary for it to be a quantity of bloodlike liquid, and since the weaker is what has a lesser share of heat in accord with nature, and the female is of this sort, as was said previously, it is necessary for the bloodlike secretion to be produced in the female to be a residue as well.[363] And the one produced that is of this sort is the so-called menstrual secretion.

That menses are a residue, therefore, and that they are the analogue in females of semen in males, is evident. The results associated with it are signs that this statement is correct.[364] For at the same time of life semen starts to appear in males and be secreted and menses to be discharged in females, and the voice changes and the breasts give signs of appearing. Also, at the time of life's declining the capacity to generate ceases in the one and the menses cease in the other.

Further, there are also the following signs that this secretion in females is a residue. For the most part neither hemorrhoids, nosebleeds, nor anything else [of the sort] occurs in women unless the menses are ceasing, and if something of this sort does occur, the menstrual purgations become more difficult, suggesting that the secretion is being diverted to it.

Further, the females have less prominent blood-vessels, less body hair, and less rough skin, because the residue that goes to these is secreted along with the menses. And this same thing must be considered as the cause of the body masses of the females being smaller than those of the males among the viviparous animals. For it is only in these that the menses are discharged externally. And among these it is most obvious in women. For woman emits more secretion than other animals. That is why she is always noticeably pale and without prominent blood-vessels, and has an evident deficiency of body as compared with the males.

Now since this is what is produced in the females as semen is in the males, and since it is not possible for two spermatic secretions to be produced at once, it is evident that the female does not contribute seed to generation.[365] For if there were seed there would be no menses. But as things stand because the latter is produced, the former is not.

Why, then, just as the seed is a residue so too are the menses has now been stated.[366] As evidence of this one may take what some of the resulting facts are for the animals. For fat animals produce less seed than non-fat ones, as was said previously.[367] (The cause is that the fat too is a residue just as seed is, namely, concocted blood, but not concocted in the same way as seed is. So it is reasonable that when the residue has been used up to make fat what has to do with the semen is deficient.) And among the bloodless animals the cephalopods and the crustaceans are at their best around the time of gestation. For since they are bloodless and produce no fat, what is analogous to fat in them is secreted to make the spermatic residue.

A sign that the female does not emit the sort of seed that the male does, and that generation is not due to the mixing of both, as some people say, is that often the female conceives without the pleasure in sexual intercourse occurring in her; and if again it occurs no less [in her], and both male and female reach it concurrently, yet often nothing comes to be unless the liquid of what is called menses is present in proportion.[368] That is why the female does not generate either when the menses are wholly absent or, for the most part, when they are present but being exuded, but rather after the purgation. For at the one time she has no nourishment or matter from which the animal will be capable of being composed by the capacity coming from the male and present in his semen, whereas at the other time it gets washed out because of the quantity being exuded. But when the menses have been produced and have departed, what remains is composed [into an embryo]. And if females conceive when the menses are not being produced, or during their production but not later, the cause is that in the former case they produce as much liquid as remains after purgation in the fertile ones, but no excess liquid is produced to depart externally, while in the latter case the mouth of the uterus closes after the purgation. When, then, what departs is plentiful but the purgation is still taking place, although not enough to wash out the seed, that is when they conceive if they have sexual intercourse. And there is nothing strange that it should continue after conception. (For the menses even recur afterward up to a point, but in small quantity and not throughout [gestation]. This, though, is a morbid condition, which is why it occurs in few females and infrequently. It is what occurs for the most part that is most in accord with nature.[369])

That what the female contributes to generation is the matter, then, that this lies in the composition of the menses, and that the menses are a residue, is clear.

I 20

The seed that some people think is contributed by the female during sexual intercourse, because a pleasure about the same as that of the males sometimes occurs in females at the same time as a liquid secre-   35
tion, is not a spermatic liquid, but is special to the place in particular females.[370] For it is a secretion from the uterus and is produced in some   **728ᵃ1**
but not in others. For it is produced in the pale-skinned and womanly, speaking for the most part, not in the dark and masculine-looking. Its quantity, when it is produced, is sometimes not in accord with that of the seed emitted, but far exceeds it. Further, one foodstuff's distinct-   5
ness from another makes a great difference to whether less or more of this sort of secretion is produced—for example, some of the bitter ones make an obvious difference to the quantity of the secretion.

The occurrence of pleasure in sexual intercourse is due to the emis-
sion not only of seed but also of pneuma, from the composition of   10
which the emission of seed results. This is clear in the case of boys who are not yet capable of its emission but are near the age for it, and in infertile men. For in all these pleasure is produced by friction. And in those who have lost the capacity to generate, the bowels are sometimes loose because of the secretion of residue that is incapable of being con-   15
cocted into the bowels.

Now a boy too is like a woman in shape, and a woman is as it were an infertile man.[371] For the female exists due to a certain incapacity, namely, in being incapable of concocting seed from the nourishment in its last stage (which is either blood or its analogue in bloodless animals) because of the coldness of her nature. Just as in the bowels non-   20
concoction produces diarrhea, then, so in the blood-vessels it produces various hemorrhages, in particular the menses. For they too are a hemorrhage, but whereas the others are due to disease, this one is natural.[372]

So it is evident that generation quite reasonably occurs from this.   25
For the menses are seed that is not pure but needs working on, just as in what has to do with the generation of fruits, when [their food] has not yet been sifted, though the nourishment is present in it, and needs working on to purify it.[373] That is why, when the former is mixed with the semen and the latter with pure nourishment, the one generates and the other nourishes.   30

A sign that the female does not emit seed is that the pleasure in sexual intercourse is produced by touch in the same place as in males. And yet they do not emit this liquid from there.

Further, this secretion is not produced in all females, but in those that are quite sanguineous, and not even in all of them, but in those   35

that do not have the uterus by the diaphragm and are not oviparous.³⁷⁴
Further, nor is it produced in those that have not blood but its ana-
728ᵇ1 logue (for the very thing that is blood in the former is a distinct secretion in the latter). The cause due to which the purgation is produced
neither in them nor in certain blooded animals, except the ones just
mentioned (namely, those whose uterus is down below and are not
oviparous), is the dryness of their bodies, which leaves little residue
5 over, enough only for generation but not for external emission.³⁷⁵ But
the ones that are viviparous without first laying an egg—these are the
human and those quadrupeds that bend the hind leg inward (for all
these are viviparous without first laying an egg)—all produce menses,
10 unless they are deformed in the process of generation like the mule,
but the purgation is not conspicuous as it is in human beings.³⁷⁶ But
how this occurs in each of the animals is described with exactness in
the *History of Animals*.³⁷⁷

Among the animals the greatest quantity of purgation is produced
15 in women, and in men the emission of seed is greatest in proportion
(*logos*) to their size. The cause is the composition of their body, which
is wet and hot. For in the ones of this sort it is necessary for the greatest
quantity of residue to be produced. Further, they do not have the sort
of parts in their body to which residue is diverted, as the others do. For
20 they do not have a great quantity of hairs on their body, nor excretions
of bones, horns, and tusks.

Here is a sign that the seed is in the menses: at the same time of life,
as was said previously, the males produce this residue and the females
25 show signs of menses, suggesting that the places receptive of the residue in each of the two become distinct at the same time, and as the
neighboring places are made permeable, a growth of pubic hair bursts
forth.³⁷⁸ And when they are about to be distinct, the places get swelled
up by the pneuma, more noticeably around the testes in males, though
it shows signs around the breasts as well, and in females more around
30 the breasts (for when they are two fingers high, then the menses are
produced in most females).

In those living things in which male and female are separated the
seed is as it were an embryo. By an embryo I mean the primary mixture of female and male.³⁷⁹ That is also why one body comes from one
35 seed—for example, one stalk from one grain of wheat, just like one
animal from one egg (for twin-eggs are two eggs). But in all genera
729ᵃ1 in which female and male are distinct, it is possible for several animals to come from one seed, suggesting that the seed in plants and
that in animals are different in nature. A sign of this is that several
young come from one mating in animals capable of generating more

than one. From this it is also clear that the semen does not come from
every part [of the body]. For separate [parts of it] would not from the
outset be secreted by the same part [of the body], nor would they, having arrived there together, become separate in the uterus. Instead, it
happens as is reasonable, since the male provides both the form and
the starting-point of movement, while the female provides the body,
that is, the matter. Like in the curdling of milk, where the body is the
milk, and the fig-juice or rennet is what contains the starting-point
of its composition, so is what comes from the male when it is partitioned in the female.³⁸⁰ But due to what cause it is partitioned here
into a larger number, here into fewer, and here is not partitioned at
all, will be for another account.³⁸¹ But because there is no difference
in the form (*eidos*) at any rate, but only the proportion between what
is divided and the matter, and neither so little that it does not concoct
or compose the matter nor so much that it dries it up.³⁸² But from the
primary thing doing the composing, from [what is] already one, only
one offspring comes to be.³⁸³

  That the female does not contribute semen to the generation, then,
but does contribute something, namely, what the menses is composed
of (or its analogue in bloodless animals), is clear both from what has
been said and is in accord with reason (*logos*) based on universal inves-
tigations.³⁸⁴ For it is necessary for there to be a progenitor and a from
which. And, even if these are one, it is necessary for them to differ at
any rate in form (*eidos*), and for the accounts of them to be distinct.
And in those that have these capacities separated, it is necessary for
both the bodies and the nature of the affecting one and the affected
one to be distinct. If, then, the male exists as mover and affecter, and
the female as affected, the female's contribution to the male's semen
would be not semen but matter.³⁸⁵ And it is evident that this is just
what happens. For the nature of the menses corresponds to the primary matter.³⁸⁶

I 21

Let these things, then, be determined in this way.³⁸⁷ At the same time,
the answer to the next question to be investigated is evident from these
considerations, namely, how it is that the male contributes to generation, and how it is that the seed from the male is a cause of what comes
to be. Is it by being present in and from the outset being a part of the
body of what comes to be, mixing with the matter from the female? Or
does the body of the seed not have a share, but only the capacity and
movement in it? For it is the latter that is the affecter, while what is

composed and takes the shape [or form] is what remains of the residue in the female.[388] This is evident both in accord with reason (*logos*) and with the facts.[389]

For if we investigate the question in universal terms, it is evident that whenever one thing comes to be *from* an affected and an affecter it is not by way of the affecter being present within what comes to be, nor quite generally is it so when one thing moves something and another is moved. But now the female, insofar as female, is a thing capable of being affected, while the male, insofar as male, is a thing capable of affecting and from which comes the starting-point of the movement. So if we take the extremes of each, in which case the one is capable of affecting, the other capable of being affected, it is not *from* these that the one thing comes to be, except in the way that the bed does so from the carpenter and the wood, or the sphere from the wax and the form. It is clear, therefore, that it is not necessary for something to come away from the male, nor, if something does come away, is it necessary because of this for what comes to be to do so from that something by way of its presence within, but only by way of being mover and form, in the way that the cured person is due to the craft of medicine.

And what happens in agreement with reason is also in agreement with the facts. For that is why some males, even though they copulate with the females, do not, it appears, insert any part into the female, but on the contrary the female inserts one into the male, as in the case of certain insects. For in those that do insert one the effect that the seed produces in the female is produced in these insects by the heat and the capacity in the [male] animal itself when the female brings into it the part that is receptive of the residue. And because of this these sorts of animals remain intertwined a long time, but when untwined generate quickly. For they copulate until [the capacity in the male] has composed [the matter in the female] in the way semen does. But after untwining they quickly emit the embryo. For they produce an incomplete thing, since all of this sort produce larvae.

But what happens in birds and in fishes of the oviparous genus is the greatest sign that the seed does not come from all parts and that the male does not emit any part of the sort that will remain present in what comes to be, but produces an animal only by a capacity in the semen, just as we said of insects in which the female inserts a part into the male.[390] For if a hen happens to be conceiving wind-eggs and is then mated before the egg has changed from being wholly yellow to turning white, the eggs become fertile instead of wind-eggs; and if it is mated with a second cock while the egg is still yellow, all the chicks turn out to be of the same genus as the second cock. That is why some

people who are serious about well-bred birds do things in this way, changing [the cocks] for the first and second matings, on the suppo-   10
sition that the seed is not mixed together with [the egg] and present within it, and that it did not come from all parts (for it would then have come from both cocks, so that the same parts would be possessed twice). Instead, by its capacity, the male seed establishes a certain state in the matter and nourishment that is in the female. For it is possible for the seed that came in second to do this by heating and concocting.   15
For the egg gets nourishment as long as it is growing.

The same happens too in the generation of the oviparous fishes. For when the female has laid the eggs, the male sheds the milt over them, and those eggs it reaches become fertile, while those it does not reach   20
are infertile, suggesting that the male's contribution to the animals is not quantitative but qualitative.

That the seed, then, does not come from all [parts] in those that emit seed, and that the female does not contribute in the same way as the   25
male to the generation of the offspring that are composed, but instead the male contributes a starting-point of movement and the female the matter, is clear from what has just been said. In fact, that is why the female does not generate by itself, since it needs a starting-point, that is, something that will cause movement and give definition—although   30
in some animals certainly, such as hens, their nature is capable of gen-erating up to a point (for these do compose something, but the things they compose are incomplete, namely, so-called wind-eggs).

I 22

It is also why the generation of what comes to be takes place in the female, although neither the male itself nor the female emits semen into the male, but rather both contribute into the female what comes to be from them, because in the female is the matter from which what   35
is handicrafted comes. And it is necessary for some to be present from   730^{b}1
the outset, gathered together, from which the embryo is composed in the first instance, whereas other matter must continually be added in order that the embryo may grow.[391] So it is necessary for birth to take place in the female. For the carpenter too is in close contact with the wood, the potter with the clay, and, in general, every working on a   5
thing and every last movement takes place in contact with the matter—for example, building takes place in what is being built.[392]

One may grasp from these cases how the male contributes to gen-eration. For not every male emits seed, and in the case of those males   10
that do emit it, it is no part of the embryo that comes to be, just as

nothing comes away from the carpenter to the matter of the pieces of wood he works on, nor is there any part of the craft of carpentry in what is being produced, but the shape—that is, the form—is produced from the carpenter by means of the movement in the matter, that is, his soul, in which the form is present, and his scientific knowledge move his hands or some other part with a certain sort of movement— distinct when what comes to be from it is distinct, the same when what comes to be from it is the same—and the hands move the instruments, and the instruments move the matter. Similarly, the nature present in the male, in those that emit seed, uses the seed as an instrument and as possessing active movement, just as in craft productions the tools are in movement. For the movement of the craft is in a way in them.

Those, then, that emit seed contribute in this way to generation. But those that do not emit it, where the female inserts some part of itself into the male, do so like someone bringing the matter to the handi-craftsman. For because of the weakness of these sorts of males their nature is not capable of producing by other means, but even when it persists the movements have scarcely enough strength, and produce like modelers, not carpenters. For it is not by means of touching some-thing else that it handicrafts what is being composed, but does so itself by using its own parts.

I 23

Now in all animals that are capable of perambulation the female is separated from the male, one animal being female and another male, though they are the same in species (*eidos*)—for example, both human or both horse. In plants, on the other hand, these capacities are mixed and the female is not separated from the male. That is why in fact they generate out of themselves and emit not semen but an embryo, which we call seeds. And this is well said by Empedocles in his poem:

Thus tall trees first lay olive eggs.[393]

For the egg is an embryo, and from a certain part of it the animal comes to be, while the remainder is nourishment. And from part of the seed the growing plant comes to be, while the remainder becomes nourish-ment for the shoot and for the first root.

In a certain way the same thing happens too in those animals that have the female and the male separated. For when there is need for them to generate they become inseparable, as in plants, and their nature tends to become one. This indeed is quite evident to the eye when they mix together and copulate, one animal coming to be from both.[394]

And for those that do not emit seed it is natural to remain inter-twined for a long time until [the male] has composed the embryo—for example, the insects that copulate. But others so remain only until the male has discharged some part of what he introduces that will com-pose the embryo in a longer time—as, for example, in the case of the blooded animals. For the former keep together for some part of a day, whereas in the latter the semen takes several days to compose the fetus, though they let go when such a thing has been released. And animals are really like divided plants: as though, when they bear seed, one were to untwine and separate them into the female and male present within them.

And nature handicrafts all this in a reasonable way. For of the sub-stance of plants there is no other function or action at all except the generation of seed, so that since this occurs through the copulation of the female and the male, nature has mixed these and arranged them together with each other. Well, plants have been investigated else-where.[395] The function of the animal, on the other hand, is not only to generate (for this is common to all living things), but also they all participate in a sort of knowledge, some in more, some in less, some in altogether little.[396] For they have perception, and perception is a sort of knowledge. And its esteem or lack of esteem differs greatly as we look at it in relation to practical wisdom and in relation to things of the inanimate genus.[397] For in comparison to being practically wise, participating in touch and taste seems like nothing at all, but in com-parison to plant or stone it seems a wondrous thing. For it seems that one would be content with even this share of knowledge, rather than lying dead and not being. It is by perception that animals differ from things that are merely living.[398] But since it is necessary for it also to be alive, if it is an animal, when there is a need for it to fulfill the function of the living thing, it then copulates, mixes, and becomes like a plant, as we said.[399]

Among the animals, though, the testaceans are intermediate between the animals and the plants, and, as being in both, perform the function of neither. For as plant they do not have the female and the male, and do not generate in another, while as animals they do not bear fruit out of themselves as plants do, but are composed and come to be from a certain earthy and wet material. But their generation must be spoken about later.[400]

15

20

25

30

35
731^{b}1

5

10

Book II

II 1

That the female and the male are starting-points of generation was said previously, as was what their capacity is and the account of their substance.[401] As for why the one becomes and is female and the other male, how it is so in virtue of necessity, of the first mover, and of a certain sort of matter, our account must try to explain as it proceeds, but how it is because of the better and the cause for the sake of which has a higher starting-point.[402]

For since some beings are eternal and divine, while others admit of both being and not being, and since the nobly beautiful and the divine is always in accord with its own nature a cause of the better in things that admit of it, while the non-eternal does admit of being and of partaking in the worse and the better, and since the soul is better than the body, and the animate than the inanimate because of the soul, and being than not being, and living than not living—due to these causes there is generation of animals.[403] For since it is impossible for the nature of this sort of genus to be eternal, what comes into being is eternal in the [only] way that is possible for it. Now in number it is not possible (for the substance of the beings is in the particular one), but if indeed it were so, it would be eternal, in form (*eidos*), however, it is possible.[404] That is why there is always a genus—of human beings, of animals, and of plants.

Since the starting-point of these is the female and the male, it would be for the sake of generation that female and male exist among the beings.[405] But the first cause of movement—in which belongs the account and the form—is better and more divine than the matter, and it is better that the more excellent be separated from the worse. That is why, in those in which it is possible, the male is as far as possible separated from the female. For the starting-point of the movement, which is where the male belongs in what comes to be, is better and more divine, whereas the female is matter. The male, however, comes together and mixes with the female for the work of generation. For this is common to both.

Something lives, then, in virtue of participating in the male and the female (which is why even plants participate in life). But the animal genus is [what it is] in virtue of perception.[406] In pretty much all of those capable of perambulation the female and the male are separated due to the causes stated.[407] And some of these, as was said, emit seed in copulation, whereas others do not.[408] The cause of this is that the more estimable animals are more self-sufficient in their nature, so that they have greater size. But this cannot be had without soul-involving heat.[409] For it is necessary for what has a greater size to be moved by a greater capacity, and the heat is something capable of causing movement. That is why, taking a general view, we may say that blooded animals are larger than bloodless ones, and those capable of perambulation larger than stationary ones. And these are just the ones that emit seed because of their heat and size.[410]

The cause due to which each of the two, the male and the female, exists has now been stated.

Of the animals, some complete and send forth externally an offspring similar to themselves—for example, those that are externally viviparous. Others bring forth something unarticulated that has not yet acquired its own shape [or form]. Among the latter sort, the blooded ones lay eggs, while the bloodless ones bring forth larvae. An egg, though, is different than a larva. For an egg is that from a part of which what comes to be comes to be (the remainder being nourishment for what comes to be), whereas a larva is that from the whole of which the whole of what comes to be comes to be.[411]

Of the viviparous animals that bring to light a complete offspring similar to themselves, some are internally viviparous from the outset (for example, human being, horse, ox, and—of the sea creatures—the dolphin, and the others of this sort). Others, though, are at first internally oviparous, then externally viviparous (for example, the so-called selachians).

Of the oviparous animals, some lay complete eggs—for example, birds, oviparous quadrupeds, and footless animals—for example, lizards, tortoises, and most of the serpent genus (for the eggs of these, once laid, do not take on growth).[412] Others, though, lay incomplete eggs—for example, the fishes, crustaceans, and so-called cephalopods, whose eggs do grow in size once they are laid.

All the viviparous animals are blooded, and the blooded ones that are not wholly infertile are either viviparous or oviparous.[413] Of the bloodless ones, insects produce a larva, whether they come to be from copulation or copulate themselves. For there are some insects of this sort, which though they come to be spontaneously, are yet female and male, and from their copulation something comes to be, even though it is incomplete.[414] The cause of this has been stated elsewhere.[415]

15   Much overlapping of genera, however, occurs. For the bipeds are not all viviparous (for the birds are oviparous) nor all oviparous (for the human is viviparous); nor are the quadrupeds all oviparous (for horse, ox, and countless others are viviparous) or all viviparous (for lizards, crocodiles, and many others are oviparous). Nor does the having
20   or not having of feet differentiate them. For there are viviparous footless animals (for example, the vipers and the selachians) and oviparous ones (for example, the fish genus and the other serpents); and of the ones having feet many are oviparous, many viviparous (for example, the quadrupeds just mentioned); and the internally viviparous include
25   both ones that have feet (for example, human) and footless ones (for example, whale and dolphin).[416] There is no dividing, then, in this way, nor are any of instruments of perambulation the cause of this difference (*diaphora*).[417] Instead, the viviparous ones are the animals that are more complete in nature and participate in a purer starting-point.[418] For nothing is internally viviparous if it does not take in pneuma and
30   draw breath. And the more complete ones are hotter in nature and wetter and not earthy. And the defining mark of natural heat is [the presence of] the lung, when it is well blooded.[419] For, in general, the ones that have a lung are hotter than those that do not, and of the former, the ones whose lung is not spongy nor firm nor poorly blooded,
35   but rather well blooded and soft. And just as the animal is complete,
733^a1   whereas the egg and the larva are incomplete, so what is complete naturally comes to be from what is complete.

The ones that are hotter due to having a lung, but drier in their nature, or are colder but wetter, either lay a complete egg or first lay
5   an egg and then are viviparous internally. For birds and horny-plated animals, because of their heat, produce a complete thing, but because of their dryness they lay an egg [only]—the selachians, though, are less hot than these, but wetter, so that they participate in both. For they are both oviparous and internally viviparous—oviparous because they are
10   cold, viviparous because they are wet. For the wet is characteristic of life, whereas the dry is farthest from the animate. And since they are neither feathered, horny-plated, nor scaled (which are signs rather of a dry and earthy nature), the egg they produce is soft. For the earthy material does not rise to the surface in the egg any more than in them-
15   selves. And that is why they lay their eggs internally. For if it were outside, the egg, not having any protection, would be destroyed.

The animals that are cold and dry rather than wet also lay eggs, but the egg is incomplete, and is hard-shelled because they are earthy, and because it is incomplete when emitted, in order that it be preserved it

has a shelly exterior to safeguard it. Fishes, then, being scaly, and crus- 20
taceans, being earthy, produce hard-shelled eggs.

The cephalopods, as themselves having bodies that are viscous in
nature, preserve in the same way the incomplete eggs they produce. For
they emit a large amount of very viscous material around the embryo.

The insects all produce larvae. Now all insects are bloodless, which
is why in fact they produce larvae externally. But the bloodless animals 25
do not all produce larvae, unconditionally speaking. For the insects,
the producers of larvae, and the producers of incomplete eggs (for
example, the scaly fishes, the crustaceans, and the cephalopods) overlap each other. For the eggs of the latter are larva-like (for they take
on growth externally), while the larvae of the former become egg-like 30
after being emitted. The way they do so we shall determine later on.[420]

We must understand how well and successively nature renders generation. For the more complete and hotter animals render their young 733[b]1
complete with respect to quality (though with respect to quantity no
animal at all does so, since all having come to be take on growth), and
these are the ones, of course, that produce animals internally from the
outset. Those that come second do not produce complete ones internally from the outset (for they are viviparous after first laying eggs), 5
but externally they are viviparous. Others [coming third] produce not
a complete animal but an egg, and this egg is complete. The next [com-
ing fourth], having a nature yet colder than these, produce an egg—not
a complete egg, though, but one that is completed externally, as with
the scaly genus of fishes, the crustaceans, and the cephalopods. The
fifth and coldest genus does not even lay eggs from itself; instead, this 10
sort of affection happens externally, as was said.[421] For the insects produce larvae at first, and after being emitted the larva becomes egg-like
(for the so-called chrysalis has the capacity of an egg), then from this
an animal comes to be, reaching in this third change the end of its 15
generation.[422]

There are, then, some animals that do not come to be from seed, as
was said previously.[423] All the blooded ones, however, come to be from
seed, when they come to be from copulation, the male emitting semen
into the female, on the entering of which the animal is composed and
takes on its own shape [or form], some within the animals themselves 20
when they are viviparous, others in eggs, {* * *} seeds, and other such
secretions.[424]

About these things there is a large puzzle as to how the plant, or any
animal, comes to be from the seed. For it is necessary for what comes
to be to come to be from something, to be due to something, and 25

to be something. Now that from which is the matter. Some animals have their primary matter within themselves, having gotten it from the female—for example, those that come to be not viviparously but as a larva or egg.[425] Others get it from the female for a long time through being suckled, as do those that come to be viviparously not only externally but also internally. That from which a thing comes to be, then, is matter of this sort.

But what is now being sought is not from what the parts come to be, but rather due to what. For either something external produces them, or something present in the semen and the seed, and is either some part of soul, or soul, or something having soul.[426] Now for something external to produce each of the viscera or other parts would seem unreasonable. For it is impossible to move a thing without making contact with it, or, without its moving it, for the thing to be affected by it.[427] In the embryo itself, therefore, something [of the relevant sort] is already present, either as a part of it or separated from it. But for it to be some other separated thing is unreasonable. For after the animal has come to be does this thing pass away or does it remain? But nothing of this sort appears to be in it, nothing that is not a part of the whole plant or animal. But then again for it to pass away after having produced either all of the parts or some of them is absurd. For if it makes [only] some, what will make the rest? For if it makes the heart and then passes away, and the heart another part, by the same argument either all pass away or all remain. Therefore, it is preserved.[428] Therefore, it is a part that is present in the seed from the outset. If, then, there is no part of the soul that is not in some part of the body, it would also be a part that is ensouled from the outset.

How, then, does it produce the other parts? For either all the parts—heart, lung, and each of the others—come to be simultaneously, or successively, as is said in the so-called Orphic poems.[429] For there he says that an animal comes to be like the weaving of a fishing net.[430] Now that it is not simultaneously is evident even to perception. For some of the parts are already noticeably present [in the embryo], others not. And that this is not because they are too small to be visible is clear. For the lung is larger than the heart but is noticeable later in the generation from the starting-point. Since, then, one is earlier and another later, does the one produce the other, and is the latter due to the contiguous one, or rather does *this* come to be [only] after *that*? I mean, for example, not that heart, having come to be, produces the liver, and it something else, but that *this* is after *that*, as after a child a man comes to be but not due to it. The reason (*logos*) for this is that, in the things that come to be by nature or by craft, what is potentially comes to be due to what is actually, so that the form and shape [of the later thing] would need to be in the earlier thing—for example, the form of the liver in the heart.[431] And in other ways too the account is an absurd fabrication.

But then too for any part of the animal or plant that comes to be to be present in the seed from the outset—whether it has the capacity to produce the other parts or not—is impossible if all come to be from seed and semen. For it is clear that it is due to what produced the seed, if indeed it is present in it from the outset. But seed must be produced beforehand, and this is the function of its progenitor. Therefore no part can be present in it. Therefore it does not contain within itself either what produces the parts. But then neither can this be external. But it is necessary for it to be one or other of these two.

We must try, then, to resolve this [puzzle]. For perhaps something of what was said is not simple—for example, in what way exactly is it not possible for the coming to be of the parts to be due to something external?[432] For there is a way in which it is possible, and another way in which it is not. Now whether we speak of the seed, or of what the seed comes from, makes no difference, insofar as the seed has within it the movement with which that other moved it. And it is possible for *this* to have moved *that*, and *that this other*, and for it to be like those wondrous automata.[433] For their parts somehow contain a capacity when at rest, and when something external has moved the first of them immediately the contiguous one becomes so actively. As, then, in the case of these automata the external thing is in a certain way moving them, not by making contact with any part now, but by having made contact with one, it is likewise in the case of what the seed came from, or that which produced the seed, it moves by having once made contact, not by making contact still. In another way, however, it is the internal movement that does this, as building does the house.[434]

That there is, then, something that produces [the parts], it does not do so as a this something nor as something present in it as a completed thing from the first, is clear.[435]

But we must grasp how each part comes to be there, first positing as a starting-point that whatever comes to be by nature or by craft comes to be due to something actively being, from something potentially being, of the relevant sort. Now the seed is of such a sort, and contains a movement and a starting-point of such a sort, that as the movement ceases each part is produced ensouled. For it is not face without having soul, nor is it flesh; rather, when they are dead, the one will be homonymously said to be a face and the other flesh, just as it would be if they were made of stone or wood.[436] And the homoeomerous parts come to be at the same time as the instrumental

35

734^b1

5

10

15

20

25

ones. And just as we would not say of an axe or other instrument that it is made of fire alone, nor likewise is foot or hand. And in the same way, neither is flesh. For of it too there is a certain function. Now heat and cold would make them hard and soft, viscous or brittle, and whatever other affections of this sort belong to the ensouled parts, but when it comes to the ratio (*logos*) in virtue of which one is already flesh and another bone, this is no longer so; rather this is due to the movement that stems from the progenitor, which is actually what the thing is potentially from which what comes to be does so, just as in the case of the things that come to be in accord with craft.[437] For heat and cold make the iron hard and soft, but what makes the sword is the movement of the instruments containing the account belonging to the craft.[438] For the craft is starting-point and form of what comes to be, but in another thing, whereas the movement belonging to the nature is in the thing itself, which stems from another nature that contains the active form.

And has the seed soul or not? The same argument applies to it as to the parts. For no soul will be in anything else whatsoever except in what it is in fact the soul of, nor will there be a part—other than homonymously, like a dead man's eye—that does not participate in soul. It is clear, then, that seed both has [soul] and is [alive]—potentially. But it is possible to be nearer and farther potentially, as the geometer asleep is farther than the one awake, and the latter than the one [actively] contemplating.[439]

Of this process of generation, then, no part is a cause, but rather the primary external mover.[440] For nothing generates itself. But once it has come to be, from that point on it causes itself to grow.[441] That is why indeed one [part] comes to be first and not all of them at the same time. And this first thing to come to be is necessarily what contains the starting-point of growth. For whether plant or animal, this belongs to all alike, namely, the nutritive part.[442] (And this is what is generative of another like oneself. For this is the function of everything that is by nature complete, both animal and plant.) And this is necessary, because once something has come to be, it is necessary for it to grow. Accordingly, though it was produced by something synonymous (for example, human being by human being), it grows because of itself. Therefore, it itself must be something if it causes growth. If, then, it is one something, and this a first thing, it necessarily comes to be first. So if the heart is the first thing to come to be in certain animals, and in those that do not have a heart the analogue of this, the starting-point would be from this in the ones that have it, and in the others from its analogue.

What the cause as starting-point is, then, in each case of generation, the primary mover and handicrafter, has been stated in response to the puzzles gone through previously.

II 2

About the nature of the seed, though, someone might raise a puzzle. For seed when it comes out of the animal is coarse-grained and white, but when it cools it becomes liquid like water and its color is that of water.[443] And this may seem strange. For while water does not become coarse-grained due to heat, the seed, on coming out of the hot [animal], is coarse-grained, and on cooling becomes water. And although watery liquids freeze, seed does not freeze if exposed to frost in the open air but liquifies, suggesting that the contrary of [cold] makes it coarse-grained. But then it is not reasonable either for it to be made coarse-grained by heat. For things that contain much earth are the ones that get composed and coarse-grained on boiling—for example, milk.[444] It should, then, solidify on cooling. But as things stand nothing of it becomes solid, instead all of it becomes water.

This, then, is the puzzle. For if it is composed of water—well, it is evident that water does not get coarse-grained due to heat, whereas the seed on issuing forth is coarse-grained and hot and the body it comes from is hot. On the other hand, if it is composed of earth, or is a mixture of earth and water, then it should not all become liquid and [like] water.[445]

Or is it that we have not distinguished all the results [of heating and cooling]. For it is not only liquids composed of water and earthy material that get coarse-grained, but also those composed of water and pneuma—for example, foam becomes more coarse-grained and white, and the smaller and less clear the bubbles in it, the whiter and firmer the mass appears. Olive oil is affected in the same way. For on mixing with pneuma it gets coarse-grained, which is why the whitening [oil] becomes more coarse-grained—the watery material in it gets disaggregated by the heat and becomes pneuma.[446] Lead ore too, when mixed with water and olive oil and beaten, makes from a smaller mass a bigger one, from something liquid something firm, and from something black something white.[447] The cause is that pneuma gets mixed in with it, and it makes the mass [bigger] and the whiteness show through, as in foam and snow. Even water itself on mixing with olive oil becomes coarse-grained and white. For due to the friction pneuma gets enclosed and the oil itself also contains much pneuma.[448] For oiliness is characteristic of pneuma, not of earth or water.[449] That is

25   also why it floats on the surface of water. For the air in it, as if in a ves-
        sel, bears it up and makes it float and is the cause of its lightness.[450] And
        in cold spells and frosts oil gets coarse-grained but does not freeze. For
        because of its heat it does not freeze (for the air is hot and not freez-
30   able), but because it is condensed and compacted by the cold the oil
        becomes coarse-grained.

        Due to these causes seed too is firm and white when it comes
        out from within, that is, due to the internal heat [of the animal] the
        pneuma contains much heat, but having come out, when the heat has
35   evaporated and the air has cooled, it becomes liquid and black. For, as
        in the case of phlegm, the water, and any small quantity of earthy mate-
        rial there may be, remain in the seed too as it dries.

        Seed, then, is jointly composed of pneuma and water, and the
736^a1   pneuma is hot air. That is why it is fluid in nature, namely, because it is
        composed of water. For what Ctesias of Cnidos said about the seed of
        elephants is quite evidently false.[451] For he says that it hardens so much
5   in drying that it becomes like amber. But this does not happen. For
        though one seed is of necessity earthier than another, and most so in
        those to which, in accord with the mass of their bodies, much earthy
        material belongs, it is coarse-grained and white because of being mixed
        with pneuma. For it is indeed white in all cases. For Herodotus is not
10   speaking the truth in saying that the semen of Ethiopians is black, as if
        it were necessary for everything belonging to someone with black skin
        to be black—and this even while seeing that their teeth are white![452]
        The cause of the whiteness of seed is that the semen is a foam, and
        foam is white, and most so that composed of the smallest particles, and
15   small in the way that each bubble is invisible, just as actually happens
        in the case when water and olive oil are mixed and beaten, as was said
        previously.[453]

        Even the ancients did not fail to notice that the nature of seed is
        foam-like.[454] At any rate, they named the goddess who is in control of
20   sexual intercourse after this capacity.[455]

        The cause of the puzzle we mentioned has now been stated, and it is
        evident that it is due to it that seed does not freeze either. For air does
        not freeze.

II 3

        The next puzzle to be stated is this. If, in the case of the animals in
25   which semen is emitted into the female, what enters is no part of the
        embryo that comes to be, where is the corporeal part of it diverted to,
        if indeed it does its work by means of the capacity it has within itself?

It is necessary to determine whether what is being composed in the female receives something, or not, from what has entered her, but also, concerning the soul in virtue of which an animal is so called (and it is an animal in virtue of the perceptual part of the soul), whether it is present within the seed and the fetus or not, and where it comes from [if it is].[456] For one could not regard the fetus as soulless, as in every way lacking in life. For both the seeds and the embryos of animals are no less alive than plants, and are fertile up to a certain point.[457] That they have nutritive soul, then, is evident (and why they must acquire this first is evident from the determinations about the soul made elsewhere), but as they proceed they also have perceptual soul in virtue of which they are animals {***}.[458] For they do not at the same time become animal and human, or animal and horse, and likewise in the case of the other animals. For the last thing to come to be is the end, and the end of the coming to be of each thing is what is special to it.[459] That is why where understanding is concerned, when, how, and from where it is acquired by those that participate in this starting-point, involves a very great puzzle, and we must try hard to get a grasp on [these things] in accord with our capacity and to the extent possible.[460]

As for the seeds and fetuses that are not yet separable, it is clear that they must be regarded as possessing nutritive soul potentially, but not actively, until, like separated fetuses, they are drawing in nourishment and performing the function of this sort of soul. For at first all things of this sort seem to live the life of a plant. And it is clear that perceptual soul and understanding soul must be spoken about accordingly. For it is necessary for all soul to be possessed potentially before being possessed actively.

For either they must all be produced [in the menses or matter] without existing beforehand, or they must all preexist, or some must, but not others; and they must be produced in the matter either without having entered in the male's seed, or having come from there; and in the male they must either all be produced [in the seed] from outside it, or none from outside, or some but not others. Now, then, that it is impossible for all to be present beforehand is evident from the following. For it is clear that it is impossible for all starting-points whose activity is bodily to be present without body (for example, walking without feet). So they cannot enter from outside. For they can neither enter by themselves, being inseparable, nor enter in a body. For the seed is a residue produced by a change in the nutriment. It remains, then, that the understanding alone enters additionally from outside and alone is divine. For bodily activity is in no way associated with its activity.[461]

Now the capacity of all soul seems to be associated with a body distinct from and more divine than the so-called elements. And as souls differ from each other in esteem and lack of esteem, so too this sort of nature differs.[462] For within the seed of everything there is present that which makes the seeds fertile, the so-called hot. This is not fire or that sort of capacity, but the pneuma enclosed within the seed and within the foamy part—that is, the nature in the pneuma, which is an analogue of the element belonging to the stars.[463] That is why fire does not generate any animal, nor, it is evident, are any composed in things affected by fire, whether wet ones or dry ones.[464] But the heat of the sun and that of animals do generate—and not only does that due to the seed do so, but also if there happens to be some other residue belonging to its nature, still it too possesses a life-giving starting-point.[465] That, then, the heat in animals is neither fire nor comes from fire is evident from these considerations.

As for the body of the semen, in which comes away part of the seed of the soul-involving starting-point, part of which is separable from the body in all the ones in which a divine something is enclosed (and what is called the understanding is of this sort) and part inseparable— this body of the semen dissolves and evaporates, having a liquid and watery nature.[466] That is why one should not look for it always to come out, nor for it to be any part of the composed shape [or form], any more than the fig-juice that composes the milk.[467] For it too changes and is no part of the mass that is being composed.

In what way, then, embryos and semen possess soul, and in what way they do not, has been determined. For they possess it potentially, but not actively.

Because the seed is a residue, then, and is being moved with the same movement as the one with which the body grows when the nourishment in its last stage is being partitioned, when it comes into the uterus it composes and moves the female's residue with just the same movement that it is moving with itself.[468] For that too is a residue, and it contains all the parts potentially, but none actively. For it even contains potentially the sorts of parts due to which there is a difference between male and female. For just as from deformed parents sometimes deformed offspring come to be and sometimes not, in the same way too from a female a female sometimes comes to be, and sometimes not a female but a male. For the female is like a deformed male, and the menses are seed, but not pure seed.[469] For there is one thing alone that they do not contain, namely, the starting-point of soul. And because of that, in those animals in which wind-eggs are produced the egg that is being composed has the parts of both, but does not have the starting-point, which is why it does not become ensouled. For this starting-point is brought in by the male's seed. But once the residue of the female has partaken of this sort of starting-point an embryo comes to be.

Things that, though liquid, are of a corporeal nature when heated get surrounded by a crust, like the crusts that form on boiled ones as they cool. For viscosity holds all bodies together. And it is just this, as they develop and become larger in size, that is acquired by what is sinewy in nature, which is just what holds together the parts of an animal, being sinew [itself] in some and its analog in others. And of the same shape [or form] are skin, blood-vessel, membrane, and everything of that genus. For these differ in the more and the less and, in general, in excess and deficiency.[470]

II 4

Among the animals having a more incomplete nature, once a complete embryo has come to be, it is emitted externally, though it is not yet a complete animal; the cause of this was stated previously.[471] A fetus is complete from the moment when it is either male or female—that is, in the case of those animals where this distinction exists among the offspring. For there are some that produce offspring that are neither female nor male, namely, the ones that neither come to be from male and female parents nor from sexual intercourse between animals. About the generation of these we shall speak later.[472]

The complete animals, the ones that are internally viviparous, until they have produced a [complete] animal and sent it forth externally, keep the animal that comes to be naturally united with and within themselves.

The ones that are externally viviparous but first internally oviparous, once they have produced a complete egg, in some cases the egg is released, just as in the externally oviparous animals, and the animal comes to be from the egg inside the female, in other cases, when the nourishment in the egg has been used up, the animal is completed by [nourishment] from the uterus, and that is why the egg is not released from the uterus. This is the difference (*diaphora*) the selachian fishes have, which later must be discussed by themselves.[473]

Now, however, we must first start with the first ones. And these are the viviparous ones, and of these the human is first.

Well, in all animals the secretion of seed comes about just like any other residue. For each is spatially moved to its proper place without being forced by pneuma or being compelled by any other cause of this sort, as some people say it is, claiming that the private parts draw the residue like cupping-glasses forcing it by means of pneuma—as if it were possible either for this residue or that of the dry or liquid nourishment to have spatially moved elsewhere without being forced, because the emission of these residues is due to the collecting together of pneuma helping to clear them out.[474] But this is common to all cases in which one must move something. For it is because of holding back the pneuma that strength springs up. Besides, even without this force the residues are secreted during sleep if the [proper] places are full of residue and relaxed. One might as well say that it is by the wind that the seeds of plants are on each occasion secreted to the places where they are in the habit of bearing fruit.[475] No, the cause of this, as was said, is that in all animals there are parts receptive of the residues, both for the useless ones (for example, for the dry and the liquid one) [and for the useful ones]; and for the blood there are so-called blood-vessels.[476]

Now in the case of females, there is the place around the uterus. The two blood-vessels, the great blood-vessel and the aorta, are partitioned higher up into many fine blood-vessels that end in the uterus.[477] When these are over-filled from the nourishment, and the female nature, because of its coldness, is not capable of concocting it, it is secreted through the finest blood-vessels into the uterus. But, because of their narrowness, these are incapable of receiving the excessive quantity, and so the affection that comes about is a sort of hemorrhage. The period is not exactly arranged in women, but tends quite reasonably to occur when the moon is waning.[478] For the bodies of animals are colder when their environment happens to become so, and the times of new moon are colder because of the moon's complete waning, which is why too the end of the month is stormier than the middle. When the residue has changed into blood, then, the menses tends to occur at the period just mentioned. But when the residue has not been concocted a small quantity is always secreted, and this is why "whites" occur in females while they are still small, in fact, children.[479] If both these secretions of residues are moderate, their bodies are preserved, inasmuch as their occurrence is a purgation of the residues that are causes of their bodies being diseased. If on the other hand they do not occur, or occur excessively, they do harm. For they either produce diseases or a diminishment of their bodies. That is why "whites," if continuous and excessive, subtract from the growth of girls.

Of necessity, then, this residue is produced in women due to the causes just stated. For since their nature is incapable of effecting concoction, it is necessary for a residue to be produced, not only from the useless nourishment, but also from the blood in the blood-vessels, which overflows when it fills the finest blood-vessels.[480] But for the sake of the better and the end, nature makes full use of it in this place 738ᵇ1 for the sake of generation, in such a way that another thing of the same genus comes to be.[481] For [the menses] is already potentially at any rate of the same sort as the body whose secretion it is.

In all females, then, it is necessary for a residue to be produced, more though in the quite sanguineous ones, and, among these, most in 5 the human. But in the others too it is necessary for some composite to be collected in the uterine place. The cause of there being more in the quite sanguineous ones and most in the human was stated previously.[482]

But though a residue of this sort exists in all females, it does not do so in all males. For some males do not emit semen, but just as the 10 ones that do emit it handicraft what is being composed from matter present in the females by means of a movement within the semen, so the ones of this sort produce and compose it by means of a movement within themselves present in that part from which the seed is emit-ted. This is the place around the diaphragm in all those that have one. 15 For the starting-point of the nature [of an animal] is the heart or its analogue, while the lower [place] is an appendage that is for the sake of this. The cause, then, of not all males having a generative residue, while all females do, is that an animal is an ensouled body. And always the female provides the matter, while the male provides the handi- 20 crafter. For this is the capacity, we say, that each of them possesses, and being female or being male consists in this. So while it is necessary for the female to provide body and mass, for the male it is not necessary. For neither is it necessary for the instruments or the producer to be present in what is coming to be. But it is the body that comes from 25 the female, the soul from the male. For the soul is the substance of a certain body.[483]

Because of this in fact if there is sexual intercourse among animals that are not of the same genus (homogenês) (and there is sexual inter-course if their times [of heat] are equal, their gestation periods are quite similar, and the sizes of their bodies not too far apart), the first offspring has a common similarity to both (for example, the offspring 30 of fox and dog, of partridge and chicken), but as time goes on and one offspring comes from another the end result takes after the female in shape, just as alien seeds do to the region.[484] For it is what provides the matter and the body for the seed. 35

And because of this the part in the females that is receptive—namely, the uterus—is not [just] a duct, but rather has dimension, whereas the males that emit seed have ducts, and these are bloodless. 739ᵃ1

Once each of the residues is in its own proper place it becomes that residue. Before then nothing is one, unless with much force, that is, contrary to nature.[485]

The cause of the secretion of the generative residues in animals has now been stated.

But when the seed from the male (in those animals that emit seed) has entered, it composes the purest part of the residue. For the greater part of the menses, being liquid, is useless too, just as the most liquid part of the male semen is, that is, of a single emission. For the earlier part is more infertile than the later in most cases. For it contains less soul-involving heat due to being non-concocted, whereas the concocted part has thickness and is more corporeal.[486]

In those cases, whether of women or of other animals, where an external emission does not occur, because there is not much useless residue present in this sort of secretion, as much is produced within them as is retained within those animals that emit it externally, namely, what is composed by the capacity of the male that is present in the seed secreted by him, or by the part analogous to the uterus being inserted into the male, just as is seen to happen in the case of certain insects.

That the liquid accompanying sexual pleasure that is produced in females contributes nothing to the embryo was stated previously.[487] It might especially seem to do so because in women too, just as in males, so-called wet dreams occur at night. But this is no sign of anything. For in fact the same thing occurs in young men who, though it is as if they are going to come, in fact emit nothing, or still more in those who emit something infertile.

Without an emission from the male in sexual intercourse, then, and without the womanly residue, whether emitted externally or whether there is [only] enough within, it is impossible to conceive. Females conceive, however, without the pleasure that usually comes about in them during sexual intercourse, if the place happens to be in heat and the uterus has descended within.[488] But for the most part pleasure does occur because when the mouth of the uterus has not closed a secretion takes place, which is usually accompanied by pleasure both in males and in women. And when this is so there is also an easier passage for the seed of the male.

The emission, though, does not take place within the uterus, as some people think (for the mouth of the uterus is narrow), but rather in front of it, just where the female emits her liquid in some cases, is where the male too emits [his semen]. Sometimes it remains in this place, sometimes, if the uterus happens to be suitably disposed and hot due to the purgation, it draws [the semen] in. A sign of this is that pessaries, though wet when applied, are dry when removed. Further, in those animals that have the uterus near the diaphragm, as birds and viviparous fishes do, it is impossible for the seed not to be drawn in there, but instead to enter when discharged.[489] And this place, because of the heat present in it, does draw in the semen. For the secretion and collection of the menses kindle heat in this part, so that it is like conical vessels which, having been washed out with something hot, draw water into themselves when the mouth is turned downward.[490] And this is the way in which the drawing up occurs—although some say that in the instrument parts involved in sexual intercourse nothing occurs in this way. And the reverse process happens in fact for those who say that the female also emits seed. For if the uterus emits any outside itself, it will have to draw it back in again, if indeed it is to be mixed with the semen of the male. But for it to occur in this way is superfluous, and nature does nothing superfluous.

When what is secreted in the uterus by the female has been composed by the semen of the male, what it does is about the same as what rennet does in the case of milk. For in fact rennet is milk that contains vital heat, which brings together what is similar into one and composes it, and the semen in relation to the nature of the menses has the same effect. For the nature of milk and menses is the same.[491] When, then, the corporeal part comes together, the liquid one is secreted and, as the earthy parts dry out, membranes form in a circle around it.[492] And this happens of necessity and for the sake of something. For it is both necessary for the extreme surfaces to dry out when heated and becoming cold, and the animal must not be in liquid but separated from it.[493] Among these [separators] some are called membranes, others choria—they differ by the more and the less.[494] They are present in ovipara and vivipara alike.

When the embryo is once composed it does things about the same way sown seeds do. For the first starting-point is also present in the seeds themselves.[495] And when this, which previously was present potentially, has been distinctly formed, the shoot and the root are sent off from it. And it is by the root that it gets its nourishment. For the plant needs growth. So too in the embryo in a certain way all the parts are present potentially, but the starting-point is farthest along the road.[496]

That is why the heart is the first to be distinctly formed actively. This is clear not only to perception (for it happens this way), but also to reason (*logos*). For when what is coming to be is distinctly formed free from both parents it must manage for itself, just like a son who has set up house away from his father. So that is why it must have a

starting-point from which even the later orderly arrangement of the
body in animals derives. For if it is to come in from the outside at
some time and be present in it later, not only might one be puzzled as
to the time, but because it is necessary, when each of the parts is being
separated out, for this starting-point to be present first, namely, the
one from whose presence both the growth and the movement of the
various parts derives.

That is why those who say, like Democritus, that the external parts of
animals become disaggregated first, and later the internal ones, do not
speak correctly.[497] It is as if they were speaking of animals made of wood
or stone. For things of this sort have no starting-point at all, whereas
all animals have one and have it within. That is why the heart is quite
evidently the first thing to become distinct in all blooded animals. For it
is a starting-point of both the homoeomerous and non-homoeomerous
parts. For this already deserves to be called the starting-point of the animal and its composition at the moment when it needs nourishment. For
what is [an animal] of course grows.[498] And for an animal nourishment
in its last stage is blood or its analogue, and of these the blood-vessels are
the receptacle.[499] That is why the heart is the starting-point of these. This
is clear from the *History of Animals* and the *Dissections*.[500]

Since the embryo is already potentially an animal, but is incomplete,
it is necessary for it to get its nourishment from elsewhere. That is why
it makes use of the uterus, that is, of the mother to get nourishment,
just as a plant makes use of the earth, until it is complete to the point
of being already an animal potentially capable of perambulation. That
is why nature has first traced out the two blood-vessels from the heart,
and from these hang smaller vessels near the uterus, forming what
is called the umbilical cord. For the umbilical cord is a blood-vessel,
consisting of one vessel in some animals, and of several in others.[501]
Round these is a skin-like sheath, because the weakness of the vessels
needs preservation and shelter. The vessels are attached to the uterus
like roots, and through them the embryo gets its nourishment. For it
is for the sake of this that the animal remains in the uterus, and not,
as Democritus says, so that the parts may be molded in accord with
the parts of the mother.[502] This is evident in the case of the oviparous
animals. For they get their disaggregation in the eggs, when they have
separated from the matrix.[503]

But one might raise a puzzle, if the blood is nourishment, and the
heart, being already filled with blood, is the first thing to come to be,
and the nourishment comes from outside, where did the first nourishment enter from?[504] Perhaps it is not true that all of it comes from

outside, but rather, just as with the seeds of plants, where there is something of this sort present in them which at first has a milky appearance,
in the same way too, the residue of the matter in animals of which they
are composed is their nourishment from the outset.

The embryo, then, grows by means of the umbilical cord in just the
same way as a plant does by means of its roots, and as animals themselves do when free of the nourishment within themselves.[505] These
issues must be spoken about later, at the opportune time for the proper
accounts.[506]

The disaggregation of the parts, however, does not come to be in the
way that some people suppose, namely, by like naturally being carried
to like.[507] For in addition to the many other difficulties involved in this
account, it follows that each of the homoeomerous parts comes to be
separately (for example, bones by themselves, and sinews, and fleshes
by themselves) if one accepts this cause. Instead it is because the residue of the female is potentially such as the animal is by nature and each
of the parts is present in it potentially, but none actively, and it is due
to this cause that each of them comes to be, and because when what
can affect and what can be affected make contact in the way in which
one can affect and the other can be affected (by "way," I mean, how,
where, and when), then straightaway the one affects and the other is
affected. Well, the female provides the matter, while the male provides
the starting-point of the movement. And as the things that come to be
due to craft come to be because of its instruments—or to put it more
truly, because of the movements of these—and this is the activation of
the craft, and the craft is the shape [or form] of the things that come
to be present in something else, so it is with the capacity of nutritive
soul.[508] Just as it also does in the animals and plants themselves later on,
it produces growth from nourishment, using heat and cold as its instruments (for in these its movements are present and a certain account
of each [part of the animal]), in the same way at the outset as well it
composes what is by nature coming to be.[509] For the matter by which
the thing grows is the same as that of which it is first composed, so that
the productive capacity [of growth] is the same as the starting-point of
[the animal]; although it is greater.[510] If, then, it is the nutritive soul, it
is also the generative one. And it is the nature of each thing, present in
all plants and animals, whereas the other parts of the soul are present
in some living things, not present in others.[511]

Now in plants the female is not separated from the male. In some of
the animals, however, it is separated, and in these the female has need
of the male in addition.

II 5

And yet one might be puzzled as to what cause this is due to. If indeed the female possesses the same soul [as the male] and the matter is the residue of the female, why has the female need of the male in addition, why does it not itself generate from itself? The cause is that animal differs from plant by perception. And it is impossible for face, hand, flesh, or any other part to exist without perceptual soul being present in it either actively or potentially, whether in some way or unconditionally.[512] For it will be like a corpse or part of a corpse. If, then, it is the male that is productive of this sort of soul, in cases where it is separated from the female, it is impossible for the female itself to generate an animal from itself. For what was just mentioned was the being for male.[513] But that there is a reason for the puzzle just stated is evident from the case of those birds that lay wind-eggs, since it shows that up to a point the female can generate. But this too involves a further puzzle as to what way we are to say their eggs are alive. For it is neither possible for it to be in the way that fertilized eggs are (for then an actually ensouled thing would come to be from them), nor again in the way that a stone one or a wood is. For there exists for these eggs as well [as for fertile ones] a sort of passing away, suggesting that previously they in a way participated in life. It is clear, then, that they possess a sort of soul potentially. But what sort of soul? It is necessary, surely, that it be the last. And this is the nutritive. For it is present alike in all animals and plants. Why, then, does it not complete the parts and the animal? Because these must possess perceptual soul. For the parts of animals are not like those of plants. That is why there is a need for the contribution of the male. For the male is separated from the female in these cases. And this is just what happens. For wind-eggs become fertile if in a certain period of time the male mates with the female. But the cause of these things will be determined later on.[514]

If there is any genus of animal that, though the female exists, contains no separated male, it is possible that this generates an animal from itself. Though this has not been observed in a reliable way up to now at least—although a case in the fish genus does make one hesitate. For among the ones called erythrinus no male has so far been seen, whereas females full of embryos have been.[515] But of this we have as yet no reliable experience. Also, ones that are neither female nor male exist in the genus the fishes belong to—for example, the eels and a genus of mullets found in marshland rivers.

In those animals, though, where the female and the male are separated, it is impossible for the female by itself to bring generation to a complete end. For otherwise the male would be pointless, and nature produces nothing pointless. That is why in animals of this sort the male always completes the generation. For he produces the perceptual soul in [the embryo] either due to himself or due to his semen.

Because the parts are present potentially in the matter, when once the starting-point of movement has come to be, just as in those wondrous automata, one thing follows another in succession.[516] And what certain of the physicists must mean when they say that "like is naturally carried to like" is not that the parts move in the sense of changing their places, but rather that they remain where they are and undergo alteration in softness, hardness, color, and the other differentiae (*diaphora*) of homoeomerous things—becoming actively the things previously present in them potentially.[517]

What comes to be first is the starting-point. This is the heart in blooded animals, and its analogue in the others, as was said often.[518] And it is evident not only to perception that it comes to be first but also around the last moments. For life leaves the heart last. And it happens in all cases that the last to come to be is the first to leave, and the first last, as if nature ran a double course, turning back to the starting-point from which it came.[519] For coming to be is from what is not to what is, and passing away from what is back again to what is not.

II 6

After the starting-point, as was said, the internal parts come to be earlier than the external ones.[520] The larger parts, though, become apparent earlier than the smaller ones, although some of them do not come to be earlier. First, the parts above the diaphragm become articulated and are superior in size, while what is below is smaller and not distinctly formed. And this happens in all cases in which the upper and the lower are distinctly formed except in the insects. In those that are produced as larvae, growth is toward the upper part. For the lower part is smaller from the start. Lack of distinction between the upper part and the lower parts, among the animals capable of perambulation, exists only in the cephalopods. And what was just said applies in the case of the plants as well: the upper body comes to be earlier than the lower. For the seeds send out roots earlier than shoots.[521]

The parts of animals are distinctly formed by pneuma—not however by that of the female progenitor or of [the embryo] itself, as some of the physicists say.[522] This is evident in the case of birds, fishes, and insects. For some of these, after being separated from the female progenitor, come to be from an egg, within which they get their articulation,

5

10

15

20

25

30

35

742ᵃ1

whereas other animals do not breathe at all, but are produced as larvae
or laid as eggs.[523] Others, though they breathe and get their articulation within the womb, do not breathe until the lung has gotten its final
[articulation], the preceding parts too getting their articulation in this
way before the animals breathe. Further, the polydactyl quadrupeds—
for example, dog, lion, wolf, fox, and jackal—all produce blind young,
and the eyelid does not divide until later on. So it is clear that it is also
the same way in the case of all the other parts: just as its quality and its
quantity come to be, pre-existing potentially but later actually, due to
the same causes due to which its quality is distinctly formed, and two
things come to be from one [eyelid]. For pneuma, though, to be present is necessary, because it is wet and hot, the hot affecting and the wet
being affected.[524]

Some of the ancient physicists attempted to state which part comes to
be after which, but had not very much experience of the facts.[525] For in the
case of the parts, as with other things, one is naturally prior to another.[526]
But actually something is prior in many ways.[527] For the for-the-sake-of-
which and what is for the sake of this are different, and of these the latter
is prior in coming to be, the former in substance.[528] But what is for the
sake of this has two differences (*diaphora*). For one is what the source of
movement is, and the other is what the for-the-sake-of-which makes use
of. I mean, for example, what is generative and what is an instrument for
what comes to be. For of these, one must be possessed prior, namely, the
one capable of affecting (for example, the teacher to the one who learns),
and other posterior (for example, the flutes to the one learning to play
them). For it is superfluous for those to possess them who do not have
the scientific knowledge of how to play them.

There are, on the one side, three things: one is the end, which we
say is [the] for-the-sake-of-which; second, the starting-point that is
capable of causing movement in, and is generative of, the things that
are for the end's sake (for what is productive and generative, insofar
as it is such, is such in relation to what is produced and comes to be);
third, what is useful, that is, what the end makes use of. On the other
side, it is first necessary for there to be present some part in which the
starting-point of the movement resides (for even from the outset this
is one part of the end, that is, the most controlling one); next after this,
the whole and the end; thirdly and finally, the instrumental parts that
these put to various uses.[529] So, if there is something of this sort that
is just what is necessarily present in animals, containing the starting-
point and end of their entire nature, it is necessary for it to come to be
first—first, insofar as it is capable of causing movement, but, insofar as
it is a part of the end, along with the whole.

So those instrumental parts that are generative in nature must always be present themselves prior [to the others] (for, as a starting-point, they are for the sake of something else); those parts that are not of this sort, but are for the sake of something else, posterior.[530] That is why it is not easy to determine which parts are prior, the ones that are for the sake of something else, or the one these are for the sake of. For the parts capable of causing movement intrude, because they are prior to the end in coming to be, and as between the parts capable of causing movement and the instrumental parts it is not easy to determine [which is prior]. And yet in accord with the present methodical inquiry we must inquire what comes to be after what.[531] For the end is posterior to some parts and prior to others. And because of this the part that contains the starting-point comes to be first, next the upper body. That is why the parts around the head and the eyes appear largest from the start in embryos, while the parts below the umbilicus—for example, the legs—appear small. For the lower parts are for the sake of the upper ones, and are neither parts of the end nor generative of it.[532]

But people do not speak correctly, not even about the necessity belonging to what it is due to, who say that "this is the way it always comes to be," and consider this to be a starting-point in these cases. Thus Democritus of Abdera says that of what is unlimited there is no starting-point, but what something is due to is a starting-point and what is always is unlimited, so that to ask for what it is due to in cases of this sort, he says, is to seek a starting-point for what is unlimited.[533] And yet according to this argument, according to which it is fitting not to seek what the thing is due to, there will be no demonstration whatsoever of what is eternal.[534] But it is evident that there are many, both of things that always come to be and of things that always are, seeing that the triangle always has angles equal to two right angles and the diagonal is eternally incommensurable with the sides, but nonetheless there is a cause and a demonstration of these things. While, then, it is correctly said that it is not fitting to seek a starting-point in all cases, it is not correctly said of all the things that always are and always come to be, but [only] of those that really are starting-points of what is eternal. For of a starting-point there is another sort of knowledge and not a demonstration.[535] A starting-point in the case of immovable things is the what-it-is, but in the case of things that come to be there are immediately several starting-points—although the way [each is a starting-point] is distinct and not the same for all. One of this number is the starting-point from which the movement comes. That is why all the blooded animals have a heart first, as was said at the start, while in the other animals it is the analogue of the heart that comes to be first.[536]

743ᵃ1   From the heart the blood-vessels extend throughout [the body], as in the mannikins drawn on the walls.[537] For the parts lie around these because they come to be from them. The generation of the homoeomerous parts is due to cold and heat. For some are composed and solidi-

5   fied by cold, others by heat. The differentiae (*diaphora*) of these have been spoken about previously elsewhere, and what sorts of things are dissolvable by liquid and by fire, and what sorts are non-dissolvable by liquid and unmeltable by fire.[538] As the nourishment oozes through the blood-vessels, then, and the ducts in each of the parts, like water

10   in unbaked pottery vessels, flesh or its analogues are composed due to the cold, which is why it is also dissolved due to fire.[539] But of the things arising [out of the blood-vessels] the ones that are too earthy, because they contain too little liquid and heat, cool as the liquid evaporates along with the heat, becoming hard and earthy in shape [or form]—for example, nails, horns, hoofs, and beaks. That is why these are soft-

15   enable by fire, whereas none is meltable by it, although some are by liquids—for example, the shells of eggs.

    Due to the internal heat the sinews and bones come to be as their liquidity dries. That is why in fact bones are non-dissolvable due to fire, just like pottery. For it is as if they have been baked in an oven due

20   to the heat present in their generation. But this heat does not produce flesh and bone from any random thing, nor in any random place, nor at any random time, but rather from what is nature, where it is natural, and when it is natural. For neither will what potentially is [produced] due to what does not actively possess the capacity to move it, nor will what actively possesses it produce it from a random thing, any more

25   than a carpenter could produce a box except from wood, nor without him will a box [be produced] from the wood. And the heat is present in the spermatic residue and the movement and the activity it possesses are of such a quantity and sort as to be proportional to each part. But to the extent that there is any deficiency or excess to that extent what

30   comes to be is completed in a worse way or is deformed, in about the same way as the one in which external things are composed due to boiling, [for example,] with a view to food's being more pleasant, or for some other work.[540] But here it is we who establish the proportion in the heat required for the movement, whereas there it is the nature of the male progenitor that provides it. In the case of those that come to be spontaneously, on the other hand, the cause is movement and heat

35   at the proper time.[541]

    Cooling is the lack of heat.[542] Nature, though, makes use of both, because of necessity they have a capacity, so that the one makes one thing *this* and another thing *that*, but, of course, in the case of what

comes to be it is for the sake of something that the one of these cools   743^b1
and the other heats and that each of the parts comes to be—flesh being
made soft on the one hand of necessity, on the other for the sake of
something, sinew dry and pullable, and bone dry and shatterable.   5

The skin is produced as the flesh dries just as so-called scum forms
on liquids in which things are boiled. This is not only because its generation occurs at the extremity of [the body], though, but also because
what is viscous stays at the surface, because it is not capable of evaporating. While in other animals the viscous is dry (which is why the
extremities of the bloodless ones are testaceous or crustaceous), in   10
the blooded ones it is more oily. And of those among the latter whose
nature is not too earthy, what is fatty gathers under the covering of
the skin, suggesting that the skin is produced from this sort of viscous material. For what is oily is somewhat viscous. And all these, as   15
we stated, must be said to come to be in one way of necessity, and in
another way not of necessity but for the sake of something.

The upper body, then, is the first thing marked off in the course of
generation, whereas, in the blooded animals, the lower gets its growth
as time goes on. All the parts have their outline shapes determined ear-   20
lier, and later get their colors and their degrees of softness and hardness,
absolutely as if they were handicrafted by an animal painter: nature.
For painters too, after having traced the animal in outline shape by
means of lines, just paint within them.⁵⁴³

Because the starting-point of perceptions is in the heart, the heart is   25
the first part of the entire animal to come to be, and because of its heat,
at the place where the blood-vessels terminate above, the cold composes the brain, as a counterpart to the heat around the heart.⁵⁴⁴ That
is why the [parts] around the head get their generation next after the
heart, and surpass the others in size. For the brain is large and liquid   30
from the start.

There is a puzzle, however, about what happens to the eyes of animals. For though at the start they appear very large in animals, whether
they walk, swim, or fly, yet they are the last of the parts to be composed
completely. For they shrink into line in the meantime.⁵⁴⁵ The cause is   35
that the perceptual organ of the eyes, like the other perceptual organs
too, is set on ducts; but while the perceptual organ of touch and taste
is just the body or some part of the body of animals, and smell and   744^a1
hearing are ducts, connected to the air outside, that are full of connate
pneuma, and terminate at the small blood-vessels around the brain
that extend from the heart, the eye, by contrast, is the only one of the
perceptual organs that has a special body of its own.⁵⁴⁶ It is liquid and   5
cold and does not pre-exist in its place potentially as the other parts

do, and then become so actively later on, but instead is the purest of
the liquid from around the brain secreted through the ducts that are
evident leading to the meninx around the brain.[547]

A proof of this is that, besides the brain, no other part in the head
is liquid and cold except the eye. Of necessity, then, this place gets
large at first, but shrinks into line later. For it also happens in the same
way where the brain is concerned. For first it is liquid and large, but
as evaporation and concoction proceed the brain too becomes more
body-like and shrinks into line, as does the size of the eyes. But at the
start, because of the brain, the head is very large, and because of the
liquid in the eye-balls, the eyes appear large. They are the last to reach
the end of their completion because the brain too is composed with
difficulty. For it is [only] later on that its coldness and liquidity come
to an end.

[And this is so] in the case of all those animals having brains, but
especially in the case of human beings. For this is why the bregma is
the last of the bones to come to be.[548] For in the case of embryos that
have come to be externally, this bone is still soft in the children. (The
cause of this happening especially in the case of human beings is that
of the animals their brain is the most liquid and largest, and the cause
of this, again, is that the heat in their heart is purest. Their thought
makes clear its good-mixture.[549] For the most practically-wise of the
animals is the human.[550]) And even children for a long time have no
control of their head, which is because of the heaviness where the brain
is concerned. And likewise too in the case of the parts that must move.
For it is [only] later on that the starting-point of movement gets control over the upper parts, and last of all over those whose movement is
not closely connected with it, like that of the limbs. And the eyelid is
a part of this sort. And since nature produces nothing superfluous or
pointless, it is clear that neither does it produce anything too late or too
soon. For otherwise what is produced will be either pointless or superfluous. So it is necessary for the eyelids to be separated at the same time
as [the animal] is capable of moving them. It is later on, then, because
of the amount of concoction required where the brain is concerned,
that the eyes of animals are completed, and they last of all the parts,
because the movement must be very controlling in order to move what
is so far away from the starting-point and so cold. And it is clear that
the eyelids have a nature of this sort. For if even any degree of heaviness whatsoever comes about in the head, due to sleep, drunkenness,
or anything else of this sort, we are incapable of raising our eyelids,
even though the weight they have is so small.[551]

Where the eyelids are concerned, then, it has been stated how and why they are produced, and due to what cause they are the last to get their articulation.

Each of the other parts is produced from the nourishment: the most estimable ones and the ones participating most in the most controlling starting-point, from the nourishment that is concocted, purest, and first; the ones that are necessary and for the sake of the former ones, from the inferior nourishment, and from the leftovers and residues.[552] For like a good household manager, nature too is not accustomed to throw anything away from which something useful can be made. In the management of households, however, the best of the nourishment produced is assigned to the free males, while the inferior nourishment and the residues of the other is assigned to the household slaves, and the worst is given to the animals that are nourished along with them.[553] Just, then, as the understanding produces from outside these things for their growth, so within the things themselves that come to be the nature produces flesh and the bodies of the other perceptual organs from the purest matter, while out of the residues it produces bones, sinews, and hair, and, further, nails, hoofs, all things of this sort.[554] That is why these are the last to get composed, namely, when a residue for the nature [to use] has already been produced.

The nature of the bones, then, is produced in the first composition from the spermatic residue, and as animals grow they get their growth from the natural nourishment (which is just what the controlling parts get theirs from), but [only] from the leftovers and residues of this. For in every case a first and a second sort of nourishment is produced, one nutritive and the other growth-productive. Nutritive is what provides the being to the whole and the parts, growth-productive is what produces increase in size. About these, determinations must be made later on.[555] The sinews are composed in the same way as the bones, and from the same things, namely, from the spermatic residue and from the nutritive. Nails, hair, hoofs, horns, beaks, the spurs of male birds, and any other part of this sort, on the other hand, are composed from the supplementary and growth-producing nourishment acquired from the female and from outside. And it is because of this that the bones get their growth [only] up to a certain point. For there is a limit of size for all animals, which is why there is also one of growth of the bones. For if these always had growth, whichever animals had bone or its analogue would grow as long as they lived, because [bone growth] is the defining mark of size for animals.[556] Due to what cause they do not always get growth must be stated later.[557] Hair, though, and things of the same genus as it, go on growing as long as they exist. And do so more during diseases, and when bodies are getting old and passing away, because more residues are left over, since less gets used up by the controlling [parts] because of old age and diseases—although when these residues too fail due to time of life, the hairs also fail. The bones, however, do the contrary. For they decay along with the body and its parts. Hair, though, goes on growing even after death, although it does not come about where it did not exist to begin with.[558]

About the teeth, however, one might raise a puzzle. For they have the same nature as the bones and are produced from the bones, whereas nails, hairs, horns, and things of that sort are produced from skin, which is why they change in color along with the skin (for they become white, black, and all sorts of colors according to the color of the skin). The teeth, though, do none of this, since they are [produced] from the bones—at any rate, in those animals that have teeth and bones. And they alone among the various bones go on growing throughout life. This is clear from teeth that turn aside and do not make contact with each other.[559] The cause of their growth, as that for whose sake it is due, is their function. For they would soon be worn down if there were not some compensating process, since even as things stand, in some aging animals that are voracious but do not have large teeth, they are entirely worn down. For their destruction proceeds at a greater rate (*logos*) than their growth. Hence in this case too nature has contrived things well with an eye to the result. For it makes old age and the decline of the teeth coincide. If life lasted for ten thousand years, though, or even for a thousand, the teeth would have to be extremely large from the start and grow anew many times. For even if they had gotten their growth continuously, they would nonetheless have been worn down and been useless for their work. What their growth is for the sake of, then, has now been stated. But it turns out that the teeth do not have the same nature as the other bones. For they all come to be in the first composition and none of them later, whereas the teeth come to be later. That is why in fact it is possible for them to grow again after [the previous ones] have fallen out. For though they make contact with the bones, they are not naturally united with them. Yet they do come to be from the nourishment that is distributed to the bones (which is why they have the same nature), and a time when the latter have already attained their full complement.[560]

The other animals come to be in possession of teeth or their analogue, unless something contrary to nature occurs, because when they are brought forth from their progenitor they are more complete than the human. But the human, unless something contrary to nature happens, does not have them.

The cause due to which some teeth come to be and fall out, while others do not fall out, will be stated later.[561]

It is because parts of this sort come from a residue that the human is the most bare-skinned of all the animals and has the smallest nails for its size. For a residue is what is non-concocted; what is earthy is what in the bodies of all animals is least concocted; and he has the smallest quantity of earthy residue.

How each of the parts is composed, then, has now been stated, as has what the cause is of their coming to be.

II 7

In viviparous animals the fetuses get their growth, as was said previously, through the umbilical cord.[562] For since the nutritive capacity of the soul, as well as the others, is present in animals, it immediately sends out the umbilical cord like a root to the uterus. The umbilical cord consists of blood-vessels in a sheath, more numerous ones in larger animals (for example, an ox and the like), two in intermediate-sized animals, and one in the smallest ones. Through it the fetus gets its sanguineous nourishment. For the uterus is the terminus of many blood-vessels.

All animals without two sets of teeth, and all those with two, whose uterus does not have one great blood-vessel running through it but many close together instead, have in their uterus so-called cotyledons.[563] The umbilical cord connects to these and is naturally attached to them. For the blood-vessels, which run through the umbilical cord on this side and on that, split up [into smaller ones] all over the uterus, and it is where they terminate that the cotyledons come to be, with their convex side toward the uterus, their concave one toward the fetus.[564] Between the uterus and the fetus are the chorion and the membranes.[565] As the fetus grows and becomes complete the cotyledons become smaller, and finally disappear when it is completed. For nature prepares the sanguineous nourishment for fetuses in this part of the uterus as in the breasts, and because the cotyledons are gradually gathered together from many into a few the body of the cotyledon becomes like an eruption or inflammation.[566] As long as the fetus is comparatively small, incapable of taking much nourishment, they are clearly visible and large, but when it has grown they shrink.

But most of the docked animals and most of those that have two sets of teeth have no cotyledons in their uterus, but the umbilical cord extends to meet a single blood-vessel that is large and extends throughout the uterus.[567] Some of these animals are uniparous, others multiparous, but the several fetuses are connected to it in the same way as one. (But one should get a theoretical grasp on these things from the paradigms drawn in the *Dissections* and in the *History of Animals*.[568]) For the animals grow out from the umbilical cord, and the umbilical cord from the blood-vessel, and they are next to each other along the stream of the blood-vessel as along a waterpipe. And around each of the fetuses are membranes and a chorion.

Those who say that children are nourished in the uterus through sucking on a bit of flesh do not speak correctly.[569] For if this were so, the same would occur in the case of the other animals, but as things stand it evidently isn't (in fact this will easily be seen by means of dissections). Also, all fetuses alike, whether of animals that fly, swim, or walk, have fine membranes that encompass them, separating them from the uterus and from the liquids that arise in it, and neither in these membranes themselves is there anything of the relevant [nourishing] sort, nor is it possible that anything of advantage will be procured through them. As for those laid as eggs, it is evident that all of them get their growth on the outside when separated from the mother.[570]

Copulation in accord with nature occurs between animals of the same genus (*homogenês*); nevertheless it also occurs between those that, though they have a close nature, do not fail to have a difference in species (*eidos*), if their size is about the same and if the times of their gestation are equal.[571] Although, in the case of other animals, such occurrences are rare, it does occur in the case of dogs, foxes, wolves, and jackals. And Indian dogs come to be from some wild dog-like animal and a dog.[572] And in the case of birds that mate frequently it has been seen to occur—for example, in the case of partridges and hens. And among the taloned birds hawks that differ in species (*eidos*) seem to have sexual intercourse with each other, and it is the same way in the case of certain other birds. In the case of sea animals nothing worth mentioning has been seen; but the so-called rhinobates especially does seem to come to be from copulation of the rhine and the batus.[573] And it is said that the proverb about Libya suggesting that "Libya is always nourishing something new" is because animals not of the same family (*homophulos*) have sexual intercourse with each other there.[574] For it is said that because of the scarcity of water they all meet at the few places with springs and have sexual intercourse, even though they are not of the same genus (*homogenês*).

Of the animals that come to be from this sort of sexual intercourse all except mules, it is evident, copulate again with each other and are

capable of generating both a female and a male, whereas mules alone
are infertile. For they do not generate either through sexual intercourse
with each other or with other animals. There is, however, a universal   15
problem as to what the cause is due to which a male or a female is
infertile. For there are both women and men who are infertile, and in
the case of the other animals there are some in each genus—for example, horses and sheep. But in this case, the case of the mules, the whole
genus is infertile. In the case of the others, though, the causes of their   20
infertility are several. For both women and men are infertile from birth
when the places used for sexual intercourse are deformed, so that the
former do not have pubic hair and the latter do not grow a beard but
remain like eunuchs.[575] But others as they advance in age are affected
in the same way, sometimes because of the well-nourishment of their   25
bodies (for in women who are too fat and in men who are in too good
condition the spermatic residue is used up by the body, and the former
do not produce menses or the latter semen), and sometimes, because
of disease, men emit semen that is cold and liquid, while the purgations [of menses] by the women are bad and full of diseased residues.   30

But in the case of many men and many women this affection occurs
because of deformations in the parts and the places used for sexual
intercourse. Some of these are curable, some incurable, but those especially remain infertile if things of this sort have come about in the first
composition.[576] For then mannish women and womanish men come   35
to be, and in the former menses are not produced, while in the latter   747^{a}1
the seed is fine-grained and cold. That is why the [semen] of males
is quite reasonably tested for infertility by trials in water. For what is
fine-grained and cold quickly disperses on the surface, whereas what
is fertile sinks to the bottom. For what is concocted is hot, and what is   5
composed and coarse-grained has been concocted. They test women,
on the other hand, by means of pessaries, to see whether its odors penetrate upward from below to the exhaled pneuma, and by colors rubbed
on the eyes to see whether they color the sputum in the mouth.[577] For   10
if these things do not result it makes it clear that, in the body, the ducts
through which the residue is secreted are commingled and grown
together. (For the place around the eyes, of all those around the head,
is the most spermatic. This is made clear by the fact that during acts of
sexual intercourse it alone changes its configuration in an obvious way,
and that those who indulge too much in sexual intercourse have quite   15
evidently sunken eyes.[578] The cause is that the nature of the semen is
similar to that of the brain. For the matter of it is watery, and the heat
acquired.[579]) Also, the spermatic purgations are from the diaphragm.
For the starting-point of the nature is there, so that the movements   20

from the sexual parts penetrate to the chest, and the odors from the chest produce a perception via the breathing.[580]

II 8

In human beings, then, and in the other genera (*genos*), as was said previously, this sort of deformation occurs in particular individuals, but in the case of the mules the whole genus (*genos*) is infertile.[581] About its cause Empedocles and Democritus speak (the first not in a perspicuous way, Democritus in a more knowable one), but they did not speak correctly.[582] For they state their demonstration alike in the case of all the animals that copulate contrary to sameness of genus (*suggeneia*).[583]

For Democritus says that the ducts of mules are destroyed in the uterus because the animals do not from the start come to be from those of the same genus (*suggenês*).[584] This latter, though, happens in the case of other animals, but this [destruction of the ducts] does not result—and yet it is necessary, if indeed this were the cause of their infertility, for all the others that have sexual intercourse in this way to be infertile too.

Empedocles, on the other hand, makes the cause be the mixture of the seeds becoming coarse-grained as a result of the semen of each being soft, since the hollows of one fit into the coarse-grains of the other, just like bronze mixed with tin—not even stating the cause correctly in the case of bronze and tin (they are spoken about in the *Problems*), nor, in general, producing his starting-points from knowable things.[585] For how do the hollows and the coarse-grains fit together to produce the mixture, for example, of wine and water? For this saying is beyond us. For the way we should understand the hollows of wine and of water is too far contrary to perception.

Further, since in fact it happens that from horses a horse comes to be, from asses an ass, and from a horse and an ass a mule does so, and in two ways, depending on whichever of the two is male or female, why is it that from these comes something so coarse-grained that what comes to be [from it] is infertile? And yet, though what is from both the male horse and the female one is soft, both a female horse and a male ass and a male horse and a female ass have sexual intercourse [that produces offspring]. And why what comes to be from both is infertile, he says, is because from the two one thing comes to be that is coarse-grained, because their seeds are soft. But so it should also be, then, when it comes to be from a male and female horse. For if only one of the two had sexual intercourse, it would be open to say that one of the two's not being a match for the semen of the ass was the cause of its not generating. But as things stand whatever sort it is in that intercourse, it is this same sort too in intercourse with an animal of the same genus (*suggenês*).

Further, the demonstration is stated alike of both the female and the male mule—the male alone, though, does generate at the age of seven years, so it is said; the female, on the other hand, is wholly infertile, and even she is so [only] because she does not nourish [the embryo] to the end, since a mule already *has* had an embryo.[586]

But perhaps a logico-linguistic demonstration might seem more convincing than the ones just mentioned—I call it logico-linguistic because in being more universal it is further away from the proper starting-points.[587] It is something like this: [P1] Suppose that from a male and a female of the same species (*homoeidês*) a male and a female naturally come to be that are of the same species (*homoeidês*) as their progenitors (for example, from a male and a female dog a male and a female dog), [P2] whereas from a pair distinct in species (*eidos*), one distinct from them in species comes to be (for example, if a dog is distinct in species from a lion, from a male dog and a female lion one distinct from them in species comes to be, also from a male lion and a female dog). So since [a] a male and a female mule come to be and are not different in species (*eidos*) from each other, and [b] a mule comes to be from a horse and an ass, and these are distinct in species (*eidos*) from mules, it is impossible for anything to come to be from mules. For [c] something of a distinct genus (*genos*) cannot come to be, because [P1] what comes to be from a male and female of the same species (*homoeidês*) is the same in species as they, and [d] a mule cannot, because it comes to be from a horse and an ass, which are distinct in species (*eidos*). Well, this argument is too universal and empty. For arguments not from the proper starting-points are empty, but rather seem to be based on the things at issue, but are not really.[588] For [arguments] from geometrical starting-points are geometrical ones, and likewise in the other cases. But what is empty, though it seems to be something, is nothing. And it is not true, because many animals that come to be from ones not of the same species (*homoeidês*) are fertile, as was said previously.[589] One should not, then, inquire in this way either concerning other things or concerning natural ones.

Rather it is from getting a theoretical grasp on what belongs to the genus (*genos*) of the horse and of the ass that one should get the cause.[590] In the first place, each of them is uniparous from animals of its own genus (*suggenês*); next, the females are not always able to conceive from the males (which is why breeders mate horses again at intervals),

because they are not continuously capable of bearing.[591] On the contrary, a female horse is not [abundantly] menstruous, but among the
quadrupeds emits the least.[592] And a she-ass is not receptive of mating, but expels the semen with her urine, which is why people follow
behind flogging her.[593] Further, the ass is a cold animal, which is why—
because its nature is sensitive to cold—it does not readily come to be in
cold climates, such as Scythia and the bordering region, or among the
Celts beyond Iberia (for it is also a cold region).[594] And it is due to this
cause that they do not put the jackasses to the females at the equinox,
as is done with horses, but around the summer solstice, in order that
the foals may come to be in warm season. For the season they come to
be in is the same as the one in which mating occurs. For the period of
gestation for a horse and an ass is a year. And because, as was just said,
its nature is cold, it is necessary for the semen of an animal of this sort
to be cold as well. Here is a sign of it: it is because of this, in fact, that
if a horse mounts a female horse that has already mated with an ass,
he does not destroy the result of the ass's mating, but if the ass mounts
second he does destroy that of the horse, due to the coldness of his
own seed. When, then, they have sexual intercourse with each other
the result is preserved by the heat of one of the two of them. For what
is secreted by the horse is hotter. For both the matter and the semen
of the mule are cold, whereas those of the horse are hotter. And when
they have sexual intercourse, whether hot [mounts] on cold or cold
on hot, the result is that the embryo that comes to be from them is
preserved and they are fertile from each other, whereas what comes to
be from them is no longer fertile, but is infertile in regard to producing
complete offspring.

In general, though, each of the two is naturally well disposed to
infertility. For the other things just mentioned belong to the ass, and
in addition if it does not begin to generate after the first shedding of
teeth, it no longer generates at all, so close does the body of the ass
come to being infertile.[595] Similarly too with the horse. For it is naturally well disposed to infertility, and all that remains to make it infertile
is for [the semen] produced from it to be colder. And this comes about
when it is mixed with the secretion of the ass. And in the same way the
ass, should it copulate with its own, comes equally close to generating something infertile, so that when in addition copulation occurs
contrary to nature (if at the same time asses are capable only with difficulty of generating a single offspring from each other), what comes to
be from the pair, being yet more infertile and contrary to nature, will
need nothing at all to make it infertile, but will of necessity be infertile.

It results too that the bodies of female mules become large in size,   20
because the secretion that goes to the menses is diverted to growth.
And since the pregnancy in animals of this sort lasts a year, the female
mule must not only conceive but also nourish [the embryo], and this
is impossible if menses are not being produced. But in female mules
none are produced, instead, the useless part [of the nourishment] is
excreted with the residue that comes from the bladder (which is why   25
male mules do not smell at the sexual parts of the female as the other
solid-hoofed animals do), while the other parts are diverted to the
growth of the body and to size. So while it is sometimes possible for
the female to conceive (which is the very thing it appears has already
happened), for her to nourish [the embryo] to the end and bring to
birth is impossible.   30

The male for his part may sometimes generate, both because the
male is hotter by nature than the female and because the male contributes no body to the mixture. And the complete thing that comes to
be is a ginnus, which is a deformed mule.[596] For ginni also come to be
from the horse and the ass when the embryo is diseased in the uterus.   35
For the ginnus is like the runts in pigs. For there too what is deformed   749^{a}1
in the uterus is called a runt. And human dwarfs come to be in a similar way. For they are deformed, both their parts and their development,
during gestation, and are like runts and ginni.

Book III

III 1

The sterility of mules has now been spoken about as have the animals that are viviparous both externally and internally. In the oviparous blooded ones things having to do with generation proceed in about the same way as those in animals that walk and one must grasp the same thing about them, although in another way they have differences (*diaphora*) both in relation to each other and in relation to the animals that walk.[597]

All of them alike, then, come to be from copulation and the emission of semen into the female from the male. But among the oviparous ones [1] birds emit a complete hard-shelled egg, unless it is deformed by disease, and the eggs of birds are all two-colored.[598] [2] The selachian fishes, as has often been said, after being internally oviparous, are viviparous, the egg changing previously from one place in the uterus to another, and their egg is soft-shelled and single-colored. One alone of these is not internally oviparous, namely, the so-called fishing-frog. The cause of this will be spoken about later.[599] [3] All the other fishes that are oviparous emit an egg of one color only, but it is incomplete. For it gets its growth outside due to the same cause that the eggs completed inside also do.

Now their uteruses, the differences (*diaphora*) they have, and due to what causes, have been spoken about previously.[600] For some of the oviparous ones have the uterus high up near the diaphragm, while others have it low down near the sexual parts. The selachian fishes have it high up; the ones that are both internally and externally viviparous (for example, human, horse, and each of the others of this sort) have it low down; and, among the oviparous ones, it is sometimes low down (as in the oviparous fishes), sometimes high up (as in the birds).

Fetuses also get composed in birds spontaneously, the ones some people call wind-eggs and *zephyria*.[601] These are produced in the ones that are neither capable fliers nor taloned, but prolific, due to the large quantity of residue these have (in the taloned ones, on the other hand, this sort of secretion is diverted to the wings and wing-feathers, and they have a small body that is dry and hot), and menstrual secretion and semen are residues.[602] Since then both the nature of the wings and that of the seed come to be from residues, nature is incapable of yielding much for both. And it is due to this same cause that the taloned birds neither mate frequently nor are prolific, whereas the heavy birds and the capable fliers that have bulky bodies are prolific, like a pigeon and those of this sort. For in those birds that are heavy and are not capable fliers—for example, chickens, partridges, and others of this sort—much residue of the relevant sort is produced. And this is why their males mate frequently and their females emit much matter, and some of this sort lay many eggs, while others do so often—for example, a chicken, partridge, and Libyan ostrich lay many, while the pigeon family lay not many but often. For these are intermediate between the taloned birds and the heavy ones. For they are capable fliers like the taloned ones, and have magnitude of body like the heavy ones. So because they are capable fliers and the residue is diverted to there, they lay few eggs, but because of the size of their bodies, because of the heat their stomach possesses and its very great capacity for concoction, and in addition because they easily procure nourishment, whereas the taloned ones do so with difficulty, they lay them often.

Small birds too mate frequently and are prolific, just as sometimes small plants are. For what is for the growth of their body becomes spermatic residue. That is why Adriatic chickens lay the most eggs.⁶⁰³ For because of the smallness of their body the nourishment is used up for procreation. Also the ones not true to their stock lay more eggs than those true to their stock.⁶⁰⁴ For their bodies are more liquid and more bulky, whereas those of the latter sort are leaner and drier. For the spirit that is true to its stock comes about more [often] in bodies of this sort.⁶⁰⁵ Further, the thinness and weakness of the legs contribute to making the nature of this sort of bird be to mate frequently and be prolific, just as in the case of human beings. For in these cases the nourishment for the legs is diverted to the spermatic residue. For what nature subtracts from one place, it adds at another. The taloned birds on the other hand have a strong foot and their legs are thick due to their [way of] life, so that due to all these causes they neither mate frequently nor are prolific. The kestrel, however, is the most prolific. For pretty much alone among the taloned birds it drinks, and the liquid, both connate and taken in, is productive of seed when combined with the heat that is present in the kestrel. But even it does not lay very many eggs, but rather four at the most.

The cuckoo, though not a taloned bird, lays few eggs, because its nature is cold (as the cowardice of the bird makes clear), whereas a spermatic animal must be hot and liquid. That it is cowardly is evident. For it is chased away by all birds, and lays its eggs in the nests of others.

Birds of the pigeon family are generally in the habit of laying two eggs. For they neither lay one egg (for no bird lays one egg except the cuckoo, and it sometimes lays two) nor many eggs, but often lay two or at the most three, generally two. For this number is intermediate between one and many.

That the nourishment in those that lay many eggs is diverted to the seed is evident from the facts. For most trees, if they bear too much fruit, dry up after the crop, when nourishment is not left over for their bodies, and this is how the annuals seem to be affected—for example, leguminous plants, corn, and the others of this sort. For they use up all the nourishment for seed. For they are of the abundant-seed genus. And some chickens after having laid very many eggs, even laying two eggs in a day, have died after the laying of so many. For just like the plants, these birds too become exhausted; and this affection is an excess excretion of residue. An affection of this sort is also the cause of the later infertility of the lioness. For at first she produces five or six cubs, then in the next year four, and again three, then the next number down to one, then none at all, suggesting that the residue is being used up and that at the same time as the seed is withering the life is abating.

In which birds wind-eggs are produced, further, what sorts of birds produce many eggs and what sorts few eggs, and due to what causes, has now been stated.

Wind-eggs are produced, as was also said previously, because while the spermatic matter is present in what is female, in birds the secretion of menses does not occur, as it does in the blooded viviparous ones (for in all those of the latter sort it does occur, more in some, less in others, and in some just enough to show signs of it).[606] Similarly, it does not occur in fishes either, any more than in birds; which is why in fishes as well [as in birds], without mating, a composition of embryos occurs, although less noticeably. For their nature is colder. The secretion corresponding to the menses in oviparous animals is produced in birds at the times appropriate for the residue, and as the place near the diaphragm is hot, the [eggs] are completed in respect of size, but are incomplete for purposes of generation, both these bird ones and those of the fishes alike, without the semen of the male. The cause of these things was stated previously.[607]

Wind-eggs are not produced, however, in birds that are capable fliers due to the very same cause as the one due to which they do not lay many eggs either. For in the taloned birds the residue is small in amount, and they need the male to provide the impulse for the excretion of the residue. The wind-eggs are produced in greater numbers than the fertilized eggs, but are smaller in size, due to one and the same cause. For because they are incomplete they are smaller in size, and because they are smaller in size they are greater in number. They are less pleasant to eat because they are more non-concocted. For in all cases what is concocted is sweeter.   25

That, then, neither the eggs of birds nor those of fishes are complete for purposes of generation without the male has been sufficiently observed, but where embryos that come to be without males in fishes are concerned, it has not been observed to a similar extent, but has been observed most in the case of river fish. For some quite evidently have eggs from the outset, as is recorded about them in the *History*   30 *of Animals*.[608] Generally speaking, though, at any rate in birds, even the eggs produced through mating are for the most part not naturally disposed to get growth if the hen is not mated continually. The cause of this is that just as in the case of women having sexual intercourse with men draws down the womanly secretion (for when the uterus has   35 been heated it draws the liquid and the ducts are opened up), so this   **751ᵃ1** happens in the case of birds as well, advancing the menses-like residue a little at a time. It is not secreted externally because of the smallness of amount and because the uterus is high up near the diaphragm, but trickles down and collects in the uterus itself. For this makes the egg   5 grow—just like the embryos of the viviparous animals are made to grow through the umbilical cord—through flowing on the inner surface of the uterus, since when the hens have been mated once, they pretty much all continue to have eggs, though altogether small ones.

That is why some people are in the habit of speaking of wind-eggs as not being produced [without the male] either, but as being leftovers   10 from previous matings. But this is false. For it has been sufficiently observed both in the case of newborn chicks and geese that wind-eggs are produced without mating. Further, female partridges, both those that are unmated and those that have been mated, when taken out to act as decoys smell the male and hear his call, the first lot become full   15 of eggs, while the second lay them at once. The cause of the affection is the very same as the one in the case of male human beings and quadrupeds. For if their bodies happen to desire sexual intercourse, some emit seed at the sight [of a female], others at the occurrence of a slight touch. The nature of birds of this sort is to mate frequently and have abundant seed, so that the movement they need is small when they   20 happen to have the desire and the excretion takes place quickly in them, so that wind-eggs are composed in the unmated ones, while in those that have been mated the eggs grow quickly and are completed.

Among the externally oviparous animals, birds emit an egg that is complete, fish one that is incomplete, but that gets its growth outside   25 [the mother], as was also said previously.[609] The cause of this is that the fish genus is prolific. Now it is impossible for a large number of eggs to reach completion inside [the mother], which is why they are laid outside. Their emission is quickly effected. For in the oviparous fishes the uterus is near the sexual parts.

30   While the eggs of birds are two-colored, those of all the fishes are single-colored. One may observe the cause of their being two-colored from the capacities of each of their parts, that of the white and of the yolk. For the secretion is produced from the blood (for no bloodless animal lays eggs), and that blood is the matter for bodies

751^{b}1   has often been stated.[610] The one part, then, is nearer the shape [or form] of what is coming into being, namely, the hot; the more earthy part, by contrast, supplies consistency for its body and is farther away [from the shape].[611] That is why in all two-colored eggs the animal

5   gets the starting-point of generation from the white (for the soul-involving starting-point is in the hot), but its nourishment from the yolk. Now in animals with a hotter nature the part from which the starting-point comes to be set apart and separate from the one from which nourishment derives, the first being white, the second yellow, and there is always more of the white and pure than of the yellow and earthy.

10   But in those that are less hot and more liquid, there is more yolk and it is more liquid. That is just what occurs in the case of marsh-birds. For their nature is more liquid and colder than the land-birds, so that the eggs of this sort of bird have more so-called "lecithus" and

15   it is less yellow, because the white is less set apart from it. And the oviparous animals, whose nature is both already cold and yet more liquid (and the fish genus is of this sort), have the white not set apart at all, both because of the smallness [of the eggs] and because of the quantity of cold and earthy material in them. (That is why all fishes' eggs are single-colored, and are white as compared with yellow, yel-

20   low as compared with white.) Even the wind-eggs of birds have this double coloring. For they contain that from which will come each of the two parts (both the one from which the starting-point comes and the one from which the nourishment does), although these are incomplete and have need of the male in addition. For wind-eggs become fertile if [the female] is mated with the male within a certain

25   period of time. The cause of the double coloring, however, is not the male and the female (as if the white came from the male and the yolk from the female)—on the contrary, both come from the female, but the latter is cold and the former hot. In those cases, then, in which there is much of the hot, it is set apart, but when there is little it cannot be. That is why the embryos of animals of this sort are single-

30   colored, as was just said.[612]

The semen, though, only composes them. And that is why an embryo in birds first appears white and small, but all yellow as it advances, and more blood-like material is continually mixed with it. In the end, as the hot is set apart, the white takes up a position all around it, equally distributed on all sides, as when a liquid boils [something]. For the white is by nature liquid and has within itself the soul-involving heat. That is why it is set apart all around, whereas the yolk and earthy part is inside. And if one pours together many eggs into a bladder or something of that sort and boils them by means of a fire that does not make the movement of the heat faster than the disaggregation within the eggs, then just as in one egg, so too in the whole composed of all the eggs, the yolk comes to be in the middle, the white around it.⁶¹³

Why some eggs are single-colored, then, while others are two-colored, has now been stated.

III 2

The starting-point coming from the male is set apart in eggs at the place where the egg is attached to the uterus, and a two-colored egg then becomes non-symmetrical, that is, not altogether round, but rather sharper at one of the two ends, because it is necessary to make the white, in which the starting-point resides, different [from the rest]. That is why the egg is harder at that point than below. For it is necessary to shelter and safeguard the starting-point. And because of this the sharp end of the egg comes out later.⁶¹⁴ For the part attached [to the uterus] comes out later, the egg is attached at the starting-point, and the starting-point is in the sharp end. It is the same way too in the seeds of plants. For the starting-point of the seed is attached in some cases to the branch, in some to the husk, and in others to the seed-case. This is clear in the case of the leguminous plants. For the point at which the two valves of beans and seeds of this sort make contact is where the seed is attached.⁶¹⁵ And the starting-point of the seed is there.

Someone might raise a puzzle, however, about the growth of the egg, as to what way it comes about from the uterus. For if animals get their nourishment via the umbilical cord, what do eggs get it via— seeing that they do not, like larvae, get their growth via themselves?⁶¹⁶ And if there is something via which they are attached [to the uterus], where does it go when the egg has reached completion? For it does not come out with the egg as the umbilical cord does in the case of animals. For when it has reached completion, its surface envelope becomes a shell. The puzzle stated, then, is quite correctly inquired into. But [the one who raises it] fails to consider the fact that when the shell is first produced it is a soft membrane, though when it has reached completion it becomes hard and brittle, though in such a measured way that when it comes out it is still soft (for otherwise laying the egg would cause pain), but when it has come out it immediately hardens when it has cooled, the liquid evaporating quickly because there is very little of it, leaving the earthy material behind. Part of this membrane, then, is at the start like an umbilical cord at the sharp end, and projects, while the egg is still small, like a pipe. It is visible in small aborted eggs. For if being wet through or chilled in some other way the bird ejects the egg too soon, the embryo appears still bloody and with a small tail running through it like an umbilical cord.[617] As the egg becomes larger this becomes more twisted around and becomes smaller. And when the egg has reached completion the sharp end of the egg [is where] this comes to its limit.[618] Underneath this is the inner membrane which divides the white and the yolk from it. When the egg has reached completion, the whole egg is released and the umbilical cord is quite reasonably not visible. For it is the last extremity of the egg itself.

Delivery, however, occurs in a contrary way with eggs than with viviparous animals. For with the latter it is head and starting-point down, whereas with an egg the delivery is as it were feet down. And the cause of this is the one that was stated, namely, that the egg is fastened at the starting-point.[619]

Generation from an egg comes about in birds due to the mother bird's incubation, that is, helping the concoction, with the part of the egg from which the animal comes being set apart, while it gets its growth and completion from the remaining part.[620] For nature puts in the egg both the matter for the animal and sufficient nourishment for its growth. For since the mother bird is not capable of completing the egg within herself she lays the nourishment along with it. For while in the case of the viviparous animals the nourishment (which is called milk) is produced in a different part (namely, the breasts), in the case of birds nature produces it within the eggs—in the contrary way, however, to the one people think and Alcmaeon of Croton states.[621] For it is not the white that is the milk but rather the yolk. For it is the nourishment for the newborn chicks, whereas they think it is the white because of the similarity of color.

The newborn chick, then, as has been said, comes to be due to the mother bird's incubation.[622] But if the season is temperate or if the place in which they are situated is sunny, the eggs get completely concocted, both those of birds and those of oviparous quadrupeds. For all of the latter lay their eggs on the ground, where they get concocted with the help of the heat of the earth, and whichever of the oviparous quadrupeds visit their eggs and sit on them do so more for the sake of safeguarding them.

Both the eggs of birds and those of the quadruped animals turn out the same way. For they are both hard-shelled and two-colored, and are composed near the diaphragm just like those of birds, and all the other things occur in the same ways both internally and externally, so that the theoretical knowledge of the causes is the same for all of them.[623] But whereas the eggs of the quadrupeds, because of their strength, get completely concocted due to the season, those of birds are more subject to disaster and need the mother. For it seems that nature tends to establish [in animals] a perception-based capacity for taking care of the young.[624] But in the inferior animals this capacity it has implanted lasts till their birth; in others till their complete development; and in those that are more practically-wise till they are brought up. Accordingly, in those that have the greatest share in practical wisdom there is intimacy and friendship toward them even after they have completely developed, as in the case of human beings and some of the quadrupeds.[625] But in the birds the capacity lasts until they have produced the chicks and brought them up. That is why females that do not incubate when they have laid get into worse condition, as if they have been deprived of things naturally a part of them.

The animal reaches completion more quickly within the egg during sunny days. For the season contributes to the work. For concoction too is [a sort] of heat. And indeed the earth helps concoct them with its heat, and the incubating female does this same thing. For she infuses [into them] as well the heat that is within herself.[626] And eggs get ruined and become so-called *ouria* more often in the hot season—and quite reasonably so.[627] For just as wines sour during sunny periods because the sediment gets stirred up (for this is the cause of their being ruined), and in eggs the yolk does. For what gets stirred up is the earthy material in each of them—which is also why wine becomes turbid when the sediment mixes with it, and eggs ruined when the yolk does so [with the white].

In the case, then, of birds that lay many eggs this sort of thing occurs quite reasonably (for it is not easy to assign the fitting amount of heat to all, instead some will get too little and others too much, making them turbid and, as it were, putrefying).[628] But in the taloned birds, which lay few eggs, this occurs to no less an extent. For often, in fact, one of a pair becomes rotten, and the third (one might almost say) always does. For their nature being hot they make the liquid in the eggs to overboil as it were. For of course the yolk and the white are of a contrary

35
753^{b}1

5

10

nature too. For the yolk gets coarse-grained in frosts but liquifies when heated.[629] That is why, when concocted in the earth or due to incubation, it liquifies, and when it is of this liquid sort it becomes nourishment for the animals being composed. When exposed to fire and baked it does not become hard, because its nature is to be earthy in the way wax is.[630] And because of this, when [the eggs] are heated more, insofar as it is not from the wet residue, it turns serous and becomes rotten.[631] The white on the other hand does not become coarse-grained due to frosts but rather liquifies (the cause has been stated previously), whereas exposed to fire it becomes solid.[632] That is why in fact when it is concocted in connection with the generation of animals it becomes coarse-grained. For it is from this that the animal is composed, whereas the yolk becomes nourishment, and the parts, as they are serially composed, get their growth from there. That is why too the yolk and the white are distinct and kept separate by membranes, as each having a distinct nature.

15

20

25

Well, for exactness about the way these parts stand to each other, both at the start of generation and during the composition of the animal, and further about the membranes and umbilical cords, one must get a theoretical grasp on what is written in the *History of Animals*.[633] But for the present investigation it is enough for this much to be evident, namely, that when the heart has been first composed and the great blood-vessel has been marked off from it, two umbilical cords extend from this blood-vessel, one to the membrane that encompasses the yolk, the other to the chorion-like membrane that encompasses the animal like a circle, and thus it goes around inside the membrane of the shell.[634] Through one of the two cords the embryo gets the nourishment from the yolk, while the yolk becomes larger. For it becomes more liquid when it is heated. For the nourishment, which is corporeal, needs to be liquid, just as it does for plants, and both the things coming to be in eggs and those doing so in animals at first live a plant's life. For they get their first growth and nourishment from something by being attached to it.

30

The other umbilical cord extends to the encompassing chorion. For in the case of the oviparously produced animals, we must suppose the bird embryo to stand in the same relation to the yolk as the viviparously produced embryo does to the mother, when they are within the mother (for since the oviparously produced ones are *not* being nourished in the mother, they take some part out with them), whereas its relation to the outermost membrane—the one that is bloody—is like that of the viviparously produced one to the uterus.[635] At the same

time the egg-shell around both the yolk and the chorion is the ana-   35
logue of a uterus that grows around the egg, as if one were to put one   754^{a}1
around both the [viviparously produced] embryo itself and around the
whole mother. It is this way because the embryo must be in the uterus,
that is, near the mother. Well, in the viviparous animals the uterus is
within the mother, but in the oviparous ones it is the reverse, as if one   5
were to say that the mother is within the uterus. For what comes from
the mother—the nourishment—is the yolk. And the cause is that the
nourishing is not within the mother.

In the process of growing, the umbilical cord going to the chorion
collapses first, because it is where the animal is to come out, while the   10
rest of the yolk and the umbilical cord going to the yolk do so later.[636]
For what has come to be must have nourishment from the outset. For it
is neither nursed by its mother nor capable from the outset of providing nourishment due to itself. That is why the yolk goes inside it along
with the umbilical cord and the flesh grows around it.

The ones, then, that come to be outside from complete eggs come to   15
be in this way both in the case of birds and in that of the quadrupeds
that lay a hard-shelled egg. These things are more clear in the larger
animals. For in the smaller ones they are non-apparent because of how
very small their dimensions are.   20

III 3

Further, the fish genus is oviparous. Of these, the ones that have the
uterus low down lay an incomplete egg, due to the cause mentioned
previously, whereas the so-called selachian fishes lay a complete egg
internally, though they are externally viviparous, with the exception
of the one they call a "fishing-frog," which alone lays a complete egg   25
externally.[637] The cause of this is the nature of its body. For its head
is many times as large as the rest of its body and is spiny and very
rough. That is why it neither takes its young in again afterward nor is
viviparous from the start.[638] For just as the size and roughness of the
head prevents their coming in, in the same way it prevents their com-   30
ing out. But since the egg of the selachians is soft-shelled (for they are
incapable of hardening and drying its surface envelope; for they are
colder than birds are), only the egg of the fishing-frog is solid and firm
so as to preserve it outside, whereas those of the others are wet and soft
in nature. For they are sheltered within and by the body of the mother.   35

The process of generation out of the egg both for the fishing-frogs,   754^{b}1
which are completed externally, and for the ones completed inside is

the same, and in these it is partly similar to and partly different from
the ones in birds. For first they do not have the other umbilical cord
which extends to the chorion that is under the encompassing shell. The
cause of this is that the surface envelope they have is not a shell, since
it is no use to them. For the mother shelters them, whereas a shell is a
defense against external harms for eggs that are laid outside. Second,
the process of generation is from the extremity of the egg in these as
well, but not [as in birds] at the place where it is attached to the uterus.
For birds come to be from the sharp end, and this is where the egg was
attached. The cause is that the egg of birds is separated from the uterus,
whereas the egg, not of all but of most, of these sorts of fishes stays
attached to the uterus when complete. And when the young animal
comes to be at the extremity, the egg gets used up, just as in the case
of the birds and the others that are detached [from the uterus], and
in the end the umbilical cord remains attached to the uterus of those
that are by this time complete. It is likewise too with those selachians
whose eggs are detached from the uterus. For in some of them the egg
is detached when it has become complete.

One might raise a puzzle, then, as to why the process of generation in birds and in fishes differs in this respect. The cause is that
in the eggs of birds the yolk and the white are separate, whereas those of
the fishes are single-colored, and what is of this sort is mixed together
throughout, so that there is nothing to prevent them from having the
starting-point be from the contrary end. For it is not only at the point
of attachment that it is of this mixed sort, but also at the opposite one,
and it is easier to draw the nourishment from the uterus by means of
certain ducts coming from this starting-point.[639] This is clear in the
case of the eggs that are not detached. For in some of the selachians
the egg is not detached from the uterus, but rather stays connected as
it is displaced downward with a view to producing the young alive; in
these cases, when the animal is completed it retains the umbilical cord
coming from the uterus after the egg has been consumed. It is evident,
then, that previously too, while the egg was still around it, the ducts
extended to the uterus. This occurs, as we have said, in the smooth
dogfish.[640]

The process of generation in birds differs in these respects from that
of fishes, then, and does so because of the causes just mentioned. But
in the other respects it occurs in the same way. For these have the other
umbilical cord in the same way, as the birds have it going to the yolk,
so the fish have it going to the whole egg (for it is not the case that part

of it is white and part yolk but rather it is all single-colored), and they get their nourishment from it, and as it gets used up the flesh likewise comes and grows around it. 5

III 4

Where the fishes that produce a complete egg within themselves but are externally oviparous are concerned, then, this is the way their process of generation proceeds. Most of the other fishes, by contrast, are externally oviparous, with all except the fishing-frog producing an incomplete egg—the cause of this was stated earlier.[641] And of the others' laying incomplete eggs the cause was also stated earlier.[642] 10

In the case of these too the process of generation from an egg proceeds in just the same way as the one in the case of the internally oviparous selachians, except that their growth is quick, from small things, and the extremity of the egg is harder. The growth of the egg is similar to that of larvae. For those animals that produce larvae also produce something small at first which grows due to itself and not due 15 to any attachment at all. The cause of this is about the same as the very one in the case of yeast. For yeast too from being small becomes large as the more solid part liquifies while the liquid part becomes pneumaticized. What handicrafts this in living things is the nature of the soul-involving heat, and within yeast is the heat of the humor blended 20 with it.[643] The eggs, then, though they grow of necessity due to this cause (for they contain a yeast-like residue), also do so for the sake of the better. For it is impossible for them to get the whole of their growth in the uterus because these animals produce so many eggs. It is because of this indeed that they are altogether small when they are 25 secreted and get their growth quickly: small—because of the narrowness of the uterus in relation to the quantity of eggs; quickly growing—in order that their genus not be destroyed because of spending a lot of time during the process of generation on growth, since even as things stand most of the embryos that are laid externally are destroyed. That is why the fish genus is prolific. For nature makes up by number 30 for the destruction. And there are some fishes—for example, the so-called *belonê*—that burst because of the size of their eggs.[644] For the embryos it holds are large instead of many. For what nature subtracts from number it adds to size. 35

That there is growth of these sorts of eggs, then, and also what cause it is due to, has now been stated. 755^b1

III 5

A sign that these fishes too are oviparous is that even the viviparous fishes, such as the selachians, are first internally oviparous.[645] For [then] it is clear that the whole fish genus is oviparous. However, none of these sorts of eggs reaches completion—namely, where there is a female and a male and they are produced from mating—unless the male sheds his milt on them.

There are, though, some who say that all fish are females except selachian ones, but this is not correctly stated. For they think that the females differ from the ones considered to be males in the same way as in those plants where the one bears fruit and the other is barren—for example, olive, oleaster, fig, caprifig. It is likewise too, they think, with the fishes, except the selachian ones—for they do not dispute the issue in the case of these. And yet there is no difference with respect to their milt-producing parts between selachian males and those in the oviparous genus, that is, it is evident that seed can be squeezed out of both at the proper season.[646] And the females, for their part, also have a uterus. But it should not be only those that produce eggs that have a uterus but also the others, although it should be different from that of the egg-producers, if indeed the whole genus was female, although some of them sterile (like mules in the genus with long hairs in their tails).[647] But as things stand one lot have milt-producing parts, the other lot uteruses, and in all except two, namely, erythrinus and channa, this difference (*diaphora*) exists.[648] And the puzzle because of which they suppose things to be this way is easily resolved by harkening to what happens. For they say quite correctly that none of the animals that mate produce many offspring. For of those that from themselves generate complete ones, either animals or eggs, none is as prolific as the oviparous fishes, for the number of their eggs is something immense. But they have overlooked the fact that the eggs of fishes do not [develop] in the same way as those of birds. For birds, whichever of the quadrupeds are oviparous, and any of the selachians that are oviparous, produce a complete egg, and it does not get its growth outside them, whereas the fishes produce an incomplete one, and their eggs do get their growth outside. Further, in the case of the cephalopods and crustaceans it is the same way, yet these are actually seen copulating, because their copulation lasts a long time. And it is evident in these cases that the one is male, while the other has a uterus. It would be strange too if this [difference in] capacity did not exist in the entire genus, just as in the viviparous animals one is male, another female. The cause of the ignorance of those who speak in the foregoing way is that the differences (*diaphora*) in the matings of animals and their processes of generation, differences that are of all sorts, are not clear to see. Instead, getting a theoretical grasp on them from a few cases, they think that the same must hold in all of them.

That is also why those who say that conceptions come from the swallowing of [male] seed by the females among the fishes have not understood some things when they speak in this way. For at about the same period of time the males have milt and the females have eggs, and the closer the female is to laying the eggs the more abundant and more liquid the milt of the males becomes. And just as the growth of the milt in the male and that of the egg in the female occurs at the same time, so it is too with their emission. For the females do not lay all their eggs at once, but a few at a time, nor do the males emit their milt at once. And all these things happen in accord with reason (*logos*). For just as in some cases among the bird genus [a female] holds eggs without impregnation (but few and seldom—rather, most come from mating), so the same occurs in the case of the fishes, but to a lesser extent. And these spontaneous eggs that are produced in both are also infertile if they are not shredded on by the male (in those genera of them in which the male exists as well).[649] Now in birds, because the eggs are complete on coming out, it is necessary for this to occur while they are still inside; but in fish, because in all cases the eggs are incomplete and get their growth outside, even if no egg within becomes fertile from mating, nonetheless the ones outside are preserved by the shedding, and it is there that the milt of the males is used up.[650] And that is why it comes down [the ducts] in smaller quantities at the same time as the eggs in the females do. For the males always follow along shedding milt on the eggs as they are laid. So there are males and females and all of them mate (unless in some genus the female and the male are not distinct), and without the semen of the male nothing of this [fish] sort comes to be.

What also contributes to the deception is the quickness of copulation among fishes of this sort, so that even many fishermen fail to notice it. For none of them observes something of this sort for the sake of knowledge. But nonetheless their copulation has been seen. For fish mate in the same way as dolphins, namely, by placing themselves side to side—that is, those whose tail prevents [belly to back copulation].[651] But ejaculation in the case of the dolphins takes a longer time, whereas in the cases of fish of this sort it happens quickly.[652] That is why, not seeing it, but seeing the swallowing of the milt and the eggs, even the

5   fishermen state the simple-minded account (*logos*) of Herodotus the
storyteller, to the effect that fish are conceived from the swallowing of
milt, not comprehending that this is impossible.[653] For the duct entered
through the mouth goes into the stomach, not into the uterus, and it is
10   necessary for what enters the stomach to become nourishment (for it
gets concocted). The uterus, however, is quite evidently full of eggs—
where did they enter it from?

III 6

It is the same way with the generation of birds. For there are some who
say that the ravens and the ibis have sexual intercourse by mouth, and
15   that among the quadrupeds, the weasel reproduces orally. For both
Anaxagoras and certain others among the physicists say these things,
speaking far too simply and without investigation.[654] Where the birds
are concerned they are deceived on the basis of a deduction, because
the mating of ravens is seldom seen, whereas they are frequently seen
20   communing with each other with their beaks, which is something all
raven-like birds do.[655] This is clear in the case of domesticated jackdaws.[656] Birds of the pigeon genus do the same thing, but because they
also quite evidently mate, they have not gained this reputation [for
having sexual intercourse by mouth]. But though the raven-like genus
25   is not overly eager for sexual intercourse (for it is among the ones that
produce few young), [it does do so,] since even it has already been seen
to mate.[657] It is a strange thing, however, that these physicists do not
deduce how the seed enters the uterus through the stomach, seeing that
it always concocts whatever comes into it, just as it does nourishment.
In fact, even these birds have a uterus, and eggs that are quite apparent
30   near the diaphragm. The weasel too, like other quadrupeds, has a uterus
in the same way as them, so how is the fetus going to make its way from
the uterus into the mouth? Still, because the weasel produces very tiny
young, just as the other cloven-hoofed animals—about which we shall
757^{a}1   speak later—also do, and often carry the newborns in their mouth,
this belief [that weasels reproduce orally] has come about.[658]

     Also very deceived are those who speak in a simple-minded way
about the trochus and the hyena.[659] For many people say that the hyena,
and Herodorus of Heraclea says that the trochus, has two private parts,
5   those of the male and those of the female, and that the trochus impregnates itself, while the hyena impregnates and is impregnated in alternate years.[660] [But this is false,] for the hyena has been seen to have only
one private part. For in some places there is no lack of opportunity for
observation of them. But hyenas have a line under their tail like the

female private part.⁶⁶¹ Both the males and the females have this sort
of sign, but males are caught more frequently. That is why on the basis   10
of these non-methodical observations the belief [about their private
parts] has been produced.

But about these things what has just been said is enough.

III 7

Where the generation of fish is concerned, however, someone might
raise a puzzle as to what on earth the cause is due to which among
the selachian-like fishes neither the females are seen shedding their   15
embryos nor the males shedding their milt, whereas among the non-
viviparous fishes both the females are seen shedding their eggs and the
males their milt. The cause of this is that the selachian-like genus does
not in general produce much seed; and, further, the females have their
uterus near the diaphragm. For males differ from the males, and the
females from the females, in a similar way. For the selachian-kinds are   20
also low-yielding as regards semen. But in the oviparous ones, the male
genus sheds its milt, just as the females lay their eggs, because of their
quantity. For they have more milt than suffices for mating. For nature
tends to use up the milt for helping to grow the eggs, once the female   25
has laid them, rather than in composing them from the start. For as
was said in the accounts farther back and in the more recent ones, the
eggs of birds are completed internally, those of fishes externally.⁶⁶² For
in a certain way the latter are like those that produce larvae. For the   30
larviparous animals discharge an embryo that is yet more incomplete.
Completion, though, in both cases, both in that of the eggs of birds and
in those of fishes, the male produces, except that in the case of birds he
does so internally (for they are completed internally), whereas in those
of the fishes he does it externally, because the egg is incomplete when
deposited outside. The *result*, however, is the same in both cases.   35

The wind-eggs of birds become fertile, and those previously fertil-   757ᵇ1
ized by mating with one genus of male change their nature to that of
the later [genus of] male.⁶⁶³ And the eggs of the original male, which
do not grow if the mating is interrupted, when he has fertilized them
by mating again, get their growth more rapidly—not however dur-   5
ing all of the time, but if the mating occurs earlier, before the change's
occurring that leads to the separation of the yolk.⁶⁶⁴ But in the eggs of
fishes nothing of this sort is determined, instead the males shed milt
on them quickly to preserve them. The cause of this is that these eggs
are not two-colored. That is why a period of time of this sort is not
fixed for them as in the case of birds. And this has come about quite   10

reasonably. For when the white and the yolk have been set apart from each other, the egg already contains the starting-point that comes from the male (for this is contributed by the male).

Wind-eggs, then, get their generation so far as is possible for them. For it is impossible for them to be completed into an animal (for there is a need of perception).[665] But both the females and the males—in fact, all the animals—possess the nutritive capacity of the soul, as has often been said.[666] That is why the egg itself, considered as the embryo of a plant, is complete, but, considered as that of an animal, incomplete. If, then, there were no male in their genus, the egg would have been produced as it in fact is in the case of certain fishes—if indeed there is any genus of fish of such a sort as to generate without a male (but about this it was said earlier too that it has not been adequately observed).[667] But as things stand there is a male and a female in all birds, so that insofar as the egg is a plant it is complete (and that is why it does not change again after being fertilized by mating), but insofar as it is not a plant, it is not complete, nor does anything else result from it. For it has neither been produced simply as a plant nor as an animal from copulation. On the other hand, eggs produced from mating that have the white set apart are produced by the first male to have fertilized them by mating. For they already contain both starting-points.[668]

III 8

The young are produced in the same way too by the cephalopods (for example, cuttlefishes and things of that sort) and by the crustaceans (for example, crayfish and things of the same genus (*suggenê*) as these).[669] For they too lay eggs from mating and the copulation of male with female is often seen. That is why those who say that all fish are female and lay eggs without mating are not speaking in a way based on methodical inquiry on this point either.[670] For to think that the former animals lay eggs from copulation while fish do not is a wondrous thing!—whereas to have been unaware that they do is a sign of lack of experience.[671] The copulation of all these lasts a long time, like that of the insects, as is quite reasonable. For they are bloodless, which is why their nature is cold.

In cuttlefishes and calamaries the eggs appear to be two, because the uterus is divided and appears cloven, whereas of octopuses there appears to be one egg. The cause is that the shape is round in visible form (*idea*) and spherical. For the cleavage is unclear when it is filled [with eggs]. The uterus of the crayfish is also cloven. All these animals also lay an incomplete embryo, and due to the same cause. The females of the crayfish family produce their young upon themselves (that is why the females of these have larger flaps than the males, namely, in order to protect the eggs), whereas the cephalopods lay them away from themselves. The male of the cephalopods sheds his milt over the females just as male fishes do over the eggs, which become continuous and viscous. But in the crayfish family something of this sort is neither seen nor reasonable. For the embryo is under the female and is hard-shelled. Both these [eggs] and those of the cephalopods get their growth outside, just as those of the fishes do.

While coming to be the cuttlefish [embryo] is attached to the eggs at its front part. For it is possible only here. For the cuttlefish alone has its front part and back part facing in the same direction. A theoretical grasp on the configuration of its position while coming to be should be gotten from the *History of Animals*.

III 9

The generation of the other animals—those that walk, fly, and swim—has now been spoken about. In accord with the methodical inquiry we are following the insects and testaceans must next be spoken about. Let us first speak, then, about the insects.

Well, that some of these come to be from copulation, others spontaneously, was said previously, and in addition that they produce larvae, and due to what cause they produce larvae.[672] For pretty much all animals seem in a certain way to produce larvae at first. For the most incomplete embryo is of this sort; and in all animals, even the viviparous ones and the oviparous ones that produce a complete egg, the embryo, being at first indistinct, gets its growth. And the nature of the larva is of this sort. After this some of the oviparous animals produce a complete embryo, others an incomplete one, but it becomes complete outside, as has often been said to be so in the case of fish.[673] In the internally viviparous animals, however, after its composition at the start the embryo becomes in a certain way egg-like. For the liquid is encompassed by a fine membrane, as if someone were to take the shell of eggs. That is why people call the destruction of embryos produced at that time "effluxions."[674]

The insects that generate, generate larvae, and those that come to be not through copulation but spontaneously, come to be at first from a composition of this sort. For one must suppose caterpillars to be a certain form (*eidos*) of larva, also what comes from spiders. And yet some even of these and many of the others seem to be like eggs because of their round configuration. We must not speak by referring to their configuration, however, or to their softness and hardness (for the embryos of some of them are hard), but to the whole thing, and not just a certain part, changing into the whole animal that will come to be.[675]

All these larva-like things having emerged, and having reached the end of their growth in magnitude, become a sort of egg. For the sheath around them hardens and they are non-moving during this period. This is clear in the case of the larvae of bees, wasps, and caterpillars. The cause of this is that their nature, because of its incompleteness, lays eggs as it were before the proper time, as if the larva, while still in the process of growing, were a soft egg. It happens in the same way too in the case of all the others that come to be, not from mating, in wool or other such materials and in water.[676] For all of them after their larva-like nature become non-moving and their sheath dries around them, and after this the sheath bursts and there emerges, as from an egg, an animal that has achieved completion at this its third process of generation. Of these, the winged ones are larger than those that walk.

Another occurrence, though in accord with reason, would also quite rightly be a cause of wonder to many people. For caterpillars at first get nourishment, but after that they no longer get it, but instead what are called chrysalises by some people are non-moving, and the larvae of wasps and bees [which get nourishment and quite evidently have excrement] after they become what are called pupae, and have nothing of this sort.[677] For the nature of eggs too, when it has reached its end, is non-growing, but at first it grows and gets nourishment until it has become distinct and a complete egg has come to be. Among larvae, some contain within themselves the sort of thing from which, as they are nourished by it, this sort of residue is produced—for example, those of bees and wasps, whereas others get it from outside, as caterpillars and certain other larvae do.[678]

Why, then, the coming to be of things of this sort occurs in three stages, and due to what cause from having been moving they become non-moving again, has been stated. And some of them come to be from mating, as birds, viviparous animals, and most fishes do, whereas others come to be spontaneously, as some plants do.[679]

III 10

The generation process of bees, though, involves much puzzlement.[680] If indeed it is a fact that in the case of some fishes there is a process of generation that generates without mating, the same seems likely to happen with bees, judging from things that seem to be the case. Or it is necessary for them either [1] to bring the brood from elsewhere (as some people say)—in which case it must either [1a] be something that grows spontaneously or [1b] that is begotten by some other animal— or [2] to generate it themselves, or [3] to bring some and generate others (for some people also say this, on the supposition that they bring only the brood of drones).[681] Again, if they [2] do generate them, they do so either [2a] by mating or [2b] without mating. And if by mating, either [2a-i] each genus must generate its own genus or [2a-ii] one genus must generate the others, or [2a-iii] one genus by copulating with another—I mean, for example, [2a-i] bees from copulating bees, drones from drones, kings from kings, or all the others from one, for example, [2a-ii] from the so-called kings and leaders or from the copulation of drones and bees (for some people say that [2a-iii] the drones are males and the bees female, while others say that [2a-iv] the bees are male and the drones female).

But all these views are impossible if we deduce things first from the facts special to bees, second from those equally common to the other animals. For if [1] they do not generate the young but bring them from elsewhere, then bees should come to be, even if not brought anywhere by bees, in those places from which they bring their seed. For why when transferred will they do so, but not do so there? For it is no less fitting for them to do so there, whether they grow in flowers spontaneously or whether some other animal produces them. And if indeed the seed belonged to some other animal, that one should come to be from it, but not bees. Further, that they should collect honey is reasonable (for it is nourishment), but that they should collect a brood that belongs to another and is not food is strange.[682] For the sake of what do they do it? For all the animals that busy themselves about the young work hard for what appears to be their own brood.[683]

But then for [2a-iii] the bees to be female and the drones male it is not reasonable either. For nature does not assign a weapon for fighting to any females, but while drones are stingless, all bees have a sting. Nor is the contrary view reasonable, that [2a-iv] the bees are male and the drones female. For no males are accustomed to work hard for their young, but as things stand the bees do this. And, in general, since it is evident that the brood of drones comes to be when there is no drone present, whereas the brood of bees does not come to be without the kings (which is why some people say that the brood of the drones alone is brought from outside), it is clear that they do not come to be from mating, either [2a-i] from each copulating with its own genus, or [2a-iii, -iv] from bees and drones doing so. (That they should [3] bring the brood of drones alone is impossible because of what was just said.

Also, it is not reasonable that a similar affection not be characteristic of the entire genus of these.[684]) But then again it is also impossible for some of the bees themselves to be males and others females. For in all the genera (*genos*) of animals the female differs from the male. Besides, if that were so, they would generate themselves. But as things stand it is evident that their brood does not come to be if the leaders are not among them, as they say.[685] An objection jointly against both bees generating from each other and from drones (that is, together with and separate from each other) is that none of them has ever been seen mating, whereas if there had been female and male among them this would often have happened.

It remains, if indeed bees come to be from mating, for [2a-ii] the kings to do the generating by copulating. But it is evident that the drones come to be even in the absence of leaders, and it is not possible either for the bees to bring the brood or to generate it themselves by copulation. It remains, then, as appears to be so in the case of certain fishes, that the bees generate the drones without mating, that is, generating them by being female, but containing within themselves, as the plants do, both the female and the male. That is also why they have the instrument for fighting. For we should not call something female in which the male is not separated. And if in the case of the drones this seems to occur, that is, that they come to be not from mating, it is necessary for the same argument (*logos*) to apply as well to the bees and the kings and that they should come to be not from mating. If, then, the brood of bees had quite evidently come to be without the kings, it would have been necessary for the bees to have come to be from themselves without copulation. But as things stand, since this is not what is said by those concerned with the care of these animals, it remains that the kings generate both themselves and the bees.

Because, then, the bee genus appears to be extraordinary and special, so too their process of generation appears to be special. For while generating without mating, as bees do, may also occur in the case of other animals, not generating the same genus of thing, by contrast, is special. For even the erythrinus generates an erythrinus and the channa a channa.[686] The cause is that bees themselves are not produced in the same way as flies and animals of this sort, but rather from a distinct though cognate genus (*suggenês*). For they are produced from the leaders. That is also why their process of generation in a way stands in proportion.[687] For the leaders are similar to the drones in size and to the bees in having a sting. The bees are like them in this respect, then, and the drones are like them in size. For it is necessary for there to be some overlapping, unless the same genus must always come from each

(but this is impossible—for then the entire genus would be leaders).
The bees, then, are similar to them in capacity, the drones in size.[688]

If the drones also had had a sting, they would have been leaders. But
as things stand a puzzle remains. For the leaders are like both genera   20
at the same time, the bees in having a sting, the drones in size.[689] On
the other hand, it is necessary for the rulers also to be produced from
something. Since, then, it is neither from the bees nor from the drones,
it is necessary for them to be produced from themselves. And their   25
cells are produced at the end and are not many in number.[690] So that
what happens is that though the leaders in fact generate themselves,
they also generate another genus (that of the bees), and the bees, while
they generate another genus, namely, the drones, no longer generate
themselves, rather this has been subtracted from them. And since what   30
is in accord with nature always has an order, because of this it is necessary for drones to have even generating another genus subtracted
from them. And it is evident that this is just what happens. For though
they are themselves produced, they generate nothing else; instead the
process of generation reaches its limit at number three [in the series].

And so nobly has nature organized this that the genera always   35
remain in existence and none of them fails, though not all generate.   760^b1
And it is also reasonable for this to happen. In good years, much honey
and many drones are produced, but in wet ones a large brood of bees
is generally produced. For the wet ones produce more residue in the
bodies of the leaders, whereas the fine ones do so in those of the bees.   5
For being smaller in size they need the good weather more.[691] It is well
too that the kings, as produced for procreation, remain inside, relieved
from necessary sorts of work, and having magnitude, as the composition of their bodies is for procreation, and that the drones be idle, as   10
they have no weapons for fighting for nourishment, and because of the
slowness of their bodies. The bees, though, are intermediate to both
(for this is useful for their work), and they are workers, as they nourish
both their children and their fathers. And it is also in agreement with
this that they attend on their kings because their generation is from   15
them (for if nothing of this sort were the case, the facts about their
leadership would not have a reason (*logos*)), and while they allow the
kings to do no work as being their parents, they discipline the drones
as their children.[692] For it is nobler to discipline children and those for
whom there exists no work.[693]   20

The fact that the leaders, though being few in numbers themselves,
generate a large number of bees seems to be about the same as what
happens in the generation of lions.[694] For the lions at first generate five,
later a smaller number, in the end one, then none at all. And the leaders

25 at first generate a multitude, later a few of themselves (the brood of the latter being smaller), and nature, since it subtracted from their number, makes up for it in their size.

On the basis of reason (*logos*), then, and on the basis of what seem to be the facts about them, matters having to do with generation of bees appear to be this way. The facts, though, have certainly not been
30 sufficiently grasped, but if at some time they are, one should take perception rather than reasonings to be what must carry conviction, and reasonings [only] if what they show agrees with what appears to be the case.

An additional sign that it is not produced from mating is the fact that the brood appears small in the cells of the comb, whereas those
35 insects produced from mating copulate for a long time, but produce
761ᵃ1 something larva-shaped and having magnitude.⁶⁹⁵

Where the process of generation of animals of the same genus (*suggenês*) as bees—for example, hornets and wasps—is concerned, it proceeds in about the same way in all of them, although what is extraordinary has quite reasonably been subtracted. For they have
5 nothing divine in them as the bee genus does.⁶⁹⁶ For the so-called "mother wasps" generate the young and mold together the first [cells] of the combs, but they generate by mating with each other. For their copulation has often been seen. As for how many differences (*diaphora*) each of these genera have either in relation to each other or in relation to the bees, a theoretical grasp on this should be gotten from what is
10 catalogued in the *History of Animals*.⁶⁹⁷

The process of generation of all the insects, then, having been spoken about, we must now speak about that of the testaceans.

III 11

And what has to do with the process of generation of the testaceans is partly like, and partly not like, that of the others. And this is quite
15 reasonably so. For compared to animals they are like plants, while compared to plants they are like animals, so that in a certain way they appear to come to be from seeds, but in another way not from seeds, and in a way they appear to come to be spontaneously, but in another way due to themselves, or some in the latter way, some in the former.
20 Because their nature is a counterpart to that of the plants, no part, or a small part, of the testacean genus—for example, snails and any others of this sort, few as they are—comes about on earth; but in the sea and in similar waters there are many and they have every sort of shape [or form].⁶⁹⁸ The plant genus, by contrast, is little—that is (one

might almost say), not at all—represented in the sea and places of that
sort, all such things coming to be on land. For their nature stands in a   25
proportion: the nature of testaceans is as far apart from that of plants
as the wet's being more characteristic of life is from the dry's and as
water's is from earth's, since the testaceans tend at any rate to be related
to the wet as plants are related to earth—as if plants were terrestrial   30
shell-fish, and shell-fish aquatic plants.

Due to this sort of cause too the testaceans in what is wet are more
varied in shape [or form] than those on earth. For the nature of the wet
is more plastic than that of earth, and not much less bodily, and the
animals in the sea are most of all of this sort. For fresh water, though   35
sweet and nourishing, is less corporeal and is cold. That is why blood-   761^{b}1
less animals whose nature is cold do not come to be in lakes nor in the
fresher among brackish waters, except to a lesser extent (for example,
testaceans, cephalopods, and crustaceans; for all of these are bloodless   5
and have a cold nature), whereas in lagoons and near the mouths of
rivers they do come to be. For they seek at the same time warmth and
nourishment, and the sea is both wet and much more corporeal than
fresh water, its nature is hot, and it has a share of all the parts, namely,   10
water, pneuma, and earth, so that the living things that come to be
participate in each of the places.[699] For plants may be assigned to land,
aquatic animals to water, terrestrial animals to air. But the more and
the less, and nearer and farther away, produce great and wondrous difference (*diaphora*).[700] As for the fourth genus, it must not be sought in   15
these places, although there certainly wants to be one corresponding
to fire in the order. For it is counted as the fourth of the [elemental]
bodies. But fire always appears to have a shape [or form] that is not
special to it; on the contrary, it is always in another of the bodies. For
what is on fire appears to be either air, smoke, or earth.[701] Instead, this   20
fourth genus must be sought on the moon. For the moon appears to
participate in [the elemental body] at the fourth remove.[702] But these
issues are for another account.

As for the nature of the testaceans, some are composed spontaneously, some emit [something with] a certain capacity from themselves,
but these also often come to be from spontaneous composition.[703]   25
We must, then, grasp the process of coming to be for plants.[704] For
some of these come to be from seed, some from slips that are planted
out, others by budding-off—for example, the onion genus.[705] This is
the way mussels come to be. For smaller ones are always outgrowing   30
alongside the starting one. But the whelks, purple-fish, and those that
are said to make combs emit a slimy liquid that is like one of a spermatic nature.[706] We must, however, consider none of these emissions

to be seed, but rather these animals as participating in the way just mentioned in a similarity to the plants.[707] That is why too a quantity of such animals comes to be when one comes to be. For though it happens that all these animals come to be spontaneously as well, proportionally (*logos*) more do if some are already composed to start with. For it is reasonable that each have some residue left over from the starting one, from which each of the animals growing alongside it buds-off. And since nourishment and its residue have about the same capacity, it is likely that the substance of the comb-makers is like that of the one composed at the start.[708] That is why it is reasonable that they also come to be from it.

The ones that neither bud-off nor make combs come to be spontaneously. And it is evident that all those composed in this way, whether on earth or in water, come to be in co-operation with putrefaction and an admixture of rainwater. For as the sweet is disaggregated into the starting-point that is being composed, the residue of the mixture takes this shape [or form].[709] For nothing comes to be by putrefaction but by concoction. For putrefaction, that is, the putrid thing, is a residue of concoction.[710] For nothing comes to be from the whole of anything, any more than in the case of what is handicrafted due to craft. For if it did, craft would have nothing to do. But as things stand, in the one case craft subtracts what is useless, and in the other nature does.

Animals and plants come to be on earth and in liquid because in earth there is water present and in water pneuma, and in all pneuma there is soul-involving heat, so that in a certain way all things are full of soul.[711] That is why they are quickly composed once it has been enclosed. And it gets enclosed and comes to be as a foamy bubble, when wet bodies heat up. And the differentiae that determine whether the genus of the thing being composed is more estimable or non-estimable lie in the enclosure of the soul-involving starting-point.[712] Now in the sea there is much earthy material present. That is why it is from such material that the nature of the testaceans is composed. For earthy material hardens all around them, solidified in the same way as bones and horns (for they are unmeltable by fire), and on the inside the body that possesses life is enclosed.[713]

The snail genus is the only one of these sorts of animals that has been seen copulating. But whether their generation is from copulation has not so far been adequately observed.

Anyone wishing to inquire correctly might well ask what corresponds to the material starting-point in the composition of animals of this sort. For in females this is a certain residue belonging to the animal, potentially of the same sort as that from which it came, that the movement-causing starting-point from the man completes into the animal. But here what should one say this sort of thing is, and where does the movement-causing starting-point corresponding to the male come from, and what is it? We must grasp, then, that even in animals that generate, it is from the incoming nourishment that the heat present in the animal makes the residue, the starting-point of the embryo, by disaggregation and concoction. Similarly too in the case of plants, except that in these, as in certain of the animals, there is no additional need of the starting-point from the male (for they have it mixed within themselves), whereas in most animals the residue does need it in addition. For some the nourishment is water and earth, for others it is things composed of these, so that the very thing that the heat present in animals produces from the nourishment is what the seasonal environmental heat aggregates and combines from sea-water by concoction. And the part of the soul-involving starting-point that is either enclosed or disaggregated in the pneuma produces an embryo and implants movement in it. The composition of [all] the plants that come to be spontaneously is the same in form (*homoeidês*). For they come to be from a part, and while one part is the starting-point, the other is the first nourishment of the outgrowths.[714]

Among the animals, on the other hand, some produce larvae, both the bloodless ones that do not come to be from animals and among the blooded ones, for example, a certain genus of mullet and of other river fishes, and further the eel genus. For all of these, even though having little blood have nonetheless a blooded nature, and have a heart, which is the starting-point of the parts, that is sanguineous. And the so-called "intestines of earth" have a larva's nature, and in these the body of the eels comes to be. That is why, even where the coming to be of human beings and quadrupeds is concerned, one might suppose that, if indeed they were really earthborn, as some people say, they come to be in one or other of two ways. For either it is by first being composed as a larva or from eggs. For it is necessary for them either to have within themselves the nourishment for growth (and an embryo of this sort is a larva) or to get it from elsewhere, and this either from the female progenitor or from part of the embryo. So if the former is impossible (namely, for it to flow from the earth as it does from the mother in the case of other animals), then it is necessary to get it from a part of the embryo. And generation of this sort, we say, is from an egg.

If indeed there was such a starting-point for the generation of all animals, then, that it is reasonable for it to be one or the other of these two is evident. But there is less reason (*logos*) for it to be from eggs.

For we see none of this sort of generation of any animal, but we do
see the other sort, both in the blooded ones just mentioned and in
the bloodless ones.⁷¹⁵ Some of the insects are of this sort as are the
testaceans that our account (*logos*) concerns. For they do not come to
be from a certain part as the oviparous animals do, and their growth
is produced in a similar way to that in larvae. For larvae grow toward
the upper part and the starting-point.⁷¹⁶ For the nourishment for the
upper parts is in the lower one. And this proceeds in a similar way in
those that come from eggs, except that these use up all of it, whereas
in the larvae-producers, when the upper part has grown from what is
composed in the lower part, the lower part gets articulated from what
is left over. The cause is that later on also the nourishment is produced
in all animals in the part below the diaphragm.

That this is the way the larva-like animals have their growth produced is clear in the case of the bees and animals of this sort. For at the
start their lower part is large, whereas their upper one is small. And in
the case of the testaceans matters having to do with growth proceed
in the same way. This is also evident in the case of the helices of the
spiral-shelled animals. For as the animal grows they always grow larger
toward the front and the so-called head.

The way the generation proceeds, then, both of these and of the
other animals that come to be spontaneously has been pretty much
stated.

That all the testaceans are composed spontaneously is evident
from such facts as the following.⁷¹⁷ They come to be on the side of
boats when the foamy mud putrefies. Also, in many places where
previously nothing of this sort existed, when later the place became
muddy through a dearth of water, so-called "lagoon shell-fish," a sort
of testacean, have come to be. For example, when a naval expedi-
tion cast anchor near Rhodes, some clay pots were thrown out into
the sea, and as time went on and mud had collected around them,
shell-fish used to be found inside them. And a proof that these sorts
of animals do not emit anything generative from themselves is this:
when certain Chians carried some live shell-fish over from Pyrrha in
Lesbos and deposited them in certain Euripus-like places in the sea
where currents clash, but though as time passed they increased in
size, they became no more numerous.⁷¹⁸ As for their so-called eggs,
they contribute nothing to generation, but are [just] a sign of being
well nourished, like fat in blooded animals.⁷¹⁹ That is also why for
purposes of eating they become well flavored at these periods.⁷²⁰ A
sign [that these are not really eggs] is that these sorts of animals—for
example, pinnae, whelks, and purple-fish—always have them, except

that sometimes they are larger, sometimes smaller.[721] Others have
them not always, but rather in the spring, in diminishing quantities
as the season advances, and in the end disappearing altogether—for
example, scallops, mussels, and so-called lagoon shell-fish.[722] For this
season is advantageous to their bodies. In others—for example, the
sea-squirts—nothing of this sort is obvious.

A theoretical grasp on the particulars concerning these and the
places in which they come to be must be gotten from the *History of
Animals*.[723]

Book IV

IV 1

The generation of the animals, then, has now been spoken about, both in common and about all of them separately. But since in the most complete of them the female and the male are separated, and since we say that these capacities are the starting-points of all plants and all animals (although some have them unseparated, others separated), we must speak first about the generation of these. For while the animals are still incomplete in their genus, the female and the male are distinct. But whether one is female and another male before the difference (*diaphora*) is clear to perception, the difference being acquired by them in the mother or earlier, is disputed. For some people—for example, Anaxagoras and others among the physicists—say that this contrariety is present in the seeds from the outset.[724] (For the seed, they say, comes from the male, while the female provides the place, and the male is from the right, and the female from the left, and whereas males are on the right of the uterus, females are on the left.[725]) Others say that it is in the mother, just as Empedocles does. (For the [seeds] that enter a hot womb become males, he says, while those that enter a cold one become females, the cause of the hotness or coldness being the flow of the menses, as it is colder or hotter, older or more recent.[726] Democritus of Abdera says that the difference (*diaphora*) of female and male is produced in the mother, nonetheless it is not because of the heat and cold that one becomes female and another male, but rather on whose seed would master whose, that is, the seed that has come from the part by which male and female are differentiated from each other.[727]

Now it is true that Empedocles made a careless assumption in thinking that female and male differ from each other only in coldness and hotness, seeing that as wholes the parts have great difference (*diaphora*), namely, that between the male private parts and the uterus. For if fabricated animals, one having the parts of the female and the other those of the male, were put into the uterus as into an oven, the one having a uterus into a hot one and the one not having it into a cold one, the one not having a uterus will be female, and the one having it will be male. But this is impossible. So in this respect what Democritus says is better. For he seeks the difference (*diaphora*) belonging to the generation of this, and tries to state it—where he does so correctly or incorrectly is another story (*logos*).[728]

Moreover, if hotness and coldness were the cause of the difference (*diaphora*) of the parts, those who speak that way should have stated this.[729] For this is (one might almost say) what speaking about the generation of male and female consists in. For it quite evidently differentiates them. And it is no small task, from hotness and coldness as starting-point, to draw conclusions about the production of the parts, as if it necessarily follows that by the animal's being cooled this part called the uterus is produced, whereas by its being heated it is not produced. It is the same way too with the parts that effect sexual intercourse. For these also differ in the way stated previously.[730]

Further, male and female twins are often produced together in the same part of the uterus—and this we have adequately observed in all the oviparous animals on the basis of dissections, both in the terrestrial ones and in the fishes.[731] If, then, Empedocles had not seen this, it is quite reasonable for him to make an error in stating this cause of his. If, on the other hand, he had seen it, it is strange to still consider the cause to be the hotness or coldness of the uterus. For, if it were, they would both become female or both male. But as things stand this is not what we see happening.

He says too that the parts are "torn asunder."[732] For some are in the male, he says, others in the female, which is also why they have an appetite for sexual intercourse with each other. It is necessary then for the magnitude of these parts also to be torn asunder and for an assembly to occur, but not because of cooling and heating.[733] But about this sort of cause for the seed there are no doubt many things to say [in criticism].[734] For, in general, this manner of cause seems to be fabricated. If, however, the facts about seed are as we have stated, and it does not come from all [parts] nor, in general, does what comes from the male provide any matter whatsoever to what is coming to be, then one must make a reply to Empedocles, Democritus, and anyone else who speaks in a similar way. For it is not possible for the body of the seed to be torn asunder, part in the female and part in the male, as Empedocles states when he says:

Torn asunder is the nature of the limbs, this part in man's . . .[735]

Neither is it possible for the totality of it to be secreted from each, and for a female or male to come to be as one part masters another.

In general, though, it is certainly better to say that the excess of one part, by its mastery, produces a female than, giving thought to nothing, to make heat alone the cause. Moreover, the fact that at the same time the shape of the private part is also distinct needs an argument for its always following along with the other.[736] For if it is because they are nearby, then each of the remaining parts should follow along too—for one of the prevailing parts is close to another part, so that the offspring, if female, would at the same time be like its mother [in all other respects], or, if male, like its father.

Further, it is also absurd to think that these parts must come to be in isolation, and not along with the whole body that is changing, and particularly and primarily the blood-vessels, around which, as around a framework, the body of the fleshes is laid.[737] It is not reasonable that these become of a certain quality because of the uterus, but rather the uterus because of them. For although each is a receptacle for a certain sort of blood, the blood-vessels are prior.[738] For the movement-producing starting-point is necessarily always prior, and by being of a certain quality is the cause of generation. The difference (*diaphora*) of these parts in relation to each other in females and males results, then, but it must not be thought of as a starting-point or a cause, but rather something else must, even if no seed is secreted either from the female or from the male, but rather what is coming to be is composed in any and every way.[739]

The very same argument may be used against those who say that the male comes from the right and the female from the left as the one used against Empedocles and against Democritus. For if the male contributes no matter at all [to the embryo], those who speak in this way would be saying nothing, whereas if, as they say, it does contribute it, it is necessary to reply in the same way as to Empedocles' argument, which distinguishes the female from the male by the hotness and coldness of the uterus. For the others do the same thing in distinguishing by their lefts and rights, while seeing the female and the male also differing by their [sexual] parts as a whole—what for them is the cause due to which the body of the uterus exists in those [embryos] that come from the left and not in those that come from the right? For if it were to come [from the left] and not possess this part, it would be a female not possessing a uterus or a male possessing one, as luck would have it. Further, as has also been said previously, a female has been seen in the right part of the uterus, a male in the left, and both in the same part, and this not only once but often, or the male one in the right, the female in the left, and no less often both come to be in the right.[740]

In about the same way, certain people who were persuaded by these things said that if the right or left testis is tied up in mating the result is a male offspring or a female offspring, respectively. For in fact Leophanes spoke this way.[741] And in a case where one or other testis is cut

out some say that the same happens, not speaking the truth but having   25
a hunch about what will happen based on likelihoods and assuming
things in advance before seeing how they turn out. Further, they do
not know that these parts contribute nothing to the generation of male
offspring and female offspring in the animals. A sign of this is that   30
many animals that are themselves both female and male, and generate females and males, do not have testes, as those not having feet do
not—for example, the fish genus and that of the serpents.

To think, then, that hotness and coldness are the cause of male and   35
female, or that the secretion coming from the right or from the left is
the cause of their coming to be, is to a certain extent reasonable (*logos*).
For the right side of the body is hotter than the left, and the concocted   765ᵇ1
seed hotter than the non-concocted, and what has been composed is
something of this sort, and what has been composed is more fertile.
But to speak in this way is to grasp the cause from too far away, and
we must most of all move on by all possible means toward the primary   5
causes.⁷⁴²

The body as a whole and its parts, what each of them is and what
cause it is due to, have been spoken about previously elsewhere.⁷⁴³ But
[1] since the male and the female are distinguished by a certain capacity and a certain incapacity (for what is capable of concocting, composing, and emitting seed containing the starting-point of the form is male   10
(*eidos*)—and by starting-point I mean not the sort from which as from
matter an offspring comes to be that is of the same sort as the progenitor, but rather the primary moving-producing one, whether capable of
producing it within itself or in something else), whereas what is receptive of seed, but incapable of composing and emitting it, is female; [2]
further, if all concoction works by heat; then [3] it is necessary, for the   15
males of the animals to be hotter than the females. For it is because
of coldness and incapacity that the female is more abundant in blood
in certain parts. And this is a sign that goes contrary to what some
people think is the very cause due to which the female is hotter than
the male, namely, because of the emission of menses. For blood being   20
hot, what has more is hotter. They suppose, however, that this affection
occurs because of an excess of blood and heat, as if it were possible for
everything and anything to be equally blood if only it is liquid and sanguineous in color, and not possible for less and purer to be produced   25
in those that are better nourished. For them it is as with the residue in
the bowels, where more rather than less, they think, is a sign of a hotter
nature. And yet it is the contrary. For just as in workings concerning
fruit, where the nourishment in its first stage is abundant, and in the
end the last stage is nothing compared to the quantity in the first stage,   30

so too in the body, the parts receive the nourishment in turn for their workings, from the entirety of which the final result is quite small.[744] In some this is blood, in others, its analogue.

Now since the one sex is capable, and the other incapable, of excreting the pure residue, and for every capacity there is an instrument, the same for the one that completes [its work] in an inferior way as for the one that does so better, and since things are said to be capable and incapable in many ways, and the female and the male are opposed in this one, it is necessary then for there to be an instrument both for the female and for the male. For the first the uterus, for the second the penis.[745] And nature assigns to each both the capacity and the instrument together. For it is better that way. That is why each of the places comes to be together with the excretions and the instruments, and just as the sight is not completed without the eye nor the eye without sight, so too the bowels and bladder come to be together with the capacity to produce the residues. And since it is from the same thing that something both comes to be and grows (and this is the nourishment), [1] each of the parts should come to be from the sort of matter and the sort of residue that it is receptive of. [2] Secondly, and contrariwise, it comes to be, we say, in some way from its contrary. [3] Thirdly, in addition to these points, we must grasp that if indeed a thing passes away to its contrary, what is not being mastered by what handicrafts it also necessarily changes to its contrary. From these principles it should presumably already be more evident what the cause is due to which one thing becomes female and another male. For when the starting-point is not doing the mastering, is not capable of concoction because of deficiency of heat, and does not lead toward its own special form (*eidos*), but is defeated in this respect, it is necessary for it to change to its contrary. Now what is contrary to the male is the female, and contrary in that respect whereby the one is male and the other female. And since it differs in the capacity it possesses, so too the instrument it possesses differs, so that it changes to its contrary. And as one vital part changes the whole composition of the animal differs greatly in form (*eidos*). This may be seen in the case of eunuchs, who, though deformed in [only] one part, utterly change their old shape and fall short [only] a little from the visible form (*idea*) of a female. The cause of this is that some of the parts are starting-points, and when a starting-point is moved [or changed] it is necessary for many of the parts that follow along with it to change in step.

If, then, [1] the male is a certain starting-point and cause, and [2] it is male insofar as it is capable of something, female insofar as it is incapable, [3] and the defining mark of the capacity, and of

the incapacity, is being capable of concocting, or being incapable of concocting, the last stage of the nourishment (which in the blooded animals is called blood and in the others its analog), and [4] the cause of this resides in the starting-point, that is, in the part of the body that contains the starting-point of the natural heat, then it is neces- 35
sary in the blooded animals for a heart to be composed, and for what comes to be to be either male or female, and in the other genera that have the female and the male, an analogue of the heart. This, then, 766^b1
is the starting-point and the cause of male and female and in this it resides. But the animal is by this time female or male when it also has the parts by which the female differs from the male. For it is not by 5
virtue of any old part whatsoever that it is male or female, any more than in the case of seeing or hearing.

To recapitulate, we say that the seed has been established to be a residue of the nourishment, namely, the last stage of it. And by "last stage" I mean what is carried to each [part], which is also why what comes to be is like its progenitor. For it makes no difference whether it comes from each of the parts or that it goes to each of them—but 10
the latter is more correct.⁷⁴⁶ But the seed of the male differs from that of the female because it contains a starting-point within itself of such a sort as to cause movement in the animal too and to concoct the last stage of the nourishment, whereas that of the female contains matter alone.⁷⁴⁷ When it has mastered [the latter] it draws [it] to itself, but when it has been mastered it changes to its contrary or comes to ruin. 15
And contrary to the male is the female, female due to the non-con-coctedness and coldness of its sanguineous nourishment. And nature assigns each of the residues to the part receptive of it. But the seed is a residue, and this in the hotter of the blooded animals—that is, the males—is moderate in quantity. That is why the parts receptive of this 20
residue are ducts. In the females, on the other hand, because of non-concoctedness, there is a [large] quantity of sanguineous material (for it is incapable of being worked up). So it is also necessary for there to be some part receptive of it, and for this to be unlike [that in the male] and to have magnitude. That is why the nature of the uterus is of this sort. And it is by this part that the female differs from the male. 25

Due to what cause, then, one thing is female and another male has been stated.

IV 2

And the facts are proofs of what has been said. For the young are more productive of females than those that are in their prime, as too are

30   those that are older. For in the former the heat is not yet complete, while in the latter it is failing.⁷⁴⁸

Also, bodies that are more liquid and more womanly are more productive of females, and liquid seeds more than those that have been more composed. For all of these are produced because of a want of natural heat, and the north winds are more productive of males

34   than are the south winds.⁷⁴⁹ For bodies are more liquid during south

34b   winds, so that they are more productive of residue. And the more res-

35   idue there is the more difficult it is to concoct. That is why the seed in males, and the menstrual excretion in females, is [then] more liquid.

767ᵃ1   Also, due to the same cause, when the menses are produced in accord with nature they occur when the moon is waning. For this time of the month is colder and more humid due to the waning and failing

5   of the moon. For while the sun in the whole year produces winter and summer, the moon does so in the month (this is not because of the solstices, but the one occurs when the light is increased, the other when it is waning).

Shepherds say too that it makes a difference to the production of females and the production of males not only if mating occurs during

10   north winds or south winds, but also if while copulating the animals look south or north. So small a thing, they say, will sometimes shift the balance, becoming a cause of cold or heat, and these a cause in generation.

In general, then, female and male are set apart from each other in relation to production of males and production of females due to the

15   causes just mentioned. Nonetheless, there must also be a proportion in their relation to each other. For all things that come to be either in accord with craft or nature exist in virtue of a certain ratio (*logos*).⁷⁵⁰ Now the hot, if it is too mastering, dries up the wet things, whereas if it is very deficient it does not compose them; instead it must stand in the mean ratio (*logos*) in relation to what is being handicrafted. If

20   it does not, just as in cooking where too much fire burns the food, while too little does not cook it, and either way the result is that what is being produced fails to be completed, likewise too in the case of the mixing of what comes from the male and what comes from the female there must be a proportion. And because of this it often happens to many [couples] that they cannot generate with each other,

25   but being separated generate [with other partners], and these contrarieties occur sometimes in young people, sometimes in older ones, alike concerning generation and infertility, and production of males and production of females.

Region differs from region, and water from water, in these respects due to the same causes. For the nourishment and especially the condition of the body become of a certain quality due both to the blend of the surrounding air and of the things that enter in, especially the liquid nourishment.^{751} For this is most brought in, and this is in all nourishment, even in dry foods. That is why hard cold waters in some cases produce sterility, in others the production of females.

IV 3

And the same causes explain why: [1] some offspring are like their procreators, others not like them; [2] some are like their father, others like their mother, both in the body as a whole and in each part; and [3] are more like them than like their ancestors; and [4] are more like these than like random people; and [5] males are more like their father, females more like their mother; and [6] some, though like none of their kin (*suggenês*), are nonetheless like some human being at least; while [7] others are not like a human in visible form (*idea*) but are already a monster. And in fact what is not like its parents is already in a certain way a monster. For nature in these cases has in a certain way deviated from the genus.^{752}

And a first starting-point is when a female comes to be and not a male—but this is necessary by nature.^{753} For the genus that is separated into female and male must be preserved, and since it is possible for the male sometimes not to master, either due to youth or age, or due to some other cause of this sort, it is necessary for production of females to occur among the animals. The monster, by contrast, is not necessary in relation to the for-the-sake-of-which and the final cause, but is necessary coincidentally.^{754}

Hence the starting-point must be grasped from the following: If the spermatic residue in the menses is well concocted, the movement from the male will produce a shape [or form] that corresponds to itself. For it makes no difference whether we say the semen or the movement that makes each of the parts grow, or again what makes them grow or what composes them at the start (for the account (*logos*) of the movement is the same [in either case]). So if this movement masters, it will produce a male, not a female, and one that is like the male progenitor and not like the mother. But if it does not master, with regard to each capacity, whatever it is, that has not mastered, it makes [the embryo] correspondingly deficient.

I mean "each capacity" in the following way. What generates is not only [the generic] male but also this sort of male, for example, Coriscus

25   or Socrates, and not only is it Coriscus, but also human.^{755} It is in this way, accordingly, that some things are closer and others farther away that belong to the male progenitor, insofar as he is generative, and not coincidentally—for example, if the male progenitor is knowledgeable in grammar or someone's neighbor.^{756} But what is special and what is

30   particular is always stronger in relation to generation.^{757} For Coriscus is both human and animal, but human is closer to what is special than animal is. Both the particular and the genus generate, but the particular more so. For this is the substance.^{758} For though what comes to be also comes to be this sort of thing, yet it also becomes a this something—and

35   this is the substance.^{759} That is why the movements existing in the seed are from capacities such as all these, and, potentially even from those of the ancestors, but especially those from a certain particular are always

768^{a}1   closer. By a particular I mean Coriscus or Socrates.

    Now since everything is shifted not into any random thing but into its opposite, and what in generation is not mastered is necessarily shifted with regard to the capacity in which the progenitor and mover has failed to master, and becomes its opposite.^{760} If, then, it has not mas-

5   tered insofar as it is male, it becomes female, if insofar as it is Coriscus or Socrates, it becomes not like its father but like its mother.^{761} For as what is opposed in general to the father is the mother, what is opposed to a particular male progenitor is a particular female progenitor. And likewise with respect to the capacities that stand next in order. For it

10   always changes more to the ancestors, whether to those of the father or to those of the mother.

    Some of the movements are present [in the semen] actively, others potentially: actively those of the male progenitor and the universal (for example, human, animal); potentially, those of the female and the ancestors. On the one hand, then, [movements], when shifted, change to their opposites, and, on the other hand, the movements

15   doing the handicrafting slacken into those near them—for example, if that of the male progenitor slackens, it changes by a very small difference to that of his father, and in the second instance to that of his grandfather. And in this way too, of course, in the case of females, the movement of the female progenitor slackens into that of her mother,

20   and if not to this, then to that of her grandmother.^{762} And likewise in the case of the more remote ancestors.

    It is most of all natural, then, for it insofar as it is male and for it insofar as it is father to master or be mastered at the same time. For the difference here is small, so that it takes no work to have both happen at the same time. For Socrates is this sort of man and this man. That is why for the most part males are like their father and females like their

mother. For the displacement to both has come about at the same time. 25
And female is opposed to male, mother to father, and displacement is
into opposites.

But if the movement from the male masters while the one from
Socrates does not, or vice versa, then the result is that males come to
be that are like mother and females like father. 30

If the movements slacken, that is, insofar as they are male stand fast,
but the movement from Socrates slackens into that of his father, the
result will be a male that is like its paternal grandfather or some other
of its more remote ancestors, in accord with the same account (*logos*).
But if insofar as it is male it is mastered, the result will be female and
most often like its mother, but if this movement too slackens, the simi- 35
larity will be to the mother's mother or some other of her more remote
ancestors, in accord with the same account (*logos*).

And it is the same way too in the case of the parts. For of the parts 768^{b}1
as well some are like the father, others like the mother, and others
like the ancestors. For some of the movements of the parts as well
are present in them actively, others present potentially, as has often
been said.[763]

But we must take the following as universal hypotheses: one, what 5
was said just now, that some movements are present actively, others
present potentially, but also two others, that if it is mastered it is shifted
into its opposite, and if it slackens it does so into the movement next
in order, and if it slackens less, into what is near, if more, into what is
farther away.[764] In the end, though, the movements are so confused 10
that there is no likeness to family members or those of like genus (*suggenês*), but only what is common remains, namely, being human. The
cause of this is that it follows along with all the particulars. For the
human is universal, whereas Socrates, father, mother, whoever she
may be, are among the particulars.[765]

And the cause of the slackening of the movements is that what 15
affects is affected by what is affected—for example, what cuts is blunted
by what is cut, what heats is cooled by what is heated, and, in general,
what moves (except for the primary mover) is moved in return with
a certain movement (for example, what is pushed is in a way pushed
in return, and what compresses is in a way compressed in return).[766]
Sometimes too it is on the whole affected more than it affects, and 20
what heats is cooled and what cools is heated, sometimes not having
affected at all, sometimes having affected less than it has been affected.
These things have been spoken about in the determinations concerning affecting and being affected, as has in what sorts of beings affecting
and being affected belong.[767]

143

25   What is affected is shifted and is not mastered, either because of a deficiency of capacity in what is concocting and causing movement or because of the large quantity and coldness of what is being concocted and distinctly formed. For by mastering at one point and not mastering at another it makes what is being composed many-shaped (*polumorphos*). For example, in the case of athletes this happens because of eating so much. For because of the quantity of nourishment the

30 nature is not capable of mastering it so as to produce proportional growth and maintain the sameness of shape.[768] The parts thus become qualitatively different, and sometimes in such a way that they are pretty much nothing like they were before.[769] And the disease called satyriasis is about the same as this.[770] For in this too, because a large quantity of non-concocted flux or pneuma is diverted to the parts of

35 the face, the face appears to be that of another animal, that is, of a satyr.[771]

    All of the following have now been determined: due to what cause

769ᵃ1 a female and a male come to be; why some resemble their parents, females female ones, males male ones, and others the reverse, female like the father and males like the mother; and, in general, why some are like their ancestors, others like none of them; and these things both

5 with regard to the whole body and each of its parts.

    Certain of the physicists, however, speak otherwise about the cause due to which offspring that are like and unlike their parents come about.[772] Indeed, they speak of the cause in two ways. For some say that the one of the two from which more seed comes is the one the offspring

10 is more like, equally for totality in relation to totality and part in relation to part, on the supposition that seed comes from the parts of each. And if an equal amount comes from each of the two, then the offspring, they say, is similar to neither. But if this is false and seed does not come from all [the parts], clearly neither can the cause of similarity and dissimilarity be the one they state. Further, how at the same time a female

15 offspring can be like her father and a male one like his mother is not something they can in a puzzle-free way determine. For while those who speak of the cause of female and male as Empedocles and Democritus do say things that are in another way impossible, those who say that it is due to the more or less [seed] coming from male or female, and that it is

20 because of this that one offspring is female and another male, could not demonstrate in what way the female is to be like the father and the male like the mother, since that more should come from both parents at the same time is impossible.[773] Further, due to what cause is an offspring for the most part like its ancestors, even the more remote ones? For none of

25 the seed has come from *them* at any rate.

But those who speak in the remaining way about the similarity and the other things speak better, especially about it. For there are certain people who say that the semen, though one, is like a universal seed-bed consisting of many [seeds].[774] It is as if someone were to mix together many juices in one liquid and then take some from it, it would be possible to take, not an equal quantity of each always, but sometimes more of this one, sometimes more of that, sometimes some of one and none at all of another—this, they say, results too in the case of the semen's being a mixture of many [seeds]. For the progenitor from whom the most comes in is the one the shape [of the offspring] is like. Though this account (*logos*) is not perspicuous and in many respects fabricated, it means to be saying something better, namely, that it is not actively but potentially that what it calls a universal seed-bed exists. For in the first way, it is impossible, but in the second it is possible.

But it is not easy, by assigning a cause in [only] one way, to state the cause of all the cases: of male and female coming to be; why the female is often similar to the father, the male to the mother; and, again, of the similarity to ancestors; further, due to what cause the offspring is sometimes human, though not similar to any of these, and sometimes, proceeding in this way, appears not even human but rather a sort of animal only, the ones that are indeed even called monsters.

And in fact, following what has been said, the next thing is to speak about the cause of these sorts of monsters. For in the end, when the movements [from the male] slacken and the matter [from the female] is not mastered, what is most of all universal stands fast—and this is [the generic] animal. Then people say that what comes to be has the head of a ram or an ox, and in other cases, in like fashion, that of another animal—for example, that a calf has a child's head, or a sheep that of an ox. But though all of these result due to the causes just mentioned, none is what it is said to be, but a likeness only—which is just what is also produced when there is no deformation involved.[775] That is why those who make jibes often liken some people who are not nobly beautiful to a fire-breathing goat, others to a butting ram.[776] And a certain physiognomist has reduced all faces to those of two or three animals, and, in so arguing, often persuaded people.

But that it is impossible for a monster of this sort to come to be (that is, one [genus of] animal inside another) is shown by the gestation-times, which are much different in human, sheep, dog, and ox. And it is impossible for each [genus] to come to be except in its proper time.

This, then, is one way things are said to be monsters, others are said to be so by having extra parts to their shape, [for example,] coming to be with extra feet or extra heads.

The accounts of the cause of what has to do with monsters are close to, indeed about the same as, those of what has to do with deformed animals. For monstrosity is a sort of deformation.

IV 4

30   Now Democritus said that monsters come to be because two semens fall [into the uterus], one setting [the menses] in movement earlier, the other later, and this latter, once it issues forth, arrives in the uterus, so that the parts [of the embryo] grow together and become confused.[777] But in the birds, he says, since mating always takes place quickly, both
35   the eggs and their color become confused.[778] But if several offspring come to be from one semen and one act of sexual intercourse, which
770^{a}1   is just what appears to be the case, it is better not to go the long way around, passing the short one by.[779] For especially in such cases it is necessary for this to occur when the seeds are not disaggregated but instead arrive together [in the uterus]. If, then, we must attribute the
5   cause to the semen from the male, that is the way we would have to state it. But, in general, we must rather think that the cause resides in the matter [contributed by the female] and in the embryos being composed.

That is why too monsters of these sorts come to be altogether rarely in uniparous animals, but more frequently in the multiparous ones, and most of all in birds, and among birds most of all in chickens. For this
10   bird is multiparous not only in laying often, like the pigeon genus, but also because it has many embryos at the same time and mates all year round. That is also why it lays many twin-eggs. For the embryos grow together because they are close to each other, as many fruits sometimes
15   do. Of these twin-eggs, when the yolks are divided by the membrane, two separate chicks come to be having nothing extraordinary about them, but when the yolks are continuous, with nothing keeping them asunder, from these, chicks that are monstrous come to be, having one
20   body and head but four legs and four wings. This is because the upper parts come to be earlier from the white, the nourishment for them being dispensed from the yolk, whereas the lower part develops later and its nourishment is one and indivisible.[780]

Also already observed is a serpent that is two-headed due to the same cause. For this genus too is multiparous and lays many eggs.
25   Monstrosities, however, are more rare in their case due to the shape of the uterus. For because of its length the large number of eggs are set in a row.[781] And where bees and wasps are concerned nothing of this sort occurs, because their offspring are in separate cells. But where

chickens are concerned the contrary is the case, which makes it clear
that we must consider the cause of these things to reside in the mat-   30
ter. For among the other animals too monstrosities occur more often
in those that are multiparous. That is why in the human they are less
common. For it is for the most part uniparous and a bearer of complete offspring, seeing that even in human beings it is in places where
the women bear more than one offspring at a time that monstrosities
occur more often—for example, in Egypt. And in goats and sheep they   35
are more common. For they are more multiparous. And it is still more
common in the multi-split-footed animals. For these sorts of animals
are multiparous and bear incomplete offspring, as the dog does. For in   770^{b}1
many cases the offspring of these are born blind.[782]

Due to what cause this happens and due to what cause they are
multiparous must be stated later.[783] But the route to the bearing of
monsters has been prepared for the nature by the fact that they generate offspring that, due to their incompleteness, are not similar to
their parents. And the monster too is among the offspring that are
not similar to their parents.[784] That is why this coincident is a point of   5
overlap in animals with this sort of nature.[785] For it is in these too that
so-called runts most frequently come to be.[786] And these have in a
certain respect been affected in the way monsters have been. For the
monster is among the things that are contrary to nature, not contrary
to all nature, though, but the one that holds for the most part.[787] For   10
concerning the nature that is always and of necessity [the way it is]
nothing comes to be contrary to nature, but rather it occurs among
the things that, though they for the most part come to be in a certain
way, admit of doing so in another way. Even in their case, though it
occurs contrary to this order, yet, since it always does so non-ran-
domly, [what comes to be] seems less a monster because even what
is contrary to nature is in a certain way in accord with nature, when-   15
ever the nature that corresponds to the form (*eidos*) has not mastered
the nature that corresponds to the matter. That is why people do not
call things of this [runt] sort monsters any more than they do in the
other cases in which something habitually comes to be, as in the case
of fruits. For there is a vine that some people call "smoky," and if it
bears black grapes they do not judge it a monster because it is in the   20
habit of doing this very often.[788] The cause of this is that its nature is
intermediate between white and black, so that the change is not from
far away nor, as it were, contrary to nature. For it is not a change to
another nature.

But in multiparous animals these things occur because the multiple
[embryos] impede each other's completion and generative movements.   25

One might raise a puzzle, though, about multiparity and having an excess of parts, and oligoparity or uniparity and having a deficiency of parts. For sometimes animals come to be having too many toes, while others have only one, and with the other parts it is the same way. For both an animal that has excess parts and one that is docked come to be.[789] Some—both among human beings and especially among goats—even have two private parts, one of a male and one of a female. For goats come to be that are called hermaphrodites because of having a female and a male private part—and a goat has even been known to have come to be with a horn on its leg.

Changes, deformations, and excesses also come about in the internal parts, by not possessing some of them, by possessing ones that have been docked, too many of them, or misplaced ones.[790] No animal, indeed, has come to be without having a heart, but rather without having a spleen, or having two spleens, or one kidney; and none without having a liver, but without having a whole one—and all these in animals complete and alive. Found too are animals not having a gallbladder that naturally have one; others having more than one. Cases of change of place are also known, the liver being on the left, the spleen on the right. And these have been seen in *complete* animals, as was just said.[791] In newborns, on the other hand, one finds much disorder of every sort. Those that depart a little from the nature usually live; those that depart a lot, when what is contrary to nature lies in the parts that have control, do not live.[792]

The investigation concerning these things is whether we must consider the cause of uniparity and having a deficiency of parts, and of having an excess of parts and multiparity, to be the same, or not the same.

First, then, why some animals are multiparous, others uniparous, is something it would seem reasonable for someone to wonder at. For it is the largest of the animals that are uniparous—for example, elephant, camel, horse, and the solid-hoofed ones. Of these some are larger than [all] the other animals, while others are very outstanding in size. Dog and wolf, on the other hand, and pretty much all the multi-split-footed animals are multiparous, even the small ones of these sorts—for example, the mouse genus. The cloven-hoofed animals, though, are uniparous, except for pig, which is among the multiparous ones. For it is reasonable that the larger ones be capable of generating more offspring and bearing more seed. But the very thing that we wonder at is a cause not to wonder.[793] For it is because of their size that they do not produce many offspring. For the nourishment in these sorts of animals is used up for growth of the body—whereas in the smaller animals nature subtracts from the size and adds the excess to the spermatic residue.

Further, it is necessary for the generating seed of a larger animal to be greater in quantity, and for that of smaller ones to be small in quantity. And though many small ones can come to be in the same [place], it is difficult for many large ones to do so. For to those intermediate in size nature has assigned the intermediate [number].

Now of there being some animals that are large, others smaller, others intermediate, we have previously stated the cause.[794] Some of the animals, though, are uniparous, others oligoparous, others multiparous. For the most part, the solid-hoofed ones are uniparous, the cloven-hoofed oligoparous, and the multi-split-footed multiparous. The cause of this is that for the most part their sizes correspond to this difference (*diaphora*). But it is not so in all cases. For it is the largeness and smallness of their bodies that is cause of their oligoparity and multiparity, but not the genus's being solid-hoofed, cloven-hoofed, or multi-split-footed. Here is evidence of this: the elephant is the largest of animals, though it is multi-split-footed, and the camel, which is cloven-hoofed, is the largest of the remaining ones. And it is not only among the animals that walk but also among the ones that fly that the large ones are oligoparous and the small ones multiparous, due to the same cause. Similarly it is not the largest plants that bear the most fruit.

Why the nature of some animals is multiparous, others oligoparous, other uniparous has been stated. As for the puzzle that has just now been stated about how one might quite reasonably wonder at those that are multiparous, seeing that these sorts of animals are often seen to conceive after a single mating. Now whether the seed of the male contributes to the matter of the embryo by becoming part of it and mixing with the seed of the female, or whether in fact it is not that way but, as we say, by bringing together and handicrafting the matter in the female, that is, the spermatic residue, just as the fig-juice does the liquid in milk—but due to what possible cause does it not complete [just] one animal having [the relevant] size, just as there in the example the fig-juice is not separated in composing a certain quantity, but rather the more it is put into and the more it is, so much the greater is what is curdled?[795]

Now to say that the places in the uterus draw the seed, and because of this several offspring come to be, is to say nothing, because of the number of the places and because of the cotyledons not being one.[796] For often two [embryos] come to be in the same place in the uterus, and in the multiparous animals, when the uterus is filled with embryos, they are seen to lie in a row. This is clear from dissections. But in fact just as when animals are completing [their growth] there is a certain size for each, both in the direction of larger and in the direction of smaller,

neither will any come to be that is larger or smaller than this; rather it
is within the intervening interval that there is an excess or deficiency
in the size they get in relation to each other, and one becomes a bigger
and another a smaller human being, or any other animal whatsoever—
so too the spermatic matter from which [the embryo] comes to be is
not so unlimited, either in the direction of more or in the direction
of less, that it comes from some random quantity. Whichever of the
animals, then, due to the cause just mentioned, emits more residue
than is the starting-point for one animal, it is not possible that from
all of it [only] one comes to be, but rather as many as is determined
by the sizes that pertain; nor will the seed of the male or the capacity
in the seed compose anything more or less than what is natural. Similarly, if the male emits more seed, or there are more capacities in the
divided-up seed, the greatest possible amount of it will not produce
anything bigger [than what is natural], but on the contrary will destroy
[the spermatic matter in the female] by drying it up. For even fire does
not heat up water more as it is itself increased; rather there is a defining
mark of the hotness, which once reached, even if one increases the size
of the fire, the water no longer becomes hotter, but instead evaporates
more and more, and in the end disappears and dries up.

Since, then, it appears that the residue of the female and that from
the male need to stand in some proportional relationship to each other
(that is, where the males emit seed), in the case of those animals that
are multiparous, the males at the outset emit [seed] capable, when
divided into parts, of composing several embryos, while the female
emits enough that several can come to be composed.[797] (In the case of
the milk example we stated it is not like that. For in the case of the heat
of the seed what is composed is not only a certain quantity but also has
a certain quality, whereas in the case of fig-juice or rennet the quantity
alone is involved.) Of many embryos coming to be, then, and not one
continuous one, this is the cause in the multiparous animals, namely,
that the embryo does not come to be from some random quantity; on
the contrary, if there is too little or too much, there will not be one. For
there is a determinate limit to the capacity, what is affected, and the
heat of what affects it.

Similarly too in the case of the large uniparous animals it is not the
case that many offspring come to be from much residue. For in them
too it is from a certain quantity that a certain quantity gets worked up.
They do not, then, emit a larger quantity of this sort of matter due to
the aforementioned cause. And what they do emit is just enough, in
accord with nature, for one embryo to come to be from. But if at some
time more of it comes, then two are produced. That is also why such

things seem to be more monstrous, namely, because they come about contrary to what holds for the most part and what is usual.

The human, however, plays a double game in all the modes of generation.[798] For it is uniparous, oligoparous, and multiparous by times, but its nature is most of all uniparous—because of the wetness and hotness of its body it is multiparous (for the nature of seed is wet and hot), but because of its size it is oligoparous and multiparous. And because of this it also happens that it is the only animal whose period of gestation is irregular. For while in the others there is a single period, in human beings there are several. For they are born at seven months, at ten months, and at the intermediate times. For even those of eight months do live, but less often. The cause may be made out on the basis of what has just been said; it has been spoken about in the *Problems*.[799]

And about these issues, let things be determined in this way.

Of the excess of parts contrary to nature and the birth of twins the cause is the same. For already in the embryos the cause occurs, whenever it composes more matter than corresponds to the nature of the part. For then the result is that one part is larger than the others—a finger, hand, foot, or some other of the extremities or limbs—or else, if the embryo is split, more parts come to be, as eddies do in rivers. For in these eddies too as the water is carried along and, having movement, collides with something, from the one [eddy] two compositions are produced that have the same movement. It happens in the same way in the case of the embryos as well.[800] The [parts] are mostly attached near each other, although sometimes they are farther away because of the movement produced in the embryos, and especially because of the excess of matter being assigned to the place it was subtracted from, while retaining the form (*eidos*) of that [part] from which it was [subtracted as] excess.

In some cases these sorts of things occur in such a way that the embryos have two private parts, one male, the other female, but when such excess occurs, one part has control and the other lacks control, and is always made weak by the nourishment, seeing that it is contrary to nature, and is attached just as tumors are (for these too get nourishment, although they are produced after birth, and are contrary to nature). If what is doing the handicrafting has gained mastery, or is wholly mastered, two similar [private parts] are produced. But should it in part master and in part be mastered, one is female, the other male. For it makes no difference whether we state the cause due to which one is female and another male in the case of the part or in the case of the whole.

772^b1

5

10

15

20

25

30

35

And wherever a deficiency occurs of these sorts of parts, for example, of an extremity or certain of the other limbs, we must consider the cause to be the very same as when the whole embryo miscarries—mis-

773ᵃ1 carriages of embryos occur frequently.[801]

Outgrowths differ from multiparity in the way just mentioned, while monsters differ from these in that most of them are due to embryos growing together.[802] In some cases, though, they also differ in this way if the [monstrosity occurs] in the larger and more controlling parts—

5 for example, some have two spleens, or several kidneys. Further, the parts may change locations because of the movements being diverted and the matter changing places. We should consider the monstrous thing to be one animal or many by reference to the starting-point. For example, if the heart is a part of this sort, what has one heart is one

10 animal, and the excess parts [mere] outgrowths, whereas those that have several hearts, will be[, for example,] two animals, though grown together due to the junction of the embryos.

It often happens, even with many animals that do not seem to be deformed and are already completely developed, that some of their ducts have grown together, while others have been diverted. And

15 in fact in some women the mouth of the uterus has been known to remain closed until the time for the menses and the subsequent pains. In some cases they broke through spontaneously, in others due to doctors having cut the mouth open. And some cases have resulted in death if the breakthrough occurred by force or could not be produced. And

20 in some boys it happens that the end-limit of the private part and the duct through which the residue from the bladder passes do not coincide, but the latter is underneath, which is also why they sit when they urinate, and since the testes have been drawn up they seem from a distance to have a female and a male private part at the same time. And the duct for dry nourishment has been known to grow closed in

25 certain animals, both sheep and others, since in fact in Perinthus an ox came to be that passes fine-grained filtered nourishment through the bladder, and when its anus was cut open it quickly grew closed again, and they could not keep it open.[803]

30 Oligoparity and multiparity, as well as outgrowths of excess parts, and, further, monstrosities, have now been spoken about.[804]

IV 5

In some animals superfetation does not occur at all, in others superfetation does occur, and among the superfetators, some are capable of bringing the embryos to birth, others are capable of doing so

sometimes, sometimes not.[805] The cause of not being a superfetator is
being uniparous. For the solid-hoofed animals and those larger than   35
these do not superfetate. For because of their size the residue gets used   773ᵇ1
up by the [one] embryo. For all these have large bodies, and of large
animals the fetuses are large in proportion (*logos*). That is why too the
fetus of elephants is as big as a calf. The multiparous animals, though,   5
do superfetate, because where there is more than one [fetus], one is a
superfetation of the other.

Of these, the ones that are large, such as a human, if the one mating occurs soon after the other, it brings the second embryo to birth.
For cases of this sort have already been seen to occur. The cause is that
just stated. For even in a single act of sexual intercourse the seed emit-   10
ted is more than enough, and when it is divided up it produces many
offspring, one later than the other. But when the embryo has already
[somewhat] grown and it so happens that mating occurs [again], superfetation sometimes takes place, although rarely, because the uterus
generally closes up in women while they are gestating. But if ever this   15
does happen (and in fact it has been known to occur), completion [of
the second embryo] is impossible, instead [such] embryos fall out in
about the same condition as so-called premature births.[806] For just as
in the case of the uniparous animals, because of their magnitude, all
the residues go to the pre-existing [embryo], so it is here too, except
that there it is so from the outset, whereas here it is when the embryo   20
has [somewhat] grown. For then they are in about the same condition
as uniparous animals. Similarly, because the human is by nature multiparous, and because there is something to spare both in the size of the
uterus and the quantity of the residue (though not enough to bring a
second embryo to birth), the only animals that admit of mating while
gestating are woman and mare, the first due to the cause just stated, the   25
mare both because of the barrenness of its nature and because there is
something to spare in the size of its uterus, which, though it has room
for more than one, is too small to superfetate another one completely).

And the mare is by nature overly eager for sexual intercourse
because they are affected in the same way as sterile females. For the latter are barren because a [menstrual] purgation does not occur (which   30
corresponds to ejaculation in males), and female horses emit very little
purgation.[807] And in all the viviparous animals the barren females are
overly eager for sexual intercourse because their condition is about the
same as that of males when the seed has collected [in the testes] but
has not been secreted. For the purgation of the menses in females is the   35
emission of seed. For the menses is seed that is non-concocted, as was   774ᵃ1
said previously.[808] That is also why those women who lack self-control

153

in relation to sexual intercourse of this sort, when they have borne many children, cease from their passionate excitement. For when the spermatic residue has been excreted it no longer produces an appetite for sexual intercourse. Among birds the females are less overly eager for sexual intercourse than the males because they have the uterus up near the diaphragm, whereas with the males things are the contrary way. For their testes are drawn up within them, so that if any genus of such animals by nature produces a lot of seed, it is always in need of sexual intercourse. In the females, then, it is the coming down of the uterus, and in the males the drawing up of the testes, that is farther along the route to mating.[809]

Due to what cause, then, some animals do not superfetate at all, while others sometimes bring the embryos to birth and sometimes do not, and due to what cause some are overly eager for sexual intercourse, others not overly eager for sexual intercourse, has now been stated.

Some of the animals that superfetate are capable of bringing the embryos to birth even when much time elapses between the matings, namely, those of a genus that produces a lot of seed, does not have a large body, and is among the multiparous animals. For because of their multiparity their uterus is spacious, because of producing a lot of seed they emit much residue for purgation, and because their body is not large, but the purgation exceeds by a large ratio (*logos*) the nourishment that goes to the embryo, they are capable both of composing the animals to a later point and of bringing them to birth. Further, the uterus in animals of this sort does not close up [during gestation] because of the spare residue for purgation.[810] This has been known to happen even in the case of women. For in some of them the purgation occurs even through to the end of pregnancy. But in these it is contrary to nature (which is why it harms the embryo), whereas in these other animals it is in accord with nature. For their body is composed in this way from the start—for example, that of hares. For this animal superfetates. For it is not one of the large animals, is multiparous (for it is multi-split-footed, and the multi-split-footed ones are multiparous), and produces a lot of seed. Their hairiness makes this clear. For the quantity of their hairs is excessive. For it alone of the animals has hairs under its feet and inside the jaws.[811] And hairiness is a sign of a large quantity of residue, which is why among human beings too the hairy ones are overly eager for sexual intercourse and produce more seed than smooth ones. As for the hare, it often has some embryos that are incomplete, but delivers others of its young complete.

IV 6

Of the viviparous ones some deliver animals that are incomplete, others animals that are complete; the solid-hoofed and cloven-hoofed animals deliver complete ones, most of the multi-split-footed animals incomplete ones. The cause of this is that the solid-hoofed ones are uniparous, the cloven-hoofed uniparous or biparous for the most part, and it is easy to bring the few to birth. But of the multi-split-footed animals that produce incomplete offspring all are multiparous. That is why, though they are capable of nourishing the embryos when they are young, but their bodies, once these embryos have grown somewhat and have attained some size, are incapable of nourishing them, and deliver them just as the larviparous animals do. And in fact some of them are pretty much non-articulated when generated, as are fox, bear, lion, and, in about the same way, some of the others. And pretty much all of them are blind—for example, not only the former ones but also, further, dog, wolf, and jackal. The pig alone is multiparous and produces complete offspring, and it alone overlaps [genera]. For it is multiparous like the multi-split-footed animals, but is solid-hoofed and cloven-hoofed (for solid-hoofed pigs exist in certain places).[812] They are multiparous, then, because the nourishment that goes to size [is diverted] to the secretion of spermatic residue (for considered as a solid-hoofed animal, the pig is not large in size), and at the same time—as if disputing the nature of the solid-hoofed ones—it is more often cloven-hoofed. Because of this, then, it is sometimes uniparous, sometimes biparous, but most often multiparous, and brings these to birth because of the good condition of its body. For it has sufficient and plentiful nourishment as rich soil does for plants.

Some birds produce incomplete and blind young, namely, the ones that are multiparous, though not having large bodies themselves (for example, crow, jay, sparrows, swallows) and those of the oligoparous ones that do not produce plentiful nourishment in the egg along with the young (for example, ring-dove, turtledove, and pigeon). And because of this if one puts out the eyes of swallows while they are still young they heal again. For the birds are still developing when they are injured, not yet developed, which is why they grow and sprout from the starting-point. And, in general, [a bird] is born prior to being completely produced, because of the inability to nourish them, and they are born incomplete because of that priority. This is clear too in the case of seven-months children. For in some of them, because they are not complete, even the ducts—for example, of the ears and nostrils—are often not yet articulated, but become articulated as the children grow. And many such children live on.

In human beings more males are born deformed than females, in the other animals, not at all so. The cause is that in human beings the male is much different from the female in the hotness of its nature, which is why male embryos move about more than female ones, and because of their movement they get more damaged. For what is young is prone to destruction because of its weakness. And it is due to this same cause too that female ones are not completed in a similar way to male ones in the case of female human beings, whereas in other animals they are completed in a similar way. For in them the female in no way much lags behind the male, as in the case of female human beings. For while within the mother, the female takes more time to become disaggregated than the male does, but once having come out everything gets completed earlier in females than in males—for example, puberty, prime of life, and old age.[813] For females are weaker and colder in nature, and we must suppose femaleness to be a natural deformation.[814] While it is within the mother, then, it gets disaggregated slowly because of its coldness (for disaggregation is concoction, it is heat that concocts, and what is hotter is easily concocted), but outside, because of its weakness, it quickly reaches its prime and old age.[815] For all inferior things reach the end more quickly, and just as they do in works that are in accord with craft, so they do too in those composed due to nature. And due to the cause just mentioned twins in human beings are also less likely to survive if they are male and female, in other animals not at all so. For in human beings it is contrary to nature for these to run an equal course, as their disaggregation does not occur in equal times; rather [if it did] it is necessary that the male be late or the female early.[816] In the other animals, though, it is not contrary to nature.

A difference also exists between human beings and other animals where gestation is concerned. For animals are in a more thriving bodily condition most of the time, whereas most women feel discomfort in connection with gestation. Now a cause of these things is also their way of life. For because they are sedentary they are filled with a greater quantity of residue, seeing that in those nations in which the life of women involves hard work, gestation is not equally obvious, and they give birth easily there, and wherever they are accustomed to hard work.[817] For hard work uses up the residues, whereas in the sedentary women a large quantity of such residues is present due to the absence of hard work and because no purgations are produced during gestation—and so childbirth is painful. But hard work exercises their pneuma so that they are capable of holding it, and in this the ease or difficulty of childbirth lies.[818]

These things, then, as was just said, contribute to the difference in how other animals and women are affected, but the most important cause is that in some animals little purgation is produced, and in others it is not obvious at all, whereas in women much more is produced than in animals, so that when, due to gestation, its excretion does not occur, it produces disturbance. For even if they are not gestating, when the purgations do not occur, diseases result. And most women are more troubled when they first conceive. For while the embryo is capable of preventing the purgations, because of its smallness it does not use up the residue in any quantity at first, but later on, when it takes its share, it eases the trouble. (In the other animals, however, because there is little [residue] it is proportional to the growth of their embryos, and as the residues that hinder growth get used up, their bodies are in better condition. And in aquatic animals and birds it is the same way.) But if by the time the embryos become big the mothers' body is no longer to be in thriving condition, the cause is that the growth of the fetus needs more nourishment than is provided by the residue. In some few women, however, their bodily condition is better during gestation— these are the ones in whose bodies the amount of residues is small, so that they get used up along with the nourishment that goes to the embryo.

IV 7

We must also speak about what is called a mole, which occurs rarely in women, but this affection does occur in some gestating ones.[819] For they produce what they call a mole. For it has been known to happen to a certain woman who had had sexual intercourse with a man, and supposed that she had conceived, that at first the bulk of her abdomen grew, and all the other things occurred in accord with reason (*logos*), yet when it was the time for the birth, she neither gave birth nor did her bulk become smaller, but instead continued in this condition for three or four years until dysentery came on, endangering her life, and she produced the fleshy mass they call a mole. In some cases too this affection continues into old age and lasts until death. The masses that come out in cases of this sort become so hard that they can scarcely be cut in two even with iron. (The cause of this affection has been spoken about in the *Problems*.[820] For the embryo is affected in the very same way in the uterus as par-boiled things are in cases of boiling, and not

776ᵃ1 because of the hotness, as some people say, but rather because of the weakness of the hotness.[821] For the nature seems to be weak and not capable of completing or putting a limit to the process of generation. That is why too the mole remains in them into old age or for a long
5 time. For it has neither the nature of something completed nor of an altogether foreign body.) For of its hardness non-concoction is the cause. For par-boiling too is a sort of non-concoction.[822]

The puzzle it involves, though, is that of why on earth this does not occur in other animals, unless it does but has entirely escaped notice. We must consider the cause to be that woman alone among
10 the animals is subject to troubles of the uterus, that is, where the purgations are concerned, she is excessively productive, and is incapable of concocting these.[823] When, then, the embryo is composed of a liquid that is difficult to concoct a so-called mole is produced in these women—quite reasonably in these alone, or most of all in these.

IV 8

15 Milk is produced in whichever females are internally viviparous as something useful at the time of birth. For nature has made it for the sake of nourishment for animals externally, so that it is neither at all deficient nor at all excessive in this time period. For this is just what we see happening unless something contrary to nature occurs. Now in the
20 other animals, because there is a single period of gestation, the time for the concoction of milk is in all cases related to it. But in human beings, since there are several periods, it is necessary for it to be present at the first one; that is why milk is useless before the seventh month in women, and then at that point becomes useful. But it also quite reason-
25 ably happens due to an of-necessity cause that it is concocted [only] in the final stages.[824] For at first the secretion of this sort of residue is used up for the generation of the fetus. Of all [secretions], though, nourishment is the sweetest and most concocted, so that when a capacity of this sort is subtracted it is necessary for what remains to be salty and
30 ill-flavored.[825] But when embryos are becoming complete, the surplus residue is greater (for less of it gets used up) and sweeter, since the well-concocted part is not being subtracted to the same extent. For it is
35 no longer going toward the molding of the fetus. For there is a sort of completion even of an embryo. That is why it comes out and changes
776ᵇ1 its process of generation, as now having the things that are its own, and no longer getting the things that are not its own, which is the time in which milk becomes useful.[826]

It is in the upper part and the breasts that milk collects because of the order of composition from the starting-point. For what is above the diaphragm is the controlling part of the animal, whereas the one below is for the nourishment and the residue, in order that those animals capable of perambulation have within them a self-sufficiency of nourishment for change from place to place.[827] From the former too the spermatic residue is secreted, due to the cause mentioned in the starting accounts.[828] But both the residue of the male and the menses of the female are of a sanguineous nature, and the starting-point of this and of the blood-vessels is the heart. And it is situated in these parts. That is why it is first there that it is necessary for a change in these residues to become obvious. It is why indeed the voices change both of males and of females when they start to bear seed (for the starting-point of the voice is there, and itself becomes altered when what moves it becomes altered).[829] And the parts around the breasts become raised up in an obvious way even in males, but more so in females. For because the excretion downward becomes great the place of the breasts becomes empty and spongy in them—and likewise in the other animals that have their breasts down below.

Now the change both in the voice and in the parts around the breasts even in the other animals becomes obvious to those who have experience with each genus, but the difference is greatest in the case of human beings. The cause is that the production of residue in proportion to size among females is greatest in these females, and among males in these males—in the former the menses, in the latter emission of seed.[830] When, then, the fetus does not take up this sort of secretion, yet prevents it from getting outside, it is necessary for all the residue to collect in those empty places that are situated on the same ducts. And in each [genus of animal] the place of the breasts is of this sort due to both causes, becoming of this sort both for the sake of the better and of necessity. It is there, then, that the concocted nourishment for [newborn] animals is at this time composed. And because of its concoction, it is possible to take either the one just mentioned, or even the contrary.[831] For it is also reasonable for the fetus, since it is larger, to take up more nourishment, so that the surplus is less around this time—and less is concocted more quickly.

That milk has the same nature as the secretion from which each animal comes to be is clear, and was stated previously.[832] For the same matter both nourishes and is what the nature composes [the animal] from in the process of generation. This is the sanguineous liquid in the blooded animals. For milk is blood that is concocted but not corrupted. As for

Empedocles, either he has interpreted things incorrectly or employed a bad metaphor when he wrote in his poem that milk is

> A white pus that comes into existence on the tenth day of the eighth
> 10   month.[833]

For putrefaction and concoction are contrary, and pus is a certain sort of putrefaction, whereas milk is concocted.

The purgations, when in accord with nature, neither occur when women are suckling children nor do they conceive when they are suckling. And if they do conceive, the milk dries up because the nature of
15 the milk is the same as that of the menses. And nature is not capable of being so productive as to play a double game; rather if the secretion occurs in one direction it is necessary for it to fail in the other, unless
20 something comes about that is forced and contrary to the nature that holds for the most part.

The process of generation of animal has also been well distinguished into periods of time. For when the nourishment coming through the umbilical cord is no longer sufficient for the embryo, because of its size, at the same time the milk is produced as something useful for becoming its nourishment.[834] And when the nourishment does not
25 enter through the umbilical cord these blood-vessels, which what is called the umbilical cord surrounds like a membrane, collapse. And because of these things and at this time the [offspring's] exit to the outside results.

IV 9

Head first is the process of generation that is in accord with nature for all animals, because the parts above the umbilical cord are larger than
30 those below. Being attached to it, then, as to the beam of a balance, they incline toward the weightier side. And the larger parts have more weight.

IV 10

The periods of gestation for each of the animals are for the most part determined in accord with their lives. For it is reasonable for the processes of generation for the longer-lived ones to be longer. Nonetheless,
35 *this* is not the cause, although it is what for the most part happens. For
777^b1 though the larger and more complete of the blooded animals do also live a long time, nonetheless the larger ones are not all longer-lived. For

the human is the longest-lived of them all except the elephant, so far as we have any reliable experience. And yet the genus of human beings is smaller than that of those with long hairs in their tails, and many others.[835] The cause, though, of long life in any sort of animal is its being blended in much the same way as the surrounding air, and because of certain other coincidents of its nature that we will speak about later on.[836] But for the times of gestation the cause is the size of the things being generated. For it is not easy for large compositions to reach their completion in a short time, whether they are animals or (one might almost say) anything else whatsoever. That is why horses and animals of the same genus (*suggenês*) as these, although living a shorter time [than human beings] gestate a longer time. For in the former birth is in a year, but in the latter in ten months at the most. And due to the same cause birth in the case of elephants is in a long period of time. For their gestation lasts two years because of their excessive size.

It is quite reasonably the case that in all animals the times of gestation, of the process of generation, and of lifespan tend in accord with nature to be measured in periods. By a period I mean a day, a night, a month, a year, and the greater periods of time measured by these; further, the periods of the moon. The periods of the moon are full moon, [completely] waning moon, and the dichotomies of the intermediate times. For it is in accord with these that it contributes in connection with the sun. For the month is a period common to both.[837] And the moon for its part is a starting-point because of its connection with the sun and its participation in the sun's light. For it becomes like another sun, a lesser one.

That is why it contributes to all processes of generation and processes of completing. For hotness and coldness, up to a certain proportion, produce the processes of generation, and afterward those of passing away. And it is the movements of these stars that fix the limit, both the starting-point and the end-point, of these processes. For just as we see the sea, and all of what is of the nature of liquids, to be settling or changing in accord with the movement of the winds, and the air and the winds in accord with the period of the sun and the moon, so too the things that grow out of these or are in these necessarily follow along.[838] For it is in accord with reason (*logos*) for the periods of things that are more lacking in control to follow along with those of the things that have more control.[839] For a wind too has a sort of life and a coming to be and passing away.[840] And of the revolutions of these stars there may perhaps be other starting-points.[841]

Nature, then, tends to measure comings to be and endings by the number of these revolutions, but cannot bring this about in an exact way because of the indefiniteness of matter, and because many starting-points exist that impede their comings to be and passings away from being in accord with nature, and often cause things to happen contrary to nature.[842]

10 The internal [to the mother] nourishment of animals and the external have now been spoken about, both about each separately and about all in common.

Book V

V 1

We must now get a theoretical grasp on the affections by which the parts of animals differ. I mean the following sorts of affections of the parts: blueness and blackness of eyes, height and depth of voice, and differences of color, whether of body and hairs or of feathers.[843] Of these sorts of affections, some are found existing throughout a whole genus, others in a random manner—for example, this happens most of all in the case of human beings. Further, in connection with the changes belonging to [different] times of life, some belong alike to all animals, whereas others do so in contrary ways, as in what has to do with the voice and the color of hair. For some do not go noticeably gray toward old age, while the human is more affected by this than any of the other animals. Also, some of these affections follow along immediately after birth, while others become clear as age advances, or in old age.

Where these affections and all the others of these sorts are concerned, however, we must no longer consider the mode of cause to be the same.[844] For none of the things that are not works of the nature, whether common or special to a given genus, either exists or comes to be for the sake of something. For though the eye is for the sake of something, it is not blue for the sake of anything, unless this affection is special to the genus. Nor, in some cases, does the affection lead to the account (*logos*) of the substance, but rather, as coming of necessity, one must refer to the matter and the moving starting-point as the causes.[845] For just as was said at the start in the first accounts, it is not because each thing comes to be of a certain sort that it is of a certain sort, when the things are ordered and determined works of nature, but rather it is because they are of *this* sort that they become of this *sort*.[846] For the coming to be follows along with the substance and is for the sake of the substance, and not for the sake of the coming to be.[847] (The ancient physicists, however, thought the contrary to be so. The cause of this is that they did not see that the causes were many, but saw only that consisting of the matter and that of the movement—and these indistinctly. But to that consisting of the account (*logos*) and that of the end they gave no consideration.[848])

Although each of the relevant things, then, is for the sake of something, it is generated at this point due to this cause and due to the remaining ones, which are present in the account (*logos*) of each thing, either as being for-the-sake-of-something or as being for-the-sake-of-which.[849] On the other hand, for things not of this sort but of which there is a process of generation, at this point the cause must be sought in the movement and in the process of generation, on the supposition that it is in the process of composition itself that they acquire what is different about them. For though an animal will of necessity have an eye (for it is hypothesized as being an animal of *this* sort), and of necessity an eye of *this* sort, the necessity is not of the same sort, but is a different mode [of necessity], namely, that is naturally such as to affect in *this* sort of way or to be affected in *this* sort of way.

Having drawn these distinctions let us speak about the things that come next in order. First, then, in the case of all animals, when the young are born, especially those born incomplete, they are in the habit of sleeping, because inside the mother too, when they first acquire perception, they are continually asleep.[850] —But there is a puzzle about the start of the process of generation as to whether wakefulness belongs to animals first or sleep does. For because it is evident that as they grow older they become more awake, it is reasonable that the contrary belong to them at the start of the process of generation, namely, sleep. Further, because the change from not being to being takes place through the intermediate, and sleep seems to be in nature among the things of this sort, being as it were a boundary between living and not living, a sleeper neither fully is not nor fully is. For living most of all belongs to being awake, because of perception.[851] On the other side, if it is necessary for an animal to have perception, and if the time it is first an animal is when perception first takes place, then we must consider its condition at the start to be not sleep but something resembling sleep, a condition of the very sort that the plant genus is also in. For at this time animals too are living the life of a plant. But for sleep to belong to plants is impossible. For there is no sleep from which it is impossible to awake, and from the affection of plants that is the analogue of sleep it is impossible to awake.—It is necessary in any case for these animals to sleep most of the time because the growth and the heaviness lie in the upper places (we have said elsewhere that this is the cause of sleep).[852] Nonetheless, it is evident that they wake up even in the uterus (this is clear in dissections and in the oviparous animals), and then immediately fall asleep again.[853] That is why when they have come out [of the mother] too they spend most of their time asleep.

Also, when they are awake infants do not laugh, but while asleep they both cry and laugh. For perceptions occur in animals even when they sleep, not only in so-called dreams, but also outside dreams, as in

the case of those who get up and do many things without dreaming. 15
For there are some who get up while sleeping and walk about, seeing
just like those who are awake. For perception of what is happening
occurs in these, though they are not awake, yet not as a dream does.
But infants, it seems, as if not knowing how to be awake, because of
being accustomed to it, perceive and live in their sleep. But as time 20
goes on and the growth changes over to the lower part, they at this
point wake up more and spend most of their time this way. At first,
though, they are more continually asleep than the other animals. For
they are born more incomplete than any other complete-at-birth animal and having growth most of all in the upper part of the body. 25

The eyes of all children are bluish immediately after birth, but later
on they change to what is going to be their natural color for them. But
in the case of the other animals this does not noticeably occur. The
cause of this is that the eyes of other animals are more of one color— 30
for example, oxen are dark-eyed, the eye of all sheep is pale gray, of
others again the whole genus is bluish-gray or blue, and some are
greenish, like the majority of the goat genus itself.[854] Those of human
beings, on the other hand, are of many colors. For they are blue, gray,
or dark in some cases, and others are greenish. So in the case of the 35
other animals, just as the individuals do not differ from each other in
this way, they do not from themselves [at different times] either. For   779^{b}1
they are not of a nature to have eyes of more than one color. But, of the
other animals, it is most of all the horse that has eyes of many colors.
For some of them in fact have eyes of different colors.[855] None of the
other animals is noticeably affected in this way, although some human
beings do have eyes of odd colors. 5

Well, we must think the following a sufficient cause of the eyes of
the other animals, young or old, not noticeably changing, but of this
occurring in the case of infants, that in the former this part is of one
color, while in the latter it is of more than one color. On the other hand,
of their being bluish and not having some other color, the cause is that 10
the parts of young infants are weaker [than those of adults], and blueness is a sort of weakness.[856]

We must, however, get a universal grasp, where the differences in
eyes are concerned, on the cause due to which some are blue, some
grayish-blue, some greenish, and some dark. To suppose that the blue
are fiery, as Empedocles says, while the dark contain more water than 15
fire, and that because of this blue ones do not see keenly in the daytime,
due to their deficiency of water, while the others do not do so at night,
due to their deficiency of fire, is not to state things correctly, if indeed
the organ of sight consists in all cases not of fire but of water. Further, it

20   is also possible to assign the cause for their colors in another way. No, rather, if indeed, it is as we stated previously in *De Sensu*, and prior to that in *De Anima*, namely, that this organ of perception is composed of water (and is composed of water and not of air or fire due to the

25   specified cause), then this must be supposed to be the cause of what was just mentioned.[857] For some eyes contain too much liquid, others too little, to be proportional to the movement, others the proportional amount.[858] Those, then, that contain too much liquid are dark because a large quantity of liquid is not easy to see through, while those that

30   contain little are blue, as is evident in the case of the sea. For the part of it that is easy to see through appears blue, the less so pale-gray, and the part that is not determined because of its depth appears black or dark-blue. As for the eyes intermediate between these, they differ at this point by the more and the less.[859]

        And the same cause, one must suppose, is also the cause of blue eyes

35   not being as keen-sighted in daytime, dark eyes at night. For blue ones,

780ᵃ1   because of the small amount of liquid, are—insofar as they are liquid, that is, transparent—moved too much by the light and by visible objects. And sight is the movement of this part insofar as it is transparent, but not insofar as it is liquid. Dark eyes, on the other hand, because of their large quantity of liquid, are moved less. For the light is weaker

5   by night, and at the same time indeed liquid in general becomes more difficult to move in the night.[860] The eye itself, then, must neither not be moved at all nor, insofar as it is transparent, be moved too much. For the stronger movement knocks aside the weaker one.[861] That is why on changing from [looking at] strong colors people do not see, or

10   on going out of the sun into the dark. For being strong, the movement pre-existing in the eye, hinders the one coming from outside—and, in general, neither strong nor weak sight is capable of seeing bright things because the liquid is affected and moved too much.

        This is made clear too by infirmities of each sort of sight. For glau-

15   coma occurs more often in those who are blue-eyed, so-called night-blindness in those who are dark-eyed. Glaucoma for its part is a sort of dryness of the eyes, which is why it occurs more in those who are getting old. For like the rest of the body these parts too become dry

20   toward old age. Night-blindness by contrast is an excess of liquidity, which is why it occurs more often in the young. For the brain of these is more liquid.

        The one that is intermediate between little and much liquid is the best sight. For it is neither so small that it gets disturbed and hinders the movement of the colors, nor so large in quantity that it is made difficult to move.[862]

But it is not only those just mentioned that are causes of dullness or   25
keenness of sight, but also the nature of the skin on the so-called eye-
jelly.[863] For this must be transparent, and it is necessary for something
of this sort to be fine, white, and even: fine, in order that movement
from outside may pass straight through; even, in order that its wrin-
kling not produce a shadow (for it is also because of this that old peo-   30
ple do not have keen sight—for like the rest of the skin that of the eye
also becomes wrinkled and coarser grained in old age); white, because
black is not transparent—for this is what black is, namely, the non-
transparent.[864] That is why even lanterns cannot give light if they are   35
made of black skin.

In old age and during the diseases in question, then, these are the
causes due to which sight is not keen; but the eyes of children appear   **780^b1**
blue at first, because of the smallness of their liquid.

And eyes of different colors come about especially in human beings
and horses due to the same cause as the one due to which the human
alone turns gray, and among the other animals the horse alone has
hairs that whiten noticeably in old age.[865] For greyness is a sort of   5
weakness and non-concoction of the liquid in the brain, as is blueness
of the eyes. For very fine-grained and very coarse-grained liquid have
the same capacity, the one as too little liquid, the other as too much
liquid. When, then, the nature is incapable of producing an even result,
whether by similarly concocting, or not concocting, the liquid in both   10
eyes, but instead concocts the one and not the other, then eyes of different colors come about.

The cause of some animals being keen-sighted and others not is of
two modes. For "keen" is said of things in pretty much two ways (as it
likewise is where hearing and smelling are concerned). For something   15
is said to see keenly in one way when it is capable of seeing what is far
away, in another way when it is capable of distinctly perceiving the
differences in the things being seen. And these capacities do not occur
together in the same individuals. For the same individual, if he shades
his eyes with his hand or looks through a tube, in no way discerns the
differences in colors either more or less well, but he does see farther. At   20
any rate, from pits and wells people sometimes see the stars. So if any of
the animals has brows projecting out a lot above its eyes, but the liquid
in the eye-jelly is not pure or proportional to the movement from outside, and the skin on its surface is not fine, this animal will not discern
the differences in colors in an exact way, but it will be capable of seeing   25
farther better than those having pure liquid and a [fine] covering, but
having no brows at all projecting over the eyes.[866] For of being keen in
this way, namely, so as to distinctly perceive the differences in colors,

30

it is in the eye itself that the cause lies. For just as on a pure [white] cloak even small stains are clearly visible, so in a pure organ of sight even small movements are clear and produce perception. But of seeing things far away and of the movements coming to the eyes from objects

35

far away, the position of the eyes is cause. For animals with prominent eyes do not see well from far away, whereas those with eyes situated in

781ᵃ1

a cavity are able to see things at a distance because the movement is not dispersed into the open but comes straight to the eye. For it makes no difference whether we say, as some do, that seeing is due to the ray of sight going out from the eye (for if there is nothing projecting over the eyes, it is necessary for the ray of sight to be dispersed, for less of it to

5

fall on the things being seen, and for the ones far away to be seen less well) or that seeing is due to the movement coming from the things being seen.⁸⁶⁷ For it is necessary for the ray of sight to resemble the movement. Things far away, then, would be seen best if there were a sort of continuous tube straight from the organ of sight to the thing being seen. For then the movement from visible objects would not be

10

dispersed; otherwise, the farther the tube extends, the more exact it is necessary for the seeing of faraway things to be.

Let these, then, be the causes of the difference in eyes.

V 2

It is the same way too where hearing and smell are concerned. For in

15

one way exactly hearing and smelling is perceiving all the differences in the underlying perceptible objects and perceiving them as well as possible, and, in another way, it is hearing and smelling from far away. Of discerning the differences correctly, then, the perceptual organ is the cause, as in the case of sight, insofar as it itself and the membrane around it are pure.⁸⁶⁸

20

For the ducts of all the perceptual organs, as has been said previously in *De Sensu*, run to the heart, or to its analogue in animals that have no heart.⁸⁶⁹ That of hearing, then, since the sense organ is composed of air, comes to an end where the connate pneuma produces in

25

some animals the beating of the heart and in others breathing.⁸⁷⁰ It is because of this too that learning comes about from what is said, so that we echo what we have heard.⁸⁷¹ For in these cases the movement that entered through the sense organ is of the sort that occurs again, since it is, as it were, of one and the same stamp as the movement that

30

comes about because of the voice, so that what was heard is what was said. Also, people hear less well while yawning or exhaling than when inhaling because the starting-point of the perceptual organ is situated near the pneumatic part and is shaken and moved at the same time as the instrument moves the pneuma.[872] For while moving it the instrument [or organ] is itself moved.[873] (And in wet seasons and blends [of the surrounding air] the affection is the same.[874]) And the ears seem to be filled with pneuma because of being a neighbor, due to the starting-point, of the pneumatic place.[875]

Exactness in discerning the differences of sounds and smells, then, depends on the purity of the perceptual organ and of the membrane on its surface. For then all the movements are distinguished in their cases too, as in the case of sight.[876]

Perception and non-perception from far away also occur in the same way as in the case of sight. For animals that have passages, as it were, passing through the relevant parts, that project a long way in front of the organ of perception, are the ones capable of perceiving from far away. That is why all animals whose nostrils are long, like Laconian hounds, are keen-scented.[877] For since the organ of perception is above them, movements from far away are not broken up but go straight through, which is just what happens when we shade our eyes with our hands.[878] It is likewise too in the case of those animals whose ears are long and jut far out like the eaves of a house, of the sort some quadrupeds have, and within which the helical passage is long. For these too catch the movement from afar and deliver it to the organ of perception.

Among animals in proportion to their size exactness of the perceptual capacities from far away is possessed (one might almost say) least in the human, but where differences are concerned he is the most capable of all of perceiving them well. The cause is that the organ of perception is pure, that is, least earthy and body-like, and by nature, among animals with respect to size, man has the finest skin.[879]

In matters concerning the seal too the nature has produced things in a quite reasonable way.[880] For although it is a viviparous quadruped it has no ears, but ducts alone. The cause of this is that its life is spent in a liquid. For the ears are a part added to the ducts to preserve the movement of the air from far away. They are of no use to it, then, but rather would even produce the contrary result by receiving a quantity of water into itself.

Seeing, hearing, and smelling have now been spoken about.

V 3

As for various sorts of hair, human beings differ in this themselves in accord with their times of life, and also from whatever genera of other animals have hair. And those that have it are pretty much all the internally viviparous ones. For even the spiny ones among these must be considered as having a form (*eidos*) of hair—for example, the spines of hedgehogs and of any other of this sort that is among the viviparous ones.[881]

782^{a}1   Hairs differ with respect to hardness and softness, length and shortness, straightness and curliness, abundance and sparseness, and in addition to these, with respect to their colors, whiteness and blackness, and the ones intermediate between these.[882] In the case of these differences animals also differ in accord with their times of life, youth and more advanced age. This is especially visible in the case of human beings. For the hairs get coarser as age advances, and some go bald in the front of the head. Also, children do not go bald, nor do women, but men do so by the time they begin to age. Also, human beings go gray on the head as they grow old, whereas this (one might almost say) never noticeably occurs in any of the other animals, though, of the others, the horse does so most. Also, though human beings go bald on the front of their head, they go gray on the temples first; no one goes bald on these or on the back of the head. As for those animals that do not have hairs but their analogue, for example, birds have feathers, and the fish genus scales, in them some of these sorts of affections come about, in accord with the same account (*logos*).

What nature has produced the genus of hairs for the sake of in animals has been spoken about previously in the causes pertaining to the parts of animals.[883] But to show due to what pre-existing things and what necessities each of these genera occurs belongs to the present methodical inquiry.[884]

Of hairs being coarse or fine, then, the principal cause is the skin. For in some animals it is coarse-grained, in others fine-grained, and in some rarified, in others dense.[885] Further, a contributing cause is the difference of the included liquid. For in some it is oily, in others watery. For in general the underlying nature of the skin is earthy. For being on the surface it becomes solid and earthy as the liquid evaporates. But both hairs and their analogue come not from the flesh but from the skin, when the liquid evaporates and is exhaled in these. That is why coarse hairs come from coarse skin, fine hairs from fine skin.[886] If, then, the skin is more rarified and more coarse, the hairs are coarse because of the large quantity of earthy material and because of the large size

782^{b}1   of the ducts [or pores], whereas if it is denser, they are fine because of the narrowness of the pores. Further, if the liquid is watery it dries up more quickly and the hairs do not get large in size, but if it is oily, the contrary occurs. For what is oily does not easily get dry.[887]

That is why animals with more coarser skin generally have hairs that are coarser. Nonetheless, the ones with skin that is most coarse do not have hairs that are more coarse [than others with such skin], due to the causes just mentioned—for example, the pig genus in relation to that of oxen, to elephants, and to many others.[888] And due to the same cause too the hairs in human beings are most coarse on the head. For the skin on it is coarsest and lies over a very great quantity of liquid, and furthermore is very rarified.[889]

The cause of hairs being long or short is the evaporating liquid not being [or being] easily dried up. And of its not being easily dried up there are two causes: its quantity and its quality. For if the liquid is large in amount, it does not dry up easily, nor if it is oily. And because of this in human beings the hairs coming from the head are longest. For the brain, being wet and cold, provides an abundance of liquid.

Straight hairs and curly hairs are due to the exhalation in the hairs.[890] For if it is smoky, it is hot and dry and makes the hair curly. For the hair gets bent due to being spatially moved with two spatial movements. For the earthy [dry] part spatially moves downward, the hot upward. And being easily bent because of its weakness it gets twisted. And this is what curliness of the hair is. It is possible, then, to grasp the cause in this way, but it is also possible that, because of containing little liquid and much earthy material, it gets dried due to the surrounding air and curls up. For what is straight becomes bent if its liquid evaporates and it shrinks up like a hair burning on a fire, implying that curliness is a contraction because of a deficiency of liquid due to the surrounding heat. A sign of this is the fact that curly hairs are harder than straight. For a dry thing is hard. And those animals that have a lot of liquid are straight-haired. For the liquid advances as a stream, not in drops. And that is why the Scythians on the Black Sea and the Thracians are straight-haired. For both they themselves and the air surrounding them are wet, whereas the Ethiopians and those in hot countries are curly-haired. For their brains and the surrounding air are dry.

Some of the animals with coarse skin, however, have fine hair, due to the cause just mentioned. For the finer the ducts [or pores] are, the finer it is necessary for the hairs to be. That is why the sheep genus has such hairs. For wool is a large number of hairs.

And there are some animals whose hair, though soft, is less fine— for example, the hare genus compared to that of the sheep. For the hair of such animals is on the surface of the skin [not deeply rooted in it]. That is why it is not long but is about the same as the scrapings from linen cloths. For these too have no length, but are soft and cannot be used for weaving.

Sheep in cold climates, though, are affected in the contrary way to human beings. For while the Scythians are soft-haired, Sarmatian sheep are hard-haired.[891] The cause of this is the same as in the case of all wild animals. For the cold hardens and solidifies by drying. For as the heat is squeezed out the liquid evaporates, and both the hair and the skin become earthy and hard. The cause, though, in the case of wild animals is their outdoor life, whereas in the others it is the place being of the sort it is. A sign of this is also what happens in the case of sea-urchins that are used to treat stranguries.[892] For these too, though small themselves, have long, hard spines due to the sea they are in being cold because of its depth (for they are found at sixty fathoms and even more). The spines are long, because the growth of the body is diverted to them (for being animals that are low in heat, and so not concocting the nourishment very much, they contain a lot of residue, and spines, hairs, and things of this sort are produced from residue), whereas they are hard and petrified because of the cold and its congealing effect. In the same way plants too are harder, earthier, and more petrified in north-facing or windy locations than in south-facing or sheltered ones. For they all get more chilled and their liquid evaporates.

Something is hardened, then, both by heat and by cold. For the liquid is evaporated due to both—intrinsically by heat, coincidentally by cold (for the liquid goes out along with the heat; for there is no liquid without heat).[893] But whereas cold not only hardens but condenses, heat makes more rarified.[894]

Due to the same cause, as animals grow older, the hairs become harder in those that have hairs, and the feathers and scales in the feathered and scaly ones. For their skins become harder and more coarse as they get older. For they become dry, and old age (*gêras*), in keeping with the name, is earthy (*geêron*) because the heat is failing and the liquid along with it.

Most of all the animals human beings go noticeably bald, although an affection of this sort is something universal. For among the plants too some are evergreen, others deciduous, and among the birds the hibernating ones shed their feathers.[895] Baldness in the case of human beings who happen to go bald is an affection of this sort. For a partial shedding of leaves occurs in all plants, and of feathers and hairs in those that have them, but it is when this affection comes about in all of them at once, it gets the names just mentioned. For then something is said to go bald, to shed its leaves, or to molt. The cause of the affection is a deficiency of hot liquid, and the oily ones among the liquids are

most of all of this sort.[896] That is why among the plants the oily ones
are more evergreen. (But the cause of this must be spoken about elsewhere.[897] For there are in fact other contributing causes of this affec-   20
tion in these.) And it is in winter that the affection occurs in plants
(for this change of season has more control than time of life), and in
animals that hibernate (for these too are in nature less hot and wet
than human beings). Human beings, on the other hand, pass through   25
winter and summer in correspondence with their ages.

That is why before the time of sexual intercourse no one becomes
bald, and why at that time it is in those of the sort whose nature is more
eager for it. For by nature the brain is the coldest part of the body, and
sexual intercourse makes one cold. For it is in fact the secretion of pure
natural heat. Quite reasonably, then, the brain feels the effect of it first.   30
For when things are weak and in poor condition small causes shift the
balance.[898] So if one reckons up that the brain itself is low in heat, further, that it is necessary for the skin around it to be more so, and for the
nature of the hairs to be more so than the skin, inasmuch as they are
farthest away, it would seem quite reasonable for it to happen to those   35
with much seed that they go bald around this time of life.[899]

And it is due to the same cause too that the front part of the head
alone goes bald and, among the animals, in human beings alone: the   784^a1
front part, because the brain is there; alone among the animals, because
the human has much the largest and wettest brain.[900] And women do
not go bald because their nature is about the same as that of children.
For both are sterile of spermatic secretion.[901] Also, eunuchs do not   5
become bald because they change to the female condition. And the
hairs that come later in life, eunuchs either do not grow these or they
lose them if they happen to, except for pubic hair. This deformation is   10
a change from the male condition to the female.

As for hibernating animals becoming hairy again and leaf-shed-
ding plants growing leaves again, but in cases of baldness the hairs
not growing back again, the cause is that for the former the seasons of
the year are the turning-points of their body more so [than in human
beings], so that since these seasons change, they change with them by   15
growing and losing feathers or hairs, and the plants their leaves. In
the case of human beings, on the other hand, winter, summer, spring,
and fall correspond to their ages, so that since the times of life do not
change, neither do the affections change that are due to these, although
the cause is similar.   20

And [color aside] the other affections of the hairs have now been
spoken about.

V 4

The cause of their colors in the other animals, and of their being single-colored or many-colored, is the nature of the skin. But in human beings it is not the cause, except of their hair going gray, not due to old age, but due to disease. For in what is called white-sickness the hairs become white, whereas if the hairs are white because of old age, whiteness in the skin does not follow along.[902] The cause is that the hairs grow out of the skin. If the skin out of which they grow is diseased and white, then, the hair is diseased along with it, and disease of hair is grayness. But the grayness of hair that is due to time of life comes about due to weakness and deficiency of heat. For every time of life shifts the balance of the body's decline, in old age toward cold. For old age is cold and dry.

We must understand, however, that the nourishment reaching each part is concocted by the proper heat present in each part, and that if the heat is incapable of doing so, the part will be ruined, and deformation or disease results.[903] (This sort of cause must be spoken about in a more exact way later on in the treatise *On Growth and Nourishment*.[904]) In those human beings, then, in whom the nature of the hairs is low in heat and too much liquid enters, the proper heat is incapable of concocting it and it becomes putrefied due to the heat in the environment. For all putrefaction comes about due to heat, but not—as was said elsewhere—due to connate heat.[905] Putrefaction, though, occurs in the case of water, earth, and all bodies of this sort, which is why it also occurs in the case of earthy vapor—for example, what is called mold.[906] For mold is in fact a putrefaction of earthy vapor. So in hairs too this sort of nourishment, because of not being concocted, putrefies and what is called grayness results. It is white because mold too, alone among putrid things (one might almost say), is white.

The cause of this is that it contains much air. For all earthy vapor has the capacity of coarse-grained air.[907] For mold is like the counterpart of hoar-frost. For if the vapor that rises up freezes, it becomes hoar-frost, if it putrefies, it becomes mold. That is also why both are on the surface of things. For vapor forms on the surface. Also, the poets make a good metaphor when jestingly calling gray hairs mold of old age and hoarfrost. For the one is in genus (*genos*), and the other in species (*eidos*), the same: hoar-frost in genus (for both are a vapor), mold in species (for both are a putrefaction).[908]

Here is a sign that going gray is a thing of this sort: as a result of diseases many people grow gray hairs, but later on, when they become healthy, grow black ones instead of these. The cause is that in sickness,

just as in the whole body there is a deficiency of natural heat, so too
the various parts, even the very small ones, share in this sickness. And
much residue is produced in their bodies and in the parts. That is why
the non-concoction of the residue in the flesh produces gray hairs.
But when they become healthy and strong they again change and, as   30
it were, from being old become young. And one might even quite correctly say that disease is an additionally acquired old age, old age a
natural disease. At any rate, some diseases produce the same effects as
old age.

The temples go gray first. For the back of the head is empty of liquid   35
because it does not have brain in it, whereas the bregma contains a large 785ᵃ1
quantity of liquid—and a large quantity does not easily putrefy.⁹⁰⁹ The
hairs on the temples, however, have neither so little liquid as to concoct nor so much as not to putrefy. For since this place on the head is
intermediate between the two others it is exempt from both affections.   5

Where the greyness of human beings is concerned, then, the cause
has now been stated.

V 5

In other animals the cause of this change not noticeably occurring due
to time of life is the very same one that was also stated in the case of
baldness: their brain is small and contains less liquid, so that the heat
is not quite incapable of effecting its concoction. In horses, of all the   10
animals we know, signs of it most appear, because the bone they have
around the brain is finer than that of all the others. A proof of this is
that a blow to this place is fatal to them. That is why Homer too has put
things as follows:

> There where the first hairs grow on   15
> the skull of horses is a place most mortal.⁹¹⁰

Hence the flow of the liquid [to these hairs] is easier because of the
fineness of the bone, and as the heat fails because of age, these hairs go
gray. And reddish hairs go gray faster than black ones. For redness too
is a sort of sickness of the hair, and all weak things age more quickly.⁹¹¹   20

Cranes, though, are said to go darker as they get older.⁹¹² The cause
of this affection would be that the nature of their feathers is whiter by
nature, and as they grow old there is more liquid in their feathers than
is easily putrefied.⁹¹³

A sign that grayness is produced by a sort of putrefaction, and that   25
it is not, as some people think, a drying-up, is that hairs protected by

hats or other coverings go gray faster (for winds prevent putrefaction, and the protection produces an absence of wind), and that anointing them with a mixture of water and oil is a help. For while the water cools them, the oil mixed with it prevents them from drying quickly (for water is quickly dried up). A sign that it is not a drying-up, that hair does not whiten as grass does by drying-up, is that some hairs grow gray from the outset, and nothing that is dried-up grows. Many hairs too are white at the tip. For into the extremities and thinnest parts the least heat comes.

In the other animals, when the hairs are white, this is produced by nature and does not come about by virtue of an affection. And the cause of the colors in the others is the skin. For if they are white, the skin is white, if they are dark, it is dark, and if they are piebald, and are produced from a mixture, it is seen to be white in the one part, dark in the other. But in the case of human beings, the skin is in no way the cause. For even white-skinned ones have very dark hair. The cause is that the human has the finest skin for its size of all the animals, which is why it has no strength for changing the hairs. Instead, because of its weakness, the skin itself also changes its color and becomes dark due to the sun and the winds, whereas the hairs do not change together with it. In the other animals, however, the skin, because of its coarseness, has the capacity of the region.^{914} That is why the hairs change in accord with the skin, but the skin does not change in accord with the winds and the sun.

V 6

Of the animals some are single-colored (and by single-colored I mean the ones whose whole genus has one color, for example, all lions are tawny, and this also applies to birds, fish, and other animals in a similar way); others, though many-colored, are whole-colored (I mean those whose whole body has the same color, for example, an ox is wholly white or wholly dark); others variegated. This latter, though, is twofold; sometimes it applies to the genus, for example, leopards, peacocks, and some fishes, for example, the ones called *thrattai*, but sometimes, though the entire genus is not variegated, variegated offspring are produced, for example, oxen and goats, and, among birds, for example, pigeons.^{915} And other genera of birds are affected in the same way.

The whole-colored, though, exhibit change much more than the single-colored, both to the simple color of the others (for example, from white parents a dark offspring comes or from dark parents a white offspring) and from both parents of both colors, mixed offspring

come.[916] This is because it is in the nature of the whole genus not to
have [only] one color. For the genus is easily moved in both directions,   30
so that it exhibits change more both to [the color] of the others and to
being variegated.

The single-colored, on the other hand, exhibit the contrary. (For
they do not exhibit change except due to an affection, and this rarely.
For a white partridge, raven, sparrow, and bear are known to have been
observed.) This results from its being distorted in the process of gen-   35
eration. For what is small is easily ruined and easily moved, and what
is coming to be is of this sort. For the starting-point of things that are   786^a1
coming to be lies in something small.

And the ones that exhibit most change are those which, though by
nature whole-colored, are in genus many-colored, due to the waters
[they drink].[917] For hot waters make the hairs white, cold ones make
them dark, just as in the case of plants. The cause is that the hot ones   5
contain more pneuma than they do water, and the air shining through
produces whiteness, as it also does in foam.[918] Hence just as skins that
are white due to an affection differ from skins that are white due to
nature, so too in hairs the whiteness due to disease or time of life differs from the whiteness of hairs due to nature, in that the causes are   10
distinct. For the natural heat produces the whiteness of the latter, alien
heat that of the former. For whiteness is produced in all things by the
vaporized air enclosed in them. That is also why those animals that are
not single-colored are all white under the abdomen. For (one might   15
almost say) all white animals are hotter and more pleasant tasting due
to the same cause. For the concoction produces the pleasant taste, and
the heat produces the concoction. And the cause is the same for the
ones that are single-colored, but either dark or white. For heat and cold
are the causes of the nature of the skin and the hairs. For each of the
parts has its own proper heat.   20

Further, tongues differ among simple-colored and variegated animals, and among those that though simple-colored differ in color—for
example, white ones and dark ones. The cause is the one mentioned
previously, namely, that the skins of the variegated ones are variegated,
and those of white-haired ones and of the dark-haired ones are white
and dark, respectively.[919] We must, though, suppose the tongue to be,   25
as it were, one of the external parts, not supposing that it is covered by
the mouth, but rather that it is like hands or feet. So, since the skin of
the variegated animals is not single-colored, this is also the cause in the
case of skin on the tongue.

Some birds and some wild quadrupeds change their colors in   30
accord with the seasons. The cause is that just as human beings change

in accord with the time of life, these change in accord with the seasons. For this is a greater difference for them than the change in accord with age.

The more omnivorous animals are more variegated, to speak in terms of what holds for the most part, and quite reasonably so—for example, bees are more single-colored than hornets or wasps. For if the nourishments are the causes of the change, it is quite reasonable for variegated nourishments to produce all sorts of movements in the residues of the nourishment from which hairs, feathers, and skin are produced.

Concerning both colors and hairs, then, let things be determined this way.

V 7

Where voice is concerned, it is low-pitched in some animals, high-pitched in others, and in others again well pitched and having a relation to both extremes that is proportional; further, some have a big voice, others a small voice, and it differs in smoothness and roughness, in flexibility and inflexibility—it must be investigated, then, due to what causes each of these belongs to a voice.

Where highness and lowness of pitch are concerned we must think the cause to be the very same one as in the case of the change from youth to age. For all the other animals when young utter a higher-pitched sound, but among oxen, the calves utter a deeper-pitched one. The same happens in the case of males and females. For in the other genera of animals the female utters a higher-pitched sound than the male (this is most noticeable, though, in the case of human beings; for it is most of all to these that nature has assigned this capacity, because they alone among the animals make use of rational speech (*logos*), and the matter for rational speech is the voice), but in the case of oxen the contrary obtains (for the females utter a lower-pitched sound than the bulls).[920]

What animals have a voice for the sake of, and what a voice is, and, in general, a sound, has been stated partly in *De Sensu*, partly in *De Anima*.[921] But since low-pitch in a voice lies in the movement being slow, and high-pitch in its being fast, whether the cause is the mover or the moved involves a certain puzzle.[922] For some people say that what is much is moved slowly, what is little quickly, and that this is the cause of lowness and highness of pitch, respectively. Up to a point this is correctly stated (for in general it seems correctly said that lowness of pitch lies in what is moved being of a certain size) but it is not wholly correct (for if it were, it would not be easy to utter a sound that is both

small and low-pitched, nor, similarly, one that is big and high-pitched).
Also, a low-pitched voice seems to be characteristic of a nobler nature,
and in melodies what is low-pitched is better than what is strained.[923]   35
For being better lies in being superior, and lowness of pitch is a sort of   787[a]1
superiority. But since the low-pitched and high-pitched in a voice are
distinct from big-voiced and small-voiced (for there are animals with
voices both high-pitched and big, and likewise with ones that are small
and low-pitched), and similarly too with respect to the pitch intermediate between these—by what else about these could one distinguish   5
them (I mean bigness and smallness of voice) except the large or small
quantity that is moved? If, then, high and low pitch are distinguished
in accord with what is said [by the people in question], the result will
be that the same animals are low- and big-voiced, high- and small-
voiced. But this is false.   10

The cause [of the puzzle] is that big and small, much and little, are
sometimes said of things unconditionally, at other times, in relation to
each other. Bigness of voice, then, lies in what is moved being unconditionally much, smallness of voice on its being unconditionally little,
whereas low-pitch and high-pitch depend on having this difference
(*diaphora*) in relation to each other. For if what is moved exceeds the   15
strength of what moves it, it is necessary for what is spatially moved
to be spatially moved slowly; if it is exceeded, quickly.[924] Sometimes,
then, the strong, moving much because of their strength, make the
movement slowly, other times, because of its superiority, quickly.[925] In
accord with the same argument (*logos*) too, sometimes weak movers,   20
moving what is for their capacity much, make the movement slowly,
but other times, moving little because of their weakness, quickly.[926]

These, then, are the causes of these contrarieties: of not all young
animals having high-pitched voices or low-pitched ones, nor all the
older ones, nor males and females; and in addition to this, of both the
sick and those having a well body uttering high-pitched sounds; and   25
further too, of people, as they approach old age, getting a more high-
pitched voice, though this time of life is the contrary of youth.

Most young animals, then, and most females, moving little air
because of their incapacity, have high-pitched voices. For the little is
spatially moved quickly, and in a voice what is quick is high-pitched.   30
But in calves and female oxen, in the one case because of time of life,
in the other because of the nature of the female, the part by which they
move [the air] does not possess strength, but because they move much,
they utter low-pitched sounds.[927] For what spatially moves slowly is
heavy [or low], and much air spatially moves slowly.[928] These animals   787[b]1
move much [air], but the others move little, because the vessel through

which the pneuma first spatially moves has in them a large opening
and is compelled to move much air, whereas in the others it is easily regulated.[929] For as their time of life advances this part that does
the moving becomes stronger in each animal, so that they change to
their contrary, and the ones with high-pitched voices come to have
lower-pitched ones that they had, and the ones with low-pitched voices
come to have more high-pitched ones. That is why bulls have a higher-
pitched one than calves and female oxen.

Now in all animals strength lies in the sinews, which is why those
in the prime of life are stronger. For the young are more unarticulated
and more without sinews. Further, in the young they are not yet tight,
while in the old the tightness by then slackens. That is why both are
weak and lacking in capacity for movement. Bulls, though, are especially sinewy, even their heart. That is why the part by which they move
[the air] has tension, just like a string made of sinew that is stretched
tight. What makes it clear that the heart of male oxen has this sort of
nature is the fact that a bone actually occurs in some of them.[930] And
bones seek the nature of sinews.[931]

When castrated all animals change to the female condition, and
because of the slackening of the sinewy strength in its starting-point
emit a voiced-sound similar to that of the females.[932] The slackening
is about the same as if one were to stretch a cord and make it tight by
hanging some weight on it, as women do who weave at the loom. For
they too stretch the warp by attaching what are called loom stones to
it. For this is how the nature of the testes too is attached to the spermatic ducts, and these to the blood-vessel whose starting-point is at
the heart near the part that moves the voice. That is why as the spermatic ducts change near the age at which they are then able to secrete
seed, this part also changes along with them. And when this changes,
the voice too changes, and though it changes more in males, the same
also happens in the case of females, though in a less obvious way, and
what some people call "bleating like a goat" results, when the voice
is uneven.[933] After this it settles into the low-pitched or high-pitched
voice of the succeeding time of life. But if the testes are removed the
stretching of the ducts slackens as when the weight is removed from
the cord and the warp. And as this slackens, the starting-point that
moves the voice is proportionally released.

It is due, then, to this cause that castrated animals change to the
female condition, both in voice and in the rest of their shape, namely,
because of the resulting slackening of the starting-point from which
the tension of the body originates, not, as some suppose, because
the testes themselves are a ganglion of many starting-points. On the

contrary, small changes are causes of big ones, not due to themselves,   10
but rather when it happens that a starting-point changes along with
them. For starting-points though small in size are great in capacity.
For this is what it is for something to be a starting-point, namely, that
it is itself the cause of many things, with nothing else above it being a
cause of it.   15

The hotness or coldness of their place [of habitation] also contributes to some animals being so composed by nature as to have in
some cases low-pitched voices and in others high-pitched ones. For
hot pneuma [or breath], because of being coarse-grained, produces
lowness of pitch in a voice, while cold pneuma, because of being fine-
grained, produces the contrary. This is clear too in the case of flutes.   20
For those who use hotter pneuma, and emit it in the same way as people who are groaning, play at a lower pitch.[934]

The cause of roughness and smoothness of voice, and of all unevenness of this sort, is that the part of the instrument [or organ] through
which the voice spatially moves is rough or smooth, or, in general, even   25
or uneven. This is clear when there is any wetness about the windpipe,
or when it becomes rough due to some affection.[935] For then the voice
too becomes uneven.

Of flexibility and inflexibility of voice the cause is the instrument's
[or organ's] being soft or hard. For a soft one is capable of being regulated and becoming of any and every sort, whereas a hard one is inca-   30
pable of this. And a soft one is capable of uttering both a small and a
big sound. That is why it can be both high-pitched and low-pitched.
For it easily regulates the pneuma [or breath], easily becoming big or
small itself. But hardness cannot be regulated.

About whatever things having to do with voice that were not previously determined in *De Sensu* and in *De Anima* let this much be said.   **788ᵇ1**

V 8

Where the teeth are concerned, it has been stated previously that they
are not for the sake of one thing, nor do all animals have them for the
sake of the same thing, but rather some have them because of their
nourishment, others also for fighting and for vocal speech (*logos*).[936]   5
But why the front teeth are produced first and the molars later, and why
the latter are not shed, while the former are shed and grow again—of
these things accounts concerned with generation must consider the
connate cause.

About these things Democritus too has spoken, but he has not spoken
correctly. For he states a universal cause without having investigated all   10

cases. For he says that the shedding is due to the fact that the teeth are produced prematurely. For it is when animals are (one might almost say) in their prime that the teeth grow in accord with nature, while of their being produced prematurely suckling is the cause assigned.⁹³⁷ And yet the pig also suckles but does not shed its teeth.⁹³⁸ Further, animals with saw-like teeth all suckle, but some of them do not shed any teeth except the canines—for example, lions.⁹³⁹ Democritus made this error, then, in speaking universally without investigating what happens in all cases. But this is what we must do. For it is necessary for the one who speaks universally to say something about all cases.

Since we assume, making our assumption on the basis of what we observe, that nature neither omits any of the things possible in each case nor produces any pointlessly, and since it is necessary, if an animal is going to get any nourishment after being weaned, for it to have instruments for working on nourishment—if, then, as Democritus says, this happened around the time of maturity, nature would omit one of the things it was possible for it to produce, and the work of nature would be contrary to nature. For what is by force is contrary to nature, but he says that the generation of the [first] teeth is contrary to nature. But that this is not true is evident from these considerations and others of this sort.

These [front] teeth are produced before the flat [molars], first because their work is earlier (for dividing comes before crushing, and the flat ones are for crushing, the others for dividing), and next because what is smaller, even if begun at the same time, naturally comes about faster than what is larger. And these teeth are smaller in size than the molars, because the bone of the jaw is flat there but narrow near the mouth. Of necessity, then, more nourishment flows from the larger part, less from the narrower one.

But though suckling itself contributes nothing to the teeth, the hotness of the milk makes them sprout more quickly. A sign of this is that even in suckling animals those that get hotter milk grow their teeth faster. For what is hot is productive of growth.

Teeth are shed after being produced, however, for the sake of the better, because what is sharp is quickly blunted. Another set must be provided, then, for the work. The flat ones, by contrast, cannot be blunted, but in time due to being pounded only become ground down. Of necessity, on the other hand, they are shed because, while the roots of the molars are situated where the jaw is flat and the bone strong, those of the front teeth are in a fine part, which is why they are weak and easily moved. And they grow again because they are shed while the bone is still growing and while it is still the time of life for teeth to

be produced. A sign of this is that even the flat ones grow for a long time. For the last ones appear at around twenty years of age. In some cases indeed people are quite aged by the time their last teeth are completely grown. This is because there is much nourishment in the wide part of the bone, whereas the front part, because of its fineness quickly   20
reaches completion, and residue is no longer produced in it; instead,   789^b1
the nourishment is used up for its own growth.

Democritus, however, omitting to mention the for-the-sake-of-which, reduces to necessity all that nature uses—but though they are such, they are nonetheless for the sake of something and in each case for the sake of what is better. So nothing prevents the teeth from being   5
produced and being shed in the way he says, but it is not because of these things, but rather because of the end, though these are causes as movers, as instruments, and as matter, since it is reasonable, indeed, for nature to make most things using pneuma as instrument. For just as some things have many uses where the crafts are concerned—as in blacksmithing are the hammer and the anvil—so does pneuma in   10
those composed by nature. Saying that the causes are [all] of necessity, however, seems similar to someone thinking that it is because of the surgeon's knife alone that water is drawn from a dropsical patient, and not because of what the knife made the cut for the sake of, namely, his being healthy.   15

The teeth, then, and why some are shed and produced again, and, in general, due to what cause they are produced, have now been spoken about. And we have also spoken about the other affections of the parts that come about not as the result of a for-the-sake-of-something, but of necessity and because of the moving cause.   20

Notes

History of Animals

BOOK I

Note 1

By genus (*genos*) I mean, for example, bird and fish. For each of these has a differentia (*diaphoran*) with respect to genus, and there are several species (*eidos*) of fishes and of birds: "Genus" (plural: "genera"), "differentia" (plural: differentiae"), and "species" are the traditional Latinate translations of *genos*, *eidos*, and *diaphora*, and are best thought of as near transliterations, with no independent semantic content beyond that conveyed by Aristotle's uses of the terms, which are (alas) many and various. In his own philosophical lexicon, for example, we find the following entry on *genos*: "Something is said to be a *genos* if: [1] The coming to be of things with the same form (*eidos*) is continuous—for example, 'as long as the *genos* of human beings lasts' means 'as long as the coming to be of human beings is continuous.' [2] It is the first mover that brought things into existence. For it is in this way that some are said to be Hellenes by *genos* and others Ionians, because the former come from Hellen and the latter from Ion as their first begetter. And more so when from the male begetter than when from the matter, although the *genos* is also sometimes named from the female—for example, the descendants of Pyrrha. [3] Further, as the plane is said to be the *genos* of plane figures and solid of solids. For each of the figures is in the one case a plane of such-and-such a sort and in the other a solid of such-and-such a sort, this being the underlying subject for the differentiae. [4] Further, as the first constituent in accounts is said to be—the one said in the what-it-is. For this is the *genos*, whose differentiae the qualities are said to be" (*Met.* V 28 1024^{a}29–^{b}5). A *genos*, then, is [1–2] a race or bloodline and [3–4] the kind of thing—the genus—studied by a single science (see Introduction, pp. xxxi–xxxii). Similarly, he uses *eidos* to refer to the species of a genus, but also to form (as opposed to matter) and to a separate Platonic Form. By the same token *diaphorai* are sometimes, as presumably here, the differentiae that divide a genus into species, and so figure in their essential definitions: "species are composed of the genus and the differentiae" (*Met.* X 7 1057^{b}7). But sometimes they are simply the different features that distinguish one kind of thing from another, without necessarily suggesting that the kinds are genera or species in the strict sense or that the differences are differentiae. To bring a semblance of order to all of this I have employed the traditional translation ("genus," "differentia," and "species"), adding the Greek term in parenthesis for clarity when needed.

Note 2
The parts, then, that the animals possess are each in this way the same or distinct: Reading τὰ μὲν οὖν μόρια ὅσα ἔχουσιν with Balme-1 for Louis κατὰ μὲν οὖν τὰ μόρια ἃ ἔχουσιν.

Note 3
Serum (*ichôr*): "The part of the blood that is watery, either because it is not yet concocted or because it has become corrupted" (*PA* II 5 651ᵃ17–18). The other part consists of fibers (*ines*), which are "in between sinew and blood-vessel" (*HA* III 6 515ᵇ27) and are "composed of earth" (*PA* II 4 651ᵃ7). See *Mete.* IV 7 384ᵃ25–30.

Note 4
Phlegm: "A residue of the useful nourishment" (*GA* I 18 725ᵃ15).

Note 5
It is a homonym related to the part when due to the shape the whole is said to be horn: Reading ὁμώνυμον γὰρ πρὸς τὸ μέρος with Pellegrin for Louis ὁμώνυμον γὰρ τὸ μέρος; Balme-1 with most mss. reads ὁμώνυμον γὰρ πρὸς τὸ γένος ("it is homonym related to the genus"). On homonymy, see *GA* I 19 726ᵇ24n.

Note 6
Beaver (*latax*): It is not entirely clear which aquatic mammal is being referred to; "beaver" is a common conjecture.

Note 7
Fishing-frog: See *GA* III 1 749ᵃ23n.

Note 8
Many of the terrestrial animals, as was said, procure their nourishment from liquid: At *HA* I 1 487ᵃ19–20.

Note 9
For example, in the case of larvae in rivers. For gnats come to be from them: Reading ἐμπίδων (see *HA* V 19 551ᵇ27) with D'Arcy Thompson for Louis, Pellegrin ἀσκαρίδων ("worms"); Balme-1 reads ἀσπίδων ("asps").

Note 10
As also seals have docked-feet (*kekolobeômenoi*): Reading ὡς καὶ τῇ φώκῃ with Balme-1 for Louis-1 and Peck-1 καὶ τῇ φώκῃ. On "docked," see *GA* I 17 721ᵇ17n.

Note 11
Swift (*drepanis*): Literally, "sickle-bird" (from the shape of its wings). Its precise identity is unclear. Perhaps, in particular, the Alpine swift.

Note 12
Whether they are footed, winged, swimmers, or play a double game: For example, both walk and swim, or fly and walk.

Note 13
And of the gregarious ones and solitary ones, some are political, whereas others are more dispersed: Reading τῶν ἀγελαίων καὶ τῶν μοναδικῶν with Louis-1 and Balme-1; D'Arcy Thompson and Peck-1 seclude καὶ τῶν μοναδικῶν, taking political and solitary to be antithetical. But solitariness is compatible with internal complexity, and that with a political life: "It is not necessary for even those cities to be inactive that are situated by themselves and have deliberately chosen to live that way, since actions can take place even among their parts. For the parts of the city have many communal relations with each other. Similarly, this also holds of any individual human. For otherwise the [primary] god and the entire cosmos could scarcely be in a noble condition, since they have no external actions beyond the [internal] ones that are proper to them" (*Pol.* VII 3 1325^{b}23–30). So it might be that Aristotle is thinking of animal communities (even families) that live in isolation from others.

Note 14
Pelamys and bonito: Varieties of tuna.

Note 15
The human, though, plays a double game: See *HA* I 1 488^{a}34–^{b}1n.

Note 16
The political animals are those among whom some one work (*ergon*) common to all is produced: See *GA* III 10 761^{a}5n.

Note 17
And some are burrowers, others non-burrowers: Reading καὶ τὰ μὲν τρηματώδη τὰ δ' ἄτρητα with Louis-1 and Balme-1; D'Arcy Thompson and Peck-1 seclude.

Note 18
Some always tame (for example, human, mule), others always wild: Reading ἄνθρωπος ("human") with Balme-1 and Pellegrin for Louis-1 ὄνος ("ass"); Peck-1 reads ἄνθρωπος but secludes "tame (for example, human, mule), others always."

Note 19
Further, there is another way [of dividing them]: Reading Ἔτι ἄλλον τρόπον with Louis-1 and Balme-1. Namely, so that, for example, tame and wild are not treated as differentiae. See *PA* I 643^{b}3–8.

Note 20
Some have speech, whereas others are unable to utter articulate sounds: "Speech" is *dialekton*; "unable to utter articulate sounds" is *agrammata*. Both words also have other meanings.

Note 21
The defensive ones are those that have some place of shelter within themselves against suffering any injury: Such as a shell.

Note 22
Spiritless (*dusthuma*): *Dusthumos* often means "melancholy," but here contrasts with *thumôdês* (*HA* I 1 488ᵇ14), which means "spirited" or "fierce." See *GA* II 1 749ᵇ33n.

Intelligent (*phronima*): See *GA* I 23 731ᵃ35n.

Servile (*aneleuthera*): *Eleutheria* is political freedom (*NE* V 3 1131ᵃ28). *Eleutheriotês* is freedom in the use of wealth, or generosity; *aneleutheria* acquisitiveness, or not being free with one's wealth. Here, though, *aneleutheros*, which is contrasted with the *eleutheria* attributed to lions (*HA* I 1 488ᵇ16), means "creeping," or "servile." More like a slave than a free person.

Serpent: Reading ὄφις with Balme-1; for Louis-1, and Peck-1 οἱ ὄφεις ("the serpents").

Note 23
Deliberation: Discussed in *NE* III 3.

Note 24
Many animals have memory and can be taught, but no other is capable of recollecting: "The cause is that recollecting is, as it were, a sort of deduction (*sullogismos*). For the one recollecting deduces that he previously saw, heard, or was affected in this sort of way, and this is a sort of inquiry. And this sort of inquiry belongs by nature only to those animals that also have a deliberative part. For deliberation is a sort of deduction" (*Mem.* 2 453ᵃ9–14).

Note 25
About each of the genera of animals, and about their characters and ways of life, we shall speak with exactitude later on: In *HA* VIII–IX.

Note 26
With which they discharge the residue of the nourishment: Secluding καὶ ᾗ λαμβάνει ("and with which they take it in") with Louis-1, Peck-1, and Pellegrin, as a dittograph of *HA* I 2 489ᵃ1.

Note 27
The parts that are for this handicrafting (*dêmiourgian*) **[of animals] differ in form** (*eidos*): The verb *dêmiourgein* is regularly used in contexts like this. Occurrences are listed in the Index.

Note 28
One has a uterus, another its analogue: "The chorion is the analogue of a uterus that grows around the egg" (*GA* III 2 754ᵃ1–2).

Note 29

[1] To all animals, though, only one perceptual capacity belongs in common, namely, touch: "Since the animal is an ensouled body, and every body is tangible, and it is what is perceptible by touch that is tangible, the body of an animal must also be capable of touch, if the animal is to preserve itself. For the other perceptual capacities—smell, sight, and hearing—perceive through other things. But anything that touches things, if it does not have perception of them, will be unable to avoid some of them and take others. And if that is so, it will be impossible for the animal to preserve itself. That is why taste too is like a sort of touch. For it is concerned with nourishment, and nourishment is a tangible body" (*DA* III 12 434^{b}11–19).

[2] so that (*hôste*) **the part in which it naturally comes to be is nameless** (*anônumon*). **[3] For it is the same part in some animals, in others the analogue:** An *onoma* is not always what we call a name, but a word more generally, or—when contrasted with a verb—a noun: "A noun or name is a composite significant voiced sound, without [a reference to] time, the parts of which are not intrinsically significant. . . . A verb is a composite significant voiced sound, involving [a reference to] time, the parts of which are not intrinsically significant" (*Po.* 20 1457^{a}10–15). A name, however, often signifies an account or (in some cases) a definition (*Met.* IV 7 1012^{a}22–24, VIII 6 1045^{a}26) of the form (VII 10 1035^{a}21) or essence (4 1029^{b}20) of the thing named. It is this that explains the *hôste* linking [1] and [2]. For if the perceptual part for touch had a name, it would have the same form or essence in all animals, which need not be the case, as [2] makes clear.

It is the same part in some animals, in others the analogue: "But there is a puzzle about . . . what the perceptual organ is of what can perceive by touch, whether it is flesh, and what is analogous to this in other beings, or whether it is not, but instead the flesh is the medium, whereas the primary perceptual organ is something else that is internal. . . . [Resolution of puzzle:] On the whole, then, it seems that as air and water are to sight, hearing, and smell, so the flesh and the tongue are to their perceptual organ as each of these is . . . From which it is also clear that what can perceive the tangible is internal. . . . So the flesh is the medium of what can perceive by touch" (*DA* II 12 422^{b}19–423^{b}26).

Note 30

Fiber and serum: Reading ἴς with Louis-1, Peck-1, Pellegrin; D'Arcy Thompson, Balme-1 read ἰός ("vein") with the mss. Serum is the analogue of blood; fiber of blood-vessel. See *HA* I 1 487^{a}3n.

Note 31

The so-called selachians: See *GA* I 8 718^{b}1n.

Note 32

One part of which comes the starting-point: The starting-point is that of embryonic development, which comes from the male. See *GA* III 2 752^{a}10–15.

Note 33
Of eggs, some are . . . two-colored: That is, they have a yolk and a white.

Note 34
These things must be spoken about with exactitude later on in *Generation [of Animals]*: See *GA* II, III.

Note 35
All [animals] have an even number [of feet]: "Every footed animal of necessity has an even number of feet. For those that make a change of place by use of jumping only do not need feet, at any rate for this sort of movement, while those that make use of jumping, but for whom this movement is not self-sufficient and they need to perambulate as well, clearly do so better with an even number of feet, or else are incapable of perambulating otherwise at all. For since this sort of change is with respect to a part and not with the whole of the body at once, as in the case of jumping, it is necessary for some of the feet to remain at rest, while the others are moving, and to make the movement in each case with opposite ones of these, shifting the weight from the ones that are moving to the ones remaining at rest. That is why no animal can use three legs or one leg to walk. For if it uses one leg it has no support at all on which to rest the weight of the body, and if it uses three it will rest it on a pair of opposite feet, so that if it tries so to move it is necessary for it to fall. Multiped animals, however, (for example, the centipede), are capable of perambulating with an odd number of feet. . . . Yet it is evident that they too would better make the change if they had an even number of feet, that is, if none were missing and they had all their feet in corresponding rows" (*IA* 8 708^{a}21–^{b}13).

Note 36
Muraena: A genus of eels.

Note 37
The fishing-frog: See *GA* III 1 749^{a}23n.

Note 38
And octopus: Reading καὶ πολύπους with Louis-1 and Balme-1; D'Arcy Thomson and Peck-1 seclude.

Note 39
The crustaceans (*sklêroderma*): Usually, *malakostraka* (literally: "soft-shelled").

Note 40
Sheatfish (*glanis*): The catfish family.

Note 41
The fliers: See *PA* I 3 642^{b}24n.
Flying-fox (*alôpêx*): "A large bat; not the animal now called flying-fox" (Peck-1, p. 28 n*b*).

Note 42
All animals—quadruped as well as multiped—move in a similar way. For they move with respect to a diagonal (*kata diagonon*): "The back legs move with respect to a diagonal in relation to the front legs. For after the right foreleg animals move the left hindleg, then the left foreleg, and after it the right hindleg" (*IA* 14 712^{a}24–27). See also *HA* II 1 498^{b}5–7.

Note 43
The chief genera (*genê megista*) **of animals:** *Megistos* can also mean "greatest," or "most important," but note *megista* at *HA* I 7 491^{a}27, where "chief" seems to best capture the meaning.
Cetaceans: Reading κήτους with Balme-1 and Peck for Louis κήτος.

Note 44
In some cases the species is simple and does not have a differentia: See *HA* I 1 486^{a}24n.

Note 45
Ginnus: Reading γίννῳ with Louis and Peck; Balme-1 reads γίννῳ καὶ ἵννῳ. A γίννος is a "deformed mule" (*GA* II 8 748^{b}34), the offspring of a mule and a mare (*HA* VI 24 577^{b}21); an ἵννος seems to be the same thing.

Note 46
Get a theoretical grasp on (*theôrein*): The verb *theasthai*, with which *theôria* is cognate, means to look at or gaze at. Thus *theôria* itself is sometimes what someone is doing in looking closely at something, or actively observing, studying, or contemplating it, and sometimes the capacity someone has to do these things (*Met.* IX 6 1048^{a}34–35, 8 1045^{a}36). When *theôria* is an exercise of understanding (*nous*), which is the element responsible for grasping scientific starting-points (*NE* VI 6 1141^{a}7–8), such as (the definition of) a right angle in the case of geometry, or (the definition of) happiness in the case of politics, it is translated as "contemplation," and the cognate verb *theôrein* as "contemplate." The corresponding capacity is translated as "theoretical knowledge," and what gives rise to it as "get a theoretical grasp on." So when we get a theoretical grasp on A, we acquire the theoretical scientific knowledge of A, which we exercise in contemplating A.

Note 47
In what follows we shall speak about them with exactitude (*di' akribeias*): In his focal discussion of *akribeia*, Aristotle makes clear that a science's degree of it is measured along three different dimensions: "One science is more *akribês* than another, and prior to it, if [1] it is both of the facts and gives their explanation, and not of the facts separately from giving the scientific knowledge of their explanation; or if [2] it is not said of an underlying subject and the other is said of an underlying subject (as, for example, arithmetic is more *akribês* than harmonics); or if [3] it proceeds from fewer things and the other from some additional posit (as, for

example, arithmetic is more *akribês* than geometry). By from an addition I mean, for example, that a unit is substance without position and a point is substance with position—the latter proceeds from an addition" (*APo.* I 27 87ᵃ31–37). The upshot is thus twofold. First, the most *akribês* version or formulation of a science is the most explanatory one—the one consisting of demonstrations from starting-points. Second, of two sciences, formulated in the most *akribês* way, one is more *akribês* than the other, if it demonstrates facts that the other deals with but does not demonstrate. Because a natural science has to posit sublunary matter in addition to such starting-points, the strictly theoretical sciences (theology, astronomy, and mathematics) are more *akribês* than any natural science. Hence it is among these that the most *akribês* one will be found. And it will be the one that explains what the others treat as a fact or undemonstrated posit. The association of *akribeia* with demonstration from starting-points makes "exact" seem a good translation of it, as does its association with abstraction (mathematics) with what we think of as pure (solid geometry) as opposed to applied sciences (mechanics), and with the idea that the *akribeia* of a science or type of argument depends on its subject matter (*NE* I 3 1094ᵇ24). As applied to craftsmen and their products, *akribês* comes closest to meaning "refinement" or "finish" or "sophistication." Applied to perceptual capacities, such as seeing or smelling (*DA* II 9 421ᵃ10), it means "discriminating." Applied to virtue and nature, it may have more to do with accuracy—hitting a target (*NE* II 5 1106ᵇ14–15)—as it may when applied to definitions (VIII 7 1159ᵃ3) or distinctions (II 9 1107ᵇ15–16) or units of measurement (*Met.* X 1 1053ᵃ1). *Top.* II 4 111ᵃ8–9 offers *saphês* ("perspicuous") as an equivalent.

Coincidental attributes (*ta sumbebêkota*): The *sumbebêkota* referred to are *ta kath hauta sumbebêkota*—the intrinsic coincidents—or *per se* accidents (as they are often called). See *PA* 1 3 643ᵃ28n.

Note 48
Methodical inquiry: See *PA* I 1 639ᵃ1n (this vol.).

Note 49
So first of all we must grasp the parts from which animals are composed: See Introduction, pp. xcv–xcvi.

Note 50
The instrumental parts (*ta orkanika*): An *organon* is often what we would naturally call a bodily "organ," but just as often it refers to some part of an animal, such as a hand, that we would not call one, or to a craftsman's tools, so that "instrument" is the best overall translation.

The homoeomerous ones: See *GA* I 1 715ᵃ10n.

Note 51
The cavity from the neck to the private parts is called the trunk: Reading τὸ ἀπ' αὐχένος μέχρι αἰδοίων κύτος, ὃ καλεῖται θώραξ with Louis and Balme-1; D'Arcy Thompson reads post θώραξ ("trunk"); Peck secludes as an interpolated explanation.

Note 52

Bregma: "This is the bone which finally grows over the space at the top of the skull known as the 'anterior fontanelle'" (Peck-3, p. 227 n*c*).

Note 53

[The cranium] of men is for the most part in three sutures, joining together at one point: For the cause, see *PA* II 7 653^{a}38–^{b}8, and on "for the most part," *GA* I 18 725^{b}17n.

Note 54

We do not speak of the face of a fish or of an ox: Although, perhaps only by transference, even Aristotle himself sometimes does. See *HA* II 8 502^{a}20, 9 503^{a}18.

Note 55

Those in whom [the forehead] is large are slower (*braduteroi*), **those in whom it is small, quicker** (*eukinêtoi*): "For the most part, slow (*bradeis*) people have a better memory, whereas those who are quick (*tacheis*) and easy learners are better at recollecting" (*Mem.* I 449^{b}7–8); "[Some] animals have more subtle thought, not because of the coldness of their blood, but rather because it is fine-grained and pure. For what is earthy exhibits neither of these features. For those animals with finer-grained liquid have quicker (*eukinêtoteran*) perception" (*PA* II 4 650^{b}19–24). Compare *Phgn.* 6 811^{b}28–30.

Note 56

Those in whom [the forehead] is broad are excitable (*ekstatikoi*), **those with a rounded one, contented** (*eukoloi*): Reading εὔκολοι (conj. Dittmeyer); Louis, Balme-1, Peck read θυμικοί ("high-spirited," "irascible"). The latter reading is difficult to square with the following text, in which *ekstatikos* and *thumoeidês* go together: "Those animals with very fibrous, coarse-grained blood are more earthy in nature, and both spirited (*thumôdê*) in character and excitable (*ekstatika*) because of their spirit" (*PA* II 4 650^{b}33–35). At *Phgn.* 3 807^{b}22–23 "a big, round, fleshy forehead" is a sign of being stupid (*anaisthêtos*), which seems closer to *eukolos* than to *thumikos*.

Note 57

A mocker (*môkou*): One who mocks or jibes. See *GA* IV 3 769^{b}18n.
A self-deprecator (*eirônos*): Socrates is, of course, the canonical *eirôn*, whose disavowal of expert craft knowledge of virtue is a commonplace in Plato's portrait of him (*Ap.* 20d6–e3, 21b4–5, *Hp. Ma.* 286c8–d2, 304d5–e3, *La.* 190b7–c5, *Ly.* 212a4–7, 223b4–8, *Men.* 71b1–3, *Prt.* 361c2–6, *Rep.* 354c1–3). As a result many of his interlocutors—especially hostile ones—charge him with *eirôneia* ("irony" as it is usually translated in this context), thinking that he must have such knowledge if he is able to refute others (*Ap.* 38a1, *Grg.* 489e3, *Rep.* 337a4, *Smp.* 216e4). Aristotle, however, takes these disavowals at face value (*SE* 34 183^{b}7–8), making "self-deprecation" a better translation.

Note 58
Eye-jelly (*korê*): Sometimes found translated as "pupil."

Note 59
Cynicism (*kakoêtheias*): "Cynicism consists in taking everything in the worst way" (*Rh.* II 13 1389ᵇ21).
Wickedness (*ponêrias*): *Ponêria* is ethical badness or vice (*NE* VII 8 1150ᵇ36–37).
Scallops: Reading οἱ κτένες (see *GA* IV 1 763ᵇ12) with Balme-1 for Louis and Peck οἱ ἰκτῖνες ("the kites"); D'Arcy Thompson reads κρεῶδες ("comb-like"). The reference, by similarity, is to the lacrimal caruncle or tear duct.

Note 60
All the viviparous [animals have eyes], except the mole: See also *DA* II 1 425ᵃ10, *HA* IV 8 533ᵃ3–15.

Note 61
In others [the eyes are] greenish: Like those of goats. See *GA* V 1 779ᵃ33–34.

Note 62
[A greenish eye] is a sign of the best character, and is best for sharpness of sight: Compare *GA* V 1 780ᵃ22–25, whose reference to the intermediate or mean may offer a clue as to why the two go together (see *HA* I 10 492ᵃ10)—if, as is perhaps not entirely clear, a greenish eye contains an intermediate amount of liquid. For "as the whole is to the whole, so too each part is to each part" (*HA* I 1 486ᵃ20–21).

Note 63
The human is the one that alone—or most of all—among the animals has eyes of many colors. The others have one species. Although some horses have blue eyes: Compare *GA* V 1 779ᵃ34–ᵇ6.

Note 64
[A tendency to blink is a sign] of instability: "Depraved people do not have anything stable about them, since they do not remain even like themselves" (*NE* VIII 8 1159ᵇ7–9).

Note 65
Alcmaeon [of Croton]: See DK 24. A phrase omitted by OCT and Ross at *Met.* I 5 986ᵃ30 describes him as flourishing ἐπὶ γέροντι Πυθαγόρᾳ ("when Pythagoras was an old man"). His views on the soul are briefly discussed at *DA* I 2 405ᵃ29–ᵇ1, and on eggs at *GA* II 2 752ᵇ25.

Note 66
But the human alone does not move them: Reading ἀλλὰ μόνον ἄνθρωπος οὐ κινεῖ with Louis and Balme-1; Peck secludes.

Note 67
All the other animals move their ears: Reading τὰ δ' ἄλλα κινεῖ πάντα with Louis and Balme-1; Peck secludes.

Note 68
Babbling (*adoleschia*): *Adoleschia* in a more technical sense is unending repetition of the same thing. See *SE* 3 165ᵇ15–17, 13 173ᵃ31–ᵇ16, 31 181ᵇ25–182ᵃ6.

Note 69
Pneumas: Here, breaths, or sorts of breath. See Introduction, pp. lxii–lxiii.

Note 70
At the same time, inhalation and exhalation occur in the chest: "Breathing is not special to the nostrils; instead, the pneuma passes through the pipe near the uvula, where the extremity in the roof of the mouth is, and as the nostrils are united by a duct, it separates, part of it going through them, part of it through the mouth, both when it comes in and when it goes out" (*Juv.* 7 474ᵃ19–23).

Note 71
Its perceptual capacity is in its tip. And if something is placed on the flat part, [its flavor is] less: "Temperance and intemperance are concerned with the sorts of pleasures that the rest of the animals share in as well (which is why they appear slavish and beast-like), namely, touch and taste. They appear, though, to make little or no use even of taste. For the use of taste is to discern flavors, as people do when testing wines, or chefs when preparing gourmet dishes. But discerning such things is scarcely what people enjoy—at any rate, intemperate ones don't. On the contrary, what they enjoy is indulging in them—which enjoyment, whether in eating and drinking or in the so-called pleasures of Aphrodite, comes about wholly through touch. That is why a certain gourmand prayed for his gullet to become longer than a crane's, showing that it was the touching that gave him pleasure. Intemperance, then, is related to the most widely shared of the perceptual capacities and so would justly seem to be disgraceful, because it characterizes us not insofar as we are human beings but insofar as we are animals" (*NE* III 10 1118ᵃ23–ᵇ3); "Even where the pleasures of taste are concerned, not all of them are attractive to wild beasts—for example, those perceived by the tip of the tongue. But those perceived by the throat are, which is a feeling more like touch than taste. That is why gluttons pray not for a long tongue, but for the gullet of a crane—as did Philoxenus, the son of Eryxis" (*EE* III 2 1231ᵃ12–17).

Note 72
The tongue also perceives all the things that other flesh can (for example, hard, hot, cold) in any part of itself, just as (*hôsper*) it also perceives flavor: Reading ὥσπερ καὶ χυμοῦ with Louis and Balme-1; Peck secludes. "Flavor is one of the objects of touch" (*DA* II 3 414ᵇ11) and the tongue "perceives all tangible objects with the same part as it does flavors" (11 423ᵃ18). Thus *hôsper* means simply that the tongue, like flesh more

generally, perceives by touching. But this is consistent with its perceiving flavors better with the tip of the tongue than with the flat of it (previous note).

Note 73

It is broad, narrow, or intermediate. But the intermediate is the best and most perspicuous [in its discriminations]: Compare: "A soft, broad tongue is useful both for the perception of flavors (for the human is the most keenly perceptive of animals, and its tongue is soft; for it is the most tactile, and taste is a sort of touch) and for the articulation of letters, that is, speech (*logos*)" (*PA* II 17 660ª18–23).

Note 74

It is detached or tightly attached, as in those who mumble or lisp: In the way that children who have not yet learned to control their tongues do: See *HA* IV 9 536ᵇ5–8.

Note 75

In the interior is another part, shaped like a hanging bunch of grapes, a pillar with prominent blood-vessels: Namely, the uvula.

Note 76

Of this the front part is the larynx, the back part, the gullet: Reading καὶ τούτου τὸ μὲν πρόσθιον μέρος λάρυγξ, τὸ δ᾽ ὀπίσθιον στόμαχος with Balme-1; Peck secludes; Louis secludes τὸ δ᾽ ὀπίσθιον στόμαχος.

Note 77

The breast (*ho mastos*) is loose-textured (*manos*): *Manos* is typically an antonym of *puknos* ("dense"), so that *ho mastos* may be in particular the female breast. For the male breast is *puknos* (*HA* I 12 493ª15), while that of the female is *somphos* ("spongy") and *porôn* ("full of ducts") (493ª16). But perhaps the idea is simply that while both male and female breasts have ducts, the latter have more, and more that are larger. See *GA* V 3 782ª26n.

Note 78

If it is cut, it does not grow back together, any more than does the jaw or the eyelid: "Because they are skin without flesh" (*PA* II 12 657ᵇ3–4).

Note 79

It gets erect (*exerchetai*) and flaccid (*eiserchetai*) in contrary ways: Literally: "it goes out and comes in in contrary ways." Secluding with Balme-1 and Pellegrin ἢ τοῖς λοφούροις ("than in pack animals"); D'Arcy Thompson, followed by Peck, conjectures αἰλούροις ("than in cats").

Note 80

The way in which all parts of this sort are possessed will be spoken about with exactitude in universal terms later on: In *HA* VIII and *GA*.

Note 81
The thumb (*daktulos . . . megas*): Literally, "the big finger."

Note 82
The palm . . . is . . . divided by lines (*arthrois*): Literally, "by joints," or "by articulations."

Note 83
Unscrupulous (*panourgoi*): An unscrupulous person is one who "greedily takes anything from anywhere" (*EE* II 3 1221^{a}36–37; also *Pr.* XVI 4 917^{a}1–2). That is to say, he takes as much as he can of money, honors, bodily pleasures, and other goods of the sort that are greed's particular targets (*NE* IX 8 1168^{b}15–21), regardless of to whom they belong.

Note 84
The upper parts and lower parts [of a human] are positioned in relation to the upper and lower parts of the universe: This is because these parts are not just spatially or relationally distinguished but functionally and absolutely so: "the part from which the distribution of nourishment and growth derives in each living thing is up and the last part toward which this travels is down—the one is a sort of starting-point, the other a limit; and up is a starting-point" (*IA* 2 705^{a}32–^{b}2). Hence a plant, whose roots are down below, not as in animals up above, is a sort of upside-down animal: "Up and down are not the same for all things as they are for the universe, but as the head is of animals, so the roots are of plants—if we are to speak of instrumental parts as distinct or the same by appeal to their functions" (*DA* II 4 416^{a}2–5; see also *PA* IV 10 686^{a}25–687^{a}2). Similarly, in animals the front is a starting-point, because it is what perception is directed toward (*IA* 4 705^{b}10–13). Even in earthworms, where right and left are more difficult to distinguish perceptually, the functional difference between them still exists: "the starting-point of the movement is the same in all animals and by nature has its position in the same place; and it is from the right that the starting-point of movement derives" (5 706^{a}10–13). Thus human beings put their left foot forward, unless they accidentally do the opposite, since "they are moved not by the foot they put in front, but by the one with which they step off" (706^{a}8–9).

Note 85
The parts visible on the outside surface of the body, then, are arranged in this way, and, as was said, they are mostly distinguished by name and are known through intimacy with them: See *HA* I 6 491^{a}23. The point about the parts being distinguished by name is new, but has been made implicitly by the use of familiar names and the reference to nameless parts (most recently at I 15 494^{a}14).

Note 86
The inner parts of human beings are especially unknown: In part, presumably, because dissection of human corpses was—for reasons explored in von Staden—forbidden.

Note 87

Two membranes encompass it, [1] the one around the bone is stronger, [2] the one around the brain itself less strong than the former: [1] is the dura mater; [2] the pia mater. The so-called arachnoid mater is between them.

Note 88

In all animals the brain has two parts: The right and left hemispheres, including the right and left cerebellar ones.

Note 89

The back of the head is empty and hollow in all animals, in keeping with the size that each has: See *GA* V 3 784ᵃ2–4n.

Note 90

It has at its center in most animals a very small hollow: Reading πᾶς κοῖλόν τι μικρόν with Balme-1 and translating with Pellegrin; Louis and Peck seclude πᾶς.

Note 91

Bregma: See *HA* I 7 491ᵃ31n.

Note 92

The largest ones are parallel and do not meet: That is, the two leading, one from each eye, to a hemisphere of the brain.

Note 93

The esophagus . . . gets its derived name (*epônumian*) from its length (*mêkous*) and narrowness (*stenotêtos*): The derived name is presumably *stomachos* ("gullet").

Note 94

Between the two apertures is what is called the epiglottis, which is capable of being folded over the orifice that leads to the mouth: That is, of the mouth and the windpipe. "The windpipe, by being positioned . . . in the front, is interfered with by the nourishment. But in relation to this nature has contrived the epiglottis . . . [which] opens during the entrance and exit of breath and closes when nourishment is being ingested, in order that nothing slip down the windpipe" (*PA* III 3 664ᵇ20–29).

Note 95

The lung tends to have two parts in all the animals that have it: That is, each lung tends to have such parts.

Note 96

They seem to have two lungs: That is, each lung seems to be split into two lungs.

Note 97
Next the intestine having breadth: Reading εἶτα ἔντερον εὖρος ἔχον with Pellegrin for Louis, Balme-1, and Peck ἐπιεικῶς πλατύ ("moderately wide"). "Il est vrai semblable que A. distingue ici intestin grêle et gros intestin" (Pellegrin, p. 129 n2).

Note 98
Bowel (*koilia*): Or "stomach."

Note 99
The omentum: The membrane that "extends over the rest of the stomach and the mass of the intestines" (*PA* IV 3 677^{b}19–20).

Note 100
The mesentery: A continuous set of tissues attaching the intestines to the abdominal wall, formed by a double fold in the peritoneum.

Note 101
The heart has three cavities: "Aristotle said that the human heart has three ventricles—right, left, and middle—a concept that has often been viewed as an astonishing error. But was it? Aristotle did not miscount ventricles. In the third century BC, all cardiac chambers were called 'ventricles,' meaning 'cavities.' The 'ears' (auricles) were distinguished from the 'cavities' (ventricles) by Herophilus of Alexandria (c 300 BC) and by Rufus and Ephesus (a contemporary of Jesus Christ). Aristotle regarded the right atrium as a venous dilatation, not as a part of the heart. Aristotle's 'right ventricle' was our right ventricle. His 'left ventricle' was our left atrium. His 'middle ventricle' was our left ventricle. Because he did not count the right atrium, Aristotle considered the human heart to be three-chambered or 'triventricular,' consisting of the right ventricle, the left atrium, and the left ventricle" (Van Praagh, p. 462). Cited by Pellegrin, p. 130 n5.

Note 102
It has three cavities, as was just said: At *HA* I 17 495^{b}4.

Note 103
All of them, even the two smaller ones, are connected to the lungs by passages: Reading ἁπάσας δ᾽ ἔχει, καί τὰς δύο μικράς, εἰς τὸν πλεύμονα τετρημένας with Aubert & Wimmer (followed by Peck and Pellegrin) for Louis καί εἰσιν εἰς τὸν πλεύμονα τετρημέναι πᾶσαι. [ἀμφοτέρας δ᾽ ἔχει τὰς δύο μικράς, καὶ τὸν πλεύμονα τετρημένας πάσας]; Balme-1 reads ἔχει δὲ τὰς δύο μικράς· καί εἰς τὸν πλεύμονα τετρημένας ἁπάσας.

Note 104
Near where the mesentery is: Reading πρὸς ἥν καὶ τὸ μεσεντέριόν ἐστι with Louis and Balme-1; Aubert & Wimmer (followed by D'Arcy Thompson and Peck) seclude.

Note 105
About the great blood-vessel and the aorta by themselves we shall speak in common later on: At *HA* II 3–4, *PA* II 5.

Note 106
In accord with nature . . . in a monstrous way: "Monstrosity is a sort of deformation" (*GA* IV 3 769ᵇ30).

Note 107
Cases have already been seen in certain quadrupeds in which the position [of liver and spleen] is exchanged: "Cases of change of place are also known, the liver being on the left, the spleen on the right" (*GA* IV 4 771ᵃ7–9).

Note 108
The liver for the most part and in most animals has a gallbladder, but in some animals it does not: Reading τὸ δ'ἧπαρ ὡς μὲν ἐπὶ τὸ πολὺ καὶ ἐν τοῖς πλείστοις ἔχει χολήν, ἐπ' ἐνίοις δ' οὐκ ἔπεστιν with Louis and Pellegrin (following Dittmeyer); Balme-1, Peck, and D'Arcy Thompson read with the mss. τὸ δ'ἧπαρ ὡς μὲν ἐπὶ τὸ πολὺ καὶ ἐν τοῖς πλείστοις οὐκ ἔχει χολήν, ἐπ' ἐνίοις δὲ ἔπεστιν ("the liver for the most part and in most animals does not have a gallbladder, but in some animals it does"). The transmitted text is incompatible with *PA* IV 2 676ᵇ16–18.

Note 109
Chalcis: Situated at the narrowest point of the Euripus Strait; the chief town in Euboea.
Naxos: The largest of the Cyclades group of islands, located in the central Aegean.

Note 110
The right [kidney] also has less fat than the left and is drier: "In all animals with kidneys the right one is higher up than the left. For because the movement is from the parts on the right side, and because of this the nature of the parts on the right is stronger, all these parts must be prepared, because of this movement, to go more upward. . . . The cause [of the right one having less fat] is that the parts on the right are dry in nature and more easily moved, and the movement is a contrary one. For it dissolves the fat more" (*PA* III 9 671ᵇ28–672ᵃ26).

Note 111
[The kidneys] have a small cavity, as was just said: At *HA* I 17 496ᵇ6. Reading ἔχουσι δὲ κοιλίαν, ὥσπερ εἴρηται, μικράν with Louis; Dittmeyer (followed by Peck) secludes. The claim is that while the body (or meat) of the kidneys contains blood-vessels, and so blood, the kidney itself (unlike the heart) does not have any blood in its cavity, since the ducts leading from the great blood-vessel and the aorta do not penetrate it.

Note 112
Others come from the aorta that are strong and continuous: The iliac arteries into which the abdominal aorta divides in the lower abdomen. These supply blood to the pelvic organs, gluteal regions, and legs.

Note 113
The way in which [males have testicles] will be determined in the common accounts: The reference is presumably to *HA* III 1. The accounts are "common" because dealing with the testicles not (as here) just in human beings but in all animals that have them.

Note 114
One must observe (*theôreisthô*) **[the uterus's appearance] on the basis of the diagrams in the *Dissections*:** DL V [25] 368 mentions a *Dissections* (*anatomôn*) in seven books, which is no longer extant. Aristotle often refers to it in the zoological treatises. See Falcon & Lefebvre (Lennox), pp. 249–272.

Note 115
The uterus too in all animals in common must be spoken about in what follows: At *HA* III 1 510^{b}5–511^{a}34.

Parts of Animals

Note 116
Theoretical knowledge (*theôrian*): See *HA* I 6 491^{a}5n.
Methodical inquiry (*methodon*): A *methodos* is a *tropos tês zêtêseôs*—a way of inquiry (*APo.* I 31 46^{a}32–^{b}36). *Hodos* means "way," "route," or "road," as at *NE* I 4 1095^{a}33. Sometimes the *met-* prefix is omitted, as at *GC* I 8 324^{b}35–325^{a}2.
More humble and more estimable alike: See *GA* I 23 731^{a}34n.
Scientific knowledge (*epistêmên*) **of the subject matter:** To understand what an Aristotelian science is we must begin with the sorts of statements or propositions that figure as premises and conclusions within it.

(1) A statement (*logos apophantikos*) is the true (or false) predication of a single predicate term A of a single subject term B, either as an affirmation (*kataphasis*) (A belongs to B) or a denial (*apophasis*) (A does not belong to B) (*Int.* 5, 8). What makes a term a single subject term, however, is not that it is grammatically singular or serves as a grammatical subject but that it designates a substantial particular—a canonical example of which is a perceptible matter-form compound, such as Socrates. Similarly, what makes a term a predicate is that it designates a universal (man, pale)—something that can have many particular instances. When the role of predicate is restricted to universals, therefore, while that of subject is left open to both particulars and universals, it is more on ontological or metaphysical grounds than on what we would consider strictly logical ones.

Subjects and predicates are thus ontological items, types of beings, rather than linguistic or conceptual ones, and logical principles, such as the principle of non-contradiction, are very general ontological principles, truths about all beings as such, or qua beings. Particular affirmations (Socrates is a man) and general affirmations (Men are mortal) have the same subject-predicate form, but when the subject is a universal, the affirmation may itself be either universal (All men are mortal) or particular (Some men are mortal)—that is to say, the predicate may be asserted (denied) of the subject either universally (*katholou*) or in part (*kata meros*) or, if the quantifier is omitted (Men are mortal), indefinitely (*adioristos*). Affirmations, as a result, are of four types: A belongs to all B (**a**AB), A belongs to no B (**e**AB), A belongs to some B (**i**AB), A does not belong to all B (**o**AB).

(2) A *science*, whether theoretical or one of the other sorts, is a state of the soul that enables its possessor to give demonstrative explanations—where a demonstration (*apodeixis*) is a special sort of deduction (*sullogismos*) from scientific starting-points and a deduction is "an argument in which, certain things having been supposed, something different from those supposed things necessarily results because of their being so" (*APr.* I 2 24^{b}18–20). The things supposed are the argument's premises; the necessitated result is its conclusion; all three are affirmations of one of the four types we looked at. In Aristotle's view, such deductions are *syllogisms* (*sullogismos*, again) consisting of a major premise, a minor premise, and a conclusion, where the premises have exactly one "middle" term in common, and the conclusion contains only the other two "extreme" terms. The conclusion's predicate term is the *major term*, contributed by the major premise; its subject is the *minor term*, contributed by the minor premise. The middle term must be either subject of both premises, predicate of both, or subject of one and predicate of the other. The resulting possible combinations of terms yield the so-called figures of the syllogism:

	First figure		Second figure		Third figure	
	Predicate	Subject	Predicate	Subject	Predicate	Subject
Premise	A	B	A	B	A	C
Premise	B	C	A	C	B	C
Conclusion	A	C	B	C	A	B

Systematic investigation of the possible combinations of premises in each of these figures results in the identification of the *moods* or modes that constitute valid deductions. In the first figure, these are as follows:

Form	Mnemonic	Proof
aAB, aBC | aAC	Barbara	Perfect
eAB, aBC | eAC	Celarent	Perfect
aAB, iBC | iAC	Darii	Perfect
eAB, iBC | oAC	Ferio	Perfect

A mood is perfect when there is a proof of its validity that is *direct*, in that it does not rely on the validity of any other mood. Only first figure syllogisms have perfect moods.

(3) Besides their logical interest as admitting of direct proof, perfect syllogisms in Barbara are also of particular importance to science. First, because "syllogisms that give the reason why, which hold either universally or for the most part, in most cases are carried out through this figure. That is why it is the most scientific of all; for getting a theoretical grasp on the reason why is most important for [scientific] knowledge" (*APo.* I 14 79^{a}20–24). Second, "only through this figure can you hunt for scientific knowledge of something's essence" (79^{a}24–25): essences hold universally, only perfect syllogisms in *Barbara* have universal conclusions, and definitions of essences, which are scientific starting-points, must hold universally.

(4) Specifically scientific starting-points are of just three types (*APo.* I 10 76^{a}37–^{b}22). Those *special* to a science are definitions of the real (as opposed to nominal) essences of the beings with which the science deals (II 3 90^{b}24, II 10 93^{b}29–94^{a}19). Because these are definitions by genus and differentia (II 13 96^{a}20–97^{b}39), a single science must deal with a single genus (I 7 75^{b}10–11, I 23 84^{b}17–18, 28 87^{a}38–39). Other starting-points (so-called axioms) are common to all or many sciences (I 2 72^{a}14–24, I 32 88^{a}36–^{b}3). A third sort of starting-point posits the existence of the genus with which the science deals, but this may often be left implicit if the existence of the genus is clear (I 10 76^{b}17–18). The source of these starting-points, in turn, is perception and experience, which lead by induction, to a grasp by understanding of them: "From perception memory comes to be, and from many memories of the same thing, experience. For, then, memories that are many in number form one experience. And from experience, or from the whole universal that has come to rest in the soul (the one over and above the many, this being whatever is present as one and the same in all of them), comes a starting-point (*archê*) of craft knowledge and scientific knowledge—of craft knowledge if it concerns production (*genesis*), of scientific knowledge if it concerns being" (II 19 110^{a}3–9).

(5) To constitute a *demonstration* a deduction must be a valid syllogism in the mood Barbara, whose premises meet a number of conditions. First, they must be immediate or indemonstrable, and so must be reached through induction. Second, our confidence in them must be unsurpassed: "If we are to have scientific knowledge through demonstration, . . . we must know the starting-points better and be better persuaded of them than of what is being shown, but we must also not find anything more persuasive or better known among things opposed to the starting-points from which a contrary mistaken conclusion may be deduced, since someone who has unconditional scientific knowledge must be incapable of being persuaded out of it (*APo.* I 2 72^{a}37–^{b}4). Finally, they must be necessary (and so, of course, true) in a special sense: the predicates in them must belong to the subjects in every case, intrinsically, and universally (*APo.* I 4 73^{a}24–27): (5a) *In every case*: A predicate A belongs to every subject B if and only if there is no B to which it fails to belong and no time at which it fails to belong to a B: "for example, if animal belongs to every man, then if it is true to say that this thing is a man, it is also true to

say that it is an animal, and if the former is the case now, the latter is also the case now" (73^a29–31). (5b) *Intrinsically:* A predicate A belongs intrinsically to a subject B just in case it is related to B in one of four ways: (i) A is in the account or definition of what B is, or of B's substance, or essence (73^a34–37); (ii) B is a complex subject φB_1, where φ is an intrinsic coincident of B_1—for example, odd number or male or female animal—and A is in the definition of φB_1's essence; (iii) A just is B's essence; (iv) A is not a part of B's essence or identical to it but stems causally from it, so that being B is an intrinsic cause of being A (73^a34–$^b24$). (5c) *Universally:* A predicate A belongs to a subject B universally just in case "it belongs to it in every case and intrinsically, that is, insofar as it is itself" (73^b26–27).

(6) Because intrinsic predicates stem in various ways from essences, the subjects to which they belong must have essences. In other words, they must be *intrinsic beings*, since—stemming as they do from essences—intrinsic predicates identify or make them clear: "The things said to be intrinsically are the very ones signified by the figures of predication" (*Met.* V 7 1017^a22–23). These figures of predication are the so-called *categories*: "Anything that is predicated (*katêgoroumenon*) of something must either be . . . a definition . . . if it signifies the essence . . . or, if it does not, a special attribute (*idion*) . . . or one of the things in the definition, or not; and if it is one of the things in the definition, it must signify the genus or the differentiae, since the definition is composed of genus and differentia. If, however, it is not one of the things in the definition, it is clear that it must be a coincident; for a coincident was said to be that which belongs to a thing but that is neither a definition nor a genus nor a special property. Next we must distinguish the kinds (*genos*) of predication in which one will find the four mentioned above. These are ten in number: what-it-is, quantity, quality, relation, when, where, position, having, doing, and being affected. For the coincidents, the genus, the special properties, and the definition will always be in one of these kinds of predication [or *categories*]" (*Top.* I 8–9 103^b7–25). For each of the intrinsic beings in these ten *categories* we can state its what-it-is (*Met.* VII 4 1030^a17–24), even if strictly speaking only substances have definitions and essences (5 1031^a7–24). Specifying these beings is one of the tasks of *Categories*, where Aristotle explains how beings in categories other than that of substance are ontologically dependent on those in the category of substance. The list of categories itself, however, has a somewhat provisional status, as Aristotle's remark about the category of *having* indicates: "Some further ways of having might perhaps come to light, but we have made a pretty complete enumeration of those commonly spoken of" (*Cat.* 15 15^b30–32).

(7) What all four types of intrinsic beings have in common, what makes them worth the attention of someone inquiring into ultimate starting-points and causes, is that they are the ontological correlates or truth-makers for scientific theorems—the beings responsible for the necessary truth of those theorems. Moreover, they would seem to be the only sorts of being that can play this role, since they constitute an exhaustive catalogue of the necessary relations that can hold between a subject (A) and something (B) predicated of it: B is part of the essence of A; A is part of the essence of B; B is the essence of A; the essence of A (being A) is an intrinsic cause of (being) B.

Note 117

It is characteristic of a well-educated person (*pepaideumenou*) **to be able to judge accurately what is well said and what is not:** "Not being well educated is just the inability to judge in each thing at issue which arguments belong to it and which are foreign to it" (*EE* I 6 1217ª7–10). Thus a person well educated in medicine, for example, is capable of judging whether someone has treated a disease correctly (*Pol.* III 11 1282ª3–7), and the "unconditionally well-educated person," who is well educated in every area, "seeks exactness in each area to the extent that the nature of its subject matter allows" (*NE* I 3 1094ᵇ23–1095ª2).

Note 118

But in one case, we consider a single individual to have the capacity to judge about (one might almost say) all things, in the other case about a definite nature: "Aristotle has distinguished three people: (1) the specialist who knows the data; (2) the educated man who, whether or not he is also a specialist, can see whether a scientific explanation is based on the appropriate principles; (3) the man who can does this for one science but not for others" (Balme-2, pp. 70–71).

A definite (*aphôrismenês*) **nature:** That is, about a definite genus which, as such, is the subject matter of a definite first-order science. Thus rhetoric, though it is a transgeneric science, "does not deal with a definite (*aphôrismenou*) genus" (*Rh.* I 1 1355ᵇ8–9), and so is not itself a "definite (*aphôrismenês*) science" (1354ª3; also 2 1355ᵇ33–34). See Introduction, pp. xxxi–xxxiv.

Note 119

It is clear in the case of inquiry into nature too that there must be certain defining marks by reference to which we can appraise its way of showing things, separately from the question of what the truth is, whether thus or otherwise: Compare: "It is also correct to judge separately the argument for the cause and what is being shown, both because of what was just said, namely, that one must not in all cases pay heed to what is due to argument, but often rather to what appears to be so (as things stand, though, when people are unable to refute [an argument], they feel compelled to be convinced by what has been stated) and because often what seems to have been shown by argument is true, yet not due to the cause that the argument says it is due to" (*EE* I 6 1217ª10–16).

Defining marks (*horous*): A common meaning of the noun *horos*, from which verb *horizesthai* ("define") derives, is "term," in the logical sense, in which a syllogism has three terms. But often a *horos* is a definition or a defining mark (a boundary marker is a *horos*) that gives definition to what would otherwise lack it. Hence the doctor's *horos* is the thing "by reference to which he discerns what is healthy for a body from what is not" (*EE* VII 15 1249ª21–22), "that is why too they make breathing the defining mark of being alive" (*DA* I 2 404ª9–10).

Its way of showing things (*ton tropon tôn deiknumenôn*): What is shown is, in particular, a scientific starting-point rather than a conclusion demonstrated from one.

Note 120

Substance (*ousian*): *Ousia* is a noun apparently formed from the present participle *ousa* of the verb *einai* ("to be"). "Substance" is the traditional translation. (1) The substance *of* something is its essence, whereas (2) *a* substance is something that has the fundamental sort of being possessed by an ultimate subject of predication—a *tode ti* ("this something")—which is not itself ever predicated of anything else (*Met.* V 8 1017ᵇ23–26). It is usually but not always clear which of (1) or (2) is intended. The reference to the *nature* of a human (*PA* I 1 639ᵃ17) as the thing being defined indicates that (1) is the meaning here.

Note 121

Genera of animals: See *HA* I 1 486ᵃ23n.

Affections (*pathôn*): What X *paschei* is what happens to him, so that he is passive with respect to it, as opposed to what he *poiei* ("does as an agent," "produces," "affects"). When Y does something to X, X is affected by it, so his *pathê* as a result are, in one sense, his affections and, in another, his passions or feelings. Often, however, while a thing's *pathê* includes its affections, they encompass its attributes more generally.

Note 122

Whenever the same ones belong to different species (*eidei*) **of animals, while they themselves have no differentia** (*diaphoran*): See *HA* I 1 486ᵃ24n.

Note 123

But presumably there are other attributes that include (*echein*) **the same predicate, but differ due to a difference in the form** (*diaperein de tê[i] kat' eidos diaphora[i]*)—**for example, the perambulation of animals**: As, for example, the attributes flying and walking include the predicate perambulate, since each is, by definition, a mode of perambulation—a way of spatially moving from place to place: "If spatial movement is a process of moving from one place to another, there are differences in form here as well—flying, walking, leaping, and so on" (*NE* X 4 1174ᵃ29–31).

Note 124

Special attributes (*tôn idiôn*): "A special attribute is what does not make clear the essence of a thing yet belongs to that thing alone and is predicated convertibly of it—for example, it is *idion* of human to be capable of learning grammar, since if someone is human he is capable of learning grammar, and if he is capable of learning grammar he is human" (*Top.* I 5 102ᵃ18–22).

Note 125

Whether just as the mathematicians show the things that astronomy is concerned with, so in that way too the natural scientist having first observed (*theôrêsanta*) **the things that appear to be so concerning the animals and the parts of each, must then state the why, that is, the cause, or else proceed in some**

other way: "The why differs from the that in another way when each is considered by means of a different science. These are sciences that are related to one another in such a way that the one is under the other, as, for example, optics is under geometry, mechanics under solid geometry, harmonics under arithmetic, and the [star-gazing that observes] the things that appear to be so [in the heavens] under astronomy. . . . For here it is for the scientists who deal with perceptibles to know the that and for the mathematical scientists to know the why. For the latter possess demonstrations of the causes, and often they do not know the that, just as people who have a theoretical grasp on (*theôrountes*) universals often do not know some of the particulars through lack of reliable experience (*anapiskepsian*)" (*APo.* I 13 78ᵇ34–79ᵃ6). That Aristotle favors following the mathematical procedure is clear from *PA* I 1 640ᵃ13–15.

The natural scientist (*phusikos*): Or natural philosopher. See *Met.* IV 1 1026ᵃ18–19 (philosopher), XI 7 1064ᵇ2 (scientist).

Note 126

Natural generation: See *GA* I 1 715ᵃ15n.
The for-the-sake-of-which and the one from which comes the starting-point of movement: The so-called final and efficient causes. See *GA* I 1 715ᵃ5n.

Note 127

For this is an account (*logos*), **and the account is a starting-point:** See *GA* I 1 715ᵃ5n.
Alike in the things composed in accord with craft and in those composed by nature: See *GA* I 22 730ᵇ11–23.

Note 128

The nobly beautiful: The adjective *kalos* is often a term of vague or general commendation ("fine," "beautiful," "good"), with different connotations in different contexts: "The contrary of *to kalon* when applied to an animal is *to aischron* ["ugly in appearance"], but when applied to a house it is *to mochthêron* ["wretched"], and so *kalon* is homonymous" (*Top.* I 15 106ᵃ20–22). (Similarly, the adverb *kalôs* often means something like "well" or "correct.")

Even in the general sense, however, *kalos* has a distinctive evaluative coloration suggestive of "order (*taxis*), proportion (*summetria*), and determinateness (*hôrismenon*)" (*Met.* XIII 3 1078ᵃ36–ᵇ1), making a term with aesthetic connotation, such as "beauty," seem a good equivalent: to bear the stamp of happiness one must have *kallos* as opposed to being "very ugly (*panaischês*)" (*NE* I 8 1099ᵇ3–4; also *Pol.* V 9 1309ᵇ23–25). Moreover, just as a thing need not have a purpose in order to be beautiful, a *kalon* thing can be contrasted with a purposeful one: a great-souled person is one "whose possessions are more *kalon* and purposeless (*akarpa*) than purposeful and beneficial" (*NE* IV 3 1125ᵃ11–12). At the same time, it seems wrong to associate *kalon* with beauty in general, since to be *kalon* a thing has to be on a certain scale: "greatness of soul requires magnitude, just as *to kallos* ('nobility of appearance') requires a large body, whereas small people are elegant and well-proportioned but not *kaloi*" (1123^{b}6–8); "any *kalon* object . . . made up of parts must not only have them properly ordered but also have a magnitude which is not random, since what is *kalon* consists in magnitude and order (*taxis*)" (*Po.* 7 1450^{b}34–37; also *Pol.* VII 4 1326^{a}33–34). It is this requirement that makes "nobility" in its more aesthetic sense a closer equivalent than "beauty."

In ethical or political contexts, the canonical application of *kalon* is to ends that are intrinsically choiceworthy and intrinsically commendable or praiseworthy (*epaineton*): "Of all goods, the ends are those choiceworthy for their own sake. Of these, in turn, the *kalon* ones are all those praiseworthy because of themselves" (*EE* VIII 3 1248^{b}18–20; also *NE* I 13 1103^{a}9–10). It is because ethically *kalon* actions are intrinsically choiceworthy ends, indeed, that a good person can do virtuous actions because of themselves (*NE* II 4 1105^{a}32) *and* for the sake of what is *kalon* (III 7 1115^{b}12–13). What makes such actions choiceworthy (VI 1 1138^{a}18–20) and praiseworthy (II 6 1106^{b}24–27), however, is that they exhibit the sort of order (X 9 1180^{a}14–18), proportionality (II 2 1104^{a}18), and determinateness (II 6 1106^{b}29–30, IX 9 1170^{a}19–24) that consists in lying in a mean (*meson*) between two extremes. This brings us full circle, connecting what is ethically *kalon* to what is aesthetically noble, lending the former too an aesthetic tinge.

Finally, what is ethically *kalon* includes an element of self-sacrifice that recommends "nobility," in its more ethical sense, as a good equivalent for it as well: "It is true of an excellent person too that he does many actions for the sake of his friends and his fatherland, even dying for them if need be. For he will give up wealth, honors, and fought-about goods generally, in keeping for himself what is *kalon*" (*NE* IX 8 1169^{a}18–22). One reason people praise a *kalon* agent, indeed, is that his actions benefit them: "The greatest virtues must be those that are most useful to others, and because of this, just people and courageous ones are honored most of all; for courage is useful to others in war, justice both in war and peace" (*Rh.* I 9 1366^{b}3–7). But since what is *kalon* is a greater good than those an excellent person gives up or confers on others, there is also a strong element of self-interest in what he does: "The greater good, then, he allocates to himself" (*NE* IX 8 1169^{a}28–29). An excellent person does *kalon* actions for their own sake, not for an ulterior motive, because it is only as done in that way that they constitute the doing well in action (*eupraxia*) that just *is* happiness.

Note 129

What is unconditionally necessary is present in the eternal things, while what is hypothetically necessary is also (*kai*) present in all generated things, as it is in the products of craft: If the account of the form or essence of an artifact A or natural being N assigns it a function that can only be achieved by something made from matter of sort m, then matter of sort m is "hypothetically necessary (*anagkê ex hupotheseôs*)" for A or N to exist. See also *PA* I 1 642^{a}1–13, 642^{a}31–^{b}4. An example of *unconditional* necessity present in natural generated things is perhaps this: "A first starting-point is when a female comes to be and not a male—but this is necessary by nature. For the genus that is separated into female and male must be preserved. . . . The monster, by contrast, is not necessary in relation to the for-the-sake-of-which and the final cause, but is necessary coincidentally (*kata sum-bebêkos*)" (*GA* IV 3 767ᵇ8–15). For discussion of whether or not *kai* has the implication, as it appears to, that this text seems to support, see Lennox-1, pp. 127–128.

Note 130
The mode of demonstration and of necessity is distinct in the case of the natural and the theoretical sciences: See *APr.* I 13 32ᵇ4–21.

Note 131
These have been spoken about elsewhere: Necessity in *Ph.* II 9, *Met.* V 5, the difference between natural and theoretical sciences in *Met.* IV 1.

Note 132
Nor is it possible to link eternally the necessity of this sort of demonstration, so as to say, "since *this* is, [it is necessary] that *that* is": The meaning may be gleaned from the following text: "If, then, it goes on without limit downward, it will not be unconditionally necessary for *this* (one of the later ones) to come to be, but hypothetically so. For always it will be necessary for there to be another before it, because of which it is necessary for it to come to be. So if there is no starting-point of what is unlimited, there will be no first thing because of which it will be necessary for it to come to be. But then even in the case of the ones that have a limit it will not be true to say that it is unconditionally necessary for it to come to be—for example, a house if a foundation has come to be. For when a foundation has come to be, if it is not always necessary for the house to come to be, the result will be something always being that admits of not always being. But *always* must belong to the coming to be, if the house's coming to be is of necessity. For *necessary* and *always* go together (for what it is necessary for there to be cannot not be), so that if it is of necessity, it is eternal, and if it is eternal, it is of necessity. If, therefore, the coming to be of something is of unconditional necessity, it is necessary for it to turn back again. For it is necessary for coming to be to have a limit or not, and if not, for it to be rectilinear or in a circle. But of these, if indeed it is to be eternal, it cannot be rectilinear, because of there being no starting-point of any sort, whether taken going downward (going toward to the future) or upward (going toward the past). But it is necessary for it to have a starting-point, and—not being limited—to be eternal. That is why it is necessary for it to be in a circle. It is necessary, therefore, for it to convert—that is, if of necessity *this*, therefore also the earlier; moreover, if the earlier, it is also necessary for the later to come to be. And this goes on always continuously. For it makes no difference whether we say it is because of two things or of more. It is in movement and coming to be in a circle, therefore, that there is unconditional necessity. And if it is in a circle, it is necessary for each thing to come to be and to have come to be, and if this is necessary, the coming to be of these things is in a circle" (*GC* II 11 337ᵇ25–338ᵃ11).
About these things too determinations have been made elsewhere, and about what sorts of things necessity is present in, what sort converts, and due to what

cause: The reference is probably to *APo.* II 12 95ᵇ36–96ᵃ8 (on conversion) and to the *GC* II 11 text just quoted.

What sort converts (*antistrephei*): The verb *antistrephein* is used to signify: (1) a logical relation between propositions, so that, for example, the universal negative converts, because if no B is A, then no A is B (*APr.* I 2 25ᵃ5–6) and so on; (2) a logical relation between terms (I 45 51ᵃ4–5), equivalent to counterpredication, where B is counterpredicated of A if and only if A is predicated of B and B of A; (3) the substitution of one term for another, without logical convertibility (*APr.* II 15 64ᵃ40); (4) the (valid) inference of (A admits of not being B) from (B admits of being A) (I 13 32ᵃ30); (5) the substitution of the opposite of a premise for a premise (II 8 59ᵇ4); (6) an argument in which from one premise in a syllogism, and the opposite of the conclusion, the opposite of the other premise is deduced (II 8–10, *Top.* VIII 14 163ᵃ32–34); (7) at *Top.* II 1 109ᵃ10, at only there it seems, A and B convert if and only if (B *belongs* to A) ⊃ (A *is* B).

Note 133
One must begin from what we said earlier, namely, that first one must grasp the things that appear to be so about each genus: See *PA* I 1 639ᵇ8–10.

Note 134
That is why Empedocles . . . when the animal was bent [in the uterus]: = DK 31 B97 = TEGP 148 F 98. See *GA* V 1 778ᵇ1–10n (this vol.).

Note 135
Prior . . . not only in account: "Things are prior in account to those things whose accounts are composed of *their* accounts" (*Met.* XIII 2 1077ᵇ3–4; see also VII 10 1035ᵇ4–6).

But also in time: Priority in time seems to be what *Met.* V 11 refers to as priority "in nature and substance" (1019ᵃ1–4). What it calls "priority in time," on the other hand, is a matter of one thing being earlier than another (1018ᵇ14–19), which it, in agreement with *Cat.* 12 14ᵃ26–28, refers to as "the strictest" sort of priority.

Note 136
It is likewise in the case of things that seem to come to be spontaneously (*automatôs*): Things that come about by chance (*to automaton*) are the ones "whose cause is indefinite and that come about not for the sake of something, and neither always nor for the most part nor in an orderly way" (*Rh.* I 10 1369ᵃ32–34). The living beings that come to be by chance are sometimes referred to as "spontaneously generated." Chance is discussed in *Ph.* II 4–6.

Note 137
Something similar to them that is capable of producing them pre-exists: Reading προϋπάρχει τὸ ποιητικὸν ὅμοιον with Louis and Langkavel; Peck secludes ὅμοιον.

Note 138

And the craft is the account of the work without the matter (and likewise with what is due to luck). For as the craft has it, so it is produced: "And all productions come either from craft, or from some capacity, or from thought. Some of them, however, may come about from chance or from luck, in a way quite similar to the ones found in those that come to be from nature. For sometimes there too some of the same things come to be either from seed or without seed. . . . From craft, though, come to be the things whose form is in the soul. And by form I mean the essence of each thing and the primary substance. For even contraries in a way have the same form. For the opposing substance is the substance of the lack. For example, health is the substance of disease, since it is by its absence that disease is made clear. And health is the account in the soul and the scientific knowledge. . . . And so it turns out that in a way health is produced from health, and a house from a house, the one that has matter from the one without matter. For the craft of medicine and the craft of building are the form of health and of a house. By the substance without matter I mean the essence. . . . What produces, then, and what the process of becoming healthy starts from, if it is from craft, is the form in the soul, but if it is from chance, it is from whatever it is that is a starting-point of producing for what produces from craft. For example, in the case of healing the starting-point is presumably from the warming, which the doctor produces by rubbing" (*Met.* VII 7 1032ᵃ27–ᵇ26).

And it is likewise with what is due to luck: Reading καὶ τοῖς ἀπὸ τύχης ὁμοίως for Louis καὶ τοῖς ἀπὸ <τέχνης τὰ ἀπὸ> τύχης ὁμοίως and Langkavel καὶ τοῖς ἀπὸ <τέχνης γίνεται τὰ ἀπὸ> τύχης ὁμοίως.

Due to luck (*apo tuchês*): What happens by luck (*tuchê*) in the broad sense is what happens coincidentally or contingently (*APo.* I 30 87ᵇ19–22), so that luck in that sense is pretty much the same as chance or spontaneity. But in a narrower sense, which is contrasted with chance, what happens by luck is what has a coincidental final cause: "Luck is a coincidental cause in things that come about in accord with deliberate choice for the sake of an end" (*Met.* XI 8 1065ᵃ30–31). Thus if a tree's being by the backdoor is the sort of thing that might be an outcome of deliberative thought, it is a candidate final cause of action—an end we aim at (*Ph.* II 5 197ᵃ5–14, 6 197ᵇ20–22). If wish, which is the desire involved in deliberation and deliberate choice, is what causes it to be there, the tree's being by the backdoor has a genuine final cause. If not, its being there has a coincidental final cause. Unlike chance, then, which applies quite generally to whatever results from coincidental efficient causes, narrow luck applies only to what could come about because of action and deliberate choice. Hence it is the sphere relevant to action: "Luck and the results of luck are found in things that are capable of being lucky, and, in general, of action. That is why indeed luck is concerned with things doable in action" (197ᵇ1–2). The sphere of narrow luck is thus that of the practical and productive sciences (*PA* I 1 640ᵃ27–33, *Rh.* I 5 1362ᵃ2).

As the craft has it, so it is produced: The craft has (or is) the account of the (essence, form, substance) of the product, and transmits it to the matter of the work or product, so that the latter comes to have that form.

Note 139

This is the essence of a human (*tout' ên to anthrôpô[i] einai*): Literally, "this is what it was to be a human." See *PA* I 1 642ª25n.

Because of this it has these things: That is, it follows from the essence of, for example, the human that it has, for example, a spine.

Note 140

Otherwise, one must say the closest thing to it, namely, either [1] in general that it is impossible to be another way or [2] that it is noble to be this way. And [3] these things follow: Suppose we want to explain [3] why a human (say) has a part P but having P is neither a part of the human essence nor an intrinsic coincidental attribute (per se accident) of human beings (see *HA* I 6 491ª10n). There are two options: [1] to demonstrate that in general (that is, not only for something that has a human essence) it is not possible to be otherwise than having P, or [2] to demonstrate that it is noble (good, better) to have P. An example of [1] is where P is a uterus. For having a uterus (being female) is neither a part of the human essence nor an intrinsic coincidental attribute of humans: "Male and female, however, are attributes that do properly belong to the animal, not in virtue of its substance [or essence] but in the matter—that is, the body. That is why the same seed becomes female or male when it is affected in regard to a certain attribute" (*Met.* X 9 1058ᵇ21–24). Nonetheless, it is impossible for a female animal to be any other way than with a uterus (or its analogue). An example of [2] is where P is testes: "If nature makes everything either because of what is necessary or because of what is better, this part should exist because of one of these two things. Well, that it is not necessary for generation is evident. For then every progenitor would have it. But as things stand neither serpents nor fish have testes. For they have been seen copulating and with their ducts full of milt. It remains, then, for it to be for the sake of what is better" (*GA* I 4 717ª15–21).

Noble: See, again, *PA* II 1 731ᵇ25n, III 10 760ᵇ20n.

Note 141

That is why of the parts *this* one comes to be first, then *that* one: See *GA* II 6 743ᵇ18–32.

Note 142

What it is (*tis*), **what sort of thing it is** (*poia tis*): The account or definition of something that states what something is consists of the thing's genus and differentiae (*Met.* VII 12 1027ᵇ29–30), of which the genus is stated first: "the genus is intended to signify the what-it-is, and is placed first of the things said in the definition" (*Top.* VI 5 142ᵇ27–29). Sometimes both elements are included in the what-it-is or essence: "genera and differentiae are predicated in the what-it-is" (VII 3 153ª17–18; also *APo.* II 5 91ᵇ28–30, 13 97ª23–25). But sometimes the genus tells us what the thing is while the differentiae tell us what sort or quality of thing it is: "a things differentia never signifies what-it-is, but rather some quality (*poion ti*)" (*Top.* IV 2 122ᵇ16–17; also 6 128ª26–27, *Met.* V 14 1020ª33).

Strife, love: Empedocles. See *GA* I 18 722^{b}15–30n.
Understanding (*nous*): Anaxagoras. See, on understanding, *GA* II 3 736^{b}5n.
Chance (*to automaton*): Probably the atomists. But see Lennox-1, p. 136, and, on chance, *PA* I 1 640^{a}27n.

Note 143
Residue: See *GA* I 18 724^{b}26–27.
Pneuma: See Introduction, pp. lxii–lxxii.

Note 144
Homoeomerous parts . . . non-homoeomerous parts: See *PA* I 1 641^{a}36n.

Note 145
A *this in this* (*tode en tô[i]de*) **or a *this such-and-such sort of thing*** (*tode toionde*): That is, this form in this matter, both taken universally: "It is clear too that the soul [= form] is primary substance, whereas the body is matter, and the human or the animal is the thing composed of both taken universally" (*Met.* VII 11 1037^{a}7); "The human and the horse, though, and things that are in this way set over the particulars, that is, [taken] universally, are not substance but rather a compound of a sort, [consisting] of this account and this matter taken universally (10 1035^{b}27–30); "For some things presumably are this in this, or these things in this state (*hôdi tadi econta*)" 1036^{b}23–24). In other words, they are like snub, not like concave. See *PA* I 1 641^{a}36–^{b}10nn.

Note 146
Nature in accord with shape [or form] is more controlling (*kuriôtera*) **than material nature:** What is *kurios* (or has control) in a sphere determines or partly determines what happens within it; it is thus one of the most estimable or important elements in the sphere, so that what is inferior or less important than it cannot control it (*NE* VI 12 1143^{b}33–35, 13 1145^{a}6–7). When Aristotle contrasts natural virtue of character with the *kurios* variety (VI 13 1144^{b}1–32), the control exerted by the latter seems to be teleological: the natural variety is a sort of virtue because it is an early stage in the development of mature virtue (compare *Met.* IX 8 1050^{a}21–23). Hence *kuria aretê* is "full virtue" or virtue in the full or strict sense of the term. Similarly, *ta kuria* are the words that are in prevalent use among listeners: "By prevalent (*kurion*) I mean [a name or word] a given group would use, and by exotic one that others would. So it is evident that the same name can be both prevalent and exotic, although not for the same groups" (*Po.* 21 1457^{b}3–5). *Kuriôs* and *haplôs* ("unconditionally") are often used interchangeably, for example, *Cat.* 13 14^{b}24, as are *kuriôs* and *kath' hauta* ("intrinsically"), for example, *Cat.* 6 5^{b}8.

Note 147
Democritus: On Democritus and his fellow atomist Leucippus, see DK 67–68 = TEGP pp. 516–685.

Note 148
Homonymously (*homônumôs*): "Things are said to be homonymous when they have only a name in common, but the account of the substance [= essence, form] that corresponds to the name is distinct—for example, both a human and a picture are animals. These have only a name in common and the account of the essence corresponding to the name is distinct. For if we are to say what-it-is for each of them to be an animal, we will give a special account to each" (*Cat.* 1 1^{a}1–6). See also, *GA* I 19 726^{b}22–24n.

Note 149
Function: See *GA* I 2 716^{a}23n.

Note 150
In too simple (*haplôs*) **a way:** See *GA* II 5 741^{a}12n.

Note 151
The physicists (*phusiologoi*): The *phusiologoi or phusikoi* (*GA* II 5 741^{b}10) were thinkers who tried to give a general account of reality that, among other things, made no reference to incorporeal beings: "They posit the elements of bodies alone, but [1] not of the incorporeal things, although incorporeal ones are also beings. And when they try to state the causes of coming to be and passing away and to give a physical account of all things, [2] they do away with the cause of movement" (*Met.* I 8 988^{b}24–26).

Note 152
What it is and what sort of thing it is: See *PA* I 1 640^{b}6.

Note 153
Soul (*psuchê*): See *GA* II 4 738^{b}27n.
Substance: That is, essence or form. See *PA* I 1 639^{a}16n.

Note 154
Philosophy (*philosophia*): Aristotle sometimes applies the term *philosophia* (or sometimes just *sophia*) to any science aiming at truth rather than action (*Met.* II 1 993^{b}19–21). In this sense of the term, all the broadly theoretical sciences count as branches of philosophy, and *philosophia* is more or less equivalent in meaning to *epistêmê* in its most exact sense. *Philosophia* also has a narrower sense, however, in which it applies exclusively to sciences providing knowledge of starting-points (*Met.* XI 1 1059^{a}18, *NE* VI 7 1141^{a}16–18). It is in this sense that there are just three theoretical philosophies: mathematical, natural, and theological (*Met.* VI 1 1026^{a}18–19). In addition to these, Aristotle occasionally mentions practical philosophies, such as "the philosophy of human affairs" (*NE* X 9 1181^{b}15). It is among these that his own ethical writings belong (*Pol.* III 12 1282^{b}18–23).

Note 155

Understanding (*nous*): In the broadest sense of the term, someone with *nous* is someone with sound common sense and the cognate verb *noein*, like *dianoeisthai*, means "to think" (*Mete.* I 3 340^{b}14, *Ph.* IV 1 208^{b}25, *NE* III 1 1110^{a}11). *Nous*, in this sense, is what enables a soul to suppose, deduce, calculate, and reason, and believe, so that it is possible to *noein* something false (*DA* III 3 427^{b}9). In the narrow sense, which is the one relevant here, *nous* is what makes possible a type of knowledge of universal scientific starting-points that, unlike scientific knowledge proper, is not demonstrable from anything further: "About the starting-point of what is scientifically known there cannot be scientific knowledge . . . since what is scientifically known is demonstrable . . . the remaining alternative is for *nous* to be of starting-points" (*NE* VI 6 1140^{b}33–1141^{a}8); "*nous* is of the terms or definitions (*horoi*) for which there is no reason (*logos*)" (8 1142^{a}25–26).

This *nous* is a divine substance (*NE* I 6 1096^{a}24–25, X 7 1177^{b}19–1178^{a}8), or anyway the most divine one in human beings (X 7 1177^{a}16), and so shares in the immortality that is characteristic of gods: "it alone [of the parts of the human soul] is immortal and eternal" (*DA* III 5 430^{a}23). Consequently, it alone of these parts is separable from the human body and can survive its death: "*Ho nous* seems to be born in us as a sort of substance, and not to pass away . . . understanding (*noein*) and contemplating (*theôrein*) are extinguished because something else within passes away, but it itself is unaffected" (I 4 408^{b}18–25; also *Long.* 2 465^{a}26–32). Among sublunary animals this *nous* is fully possessed only by human beings (*PA* II 10 656^{a}7–8, *NE* X 8 1178^{b}24–25), and thus is special to them. In fact, a human is most of all his *nous* (*NE* IX 8 1168^{b}31–32, X 7 1178^{a}2–8).

No English term is a precise equivalent for *nous* or *noein* in this narrow sense. "Intellect," which is in many ways the best choice, lacks a cognate verb in current use. "Understanding" is better in this respect but shares with "intellect," "intelligence," "intuitive reason," "apprehension," and other common translations the defect of not being factive or truth entailing, since *nous* is one of the five states of the soul "in which the soul grasps the truth by way of affirmation and denial" (VI 3 1139^{b}15–17).

Intelligible objects (*noêtôn*): As objects of understanding in the strict sense these are definitions of essences, or the essences themselves. And essences are of two sorts: "But we must not neglect to consider the way the essence or its account is, because, without this, inquiry produces no result. Of things defined, however, that is, of the 'whats' that things are, some are the way the snub is, others the way the concave is. And these differ because the snub is grasped in combination with the matter (for the snub is a concave nose), whereas the concavity is without perceptible matter. If, then, all natural things are said the way the snub is (for example, nose, eye, face, flesh, bone, and, in general, animal, and leaf, root, bark, and, in general, plant—for the account of none of these is without [reference to] movement, but always includes matter), the way we must inquire into and define the what-it-is in the case of natural things is clear" (*Met.* VI 1 1025^{b}28–1026^{a}5). Thus natural sciences are distinguished from the strictly theoretical sciences by the sorts of essences that are their starting-points. See Introduction, pp. lxxxvii–xcvii.

Note 156

Someone might raise a puzzle, though, in view of what was said just now, as to whether it belongs to natural science to speak about all soul, or about a certain part of it. For if it is about all of it, beyond natural science there is no philosophy left. For understanding (*nous*) is of the intelligible objects. So natural science would be knowledge of all things: When the understanding actively understands an essence that is like concave rather than snub, it is identical to that essence: "And [the understanding] is an intelligible object in just the way its intelligible objects are, since, in the case of those things that have no matter, what understands and what is understood are the same, since theoretical scientific knowledge and what is known in that way are the same" (*DA* III 4 430ª2–5); "The being for an act of understanding is not the same as the being for a thing understood. Or is it that in some cases the scientific knowledge is the thing? In the case of the productive sciences isn't it the substance and the essence without the matter? In the case of the theoretical sciences isn't it the account the thing and its active understanding? In the cases, then, where the thing understood and the active understanding of it are not distinct, namely, in those where the thing understood has no matter, they will be the same, and the active understanding will be one with the thing understood" (*Met.* XII 9 1074ᵇ38–1075ª5). Thus if natural science dealt with all soul, it would deal with the understanding too, and so would deal with the essences that, like concave, have no matter, to which the understanding is identical. But then it would deal with all essences, and so natural science would be the science of all things: "If . . . there is no other substance beyond those composed by nature, natural science will be the primary science" (*Met.* VI 1 1026ª27–29).

Note 157

For it belongs to the same science to get a theoretical grasp on understanding and on the intelligible objects, if indeed they are in relation to each other and the theoretical knowledge of things that are in relation to each other is in all cases the same knowledge, just as is also the case with perception and perceptible objects: Understanding is similar in structure to perceiving, so that when it is active the understanding "must be unaffectable . . . , but receptive of the form, and potentially such as it is, although not the same as it, and as what is capable of perceiving is in relation to the perceptible objects, so the understanding must be in relation to the intelligible ones" (*DA* III 4 429ª13–18). Thus the route to understanding, as to perceptual capacities generally, is via the forms or essences (intelligible in the one case, perceptible in the other) that are their special objects (as color is the special object of sight, sound of hearing). That is why the grasping of understanding's special objects (essences that are like concave) is grasping understanding itself.

The element in the understanding that receives the intelligible form is like the eye-jelly (*HA* I 9 491ᵇ21). For, as in the case of seeing, what this element takes on is the form of the intelligible object without its matter (*DA* III 4 430ª7–8). The element in question is "passive understanding (*pathêtikos nous*)" (5 430ª24–25). It "serves as matter for each kind of thing," and is "what is potentially each of them." In addition, "there is also something else that is understanding's cause and that is productive, in that it produces it—the two being related as, for example, a craft to its matter [or materials]" (430ª10–13). This second element is productive (or active) understanding (*nous poiêtikos*). This helps us to see why Aristotle thinks that active understanding is identical to its objects in some but not in other cases. So consider a case of an intelligible object F that is like snub, so that its structure is this form G in this matter m. When a person X has learned what F is, but is not now actively thinking about F, F is a potentiality present in X's passive understanding, which he is capable of activating by himself (*DA* III 4 429ᵇ7–9). Since X can activate F on numerous occasions, F is a universal—something that is one and the same on many different occasions. As present in X's passive understanding, then, F is this form G in this matter m, both taken universally. When activated or actualized in X's productive understanding, however, F is an intelligible particular F*: "Scientific knowledge, like knowing scientifically, is twofold, one potential, the other active. The capacity [or potentiality], being as matter, universal and indefinite, is of what is universal and indefinite, whereas the activity, being determinate, is of what is determinate—being a this something it is of a this something" (*Met.* XIII 10 1087ª15–18). But because F is this form G in this matter m, both taken universally, F* must be this form G in this particular bit of perceptible matter m. F* is thus a particular matter-form compound—a particular snub nose, for example. As such it obviously cannot be present in X's understanding, and his active understanding of F cannot be identical to F*. It follows, then, as (3) claims that it is only when an intelligible object does not have a structure like snub that the active understanding of it is identical to it.

The theoretical knowledge of things that are in relation to each other (*pros allêla*) **is in all cases the same knowledge:** "We call relatives all such things as are said to be just what they are, *of* or *than* other things, or in some other way in relation to something else. For example, what is larger is said to be *than* something else, since it is said to be larger than something, and what is double is said to be *of* something else, since it is said to be double of something. Similarly with all other such cases" (*Cat.* 7 6ª36–ᵇ2) Hence scientific knowledge is a relative: "Scientific knowledge, a genus, is said to be just what it is *of* another thing (it is said to be scientific knowledge *of* something)" (8 11ª24–26). Thus to know what scientific knowledge is to know what it is of, and to know what it is of is to know what it is.

Note 158

Not all soul, however, is a starting-point of movement, nor are all its parts, rather of growth it is the very part that is also present in plants: Namely, the nutritive part (*threptikon*). See *GA* II 1 735ª17n.

Of alteration it is the perceptual part: See *GA* I 23 731ᵇ4n.

And of spatial movement some other part, and not the one capable of understanding: "Both of these, therefore, are capable of causing movement with respect to place, namely, understanding and desire—understanding, however, that is of the practical sort, which rationally calculates for the sake of something, and differs from the theoretical sort in respect of the end. And every desire too is for the sake of something. For the object of desire is the starting-point of practical understanding, and the last thing is the starting-point of the action. So it is reasonable that these two things—desire and practical thought—appear to be the causes of movement. For the object of desire moves us, and, because of this, thought causes movement, because its starting-point is the object of desire. Also, when the imagination causes movement it does not cause movement in the absence of desire. There is, then, one thing that causes movement, namely, the desiring part. For if there were two things that caused movement, understanding and desire, they would cause movement in virtue of some common form. But as things stand the understanding evidently does not cause movement without desire (for wish is a desire, and when something is moved in accord with rational calculation, it is moved in accord with wish), and desire causes movement even contrary to rational calculation, since appetite is a sort of desire" (*DA* III 10 433ª9–26); "Thought by itself, however, moves nothing. But the one that is for the sake of something and practical does" (*NE* VI 2 1139ª35–36).

Note 159

Thought (*dianoia*): *Dianoia* is often contrasted with the body (*Pol.* II 9 1270ᵇ40, VII 16 1335ᵇ16), making "mind" seem a natural translation of it. But unlike the mind, which includes perception, imagination, belief, knowledge, desire, virtues of character, and other such things, *dianoia* is contrasted with each of these. It is not perception, because all animals have that, whereas "the majority of animals do not have *dianoia*" (*DA* I 5 410ᵇ24). It is not imagination, because, as we might put it, *dianoia* is propositional, or operates on things that can be true or false, affirmed or denied (*Pol.* II 11 1273ª22), whereas imagination is a representational state that is more like perception, more "imagistic." Thus "what affirmation and denial are in the case of thought, that, in the case of desire, is precisely what pursuit and avoidance are" (*NE* VI 2 1139ª21–22). Unlike belief and knowledge, however, "thought is in fact not yet affirmation" (VI 9 1142ᵇ12–13), making it natural to think of it, or some of it anyway, as the process of reasoning that can culminate in a belief or an affirmed proposition. And this is further evidenced by the fact that the virtues of thought, which are theoretical wisdom and practical wisdom (*NE* I 13 1103ª4–6), are (respectively) those of the scientific sub-part and the rationally calculative sub-part, of the part of the soul that has reason (VI 1 1139ª5–12). At the same time, the fact that scientific knowledge includes both demonstrative reasoning and a grasp of scientific starting-points by the understanding implies that not all thinking need be in any sense inferential, since understanding is non-inferential—a grasping of something rather than something process-like (see *PA* I 1 641ª36n). *Dianoia* is not desire, because, while desire can cause animal movement, without thought, as it does in the case of non-rational animals, "thought by itself . . . moves nothing" (*NE* VI 2 1139ª35–36). As a result, it is not character (*Pol.* VIII 2 1337ª38–39), since the latter, as involving desire, is cultivated by habituation, whereas *dianoia* is cultivated by teaching (*NE* II 1 1103ª14–18)—hence the common contrast between thought and character (*Pol.* III 11 1281ᵇ7).

Note 160

Not all soul is a nature, although some part of it—whether one part or several—is: "It belongs to the natural scientist to get a theoretical grasp even on some of the soul, that is, on as much of it as is not without matter" (*Met.* VI 1 1026ª5–6).

Note 161

Of the results of abstraction (*ex aphaireseôs*) **none is an object of theoretical natural science, since nature does everything for the sake of something:** The results of abstraction referred to are mathematical objects (see Introduction, pp. xxxix–xl), and in mathematics, as opposed to natural science, no appeal is made to a final cause: "Further, to many beings not all the starting-points pertain. For in what way can there be a starting-point of movement for immovable things? Or in what way can the nature of the good be such a starting-point, if indeed everything that is good intrinsically and because of its own nature is an end and a cause in this way, namely, that for its sake the other things both come to be and are, and if the end—that is, the for-the-sake-of-which—is an end of some action, and all actions involve movement? So in the case of immovable things this starting-point could not exist, nor could there be any good-itself. That is why in mathematics too nothing is shown through this cause, nor is there any demonstration where the cause is this: 'because it is better or worse.' Indeed no one mentions any such thing at all" (*Met.* III 2 996ª21–32).

Nature (*hê phusis*) **does everything for the sake of something:** (1) Many of the things Aristotle means by *phusis* ("nature") are discussed in *Met.* V 4. But he uses the term more widely than that discussion suggests. In the "primary and full way" a being that is or does something by nature has a nature—an internal starting-point of movement and rest (1015ª13–15; *Cael.* III 2 301ᵇ17–18). The world of nature, investigated by natural science, is a world of such beings, all of which have perceptible matter as a constituent (*Met.* VI 1 1025ᵇ30–1026ª6). This world is roughly speaking the sublunary one. Beyond it lies the world of the heavens studied by astronomy and theology (1026ª7–22), where beings either have no matter, or matter of a different sort (*Cael.* I 2 269ᵇ2–6, 3 270ᵇ19–25, *Mete.* I 3 339ᵇ25–27). Although, strictly speaking, these beings do not have natures, since "nature is the proper order of perceptible things" (*Cael.* III 2 301ª5–6), Aristotle nonetheless speaks of them as if they do (III 1 298ᵇ23, *Met.* VI 1 1026ª20, 25 are nice, because particularly unfortunate, examples, as in *GA* itself is IV 4 770ᵇ9–17). We use the term "nature" in a similar way when we speak of the nature of the numbers or the nature of fictional entities, not meaning to imply at all that these things are parts of the natural world (compare XIII 4 1078ª10). (2) Sometimes, instead of using *phusis* to refer to the or a *phusis of* X, Aristotle uses the term and its plural *phuseis* to mean something we translate as "a nature" (Greek has no indefinite article) or "natures." The thing or things referred to may or may not have natures in the strict sense; they are pretty much just entities of some sort. (3) He also speaks, as he does here, of *phusis* or *hê phusis* in agentive terms—for example, when he says, as he frequently does, that nature does nothing pointlessly (for example, *Cael.* I 4 271ª33, *DA* II 5 415ᵇ16–17, III 9 432ᵇ21, 12 434ª31, *PA* I 1 641ᵇ12–29) or that it does something correctly (*Cael.* I 3 269^{b}20), or for the best (II 5 288^{a}3). Just as when he speaks of "the nature of the All" (I 2 268^{b}11) or "the nature of the whole" (*Met.* XII 10 1075^{a}11) it is not entirely clear how exactly or how literally these words are to be taken. He also speaks of it as having psychological attitudes, such as wish (*boulêsis*) (*Sens.* 3 441^{a}3, *GA* IV 10 778^{a}4, *Pol.* I 6 1255^{b}3), but here *bouleuesthai* is usually, and best, translated as "tend." That this is not an a priori but rather an empirically based assumption is made clear at *GA* V 8 788^{b}20–22: "we assume, making our assumption on the basis of what we observe, that, nature neither omits any of the things possible in each case nor produces any pointlessly." (4) Since *hê phusis* is also spoken of agentively when it refers to a particular nature it is sometimes unclear whether *hê phusis* refers to nature generally or to a particular nature, though context usually favors one alternative over another. When it refers (or most likely refers) to a particular nature the definite article is translated, but not when the reference is (or most likely is) to nature generally.

Note 162

Craft is present in the products of craft: Because "the craft of building is the form of a house" (*Met.* XII 4 1070^{b}33), and the form is in the product. See also *PA* I 1 640^{a}31–32n.

Note 163

The heaven (*ton ouranon*): "[1] In one way, we say that the substance belonging to the outermost circumference of the universe is heaven, or the natural body that is on the outermost circumference of the universe, since more than anything else it is the last upper region that we usually call heaven, the one in which we say that everything divine also has its seat. In another way, [2] it is the body that is continuous with the outermost circumference of the universe, in which we find the moon, the sun, and some of the stars, since we say that these bodies too are in the heaven. Further, [3] we say that the body that is encompassed by the outermost circumference is heaven, since we are accustomed to say that the whole and the universe is heaven" (*Cael.* I 9 278^{b}9–21). Here the heaven referred to, since it is contrasted with the sublunary sphere around us (*PA* I 1 641^{b}19), is [2].

Note 164

Some people say, though, that each of the animals is and came to be by nature, while the heaven, in which no chance or disorder whatsoever is evident, was composed in that way by luck and chance: "Other people make chance the cause of this heaven and of all the cosmoses. For they say that the rotation came to be by chance, as did the movement that separated things out and put in place the present order of the universe. And this itself merited yet more surprise. For on the one hand they say that animals and plants neither are nor come to be by luck, but that nature, understanding, or something else of that sort is the cause (since it is not just any random thing that comes to be from a given sort of seed, but an olive tree from one sort and a human from another), whereas on the other hand they say that the heaven and the most divine of visible things came to be by chance, and have no cause of the sort that animals and plants have. And yet if such is the case, this very fact merits attention, and something might well have been said about it. For in addition to the other respects in which what they say is strange, it is even stranger to say it when they see nothing in the heaven coming to be by chance, whereas among the things that [in their view] are not by luck many do come to be by luck. And yet for the contrary to happen would surely have been likely" (*Ph.* II 4 196^{a}25–^{b}5).

Note 165
The seed is becoming (*genesis*), **the end is substance** (*ousia*): To be a seed of substance X is to be something that, everything else being equal, will become an X.

Note 166
We know how potentiality is related to actuality (*entelecheian*): See *GA* I 19 726^{b}17n.

Note 167
For of two of the modes distinguished in the works in philosophy (*tois kata philosophian*) **neither can apply. The third, though, does apply, at any rate to the things that have a process of generation:** The reference is not to the work *On Philosophy* referred to as *tois peri philosophias* at *Ph.* II 2 194^{a}36, which survives only in fragments (see F1–27 R3 = Barnes, pp. 2389–2397), but otherwise is unclear. The following texts are likely candidates: "Necessity is twofold: one is in accord with nature and impulse (*hormên*); the other by force and contrary to impulse—for example, a stone spatially moves upward and downward of necessity, but not because of the same necessity. And among the things that are due to thought, some (for example, a house or a statue) never occur due to chance, nor because of necessity, whereas others occur due to luck as well (for example, health and preservation). But it is especially among those that admit of being this way and otherwise, when, not due to luck, their coming to be is such that the end is good, that things come to be for the sake of something, and is by nature or by craft. Due to luck, though, nothing comes to be for the sake of something" (*APo.* II 11 94^{b}36–95^{a}9); "Something is said to be necessary: [1] If it is that without which, as a contributing cause, living is impossible—for example, breathing and nourishment are necessary for an animal, since it cannot exist without these. Also, if it is anything without which it is not possible for the good to be or come to be, or for the bad to be got rid of or taken away—for example, drinking the medicine is necessary in order not to be sick, as is sailing to Aegina in order to get the money. [2] Further, if it is forced or is force (that is, what is contrary to the impulse or the deliberate choice impedes or tends to hinder). For what is forced is said to be necessary, which is why it is also painful. . . . And it seems that necessity is something that cannot be persuaded, and correctly so, since it is contrary to the movement that is in accord with deliberate choice and in accord with rational calculation. [3] Further, we say that it is necessary for what does not admit of being otherwise to be the way it is. And it is in accord with this sort of necessity that all the others are in some way

said to be necessary" (*Met.* V 5 1015ᵃ20–36). Here [1] is the "third" mode of necessity; [2] and [3] the modes that do not apply.

Note 168
It is clear, then, that there are two modes of cause, and that as far as possible one must succeed in stating both, but if not, at any rate try to do so: Reading εἰ δὲ μή, γε πειρᾶσθαι ποιεῖν, δῆλόν with Ogle for Louis εἰ δὲ μή, δῆλόν γε πειρᾶσθαι ποιεῖν; Balme-2 reads εἰ δὲ μή, δῆλόν γε πειρᾶσθαι ποιεῖν, δῆλόν.

Note 169
Even Empedocles stumbled onto this, led by the truth itself, and is compelled to say that the substance and the nature is the ratio (*logos*)—for example, when he says what bone is: "For early philosophy concerning all things seemed to speak inarticulately, because it was young and at the starting-point, since even Empedocles says that bone exists as a result of its ratio, and this is the essence and the substance of the thing" (*Met* I 10 993ᵃ15–18).

Note 170
Essence (*to ti ên einai*): *To ti ên einai* is a phrase of Aristotle's coinage, of which "essence," from the Latin verb *esse* ("to be"), is the standard translation. The imperfect tense ên ("was") may—as in the Latin phrase *quod erat demonstrandum* ("which was to be proved")—stem from an original context (such as a Socratic conversation) in which someone is asked to say or define what X is, and concludes by giving his answer in the imperfect tense to signal that he is giving the answer that was asked for (*ên* at *Met.* VII 4 1030ᵃ1 may be a case in point). Apart from that it seems to have no special significance, so we could equally well translate *to ti ên einai* as "the what-it-*is*-to-be."

Note 171
In the time of Socrates, however, [interest in] it grew, but inquiry concerning natural things abated, and philosophers turned instead to useful virtue and political science: "It" is definition of the essence and substance: "The work Socrates did, on the other hand, was concerned with ethical issues, not at all with nature as a whole. In these, however, he was inquiring into what is universal and was the first to fix his thought on definitions" (*Met.* I 6 987ᵇ1–4); "Socrates, on the other hand, busied himself about the virtues of character, and in connection with these was the first to inquire into universal definition. (For among the physicists Democritus latched on to this only a little, and defined, after a fashion, the hot and the cold, while the Pythagoreans had previously done this for a few things, whose accounts they connected to numbers—for example, what opportune is, or the just, or marriage.) It was reasonable, though, that Socrates was inquiring into the what-it-is. For he was inquiring in order to deduce, and the what-it-is is a starting-point of deductions. For at that time there was not yet the strength in dialectic that enables people, even separately from the what-it-is, to investigate contraries, and whether the same science is a science of contraries. For there are two things that

may be fairly ascribed to Socrates—inductive arguments and universal definition, both of which are concerned with a starting-point of scientific knowledge" (XIII 4 1078^{b}17–30).

Note 172

The beating back of the internal heat in the process of the cooling of the external air is inhalation: Reading ἡ εἴσοδος with Louis; Peck (followed by Lennox-1) reads ἡ εἴσοδος καὶ ἡ ἔξοδος ("the beating back of the internal heat during the cooling of the external air is inhalation and exhalation"). "The example unfortunately is highly compressed and does not appear to represent Aristotle's own theory, according to which the lung is expanded by the organism, air naturally flows in to 'fill the void' caused by the expansion, and being cool this air reduces the heat around the heart. The lung then contracts, forcing the warm air out (*Juv.* 27 . . . 480^{a}25–^{b}4)" (Lennox-1, p. 151).

Note 173

Some people: Plato uses dichotomous division as a method of definition in the *Statesman* and *Sophist*, and the reference may be to him. On the topic of this chapter more generally, see Introduction, pp. lxxxvii–xcvii.

[Try to] grasp the particular [species] by dividing the genus into two differentiae: Particulars, as things that are severally one in number and jointly many (*Met.* III 4 999^{b}34–1000^{a}1), are usually contrasted with universals, which belong to many numerically distinct particulars (VII 13 1038^{b}11–12), and the usual route is the inductive one from particulars to universals. But sometimes (as here, where it is the species into which the genus is divided by the differentiae) what is *kath' hekaston* is what is less universal than something else. Thus while genuine particulars are indefinable (15 1039^{b}27–29, 1040^{a}27–^{b}4), it is "easier to define *to kath' hekaston* than the universal" (*APo.* II 13 97^{b}28), and a definition of a universal divides into *kath' hekasta* (*Ph.* I 1 184^{a}23), where these are things that are particular in the sense of being "indivisible in species" (*PA* I 4 644^{a}30–31). See also *PA* I 3 643^{b}26–27.

Note 174

Of some things there will be only one differentia, the others being superfluous— for example, footed, two-footed, split-footed: Omitting ἄπουν ("footless") with Louis, Ogle, and Peck (see *PA* I 3 644^{a}5–6, where "footless" is omitted). Balme-2 retains ἄπουν, but reads δίπουν ἢ σχιζόπουν ("two-footed or split-footed"), so that the first division is footless/footed, footed/two-footed, and the second footless/footed, footed/split-footed.

For this one differentia is a controlling one. Otherwise, it is necessary to say the same thing many times: For in a case like this "it is evident that the ultimate differentia will be the substance of the thing and its definition, if indeed we should not state the same thing many times in the definitions, since that would be wasted work" (*Met.* VII 12 1038^{a}18–21). So the ultimate differentiae should be the controlling one. But notice that "split-footed" does not entail "two-footed."

Note 175

The diagrammed divisions: A reference, presumably, to a diagram in which the genus of birds is torn asunder.

Note 176

Lack (*sterêsis*): "[1] Something is said to lack something in one way if it does not have one of the attributes that something or other naturally has, even if this thing itself does not naturally have it—for example, a plant is said to lack eyes. [2] In another way if what it or its genus naturally has, it itself does not have—for example, a human who is blind and a mole lack sight in different ways, the one in contrast to its genus, the other intrinsically. [3] Further, if it does not have what it is natural for it to have when it is natural for it to have it. For blindness is a sort of lack, but a being is not blind at any and every age, but only if it does not have sight when it is natural for it to have it. Similarly, if it does not have sight in that in which, and in virtue of which, and in relation to which, and in the way in which, is natural. [4] Further, a thing forcefully taken away is said to be lacked" (*Met.* V 22 1022^{b}22–32).

Note 177

Further, [1] it is necessary to divide by a lack, and those who dichotomize do divide by it. But [2] there is no differentia of a lack insofar as it is a lack. [3] For it is impossible for there to be forms (*eidos*) **of what is not (for example, of footless or wingless), as there are of winged and of footed:** The argument is: [1] Division is into F and lack-of-F. And those who define species by division do so. Therefore, they must treat F and lack-of-F as differentiae. But [2] there are no differentia of a lack as such. [3] gives the reason "in a form a Platonist would understand" (Lennox-1, p. 155), but is in any case intuitively acceptable. So further division of lack-of-F is impossible. Thus there need be nothing wrong with [1], and in fact Aristotle allows that lacks can be differentiae. See *PA* I 3 643^{b}24–26.

Winged (*pterôseôs*): *Pterôsis* "translated as 'winged' primarily refers to feathers. It was extended to refer to feathered wings, and sometimes (as here) it is used simply to refer to wings. . . . The ambiguity of the term can make for some odd claims, as in the following assertion about winged insects: 'Their wing is unsplit and without a shaft; for it is not a feather [literally: 'not a wing'] but a skin-like membrane' ([*PA* IV 6] 682^{b}18–19). In either case the differentiation is clear—feathers are 'split' into individual fibers, and bird wings are 'split' into feathers; and whether one imagines the insect wing as analogous to a feather or to a bird wing, it is unsplit by comparison. Functionally, nevertheless, it is a wing" (Lennox-1, pp. 156–157). See also *HA* IV 7 753^{a}19–25, on flying insects, and *PA* IV 6 682^{b}7–21 on insect wings.

Note 178

Why would it be a universal and not a particular [species]: See *PA* I 2 642^{b}5n. Similarly, when Aristotle refers to animals in this chapter, he means species of animals.

Note 179

Cloven-hoofed (*dichala*) . . . **solid-hoofed** (*monucha*): "The cloven-footed animals have two splits behind; in the solid-hoofed, this part is continuous" (*HA* II 1 499^{b}14–15).

Note 180
The bloodless ones: Reading εἰς τὰ ἄναιμα with Balme-2, Lennox, and the mss. for Louis τὰ ἀντικείμενα ("the opposite ones"); Peck reads τὰ ἀντικειμένας, which he translates as "the opposite lines of differentiation."

Note 181
But [1] most difficult of all, or else impossible, is to distribute them into [, for example,] the bloodless ones. For [2] it is necessary for each of the differentiae to belong to one of the particular [species], so that the opposing one does so too. But [3] it is not possible for some indivisible species that is part of the substance to belong to animals that differ in species, instead it will always have a differentia—for example, bird differs from human being (for their two-footedness is other and different), and even if they are blooded, their blood is different, or blood must be supposed to be no part of their substance. But [4] if this is so, one differentia will belong to two [species of] animals. And if *this* is so, [5] it is clear that it is impossible for a lack to be a differentia: Suppose that a lack, bloodlessness, has a differentia D_b. [2] Since D_b is a differentia it divides a genus G into two species, S_1, which has D_b, and S_2, which has D_{ob}, which is the opposite of D_b. [3] Now look at the definitions of S_1 and S_2, which will be GD_b and GD_{ob} (respectively). But D_b and D_{ob} are differentiae of bloodlessness, which is a lack, and so has no differentiae (*PA* I 1 642ᵃ22). So GD_b does not differ from GD_{ob}. But that means that the indivisible species that are parts of the substances (here = essences) they define do not differ either. But it is impossible for two distinct species S_1 and S_2 to be parts of the same indivisible substance or essence. [4] Since D_b belongs to S_1 and D_{ob} belongs to S_2, and D_b and D_{ob} do not differ, it follows that bloodlessness (of which they were supposed to be distinct differentiae) belongs to both S_1 and S_2. So that one differentia will belong to two distinct species. But this is impossible. Therefore, [5] it is impossible (now on the basis of [4]) for a lack to be a differentia.
Some indivisible species that is part of the substance (*eidos ti tês ousias atomon*): The genitive *tês ousias* is best understood as partitive, so that the substance does not belong to the species (as "species of substance," understood like "species of animal," implies), but rather the species to the substance or essence. The essence is defined by the genus + differentiae; the genus + differentiae = the species.

Note 182
The differentiae will be equal in number to the indivisible [species of] animals, on the assumption that both the [species of] animals and the differentiae are indivisible: See Introduction, pp. lxxxvii–xcvii.

Note 183
If it is possible for [a differentia] that is in fact common to be present: Reading εἰ δ' ἐνδέχεται ὑπάρχειν καὶ κοινήν with Ogle and Peck for Louis and mss. εἰ δ' ἐνδέχεται μὴ ὑπάρχειν † . . . καὶ κοινήν.

It is clear that, in accord with the common one at any rate, animals that are distinct in species, are in the same differentia: Clear because of the argument of *PA* I 3 642ᵇ34–643ᵃ6.

Note 184
Special: See *PA* I 1 639ᵃ5.

Note 185
The species is the differentia in the matter: Because the matter is here the genus: "Something is said to be a genus . . . as matter, since that to which the differentia or quality belongs is the underlying subject, which we call the matter" (*Met.* V 28 1024ᵇ6–9); "the genus is the matter of what it is said to be the genus of—not as in 'the genus of the Heraclidae' but as in 'the genus that is included in the nature of that thing'" (X 8 1058ᵃ23–25).

Note 186
A body in any and every condition will not be an animal, nor any of its parts, as has often been said: Most recently at *PA* I 1 641ᵃ17–21.

Note 187
The intrinsic coincidents (*tois sumbebêkosi kath' hauto*): The *kath' hauta sumbebêkota* (or per se accidents) are attributes that belong to a subject intrinsically and thus demonstrably, but are not part of its *ousia*, or essence (*APo.* I 7 75ᵇ1, 22 83ᵇ19, *Met.* V 30 1025ᵃ30–32, XIII 3 1078ᵃ5–9). They are contrasted with the non-intrinsic coincidents (or coincidents proper) which belong to a subject contingently, and so non-demonstrably. Thus it follows from the definition of the substance or essence of the triangle that its interior angles equal to two right angles, but it is not part of its substance or essence.

Note 188
Opposites (*antikeimenois*): "Things said to be opposites (*antikeimena*) include contradictories, contraries, relatives, lacking and having, and the extremes that comings to be and passings away are from and to. And all things that cannot be present at the same time in what is receptive of both are said to be opposed—either themselves or their components (for gray and white do not belong at the same time to the same thing, because their components [namely, black and white] are opposed)" (*Met.* V 10 1018ᵃ20–25). Here the opposites are contradictories.

Note 189
[1] Animate beings (*empsucha*) **at any rate must not be divided by the common** (*koinois*) **functions of the body and the soul—[2] for example, in the divisions mentioned just now, walkers and fliers (for there are certain genera to which both differentiae belong and are fliers and wingless, just like the ant genus):** The reference in [2] is to the division of animals into footed (here walkers) and winged (here fliers) at *PA* I 3 642ᵇ23–24. And the problem with the division raised

here is that ants are both wingless and fliers. Its relevance to [1] is that the function of perambulation (of moving around in space under one's own steam), for which feet and wings are instrumental parts, is not so divided by those parts that all and only the walkers are footed and all and only the fliers are winged. For ants are wingless fliers. Turn now to [1] which tells us that to be a (ultimate) differentia of animate or ensouled beings D must not be a common (*koinos*) function of the body and the soul. But this is ambiguous between at least two things. It could mean [2a] that D must not be a function shared by the body and soul (which is the meaning at *DA* III 10 433ᵇ10, *Sens.* 1 437ᵃ7, *Somn.* 1 453ᵇ13) or [2b] that D must not be common to the species into which it divides the animals (which is what *koinos* means elsewhere in *PA* I 3). What our interpretation of [2] shows, however, is that both [2a] and [2b] are probably in play. For it is because perambulation is a function common to body and soul that different bodily parts can be instrumental for it, but it is because the parts that are instrumental for it in one species or genus need not in fact be instrumental for it in another, that an attempt to differentiate the function (flying) via the instrumental parts (being winged) fails. For flying is common to both the winged and the non-winged.

Note 190

Indian dogs: See *GA* II 7 746ᵃ34n.
For (one might almost say that) whatever is tame is also wild: "Tame animals are by nature better than wild ones, and it is better for all of them to be ruled by human beings, since in this way they secure their preservation" (*Pol.* I 5 1254ᵇ10–13).

Note 191

Homonymous: Reading εἰ μὲν ὁμώνυμον with Louis; Balme-2 reads εἰ μὴ ὁμώνυμον ("if not homonymous"). See *GA* I 19 726ᵇ24n.

Note 192

There will be only one differentia, and this one, whether simply or the result of interweaving (*sumplokê*) will be the final species (*eidos*): *Sumplokê* is used by Plato to refer to the interweaving of Forms (*Sph.* 259e6), which is presented as occurring through division (253d–e).

Note 193

If, on the other hand, one does not take the differentia of a differentia: See Introduction, pp. lxxxvii–xcvii.
One will necessarily make the division continuous in the same way that one makes the account (*logos*) one by being bound together (*sundesmô[i]*): The account is the definition of the species essence: "A definition, however, is an account that is one not by being bound together (*sundesmô[i]*), like the *Iliad*, but by being of one thing. What is it, then, that makes the human one, and why one and not many—for example, both the animal plus the two-footed?" (*Met.* VIII 6 1045ᵃ12); "The essence is just what something is. But when one thing is said of another, it is not just a this something—for example, the pale human is not just a this

something, if indeed the 'this' belongs only to substances. And so there will be an essence only of those things whose account is a definition. We have a definition, however, not when a name and an account signify the same thing (for then all the accounts would be definitions, since there will be a name answering to any account whatever, so that even the *Iliad* will be a definition), but when the account is of something primary; and primary things are those that are said *not* by way of saying one thing of another. Hence the essence will belong to things that are species of a genus and to nothing else" (VII 4 1030ᵃ3–13).

Note 194

In this way too lacks will produce a differentia, whereas by dichotomy they will not produce one: The way referred to is W, which is dividing a genus G into many differentiae $D_1 \ldots D_n$ from the outset, and then taking the differentiae of D_1, D_2, $D_3 \ldots D_n$. Suppose D_1 is a differentia whose lack is $D_{1\text{-L}}$, will $D_{1\text{-L}}$ be a differentia? If the divisions in the scheme are dichotomous and D_1 is a differentia, it must be (or in general will be) a universal one, since it is at the highest level of differentiating. As a result $D_{1\text{-L}}$ will not be a universal differentia, since no differentia of $D_{1\text{-L}}$ exists, because nothing can be below it in the scheme (see *PA* I 3 642ᵇ21–643ᵃ7). But if division proceeds in way W, $D_{1\text{-L}}$ will be a differentia (even if one that does not admit of further differentiation and even if empty), because some other differentia, D_2 or D_3 or . . . , through admitting of further differentiation, allows the scheme to continue downward. And what applies to D_1 applies to any other differentia in the scheme that are not themselves lacks.

Note 195

Whatever genera differ by excess (*kath' huperochên*): Usually, as at *GA* II 3 737ᵇ6, coupled with "or deficiency." See *HA* I 1 486ᵃ14–ᵇ22 (this vol.).

And by the more and the less (*mallon kai hêtton*): The more and the less corresponds to our notion of degree, and so is connected to the notion of increasing and decreasing—tightening and loosening (*epiteinein kai aniêsin*). Thus as a musician tightens or loosens his instrument's strings until a certain target note is struck (*Pol.* IV 3 1290ᵃ22–29), so too with vocal cords, sinews, and other string-like things (*GA* V 7 787ᵇ10–24). Hence Aristotle employs the notion of tightening and loosening wherever a certain tripartite structure is thought to exist, consisting of a continuous underlying subject (*to mallon kai hêtton*), a pair of opposed attributes that can vary in degree, and a target, typically a mean condition of some sort, that can be achieved by tightening or loosening the underlying subject to change the degree of the attributes. As a result, he speaks of tightening and loosening in characterizing a wide range of phenomena, from the parts of animals to political constitutions (*Pol.* V 9 1309ᵇ18–31, *Rh.* I 4 1360ᵃ23–30). In the case of noses and other such parts, the continuous underlying subject is flesh and bone (or its shape), the pair of opposite attributes is hooked and snub, and the target—which lies somewhere in between the two, and so (as in political constitutions) in a mean of some sort—is being a straight nose, or at the very least a nose of some sort. In the case of colors too, while many are constituted out of white and black in some definite ratio, others are constituted in "some incommensurable ratio of excess or deficiency," and so are apt for tightening and loosening (*Sens.* 3 439^{b}30). Because *to mallon kai hêtton* is found in many different genera, it cannot be the subject matter of any of the first-order sciences, since these are restricted to a single genus (*Rh.* I 2 1358^{a}10–17), but is instead studied by dialectic (*Top.* II 10 114^{b}37–115^{a}24) and rhetoric (*Rh.* II 23 1397^{b}12–29), which are transgeneric sciences.

Note 196
By analogy: See *HA* I 1 486^{a}14–^{b}22 (this vol.).

Note 197
But since it is the ultimate species (*eidos*) that are the substances, and these are undifferentiated with respect to form (*eidos*) (for example, Socrates, Coriscus): The substances referred to are essences, which "belong to things that are species of a genus and to nothing else" (*Met.* VII 4 1030^{a}12–13). Socrates and Coriscus are examples not of these, but of things undifferentiated with respect to form. See Introduction, pp. lxxxiv–lxxxvii.

Note 198
Estimable (*timias*): The core sense of *timios* ("estimable") is captured in the remark that ordinary people "commonly say of those they find especially estimable and especially love that they 'come first'" (*Cat.* 12 14^{b}5–7). Something is thus objectively *timios* when—like starting-points and causes—it "comes first by nature" (14^{b}3–5). To say that something is estimable is thus to ascribe a distinct sort of goodness or value to it: "By what is estimable I mean such things as what is divine, what is superior (*beltion*) (for example, soul, understanding), what is more time-honored (*archaioteron*), what is a starting-point, and so on" (*MM* I 2 1183^{b}21–23). Thus happiness is "something estimable and complete . . . since it is a starting-point . . . and the starting-point and the cause of goods is something we suppose to be estimable and divine" (*NE* I 12 1102^{a}1–4).

Note 199
Since where these [divine things] are concerned we are through with stating what seems to be so to us: Presumably, in *De Caelo* and in the *Metaphysics*, especially Book XII.

Note 200
We must not be childishly disgusted at the investigation of the less estimable animals: "The differentiae that determine whether the genus of the thing being composed is more estimable or non-estimable lie in the enclosure of the soul-involving starting-point" (*GA* III 11 762^{a}24–26).

Note 201
Heraclitus is reported to have said to those strangers who wished to meet him but stopped as they were approaching on seeing him warming himself at the

oven. For he told them to enter confidently (*tharrountas*), **"for there are gods even here":** = DK 22A9 = TEGP 162.

Heraclitus: Heraclitus of Ephesus (fl. c. 500 BC), one of the greatest of the Presocratic philosophers, was originator of the doctrine that everything flows or is in flux. See DK 22 = TEGP pp. 135–200.

Warming himself at the oven (*theromenon pros tô[i] ipnô[i]*): "Possibly a polite euphemism for visiting the lavatory" (Balme-2, p. 123). This would explain the story's relevance to disgust, which is difficult to do otherwise. The idea would be that as the strangers came within sight of Heraclitus they saw him going into the lavatory (which may have been an outhouse). He told them to enter (not the lavatory or outhouse, of course, but the house) confidently, since even in the place he was going to there are gods present (to those capable of seeing causes clearly). There is additional evidence for understanding *theromenon pros tô[i] ipnô[i]* in this way (see Henderson, pp. 191–92), but it is not as weighty as one might wish (see Gregoric, pp. 76–78).

Note 202

Nobly beautiful: See *PA* I 1 639^{b}20n.

Note 203

The end for the sake of which each has been composed or has come to be has taken the place of the nobly beautiful: As painters and sculptors aim to produce nobly beautiful painting or sculptures of animals, so nature aims at the end that has the same explanatory role as the nobly beautiful.

Note 204

Those things that do not occur in separation from their substance: That is, the functional parts of the animal whose parts they are: "Now since the soul of animals (for this is substance of the animate) is the substance that is in accord with the account and is the form and the essence of such-and-such sort of body (certainly each part, if it is to be defined correctly, will not be defined without its function, which it could not have without perception), it follows that the parts of this are prior, either all or some, to the compound animal, and similarly, then, to each particular animal, whereas the body and its parts will be posterior, and what is divided into these as into matter is not the substance but the compound. These bodily parts, then, are in a way prior to the compound, but in a way not, since they cannot even exist when they are separated. For it is not a finger in any and every state that is the finger of an animal, rather, a dead finger is only homonymously a finger" (*Met.* VII 10 1035^{b}14–25).

Note 205

The coincidental attributes that belong intrinsically to all the animals: See *PA* I 3 643^{a}28n.

Note 206

It has been said previously too that many things belong in common to many animals: See *PA* I 639^{a}19–22.

Note 207
To speak separately about each of the particular [species], though, as was also said before, will result in saying the same things many times: See *PA* I 1 639ª23–29.

Note 208
Instrument: See *HA* I 6 491ª26n (this vol.).

A sort of whole action (*praxis tis*): The noun *praxis* (verb: *prattein*) is used (1) in a broad sense to refer to any intentional action, including one performed by a child or wild beast (*NE* III 1 1111ª25–26, 2 1111ᵇ8–9), and (2) in a narrower one, to refer exclusively to what results from deliberation (*bouleusis*) and deliberate choice (*prohairesis*), of which neither beasts nor children are capable (*NE* I 9 1099ᵇ32–1100ª5, *EE* II 8 1224ª28–29). What distinguishes a *praxis* from a *poiêsis* ("production") is that the latter is always performed for the sake of some further end, whereas a *praxis* can be its own end: "Thought by itself, however, moves nothing. But the one that is for the sake of something and practical does. Indeed, it even rules productive thought. For every producer produces for the sake of something, and what is unconditionally an end (as opposed to in relation to something and for something else) is not what is producible but what is doable in action. For doing well in action (*eupraxia*) [= eudaimonia or happiness] is the end, and the desire is for it. That is why deliberate choice is either desiderative understanding or thought-involving desire, and this sort of starting-point is a human being" (*NE* VI 2 1139ª35–ᵇ5). Thus the distinction between a *praxis* and a *poiêsis* is a special case of a more general distinction that Aristotle draws between an *energeia* ("activity") or *entelecheia* ("actuality") and a *kinêsis* ("movement")—on which, see *GA* I 19 726ᵇ17n (this vol.). Since living bodies in general are under discussion, and not just adult human ones, this might seem to imply that (1) is the intended meaning of *praxis* here. But the pronoun *tis* is almost certainly intended to cancel that implication, so that the relevant *praxis* is a sort of (2), and so is an end of some sort.

The whole body too has been composed for the sake of a sort of full action: Reading πλήρους with Balme-2 and some mss. for Louis-2 πολυμεροῦς ("multipartite"). The reference is to "the coordinated activity of the animal as a whole organism, not merely the aggregation of the parts" (Balme-2, p. 124).

Note 209
Those whose differentiae in relation to each other we see to [differ] by excess: See *PA* I 4 644ª16–19.

Everything that in accord with its universal account has no differentia at all: As human being is not further divided by a differentia.

Note 210
[1]–[3]: See *PA* I 1 642ª31–ᵇ2.

[3] things whose existence necessitates the presence [of other things]: See *PA* I 1 640ª35–ᵇ1n.

Generation of Animals

BOOK I

Note 211

Genus: See *HA* I 1 486ᵃ23n.

The other parts present in animals have been spoken about: See *HA* I 1 486ᵃ23–25n.

The for-the-sake-of-which as end (*to hou heneka hôs telos*): The so-called final cause.

Note 212

There are four underlying causes (*aitiai*): One difference between *aition* (neuter), and *aitia* (female), used here, is that an *aitia* is an explanatory argument (a type of deduction) that identifies causes, whereas an *aition* may be an item in the world that is causally efficacious. Aristotle does not seem to observe the distinction, though it is *aitia* that figures in his definitions of craft knowledge and scientific knowledge (*APo.* I 2 71ᵇ9–12, II 11 94ᵃ20–27). Both *aition* and *aitia* are translated as "cause." The four causes are discussed in *Ph.* II 3.

The account (*ho logos*): A *logos* in ordinary Greek is a word or organized string of words constituting an account, argument, explanation, definition, principle, reason, or piece of reasoning, discussion, conversation, or speech; what such words or their utterances mean, express, or refer to, such as the ratio between quantities (*NE* V 3 1131ᵃ31–32); the capacity that enables someone to argue, give reasons, and so on (*Pol.* VII 13 1332ᵇ5). Aristotle also uses the word in a more technical sense: "A *logos* is a significant voiced sound some part of which is significant when separated—as an annunciation (*phasis*), not as an affirmation (*kataphasis*). I mean, for example, that human signifies something, but not that the thing is or is not (though it will be an affirmation or denial if something is added); the single syllables of human, by contrast, signify nothing" (*Int.* 4 16ᵇ26–31). "Account" and "argument" translate *logos*; in other cases *logos* is added in parenthesis. Here *logos* is equivalent in meaning to "definition." As we can see, then, Aristotle is not always careful to distinguish linguistic items, such as accounts or definitions from their ontological correlates. Thus he speaks of Socrates as not separating "the definitions" from perceptibles, when it is the essences that are the ontological correlates of the definitions to which he is referring (*Met.* XIII 4 1078ᵇ30–31), and of the account of X as composed of the matter and the activation (= form), when it is X itself—the ontological correlate of the account—that is so composed (VIII 6 1045ᵃ34–35).

Of the substance (*tês ousias*): See *PA* I 1 639ᵃ16n (this vol.).

The for-the-sake-of-which as end, the account of the substance (and these must be taken pretty much as one): See *PA* I 1 639ᵇ11–21 (this vol.).

Note 213

The matter for the animals is their parts—for the animal as a whole, the non-homoeomerous parts, for the non-homoeomerous parts, the homoeomerous ones, and for these, the so-called elements of bodies: "By homoeomerous bodies, I mean, for example, 'metals' (bronze, gold, silver, tin, iron, stone, and others of this sort, and those that come to be segregated out of these) and the ones in animals and plants (for example, flesh, bone, sinew, skin, visceral body, hair, blood fiber, veins), from which the non-homoeomerous parts (for example, face, hand, foot, and others of this sort) are forthwith composed (and in plants, wood, bark, leaf, root, and things of this sort)" (*Mete.* IV 10 388^{a}13–20); "We grasp what the nature of the homoeomerous things is composed of, the genera of them, and which genus each belongs to, through their coming to be. For the homoeomerous things are composed of the elements, and of these as matter all the works of nature are composed" (12 389^{b}24–28). Something is homoeomerous in the strict sense if "a part is synonymous with the whole" (*GC* I 1 314^{a}20; also *PA* II 9 655^{b}5–6), so that part and whole have the same name and their essences have the same account (see *GA* I 16 721^{a}3n). But Aristotle recognizes that, for example, the heart is "in one way homoeomerous and in another non-homoeomerous" (*PA* 1 647^{b}8–9; also 2 647^{b}17–20). It is homoeomerous at the level of the "chemical" formula of heart stuff, but because of "the shape of its configuration (*tên tou schêmatos morphên*), it is non-homoeomerous" (647^{a}33). "It may sound odd to us; but it seems we are being told that certain 'parts' are *proto*-structural, of an intermediate nature or at an interface between uniform and non-uniform: the same nature somehow doubling as stuff and as structure" (Furth, p. 81). See also *GA* I 18 724^{b}29n.

Elements (*stoicheia*): A *stoicheion* was originally one of a row (*stoichos*) of things and later a letter of the alphabet or an element of any complex whole (Plato, *Tht.* 201e). Aristotle uses it in these ways, and to refer to the elemental bodies (earth, water, air, fire, ether), from which all others are composed: "Let an element of bodies be (1) that into which other bodies are divisible, (2) present (*enuparchon*) in them potentially or actually (which of the two is a matter of dispute), and (3) something that is itself indivisible into things of another form (*eidos*). Something like this is what everybody in any context means by 'element'" (*Cael.* III 3 302^{a}15–19). **The so-called elements of bodies:** See Introduction, pp. lx–lxxvii.

Note 214

The generation (*genesin*) of animals: The noun *genesis* (verb: *gennan*) applies to two apparently different processes in animals: (1) the development of an animal from embryo to mature adult; (2) the reproductive process in which a mature animal reproduces itself by generating another of the same kind as itself. By assigning the process of nutrition and growth on the one hand with that of reproduction on the other to the same capacity in the soul (*DA* II 4 415^{a}23–26, 416^{a}18–21), Aristotle ties together (1) and (2), since development and reproduction both involve the transmission of form into new matter. In the one case through digestion and nourishment; in the other through sexual intercourse (or its analogues). See Falcon & Lefebvre (Pellegrin), pp. 77–88. Nonetheless, as is usual, I have for the most part translated *genesis* (and cognates), when it refers to *active* reproduction of animals or their parts, as "generation," but otherwise as "coming to be." In other cases, *gennan* is often translated as "produce." Thus, while animals typically *generate*, or are capable of *generation*, they typically *produce* embryos, eggs, residues, and the like.

What sort of starting-point is cause of the movement (*aitias de tês kinousês tis archê*): That is, "from where the starting-point of the movement comes" (I 1 715^{a}7).

Note 215

To investigate [the cause of the movement] and to investigate the generation of each animal is in a way the same: Only in a way the same because there is also a material cause involved.

Note 216

That is why the account has brought them together as one, by putting these parts at the end of our accounts of the parts, and the accounts of the starting-point of generation (*tôn de peri geneseôs tên archên*) **next after them:** I take *archê* to have the same reference here as at I 1 715^{a}7, 14. Balme-2, Louis-3, Platt, and Peck-3 take it to refer instead to the starting-point of the account of generation. See Falcon & Lefebvre (Lefebvre), pp. 47–50.

The accounts of these parts: In *Parts of Animals*, *Movement of Animals*, and *Progression of Animals*. "We have now stated the causes of the parts of each animal, the soul, perception, sleep, memory, and movement in general. It remains to speak about their generation" (*MA* 11 704^{a}2–^{b}3).

Note 217

The female (*to thêlu*) **and the male** (*to arren*): The article is neuter in both cases, so I have preserved it in the translation. The reference is to males and females, but also to the female and male factors or starting-points, that make males and females what they are. See *GA* I 2 716^{a}5–7, 13–15, and especially 27–31. On the puzzle of how it is that male and female, though quite different, nonetheless belong to the same species, see Introduction, pp. lxxvii–lxxxiii.

Note 218

Those blooded ones, with few exceptions, in which the female and the male are completed . . . produce offspring of the same genus as themselves: The exceptions are the erythrinus (II 5 741^{a}35) and the channa (II 5 755^{b}21, III 10 760^{a}8), two species of fish, mentioned also in this regard at *HA* VI 13 567^{a}27 ("but one is puzzled about the erythrinus and channa, since those caught are always pregnant").

Blooded (*enaimois*) . . . **bloodless** (*anaimôn*): By "blood" Aristotle means red blood only, so that "these two classes do not quite coincide with vertebrates and invertebrates, for there are some invertebrates which have red blood, e.g., mollusks (*Planorbis*), insect larvae (*Chironomus*), and worms (*Arenicola*). In other invertebrates the blood may be blue (Crustacea and most mollusks) or green (Sabellid worms), or there may be no respiratory pigment at all (most Insects)" (Peck-3, p. lxix n73). The blooded animals are: Human beings, oviparous quadrupeds and footless animals (reptiles and amphibians), birds, fish. The bloodless ones are: crustaceans, cephalopods, insects, testaceans.

Of the same genus (*homogenê*): Homogenês here = *suggenês* at I 1 715^{b}3.

Note 219

The ones that come to be not from animal copulation but from putrefied earth: Aristotle thinks that insects (*GA* I 16 721^{a}7–9, *HA* V I 539^{a}21–26), testaceans (15 547^{b}18–32), and eels (VI 16) come about in this way. "It is not in the process of concoction that living things come to be, as some people say, but rather they come to be in the excreta [= residues] that putrefy in the lower intestines, and then ascend" (*Mete.* IV 3 381^{b}9–11). The living things in question are probably "bowel or intestinal worms (*terêdones*)" (Alex. 197.15 = Lewis, p. 87). See also *Mete.* X 11 389^{b}5–8.

And residues (*perittômatôn*) **are of this sort:** "By a residue (*perittôma*) I mean a leftover (*hupoleimma*) of the nourishment" (*GA* I 18 724^{b}26–27).

Putrefying (*sêpomenês*): See V 4 784^{b}6–7n.

Note 220

Whether they are capable of swimming . . . : Reading ἐστὶ with Peck-3 for OCT †ὄντα τὰ μὲν νευστικά.

Note 221

The cephalopods (*malakiois*) **and crustaceans** (*malakostrakois*): The cephalopods (*ta malakia*) (literally: "the softies") include the squid and the octopus; the crustaceans (*ta malakostraka*) ("the soft-shelled ones") include the crab and the lobster. The hard-shelled ones are *ta ostrakoderma* ("the pottery-skinned ones").

Note 222

Those that come to be not from animals but from putrefying matter produce something of a distinct genus, and what comes to be is neither female nor male. Some of the insects are of this sort: See II 1 732^{b}11–14, III 9 758^{b}6–759^{a}7.

Note 223

Nature (*hê phusis*), **however, avoids** (*pheugei*) **the unlimited:** See *PA* I 1 641^{b}12n (this vol.).

The unlimited (*to apeiron*): Discussed in *Ph.* III 4–8.

Note 224

The testaceans (*ta ostrakoderma*): This class includes "a number of shelled invertebrates, comprising Gastropods, Lamellibranches, and some Echinoderms. Modern zoologists apply the term Testacea to the Foraminifera, which are shelled Protozoa. The term Ostracoderms (a transliteration of Aristotle's word) is now given by zoologists to a group of primitive fossil fishes" (Peck-3, p. lxix n*a*).

In these, the female and male do not exist—although they are immediately said to be male or female by way of similarity and by analogy: See *HA* I 1 486ª14–ᵇ22 (this vol.).

Note 225
The difference (*diaphoran*) of this sort that they have is small: See *HA* I 1 486ª24n.

Note 226
The concocting (*pettein*) of what is borne by the others: "Concoction . . . is what everything is affected by when its matter—that is, its liquid—is mastered. For this is what is determined by the heat in its nature. For as long as the ratio [*logos* = form, essence] is in this, the thing has its nature" (*Mete.* IV 2 379ᵇ32–35). The various sorts of concoction—ripening, boiling, broiling—are discussed in *Mete.* IV 3. **Some trees that bear fruit and others that, while not bearing fruit themselves, contribute to the concocting of what is borne by the others, as happens, for example, with the fig and the caprifig:** "The fig tree commonly cultivated in S. Europe is *Ficus carica*. This species includes two kinds of individual trees: (1) those whose inflorescences contain fully-developed female flowers only; (2) those whose inflorescences contain male flowers near the opening and lower down aborted female flowers known as 'gall-flowers' owing to their being specially prepared to receive the eggs of the fig-wasp (*Blastophaga grossorum*), which turn the ovary of the flower into a 'gall.' The latter trees are known as *Caprificus*. The female wasps after impregnation by the male wasps within the gall, emerge from it and get dusted with pollen from the male flowers as they leave the inflorescence, and then pollinate female flowers elsewhere. Caprification is the name given to the artificial assistance of this process by hanging inflorescences of the caprifig on to trees of class (1)" (Peck-3, pp. 8–9 nb). At *HA* V 32 557ᵇ25–31 Aristotle describes this process. See also *GA* II 5 759ᵇ9–11.

Note 227
The spontaneous operations (*automatizousês*) of nature: See *PA* I 1 640ª27n (this vol.).

Note 228
Some [plants] are not composed separately by themselves but come to be on other trees—for example, mistletoe: See also III 11 762ᵇ18–21, *HA* V 1 539ª15–25. **Composed** (*sunistanai*): "The noun σύστασις [translated as 'composition'] refers to a state of matter, which is often in the right or appropriate density or constitution for a certain outcome or has that appropriate constitution dissolved and destroyed by some external agency. It is used both for dry exhalations . . . and wet exhalations. Dry συστάσεις are at the right density for ignition; a majority of the wet συστάσεις (eight of thirteen) concern reflection, for which the vapor has to attain the right density. The cognate verb συνίστασθαι can mean 'gather' (I 10 347ª27), and as such is similar to ἀθροίζειν [next note] (I 10 347ᵇ10 . . .). More commonly, though, the verb refers to the process by

which the wet exhalation turns into rain (though we should be wary of calling it 'condensation'). The noun, σύστασις, by contrast is never used to describe this process. . . . The sole cause of συνίστασθαι is the cold (I 9 346ᵇ29, II 4 360ᵃ1, 360ᵇ35, 6 364ᵇ27). The process of συνίστασθαι, then, is the opposite of διαλύεσθαι (II 2 355ᵃ32) or διακρινέσθαι ['disaggregate'] which can oppose or undo the process of συνίστασθαι (I 7 344ᵇ24, 345ᵃ8, 8 346ᵃ16)" (Wilson, p. 65). **It is the same way in plants too . . . for example, mistletoe:** Peck-3, p. 9 nc, argues that this paragraph is out of place here, but "would be relevant if transferred to 715ᵃ25."

Note 229

Well, plants must be investigated separately by themselves: Secluded in Balme-2. See also I 23 731ᵃ29–30, V 3 783ᵇ20–24. The reference is to a lost treatise; the extant *On Plants* (Barnes, pp. 1252–1271) is not by Aristotle.

Note 230

The male one as containing the starting-point of the movement and the generation, the female one as containing that of the matter: See also I 21 729ᵇ12–14.
Starting-point (*archas*): An *archê* ("starting-point," "first principle") is a primary cause: "This is what it is for something to be a starting-point, namely, that it is itself the cause of many things, with nothing else above it being a cause of it" (*GA* V 7 788ᵃ14–16).

Note 231

Getting a theoretical grasp on (*theôran*): See *HA* I 6 491ᵃ5n.
Seed (*sperma*): See I 17 721ᵇ6–722ᵃ1, 18 724ᵃ14–ᵇ19.

Note 232

It is because a part (*morion*) **of this sort is secreted** (*apokrinesthai*) **from the female and the male:** The *moria* of an animal include not just the non-homoeomerous things that we would naturally call parts, but also the homoeomerous ones, such as blood, seed, and so on.
Secretion (*apokrisin*): The noun *apokrisis* is used to refer exclusively to spermatic (I 19 727ᵃ27) or generative (II 4 739ᵃ5) residues, or to related things, such as milk (IV 8 776ᵃ27, 776ᵇ29, 777ᵃ4) and the cognate verb *apokrinein*, with one exception (II 6 744ᵃ9), to their expulsion. These are translated invariantly as "secretion" and "secrete." Another noun, *ekkrisis* (verb: *ekkrinein*) is used a few times to refer to the expulsion of spermatic residues (III 1 751ᵃ22, IV 1 765ᵇ31, 2 767ᵃ7, 5 774ᵃ5, 6 775ᵇ8) and milk (IV 8 776ᵇ20), but is also used for the expulsion of waste products (I 13 719ᵇ32, 720ᵃ6, III 1 750ᵃ30, ᵇ20) and for the outgrowth of bones, horns, and teeth (I 20 728ᵇ20). It is translated as "excretion" or "excrete."

Note 233

By a male animal we mean what generates in another, by a female what does so within itself: Compare *HA* I 3 489ᵃ11–12.

Note 234
Heaven (*ouranon*): See *PA* I 1 641^{b}16n (this vol.).

Note 235
The male and the female, however, differ with respect to their account, because each is capable of a distinct thing, and with respect to certain of their perceptible parts: Compare: "All these [homoeomerous] things differ from each other with regard to the special objects of the perceptual capacities, in virtue of which the things are capable of affecting the capacities in a certain way (for a thing is white, fragrant, resonant, sweet, hot, or cold, in virtue of being capable of affecting the perceptual capacity in a certain way), and also with regard to other affections more proper to themselves, in virtue of which they are said to be affectable—I mean, for example, being dissolvable, solidifiable, bendable, and whatever others are of this sort" (*Mete.* IV 8 384^{b}34–385^{a}6).
The male has the capacity to generate in another, as was said previously: At I 2 716^{a}14.
The thing produced, which was present in the progenitor: On the way in which it is thus present, see II 1 734^{a}33–36.
Comes to be from (*ex hou*): That is, the sort of matter it comes to be from. See II 1 733^{b}24–31.

Note 236
Capacity (*dunamei*): The term *dunamis* (plural: *dunameis*) is used by Aristotle to capture two different but related things. (1) As in ordinary Greek, it signifies a power or capacity something has, especially to cause movement in something else (affecting *dunamis*) or to be caused to move by something else (affected *dunamis*). (2) It signifies a way of being, namely, potential (*dunamei*) being as opposed to actual (*entelecheia[i]*) or active (*energeia[i]*) being. See also *Met.* V 12 and *GA* I 19 726^{b}18–19n.
Function (*ergon*): A function is (1) an activity that is the use or actualization of a state, capacity, or disposition; (2) a work or product that is the further result of such an activity (*NE* I 1 1094^{a}5–6). It is intimately related to its possessor's end or final cause: "The function is the end, and the activity is the function" (*Met.* VIII 8 1050^{a}21–22); "each thing of which there is a function is for the sake of its function" (*Cael.* II 3 286^{a}8–9). Moreover, a thing's good or doing well "seems to lie in its function" (*NE* I 7 1097^{b}26–27). But this holds only when the thing itself is not already something bad (*Met.* VIII 9 1051^{a}15–16). Finally, a thing's function is intimately related to its nature, form, and essence. For a thing's nature is its "for-the-sake-of-which" (*Ph.* II 2 194^{a}27–28), its form is more its nature than its matter (1 193^{b}6–7), and its essence and form are the same (*Met.* VII 7 1032^{b}1–2). Hence "all things are defined by their function" (*Mete.* IV 12 390^{a}10), with the result that if something cannot function, it has no more than a name in common with its functional self (*Met.* VII 10 1035^{b}14–25, *Pol.* I 2 1253^{a}20–25, *PA* I 1 640^{b}33–641^{a}6). Functions are thus attributed to a wide variety of things, whether living or non-living. These include plants (*GA* I 23 731^{a}24–26) and animals generally (*NE* X 5 1176^{a}3–5),

including divine celestial ones (*Cael.* II 3 286ª8–11), parts of their bodies and souls (*PA* II 7 652ᵇ6–14, IV 10 686ª26–29), instruments or tools of various sorts (*EE* VII 10 1242ª15–19), crafts, sciences (II 1 1219ª17), philosophies (*GC* I 3 318ª6) and their practitioners (*NE* VI 7 1141ᵇ10), cities (*Pol.* VII 4 1326ª13–14), and nature itself (I 10 1258ª35).

Instruments (*organôn*): See *HA* I 6 491ª26n (this vol.).

Note 237

It is not in virtue of the whole of it that it is female or male, but in virtue of a certain capacity and in virtue of a certain part: See also IV 1 766ᵇ3–7.

Capable of perambulation (*poreutikon*): Or, so-called progressive movement, as in the treatise, *The Progression of Animals.*

Note 238

The penis (*perineous*): At *HA* I 14 493ᵇ10 the *perineous* is the perineum, the part between the anus and scrotum, or anus and vagina. But here, as at IV 1 766ª3–5, the *perineous* is the instrumental part that is special to the male and the counterpart of the uterus in the female: so, the penis.

Note 239

Some of them have testes and others spermatic ducts: See I 3 716ᵇ15–17n.

Ducts (*porous*): No English word matches Aristotle's use of *poros* perfectly in every context. But because the notion is an important one, it requires consistent handling in translation. Overall "duct" seems to work better than "passages," "pores," "channels," and so on, though these give a more natural reading in some cases.

Note 240

This contrariety: Between male and female. Contrariety is discussed in *Met.* X 4.

Differ in their configurations (*schêmasin*): As womb differs from penis in human beings.

Note 241

Shape [or form] (*morphê*): *Morphê* is often—though surely not here (since male and female of the same species have the same form)—used by Aristotle as a substitute for *eidos* ("form"). "Form" is added in square brackets when needed for clarity.

Note 242

The female appears (*phainetai*) **to be a sort of starting-point:** The verb *phainesthai* ("appear") with (1) a participle endorses what appears to be so and is translated "it is evident," "or it is seen to be," or the like, and the cognate adjective *phaneron* as "evident." *Phainesthai* with (2) an infinitive, as here, neither endorses nor rejects what appears to be so and is translated "appears." When *phainesthai* occurs without a participle or an infinitive, it may either endorse or reject. Appearances (*phainomena*) are things that appear to be so but that may or may not be so. Things that appear so to everyone or to wise people who have investigated them are *endoxa,* or reputable beliefs.

Note 243
Some animals of this sort do not have testes at all (for example, the fish genus and the serpent genus), but only two spermatic (*spermatikous*) ducts: "These are in fact testes, but Aristotle reserves the name for the firm, oval-shaped testes. This negative statement does not of course include the cartilaginous fishes, the Selachia, many of which are viviparous" (Peck-3, p. 15 n*b*).

Note 244
Oviparous quadrupeds: Reptilians and amphibians, which Aristotle "does not separate from each other. . . . Of the oviparous monotremes, duck-bill and echidna, he was naturally ignorant" (Platt, n2).

Note 245
All the viviparous ones have their testes in the front: That is, they would have them in front if, like human beings, they had the best animal posture and stood up straight: "Instead of having forelegs and forefeet, the human has arms and so-called hands. For the human is the only animal that stands upright, and this is because its nature, that is, its substance is divine. Now the function of that which is most divine is understanding and thinking; and this would not be easy if there were a great deal of the body at the top weighing it down, for weight hampers the movement of understanding and of the common sense. Thus when the weight and the body-like quality becomes too great, the body itself must lurch forward toward the ground; and then, for preservation's sake, nature provides forefeet instead of arms and hands—as has happened in quadrupeds . . . because their soul could not sustain the weight bearing it down. . . . In fact, compared with man, all other animals are dwarf-like [that is, top-heavy]. . . . That is why all animals are less wise than man. Even among human beings, indeed, children, . . . though possessing some other exceptional potentiality, are inferior in the possession of understanding as compared to adults. The cause . . . is that in many of them the starting-point of the soul is movement-hampered and body-like in quality. And if the heat that raises the organism upright wanes still further and the earthly matter waxes, then the animals' bodies also wane, and they will be many-footed; and finally they lose their feet altogether and lie full length on the ground. Proceeding a little further in this way, they actually have their starting-point down below, and finally the head part comes to have neither movement nor sensation and what you have is a plant, which has its upper parts below and its lower parts above. For in plants the roots have the capacity of mouth and head, whereas the seed counts as the opposite, being produced in the upper part of the plant on the ends of the twigs" (*PA* IV 10 686^{a}25–687^{a}2).
Private part (*aidoion*): An *aidoion* can be a penis (*HA* I 13 493^{a}25), a vagina (I 14 493^{b}2), a uterus (*GA* IV 1 764^{b}23), or an excretory organ (I 13 719^{b}30–31).
Ox-fish (*boes*): A cartilaginous fish, one of the selachians. See *HA* V 5 540^{b}17, VI 12 566^{b}4.

Note 246
I have made more exact determinations about these in the *History of Animals*: Especially *HA* III 1. On exactness, see *HA* I 6 491^{a}9n.

Note 247
Uterus: This includes "what are now known as oviducts" (Peck-3, p. 17 n*e*).

Note 248
Diaphragm (*hupozômati*): The division between the thorax and the abdomen, which is the diaphragm proper in mammals, and its analogue in other animals, such as the waist in insects. It is discussed in *PA* III 10.

Note 249
For the membranes encompassing their so-called eggs have a uterus-like quality: Reading τὰ γὰρ with Balme-2, Peck-3, and most mss. for OCT καὶ τὰ.

Note 250
The octopuses (*polupodôn*): See *HA* V 18 548^{b}31–550^{a}16.

Note 251
Nature makes everything either because of what is necessary or because of what is better: See I 1 715^{a}16n.

Note 252
They have been seen copulating and with their ducts full of milt: On these ducts, which are in fact testes, see I 3 716^{b}15–17n, and, on the copulation of fishes, 6 717^{b}36–718^{a}2n.

Note 253
The function of most animals: See I 2 716^{a}23n.

Note 254
Animals with straight intestines are greedier in their appetite for food: "The entire genus of fish, because the parts involved in the functioning of nourishment are so deficient that they excrete it non-concocted, is greedy for food—especially those with straight intestines. For since they excrete quickly, their enjoyment of these things is brief, it is necessary for their appetite also to come about again quickly" (*PA* III 14 675^{a}18–24).
Activity (*energeian*): See I 19 726^{b}17n.

Note 255
Those that need to be more temperate: Temperance in its full form requires the possession of practical wisdom (*phronêsis*) and understanding (*nous*), which, in their full forms, are possessed only by human beings (or, in the latter case, gods). But Aristotle sometimes attributes a weaker form (*HA* VII 1 588^{a}18–31, IX 1 608^{a}11–21) of these to non-human animals, such as deer, hare, cranes, bees, and ants (I 2 488^{b}15, IX 5 611^{a}15–16, IX 10 614^{b}18, *PA* II 2 648^{a}5–8, 4 650^{b}18–27, *GA* III 2 753^{a}10–17). It is in this sense, for example, that dogs are "remarkable for courage" (*HA* IX 1 608^{a}31) and elephants differ from one another in how courageous they are (610^{a}18).

In the one case have non-straight intestines and in the other have helices in their ducts, with a view to their appetite being neither quick nor greedy: "Those animals that need to be more temperate in relation to the production of nourishment do not have large open spaces in their lower intestines, but rather it contains many helices and is not straight. For an open space produces an appetite for much food, and straightness makes for quickness [in the return] of appetite. That is why animals with simple or spacious receptacles are greedy, the latter in terms of the quantity they eat, the former in terms of quickness" (*PA* III 14 675ᵇ23–28).

Note 256
They do this by preserving the doubling-back [of the ducts] (one should get a theoretical grasp on the way they do this from the *History of Animals*): See *HA* III 1 510ᵃ12–ᵇ4, also *GA* I 6 718ᵃ9–14. The ducts are the epididymis and the vasa differentia (Fig. 1):

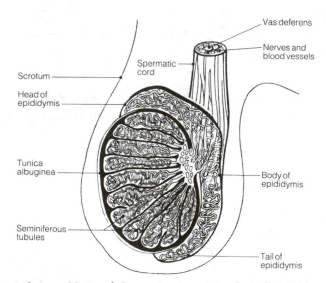

Fig. 1. Source: National Cancer Institute Visuals Online Library.

Note 257
Just like the stone weights that women attach to their looms when weaving: These keep the warp steady.

Note 258
This is evident in the case of birds. For their testes are much larger around mating time: See *HA* III 1 509ᵇ35–510ᵃ7.

Note 259
Whereas for birds it is not possible [to have an instrument for copulation]: However: "In the case of the larger [oviparous animals]—for example, in the goose

and the like—[the private part] becomes quite evident just after mating" (*HA* III 1 509^{b}30–32).

Note 260

[Hedgehogs] have intercourse standing upright because of their spines: In fact the female hedgehog adopts a special body position with her spines flattened and the male mounts her from behind.

Note 261

Fishes mate by placing themselves side to side and ejaculating: This is "totally untrue of the great majority of fish in which the female deposits eggs unfertilized and the male fertilizes them afterwards by shedding his milt upon them. A. knew of this latter process, but regarded it as merely supplementary to the supposed original copulation" (Platt, n3).

Ejaculating (*apoluontai*): The verb *apoluesthai* is translated as "separating again quickly" by Platt, followed by Lefebvre. Peck-3, followed by Louis-3, uses "ejaculate."

Note 262

Just as in the case of human beings and in all the others of this sort: That is, all air-breathers.

Pneuma: See Introduction, pp. lxii–lxxii.

Fishes at such times must not take in sea-water: "A certain genus of animals have a lung because they are terrestrial. For it is necessary for the heat to be cooled, and the blooded animals must be cooled from outside, since they are hotter, whereas those that are not blooded are capable of doing so by means of their connate pneuma (*sumphutô[i] pneumati*). And it is necessary for cooling from outside to be either by water or by air. That is why none of the fishes has a lung, but instead of this has gills. . . . For fish cool themselves by means of water, while the breathers do so by means of air. That is why all the breathers have a lung" (*PA* III 6 668^{b}33–669^{a}6). See also *Juv.* 16 476^{a}6.

And they easily pass away if they do not do this: That is, when they stop taking in sea-water. This is another reason why their mating has to be quick.

Note 263

[Fish] must not concoct their seed during copulation, as the viviparous terrestrial animals do: See I 5 717^{b}23–26.

Note 264

Of the part of the duct that is doubled back one part is blooded and another bloodless: The latter is the vas deferens, the former the epididymis. See Fig. 1 in I 4 717^{a}33n.

Note 265

Serpents mate by twisting around each other, but do not have testes or even a private part, as was said previously: I 4 717^{a}18 mentions a lack of testes but not of a genital organ. Serpents in fact have two testes and two genital organs or hemipenes.

Note 266

The great care taken (*skeuôrian*): "And some of the male [chickens] have been seen before now, after the death of the female, taking great care (*skeuôrian*) of the chicks, leading them around and rearing them" (*HA* IX 49 631^b13–15).

Note 267

Selachians: Cartilaginous fish, including sharks.

Note 268

Some eggs are incomplete when emitted—for example, those of fish. For these are completed and do their growing outside the fish: The eggs of fish, unlike the so-called cleidoic ones of reptiles and birds, which are only gas permeable, are permeable to water and inorganic materials which they absorb from the environment. Their "growing" is mostly due to the water they take in.

Note 269

The cause is that fish are prolific; in fact, this is their function just as it is of plants: See also I 4 717^a21–22 and, on function, I 2 716^a23n.

Note 270

These are the most prolific of all, just as in the case of other things—both among plants and among animals—that have a nature analogous to theirs: That is, that are small compared with others of the same species. See IV 4 771^b24–27.

Note 271

Growth in size turns in them to seed: Because both blood and seed are residues from nourishment, which is what produces growth. See I 9 726^b1–11 and *GC* I 5 322^a26–28: "Insofar as what enters is potentially so-and-so-much flesh, it is by it that a growth-producer [produces] flesh, but insofar as it is potentially flesh alone, nourishment."

Note 272

[The place around the diaphragm] in fact concocts the nourishment: Which requires heat. See I 1 715^b24n.

Note 273

The limit point of the uterus is low down too, and the uterus is where its function is: "The function of the uterus is to give birth to young, but this function is performed low down in the body; therefore naturally the uterus is low. But if Nature finds it desirable to cover the egg with a hard shell, she moves the uterus or oviducts higher up to secure the heat required for this purpose. Therefore the uterus of fish may remain low in its natural position, but with birds and reptiles it must go higher up" (Platt, n1).

The limit (*peras*): Probably, the opening from which the eggs emerge. Compare *HA* I 1 495^{a}30. But *peras* and *telos* (always "end") are closely associated, as are *telos* and *ergon* ("function"): "The function is the end, and the activity is the function" (*Met.* VIII 8 1050^{a}21–22).

Note 274

Some produce their young alive, not only externally, but also internally: That is, without first producing an egg. The microscopic mammalian egg was unknown to Aristotle. **Cetaceans** (*kêtê*) **of this sort:** That is, "the ones having not gills but a blowhole" (*HA* VI 12 566^{b}2–3).

Note 275

They do not lay eggs externally because of the coldness of their nature, and not, as some people say, because of its heat: "Empedocles is incorrect when he says that those animals that have the most heat and fire live in water to avoid the excess of heat in their nature, in order that, since they are deficient in cold and liquid they may be preserved by the contrary character of the place they occupy. For water has less heat than air" (*Juv.* 20 477^{a}32–^{b}5).

Note 276

Viviparous from the outset: That is from the start of the process of generation. See I 9 718^{b}27–32n.

Note 277

One must get a theoretical grasp on the way this and the other sorts of uterus are possessed from the *Dissections*: See *HA* I 17 497^{a}32n (this vol.).
And the *History of Animals*: See III 1 510^{b}5–511^{a}34.

Note 278

No function of nature impedes this: See I 8 718^{b}25–27.
Nor do they double-bear (*dittogonei*): That is, they are not both oviparous and viviparous.

Note 279

Fetuses (*embrua*) **necessarily possess heaviness and movement:** See I 13 719^{b}33n.

Note 280

But because: Reading διὰ <δὲ> and secluding διόπερ at I 12 719^{b}4 with Peck-3; OCT marks a lacuna prior to διὰ and reads διόπερ.

Note 281

This is a cause in all these cases [of their having their testes inside] that is in addition to the others mentioned previously, stemming from facts about the necessities of mating: See I 4 717^{a}15–5 717^{b}33.

Note 282

The skin is not naturally well-disposed (*euphuês*) **to keeping the protective part separate:** Something is *euphuês* if it is well (*eu*) grown (*phuê*), or favored by nature in capacities, appearance, or some other respect: the situation of a body can be *euphuês* (*PA* III 4 666ª14), as can that of a city (*Pol.* V 3 1303ᵇ8); an animal can be *euphuês* as regards a function, such as reproduction (*GA* II 8 748ᵇ8, 12), or the acquisition of a capacity, such as bearing the cold (*Pol.* VII 17 1336ª20), becoming a poet (*Po.* 17 1455ª32), or a musician (*EE* VIII 2 1247ᵇ22).

Note 283

{Contrary positions . . . that no weight be put on the uterus}: Platt thinks this paragraph should be secluded as "an incorrect reminiscence of preceding chapters" (n6); Peck-3 describes it as "simply a hash-up of parts of the preceding chapters" (p. 37 n*b*).

Note 284

Dry (*xêra*) **. . . wet** (*hugra*): "Things, though, are said to be dry and wet in many ways. For both wet (*hugron*) and moist (*dieron*) are opposed to dry, and, in turn, both dry and solid (*pepêgos*) are opposed to wet. But all these belong to the wet and the dry said in the primary way. For since dry is opposed to moist, and moist is what has alien liquid (*hugrotêta*) on its surface, whereas soaked is what has it to its depths, and dry is what is deprived of it, it is evident that moist will belong to the wet, and the dry that is opposed to it to what is dry in the primary way. Again, wet and solid are the same way. For wet is what has its own liquid down to its depths (whereas soaked is what has alien liquid down to its depths), and solid is what is deprived of this, so that these too belong, the one to the dry, the other to the wet" (*GC* II 2 330ª12–24). Generally, then, I have translated *hugros* as "wet," or "liquid," even when "moist" or "moisture" might seem more natural; and *xêros* as "dry," not "solid."

Note 285

The embryo (*to kuêma*): "By *kuêma* I mean the primary mixture of male and female" (I 20 728ᵇ34). The fertilized ovum of viviparous animals are *kuêmata*, but so too are complete and incomplete eggs (II 1 733ª24), larvae (III 8 758ª12, 9 758ª33), and fish roe (II 5 741ª37), so that "embryo," which is the usual translation, is no better than an approximation. Similar considerations apply to *embruon*, translated as "fetus," since *embrua* "necessarily possess heaviness and movement" (I 11 719ª15–16). And even though *embruon* and *kuêma* often seem to be more or less interchangeable, the former seems to be a later stage in the development of the latter. Thus in IV 8 we find *embruôn* at 776ª25, *kuêmatôn* at 31, *embruou* at 34 and *kuêmatos* at ᵇ1, but the sense even there is that an *embruon* is further along in the gestation process, making it natural to say that "there is a sort of completion even of an embryo" (776ª35–ᵇ1).

Note 286

The duct for [the excretion] of the dry nourishment: That is, for the dry or solid waste left over after the concoction of the nourishment (digestion of food).

Note 287
{**Oviparous animals . . . develops outside**}: This sentence clearly belongs with the other bracketed material at the end of I 12, and is in fact read there by Louis-3. Platt consigns it to a footnote.

Note 288
The duct is the same as that for the solid nourishment in those animals that have no generative (*gennêtikon*) **private part:** Secluding καὶ ante ἐν τοῖς μὴ ἔχουσι γεννητικὸν αἰδοῖον with Platt and Peck-3.

Note 289
Its continuation is low down near the abdomen: Reading προϊοῦσα with Platt and Peck-3 for OCT †προϊούσης. See I 11 719ᵃ7–8.

Note 290
None of them has a private part, as was said previously, hanging down: At I 3 716ᵇ13–32, *HA* III 1 509ᵃ31–ᵇ24.

Note 291
Fourth, the testaceans: See I 23 731ᵇ8–14.
It is evident that most of them do not copulate: Reading οὐ συνδυάζεται with OCT, Peck-3. Louis-3; Platt secludes οὐ ("most of them do copulate").
In what way they get composed must be stated later: See III 11.

Note 292
Nature has turned around the end of the duct for residues and brought it near the mouth, as was said previously: At *PA* IV 9 684ᵇ35–685ᵃ3. Secluding ἐν τοῖς περὶ τῶν μορίων λόγοις ("in the accounts of the parts" [= *PA*]) with OCT.

Note 293
In fact it is through this duct that the animal releases its ink: Reading ἔστι γὰρ ᾗ τὸν θολὸν ἀφίησι διὰ τοῦ πόρου with Louis-3; Peck-3 secludes. And τοῦτο δ᾽ with Peck-3 for OCT †ἔστι γὰρ ᾗ τὸν θολὸν ἀφίησι διὰ τοῦ πόρου. ταῦτα δ᾽ ἐστὶν†.
Dirt (*tholon*): *Tholos* is mud or dirt, especially in water. But it is also the ink of a cephalopod (*PA* IV 5 679ᵃ4–7), which is released through the same orifice (*HA* IV 1 524ᵇ20–21).

Note 294
If indeed the male releases something, whether seed or part: The part referred to may be the so-called hectocotylized tentacle, which "becomes detached from the male and remains within the mantle of the female" (Peck-3, p. 44 n*d*). On "part," see I 2 716ᵃ11n.
Or some other capacity: See I 21 729ᵇ1–8.

Note 295
Synonymous: "Things are said to be *synonymous* when they have a name in common and when the account of the essence that corresponds to the name is the same—for example, both human and ox are animals. Each of these is called by a common name 'animal,' and the account of the essence is also the same, since if we are to give the account of what-it-is for each of them to be an animal, we will give the same account" (*Cat.* 1 1ᵃ6–12).
Spiders (*phalaggia*): "Spiders were included among the insects until the time of Lamarck (1800)" (Platt, n1).

Note 296
[Those that do not come to be] from animals, but rather from putrefying liquids, and some from putrefying dry materials: See I 1 715ᵃ25n.

Note 297
Gnats (*empides*), **mosquitoes** (*kônôtes*): It is not certain which insects are meant.

Note 298
In most of the sorts that copulate, the females are larger than the males; and the males do not appear to have any spermatic ducts: Balme-2 reads this at I 16 721ᵃ17 post "divide them by genus."

Note 299
This has been observed in many cases: Secluding καὶ περὶ τοῦ ἀναβαίνειν ὡσαύτως ("and similarly as concerns the male mounting the female") with OCT, Peck-3, and Lefebvre; Platt and Louis-3 retain. In fact, it has not been observed at all, since "all insects copulate in the usual way, and the males have 'spermatic passages' which A. could not make out" (Platt, n4).

Note 300
The generative instruments in animals, which were not spoken about previously: That is, in *PA*. See I 1 715ᵃ1–14.

Note 301
These, then ... in what follows: Secluded in Balme-2 as an interpolation.
[We shall speak] about milk in what follows: In IV 8.

Note 302
That is why some people say that it [seed] comes from all the body: See Democritus DK A141 = TEGP 90; Hippocrates, *On Generation* and *The Nature of the Child* (Littré VII.472–542 = Lonie, pp. 1–21). This view is usually referred to as pangenesis.

Note 303
There are pretty much four things that someone might use as proofs: Secluding with OCT ὡς ἀφ' ἑκάστου τῶν μορίων ἀπιόντος τοῦ σπέρματος ("that the seed comes from each of the parts"); Platt, Peck-3, Louis-3, and Lefebvre retain.

Proofs (*tekmêriois*): "A necessary sign is a proof (*tekmêrion*). . . . I call necessary those from which a deduction comes about" (*Rh.* I 2 1357ᵇ4–6).

Note 304
The intensity of the pleasure involved: "Sexual intercourse is a minor seizure. For human being bursts forth from human being and is torn away, separated by a sort of blow" (Democritus DK B32 = TEGP 319 F188).

Note 305
From docked things (*kolobôn*) **docked things come to be:** The adjective *kolobos* means "docked" (as in docking a puppy's tail, or docking someone's salary), "curtailed," "stunted," "truncated"—the central idea is that of cutting off a projecting part, typically a non-essential one. None of these English terms fits all the cases Aristotle cites in his discussion of the notion in *Met.* V 27 in an entirely natural way. "Mutilated" is the traditional rendering but suffers the disadvantage of not capturing the central idea: mutilation need not involve the cutting off of a part; cutting off a part need not result in mutilation. Compare: "a short syllable, because of its incompleteness, produces something docked" (*Rh.* III 8 1409ᵃ18–19).

Note 306
Because the thing is missing the part, no seed, they say, proceeds from there, with the result that the part that would have come from there does not come to be: The progenitor is docked, for example, a finger. So no seed comes from there to form that finger in his offspring. So the offspring too is docked in that regard.

Note 307
Just as there is also some primary thing from which the whole comes to be, it is this way too with each of the parts: That is, some primary matter. See I 20 729ᵃ32–33, II 1 733ᵇ26.

Note 308
Similarity is no sign (*sêmeion*) **that the seed comes from all the body:** That is, no necessary sign or proof. See I 17 721ᵇ13n and I 19 727ᵃ4n.
Voice (*phônê*): See V 7 786ᵇ18–22n.

Note 309
The woman in Elis who had intercourse with an Ethiopian . . . : The woman was white, the man black. Their daughter was white, her son black. So the color skipped a generation. Elis was a city in the northwestern Peloponnese.

Note 310
The non-homoeomerous ones, such as face, hands, and feet: Reading ἃ ἀνομοιομερῆ οἷον πρόσωπον καὶ χεῖρας καὶ πόδας; OCT secludes.

Note 311

It is more fitting for it to come from the homoeomerous ones because they are prior and the non-homoeomerous ones are composed of them: "Because there are three compositions (*suntheseôn*), one might put first the one from what some people call the elements—for example, earth, air, water, and fire. And yet perhaps it is better to speak of composition from the capacities, and not from all of them, but as stated previously in other works. For wet, dry, hot, and cold are matter of the composite bodies, while the other differentiae—for example, heaviness and lightness, density and rarity, roughness and smoothness, and the other corporeal affections of this sort—follow along with these. The second sort of composition is that of the nature of the homoeomerous parts in animals—for example, bone, flesh, and other things of this sort—from the primary things (= the elements). Third and last in the series is the composition of the nature of the non-homoeomerous parts—for example, of face, hand, and others of this sort. But in coming to be things are a contrary way to the way they are in substance. For things posterior in coming to be are prior in nature, and the final stage (*teleutaion*) in coming to be is primary in nature (for the house is not for the sake of the bricks and stones, but rather these are for the sake of the house—and this holds in the same way of other sorts of matter)" (*PA* II 1 646ᵃ12–29).

Note 312

The elements: See I 1 715ᵃ11n.

Note 313

If something handicrafts (*dêmiourgei*) this later, it would be the cause of the similarity: The verb *dêmiourgein* is regularly used in contexts like this. Occurrences listed in the Index.

Note 314

What about what belongs to the private parts? For what comes from the male and what comes from the female are not similar: "How could female organs come from the male parent and vice versa. The theory fails to account for the resemblance between daughter and father, or son and mother" (Balme-2, p. 142).

Note 315

Empedocles: See DK 31 = TEGP pp. 326–433.
Seems to speak most in agreement with this account: Secluding τό γε τοσοῦτον, ἀλλ᾽ εἴπερ ἑτέρᾳ πῃ, οὐ καλῶς ("at any rate up to a point, but if indeed [we look] anywhere else he seems not to speak correctly") with OCT. Balme-2, Peck-3; Louis-3, Lefebvre, Platt retain.

Note 316

A sort of token (*hoion sumbolon*): *Sumbola* were originally two pieces of a bone or coin that uniquely fitted together, enabling a person with one to recognize a person with the other. In *GC* II 4 Aristotle uses the term to refer to a differentia shared by two consecutive elements, like the cold in earth and water. Thus when water becomes earth only one differentia has to be changed (dry to wet), which makes that change easier than one in which both differentiae have to be changed. **Torn asunder is the nature of the limbs, part in man's** . . . : DK B63 = TEGP 126 F77. See also IV 1 764ᵇ3–20.

Note 317
Which is how Empedocles speaks of them as coming to be under the influence of love: "But since it was evident that the contraries of good things were also present in nature (not only order and nobility but also disorder and baseness, and more bad things than good ones, and more base things than noble ones), someone else accordingly introduced love *and* strife as each singly the cause of one of the two sorts of things. For if we were to follow and grasp the *thought* and not the inarticulate words of Empedocles, we would find that love is the cause of good things and strife of bad ones. So, if we were to claim that Empedocles in a way says, and was the first to say, that the good and the bad are starting-points, we would perhaps be right—if indeed the cause of all good things is the good itself" (*Met.* I 4 984ᵇ32–985ᵃ10).
As many heads sprouted without necks: DK B57 = TEGP 118 F71.

Note 318
Soul (*psuchên*): See II 4 738ᵇ26–27.

Note 319
Hardness and softness: "Hard is that whose surface cannot be pressed into itself; soft is that whose surface can be pressed in, but not by being replaced" (*Mete.* IV 4 382ᵃ11–14); "A soft thing is what can be pressed into itself, whereas a hard one is what cannot be pressed in" (*Cael.* III 1 299ᵇ13–14).

Note 320
What has come from them cannot be synonymous with the parts: See I 16 721ᵃ3n.

Note 321
Anaxagoras: See DK 59 = TEGP pp. 271–325.

Note 322
Anaxagoras quite reasonably says that [particles of] flesh (*sarkas*) **from the nourishment are added to [particles of] flesh** (*sarxin*): The nouns are plural. On Anaxagoras' theory there is a little bit of everything in everything (DK B3–4 = TEGP 12–13 F3–5). Thus flesh is already present as such in nourishment. When segregated out from there it gets added to flesh that has already segregated out, resulting in growth (DK A46 = TEGP 29).

Note 323
"[Seeds] were poured . . . cold": Empedocles, DK B65 = TEGP 131 F81. See IV 1 764ᵃ2–6.

Note 324
It is clear, therefore, if we assume it to be this way, that a female is not due to the seed's coming from a certain thing: Reading οὗτος<,> with Balme-2, Louis-3, Peck-3 for OCT οὗτος.
The part specially possessed by the male or the one specially possessed by the female: The penis in the one case, and the uterus (considered as a source of female seed) in the other.

Note 325
Certain animals come to be neither from those of the same genus nor from those of a different genus—for example, the flies and the genera called fleas: See I 1 715ª25n, 16 721ª5–10.

Note 326
And the plants in fact do so always—for it is clear that due to one movement these bear all their yearly fruit: Aristotle "does not mean that one plant is fertilized by another as a single act, for he knew nothing about their fertilization. He can only mean that the plant as a whole produces fruit all over itself in consequence of a single impulse at its heart, so to say" (Platt, n3).

Note 327
It is not possible for it to get separated up in the uterus: See I 20 729ª6–20.

Note 328
For by then the separation would be, as it were, from an animal, not from seed: Since the seed would already have begun forming a fetus.

Note 329
That is why [the insects] mate, as we said previously, the way they do: Peck-3 secludes.
As we said previously: At I 16 721ª9–17.

Note 330
It is evident, even in those males that emit semen, that the seed's coming from all the body is not the cause of generation, but it occurs in some other way that must be investigated later on: See I 21.

Note 331
We must get a theoretical grasp on the cause of [inherited similarities] later on: In IV 3.

Note 332
Not from that thing which is the producer—for example, the human (for they come to be from it because the seed belongs to it): OCT reads but obelizes οὐ τῷ

ἐξ ἐκείνου τι εἶναι τὸ ποιοῦν οἷον τοῦ ἀνθρώπου· γίγνεται γὰρ ἐκ τούτου ὅτι τοῦτό ἐστι τὸ σπέρμα; Peck-3 secludes; Balme-2, Lefebvre, and Louis-3 read.

That from which (*ex hou*) the things composed in accord with nature first come to be: "For in every case there is something that underlies, from which the thing comes to be—for example, plants and animals come to be from seed" (*Ph.* I 7 190ᵇ3–5).

For they come to be from it because the seed belongs to it: Reading τούτου with some mss. for OCT τοῦτό. See I 2 716ᵃ7–10, 17 721ᵇ6–7.

Note 333

But there are many ways in which one thing comes to be *from* another: Similar lists with some of the same examples are given at *Ph.* I 7 190ᵃ21–30, *Met.* V 24.

Note 334

Non-musical comes to be from musical: As when someone who used to be able to sing loses the ability, and so persists as one and the same through the change.

Note 335

Epicharmus: An early fifth-century writer of comedies from Sicily. A quotation of some of his lines (of which Aristotle gives the gist) exemplifies the building to a climax attributed to him: "After the sacrifice, a feast; after the feast, drinking; after the drinking, derision; after derision, swinish insults; after the insults, a law suit; after the verdict, chains, stocks, a fine" (Athenaeus, II.3). See also *Rh.* I 7 1365ᵃ16.

Note 336

The crafts [are the starting-point of movement] for things handicrafted: See *PA* I 1 640ᵃ31–33n (this vol.).

Note 337

The primary mover (*prôtou kinêsantos*): That is, the proximate mover—the first of the movers one encounters in proceeding from what is moved.

Note 338

Panathenaean festival: A festival in honor of Athena as patron goddess of Athens.

The sea voyage: Legend had it that Athens was once obliged to send King Minos of Crete an annual tribute of seven young men and seven maidens to be given to the Minotaur—a monster, half man and half bull, that he kept in a labyrinth. With the help of a thread given to him by Minos' daughter Ariadne, Theseus, a legendary king of Athens, made his way through the labyrinth, killed the Minotaur, and escaped, thus ending the tribute. Each year, Athens commemorated these events by sending a mission of thanks to the sanctuary of Apollo on the sacred island of Delos. This is the sea voyage referred to. No executions could take place in Athens until the mission returned from its voyage. See Plato, *Cri.* 43c, *Phd.* 58a–c.

There must be some other subject underlying and remaining present from which it will first come to be: As a man underlies the change from non-musical to musical. See I 18 724ᵃ26–27n.

Note 339

Like the seeds of plants and of certain animals in which male and female are not separated: Reading οἷον τά τε τῶν φυτῶν καὶ ἐνίων ζῴων ἐν οἷς μὴ κεχώρισται τὸ θῆλυ καὶ τὸ ἄρρεν, which Platt secludes as a near repeat of I 18 724^{b}10–12.

Note 340

The prior and the posterior: See *Met.* V 11.

Note 341

Now what comes away from the progenitor . . . it must be stated again what the primary nature is of what is called seed: Secluded by Peck-3.

But it must be stated again what the primary nature is of what is called seed: Secluded in Balme-2.

Note 342

By a residue I mean a leftover of the nourishment (*trophês*), **by a colliquescence** (*suntêgma*) **what has been secreted from a growth-producer** (*auxêmatos*) **by contrary-to-nature dissolution:** The difference between nourishment and a growth-producer is explained in the following two texts: "Nourishment and that by which something will grow (*tê[i] auxêsei*), though they are the same, are distinct in being. For insofar as what enters is potentially so-and-so-much flesh, it is by it that a growth-producer [produces] flesh (*auxêtikon*), but insofar as it is potentially flesh alone, nourishment" (*GC* I 5 322^{a}25–28); "The being for nourishment, however, is distinct from the being for a growth-producer (*auxetikô[i]*). For it is insofar as the ensouled thing has some quantity that a growth-producer exists for it, whereas it is insofar as it is a this something and a substance that nourishment does. For the ensouled thing preserves its substance and lasts just as long as it is nourished, and it is generative not of what is being nourished, but of something of the same sort as what is being nourished. For its own substance already exists, and nothing generates itself, but rather preserves itself. So this sort of starting-point of the soul is a capacity of the sort that preserves what has it, insofar as it has it, whereas nourishment equips it to be active. That is why, if deprived of food it cannot exist. But since the end is what determines what it is right to call everything, and the end is to generate something of the same sort as itself, the primary soul will be one that can generate something of the same sort as itself" (*DA* III 4 416^{b}11–25a). Nourishment that is not concocted (useless residue) is (1) excreted as waste product (urine, feces, or their analogues), while (2) what remains, when (2a) properly concocted is (in part) a growth-producer (useful residue) and (2b) when improperly (or non-naturally) concocted, a colliquescence: "the colliquescence is produced as non-concocted nourishment" (*Somn.* 3 456^{b}35–437^{a}1). The one example Aristotle gives is in *PA* IV 2 677^{b}11–15: "But just as bile (*cholê*), when it is produced throughout the other part of the body, seems to be a residue, or rather [3] a colliquescence (*suntêxis*), so too [4] the bile near the liver seems to be a residue and not to be for the sake of something, just like too the excretions in the bowels and the intestines." Notice that [4] has a definite location in the body, whereas [3] occurs throughout. This is a mark of a colliquescence: "no place is assigned to a colliquescence in accord with nature, rather it flows wherever there is an easy route in the body" (*GA* I 18 725ª33–35).

Note 343
[Seed] is homoeomerous: "Just as horn, which is homoeomerous in respect of its material make-up, is, when its function is taken into account, inseparable from its configuration, so semen [seed], which is homoeomerous in composition, would be inseparable from the movement on which its *function* depends" (Falcon & Lefebvre (Rashed), p. 110). See I 1 715ª10n.

Note 344
Neither is it separated, whereas all the other parts are: "This may mean that it is not present continuously as such, but has to be 'collected' and 'concocted' on each occasion for which it is required: see 717ᵇ25" (Peck-3, p. 78 n*c*).

Note 345
Deformation (*pêrôma*): A *pêrôma* or *anapêria* (adjective: *anapêros*) can have an effect on functioning and may be a part of a thing's nature. Being female, for example, is "like a natural *anapêria*" (*GA* IV 6 775ª15–16), affecting the ability to reproduce (I 20 728ª18–21). On the other hand, someone may be *pêros* (blind, for example) not by nature but simply as a result of an accident or a condition such as drunkenness (*NE* III 5 1114ª25–28). Neither "deformity" nor "mutilation," which are common translations, capture these meanings, and I have elsewhere usually opted for "disability" as a less misleading alternative. In *GA*, however, "deformation" seems the better option all things considered. Here a *pêrôma* is presumably the same thing as the *phuma* ("tumor") mentioned at *GA* I 18 724ᵇ25.

Note 346
Saying that it comes from all the body because of the heat from the movement [in copulation]: "There are veins and nerves which extend from every part of the body of the penis. When as result of gentle friction the vessels grow warm and become congested, they experience a kind of irritation, and in consequence a feeling of pleasure and warmth arises over the whole body. Friction on the penis and the movement of the whole man cause the fluid in the body to grow warm: becoming diffuse and agitated by the movement it produces a foam in the same way as all other fluids produce foam when they are agitated. But in the case of the human what is secreted as foam is the most potent and richest part of the fluid. This fluid is diffused from the brain into the loins and the whole body, which enable the fluid to pass to and from the spinal marrow. Once the sperm has entered the spinal marrow it passes on its course through the veins along the kidneys. . . . From the kidneys it passes via the testes into the penis—not however by the urinary tract, since it has a passage of its own next to the urinary tract" (Hippocrates, *On Generation* 1 (Littré VII.472 = Lonie, p. 1)).

Note 347

By useless [nourishment] I mean that from which nothing further is contrib-uted to the nature: That is to the nature of the thing consuming the nourishment, either by sustaining it or by contributing to its natural growth.

Note 348

The [residue] from the first stage of the nourishment is phlegm and anything of that sort: After eating nourishment rises as vapor to the brain, where it is cooled and condenses into serum and phlegm. Unlike urine and stool, which are useless, these are (or are on the whole) useful.

Note 349

We say that [the seed] is what naturally goes to all of it: Because it is a part of the residue of the useful nourishment that goes to all the body's parts.

Note 350

For the most part (*hôs epi to polu*): Aristotle associates what holds always with what holds by necessity: "*necessary* and *always* go together (for what it is necessary for there to be cannot not be)" (*GC* II 11 337^{b}35–36). He associates what holds *hôs epi to polu* with what rarely fails to happen (*Top.* II 6 112^{b}10–11), and attributes its exis-tence to matter: "Nature tends to measure comings to be and endings by the regular movements of these bodies [the sun and moon], but cannot bring this about rigor-ously because of the indefiniteness of matter, and because many starting-points exist which impede coming to be and passing away from being according to nature, and often cause things to come about contrary to nature" (*GA* IV 10 778^{a}4–9). Since the "indefiniteness of matter" seems to be a standing condition, while the "many starting-points . . . which impede" are not, we should presumably divide things up as follows. The indefiniteness of matter explains why laws or theorems of natural science hold *hôs epi to polu*, and so have contraries that are rarely true, while impedi-ments explain why what otherwise would occur rarely may occur quite often. All human beings are bipeds, and this would remain true even if some freak accident or genetic disorder resulted in all or most human beings having only one leg. Nonethe-less, it would still hold *hôs epi to polu*, since even under normal conditions a human offspring may be born with only one leg, simply due to facts about his father's seed (form) and his mother's menses (matter). See also *Met.* VI 2.

Note 351

Becoming very fleshy and rather too fat: Reading πολύσαρκοι ἢ πιότεροι μᾶλλον with OCT; Balme-2 reads πολύσαρκοι μᾶλλον ἢ πρότερον ("becoming more fleshy than before").

Note 352

Some, though, bear no seed at all—for example, the willow and the poplar: "A popular delusion among the ancients. That is why the trees are connected with the dead—ἰτέαι ὠλεσίκαρποι ["fruit-perishing willows"], *Odyssey* X.510" (Platt, n5).

Note 353
This affection too has both sorts of cause: Reading καὶ ἑκάτεραι αἰτίαι with Balme-2, Louis-3, Peck-3, and Platt for OCT καὶ †ἕτεραι αἰτίαι.

Note 354
Through incapacity they do not concoct [their nourishment] and through capacity they use it up, as was mentioned: At I 18 725^{b}30.

Note 355
Prolific [seed] (*poluchoa*) **and abundant seed:** *Poluchoa* usually means "prolific," that is, producing many offspring. But here it seems to refer to a feature of seed. If so, capacity of seed (to produce many offspring) and quantity of seed are being contrasted. Some mss. have πολυχρόνια ("long lifetime"), so there may be corruption in the text.

Note 356
When there is no easy route the evacuation of these (*autôn*): Reading ταύτῃ with ms. Z for OCT αὐτῶν.

Note 357
For much useless residue is mixed together with it. . . . But as things stand it does not do this: OCT secludes. For a reason to preserve the text, see Balme-2, p. 146.
Further, a colliquescence is always morbid. . . . But as things stand it does not do this: Bracketed as an interpolation by Peck-3 (p. 86 n*a*) and ticketed for rejection by Platt, n1.

Note 358
That blood is the last stage of the nourishment in blooded animals, and its analogue in bloodless ones, has been said previously: At *PA* II 3 650^{a}34, 4 651^{a}15, IV 4 678^{a}8.

Note 359
Actively (*energeia[i]*): The term *energeia*, which is used only a few times in *GC* (at I 3 318^{a}20, 10 327^{b}23), is an Aristotelian coinage, translated as "activity," with the dative or adverbial form *energeia[i]* translated as "active" or "actively," in order to signal its relation to *energeia*. The etymology of the coinage is unclear, but Aristotle is explicit that it has been extended from movement to other things (*Met.* IX 1 1046^{a}1–2, 3 1047^{a}30–32), and that it is related to another term with an *erg-* root, namely, *ergon*: "The *ergon* ('function', 'work') is the *telos* ('end'), and the *energeia* is the *ergon*, and that is why the name *energeia* is said [of things] with reference to the *ergon* and extends to the *entelecheian* ('actuality')" (8 1050^{a}21–23). *Entelecheia*, used in a parallel context at *PA* I 1 642^{a}1, is also an Aristotelian coinage. It is mostly used as a synonym of *energeia*, but with a slightly different connotation: *energeia* is

action, activity, and movement oriented; *entelecheia*—as the *tel-* suggests—is end or *telos* or completion (*enteles*) oriented (*Met.* V 16 1021^{b}24–30). The dative or adverbial form *entelecheia[i]* is translated as "actual" or "actually." The *entelecheia of* something is thus "the actualization" of it. Putting all this together: the activation or actualization of X is an activity, which is X active or actual, which is X achieving its end, which—since "the for-the-sake-of-which is the function" (III 2 996^{b}7)—is X fulfilling its function, and being actively or actually X, and so being complete.

It is natural to wonder why Aristotle coined two terms with such similar meanings. One suggestion is that the need stems from psychology. Aristotle has to distinguish (a) a dead animal from an animate one and (b) a dormant or sleeping live animal from an active or awake one. *Energeia* recommends itself for (b). But how, then, to distinguish the level of activity in (a) that constitutes the possession of a soul? That is where *entelecheia* comes in: the soul is "the first *entelecheia* of a natural body that has instrumental parts" (*DA* II 2 412^{a}27–^{b}6). This may well be true, but it is interesting that in a case where *energeia* seems yet more unfortunate in its connotations, Aristotle uses it anyway: "What is stillness? Quietness in a large quantity of air. The air is matter; the quietness is *energeia* and substance" (*Met.* VIII 2 1043^{a}23–24). In fact, he also uses it for the soul, which is the *energeia* of a certain sort of body (3 1043^{a}35–36).

Potentially (*dunamei*): See I 2 716^{a}23n.

Note 360

Neither the hand nor any other part, without being soul-involving (*psuchikês*) **or having a certain other capacity, is a hand or any other part whatsoever except homonymously:** "For if the eye were an animal, sight would be its soul. For that is the substance of an eye, the one in accord with the account. And the eye is matter for sight, and if this fails, it is no longer an eye, except homonymously, like an eye in stone or in a picture" (*DA* II 1 412^{b}18–22); "A corpse is a human homonymously. In the same way, therefore, the hand of a dead man is homonymously a hand, just as stone flutes too might be called flutes. For these [bodily parts] also seem to be instruments of sorts" (*Mete.* IV 12 389^{b}31–390^{a}2); "Bodily parts . . . cannot even exist when they are separated. For it is not a finger in any and every state that is the finger of an animal, rather, a dead finger is only homonymously a finger" (*Met.* VII 10 1035^{b}23–25).

Homonymously (*homônumon*): See *PA* I 1 640^{b}36n.

Note 361

{It is also evident that . . . the first colliquescence}: This should be read post I 18 726^{a}25.

Note 362

And let these things be determined in this way: Secluded in Balme-2.

Note 363

The weaker is what has a lesser share of heat in accord with nature, and the female is of this sort, as was said previously: At *PA* II 2 648^{a}12, also *GA* IV 1 765^{b}6–766^{b}28.

Note 364

The results associated with it are signs (*sêmeia*) **that this statement is correct:**
Aristotle often declares something to be a sign (*sêmeion*) of something both in
GA (see Index) and in other treatises (more than thirty times, for example, in
Rh.). But just what a sign is takes a bit of working out. The first thing to note is
that signs are of two sorts: related as (1) particular to universal or (2) as universal
to particular (*Rh.* I 2 1357^{b}1–3). An example of (1): "if someone were to say that
since Socrates is wise and just it is a sign that the wise are just" (1357^{b}11–13);
an example of (2): "if someone were to say that there is a sign that a person is
feverish, since he is breathing rapidly" (1357^{b}18–19). Both of these are refutable
(1357^{b}13, 19–20). Yet, as Aristotle puts it in the *Prior Analytics*, "truth may be
found in signs whatever their sort" (II 27 70^{a}37–38). The question is what sort of
truth? Not necessary truth: signs are not proofs. But is it contingent truth or the
sort of gappy necessary truth found in things that hold for the most part (*APr.*
I 13 32^{b}6)? And if it is the latter, are signs distinct from things that hold for the
most part or the very same thing? The answer becomes clear once we reflect
on the fact that only a universally quantified proposition can hold for the most
part, as in the examples Aristotle gives about crabs: "for the most part all crabs
have the right claw bigger and stronger than the left" (*HA* IV 3 527^{b}6–7). For
it certainly cannot hold for the most part that *some* crabs have their right claw
bigger than their left. Their right claw is either bigger than the left or it isn't. The
same goes for any particular crab. With signs, by contrast, there are some that
are related as particular to universal, as the fact that Socrates is wise and just is a
sign that the wise are just. Therein lies the difference we were looking for. A sign
can be a particular proposition; one that holds for the most part cannot. At the
same time, though, it is not just a contingent fact that Socrates is both wise and
just, as it might be that he was married to Xanthippe, but something (putatively)
more robust than that, namely, a gappy necessity.

Note 365

It is not possible for two spermatic secretions to be produced at once: "Why
not two? Presumably because spermatic residue comes from a regular source or
set of sources; all that Aristotle has said above about the female residue will apply to all the production from these sources; there cannot also be other sources,
or other conditions of production" (Balme-2, p. 148); "Because A. has found
that everywhere Nature is economical, and does not use superfluous methods"
(Platt, n1).
It is evident that the female does not contribute seed to generation: This is one
of several places in which Aristotle denies that females emit seed (also I 20 728^{a}31).
But by this he clearly means pure seed (728^{a}26–27) or semen (729^{a}22), since the
menses are themselves seed (728^{a}26), as are eggs (I 8 718^{b}15).

Note 366

**Why, then, just as the seed is a residue so too are the menses has now been
stated:** Secluded in Balme-2.

Note 367
Fat animals produce less seed than non-fat ones, as was said previously: At I 18 725^{b}32–34.

Note 368
The female does not emit the sort of seed that the male does: That is, "a white fluid sent forth at sexual climax" (Connell, p. 101). But she does of course contribute seed of another sort (*GA* I 2 716^{a}5–14).
Unless the liquid of what is called menses is present in proportion: See I 18 723^{a}29–30.

Note 369
It is what occurs for the most part that is most in accord with nature: See I 18 725^{b}17n.

Note 370
This liquid is not spermatic but is special to the place in each female: The place is in front of the mouth of the uterus (II 4 739^{a}37). This, together with the fact that it is produced at the same time as orgasm (I 20 727^{b}35), suggests that the liquid may be vaginal mucus and the "sweating" produced during sexual arousal and vasocongestion. But its quantity seldom if ever "far exceeds" that of the (male?) seed (I 20 728^{a}4–5). Another possibility is that it is leucorrhea, which can be quite copious. But this is not produced at the same time as orgasm and occurs even in small girls (II 4 738^{b}25). A third possibility is that it is so-called female ejaculate, believed to be produced by the Skene's gland (which is made of the same tissue as the male prostate) and seems to be similar in chemical composition to male semen, though containing no sperm. But though this is emitted at orgasm, it is small in quantity. In some women, urine mixed with prostatic-specific enzyme (PSA) is emitted during orgasm and can be quite copious.

Note 371
A boy too is like a woman in shape (*morphê*): That is, in form.

Note 372
[Menses] too are a hemorrhage: See II 4 738^{a}16.

Note 373
Just as in what has to do with the generation of fruits, when [their food] has not yet been sifted, though the nourishment is present in it, and needs working on to purify it: "A mixture of impure food mixed with the pure sort makes the whole thing more useful than a little [of the latter]" (*Pol.* III 11 1281^{b}36–37). Here, it is the reverse. The impure food has nourishment (pure food) in it, but this needs to be sifted out. Compare, "Even the very things that might seem to be nourished by only one thing, like plants by water, are in fact nourished by several. For earth is mixed with the water. That is why farmers try to mix

in something when watering" (*GC* II 8 335ª11–14); "Farmers mix in not just any random earth, but manure, which partakes of fiery and airy substances, and, having mixed, he says, use it in this way in watering" (Philop. 280.8–10 = Kupreeva, p. 72).

Note 374
Those that are quite sanguineous (*tois haimatikois*): The reference is "to only some of the class of blooded animals" (Balme-2, p. 150). Similarly, at II 4 738ᵇ5, IV 8 776ᵇ12.

Note 375
The purgation is produced neither in them nor in certain blooded animals, except the ones just mentioned: Reading τοῦ δὲ μήτε τούτοις γίγνεσθαι κάθαρσιν μήτε τῶν αἷμα ἐχόντων <τισὶ πλὴν> τοῖς εἰρημένοις, τοῖς κάτω ἔχουσι καὶ μὴ ᾠοτοκοῦσιν with Balme-2 for OCT τοῦ δὲ μήτε τούτοις γίγνεσθαι κάθαρσιν μήτε τῶν αἷμα ἐχόντων τοῖς εἰρημένοις, [τοῖς κάτω ἔχουσι καὶ μὴ ᾠοτοκοῦσιν] ("the purgation is produced neither in them nor in the just mentioned blooded animals [those whose uterus is down below and are not oviparous]").

Note 376
These are the human and those quadrupeds that bend the hind leg inward (for all these are viviparous without first producing an egg): Secluded in Balme-2.
Those quadrupeds that bend the hind leg inward: That is, so that the foot is brought in toward the body. See *PA* IV 12 693ᵇ3, *IA* 1 704ª23.
Unless they are deformed (*pepêrôtai*) **in the process of generation like the mule:** See I 18 724ᵇ32n and, on mules, II 8.

Note 377
How this occurs in each of the animals is described with exactness in the *History of Animals*: See *HA* III 19 521ª21–ᵇ3, VI 18 572ᵇ29–573ª16, 20 574ª31–ᵇ3, VII 1 581ᵇ1–11, 2 582ª34–583ª12 (but only some cases are described in these passages). The sentence is secluded in Balme-2.

Note 378
At the same time of life, as was said previously, the males produce this residue and the females show signs of menses: See I 19 727ª5–10.

Note 379
By an embryo (*kuêma*) **I mean the primary mixture of female and male:** See I 13 719ᵇ34n.

Note 380
The fig-juice or rennet is what contains the starting-point of its composition: Like rennet, the acidic juice of the fig tree is used to curdle milk in making cheese.

Note 381
Due to what cause it is partitioned here into a larger number, here into fewer, and here is not partitioned at all, will be for another account: See IV 4 771^{b}14–772^{b}12.

Note 382
The proportion between what is divided and the matter, and neither so little that it does not concoct or compose the matter nor so much that it dries it up: See IV 4 772^{a}10–12.

Note 383
The primary thing doing the composing, from [what is] already one, only one offspring comes to be: The primary thing doing the composing is the now unified result of partitioning the male semen that acts directly on the menses to compose it, that is, the single proximate cause of its composition.

Note 384
Reason (*logos*) **based on universal investigations:** Namely, on investigations into generation (coming to be) generally, not just animal generation. See also I 21 729^{b}9–21.

Note 385
The female as affected: Secluding ἡ θῆλυ with OCT, Balme-2, and Lefebvre; Louis-3, Peck-3, and Platt retain ("the female, insofar as female, . . ."). See I 21 729^{b}12.

Note 386
The nature of the menses corresponds to the primary matter: "And nature is both the primary matter—and this in two ways, either primary relative to the thing itself or primary in general (for example, in works of bronze the bronze is primary relative to themselves, but in general perhaps water is primary, if all meltable things are water) and the form and the substance, which is the end of their coming to be" (*Met.* V 4 1015^{a}7–13). Here the menses is the analogue of bronze in works of bronze, since it is the matter on which the male semen first works directly (in other words, the proximate matter).

Note 387
Let these things, then, be determined in this way: Secluded in Balme-2.

Note 388
What remains of the residue in the female: After the rest has been expelled externally.

Note 389
Facts (*ergôn*): *Ergon*, which is usually translated as "work" or "function," here means "fact."

Note 390
The male produces an animal only by a capacity in the semen, just as we said of insects in which the female inserts a part into the male: At I 21 729ᵇ26–28.

Note 391
It is necessary for some to be present from the outset, gathered together, from which the embryo is composed in the first instance: This is the primary matter. See I 20 729ᵃ32–33, II 1 733ᵇ26.

Note 392
Every working on a thing and every last movement takes place in contact with the matter—for example, building takes place in what is being built: "For the activity of building is in what is being built and comes to be and is at the same time as the house. In the cases, then, where what comes to be is some other thing beyond the use, in those cases the activity is in what is being produced—for example, the activity of building is in what is being built, the activity of weaving is in what is being woven, and similarly in the other cases, and in general the movement is in what is being moved" (*Met.* IX 8 1050ᵃ28–34); "In the case of all capacities the activities are external, either in something other than the agent himself, or in himself insofar as he is other [as when a doctor makes himself healthy]" (*EE* VII 2 1237ᵃ36).
Last movement (*eschatê*): That is, the last one in the chain of movements that begins with the first mover and ends with movement in the matter.

Note 393
"Thus tall trees first lay olive eggs": DK B79 = TEGP 142 F91.

Note 394
One animal coming to be from both: Retaining ἕν τι ζῷον γίγνεσθαι ἐξ ἀμφοῖν with Balme-2, Lefebvre, Louis-3, and Platt; OCT and Peck-3 seclude. The one animal is the two-backed one, as we say.

Note 395
Well, plants have been investigated elsewhere: Secluded in Balme-2. This lost treatise is also referred to at I 1 716ᵃ1–2 and V 3 783ᵇ20–24.

Note 396
The function of the animal . . . is not only to generate (for this is common to all living things): This presupposes, as *NE* I 7 1097ᵇ33–34 asserts in the case of the human function, that the function of X is special to X. The justification for this claim lies in the connection between X's function and what X does best: "People whose function, that is to say, the best thing to come from them, is to use their bodies . . . are natural slaves" (*Pol.* I 6 1254ᵇ17–19); "If the human is a simple animal and his substance is ordered in accord both with reason and with understanding, he has no other function than this alone, namely, the attainment of the most exact truth

263

about the beings. But if he is naturally co-composed of several potentialities, and it is clear that he has by nature several functions to be completed, the best of them is always *his* function, as health is the function of the doctor, and safety of a ship's captain" (*Protr.* B65). Since human beings are not naturally simple (*NE* VII 14 1154b20–22) and do have several functions (I 10 1100^{b}12–13), the best one will be the one that is special to them. But because human beings have not just a complex nature but also a compound one consisting of a divine element (understanding) and a human one (X 7–8 1177^{b}26–1178^{a}23), their special function may—like that of the part of the soul that has reason (VI 1 1139^{a}17, 2 1139^{a}29–31, ^{b}12)—be compound too. Moreover, it will matter whether we are considering male or female human beings, since these have different special functions: "straight from the beginning their functions are divided, those of a man being different from those of a woman, so they assist each other by putting their special ones into the common enterprise (VIII 12 1162^{a}22–24); "his function [in household management] is to acquire property and hers to preserve it" (*Pol.* III 5 1277^{b}24–25).

Sort of knowledge (*gnôseôs tinos*): Although there may be little difference between *gnôsis (verb: gnorizein)* and *epistêmê (verb: epistasthai)*, *epistêmê* is usually applied only to demonstrative sciences, crafts, or other bodies of systematic knowledge, so that *epistêmê* is specifically *scientific* knowledge. *Gnôsis* is weaker and is used for perceptual knowledge and knowledge by acquaintance—something familiar is *gnôrimos*. If X knows that p, it follows that p is true and that X is justified in believing it. Similar entailments hold in the cases of *epistasthai* and *eidenai* but may not hold in that of *gignôskein*.

Note 397

Esteem (*to timion*): See *PA* I 5 644^{b}24n (this vol.).

Practical wisdom (*phronêsin*): *Phronêsis* (verb *phronein*) is used: (1) in a broad sense to refer to thought or (roughly speaking) intelligence of any sort (as at *Met. IV* 5 1009^{b}13, 30); (2) in a narrower sense to refer to the distinctively practical wisdom discussed in *NE* VI 5, which is the virtue or excellence of the rationally calculative or deliberative part of the soul, which ensures that we aim at and hit the best good—happiness; and (3) as equivalent in meaning to *sophia* or theoretical wisdom (*Met. XIII* 4 1078^{b}15, and throughout *Protr.*). (2), in its fullest form, and (3) are distinctively human possessions. But Aristotle does sometimes attribute a weaker form (*HA* VII 1 588^{a}18–31) of (2) to non-human animals, such as deer, hare, cranes, bees, and ants (I 2 488^{b}15, IX 5 611^{a}15–16, IX 10 614^{b}18, *PA* II 2 648^{a}5–8, 4 650^{b}18–27, *GA* III 2 753^{a}10–17).

Note 398

It is by perception that animals differ from things that are merely living: "We say, then, to make a start to the inquiry, that what has soul is distinguished from what lacks soul by living. But things are said to be living in many ways, and we say that a thing is alive if any one of these alone is present, for example, understanding, perception, movement and rest with respect to place, further the movement involved in nourishment, and also both withering and growth. That is why all plants too seem to be alive. For they evidently have within themselves a capacity and starting-point of this sort, through which they come to grow and decay in contrary directions. For they do not grow upward without growing downward, but grow in both directions alike, indeed in all directions, if they are constantly nourished and continue to live for as long as they are capable of taking nourishment. This can be separated from the others, but in the case of the mortal beings the others cannot be separated from it. This is evident in the case of plants, since they have no other capacity of soul. It is due to this starting-point, then, that life belongs to living things, whereas being an animal is due primarily to perception. For even what does not move or change its place, but which does have perception, is said to be an animal and not just a living thing. Now the primary sort of perception that belongs to all animals is touch. And just as the nutritive can be separated from touch and every perceptual capacity, in the same way touch can be separated from the other perceptual capacities" (*DA* II 2 413ª20–ᵇ7); "Animals, though, must have perception, and without this nothing can be an animal, if nature does nothing pointlessly. For all things that are by nature are for the sake of something or will be concomitants of those things that are for the sake of something. Every body that can perambulate, then, if it did not have perception, would perish and fail to arrive at its end, which is the function of nature. For how would it be nourished? For the stationary ones this is indeed present where they have grown. However, if a body is not stationary and is generated, it is not possible for it to have a soul and an understanding that is capable of judging but not to have perception—indeed, even if it is not generated. For why would it not have this? For either it would be better for the soul or for the body, but in fact it would be better for neither. For the soul would not understand any better and the body would be no better because of that. No body, therefore, that is not stationary has a soul without perception" (III 12 434ª30–ᵇ8).

Note 399
[The animal] becomes like a plant, as we said: At I 22 731ª21–24.

Note 400
But [testaceans'] generation must be spoken about later: In III 11.

Book II

Note 401
That the female and the male are starting-points of generation was said previously, as was what their capacity is: See I 1 716ª5–7 (starting-points), 2 716ª20–22 (capacity).
And the account of their substance (*logos tês ousias*): The phrase *logos tês ousias* is found at I 1 715ª5, though not applied directly to male and female. But see I 2 716ª17–ᵇ12 and, on substance, *PA* I 1 639ª16n (this vol.).

Note 402
A higher starting-point: See II 1 732^{b}29n.

Note 403
The nobly beautiful (*to kalon*): See *PA* I 1 639^{b}20n (this vol.).
The nobly beautiful and the divine is always in accord with its own nature a cause of the better in things that admit of it: "For of many things the starting-point both of knowledge and of movement is the good and the nobly beautiful" (*Met.* V 1 1013^{a}21–23); "Since the good and the nobly beautiful are distinct, however (for the good is always found in action, whereas the noble is found also in immovable things), those who assert that the mathematical sciences say nothing about the nobly beautiful or the good are speaking falsely" (XIII 3 1078^{a}31–34). See also III 10 760^{b}20n.
The non-eternal does admit of being: Rejecting with Balme-2 and Lefebvre the addition of καὶ μὴ εἶναι ("the non-eternal does admit of being and of not being"), accepted by OCT, Louis-3, Peck-3, and Platt.
Living [is better] than not living: "It is clear that most human beings are willing to endure much misery in order to cling to living, on the supposition that there is a sort of joy in it and a natural sweetness" (*Pol.* III 6 1278^{b}27–30); "Even if no other good should follow, living is intrinsically choiceworthy" (*Rh.* I 6 1362^{b}26–27).

Note 404
In number it is not possible: "Whether we say 'one in number' or 'particular' makes no difference, since by 'particular' we mean 'one in number', and by 'universal' we mean 'what is over particulars'" (*Met.* III 4 999^{b}33–1000^{a}1). The claim, then, is that particular living things are not eternal.
For the substance of the beings is in the particular one: Substance here is essence: "In one way, the essence of each thing is what it is intrinsically—for example, Callias is intrinsically Callias, and the essence of Callias. In another way, anything that is present in the what-it-is—for example, Callias is intrinsically an animal. For animal is present in his account, since Callias is a sort of animal" (*Met.* V 19 1022^{a}25–29).
In form (*eidos*)**, however, it is possible:** "We must first speak about nourishment and generation. For the nutritive soul belongs to the others as well [as to plants], and it is the first and most common capacity of soul, in virtue of which life belongs to every one. Its functions are generation and the making use of nourishment. For it is the most natural function in those living things that are complete and not deformed or spontaneously generated, to produce another like itself—an animal producing an animal, a plant a plant—in order that they may partake in the eternal and divine insofar as they can. For all desire that, and it is for the sake of it that they do whatever they do by nature. . . . Since, then, they cannot share in what is eternal and divine by continuous existence, because nothing that admits of passing away can persist as the same and numerically one, they share in them insofar as each can, some more and some less. And what persists is not the thing itself but something like itself, not one in number but one in form" (*DA* II 4 415^{a}22–^{b}7).

Note 405
It would be for the sake of generation that female and male are present among the beings: Reading ἕνεκα τῆς γενέσεως ἂν εἴη τὸ θῆλυ καὶ τὸ ἄρρεν ἐν τοῖς οὖσιν with Louis and the mss. for OCT ἕνεκα τῆς γενέσεως ἂν εἴη τὸ θῆλυ καὶ τὸ ἄρρεν ἐν τοῖς <ἔχ>ουσιν ("it would be for the sake of generation that female and male exist in the ones that have them"). The implications of the transmitted text have been understood to be quite general: "This seems to produce a framework in which all caused reality is the result of a female (material) principle that receives being thanks to the form-giving power emanating from the male" (Bos-2, p. 239). But so understood male and female seem to have lost their specifically biological significance and become little more than surrogates for matter and form. For there are species in which biological males and females do not exist, and there is a possibility, at least, of species in which females but not males are found. See Introduction, pp. lxxvii–lxxxiii.

Note 406
The animal genus is [what it is] in virtue of perception: See I 23 731^{b}4n.

Note 407
The female and the male are separated due to the causes just mentioned: At II 1 732^{a}3–9.

Note 408
Some of these, as was said, emit seed: At I 17 721^{a}30–^{b}6.

Note 409
Soul-involving heat (*thermotêtos psuchikês*): See Introduction, pp. lxii–lxxii.

Note 410
Something lives, then, in virtue of participating . . . heat and size: Peck-3 secludes this passage as "consisting of various remarks which are irrelevant here" (p. 132 n*d*).

Note 411
An egg . . . a larva: Compare *HA* I 5 489^{b}6–10 (this vol.).

Note 412
Of the oviparous animals, some lay complete eggs—for example, . . . most of the serpent genus: Vipers are the exception. See II 1 732^{b}21.

Note 413
All the viviparous animals are blooded: Secluding ἢ ᾠοτοκοῦντα with Lefebvre, Louis-3, Peck-3, and Platt; OCT retains ("all the viviparous or oviparous animals are blooded").

Note 414
They come to be spontaneously: See *PA* I 1 640ª27n (this vol.).

Note 415
The cause of this has been stated elsewhere: The phenomenon of incomplete things being produced through the copulation of insects that are themselves spontaneously generated is mentioned at *GA* I 16 721ª3–10 and *HA* V 1 539ᵇ7–14, but the cause referred to it is not given.

Note 416
The internally viviparous include both ones that have feet . . . and footless ones: Reading πόδας ἔχοντα with Louis-3, Peck-3, and Platt for OCT (followed by Lefebvre) δίποδα ("the internally viviparous include both biped ones and footless ones").

Note 417
There is no dividing, then, in this way: That is, by dichotomous division into, for example, animals having feet and animals not having feet. For the reason and the alternative, see *PA* I 3 643ᵇ10–644ª11 (this vol.).

Note 418
The viviparous ones are the animals that are more complete in nature and participate in a purer starting-point: The starting-point in question is pretty certainly blood. See *Juv.* 13 477ª13–22, Introduction, pp. lxii–lxxii.

Note 419
The defining mark: See *PA* I 1 639ª13n (this vol.).
Of natural heat is [the presence of] the lung, when it is well blooded (*enaimos*): *Enaimos* usually means simply "blooded," but is here an antonym of *oligaimos* ("poorly blooded") at *GA* II 1 732ᵇ35. Compare I 20 728ª35n.
Natural heat (*thermotêtos tês phusikês*): Namely, the soul-involving heat mentioned at II 1 732ª18.

Note 420
The way they do so we shall determine later on: In III 9.

Note 412
The fifth and coldest genus does not even lay eggs from itself; instead, this sort of affection happens externally, as was said: At II 1 733ª31.

Note 422
Reaching in this third change the end of its generation: We count two changes, from larva to egg, from egg to animal. The Greeks count the first as well as the last member of the series—larva, egg, animal.

Note 423
Some animals that do not come to be from seed, as was said previously: At I 1
715ᵇ26–30.

Note 424
Others in eggs, {* * *} seeds, and other such secretions: Reading * * * καὶ σπέρμασι
καὶ τοιαύταις ἄλλαις ἀποκρίσεσιν with OCT (followed by Lefebvre); Peck-3 and Platt
seclude. The hiatus is required because what follows it —"seeds and other such secretions"—is "obviously unintelligible when the question is only of vertebrates" (Platt, n2).

Note 425
Their primary matter: See I 20 729ᵃ30–33n.

Note 426
**But what is now being sought is not from what the parts come to be, but rath-
er due to what. For either something external produces them, or something
present in the semen and the seed, and is either some part of soul, or soul, or
something having soul:** Preformationism is the view that a miniature version of
the complete embryo preexists inside the semen or female seed. One form of epi-
genesis (the view opposed to preformationism) is that the form and structure of
the embryo emerge gradually from seed that is not itself formed and structured in
that way. Another, expressed in the language of modern biology, is that "develop-
mental pathways are not fixed ahead of time by the genetic program. Rather, the
genes represent a set of potential pathways. And which pathways are actualized is
determined in real time as the process unfolds in response to environmental cues
(including factors internal to the developing system but external to the genome).
On this view, then, all the information needed to build a new individual is not
already contained in the genome." Aristotle was almost certainly an epigenesist of
the first sort, but not of the second. See *GA* II 1 734ᵇ9–13, 5 741ᵇ7–15, and Falcon
& Lefebvre (Henry), pp. 89–107 (the previous quotation is from p. 90).

Note 427
It is impossible to move a thing without making contact with it: See I 22 730ᵇ4–8,
II 4 740ᵇ18–24.

Note 428
**If it makes the heart and then passes away, and the heart another part, by the
same argument either all pass away or all remain. Therefore, it is preserved:** If
X makes the heart and then passes away, then non-arbitrariness requires that the
heart, having made the next part, should also pass away. If it does not (as is in fact
the case), then X does not pass away either.

Note 429
The so-called Orphic poems (*tois kaloumenois Orpheôs epesin*): Aristotle uses
the same phrase at *DA* I 5 410ᵇ28, on which Philoponus comments, "He says

'so-called,' because it seems that these verses are not by Orpheus, as indeed he himself says in *On Philosophy*; for it is the doctrines that are Orpheus', and they say that it was Onomacritus who put them into verse" (*In. de An.* 186.24–26).

Note 430
There [Orpheus] says that an animal comes to be like the weaving of a fishing net: DK 10a.

Note 431
The things that come to be by nature or by craft, what is potentially comes to be due to what is actually, so that the form and shape [of the later thing] would need to be in the earlier thing—for example, the form of the liver in the heart: See I 18 724^{a}14–^{b}12.

Note 432
Perhaps something of what was said is not simple (*haploun*): In other words, perhaps it is said in many ways.

Note 433
Those wondrous automata: These were puppets operated by a concealed inner mechanism (*Mech.* 848^{a}3–37), mentioned at Plato, *Rep.* 514b, at *GA* II 5 741^{b}9, *Met.* I 2 983^{a}14, and—with the most details—in *MA* 7 701^{b}1–32 (Introduction, pp. lxxxi–lxxxii).

Note 434
In another way, however, it is the internal movement that does this, as building does the house: See I 18 730^{b}5–8n.

Note 435
There is, then, something that produces [the parts], it does not do so as a this something: That is, as some substantial thing or part that comes away from the producer or progenitor of the seed. See I 22 730^{b}11–23.
This something (*tode ti*): *Tode ti* involves a particularizing element and a generalizing element. I take the demonstrative pronoun *tode* as particularizing (as suggested by *Met.* VII 4 1030^{a}5–6) and the indefinite pronoun *ti* as generalizing, but since *tode* need not be particularizing (as it may not be in 7 1032^{b}6–21) and *ti* may be, it is possible to go the other way and translate as "thing of a certain sort." Often *tode ti* appears in translations simply as "a this," and in at least one place Aristotle himself suggests that *tode* and *ti* are interchangeable (XII 2 1069^{b}9, 11).
    (1) In very many cases, as in the present one, being a *tode ti* is a distinctive mark of *ousia* ("substance"), and so has some share in the ambiguity of the latter, as between (1a) an ultimate subject of predication and (2a) the substance or essence of something (*PA* I 1 639^{a}16n [this vol.]). This is reflected in the fact that (1b) a particular man and a particular horse are primary substances (*Cat.* 5 2^{a}11–14), so that "it is indisputably true that each of them

signifies a *tode ti*" (3ᵇ10–12), while at the same time (2b) what is separable and a *tode ti* is "the shape or form of each thing" (*Met.* V 8 1017ᵇ24–26; also VIII 1 1042ᵃ27–29, IX 7 1049ᵃ35, XII 3 1070ᵃ11). Some things, to be sure, are one and the same as their forms or essences—which would remove the ambiguity at least in their cases—but it is not true that all are (VII 11 1037ᵃ33–ᵇ7).

(3) As strong as the connection between substance and being a *tode ti* is the disconnection between being a *tode ti* and being a universal—"no common thing signifies a this something, but rather a such-and-such sort of thing" (*Met.* III 6 1003ᵃ8–9; also VII 13 1039ᵃ15–16)—and the connection between being substance and being a *kath' hekaston*: "If we do not posit substances to be separate, and in the way in which the *kath' hekasta* are said to be separate, we will do away with the sort of substance we wish to maintain" (XIII 10 1086ᵇ16–19). Apparently, then, a form that is (2b) a primary substance—as some are explicitly said to be (VII 7 1032ᵇ1–2)—must be a *kath' hekaston*.

(4) A *kath' hekaston*, in turn, is "what is numerically one" (*Met.* III 4 999ᵇ34–1000ᵃ1), and so, (4a) taking "numerically one" to mean that no two things can be one and the same *kath' hekaston*, as no two things can be you or Socrates (VII 14 1039ᵃ34), it is translated as "particular." But is also possible to take "numerically one" to mean (4b) "indivisible" or "individual," so that like an ultimate differentia—identified with form and substance at VII 12 1038ᵃ25–26—something is *kath' hekaston* because it cannot be further divided or differentiated.

(5) As we try to disambiguate *tode ti*, then, we run into ambiguities that parallel the initial one in substance itself, or that are related to it. That this may be no accident but rather the heart of the issue is suggested by *Met.* XIII 10 1087ᵃ19–21.

(6) Finally a point about matter. What *Ph.* I 7 190ᵇ24–26 refers to as "countable matter (*hulê arithmêtikê*)," and treats as a generalization of such things as the human and the bronze, is "more of a this something," as, no doubt, is the "this wood (*todi to xulon*) of this [box]" at *Met.* IX 7 1049ᵃ24 and the "this (*toudi*), which is bronze" at VII 8 1033ᵇ2, from (some or all of) which the smith makes this brazen sphere. But these are particular identifiable and countable parcels of matter—minimally shaped up by form, perhaps, but enough to count as (anyway low-grade) *tade tina*. Matter taken more generally, however, is "what not being actually a this something, is potentially a this something" (VIII I 1042ᵃ27–28).

Note 436

It is not face without having soul, nor is it flesh; instead, when they are dead, the one will be homonymously said to be a face and the other flesh, just as it would be if they were made of stone or wood: See I 19 726ᵇ15–24n.

Note 437

When it comes to the ratio (*logos*) in virtue of which one is already flesh and another bone: "We must grasp the workings . . . of the ones capable of affecting, and the species of the affectable ones. First off, then, universally [speaking], unconditional coming to be and natural change is the function of these capacities, as is the opposite passing away that is in accord with nature. And these processes occur both in plants and in animals and their parts. Unconditional and natural coming to be is a change due to these capacities—when they stand in the right ratio (*logos*)—in the matter that by nature underlies a given thing, these being the capacities to be affected that we have just mentioned" (*Mete.* IV 1 378^{b}26–34); "Concoction, in fact, is what everything is affected by when its matter—that is, its liquid—is mastered. For this is what is determined by the heat in its nature. For as long as the ratio (*logos*) is in this, the thing has its nature" (2 379^{b}32–35); "If one wished to take the extreme cases, matter is nothing beyond itself, and substance nothing other than a ratio (*logos*)" (12 390^{a}5–6).

Note 438

What makes the sword is the movement of the instruments containing the account belonging to the craft: See I 22 730^{b}11–23.

Note 439

It is clear, then, that seed both has [soul] and is [alive]—potentially. But it is possible to be nearer and farther potentially, as the geometer asleep is farther than the one awake, and the latter than the one [actively] contemplating: Female menses is a complex structure of capacities or potentialities to move in certain ways. As such, it is lifeless and soulless—unmoving. When the male semen enters it and causes ongoing movements within it, the resulting embryo acquires nutritive soul (*GA* II 3 736^{a}35–36). Hence the seed has the *capacity* to take in nourishment and grow when it is in a functioning female uterus where menses are available to it. And because it does Aristotle can define soul of every sort—whether nutritive or perceptive or rational—as "the first actualization of a natural body that has life potentially" (*DA* II 1 412^{a}27–28) or, more expansively, as "the first actualization of a natural instrumental body" (412^{b}5–6). For a first potentiality is like the capacity someone has to learn geometry. When that capacity is actualized through the acquisition of the ability to do geometry, that is its *first* actuality—the first stage in the actualization of the capacity. The acquired capacity he now has to exercise his acquired ability in actively doing geometry is a second potentiality—a second stage in the development of the original first potentiality (he is now like the sleeping geometer). Actualizing that second potentiality in actively doing geometry, in turn, is a *second* actualization (II 5 417^{a}21–29) or activity (*energeia*) (III 4 429^{b}6–7) (he is now like the geometer actively exercising his geometrical knowledge in contemplating some geometrical truth). Thus in a mature animal the potentiality for nourishment and growth is always possessed as a *first* actuality as long as the animal is alive. It is only in the seed from which it develops that nutritive soul is present as a *first* potential: "It is not what has lost its soul that is potentially such as to live, but what has it. The seed and the fruit are potentially bodies of this sort" (II 1 412^{b}26–27).

Note 440

The primary external mover: That is, the proximate one.

Note 441

Nothing generates itself. But once it has come to be, from that point on it causes itself to grow: See I 18 724ᵇ26–28n.

Note 442

For whether plant or animal, this belongs to all alike, namely, the nutritive part (*to threptikon*). **(And this is what is generative of another like oneself):** "The nutritive soul, then, must be possessed by everything that is alive and has a soul from its birth until its death. For what has been born must have growth, a prime of life, and a time of withering away, and these things are impossible without nourishment. The nutritive capacity must therefore be present in all things that grow and wither away" (*DA* III 12 434ᵃ22–26). The reproductive system, however, is in many ways simply a means of transmitting the form-preserving nutritive system (of which blood and the heart are parts) into new matter, thereby initiating the formation of a new self-maintaining creature. That is why both functions are assigned to the nutritive part of the soul: "the same capacity of the soul is nutritive and generative" (II 4 416ᵃ19).

Note 443

Coarse-grained (*pachu*): "What has small parts is fine-grained and what has large parts is coarse-grained" (*Cael.* III 5 303ᵇ26–27). It is somewhat misleading, therefore, to translate *pachus* as "dense" or "thick," and the corresponding verb *pachunein* as "thicken" or "increase in density." See *GA* II 2 735ᵇ7–16. When applied to things such as skin, membranes, or the bone surrounding the brain, however, coarse-grainedness implies thickness (and vice versa), since a single layer of coarse-grained material is perforce thicker than a single layer of fine-grained material. Sometimes, then, *pachus* is translated as "coarse," *leptos* as "fine." The discussion of hairs in V 3 is a revealing case in point, since what explains their fineness or coarseness is the size of the ducts or pores in the skin—in other words, the skin's fineness (fine-grainedness) or coarseness (coarse-grainedness).

Note 444

Things that contain much earth are the ones that get composed and coarse-grained on boiling: See IV 7 776ᵃ1n.

Note 445

It should not all become liquid and [like] water: Retaining καὶ ὕδωρ with Lefebvre, Louis-3, Peck-3, and Platt; OCT secludes.

Note 446

Olive oil is affected in the same way. For on mixing with pneuma it gets coarse-grained, which is why the whitening [oil] becomes more coarse-grained—the watery material in it gets disaggregated by the heat and becomes pneuma: "The nature of olive oil, however, is most puzzling. For if it contains more water, it should be solidified due to cold, but if more earth, due to fire. But as things stand it is solidified due to neither, but becomes coarse-grained due to both. The cause is that it is full of air. That is also why it rises to the surface of water, since in fact air spatially moves upward. Cold makes it coarse-grained by producing water from the pneuma within it. For when water and olive oil are mixed, the two together become more coarse-grained. Due to fire and time olive oil becomes coarse-grained and whitens. It whitens, though, due to the evaporation of any water there was within it, whereas it becomes coarse-grained because as its heat dies out air comes to be from the water. In both ways, then, the same affection comes about, and due to the same thing, but not in the same way. It becomes coarse-grained, then, due to both [heat and cold], but it does not become dry due to either (for neither the sun nor cold dries it), not only because it is viscous but because it contains air. For the water does not get dried out or boiled off due to the fire, because, due to the viscosity, it does not evaporate" (*Mete.* IV 7 383^{b}20–384^{a}2). On disaggregation, see *GA* IV 6 775^{a}17–18.

Note 447
Lead ore: "This is no doubt galena (lead sulphide), the chief ore found in the Attic mines at Laurium, although these were more famous for their silver output. The reference to the mixing of the ore with water *and oil* [Platt reads ἢ καὶ ('or even with oil')] . . . must imply an early process of 'flotation,' a stage which follows the mechanical crushing of the ore and precedes the metallurgical extraction of the metal, its object being to separate the metalliferous from the non-metalliferous constituents of the ore by means of the production of a froth" (Peck-3, p. 160 n*a*).
When mixed with water and olive oil and beaten: Reading καὶ τριβομένη ("and beaten") with OCT and Lefebvre; Louis-3, Peck-3, and Platt omit with other mss.

Note 448
Due to the friction pneuma gets enclosed (*egkatakleietai*)**:** Namely, in bubbles. See II 2 736^{a}13–18, III 11 762^{a}18–32.

Note 449
Oiliness (*to liparon*) **is characteristic of pneuma, not of earth or water:** The oiliness is responsible for the sheen or shine, so that *to liparon* is sometimes translated as "shininess."

Note 450
The air in it: Olive oil has pneuma in it and "pneuma is hot air" (II 2 736^{a}1). That is also why the air in it is hot (735^{b}29–30). But the heat, unlike that of fire, is generative (3 736^{b}37).

Note 451
Ctesias of Cnidos: A contemporary of Xenophon, who "belonged to an old medical family, and was physician to the Persian king Artaxerxes Mnemon (405–362 BC). His chief work was his Περσικά, in 23 books, containing a history of the East down to 398–397 BC. Most of his zoological matter, however, seems to have been

contained in his᾽Ινδικά" (Peck-3, p. 162 n*b*). Aristotle also refers to him (disparagingly) at *HA* II 1 501ᵃ25, VIII 28 608ᵃ8, and, again, to the falsehood of his views on the seed of elephants at III 22 523ᵃ26.

Note 452
Herodotus is not speaking the truth in saying that the semen of Ethiopians is black: See Herodotus III.101.

Note 453
Just as actually happens in the case when water and olive oil are mixed and beaten, as was said previously: At II 2 735ᵇ21–23.

Note 454
Even the ancients did not fail to notice that the nature of seed is foam-like: See Diogenes of Apollonia DK A24 = TEGP 36: "Some also suppose that the seed of an animal is in substance a foam of blood, which because of the innate heat of the male, by being stirred up and agitated in copulation, is made foamy (*exaphrountai*) and deposited in the spermatic vessels. From this Diogenes of Apollonia derives the term *aphrodisia* [for sexual intercourse]." Also DK B6 = TEGP 34 F8 = *HA* III 2 511ᵇ31–512ᵇ11.

Note 455
They named the goddess who is in control of sexual intercourse (*mixeôs*) after this capacity: The capacity is that stemming from being foam-like (*aphrôdês*); the goddess is Aphrodite.

Note 456
It is an animal in virtue of the perceptual part of the soul: See I 23 731ᵇ4n. Balme-2 secludes this clause.

Note 457
Both the seeds and the embryos of animals are no less alive than plants, and are fertile up to a certain point: Like the wind-eggs of birds. See I 21 730ᵃ4–9.

Note 458
Why seed and fetuses must acquire [nutritive soul] first is evident from the determinations about the soul made elsewhere: In *DA* II 4. See also *GA* II 735ᵃ12–26. {***}: OCT, Balme-2, and Lefebvre mark a lacuna in the mss. at this point.

Note 459
The last thing to come to be is the end, and the end of the coming to be of each thing is what is special to it: See IV 3 767ᵇ29–36 and, on what is special, *PA* I 1 639ᵇ5n.

Note 460
Understanding (*nou*): See *PA* I 1 641ᵃ36n.

Note 461
For either they must all be produced [in the menses or matter] . . . bodily activity is in no way associated with its activity: This complex text is analyzed in the Introduction, pp. lxxii–lxxv.

Note 462
As souls differ from each other in esteem: See *PA* I 5 644ᵇ24n (this vol.).

Note 463
Now the capacity of all soul seems to be associated . . . the element belonging to the stars: See Introduction, pp. lxxiv–lxxv.

Note 464
Fire does not generate any animal, nor, it is evident, are any composed in things affected by fire, whether wet ones or dry ones: See III 11 761ᵇ15–22n.

Note 465
The heat of the sun and that of animals [unlike that of fire] do generate: "The heat and light from the stars come about when air is chafed by their spatial movement" (*Cael.* II 7 289ᵃ19–21).

Note 466
The body of the semen, in which comes away part of the seed of the soul-involving starting-point: Reading τὸ σπέρμα τὸ τῆς ψυχικῆς ἀρχῆς with Lefebvre and most mss.; OCT obelizes τὸ σπέρμα; Louis-3 and Peck-3 seclude it; Platt reads τὸ πνεῦμα ("the pneuma"). At II 3 736ᵇ36, however, it is seed in which something is enclosed (ἐμπεριλαμβανόμενον), making it likely that it is again seed in which here "the soul-involving starting point" is enclosed (ἐμπεριλαμβάνεταί).
The soul-involving (*psuchikês*) **starting-point:** Referred to as a "life-giving (*zôtikên*) starting-point" at II 3 737ᵃ5.
Part of which is separable from the body in all the ones in which a divine something is enclosed (and what is called the understanding is of this sort) and part inseparable: As explained at II 3 736ᵇ21–29. See also III 10 761ᵃ5.

Note 467
The fig-juice that composes the milk: See I 20 729ᵃ11–14.

Note 468
When the nourishment in its last stage is being partitioned: The nourishment in its last stage is "the one from which each of the parts comes to be from the outset" (I 18 725ᵃ12). This is the partitioning referred to. Compare I 20 729ᵃ14–16.

Note 469
The female is like a deformed male: See I 18 724^{b}32n.

Note 470
The more and less (*to mallon kai hêtton*): See *PA* I 4 644^{a}16–18n (this vol.).
Things that, though liquid . . . excess and deficiency: Double-bracketed in OCT as out of place and bracketed as "irrelevant here" by Peck-3 (p. 175 n*e*), and noted as "*hors de sujet*" by Louis-3 (p. 216).

Note 471
A complete embryo: That is, an egg.
Once a complete embryo has come to be, it is emitted externally, though it is not yet a complete animal; the cause of this was stated previously: At II 1 732^{a}24–733^{b}23.

Note 472
About the generation of [the ones that neither come to be from male and female parents nor from sexual intercourse between animals] we shall speak later on: In III 8 (insects), 11 (testaceans).

Note 473
The selachian fishes . . . later must be discussed by themselves: At III 3.

Note 474
Proper place (*oikeiôn topon*): See Introduction, p. lxvi.
The collecting together of pneuma: As happens in holding the breath.

Note 475
It is by the wind (*pneumatos*): See IV 10 778^{a}32n.

Note 476
As some people say it is, claiming that the private parts draw the residue like cupping-glasses forcing it by means of pneuma: Hippocrates, *On Ancient Medicine* 22 = Littré I.626 = Schiefsky, pp. 105–9.
The cause of this, as was said, is that in all animals there are parts receptive of the residues: See II 4 737^{b}28–30.
For example, for the dry and the liquid one: Retaining οἷον τῇ τε ξηρᾷ καὶ τῇ ὑγρᾷ with Lefebvre, Louis-3, and Platt; OCT obelizes and Peck-3 brackets as an interpolation.

Note 477
The great blood-vessel and the aorta: "By the great blood-vessel A. means the *vena cava* and the whole venous system, by the aorta he means the aorta and the whole arterial system. He does not distinguish between their functions, holding that both alike nourish the body by carrying the blood to all parts of it. The fine

vessels are the smallest veins and arteries visible to the naked eye, not the capillaries, which were unknown even to Harvey" (Platt, n1).

Note 478
The period is not exactly arranged in women, but tends to occur, as is reasonable, when the moon is waning: There is in fact no correlation between the lunar cycle and the menstrual cycle.

Note 479
"Whites": That is, leucorrhea.

Note 480
It is necessary for a residue to come about, not only from the useless nourishment, but also from the blood in the blood-vessels: Reading τοῦ αἵματος with OCT. The blood in the blood-vessels is a useful residue (II 4 738ᵇ1).

Note 481
This place: Namely, the uterus.

Note 482
The cause of there being more [residue] in the quite sanguineous ones and most in the human was stated previously: See I 19 727ᵃ21–25, II 4 728ᵃ30–ᵇ14.

Note 483
The soul is the substance of a certain body: "The soul is the first actuality (*entelecheia*) of a natural body that has life potentially. And something will be such insofar as it has instrumental parts (*organikon*). . . . If, then, we are to speak of something common to all soul, it will be the first actualization of a natural body that has instrumental parts" (*DA* II 2 412ᵃ27–ᵇ6).
Substance: See *PA* I 1 639ᵃ16n (this vol.).

Note 484
If there is sexual intercourse among animals that are not of the same genus (*homogenês*): Compare II 7 746ᵃ29–8 749ᵃ6.

Note 485
Before then nothing is [a residue], unless with much force, that is, contrary to nature: "By force and contrary to nature are the same" (*Cael.* III 2 300ᵃ23); "What is forced [is] contrary to natural impulse" (*Met.* XII 7 1072ᵇ12; also V 5 1015ᵇ15).

Note 486
[The earlier part of a seminal emission] contains less soul-involving heat due to being non-concocted: The viviparous terrestrial animals concoct their seed during copulation. See I 5 717ᵇ23–26, 6 718ᵃ5–7.
More corporeal (*sesômatôtai mallon*): That is, denser, more substantial.

Note 487
That the liquid accompanying sexual pleasure that is produced in females contributes nothing to the embryo was stated previously: At I 20 727^{b}33–728^{a}1.

Note 488
The uterus has descended within: This does not in fact occur.

Note 489
In those animals that have the uterus near the diaphragm, as birds and viviparous fishes do, it is impossible for the seed not to be drawn in there, but instead to enter when discharged: "It must be remembered that A. calls the ovarian passages of birds and fishes 'uterus'" (Platt, n5).

Note 490
It is like conical vessels which, having been washed out with something hot, draw water into themselves when the mouth is turned downward: As in cupping.

Note 491
The nature of milk and menses is the same: Since both are late stages in the concoction of nourishment.

Note 492
The earthy parts dry out: Drying, by removing liquid, results in solidification.

Note 493
The animal: That is, the fetus.

Note 494
Choria: The term "chorion" now refers to the exterior envelope of the embryo in mammals, birds, and reptiles. Aristotle, however, seems to use it to refer to what is now called the allantois, a membrane lying below the chorion and forming part of the placenta in certain mammals. See *HA* VI 1 561^{b}31–562^{a}1.
They differ by the more and the less: See *PA* I 4 644^{a}18n (this vol.).

Note 495
The first starting-point is also present in the seeds themselves: Namely, nutritive soul. See II 3 736^{a}33–35.

Note 496
In a certain way all the parts are present potentially, but the starting-point is farthest along the road: See II 1 735^{a}9–11.

Note 497
That is why those who say, like Democritus, that the external parts of animals become disaggregated first, and later the internal ones, do not speak correctly: = DK 68A145 = TEGP 98.

Note 498
For what is [an animal] of course grows: See II 1 735ª21.

Note 499
Of [blood or its analogue] the blood-vessels are the receptacle: See II 6 743ª1–17.

Note 500
History of Animals: See *HA* III 3.
Dissections: See *HA* I 17 497ª32n.

Note 501
The umbilical cord is a blood-vessel, consisting of one vessel in some animals, and of several in others: See II 7 745ᵇ24–746ª19.

Note 502
The vessels are attached to the uterus like roots, and through them the embryo gets its nourishment. For it is for the sake of this that the animal remains in the uterus, and not, as Democritus says, so that the parts may be molded in accord with the parts of the mother: = DK 68A144 = TEGP 96.

Note 503
The matrix (*mêtras*): The cervix including the orifice of the womb. See *HA* II 1 510ᵇ14.

Note 504
The first nourishment: That is, the blood already in the heart when it first came to be.

Note 505
As animals themselves do when free of the nourishment within themselves: See II 4 740ᵇ7–8. Peck-3 brackets this clause as an interpolation; Platt thinks that ἐν αὐτοῖς ("within themselves") is corrupt. The reference, however, seems to be to the residue of the matter that went to compose the animals, and, since it was then inside them, served to nourish them before the umbilical cord was operative.

Note 506
These issues must be spoken about later, at the opportune time for the proper accounts: See III 2 752ª11–754ª20.

Note 507
The disaggregation of the parts, however, does not come to be in the way that some people suppose, namely, by like naturally being carried to like: "As the flesh grows it is formed into distinct members by pneuma, each thing in it goes to its like—the dense to the dense, the rare to the rare, the liquid to the liquid. Each settles in its appropriate place, corresponding to the part it came from and is akin

to. I mean that those parts that came from a dense part in the parent body are themselves dense, while those from a liquid part are liquid, and the others come to be in accord with the same account in the process of their growth. The bones grow hard due to solidification by the heat, and what is more they send out branches like a tree. Both the interior and exterior of the body now begin to separate into parts more distinctly" (Hippocrates, *The Nature of the Child* 17.1–9 = Littré VII.499 = Lonie, p. 9).

Note 508
The craft is the shape of the things that come to be present in something else: Namely, in the understanding of the craftsman. See I 22 730^{b}11–23.

Note 509
[Nutritive soul's] movements are present and a certain account (*logos*) **of each [part of the animal]:** *Logos* here is a stand-in for the form or shape that is its ontological correlate.

Note 510
Although it (*hautê*) **is greater** (*meizôn*): Reading μείζων δὲ αὕτη ἐστίν with OCT, Lefebvre, and Louis-3; Peck-3 secludes. *Hautê* refers to the capacity productive of growth (nutritive soul), which, as part of a developed animal, is greater (since it is moving more matter) than the one that composes the tiny embryo at the outset.

Note 511
[The nutritive soul or generative soul] is the nature of each thing, present in all plants and animals: "Nature is a sort of starting-point and cause of moving and being at rest in that to which it belongs primarily, intrinsically, and not coincidentally" (*Ph.* II 1 192^{b}21–23); "nature is a starting-point of movement within the thing itself" (*Cael.* III 2 301^{b}17–18). The movement of nutritive soul is growth and maintenance, other sorts of souls, such as perceptual soul, which are present in animals, but not in plants are responsible for other sorts of movement.
The other parts of the soul are present in some living things, not present in others: For example, perceptual soul is present in animals but not in plants. See I 23 731^{b}4n.

Note 512
Unconditionally (*haplôs*): The adjective *haplous* means "simple" or "single-fold." The adverb *haplôs* thus points in two somewhat opposed directions. (1) To speak *haplôs* sometimes means to put things simply or in general terms, so that qualifications and conditions will need to be added later. (2) Sometimes, as here, to be F *haplôs* means to be F in a way that allows for no ifs, ands, or buts (*Top.* II 11 115^{b}29–35). In this sense, things that are F *haplôs* are F in the strictest, most absolute, and most unqualified way (*Met.* V 5 1015^{b}11–12).

Note 513

What was just mentioned: Namely, being productive of perceptual soul. At II 4 729ᵃ25–26 the male is claimed to be the source of all soul. Here a puzzle about this, focusing on nutritive soul, is being explored.

Was the being (*einai*) **for male** (*arreni*): Reading ἦν τὸ ἄρρενι εἶναι with Peck-3 and Platt for OCT, Louis-3 ἦν τὸ ἄρρεν εἶναι. *Arreni* is dative and *einai* + dative refers to what something is intrinsically, or to that thing's essence (*Met.* VII 4 1029ᵇ13–1030ᵇ13). At I 2 716ᵃ13–14, however, a male animal was defined as "what generates in another."

Note 514

Wind-eggs become fertile if in a certain period of time the male mates with the female. But the cause of these things will be determined later on: See III 1 750ᵇ3–751ᵃ30, 7 757ᵇ1–30.

Note 515

Among the ones called erythrinus no male has so far been seen: "Probably the *Serranus anthias*, a kind of sea-perch. This fish is hermaphrodite, and the male organs are difficult to make out" (Platt, n2).

Note 516

Just as in those wondrous automata: See II 1 734ᵇ10n.

Note 517

What certain of the physicists (*phusikôn*): See *PA* I 1 641ᵃ7n.

Must mean when they say that "like is naturally carried to like": See II 4 740ᵇ13–14n.

The other differentiae of homoeomerous things: See *Mete.* IV 8 385ᵃ8–19.

Note 518

[The starting-point] is the heart in blooded animals, and its analogue in the others, as was said often: For example, at II 4 738ᵇ16–17, 740ᵃ3–4, 17–18, 22–23.

Note 519

It happens in all cases that the last to come to be is the first to leave, and the first last: Like all truths of natural science this holds only for the most part, tortoises being an exception, since they continue to move "even after the heart has been extracted" (*Juv.* 2 468ᵇ14–15; also 23 (17) 479ᵃ3–7).

Note 520

After the starting-point, as was said, the internal parts come to be before the external ones: At II 740ᵃ12–23.

Note 521

What was just said applies in the case of the plants as well: the upper body comes to be earlier than the lower. For the seeds set out roots earlier than

shoots: This counterintuitive claim (aren't the shoots above and the roots below?) is a consequence of Aristotle's view that in living things, up and down, front and back, right and left are not just spatially or relationally distinguished but functionally and absolutely so: "the part from which the distribution of nourishment and growth derives in each living thing is up and the last part toward which this travels is down—the one is a sort of starting-point, the other a limit; and up is a starting-point" (*IA* 2 705ª32–ᵇ2; also *DA* II 4 416ª5). Similarly, the front is a starting-point, because it is where the organs of perception are located (4 705ᵇ10–13). Even in earthworms, where right and left are more difficult to distinguish perceptually, the functional difference between them still exists: "the starting-point of the movement is the same in all animals and by nature has its position in the same place; and it is from the right that the starting-point of movement derives" (*IA* 5 706ª10–13).

Note 522
The parts of animals are distinctly formed by pneuma—not however by that . . . of [the embryo] itself, as some of the physicists say: See II 4 740ᵇ13–14n and, on the physicists, *PA* I 1 641ª7n.

Note 523
Other animals do not breathe at all: Fishes and insects. Hence they do not take in pneuma themselves.

Note 524
For pneuma, though, to be present is necessary, because it is wet and hot, the hot affecting and the wet being affected: This is the pneuma enclosed in the foamy part of the seed, which is "jointly composed of pneuma and water, and the pneuma is hot air" (II 2 735ᵇ37–736ª1). On the hot as an affecting or active capacity, and the wet as affected or passive one, see Introduction, pp. lxxv–lxxvii.

Note 525
Experience (*empeirikôs*): *Empeiria* is not quite what we mean by experience: for us experience gives rise to memory; for Aristotle memory gives rise to *empeiria*. Thus suppose A perceives that when X_1 is sick with a fever giving him honey-water is followed by a reduction in fever (*Met.* VI 2 1027ª23–24), and he retains this connection in his memory. Then he perceives that giving honey-water to $X_2, X_3, \ldots X_n$ is also followed by a reduction in their fever. A also retains these connections in his memory. When as a result of retaining them A associates drinking honey-water with fever reduction, he has "one experience," since "from memory (when it occurs often in connection with the same thing) comes experience. For memories that are many in number form an experience that is one in number" (*APo.* II 19 100ª4–6).

Note 526
In the case of the parts, as with other things, one is naturally prior to another: A is naturally prior to (earlier than) B if A can be without B, but not B without A (V 11 1019ª3–4).

Note 527
But actually (*êdê*) something is prior in many ways: These are discussed in *Met.* V 11.

Note 528
The for-the-sake-of-which and what is for the sake of this are different, and of these the latter is prior in coming to be, the former in substance: "Now since the soul of animals (for this is substance of the animate) is the substance that is in accord with the account and is the form and the essence of such-and-such sort of body (certainly each part, if it is to be defined correctly, will not be defined without its function, which it could not have without perception), it follows that the parts of this are prior, either all or some, to the compound animal, and similarly, then, to each particular animal, whereas the body and its parts will be posterior, and what is divided into these as into matter is not the substance but the compound. These bodily parts, then, are in a way prior to the compound, but in a way not, since they cannot even exist when they are separated. For it is not a finger in any and every state that is the finger of an animal, rather, a dead finger is only homonymously a finger. Some of these parts, however, are simultaneous, namely, the ones that are controlling and in which the account and the substance are first found—for example, the heart, perhaps, or the brain (for it makes no difference which of them is of this sort)" (*Met.* VII 1035^{b}14–27).

Note 529
For even from the outset this is one part of the end, that is, the most controlling one: Namely, the heart, or its analogue in bloodless animals, which is the first part of the embryo to be formed. On why it is a part of the end, see II 6 742^{b}17n. **Most controlling** (*kuriôtaton*): See *PA* I 1 640^{b}28n.

Note 530
Those parts that are not of this sort: That is, not generative.

Note 531
Methodical inquiry: See *PA* I 1 639^{a}1n (this vol.).

Note 532
The lower parts are for the sake of the upper ones, and are neither parts of the end nor generative of it: "The lower parts of the body are a part of the body indeed as a whole, but they only exist to subserve the upper part where all the important functions of life are performed. It is this upper part then that is the true end (τέλος) of Nature, and thus the lower part are not 'parts of the end', but fall into the third class of mere instruments for the use of the end" (Platt, n1).

Note 533
Democritus of Abdera says that of what is unlimited there is no starting-point: Secluding ἀεὶ καὶ ("of what is always and unlimited")—which OCT, Lefebvre, and Louis-3 read—with Platt, followed by Peck-3. See DK 68A56 = TEGP 27.

Note 534

There will be no demonstration whatsoever of what is eternal: Compare: "In general, to think that this is an adequate starting-point, namely, the fact that something always is or comes to be in this way, is an incorrect assumption to make. Thus Democritus refers back causes concerned with nature to the fact that this is how things also happened previously. Of what always happens, however, he does not think it fitting to seek a starting-point, which in some cases is a correct thing to say, but that it holds in all cases is not correct. For a triangle has its angles always equal to two right angles as well, but nonetheless there is some other cause of the eternality of this, although of starting-points that are eternal there is no other cause" (*Ph.* VII 1 252^{a}32–^{b}5).

Note 535

For of a starting-point there is another sort of knowledge (*gnôsis*): Namely, understanding. See *PA* I 1 641^{a}36n.
And not a demonstration (*apodeixis*): See *PA* I 1 639^{a}3n(5) (this vol.).

Note 536

That is why all the blooded animals have a heart first, as was said at the start: For example, at II 4 740^{a}3–4.

Note 537

The heart the blood-vessels extend throughout [the body], as in the mannikins (*kanabous*) **drawn on the walls:** "The blood-vessels, as in the drawn mannikins, have the figure of the entire body" (*HA* III 5 515^{a}34–35). The wall, presumably, of Aristotle's "lecture room." See also *GA* IV 1 764^{b}29–31.

Note 538

The differentiae of [the homoeomerous parts] have been spoken about previously elsewhere, and what sorts of things are dissolvable by liquid and by fire, and what sorts are non-dissolvable by liquid and unmeltable by fire: At *Mete.* IV 7–10. See also I 2 716^{a}17–23n.

Note 539

Flesh or its analogues are composed due to the cold, which is why it is also dissolved due to fire: Cold and hot (fire), being contraries, have contrary effects: composition, dissolution.

Note 540

External things: Things outside the uterus.

Note 541

Those that come about spontaneously: See *PA* I 1 640^{a}27n (this vol.) and *GA* III 11.
At the proper time (*hôras*): See I 6 718^{a}7.

Note 542
Cooling is the lack of heat: See also *Mete.* IV 2 380^{a}7–8, *PA* II 2 649^{a}18–19 (on which, see Lennox, pp. 194–195), IV 4 784^{a}33, *Met.* XII 4 1070^{b}11–12.
Lack (*sterêsis*): See *PA* I 3 642^{b}21n.

Note 543
An animal painter (*zôgraphou*): A *zôgraphos* is someone who paints from life; a *zôion* is both a painting (not necessarily of animals) and an animal (*Cat.* 1 1^{a}1–6). "Animal painter" attempts to capture Aristotle's pun.

Note 544
Counterpart (*antistrophon*): In the choral odes familiar from Greek tragedies the antistrophe answers a preceding strophe.

Note 545
Though at the start they appear very large in animals, . . . they shrink into line (*sumpiptousin*) **in the meantime:** At the start, the eyes are large relative to the other parts of the embryo, but later they shrink so that their size is in line with that of the other parts.

Note 546
Smell and hearing are ducts, connected to the air outside, that are full of connate pneuma: "What has a sound, then, is what can cause a movement in air that is one by continuity and that reaches up to the organ of hearing. But the organ of hearing has connate air. And because this organ is in air, when the air outside is moved, the air inside is moved. That is why the animal does not hear in every part of it, nor does the air enter every part. For it is not in every part that it has air, but the part that is going to be moved and is animate" (*DA* II 8 420^{a}3–7). See also *GA* V 1 781^{a}20–^{b}1.
Connate pneuma (*sumphutou pneumatos*): See Introduction, pp. lxii–lxxii.
The eye, by contrast, is the only one of the perceptual organs that has a special body of its own: Namely, the *korê*, or eye-jelly: "Just as the eye-jelly (*korê*) and sight are an eye, so . . . the soul and the body are an animal" (*DA* II 1 413^{a}2–3).

Note 547
The ducts that are evident leading to the meninx around the brain: Namely, the optic nerves.
Meninx (*mênigga*): See *HA* I 16 494^{b}8–9 (this vol.).

Note 548
The bregma: The anterior fontanelle. See *HA* I 7 491^{a}31n (this vol.).

Note 549
The thought (*dianoia*): See *PA* I 1 641^{b}8n.

Note 550
Most practically-wise (*phronimôtaton*): See I 23 731ᵃ35n.

Note 551
Sleep (*hupnon*): "Sleep is not every disability of the perceptual part but, rather, this affection arises from the evaporation that attends eating food. For that which is vaporized must be driven on to a given point and then must turn back and change, just like the tide in a narrow strait. In every animal the hot naturally rises, but when it has reached the upper parts, it turns back and moves downward in a mass. That is why sleepiness mostly occurs after eating food, since then a large watery and earthy mass is carried upward. When this comes to a stop, therefore, it weighs a person down and makes him nod off; but when it has actually sunk downward, and, by its return, has driven back the hot, then sleepiness comes on and the animal falls asleep" (*Somn.* 3 456ᵇ17–28).

Note 552
The nourishment that is concocted, purest, and first: Not first-stage nourishment, but rather last-stage, the one from which each of the parts first comes to be (I 18 725ᵃ11–21).

Note 553
The household slaves . . . the animals that are nourished along with them: "To poor people an ox takes the place of a servant" (*Pol.* I 2 1252ᵇ12).

Note 554
The understanding produces from outside these things for their growth: Reading θύραθεν with Louis-3; OCT obelizes. Presumably, as Louis-3 (p. 220) suggests, the understanding is that of the household manager, and "from outside" means from outside the human beings and animals that constitute the household.

Note 555
Nutritive is what provides the being to the whole and the parts, growth-productive is what produces increase in size: See I 18 724ᵇ27n.
About these, determinations must be made later on: Reference unclear.

Note 556
Defining mark (*horos*): See *PA* I 1 639ᵃ13n (this vol.). Here *horos* means much the same as *peras* ("limit") used a few lines earlier at II 6 745ᵃ6.

Note 557
Due to what cause [animals] do not always get growth must be stated later: The reference is uncertain, but the following passage is germane: "Some people think that it is the nature of fire to be the unconditional cause of nourishment and growth. For among the bodies fire alone is something that is nourished and grows. That is why we might suppose that in both plants and animals it is this that

performs the function. But, though it is in a way a contributing cause, it is certainly not an unconditional cause. On the contrary, it is rather the soul that is this. For the growth of fire is unlimited, as long as there is fuel, but there is a limit and an account of size and growth for things that are put together by nature; and these are characteristic of soul but not of fire, and of the account rather than of the matter" (*DA* II 4 416ª9–18).

Note 558
Hairs . . . go on growing even after death: Nails and hairs appear to keep growing, but this is due to the shrinkage of the flesh as it dries out, which makes the nails and hairs appear longer. After the heart stops beating, though, cells that need less oxygen can live a bit longer, so nails and hairs could then grow a tiny bit more.

Note 559
[Teeth] alone among the various bones go on growing throughout life. This is clear from teeth that turn aside and do not make contact with each other: "This is true of the incisors of rodents and tusks of elephants; A. extends the principle to all teeth [but it is false of them]" (Platt, n4).

Note 560
Their full complement (*ton arithmon to autôn*): Literally, "the number that is theirs."

Note 561
The cause due to which some teeth come to be and fall out, while others do not fall out, will be stated later: At V 8 788ᵇ3–15.

Note 562
Animals without two sets of teeth: That is, ruminants. "But it is hard to see what A. means by the animals he goes on to describe" (Platt, n2).

Note 563
In viviparous animals the fetuses get their growth, as was said previously, through the umbilical cord: At II 4 740ª24–ᵇ2.
Cotyledons: "The cotyledons are pits in the modified wall of the uterus into which fit the villi of the outside membrane of the embryo. In modern works the term is applied to the tufts of villi themselves, but A. plainly uses it of the pits into which they fit, as one would expect from the derivation. They were called 'cotyledons' from the suckers on the arms of cuttlefish" (Platt, n3).

Note 564
745ᵇ33a–c: The lines are absent from some mss.

Note 565
Chorion: See II 4 739ᵇ31n.

The membranes: "The amnion, and perhaps . . . that part of the allantois which is not united with the chorion" (Platt, n5).

Note 566
The body of the cotyledon becomes like an eruption or inflammation: "By the 'body' A. means the 'caruncle' or 'swelling' in the wall of the uterus in which is the cotyledon. The [gradual gathering together] is unintelligible, but the caruncle does become 'like an inflammation'" (Platt, n2).

Note 567
The docked animals: Here, apparently, the hornless ones. On docked, see I 17 721^{b}17n.
A single blood-vessel that is large and extends throughout the uterus: No animal has such a blood-vessel.

Note 568
One should get a theoretical grasp on these things from the paradigms drawn in the *Dissections*: See *HA* I 17 497^{a}32n.
And in the *History of Animals*: The reference is probably to *HA* VII 8, which presumably included diagrams.

Note 569
Those who say that children are nourished in the uterus through sucking on a bit of flesh: "Democritus and Epicurus say that the fetus in the womb is nourished through the mouth. Hence as soon as it is born it goes to the teat with its mouth. For in the womb too there are nipples and orifices through which it is nourished" (DK 68A144 = TEGP 97 = Aëtius P 5.16.1). According to Diocles of Carystus, who was associated with Aristotle in the Lyceum, the fetus sucked on the cotyledons (fr. 27 Wellmann).

Note 570
. . . when separated from the mother: Rejecting with Lefebvre, Louis-3, Peck-3, and Platt the OCT addition of ὥστε λέγουσιν οὐκ ὀρθῶς οἱ λέγοντες οὕτως ὥσπερ Δημόκριτος ("so they do not speak correctly who speak in this way, as Democritus does").

Note 571
Copulation in accord with nature occurs between animals of the same genus (*homogenês*); nevertheless it also occurs between those that, though they have a close nature, do not fail to have a difference in species (*eidos*): "Another term later used by Aristotle ὁμόφυλα (746^{b}9: 'of the same family'), clearly shows that terminological consistency is just not at stake here: for Aristotle, all three terms 'species' or 'genus' or 'family' can refer to a group of animals inside which generation is considered natural and it is only according to an anachronistic convention, rather than Aristotelian usage, that we speak of hybridity as generation between

different species" (Falcon & Lefebvre (Groisard), p. 155). Greek terms are added in parentheses to register this.

It also occurs between those that, though they have a close nature, are not without difference in species (*eidos*), if their size is about the same and if the times of their gestation are equal: Compare II 4 738^{b}27–30.

Note 572

Indian dogs come to be from some wild dog-like animal and a dog: "The say that the Indian dog comes to be from a tiger and a bitch" (*HA* VIII 28 607^{a}3–4).

Note 573

The so-called rhinobates especially does seem to come to be from copulation of the rhine and the batus: "The rhine is probably some kind of shark, the batus a ray, the former having a thick tail, the latter a thin one. A rhinobates was a fish with a thick tail but the forepart of the body like a batus. . . . I incline to think it was the angel fish, *Squantina vulgaris*" (Platt, n4).

Note 574

The proverb about Libya: "Proverbs . . . are witnesses" (*Rh.* I 15 1376^{a}2–3).

Note 575

The places used for sexual intercourse are deformed: See I 18 724^{b}32n.

Note 576

The first composition: The one from the spermatic residue. See II 6 744^{b}27, 745^{b}4.

Note 577

They test women, on the other hand, by means of pessaries: These were scented with various fragrant herbs.

To see whether its odors penetrate upward from below to the exhaled pneuma, and by colors rubbed on the eyes to see whether they color the sputum in the mouth: "The pessary sets up movements which, like all movements, in any part, are passed on the center of the body as the seat of life. As the pessary is highly scented these scents passed up along with movements, and entering the cavity of the chest are then expelled with the breath through the mouth" (Platt, n6).

Note 578

The place around the eyes, of all those around the heat, is the most spermatic. This is made clear by the fact that during acts of sexual intercourse it alone clearly changes its configuration, and that those who indulge too much in sexual intercourse have quite evidently sunken eyes: "Why do the eyes and the buttocks of those who indulge too much in sexual intercourse clearly sink in, though the latter are near and the former far away [from the sexual organs]? Is it because even during sexual intercourse itself these parts clearly co-operate in the work by contracting around the time of the emission of the seed? It is most of all from there, then, that any easily melted nourishment present is pressed out because of the pressure. Or is it because things that are overheated melt most of all, and sexual intercourse produces heat, and those parts that are moved during the work get most heated? Now the eyes and the buttocks clearly co-operate during sex. For it is not possible to emit seed without drawing the buttocks together and closing the eyes. For the contraction of the buttocks exerts pressure (just as liquid can be expelled from the bladder by the pressure of the hand), while the closing of the eyes exerts pressure on the [secretions] from the brain. And that the eyes and the place around them have a great capacity with a view to generation is made clear from the trials on both childless and fertile women, on the supposition that the capacity [to generate] must pass by this way into the seed. Now both the rectum and the eyes are always fat in everyone. Because, then, of their co-working in sex they share in the heat, and because of this reason they become leaner and much [of the fat] is secreted into the seed" (*Pr.* IV 2 876^{a}36–^{b}17).

Note 579

The nature of the semen is similar to that of the brain. For the matter of it is watery, and the heat a supplementary acquisition (*epiktêtos*): The semen, as a blood product or derivative, is heated by the heart, just as the blood is: "It is evident that blood is in a way hot, that is, insofar as the being for blood itself is concerned [reading οἷον ἦν αὐτῷ τὸ αἵματι εἶναι with ms. E and Düring]. For just as if a certain name signified boiling water, in that way something is said to be blood. But the underlying subject, that is, whatever it is that is blood, is not hot. And intrinsically blood is in one way hot, and in another way not. For heat will belong in its account, just as pale belongs in that of pale human being. But insofar as it is so in virtue of an affection, blood is not intrinsically hot" (*PA* II 3 649^{b}21–27).

Note 580

The spermatic purgations are from the diaphragm. For the starting-point of the nature is there: "All the blooded animals have a diaphragm, just as they have a heart and a liver. The cause of this is that the diaphragm is there for the sake of dividing the part around the stomach from the part around the heart, in order that the starting-point of perceptual soul will be unaffected and not be quickly overwhelmed because of the fumes coming from the nourishment and the great quantity of heat introduced. For this nature divided them" (*PA* III 10 672^{b}13–19).

Note 581

In human beings, then, and in the other genera (*genos*), **as was said previously, this sort of deformation occurs in particular individuals, but in the case of the mules the whole genus** (*genos*) **is infertile:** At II 7 746^{b}12–20.

Note 582

Not in a perspicuous way (*saphôs*): *Saphêneia* ("perspicuousness") is associated with explanation, which is ultimately from starting-points: "Beginning with things that are truly stated but not perspicuously, we proceed to make them perspicuous as well. . . . That is why even politicians should not regard as peripheral to their work the sort of theoretical knowledge that makes evident (*phaneron*) not only the fact that but also the explanation why" (*EE* I 6 1216ᵇ32–39).

In a more knowable way (*gnôrimôs*): "It advances the work to proceed toward what is more knowable. For learning comes about for all in this way—through things by nature less knowable toward ones that are more knowable. . . . But the things that are knowable and primary for particular groups of people are often only slightly knowable and have little or nothing of the being in them. Nonetheless, beginning from things that are poorly known but known to ourselves, we must try to know the ones that are wholly knowable, proceeding, as has just been said, through the former" (*Met.* VII 3 1029ᵇ3–12). Notice "nor, in general, producing his starting-points from knowable things" (*GA* II 8 747ᵇ5–6), and producing them from "things too far contrary to perception" (747ᵇ9–10), as criticisms of Empedocles.

Note 583
Demonstration: See *PA* I 1 639ᵃ3n(5) (this vol.).

Note 584
Democritus says that the ducts of mules are destroyed in the uterus because the animals do not from the start come to be from those of the same genus (*suggenês*): = DK 68A149. See also DK 68A151 = TEGP 99.

Note 585
[Bronze and tin] are spoken about in the *Problems*: There is nothing about this in the extant *Problems*, but see *GC* I 10 328ᵇ6–14.

Note 586
Since a mule already *has* had an embryo: The implication being that instances of embryos in mules have been known to occur.

Note 587
Perhaps a logico-linguistic demonstration (*apodeixis . . . logikê*) **might seem more convincing than the ones just mentioned:** (1) The adjective *logikos* is used to distinguish a set of propositions and problems from those belonging to natural science or ethics: "Propositions such as this are ethical—for example, whether one should obey our parents or the laws, if they disagree. *Logikos*, whether contraries belong to the same science or not. Natural scientific, whether the cosmos is eternal or not. And similarly for the problems" (*Top.* I 14 105ᵇ21–25). Since the question about a science of contraries is a philosophical one (*Met.* III 2 996ᵃ18–21), *logikos* problems overlap with philosophical ones. At the same time, "if an argument depends on false but reputable beliefs, it is *logikos*" (*Top.* VIII 12 162ᵇ27), suggesting that *logikos* arguments overlap with dialectical ones, since both may rely on reputable beliefs (*endoxa*) or—more or less equivalently—on things said (*legomena*)

about the topic (*Ph.* I 2 185^{a}2–3n). Indeed, the question about a science of contraries is itself identified as one for dialectic (*Met.* XIII 4 1078^{b}25–27).

(2) When Plato, unlike previous thinkers, is accorded a share of dialectic it is due to his investigation of *logoi* or accounts (*Met.* I 6 987^{b}31–33), which he almost always undertook through staged Socratic conversations, whose aim was to discover the correct definition (XIII 4 1078^{b}23–25) of what something essentially or intrinsically is, or is itself-by-itself (*auto kath' hauto*)—the "itself" in the name of a Form probably stems from its being the ontological correlate of such a definition (*Met.* III 2 997^{b}8–9). One core meaning of *logikos*, in fact, relates it to conversation and speaking, while another relates it to reason—the *logikai aretai* are the virtues of reason or thought (*NE* II 8 1108^{b}9–10). When we ask *logikôs* (adverb) why it is that these bricks and stones are a house, what we are asking for is a formal cause or an essence (*Met.* VII 17 1041^{a}26–28), which is presumably why a deduction of the essence is a *logikos sullogismos* (*APo.* II 8 93^{a}15).

(3) When dialecticians are contrasted with natural scientists it is on the grounds that "the scientist gives the matter, whereas the dialectician gives the form and the account" (*DA* I 1 403^{b}1–2)—again associating dialectic with proceeding *logikôs*. The dialectician proceeds *logikôs*, the natural scientist *phusikôs*—looking to matter but also to form, when the relevant essence requires it (notice *tôn phusikôn* at *GA* II 8 747^{a}14): "that is why it belongs to the natural scientist to get a theoretical grasp even on some of the soul, that is, on as much of it as is not without matter" (*Met.* VI 1 1026^{a}5–6). So to proceed in a strictly *logikôs* way, when there is empirical evidence bearing on the subject, is bad scientific practice: "It seems that the knowledge of the what-it-is is not only useful for getting a theoretical grasp on the causes of the coincidents connected to the essences [= intrinsic coincidents] . . . but also, conversely, knowing these coincidents contributes in great part to knowing the what-it-is. For when we can give an account of the way either all or most of these coincidents appear to be, we will then be able to speak best about the essence. For the starting-point of all demonstration is [the definition of] the what-it-is, so that insofar as definitions do not lead us to know the coincidents, or fail even to facilitate a likely conjecture about [how to demonstrate] them, it is clear that they have all been stated in a dialectical and empty way (*kenôs*)" (*DA* I 1 402^{b}16–403^{a}2). Notice *kenos* and *kenoi* at *GA* II 8 748^{a}8–9 and the coupling of *logikôs* and *kenôs* at *EE* I 8 1217^{b}21.

(4) Before we start defining essences logico-linguistically, then, we should have intimate knowledge of the empirical data that they are supposed to explain: "The cause of our being incapable of taking a comprehensive view of the agreed-upon facts is lack of experience. That is why those who are at home among natural things are better able to posit the sort of starting-points that can collect together a good many of these, whereas those who from their many arguments do not get a theoretical grasp on the facts, but look at only a few, make their declarations too recklessly. One can see from this too how much difference there is between investigating in the way appropriate to natural science and in a logico-linguistic one" (*GC* I 2 316^{a}5–11). Thus a frequent criticism of Plato and the Platonists is that in proceeding logico-linguistically they leave the earth and the world of facts too far behind and proceed at too abstract and general a level (*Met.* I 2 987^{b}29–988^{a}7, XII 1 1069^{a}26–28).

(5) When the perceptual data are scarce, however, it is still possible to make some scientific headway. Astronomy is a case in point. Our theoretical knowledge of the heavenly bodies is relatively slight, "since as regards both those things on the basis of which one would investigate them and those things about them that we long to know, the perceptual appearances are altogether few" (*PA* I 5 644ᵇ25– 28). There are many puzzles in astronomy, therefore, about which we can do little but conjecture, since "where things not apparent to perception are concerned, we think we have adequately shown our case to be in accord with reason if we have brought things back to what is possible, given the available appearances" (*Mete.* I 7 344ᵃ5–7). To become a "little less puzzled" in areas like these is—until further perceptual data becomes available—the most we can hope for (*Cael.* II 12 291ᵇ24–28). In the case of hybridization, however, we already have sufficient perceptual data to show that [P1] and [P2] are false (*GA* II 8 748ᵃ12–13). So to the degree that they are reputable enough as they stand, without gaining their reputability from some authority (none is named), to make an argument of them more convincing (presumably to people unaware of the perceptual evidence against them), a demonstration based on them might count as logico-linguistic for this reason too. For, as we saw in (2), an argument based on false but reputable beliefs is logico-linguistic. At the same time, to count as reputable a belief held by acknowledged wise people cannot be contradoxical (*Top.* I 10 104ᵃ8–11), it cannot go contrary to things already believed. Thus the principles appealed to by Democritus and Empedocles, though held by acknowledged wise people, are presumably not themselves reputable beliefs. For the one adopted by Democritus would rule out all hybrids, whereas it is well known that there are such things, while the one adopted by Empedocles is "too far contrary to perception" (*GA* II 8 747ᵇ9–10) to be knowable.

I call it logico-linguistic because in being more universal it is further away (*porrôterô*) **from the proper starting-points:** In what way are [P1] and [P2] further away from proper starting-points than (presumably) the ones appealed to by Democritus and Empedocles? The obvious answer seems like the right one. That of Democritus appeals to spermatic ducts being destroyed in the uterus, while that of Empedocles appeals to seeds becoming more coarse-grained, and both of these notions are closer to the things at issue (II 8 748ᵃ9) than that of the sameness of species employed in [P1] and [P2], which are, of course, more universal in application. By the same token we might see [P1] and [P2] as appealing to form (*eidos*) alone, without any appeal to matter (spermatic, ducts, seeds, and so on), and so on that ground too, as supporting a logico-linguistic rather than natural scientific demonstration, as (3) above suggests. See also IV 1 765ᵃ34–ᵇ6.

Note 588

Arguments not from the proper starting-points are empty, but rather seem to be based on the things at issue, but are not really: "In each methodical inquiry arguments (*logos*) stated in a philosophical way differ from those not stated in a philosophical way. That is why even politicians should not regard as peripheral to their work the sort of theoretical knowledge that makes evident not only the that but also the why. For this is the sort of methodical inquiry about each thing that is philosophical. Yet much caution is needed here. For certain people, because it seems to be characteristic of the philosopher never to speak at random but always in accord with argument (*logos*), often escape notice when they state arguments that are foreign to the thing at issue and empty" (*EE* I 6 1216ᵇ35–1217ᵃ3).

Note 589
Many animals that come to be from ones not of the same species (*homoeidês*) **are fertile, as was said previously:** At II 7 746ᵃ29–ᵇ11, 8 747ᵃ31–33.

Note 590
It is from getting a theoretical grasp on what belongs to the genus (*genos*) **of the horse and of the ass that one should get the cause:** Failing to do this, though they differ in other respects, is what the demonstrations of Democritus, Empedocles, and the unattributed logico-linguistic demonstration have in common.

Note 591
Because they are not continuously capable of bearing: Reading διὰ τὸ μὴ δύνασθαι συνεχῶς φέρειν with Louis-3 and Lefebvre; OCT, Peck-3, and Platt seclude.

Note 592
A female horse is not [abundantly] menstruous (*katamêniôdês*)**, but among the quadrupeds emits the least:** In proportion to size (*HA* VI 18 573ᵃ11).

Note 593
A she-ass is not receptive of mating, but ejects the semen (*ton gonon*) **with her urine, which is why people follow behind flogging her:** "It has happened before now that a she-ass has conceived when a year old and brought [the foal] to birth. She expels the semen (*tên gonên*) with her urine, unless she is prevented, that is why she is beaten directly after mating and chased about [preventing her from urinating]" (*HA* IV 23 577ᵃ21–24).

Note 594
Celts: Herodotus, II.23, IV.49, mentions Celts as living near the head of the Danube and in the far west of Europe. They are also mentioned as living near present-day Marseille.

Note 595
The other things just mentioned belong to the ass: Paucity of menses, expulsion of semen with urine, and a cold nature.
The first shedding of teeth: At thirty months (*HA* VI 23 577ᵃ18).

Note 596
A ginnus (*ginnos*) **is a deformed mule:** A ginnus is the offspring of a mule and a mare (*HA* VI 24 577ᵇ21). On deformation, see I 18 724ᵇ32n.

BOOK III

Note 597
The animals that walk (*ta peza*): "The walking animals must here mean only land animals. The ovipara are mostly flying or swimming animals, but A. seems to forget all about the land reptiles and amphibia" (Platt, n1).

Note 598
The eggs of birds are all two-colored: White and yolk. Single-colored ones have no difference between white and yolk. See III 1 751ª31–33.

Note 599
One alone of these is not internally oviparous, namely, the so-called fishing-frog (*batrachos*): Probably *Lophius piscatorius*. The popular names are "fishing-frog," "angler fish," "sea-devil," and "monkfish." "These fish are teleostean, not cartilaginous, and spawn very abundantly" (Platt, n4).
The cause of this will be spoken about later: At III 3 754ª25–31.

Note 600
Their uteruses, the differences (*diaphora*) **they have, and due to what causes, have been spoken about previously:** At I 3.

Note 601
Spontaneously: See *PA* I 1 640ª27n (this vol.).
Zephyria: Wind-eggs produced in spring (*HA* IV 2 560ª6).

Note 602
The taloned ones . . . have a small body that is dry and hot: "The bodies—without the wings—of taloned birds are small because the nourishment is used up in their weapons and their defense" (*PA* IV 12 694ª8–10).

Note 603
Adriatic chickens: Perhaps a kind of bantam; also mentioned at *HA* VI 1 558ᵇ16–17.

Note 604
The ones not true to their stock (*agenneis*) **lay more eggs than those true to their stock** (*gennaiôn*): "An animal is well-bred (*eugenes*) if it comes from good stock; it is true to its stock in not being a degeneration from its own nature" (*HA* I 1 488ᵇ18–20); "Good breeding (*eugenes*), though, is in accord with the virtue of the stock (*genos*), whereas being true to one's stock (*gennaios*) is in accord with not being a degeneration from nature" (*Rh*. II 15 1390ᵇ21–23).

Note 605

The spirit (*thumos*): Aristotle often uses *thumos* and *orgê* ("anger") interchangeably (*Rh.* I 10 1369^{a}7, ^{b}11) and very often uses *thumos* in contexts where its aggressive side is highlighted (*NE* III 8 1116^{b}15–1117^{a}9). In other places, however, he says only that anger is "in (*en*)" the spirited part of the soul (*Top.* II 7 113^{a}36–^{b}1, IV 5 126^{a}10), alongside other feelings, such as fear and hatred (IV 5 126^{a}8–9). In one passage, indeed, he identifies spirit as the source not just of "negative" feelings but also of love and friendship: "spirit (*thumos*) is what produces friendliness (*philêtikon*), since it is the capacity of the soul by which we love (*philoumen*)" (*Pol.* VII 7 1327^{b}40–1328^{a}1). This is in keeping with his claim that if hatred is in the spirited part, then love, as its contrary, must be there too (*Top.* II 7 113^{a}33–^{b}3). Presumably, then, we should think of spirit as passionate—as "hot and hasty" (*NE* VII 6 1149^{a}30)—rather than as always aggressive. Nonetheless, it is surely its aggressive side that is most relevant in the case of birds bred for fighting.

Note 606

Wind-eggs are produced, as was also said previously: At II 5 741^{a}16–32, III 1 749^{a}34–^{b}3.

Note 607

[The eggs of birds and fishes] are incomplete with a view to generation ... without the semen of the male. The cause of these things was stated previously: At II 5.

Note 608

Some [river fish] quite evidently have eggs from the first, as is recorded about them in the *History of Animals*: At *HA* VI 13 567^{a}30–31.

Note 609

Fish [emit an egg] that is incomplete, but that gets its growth outside [the mother], as was also said previously: At II 1 749^{a}25–27.

Note 610

For no bloodless animal lays eggs: This clause is secluded by Platt (followed by Peck-3), since "A. says over and over again that many invertebrates lay eggs" (n1). **That blood is the matter for bodies has often been stated:** See, for example, II 4 740^{b}34–35.

Note 611

The one part ... the hot: Namely, the white.

Note 612

That is why the embryos of animals of this sort are single-colored, as was said: At III 1 750^{b}10–19. Embryos in this case are within eggs, and the relevant sort of animal is the one whose nature is colder and more liquid.

Note 613
If one pours together many eggs into a bladder or something of that sort and boils them by means of a fire that does not make the movement of the heat faster than the disaggregation within the eggs: The eggs are apparently poured in gently, so that the yolks do not break. As the yolks and whites begin to separate, they are gently heated, so that neither gets cooked until the movement of the yolks to the center and the whites to the outside is complete. When removed from the bladder, the cooked yolks should be surrounded by the cooked whites. See also *HA* VI 2 560ᵃ30–ᵇ3.

Note 614
That is why the egg is harder at [the sharp end] than below. For it is necessary to shelter and protect the starting-point. And because of this the sharp end of the egg comes out later: "'Below' means the blunter end, which A. [rightly] supposes to be lower in the passage downwards. . . . This was quite unknown to modern writers till recently. . . . The blunt end is softer, as A. says; this is because the young bird is to break its way out there" (Platt, n5).

Note 615
The point at which the two valves (*dithuron*) of beans and seeds of this sort make contact is where the seed is attached: "Generation from seeds always occurs from the middle. For all of them are bi-valvular (*dithurôn*), and it is at the natural join or middle of the two parts that both root and stem of growing things grow out, and the starting-point is the middle of them" (*Iuv.* 3 468ᵇ18–23).

Note 616
[Eggs] do not, like larvae, get their growth via themselves: See II 1 732ᵃ29–32.

Note 617
With a small tail running through it like an umbilical cord: The small tail is probably one of the two chalazae (the two twisted membranous strips joining the yolk to each of the two ends of the shell).

Note 618
When the egg has reached completion the sharp end of the egg [is where] this comes to its limit: That is, where the umbilical-cord-like tail in the egg reaches the limit of its ever-decreasing size.

Note 619
With an egg the delivery is as it were feet down. And the cause of this is the one that was stated, namely, that the egg is fastened at the starting-point: See III 2 752ᵃ10–18.

Note 620

Generation from an egg comes about in birds due to the mother-bird's incubation: The female is the only incubator in some species (such as hummingbirds and all North American polygynous species). In polyandrous species, on the other hand, it is common for the male to be the only incubator (for example, the ostrich, which Aristotle mentions at III 1 749^{b}17). But in most species the male and the female share the incubation. But there are some (for example, the Australian bush turkey) where the incubation is done not by either male or female but by the enclosed nest whose temperature they control.

Note 621

Alcmaeon of Croton: See HA I 11 492^{a}14n (this vol.).

Note 622

The newborn chick, then, as had been said, comes to be due to the mother bird's incubation: At III 2 752^{b}15–17.

Note 623

Theoretical knowledge (*theôria*): See HA I 6 491^{a}6n.

Note 624

A perception-based capacity for taking care of the young (*tên tôn teknôn aisthêsin epimelêtikên*): *Epimelêtikos* means "able to take charge," or "able to manage," "or able to take care." *Aisthêsis* is at once "perception" and a "perceptual capacity" or "sense." The idea here, however, is not that there is a special sense devoted to care of the young, but that there is a capacity, based in the various senses, for this.

Note 625

In those that have the greatest share in practical wisdom . . . as in the case of human beings and some of the quadrupeds: See I 23 731^{a}35n.

Note 626

She infuses into [them] as well the heat that is within herself: Reading προσεγχεῖ ("pour in besides," "infuse into . . . as well") with OCT, Louis-3, and Peck-3; Platt reads προσέχει ("applies").

Note 627

Eggs get destroyed and become so-called *ouria*: That is, wind-eggs produced mostly in the summer. See III 1 749^{b}1n. *Ourios* means "of urine," or "like urine," so "rotten" at III 2 753^{a}33 and 753^{b}7.

Note 628

Putrefying: See I 1 715^{a}25n.

Note 629

Coarse-grained: See II 2 735^{a}31n.

Note 630
When exposed to fire and baked it does not become hard: "Due to fire the white becomes coarse-grained, whereas the yolk does not become coarse-grained but remains soft, unless it is thoroughly burned, and it is more by boiling than by baking that it becomes composed and dry" (*HA* VI 2 560ᵃ24–27).
[The yolk's] nature is to be earthy in the way wax is: "Now since things meltable by fire at any rate must be put down as meltable, these are mostly composed of water, though some are in fact a compound of water and earth—for example, wax" (*Mete.* IV 10 388ᵇ33–389ᵃ1).

Note 631
And because of this, when [the eggs] are heated more, insofar as [1] it is not from the wet residue, [2] it turns serous and becomes rotten: Reading καὶ διὰ τοῦτο θερμαινόμενα μᾶλλον ἐὰν ᾖ μὴ ἐξ ὑγροῦ περιττώματος διοροῦται καὶ γίγνεται οὔρια with the mss. OCT obelizes ἐὰν ᾖ μὴ; Louis-3 obelizes, while Platt and Peck-3 seclude ἐὰν ᾖ μὴ ἐξ ὑγροῦ περιττώματος. We have just been told that the properly concocted yolk liquifies and becomes nourishment for the developing embryonic chick. Since what serves as nourishment is a (useful) residue, this is the wet residue referred to in [1]. But when the eggs are heated more (than in successful incubation), the part of the yolk that does not remain liquid and serve as nourishment, [2] is turned serous (earthy and thick like the serum in blood), since, as we have again just been told, the yolk is like wax, and responds to heat as wax does.

Note 632
The white on the other hand does not become coarse-grained due to frosts but rather liquifies (the cause has been stated previously): At any rate, in the analogous case of seed. See II 2 735a34–36.

Note 633
For exactness about the way these parts stand to each other, both at the start of generation and during the composition of the animal, and further about the membranes and umbilical cords, one must get a theoretical grasp on what is written (*gegrammenôn*) **in the** *History of Animals*: The reference is to *HA* VI 3 561ᵃ3–562ᵇ2. The account there is no more exact than the one given in *GA*, but may have been accompanied by detailed illustrations, to which *gegrammena*, which can also mean "drawings," might rather be taken to refer. See *GA* III 8 758ᵃ23–25.

Note 634
Two umbilical cords extend from this blood-vessel, one to the membrane that encompasses the yolk, the other to the chorion-like membrane that encompasses the animal like a circle, and thus it goes around inside the membrane of the shell: "This description seems to be of a chick of about the sixth to the tenth day. The great blood-vessel is the dorsal aorta running from the heart towards the tail. The 'umbilical cords' are (1) the 'umbilical stalk' by which the yolk-sac hangs from the embryo, (2) the stalk of the allantois, a sac which, growing out from the

embryo, lies close under the shell. . . . But the description of these as 'running from the vessel' is hardly correct" (Platt, n5).

The chorion-like membrane: See II 4 739^{b}31n.

Note 635

Since the oviparously produced ones are *not* nourished in the mother, they take some part out with them: Namely, the yolk.

[The oviparously produced embryo's] relation to the outermost membrane—the one that is bloody—is like that of the viviparously produced one to the uterus: The outermost membrane is the allantois, which "can scarcely be compared to the uterus; the allantois serves mainly for respiration in both bird and mammals" (Platt, n3).

Note 636

The umbilical cord going to the chorion collapses first: "This is not correct; the yolk-sac with its stalk is drawn onto the abdominal cavity of the chick on the nineteenth day, but the allantois shrivel up and the umbilicus closes on the twentieth or thereabouts" (Platt, n2).

Note 637

[The fishes] that have the uterus low down lay an incomplete egg, due to the cause mentioned previously: At I 8 718^{b}23–27.

The one they call a "fishing-frog": See III 1 749^{a}23n.

Note 638

Takes its young in afterward: "The young have the habit of swimming into the mouth of the parent for protection" (Peck-3, p. 298 n*a*): "Dogfish with one exception can release [from their mouth] and take in again their young: the angelfish and the torpedo-fish can do it (for a large torpedo-fish has been known to have around eight embryos inside it), but the spiny dogfish, because of the spines, is the only one of the dogfish that cannot take them back in. Of the broad selachia, the stingray and the *batos* [ray] cannot take them in again because of the roughness of their tails. Nor can the fishing-frog take them back in, because of the size of their heads, and their spines, it is the only one of the selachians that is not oviparous" (*HA* VI 10 565^{b}23–31).

Note 639

It is not only at the point of attachment that it is of this mixed sort, but also at the opposite one, and it is easier to draw the nourishment from the uterus by means of certain ducts coming from this starting-point: Reading ῥᾷον ("easier") with OCT and Louis-3; Platt followed by Peck-3 and Lefebvre read ῥάδιον ("easy"). The ducts are "blood-vessels running from the germinating vesicle through the egg to the uterus, corresponding to the umbilical cord of mammals and allantoic stalk in birds" (Platt, n3). Aristotle's point is surely this: In birds' eggs the starting-point is at the blunt end of the egg, the attachment point at the sharp end, and so it is farther away from where nourishment is drawn from the uterus. In fishes, by contrast, the starting-point can be at the attachment point, making the drawing in of nourishment easier.

Note 640

This occurs, as we have said, in the smooth dogfish: The *Mustelus laevis*. "In this shark the young are connected with the uterus by a kind of placenta. This extraordinary fact remained unknown to modern science till . . . 1840" (Platt, n7). The reference is to the very detailed description at *HA* VI 10 565^{b}2–17.

Note 641

The cause of [the fishing-frog producing a complete egg] was stated earlier: At III 3 754^{a}26–31.

Note 642

Of the others' laying incomplete eggs the cause was also stated earlier: At I 8 718^{b}8–15.

Note 643

The soul-involving heat: See Introduction, pp. lxii–lxxii.

Humor (*chumos*): Aristotle uses the word *chumos* to refer to a number of apparently different things: (1) the "juice" in plants (*HA* V 22 554^{a}13, VIII 11 596^{b}17); (2) animal juices (V 31 556^{b}22, *PA* III 15 676^{a}16); (3) the special object of taste (*DA* II 6 418^{a}13), which is a sort of touch for Aristotle (3 414^{b}11); (4) a sort of seasoning that adds flavor (414^{b}13). The somewhat technical term "humor" seems to best capture its overall meaning.

Note 644

The so-called *belonê*—**that burst because of the size of their eggs:** "One of the 'pipe-fishes,' perhaps *Sygnatus acus*. In this group (of which the well-known 'seahorse' is another member) the male incubates the eggs in a brood-pouch formed by the pelvic fins" (Peck-3, pp. 304–5 n*e*). After the burst "the sides grow together again" (*HA* VI 13 567^{b}21–26).

Note 645

A sign: See I 19 727^{a}4n.

These fishes too: Apparently, the ones other than the (Aristotelian) selachians.

Note 646

Their milt-producing parts: The spermatic ducts mentioned at I 3 716^{b}17.

Note 647

Like mules in the genus with long hairs in their tails: Reading ὥσπερ αἱ ἡμίονοι ἐν τῷ γένει τῷ τῶν λοφούρων here with Louis-3, Platt; Lefebvre reads it, while OCT and Peck-3 seclude it, post τῶν ᾠοτοκούντων ("of the egg-producers"). The genus is *Equus*.

Note 648
Erythrinus and channa: See I 1 715ᵃ21n, II 5 741ᵃ36n.

Note 649
Spontaneous eggs: See *PA* I 1 640ᵃ27n (this vol.).

Note 650
But in fish, because in all cases the eggs are incomplete and get their growth outside: The text here is corrupt, though the meaning is tolerably clear.
Even if no egg within becomes fertile from mating: Reading εἰ καὶ μη<δὲν> ἐντὸς ἐξ ὀχείας γένηται γόνιμον with OCT; Louis-3 and Platt read κἂν ἐξ ὀχείας γένηται τὸ ᾠόν ("even if the egg has come to be from mating").

Note 651
Those whose tail prevents [them from mating in another way]: Reading ὅσοις ἐμποδίζει τὸ οὐραῖον with OCT, Louis-3, and Lefebvre; Platt, followed by Peck-3, reads and secludes ὅσοις μὴ ἐμποδίζει τὸ οὐραῖον ("those whose tail does not prevent them"). See *HA* V 5 540ᵇ6–11: "All fishes, except for the flat selachians, place themselves side to side and copulate belly to belly. But fish that are flat and have tails—for example the *batos* [ray], the stingray, and such—copulate not only by placing themselves side to side but also by the mounting belly to back of the male upon the female, in those where the tail is not so thick as to prevent it."

Note 652
Ejaculation (*apolausis*) in the case of the dolphins takes a longer time: On the meaning of *apolausis*, see I 6 718ᵃ1n.

Note 653
The simple-minded account (*logos*) of Herodotus the storyteller to the effect that fish are conceived from the swallowing of milt: See Herodotus II.93.

Note 654
For there are some . . . without investigation: = DK 59A114.
Physicists: See *PA* I 1 641ᵃ7n.

Note 655
On the basis of a deduction (*ek sullogismou*): See *PA* I 1 639ᵃ3n(2) (this vol.).

Note 656
Domesticated jackdaws (*koloiôn*): "Of the jackdaws there are three species. One is the chough, which is the size of a crow, with a red beak. Another is the so-called 'wolf.' Further, the small one, the 'joker.' And also yet another genus of jackdaws

found around Lydia and Phrygia, which is web-footed" (*HA* IX 24 617ᵇ16–19). The last mentioned is probably the little cormorant, *Phalacrocorax pugmaeus*.

Note 657
Eager for sexual intercourse (*aphrodisiastikon*): Or "lecherous," "amorous," or "overly sexual."

Note 658
The other cloven-hoofed animals—about which we shall speak later: At IV 4 771ᵃ21–ᵇ14.

Note 659
Trochus: It is not clear what animal Aristotle is referring to.
Hyena: That is, the striped hyena.

Note 660
Herodorus of Heraclea: A contemporary of Herodotus, father of the sophist Bryson, and author of mythological works on Heracles and on the Argonauts, he is mentioned in connection with similar errors about vultures at *HA* VI 5 563ᵃ5–12, IX 11 615ᵃ8–14. Many Greek cities were named "Heraclea," after the hero Heracles. This is the one on the Black Sea, which was founded by Megara c. 560 BC.
Says that the trochus has two private parts: 31 Fr. 58 Jacoby.

Note 661
Hyenas have a line under their tail like the female private part: "The part which seems to be like that of a female is under the tail and in configuration is about the same as that of the female, but it has no duct at all, and the duct for the residue is underneath it. The female hyena does have what is said to be similar to a female private part, but as in the male it is underneath the tail and has no duct; after that there is the duct for the residue, and underneath it the true private part" (*HA* VI 32 579ᵇ19–26).

Note 662
As was said in the accounts farther back and in the more recent ones, the eggs of birds are completed internally, those of fishes externally: See I 8 718ᵇ5–27, III 4 755ᵃ11–ᵇ1.

Note 663
In the case of birds wind-eggs become fertile, and those previously impregnated by one genus of male change their nature to that of the later male: "If [the female] is mated with the male within a certain period of time" (I 1 751ᵇ24–25).

Note 664
Which do not grow if the mating is interrupted, when he has fertilized them by mating again: Reading ἀναύξητα ὄντα ἂν διαλείπῃ τὴν ὀχείαν, ὅταν ὀχευθῇ with

Louis-3; OCT obelizes; Platt, followed by Peck-3, reads διαλίπη ("if the male has left off mating"), and suggest as an alternate possibility ὅταν ὀχεύσῃ, which Peck-3 adopts.

Note 665
It is impossible for them to be completed into an animal (for there is a need of perception): Since the male is needed to produce perceptual soul. See II 5 741ᵃ10–16.

Note 666
All the animals possess the nutritive capacity of the soul, as has often been said: For example, at II 5 740ᵇ36–741ᵃ3.

Note 667
If indeed there is any genus of fish of such a sort as to generate without a male (but about this it was said earlier too that it has not been adequately observed): At II 5 741ᵃ35–37.

Note 668
They already contain both starting-points: That of perceptual soul, from the male, and that of nutritive soul, from the female.

Note 669
Cuttlefishes (*sêpia*): Sepia is actually the genus of cuttlefish in the family *Sepiidae*, which includes most of the common species.
Crayfish (*karaboi*) **and things of the same genus** (*suggenê*) **as these:** "The crustaceans are all perambulatory, which is why they have numerous feet. There are four greatest genera of them, called crayfish, lobsters, prawn and crabs" (*PA* IV 8 684ᵇ25–28).

Note 670
That is why those who say that all fish are female and lay eggs without mating are not speaking in a way based on methodical inquiry on this point either: See III 6 757ᵃ11–12.

Note 671
Lack of experience (*apeirias*): See II 6 758ᵃ3n.

Note 672
That some [insects] come to be from copulation, others spontaneously, was said previously: At I 16 721ᵃ5–16, II 1 732ᵇ10–14, 733ᵃ24–32. On spontaneous coming to be, see *PA* I 1 640ᵃ27n (this vol.).
And in addition that they produce larvae, and due to what cause they produce larvae: See *GA* I 21 729ᵇ25–33, II 1 733ᵃ24–32, III 4 755ᵃ14–21.

Note 673
Some of the oviparous animals produce a complete embryo, others an incomplete one, but it becomes complete outside, as has often been said to be so in the case of fish: For example, at III 1 749ª24–27.

Note 674
That is why people call the destruction of embryos produced at that time "effluxions" (*ekruseis*): "What is called an effluxion is the destruction of the embryo up to seven days [in a woman], miscarriages for those up to forty days" (*HA* VII 3 583ᵇ11–12).

Note 675
We must . . . speak by referring to the whole thing, and not just a certain part, changing into the whole animal that will come to be: Because this is precisely the difference between a seed and a larva. See II 1 732ª29–32.

Note 676
All the others that come to be, not from mating, in wool or other such materials: For example, clothes-moths: "Other tiny animals come to be, some in wool and whatever things are made of wool—for example, the clothes-moth (*sêtes*). And these grow more abundantly when the woolens are dusty, and particularly if a spider is shut up inside them. For it drinks up any liquid there may be in them, and dries them. This larva is also found in men's tunics" (*HA* V 32 557ᵇ1–5).

Note 677
The larvae of wasps and bees [which get nourishment and quite evidently have excrement] after they become what are called pupae, and have nothing of this sort: OCT reads καὶ τῶν σφηκῶν οἱ σκώληκες καὶ τῶν μελιττῶν *** μετὰ ταῦτα αἱ καλούμεναι νύμφαι γίγνονται, καὶ τοιοῦτον οὐδὲν ἔχουσιν; Platt secludes καὶ τοιοῦτον οὐδὲν ἔχουσιν ("and have nothing of this sort"). Following Louis-3, I have added material from *HA* V 19: "The larvae of bees, hornets, and wasps, when they are young get nourishment and quite evidently have excrement; but when they have passed from what are larvae to their marked shape (*diatupôsin*), being then called pupae, they get no nourishment and have no excrement" (551ª29–ᵇ3).

Note 678
This sort of residue is produced: That is, excrement.

Note 679
Others come to be spontaneously, as some plants do: For example, mistletoe. See I 1 715ᵇ25–30.

Note 680
The generation process of bees, though, involves much puzzlement: "The facts are briefly as follows. There are three kinds, (1) perfect [or complete] males

or drones, (2) perfect females or queens, (3) undeveloped females or workers. The queen lays eggs before she has been fertilized by a drone; this is known as parthenogenesis; these eggs produce drones. The fertilized eggs of the queen produce workers or queens, according to the way the grub is fed by the workers. . . . The workers also, in spite of being sexually undeveloped, do occasionally lay parthenogenic eggs, which always produce drones. It will be evident to any reader of this chapter that A. knew next to nothing about the truth. He does indeed hit upon the fact that workers may (but he says always do) parthenogenically produce drones; he gets at this by hard thinking, and the whole chapter is greatly to his credit. But it is not to the credit of any modern writer that he should assert that the Greeks were well acquainted with the internal economy of the hive" (Platt, n1).

Note 681
The brood (*ton gonon*): Consisting of the larvae.

Note 682
That they should collect honey is reasonable (for it is nourishment): In fact they collect nectar and turn it into honey.

Note 683
All the animals that busy themselves about the young work hard for what appears to be their own brood: For example, the cuckoo. See III 1 750ᵃ15.

Note 684
It is not reasonable that a similar affection not be characteristic of the entire genus of these: That is, if drones are brought from outside, bees and kings should be as well, since they do in fact all belong to the same genus.

Note 685
The leaders: That is, the kings (really queens) (III 10 759ᵃ21).

Note 686
Erythrinus . . . channa: See I 1 715ᵃ18–25n.

Note 687
That is also why [the bees'] process of generation in a way stands in a proportion: Kings generate two kinds: themselves and bees; bees generate one kind: drones; drones generate no kind, so that the process of generation reaches its limit with them (III 10 760ᵃ34–35).

Note 688
The bees, then, are similar to them in capacity: Secluding καὶ τῷ τίκτειν ("and by producing") with Louis-3 and Peck-3; OCT, Platt, and Lefebvre retain.

Note 689
If the drones also had had a sting, they would have been leaders. But as things stand a puzzle remains. For the leaders are like both genera at the same time, the bees in having a sting, the drones in size: Reading εἰ δ’ εἶχον καὶ κέντρον ἡγεμόνες ἂν ἦσαν. νῦν δὲ τοῦτο λείπεται τῆς ἀπορίας· οἱ γὰρ ἡγεμόνες ἀμφοτέροις ἐοίκασιν ἐν τῷ αὐτῷ τοῖς γένεσι, τῷ μὲν κέντρον ἔχειν ταῖς μελίτταις τῷ δὲ μεγέθει τοῖς κηφῆσιν with Louis-3 and Lefebvre; OCT and Peck-3 seclude; Platt reads λέλυται ("has been resolved") for λείπεται.

Note 690
Their cells (*kuttaroi*) are produced at the end and are not many in number: Reading γίγνονται δ’ ἐπὶ τέλει οἱ κύτταροι αὐτῶν καὶ οὐ πολλοὶ τὸν ἀριθμόν here with OCT, though Peck-3 thinks it misplaced and "more relevant if moved to 760ᵇ27" (p. 341 n*d*). The cells are those of the honeycomb. "This sentence is correct. After a great number of drones and workers have been brought up, the workers build one or several larger cells in each of which an egg . . . is laid by the queen. The grub is fed upon 'royal jelly,' and it seems that this special food causes it to develop into a queen" (Platt, n1).

Note 691
Being smaller in size they need the good weather more: Smaller bodies mean less internal heat, and so a greater need for external heat, to concoct nourishment for the purposes of growth and reproduction.

Note 692
[Bees] attend on their kings because their generation is from them: "It would seem, though, that in matters of sustenance we should assist our parents most, on the grounds of owing them this, and that it is a nobler thing to assist the causes of our existence in this way than to assist ourselves" (*NE* IX 3 1165ᵃ21–24); "The friendship of children toward parents, as of human beings toward gods, is as toward something good and superior, since they are the producers of the greatest goods and the cause of their existence and nurture as well as of their education, once born" (VIII 12 1162ᵃ4–7).

Note 693
It is nobler (*kallion*) to discipline (*kolazein*) children and those for whom there exists no work: It is because *kalon* things are done for their own sake (see *PA* I 1 639ᵇ20n [this vol.]), it is because they are purposeless or useless, that they are contrasted with necessary things, things we *have* to do, even though they have no intrinsic value. This contrast is particularly clear in the following text: "And we say . . . that happiness is a complete activation and use of virtue, and this not on the basis of a hypothesis but unconditionally. By on the basis of a hypothesis I mean what is necessary, by unconditionally I mean those that are done nobly. For in the case of just actions, for example, just penalties and punishments spring from virtue, but are necessary, and their nobly done has the character of necessarily done.

For it is a more choiceworthy situation if no man or city needs any such things. By contrast, just actions that aim at honors and prosperity are unconditionally noblest. For the former involve choosing something bad, whereas the latter are the contrary, since they establish and generate good things" (*Pol.* VII 13 1332ᵃ7–18). What makes it nobler, then, "to discipline children and those for whom there exists no work" is that discipline is not a punishment (though *kolazein* can also mean "punish") imposed of necessity on someone who fails to do his work. In fact, though, the bees kill all the drones at the end of the summer, "which carries nobility to extreme lengths" (Platt, n3).

Note 694
The generation of lions: See III 1 730ᵃ31–ᵇ1.

Note 695
An additional sign . . . having magnitude: OCT, following Peck-3, double-brackets this as misplaced.

Note 696
For they have nothing divine (*theion*) **in them as the bee genus does:** The divine element is understanding (*nous*) (II 3 737ᵃ10), and it—perhaps in an attenuated form (I 23 731ᵃ35n)—is something Aristotle thinks bees possess: "Coarser-grained and hotter blood is more productive of strength, finer-grained and colder blood is more perceptive and more understanding (*noerôteron*). And the same difference obtains among things possessing the analogue of blood. That is why both bees and other animals of this sort are more practically-wise (*phronimôtera*) in their nature than many blooded animals, and why among blooded animals those having cold and fine-grained blood are more practically-wise than their contraries" (*PA* II 2 648ᵃ3–8). But Aristotle also thinks that, like human beings, though again in an attenuated way, bees, wasps, ants, and cranes are political animals, because "some one work (*ergon*) common to all is produced" (*HA* I 1 488ᵃ7–8). The common work in the case of human beings is the *polis* or city, making them the political animals *par excellence* (*Pol.* III 6 1278ᵇ15–30, *NE* VIII 12 1162ᵃ17–19). Since Aristotle's (primary) god is himself simply an understanding (*Met.* XII 9 1074ᵇ34–35), and is the good of the whole universe both as something "separated and intrinsic," like the general of an army, and as its "order," like the army itself (10 1075ᵃ11–15), we might suspect that the divine something is, in the case of bees, as much present (if not more present) in the hive as in the individual bees. See *HA* IX 40.

Note 697
As for how many differences (*diaphora*) **each of these genera have in relation to each other or in relation the bees, a theoretical grasp on this should be gotten from what is catalogued** (*anagegrammenôn*) **in the** *History of Animals***:** The reference is to *HA* IX 41.

Note 698
Because [the testaceans'] nature is a counterpart to that of the plants: See II 6 743^{b}28n.
On earth . . . in the sea: The preposition is *en* in both cases.

Note 699
[The sea] has a share of all the parts—water, pneuma, and earth: All the parts, that is, of the sublunary world.
The living things that come to be participate in each of the places: Reading ἐν τοῖς τόποις ζῴων with OCT; Platt, followed by Peck-3, secludes.

Note 700
The more and the less, and nearer and farther away, produce great and wondrous difference: How fresh or how salty the water, how near land or how far away, have large effects on the features (or perhaps differentiae) of the living things found there. On the more and the less, see *PA* I 4 644^{a}18n (this vol.).

Note 701
What is on fire appears to be either air, smoke, or earth: See Introduction, pp. lx–lxii.

Note 702
This fourth genus [of living thing] must be sought on the moon. For the moon appears to participate in [the elemental body] at the fourth remove [namely, fire]: Compare: "In Cyprus, in places where copper ore is smelted, with more thrown in day after day, an animal comes to be in the fire, a little larger than a large fly, with wings, that can walk or crawl through the fire. . . . The salamander makes this clear, since it, so they say, by walking through the fire puts the fire out" (*HA* V 19 552^{b}10–17); "If, then, ice is the solidification of wet and cold, fire will be the boiling of dry and hot. That is why nothing comes to be either from ice or from fire" (*GC* II 3 330^{b}28–30); "Fire generates no animal, and none appears to be composed in wet or dry things under the influence of fire" (*GA* II 3 737^{a}1–3); "It is only in earth and in water that there are animals, and not in air or fire, because these are the matter of their bodies" (*Mete.* IV 4 382^{a}6–8). A way to resolve the tensions between these various claims is to recall that all of them, as belonging to natural science, rather than to a strictly theoretical one, hold only for the most part. But it is also important to remember that so-called (or non-elemental) fire's "underlying subject is smoke or charcoal," that "smoke is a vapor" (*PA* II 2 649^{a}18–22), and that vapor is "disaggregated water" (*Mete.* I 3 340^{b}3). We are in an area, in other words, where "the more and the less and nearer and farther" do indeed "make a wondrous difference" (*GA* III 11 761^{b}14–15).
The moon appears to participate in [the elemental body] at the fourth remove [namely, fire]: The fourth place, but third remove (from the earth), in our way of counting: "Since the simple bodies are four in number, two each belong to each of the two places (fire and air belong to what spatially moves toward the limit,

earth and water to what spatially moves toward the center). And earth and fire are the extremes and the purest, whereas water and air are intermediates and more mixed" (*GC* II 3 330^{b}30–331^{a}1).

Note 703
Some emit [something with] a certain capacity from themselves: See III 11 762^{a}5–8. **Spontaneous composition:** See *PA* I 1 640^{a}27n (this vol.).

Note 704
We must, then, grasp the process of coming to be for plants: Because testaceans are like plants (III 11 761^{a}16–17).

Note 705
Others by budding-off (*parablastanein*)—**for example, the onion genus:** "Bulbs often send off a little bulb from themselves, which being freed from the parent grows into a new plant" (Platt, n8).

Note 706
Those that are said to make combs: "Because a mass of whelks' eggs . . . looks like a wasp-comb" (Platt, n10).

Note 707
We must, however, consider none of these emissions to be seed, but rather these creatures as participating in the way just mentioned in a similarity to the plants: The slimy liquid they emit is not properly seed but "merely so much stuff homogeneous with the body of the animal, like the cutting of a plant" (Platt, n1).

Note 708
The substance of the comb-makers: That is, their essence.

Note 709
It is evident that all those composed in this way, whether on earth or in water, come to be in co-operation with putrefaction and an admixture of rainwater. For as the sweet is disaggregated into the starting-point that is being composed, the residue of the mixture takes this shape [or form]: Rainwater, as fresh rather than salt, is sweet (*HA* I 5 490^{a}25, VIII 13 598^{b}5), and hence provides the sweet material that, as it gets disaggregated or separated off from the other materials, leaves behind a residue that takes on the shape or form of putrefaction, as its internal heat passes away under the influence of the alien heat in the surrounding earth or sea, both of which are naturally hot. See *GA* III 2 758^{a}19–20 (earth), 11 761^{b}10 (sea water), and on putrefaction, I 1 715^{a}25n.

Note 710
Putrefaction, that is, the putrid thing, is a residue of concoction: Reading τὸ σαπρὸν with OCT; Louis-3 and Peck-3 read τὸ σηπτὸν. The meaning is the same on either reading.

Note 711
In a certain way all things are full of soul: See Introduction, p. lxix.

Note 712
More estimable . . . non-estimable: See *PA* I 5 644^{b}24n (this vol.).

Note 713
Earthy material hardens all around them, solidified in the same way as bones and horns (for they are unmeltable by fire): See II 6 743^{a}3–17.

Note 714
Now the composition of [all] the plants that come to be spontaneously is the same in form (*homoeidês***). For they come to be from a part, and while one part is the starting-point, the other is the first nourishment of the outgrowths:** "For they come to be when either the earth or certain parts of [other] plants putrefy. For some of them are not composed separately by themselves but come to be on other trees—for example, mistletoe" (I 1 715^{b}27–30).

Note 715
This sort of generation: That is, animals coming to be from eggs that are spontaneously generated.
The blooded ones just mentioned: Mullets and eels (III 11 762^{b}23–24).

Note 716
Larvae grow toward the upper part and the starting-point: See II 6 741^{b}34–37n.

Note 717
All the testaceans are composed spontaneously: Compare III 11 761^{b}23–26.

Note 718
Chians: Inhabitants of Chios, the fifth largest of the Greek islands, just over four miles from the Anatolian coast.
Euripus-like (*euripôdeis***):** The Euripus is a narrow strait in the Aegean, between the island of Euboea and the mainland of central Greece. It has strong tidal currents that reverse direction seven or more times a day. Aristotle often uses it as a simile for psychological turbulence (see *Somn.* 3 456^{b}17–28, *NE* IX 7 1167^{b}6–7), and refers to it directly at *Mete.* II 8 366^{a}23, *HA* V 15 547^{a}6.

Note 719
As for their so-called eggs, they contribute nothing to generation, but are [just] a sign of being well nourished, like fat in blooded animals: "These are the ovaries and their contents, which A. wrongly denies to be eggs; no invertebrate has fat, and so he held these to be the analogue of fat" (Platt, n2).

Note 720
They become well flavored at these periods: That is, when they have the eggs that Aristotle thought to be an analogue of fat.

Note 721
Pinnae: The *Pinna nobilis* or fan mussel is a species of large (1–4 feet in length) Mediterranean clam.

Note 722
Scallops (*ktenes*): See *HA* I 9 491^{b}26.

Note 723
A theoretical grasp on the particulars concerning these and the places in which they come to be must be gotten from the *History of Animals*: On the testaceans in general, see *HA* IV 4; on their generation, V 15; on their nourishment, VIII 2 590^{a}18–^{b}3.

Book IV

Note 724
The physicists: See *PA* I 1 641^{a}7n.

Note 725
The male is from the right, and the female from the left: See DK 59A42.12 = TEGP 38.12, A111, also DL II [9] 47–48. The right and left testis may be meant. See *GA* IV 1 765^{a}21–25.
And whereas males are on the right of the uterus, females are on the left: Secluded by Peck-3 as an interpolation.

Note 726
[Seeds] that enter a hot womb become males, he says, while those that enter a cold one become females: See I 18 723^{a}25, where the relevant verses of Empedocles are quoted.

Note 727
Democritus of Abdera . . . from each other: = DK 68A143 = TEGP 93.

Note 728
[Democritus] the difference (*diaphora*) **belonging to the generation of this** (*tautês*): Namely, the difference that explains why a uterus is produced rather than male genitalia. Alternatively: "the difference belonging to this generation," that is, the sort that results sometimes in females, sometimes in males. It seems, however, that the uterus is the main focus.

Note 729

If hotness and coldness were the cause of the difference (*diaphora*) of the parts, those who speak that way should have stated (*lekteon*) this: Not just stated or asserted it, but stated it so as to explain how heat and cold produce the difference between male and female, and their different reproductive capacities.

Note 730

It is the same way too with the parts that effect sexual intercourse. For these also differ in the way stated previously: Especially in I 2.

Note 731

Male and female twins are often produced together in the same part of the uterus: "Twins" being understood to cover all cases in which at least one male and one female embryo are produced in the same part (left or right) of the uterus.

Note 732

[Empedocles] says too that the parts are "torn asunder": See I 18 722^{b}12, IV 1 764^{b}18.

Note 733

It is necessary then for the magnitude of these parts also to be torn asunder and for an assembly to occur, but not because of cooling and heating: The parts of the embryo (such as the heart) cannot be already assembled in the seeds of the male and female progenitors. Hence they (as things with magnitude) must be divided there and assembled in the uterus. But this cannot be due to cooling and heating, because cooling produces female parts and heating male ones, but many parts are the same for both.

Note 734

This sort of cause for the seed: Reading τοῦ σπέρματος with OCT and Louis-3; Peck-3 secludes; Platt reads it post "heating" in the previous sentence: "It is necessary then for the magnitude of these parts also to be torn asunder and for an assembly to occur, but not because of cooling and heating of the seed."

Note 735

Torn asunder is the nature of the limbs, this part in man's . . . : DK B63 = TEGP 126 F77.

Note 736

The fact that at the same time the shape of the private part is also distinct needs an argument for its always following along with the other: Of why, in other words, the uterus and the female external genitalia always go together.

Note 737

The blood-vessels around which, as around a framework, the body of the fleshes is laid: See II 6 743^{a}1–2.

Note 738

Although each is a receptacle for a certain sort of blood: The uterus is the receptacle for menstrual blood, the blood-vessels for ordinary blood.

The blood-vessels are prior: That is, they—especially the heart (II 4 740ᵃ17–19)—are formed prior to the uterus in embryological development.

Note 739

The difference (*diaphora*) of these parts in relation to each other in females and males results (*sumbainei*), then, but it must not be thought of as a starting-point or a cause: *Sumbainei* is translated as "is a contingent phenomenon" by Peck-3, and as "*accidentel*" by Louis-3. But what Aristotle seems to be saying is simply that the distinction is something caused by the movement-producing starting-point (whether coming from the male or not), not something that is itself a starting-point or cause.

Note 740

As has also been said previously, a female has been seen in the right part of the uterus, a male in the left, and both in the same part: At IV 1 764ᵃ33–36.

Or the male one in the right, the female in the left, and no less often both come to be in the right: Reading ἢ τὸ ἄρρεν μὲν ἐν τοῖς δεξιοῖς τὸ θῆλυ δ' ἐν τοῖς ἀριστεροῖς· οὐχ ἧττον δὲ ἀμφότερα γίγνεται ἐν τοῖς δεξιοῖς with Louis-3 and Lefebvre; OCT, Peck-3, and Platt seclude.

Note 741

Leophanes: "Leophanes is quoted by Theophrastus, *De Causis Plantarum* II.4.11; and the fact that in Aëtius' *Placita* V.7.5 (*Doxogr.* 420a7) he comes between Anaxagoras and Leucippus may give a rough indication of his date" (Peck-3, pp. 382–83 nc).

Note 742

We must most of all move on by all possible means toward the primary causes: That is, proximate causes, that are closer to their effects than those that are farther away, as causes that are primary by being first in the causal chain leading to the effects would be.

Note 743

The body as a whole and its parts, what each of them is and what cause it is due to, has been spoken about previously elsewhere: In *PA* II–IV and (in the case of the generative parts) *GA* I.

Note 744

Workings (*ergasiais*) concerning fruit: See I 20 728ᵃ25–30.

Note 745

Things are said to be capable and incapable in many ways: These are discussed in *Met.* V 12 and IX.

The penis (*perineos*): Here probably the penis and testicles.

Note 746

We say that the seed has been established to be a residue of the nourishment, namely, the last stage of it. . . . For it makes no difference whether it comes from each of the parts or that it goes to each of them—but the latter is more correct: See I 18 725ª21–726ª28.

Note 747

It contains a starting-point within itself of such a sort as to cause movement in the animal too and to concoct the last stage of the nourishment: Reading καὶ ἐν τῷ ζῴῳ ("in the animal too") with Louis-3 and Lefebvre; OCT obelizes and Peck-3 secludes. The animal referred to is, as often, the embryo.

Note 748

The heat is not yet complete: That is, the soul-involving natural heat whose starting-point is in the male semen. See IV 1 766ª35–36, 2 766ᵇ34.

Note 749

The north winds are more productive of males than are the south winds: "For the air is wetter when the wind is in the south" (Platt, n3).

Note 750

All things that come to either in accord with craft or nature exist in virtue of a certain ratio (*logos*): See II 1 734ᵇ19–735ª4.

Note 751

The blend of the surrounding air: See IV 10 777ᵇ6–7.

Note 752

Nature in these cases has in a certain way deviated from (*parekbebêke*) **the genus:** Deviation is a matter of degree: "Just as a nose that deviates (*parekbebêkuia*) from the most noble straightness toward being hooked or snub can nevertheless still be noble and please the eye, if it is 'tightened' still more toward the extreme, the part will first be thrown out of due proportion, and in the end will appear not to be a nose at all, because it has too much of one and too little of the other of these contraries" (*Pol.* V 9 1309ᵇ23–29). The same is true of the verb *existasthai*, which Aristotle uses at GA IV 3 768ª2, 15, ᵇ8, and which can simply mean "change," but can also mean "change for the worse" or "degenerate": "Good breeding, though, is in accord with the virtue of the stock (*genos*), whereas being true to one's stock (*gennaios*) is in accord with not being a degeneration (*existasthai*) from nature. For the most part, this degeneration does not happen to the well-born, although there are many who are worthless people. . . . Naturally clever stock degenerates (*existatai*) into rather manic characters . . . , whereas steady stock degenerates into stupidity and sluggishness" (*Rh.* II 15 1390ᵇ21–30). So in the present context I have used "deviate" for *parekbainein*, and "shifted" for *existasthai*, understanding that both deviation and shifting may involve only a relatively small change or a much larger one. See also Connell, pp. 340–52.

Note 753

And a first starting-point is when a female comes to be and not a male—but this is necessary by nature: The point of the final clause is to distinguish the generation of female offspring, as something necessary by nature (a "natural deformation" as IV 6 775^{a}15–16 puts it), from cases, such as the birth of "monsters," where nature "has in a certain way deviated from the genus" (IV 3 767^{b}6–7). A female is not such a deviation, obviously, since to be such a deviation must result in an offspring that is not like its "parents (*goneusin*)" (767^{b}6)—which is not a description that fits normal female offspring.

Note 754

The monster, by contrast, is not necessary in relation to the for-the-sake-of-which and the final cause, but is necessary coincidentally: Again, this contrasts the case of the monster with that of the female. The production of females is by nature for the sake of something, and is necessary to the achievement of nature's ends; the production of monsters is necessary only coincidentally.

Note 755

This sort of (*toion*) male: That is, a human one. *Toios* is a demonstrative pronoun corresponding to the relative *hoios*, and interrogative *poios*. Thus *poion ti* ("this sort of thing") is contrasted with *tode ti* ("this something").
Coriscus: Coriscus of Scepsis was a member of a school of Platonists with whom Aristotle was probably acquainted while at the court of Hermias in Assos (c. 347–344 BC). Like Socrates, he is frequently used as an example.

Note 756

Some things are closer and others farther away [1] that belong to the male progenitor, insofar as he is generative, and [2] not coincidentally—for example, if the male progenitor is knowledgeable in grammar or someone's neighbor: [2] excludes Coriscus' coincidental attributes (such as knowing grammar) from playing a causal role in generation, since what is coincidental is excluded from the realm of causes open to scientific explanation. See IV 1 764^{b}36–765^{a}3n. For a proposal about what is included in [1], see Introduction, pp. lxxvii–lxxxiii, Falcon & Lefebvre (Salmieri), pp. 188–206.

Note 757

What is special . . . what is particular: On special, see II 3 736^{b}4n, and, on particular, II 1 734^{b}18n(4).

Note 758

This [the particular] is the substance: See II 1 734^{b}18n.

Note 759
This something: See II 1 734^{b}18n.

Note 760
Everything is shifted not into any random thing but into its opposite: "Things that are neither contraries nor composed of contraries could not displace (*existêsi*) each other from their nature. But since no random thing is naturally disposed to be affected and to affect, but rather things that have a contrariety or are contraries, it is necessary for the affecter and the affected to be like—in fact, the same—in genus (*genos*), but unlike and contrary in species (*eidos*)" (*GC* I 7 328^{b}28–34).

Note 761
It becomes (*gignetai*) female, if insofar as it is Coriscus or Socrates, it becomes not like its father but like its mother: The subject of *gignetai* (3rd person singular) is unspecified. Sometimes it refers to a movement, sometimes to an embryo or offspring of some sort. Usually context makes clear which is intended. When a grammatical subject is needed I have added "the result" as suitably neutral.

Note 762
And in this way too, of course, in the case of females: Secluding καὶ ἐπὶ τῶν ἀρρένων with OCT and Peck-3; Louis-3, Platt, and Lefebvre retain to give, "And in this way, of course, both in the case of males and in the case of females."

Note 763
Some of the movements of the parts as well are present in them actively, others potentially, as has often been said: See, for example, II 3 737^{a}18–30.

Note 764
We must take the following as universal hypotheses (*hupotheseis*): "The hypotheses are the starting-points of demonstrations" (*Met.* V 1 1013^{a}15–16).

Note 765
Socrates, father, mother, whoever she may be, are among the particulars: See again II 1 734^{b}18n(4).

Note 766
What moves (except for the primary mover) is moved in return with a certain movement: The primary mover must be unmoved, otherwise it would not be primary.

Note 767
These things have been spoken about in the determinations concerning affecting and being affected: The reference—also found at *DA* II 5 407^{a}1—is probably to *GC* I 6–7, in particular the following passage from I 7: "The same account,

though, must be assumed to apply to affecting and being affected, just as to being moved and moving. For something is also said to be a mover in two ways. For [1] that in which the starting-point of movement is present seems to move things (for the starting-point is primary among the causes), and again [2] the last [mover] in relation to the moved and the [thing's] coming to be. Likewise where the affecter is concerned. For we also say that a doctor cures and that wine does. Now in the case of movement nothing prevents the first mover from being immovable, in some cases this is even necessary, but the last is always a moved mover. And in the case of affection, while the first is unaffectable, the last is also itself affected. For things that do not have the same matter affect while being unaffectable, for example, the craft of medicine (for this produces health but is not at all affected by what is being cured), whereas the food affects and is itself somehow affected. For it is heated, cooled, or affected in some other way at the same time as it affects. The craft of medicine, though, serves as starting-point, while the food serves as the last thing and the one making contact. So things capable of affecting that do not have their shape in matter are unaffectable, whereas those that do have it in matter are affectable. For the matter, we say, is in alike, (one might almost say) the same, for either of the two opposites, being, as it were the genus, and something capable of being hot is necessarily heated if what is capable of heating is present and comes near. That is why, as has just been said, some things capable of affecting are unaffected while others are affectable. And it is the same way in the case of things capable of affecting as in the case of movement. For there the first mover is unmoved, and in the case of the affecters, the first is unaffectable" (324^{a}24–^{b}13).

Note 768

Maintain the sameness of shape: Reading διαμένειν ὁμοίαν τὴν μορφήν with OCT; Louis-3 and Peck-3 read διανέμειν ὁμοίως τὴν τροφήν ("distribute the nourishment evenly throughout"); Platt reads διανέμειν ὁμοίαν τὴν μορφήν ("arrange their shape symmetrically").

Note 769

The parts thus become qualitatively different (*alloia*): *Alloiôsis* is in particular qualitative change or alteration: "There is alteration (*alloiôsis*) when the underlying subject persists and is perceptible but change occurs in the attributes that belong to it, whether these are contraries or intermediates" (*GC* I 4 319^{b}10–12); "There is alteration only in things that are said to be intrinsically affected by perceptibles" (*Ph.* VII 3 245^{b}4–5).

Note 770

The disease called satyriasis: Perhaps elephantiasis or a stage thereof.

Note 771

For in this too, because a large quantity of non-concocted flux or pneuma is diverted to the parts of the face, the face appears to be that of another animal, that is, of a satyr: Reading καὶ γὰρ ἐν τούτῳ διὰ ῥεύματος ἢ πνεύματος ἀπέπτου πλῆθος εἰς μόρια τοῦ προσώπου παρεμπεσόντος ἄλλου ζῴου καὶ σατύρου φαίνεται τὸ πρόσωπον with Louis-3 and Lefebvre; OCT brackets ἢ πνεύματος ("or of pneuma"); Peck-3 brackets the entire sentence as "probably a marginal note which has crept into the text" and because he thinks "non-concocted pneuma" to be meaningless (p. 413 n*a*).

Note 772
Certain of the physicists: See *PA* I 1 641ᵃ7n.

Note 773
Those who speak of the cause of female and male as Empedocles and Democritus do say things that are in another way impossible: See IV 1 764ᵃ1–765ᵃ3.

Note 774
There are certain people who say that the semen, though one, is like a universal seed-bed (*panspermian*) consisting of many [seeds]: The notion of a *panspermia* comes from Anaxagoras. See DK 59B4a = TEGP 13 F4: "There are many things of all sorts in all composites, namely, seeds of all things having all sorts of forms, colors, and tastes." But Aristotle applies the notion to Democritus as well (*Ph.* III 4 203ᵃ21–23).

Note 775
Which is just what is also produced when there is no deformation involved: See I 18 724ᵇ32n.

Note 776
Those who make jibes (*hoi skôptontes*): *Skôptein* is often translated as "joking" but seems closer in meaning to "jibing" or "mocking," or "putting down," since "the person who jibes (*skôptôn*) is the one who aims to expose faults of soul or body" (*Po.* II = Janko, p. 37). Wit—jibing well—is thus "well-educated wanton aggression (*pepaideumenê hubris*)" (*Rh.* II 12 1389b11–12). It is discussed at *NE* IV 8.

Note 777
Now Democritus said that monsters come to be because two semens fall [into the uterus], [1] one setting [the menses] in movement earlier, [2] the other later, and this latter, once it issues forth, arrives in the uterus, so that the parts [of the embryo] grow together and become confused: = DK 68A146. Reading δύο γονὰς πίπτειν, τὴν μὲν πρότερον ὁρμήσασαν τὴν δ' ὕστερον καὶ ταύτην ἐξελθοῦσαν ἐλθεῖν εἰς τὴν ὑστέραν with Louis-3 for OCT τὴν μὲν πρότερον ὁρμήσασαν <καὶ μὴ ἐξελθοῦσαν> τὴν δ' ὕστερον καὶ ταύτην [ἐξελθοῦσαν] ἐλθεῖν εἰς τὴν ὑστέραν; Peck-3 obelizes καὶ ταύτην ἐξελθοῦσαν ἐλθεῖν εἰς τὴν ὑστέραν, which Platt also thinks to be corrupt (he reads συμπίπτειν for πίπτειν and ἐπελθοῦσαν for ἐξελθοῦσαν). The idea is that movements started by [1] get confused by those later started by [2] (see IV 3 768ᵇ10), so that together they end up misshaping the embryo's parts.

Note 778
But in the birds, he says, since mating always takes place quickly, both the eggs and their color become confused: = DK 68A146. Color being, as usual, that of yolk and white. Multiple matings occurring quickly are like single matings producing two semens.

Note 779
It is better not to go the long way around, passing the short one by: The thought seems to be that Democritus practices economy of explanation by explaining confusion in egg color in essentially the same way as monsters.

Note 780
When the yolks are continuous, with nothing keeping them asunder, from these, chicks that are monstrous come to be, having one body and head but four legs and four wings. This is because the upper parts come to be earlier from the white, the nourishment for them being dispensed from the yolk, whereas the lower part develops later and its nourishment is one and indivisible: "The last words are obscurely expressed but the argument runs thus: 'The head and the body are formed from one spot in the white, the yolk only serving as further nourishment to them; hence the double yolk does not cause the head and body to be doubled. But the limbs are formed later, drawing their nourishment and material from the yolk *alone*; hence, as there are two yolks, the limbs are doubled'" (Platt, n6).

Note 781
The large number of eggs are set in a row: And so are less likely to grow together.

Note 782
In many cases the offspring of these are born blind: And are incomplete until their eyes open.

Note 783
[1] Due to what cause [animals produce complete or incomplete offspring] happens and [2] due to what cause they are multiparous must be stated later: [1] at IV 6; [2] at IV 4 771^{a}17–^{b}14.

Note 784
The monster too is among the offspring that are not similar to their parents: See IV 3 767^{b}5–6.

Note 785
Coincident (*sumptôma*): As at *Top.* IV 5 126^{b}36, 39, *Ph.* II 8 199^{a}1, and *Rh.* I 9 1367^{b}25 (where it is equivalent to "by luck"). Here the coincident is a monstrous birth.

Note 786
So-called runts: See II 8 749^{a}1–6.

Note 787
The monster is among the things that are contrary to nature, not contrary to all nature, though, but the one that holds for the most part: See, on nature, *PA* I 1 641ᵇ12n, and on holding for the most part, *GA* I 18 725ᵇ17n.

Note 788
There is a vine that some people call "smoky," and if it bears black grapes they do not judge it a monster because it is in the habit of doing this very often: See Theophrastus, *Enquiry into Plants* II.3.2.

Note 789
Docked: See I 17 721ᵇ17n.

Note 790
And excesses: Accepting OCT's addition of καὶ πλεονασμοί.

Note 791
These have been seen in *complete* animals, as was just said: At IV 4 771ᵃ5–6.

Note 792
The parts that have control: See II 6 742ᵃ32–ᵇ3.

Note 793
The very thing that we wonder at is a cause not to wonder: Compare: "Nothing would make a man who knows geometry wonder more than if the diagonal *were* to turn out to be commensurable" (*Met.* I 2 983ᵃ19–21).

Note 794
Of there being some animals that are large, others smaller, others intermediate, we have previously stated the cause: A reference, perhaps, to *PA* IV 10 686ᵇ29–32: "And, further, as the heat that rises becomes less and the earthy material becomes greater animals grow smaller and many-footed, and in the end become footless and stretched out on the ground."

Note 795
Due to what possible cause does it not complete [just] one animal having [the relevant] size, just as there in the example the fig-juice is not separated in composing a certain quantity, but rather the more it is put into and the more it is, so much the greater is what is curdled: Reading διὰ τίνα ποτ' αἰτίαν οὐχ ἓν ἀποτελεῖ ζῷον μέγεθος ἔχον, ὥσπερ ἐνταῦθα ὁ ὀπὸς οὐ κεχώρισται τῷ συνιστάναι ποσόν τι, ἀλλ' ὅσῳπερ ἂν εἰς πλεῖον ἔλθῃ καὶ πλείων τοσούτῳ τὸ πηγνύμενόν ἐστι μεῖζον; with OCT; Peck-3 reads ἀλλ' ἐν τούτῳ τῷ περριτώματι πλείω γίνεται; ("but instead several offspring are formed out of the residue") post ὁ ὀπὸς and secludes οὐ κεχώρισται τῷ συνιστάναι ποσόν τι, ἀλλ' ὅσῳπερ ἂν εἰς πλεῖον ἔλθῃ καὶ πλείων τοσούτῳ τὸ πηγνύμενόν ἐστι μεῖζον.

Note 796
Cotyledons: See II 7 745^{b}33n.

Note 797
It appears that the residue of the female and that from the male need to stand in some proportional relationship to each other: See IV 2 767^{a}15–28.

Note 798
The human, however, plays a double game (*epamphoterizei*) **in all the modes of generation:** The verb *epamphoterizein* is used to characterize ambiguous statements (Plato, *Rep.* V 479c3) and to describe things that lie halfway between others. Thus water and "play a double game," because they have tendencies to move up (relative to earth) and down (relative to fire) (*Ph.* III 5 205^{a}28). See also *Pol.* VII 13 1332^{b}1–3.

Note 799
For [children] come to be at seven months, at ten months, and at the intermediate times. For even those of eight months do live, but less often: "The other animals bring birth to completion in one way. For there is one time determined for the birth in all cases. But for humankind, alone among animals, there are many times. For there are seven-month, eight-month, and nine-month births, and most of all ten-month ones. But some women even reach the eleventh month. Those that are born earlier than seven months are never capable of life. The seven-month ones become viable (*gonima*) first, but most are weak (that is why too they swaddle them in wool), and many have some of the ducts undivided—for example, those of the ears and nostrils. But as they grow they become articulated, and many such babies live. As for the eight-month ones, around Egypt and in certain places where the women are good at bringing forth timely births, and bear and deliver many children easily, and where once born they are capable of living, even if they are born monstrous, there the eight-month ones live and are reared, whereas in the places around Greece few in all are preserved, and the majority perish" (*HA* VII 584^{a}33–^{b}12). The months referred to are lunar months. The Hippocratic view was that some seven-month babies live, while all eight-month ones die. See Littré VII.438, 452, VIII.612.
The cause may be made out on the basis of what has just been said; it has been spoken about in the *Problems*: No such discussion is found in our *Problems*.

Note 800
In these eddies too as the water is carried along and, having movement, collides with something, from the one [eddy] two compositions are produced that have the same movement. It happens in the same way in the case of the embryos as well: "Suppose the water in an eddy to be whirling round the same way as the hands of a clock; if this eddy strikes a stick standing up in the river it will be split into two new smaller eddies still whirling in the same way. The movements which take place in the embryo are like such an eddy, and if e.g. the cells which are to form the little

finger in the embryo are 'split,' they will form two such fingers, the same movement going on in each set of cells" (Platt, n4). See also *Insomn.* 3 461^{a}8–13.

Note 801
Miscarriages (*amblôseis*): See III 9 758^{b}6n.

Note 802
Outgrowths are different from multiparity in the way just mentioned: At IV 4 772^{b}13–773^{a}2.

Monsters (*terata*) **differ from these in that most of them are due to embryos growing together:** *Terata* here must be out-and-out monsters, not merely offspring that, though otherwise normal, are not like their parents (see IV 3 767^{b}5–6). Monstrosity is a matter of degree. Peck-3 secludes the entire sentence ("Outgrowths . . . together").

Note 803
Dry nourishment . . . fine-grained filtered nourishment: More exactly, the useless residues from the nourishment.
Perinthus: A town in Thrace.

Note 804
As well as outgrowths of excess parts: Secluding ἢ ἐλλειπόντων ("as well as outgrowths of excess parts or of their deficiency") with OCT; Louis-3, Peck-3, and Platt retain.

Note 805
In some animals superfetation does not occur at all: "There are two kinds of superfetation; either ova produced at the same period may be fertilized by two different impregnations, or the ova may themselves be produced at two different periods and the earlier and later ova may then be fertilized by earlier and later impregnations. A. speaks only of the latter (the former is now generally called superfecundation)" (Platt, n3).

Note 806
Instead [such] embryos fall out in about the same condition as so-called premature births: Reading ἐκπίπτει with OCT and Louis-3; Peck-3 reads ἐκπέμπει for ("[the mother] ejects such embryos"].

Note 807
Purgation [of menses] . . . corresponds to ejaculation (*aphrodidiasai*) **in males:** *Aphrodisiazein* usually means "have sexual intercourse," but here more probably refers to ejaculation or the emission of semen.

Note 808
Menses is seed that is non-concocted, as was said previously: At I 19 726^{b}30–727^{a}4.

Note 809

In the females, then, it is the coming down below of the uterus, and in the males the drawing up of the testes, that is farther along the route (*pro hodou*) to mating: For a partial explanation in the case of the males, see I 12 719^{b}2–4, and in that of the female, III 1 750^{b}35.

Note 810

The uterus in animals of this sort does not close up [during gestation] because of the spare residue for purgation: The spare residue needs an opening from the uterus in order to be emitted.

Note 811

[The hare] alone of the animals has hairs under its feet and inside the jaws: Though a certain whale has one of these features: "The moustache-whale instead of teeth has hairs in its mouth resembling pigs' bristles" (*HA* III 12 519^{a}23–24).

Note 812

Solid-hoofed pigs exist in certain places: "The pig genus plays a double game. For in Illyria and Paeonia there are solid-hoofed pigs" (*HA* II 1 499^{b}11–13).

Note 813

775^{a}11a–c: Added in OCT, as in most editions, from the Latin and Arabic translations.

While inside the mother, the female takes more time to get disaggregated than the male does, but once having come out everything gets completed earlier in females than in males—for example, puberty, prime of life, and old age: "It is fitting for the women to marry when they are around eighteen years of age, the men when they are thirty-seven, or a little before. For, at such an age, sexual union will occur when their bodies are in their prime, and, with respect to losing their capacity to procreate, they will also decline together at the appointed times" (*Pol.* VIII 16 1335^{a}28–32); "Since we have determined the starting-point of the age at which men and women should start their sexual coupling, let us also determine for how long a time it is fitting for them to render public service by procreating. For the offspring of parents who are too old, like those of parents who are too young, are imperfect in both body and in thought, whereas those of people who have reached old age are weak. That is why the length of the time in question should be in accord with the time when thought is in its prime. In most cases, this occurs—as some of the poets who measure age in periods of seven years have said—around the time of the fiftieth year. So when they have exceeded this age by four or five years they should be released from bringing children into the light of day" (1335^{b}26–37).

Note 814

We must suppose femaleness to be a natural deformation: Unlike the case in males where, though deformities are more common, they are not natural. See IV 3 765^{b}8–15n.

Note 815
Disaggregation is concoction: "Disaggregating . . . is the aggregating of things of the same genus, since this results in removing what is alien" (*GC* I 2 329ᵇ27–28). Thus in embryogenesis disaggregation results in the articulation of the various parts of the embryo, including those that distinguish males from females.

Note 816
Their disaggregation does not occur in equal times; rather [if it did] it is necessary that the male be late or the female early: The female develops more slowly, so if the male twin developed at the same rate as the female, he would be born later than normal for a male, whereas the female twin would be born earlier than normal for a female if she developed at the same rate as the male one.

Note 817
Nation (*ethnos*): A nation occupied a larger territory than a city (*polis*), had a larger population, and a less tight political order. It did not need to have a single town or urban center, and could consist of many scattered villages. See *Pol.* VII 2 1324ᵇ11–12 for examples.

Note 818
Hard work exercises their pneuma so that they are capable of holding it: Here, as often elsewhere, pneuma is, or is a sort of, breath.

Note 819
A mole: A uterine hydatidiform mole is a rare mass or growth that forms inside the uterus at the beginning of a pregnancy. It results from the abnormal fertilization of the egg, resulting in an abnormal fetus. There is little or no growth of fetal tissue. But the placenta grows in the usual way, eventually forming a mass of placental tissue.

Note 820
The cause of this affection [uterine moles] has been spoken about in the *Problems*: There is nothing about this in the extant *Problems*.

Note 821
The embryo is affected in the very same way in the uterus as par-boiled things are in cases of boiling (*hepsomenois*): "Boiling in general is concoction by wet heat of the [matter] present in the liquid in the thing being boiled, but the name is said in the strict sense only of things being cooked by boiling. This, as was stated [at *Mete.* IV 3 380ᵃ23–25], is either pneumaticized or watery. The concoction comes about due to the fire in the liquid. For what is cooked on griddles is broiled (for it is affected by the external heat and, as for the liquid [that is, the fat] in which it is contained, it dries this up, taking it into itself). But what is boiled produces the contrary effect (for its water is segregated out of it due to the heat in the water outside it). That is why boiled meats are drier than broiled ones. For

boiled things do not draw liquid into themselves, since the external heat masters the internal. But if a thing's internal heat did master, it would draw it into itself" (*Mete.* IV 3 380ᵇ13–24); "Things can be boiled that are capable of becoming more coarse-grained, smaller, heavier, or of which a part is of this sort, while a part is the contrary sort, and because of this disaggregating, part becomes coarse-grained and part fine-grained, as milk disaggregates into whey and curd" (381ª4–8). On par-boiling, see next note.

Note 822

Par-boiling too is a sort of non-concoction: "Par-boiling is the [species of] non-concoction contrary to boiling. And so the contrary of boiling, and the primary sort of par-boiling, would be non-concoction of the [matter] in the body due to a deficiency of heat in the surrounding liquid. (That deficiency of heat is presence of cold has already been stated [at *Mete.* IV 2 380ª8].) This comes about because of another sort of movement. For the heat doing the concocting is expelled, and the deficiency of heat is due either to the quantity of cold in the liquid or due to the quantity of it in the thing being boiled. For then the result is that the heat in the liquid is too great to cause no movement at all, but too small to make it even and concoct throughout. That is why things are harder when they are par-boiled than when they are boiled, and the liquid parts more distinguished" (*Mete.* IV 3 381ª12–22).

Note 823

Woman alone among the animals is subject to troubles of the uterus (*husterikon*): Hence our word "hysterical."

Note 824

It also quite reasonably happens due to an of-necessity cause: That is, as well as from a final cause, or for the sake of something. See, for example, *GA* II 4 755ª22–24, *PA* I 1 642ª1–3.

Note 825

Of all [secretions], though, nourishment is the sweetest and most concocted, so that when a capacity of this sort is subtracted it is necessary for what remains to be salty and ill-flavored: "In those animals with a bladder, when the residue comes out, an earthy salt is deposited in their cavities. For the sweet and drinkable part gets used up, because of its lightness, for the flesh" (*PA* IV 1 676ª33–36).

Note 826

That is why [the fetus] comes out and changes its process of generation, as now having what is its own, and no longer getting what is not its own, which is the time in which milk becomes useful: Before the fetus comes out of its mother as a newborn infant, it is still incomplete, in the sense of not yet having everything it needs to be a complete human being, that is, the things that are its own. When it is born it has these and is now no longer getting what would at that point have to be things that are not its own, since it is already fully equipped with the ones that are its own. Yet there is a sense in which, as not yet able to feed itself and needing its mother's milk, rather than, as before, the formative or molding growth factor from her residues, it is still incomplete.

Note 827
The controlling part of the animal: See *PA* I 1 640^{b}28n.

Note 828
From the [upper part] too the spermatic residue is secreted, due to the cause mentioned in the starting accounts: See II 4 738^{b}15–18, 7 747^{a}19–20.

Note 829
The starting-point of the voice is there, and itself becomes altered when what moves it becomes altered: See V 7, especially 787^{b}19–788^{a}16.

Note 830
In the former the menses, in the latter emission of seed: Reading ταῖς μὲν τὴν τῶν καταμηνίων, τοῖς δὲ τὴν τοῦ σπέρματος πρόεσιν with Louis-3, Lefebvre, and Platt; OCT and Peck-3 seclude.

Note 831
As because of its concoction, it is possible to take either the one just mentioned: Namely, the fetus no longer taking up the large quantity of residue produced (IV 8 776^{b}25).

Note 832
That milk has the same nature as the secretion from which each animal comes to be is clear, and was stated previously: At II 4 739^{b}25–26.

Note 833
"A white pus that comes into existence on the tenth day of the eighth month": = DK31 B68 = TEGP 134 F84.

Note 834
The milk is produced as something useful for becoming its nourishment: Reading πρὸς τὴν γιγνομένην τροφήν with OCT, Louis-3; Peck-3 secludes; Platt reads πρὸς τὴν γενομένου τροφήν ("for the nourishment of the newborn").

Note 835
[The genus] of those with long hairs in their tails: See III 5 755^{b}18n.

Note 836
The cause, though, of long life in any sort of animal is its being blended in much the same way as the surrounding air: See IV 2 767^{a}28–35.

And because of certain other coincidents of its nature that we will speak about later on: In *On Length and Shortness of Life*.
Coincidents (*sumptômat*): See IV 4 770ᵇ6n.

Note 837

For the month is a period common to both: Reading ὁ γὰρ μεὶς κοινὴ περίοδός ἐστιν ἀμφοτέρων with OCT; Platt secludes on the grounds that "a period common to both sun and moon would be one which contained both the solar and lunar periods exactly" (n7). But, as Peck-3 explains, "The month, taken in the sense of a lunation, *i.e.*, the period from one new moon to another, or the time required by the moon to go through all its phases once, is, literally and properly speaking, not a private period of the *moon's*, but, as Aristotle says, a joint period of the *moon and sun*, since it is the moon's position relative to the sun which determines how much of the moon's disk is illuminated. If the moon were self-luminous, there would be no phases, and therefore there could be no 'phase-period.' This is made even more clear if we consider that the moon does not in fact possess a 'period' proper to itself, pertaining to the moon's own actual motion, and not to the mere illumination of its own surface by another body, and it is a period which differs in length from the lunation or 'phase period' . . . This is the period known in astronomy as the 'sidereal period,' i.e., the time taken by the moon to return again to its same apparent position among the stars—*not* to return into conjunction with the sun. The duration of this period is roughly 27 days 8 hours, as against the 29 days 13 hours for the 'phase period.' Aristotle is therefore quite correct in stating that the 'month,' by which, as the context clearly shows, he means the 'phase period,' is a joint period of the sun and moon" (Peck-3, pp. 478–479 n*c*).

Note 838

In accord with the movement of the winds (*pneumatôn*): See IV 2 766ᵇ31–767ᵃ13.
The things that grow out of these or are in these (*toutois*): That is, in the sea and in things that are of the nature of liquid, since "the wet is characteristic of life" (II 1 733ᵃ11).

Note 839

Lacking in control . . . have more control: See *PA* I 1 640ᵇ28n.

Note 840

A wind too has a sort of life and a coming to be and passing away: A wind, such as the north wind or south wind, is analogized to a river or spring, and is not just air in movement, but has a specific source and a distinctive cause (*Mete.* II 4 360ᵃ17–ᵇ26). Hence "wind and air are more a this something and a form than earth is" (*GC* I 3 318ᵇ33–34).

Note 841

And of the revolutions of these stars there may perhaps be other starting-points: Namely, the immovable mover.

Note 842
Nature, then, tends to measure ... but cannot bring this about in an exact way:
See I 18 725^{b}17n.

BOOK V

Note 843
Differences of color, whether of body and hairs or of feathers: Reading καὶ
χρώματος ἢ σώματος καὶ τριχῶν ἢ πτερῶν διαφοράς; OCT, Louis-3, and Peck-3
seclude ἢ σώματος ("whether of body").

Note 844
**Where these affections and all the others of these sorts are concerned, however,
we must no longer consider the mode of cause to be the same:** The processes of
generation and gestation discussed previously are the same, and have the same
cause, in the case of each individual member of a kind, but we should no longer
consider that to be so in the case of eye color, hair color, and so on.

Note 845
**Nor, in some cases, does the affection lead to the account (*logos*) of the sub-
stance:** That is to the account of the essence, that is, the formal cause. See *PA* I 1
639^{a}16n (this vol.).
**But rather, as coming of necessity, one must refer to the matter and the moving
starting-point as the causes:** That is, to the material cause (the menses) and the
efficient cause (the male semen).

Note 846
Just as was said at the start in the first accounts: The reference is to *PA* I, especially 1 640^{a}3–^{b}4.
**It is not because each thing comes to be of a certain sort (*poion ti*) that it is of a
certain sort (*poion ti*):** See *PA* I 1 640^{b}6n.

Note 847
**The coming to be follows along with the substance and is for the sake of the
substance, and not it for the sake of the coming to be:** It is the form (essence,
substance) in the male semen that handicrafts the matter (the female menses) to
produce an offspring with that form, thereby functioning as the major determi-
nant of the process of its coming to be, which process is for the sake of the offspring, not the offspring for the sake of the process.

Note 848
**The ancient physicists, however, thought the contrary to be so. The cause of this
is that they did not see that the causes were many, but saw only that consisting
of the matter and that of the movement—and these indistinctly. But to that**

consisting of the account and that of the end they gave no consideration: The following texts elaborate: "We have, then, briefly and in summary fashion gone through which thinkers have spoken and in what ways about the starting-points and about the truth. Nonetheless we have got this much at least from them, that of those who have spoken about a starting-point and a cause none has mentioned any outside of those we distinguished in our works on nature, rather it is evident that they are all in some vague way touching upon these. For some speak of the starting-point as matter, whether they posit one or many. . . . All these thinkers, then, latched on to this sort of cause, and so too did those who spoke of air, fire, water, or something denser than fire and more fine-grained than air—for some have also said that the primary element is like this. So these thinkers latched on to this cause alone, and certain others onto the starting-point from which movement derives—for example, those who made love and strife or understanding and love a starting-point. But the essence and the substance no one has presented in a perspicuous way. . . . And that for the sake of which actions, changes, and movements take place they speak of as in a way a cause, but not in this way—that is, not in the way in which it is its nature to be a cause. For those who speak of understanding or love posit these causes as good, but they do not speak as if anything is or comes to be for the sake of these things, but as if movements arise from them. In the same way too those who say that the one or being is such a nature say that it is a cause of the substance, but not that anything is or comes to be for its sake, so that in a way they do and in a way they do not say that the good is a cause, since they do not say it is so unconditionally but coincidentally" (*Met.* I 7 988ᵃ18–ᵇ16); "It is clear even from what we previously said that all thinkers seem to have been inquiring into the [four] causes that we mentioned in the *Physics*, and that we cannot mention any outside these. But [they touched upon] these vaguely, and so in a way they have all been discussed before, and in a way they have not been discussed at all. For early philosophy concerning all things seemed to speak inarticulately, because it was young and at the starting-point" (10 993ᵃ11–17). On the ancient physicists, see *PA* I 1 641ᵃ7n.

Note 849
Either as being for the sake of something or as being for-the-sake-of-which: Either as a means or as an end.

Note 850
When the young are born, especially those born incomplete, they are in the habit of sleeping, because inside the mother too, when they first acquire perception, they are continually asleep: Only what has perception can sleep, because "sleeping and waking are affections of this perceptual organ [namely, touch]" (*Somn.* 2 455ᵃ25–26).

Note 851
Living most of all belongs to being awake, because of perception: "'Living' is said of things in two ways, and we must take the one in accord with activity, since

it seems to be called 'living' in a fuller sense" (*NE* I 7 1098ª5–7). See also *GA* I 23 731ᵇ4n.

Note 852
It is necessary in any case for these animals to sleep most of the time because the growth and the heaviness lie in the upper places (we have said elsewhere that this is the cause of sleep): The reference is to *Somn.* 3 456ᵇ17–28 (II 6 744ᵇ7n).

Note 853
It is evident that they wake up even in the uterus (this is clear in the *Dissections* and in the oviparous animals): "A. means that the embryo may be extracted in a wakeful condition from the eggs of ovipara or from being cut out from the mother in mammalia" (Platt, n3).

Note 854
Some are greenish (*aigôpa*): Literally, "like those of a goat."

Note 855
[Some horses] have eyes of different colors (*heteroglaukoi*): Literally, "have one eye that is blue."

Note 856
Blueness is a sort of weakness: See V 1 779ᵇ21–34.

Note 857
If indeed, it is as we stated previously in *De Sensu*, and prior to that in *De Anima*, namely, that this organ of perception is composed of water: The reference is to *Sens.* 2 and to *DA* III 1 425ª3–6: "The perceptual organs are composed of two of these simple bodies [or elements] only, namely, air and water (for the eye-jelly is composed of water, the organ of hearing of air, and the organ of smell of one or the other of these), whereas fire either belongs to none or is common to all (for nothing is capable of perceiving without heat)."

Note 858
Some eyes contain too much liquid, others too little, to be proportional to the movement, others the proportional amount: See V 1 780ª1–7.

Note 859
As for the eyes intermediate between these, they differ at this point by the more and the less: See *PA* I 4 644ª18n (this vol.).

Note 860
The light is weaker by night, and at the same time indeed (*hama gar kai*) liquid in general (*holôs*) becomes more difficult to move in the night: The meaning, though a bit obscure—"I do not see what these words mean" (Platt, n4)—is

presumably something like this: "Light is the activity of this, of the transparent insofar as it is transparent . . . when it is made actually transparent by fire or something of that sort, such as the body above" (*DA* II 7 418ᵇ11–13). Thus to the extent that any liquid, whether in the eye or elsewhere, is transparent (that is, potentially transparent), it is made actually transparent, and so is in that way moved, by the light of, for example, the sun. As less actually transparent at night, then, the liquid in the eye is less easily moved by (normally) visible objects, and so its sight of them is less keen.

Note 861

The stronger movement knocks aside the weaker one: See also *Sens.* 7 477ᵃ15, 22, and, for different applications of the principle, *NE* VII 14 1154ᵃ27, X 5 1175ᵇ8. The point here is that if the movement of the transparent fluid in the eye, insofar as it is transparent, is much stronger than the movement caused by the visible object, it will knock aside the latter, making the object invisible. A similar explanation is given in the case of memory: "A problem might be raised as to how, when the affection is present but the thing producing it is absent, what is not present is ever remembered. For it is clear that one must understand the affection, which is produced by means of perception in the soul, and in that part of the body in which it is, as being like a sort of picture, the having of which we say is memory. For the movement that occurs stamps a sort of imprint, as it were, of the perceptible object, as people do who seal things with a signet ring. That is also why memory does not occur in those who are subject to a lot of change, because of some affection or because of their age, just as if the change and the seal were falling on running water. In others, because of wearing down, as in the old parts of buildings, and because of the hardness of what receives the affection, the imprint is not produced" (*Mem.* 1 450ᵃ25–ᵇ5).

Note 862

The one that is intermediate between little and much liquid is the best sight. For it is neither so small that it gets disturbed and hinders the movement of the colors, nor so large in quantity that it is made difficult to move: The intermediate in question is the so-called "perceptual mean" (*DA* III 7 431ᵃ11), which is the constituent in a perceptual part that functions like a laboratory balance or weighing scale enabling it to detect differences in proper perceptibles, which activate it by tilting it, as it were, one way or another: "The mean is capable of discerning, since in relation to each extreme it becomes the other. And just as what is to perceive white and black must be neither of them actively, although both potentially (and similarly too in the case of the other perceptual capacities), so in the case of touch it must be neither hot nor cold" (*DA* II 11 424ᵃ5–10). Depending on the makeup of these perceptibles, the activation of the perceptual part is either pleasant or painful: "Things—for example, the high-pitched, sweet, or salty—are pleasant when, being pure and unmixed, they are brought into the ratio, since they are pleasant then. And in general a mixture, a consonance, is more pleasant than either high or low pitch, and for taste what can be [further] heated or cooled. For the perceptual capacity is a ratio, and excessive things dissolve or destroy it" (III 2 426b3–7). The perception of a proper perceptible is pleasant, then, provided it is within the limits determined by—or consonant with—the structural ratio of the perceptual capacity (and is painful otherwise). More precisely, since a perceptual capacity functions better within some areas of its range of operation than others, so that we see better in brighter light than in dimmer, perception is pleasant in the optimal range, the range of maximal consonance: "in the case of each perceptual capacity, the best activity will be . . . the activity of the subject that is in the best condition in relation to the most excellent of its objects. And this activity will be the most complete and most pleasant" (*NE* X 4 1174^{b}18–20). See also *HA* I 10 492^{a}4.

Note 863
Eye-jelly (*korê*): See *HA* I 9 491^{b}20–21 (this vol.).

Note 864
White (*leukon*), **because black is not transparent—for this is what black is, namely, the non-transparent:** Thus *leukon* here means "clear," or "the color of light."

Note 865
The human alone turns gray, and among the other animals the horse alone has hairs that whiten noticeably in old age: "It is strange that A. should not have known that dogs go grey. Even sea-lions do" (Platt, n1).

Note 866
It will be capable of seeing farther: Secluding ὥσπερ εἰ καὶ ἐγγύθεν ("just as it can from close at hand") with OCT; Louis-3, Peck-3, and Platt retain.

Note 867
The ray of sight: *Opsis* means "sight," or "organ of sight," but here seems to refer to a ray of some sort.
[Some say] that seeing is due to the ray of sight going out from the eye: See Empedocles DK B84 = TEGP 151 F105 = *Sens.* 437^{b}26–438^{a}2, and Plato, *Ti.* 45b–46c. Both theories involve rays emitted from the eyes passing through a transparent medium and being reflected back.

Note 868
Of discerning the differences correctly, then, the perceptual organ is the cause, as in the case of sight: See V 1 780^{b}29–31.

Note 869
The ducts (*poroi*) **of all the perceptual organs, as has been said previously in De Sensu, run to the heart, or to its analogue in animals that have no heart:** The term *poros* occurs but rarely in the *Parva Naturalia* (at *Sens.* 2 438^{b}14, *Somn.* 3 457^{a}13, 26, ^{b}13, *Juv.* 13 473^{b}3, 27 480^{b}16), and only once in *De Anima* (at II 9 422^{a}3). But the connection of sense organs to the heart is firm doctrine there (*Sens.*

2 439^{a}1–2, *Juv.* 3 469^{a}2–23) as elsewhere (*PA* II 1 647^{a}24–31, 10 656^{a}27–29). Compare *GC* I 9 327^{b}34–327^{a}1: "One would more properly speak about ducts in this connection as veins of susceptibility to affection, just like [veins of ores] stretching continuously in mines."

Note 870
The perceptual organ of hearing . . . is composed of air: See II 6 743^{b}35–744^{a}5.
The connate pneuma: The pneuma internal and essential to the sense organ as opposed to that outside.
Breathing: Omitting καὶ εἰσπνοήν ("and inhalation") with some mss.

Note 871
It is because of [the structure of the ear duct] that learning comes about from what is said, so that we echo what we have heard: See V 7 786^{b}23–25n.

Note 872
The pneumatic part (*pneumatikô[i] moriô[i]*): Presumably, the lungs.

Note 873
For while moving [the pneuma] the instrument [or organ] is itself moved:
Reading κινεῖται γὰρ κινοῦν τὸ ὄργανον with OCT; Peck-3 secludes. The instrument is the pneumatic part (lungs), which in moving the pneuma is itself moved. The starting-point of the perceptual organ of hearing (the ear) is the heart (V 2 781^{a}20–23). Because the latter is situated near the former it is excessively moved during yawning or exhaling, distorting the sound-transmitting movements in the ear's connate pneuma, making it harder to hear than in (normal) inhalation. It is not clear why (normal) exhaling creates more movement in the lungs than in (normal) inhaling, but Aristotle may be thinking of cases in which, as in male ejaculation, the pneuma (breath) is forcefully expelled: "In the emission of seed, pneuma first leads it. And the actual emission makes it clear that it occurs due to pneuma. For nothing is thrown a long way without a pneumatic force (*bias pheumatikês*)" (*HA* VII 586^{a}15–17). See also *GA* II 4 737^{b}35–738^{a}1, IV 6 775^{b}1–2.

Note 874
Blends [of the surrounding air]: See IV 2 767^{a}29–32.

Note 875
And the ears seem to be filled with pneuma because of being a neighbor, due to the starting-point, of the pneumatic place: Reading καὶ τὰ ὦτα πληροῦσθαι δοκεῖ πνεύματος διὰ τὸ γειτνιᾶν τῇ ἀρχῇ τοῦ πνευματικοῦ τόπου for OCT * * * καὶ τὰ ὦτα πληροῦσθαι δοκεῖ πνεύματος διὰ τὸ γειτνιᾶν †τῇ ἀρχῇ τοῦ πνευματικοῦ τόπου†. Louis-3, Peck-3, and Platt read τὴν ἀρχὴν for τῇ ἀρχῇ ("because of its starting-point being a neighbor"), but the mss. reading, which gives the same meaning, can, I think, be preserved. The phrase τὸν πνευματικὸν τόπον is also used at *Pr.* XXXIII 5 962^{a}11, and refers, as here, to the location of the pneumatic

part (lungs), to which the starting-point of the perceptual organ of hearing (the ears)—namely, the heart—is a neighbor. The sentence, so understood, is best taken as continuing the discussion of hearing less well while yawning and exhaling, with the comment about seasons and environment treated as parenthetical.

Note 876
For the ducts of all the perceptual organs . . . , as in the case of sight: Secluded by Peck-3.

Note 877
Laconian hounds: See *HA* VI 20, which is devoted to these.

Note 878
The organ of perception is above (*anô*) them: "The sensitive part of the nose being above the nostrils in man, A. uses the term 'above' loosely for the position in any animal; he should rather have said 'behind'" (Platt, n5).

Note 879
The organ of perception is pure, that is, least earthy and bodily, and by nature, among animals with respect to size, man has the finest skin: Since the exactness under discussion is the exactness of the "perceptual capacities" (*tên aisthêseôn*) (V 2 781^{a}17), the organ of perception referred to is presumably that associated with the relevant capacity, whatever it is. The fineness of human skin presumably carries over to the membrane on the surface of this organ (781^{b}3–4).

Note 880
In matters concerning the seal too the nature (*hê phusis*) has produced things in a quite reasonable way: I take *hê phusis* to refer to the nature of the seal, but it might also be reasonably taken to refer to nature in general. See *PA* I 1 641^{b}12n.

Note 881
Hedgehogs (*chersaiôn echinôn*): Literally, "land echinus," as opposed to a sea echinus, or sea-urchin (V 3 783^{a}20).

Note 882
Whiteness and blackness, and the ones intermediate between these: "The [intermediate] colors result from the mixture of white and black" (*Sens.* 4 442^{a}12–13).

Note 883
What nature has produced the genus of hairs for the sake of in animals has been spoken about previously in the causes pertaining to the parts of animals: "Hairs are present in those that have them for the sake of shelter" (*PA* II 14 658^{a}18–19).

Note 884
The present methodical inquiry: See *PA* I 1 639^{a}1n (this vol.).

Note 885
Coarse . . . fine: See II 2 735ᵃ31n.
In some rarified (*manon*), in others dense (*puknon*): "The starting-point of all affections is condensation and rarefaction (*puknôsis kai manôsis*). For heavy and light, soft and hard, hot and cold, seem to be sorts of density or rarity. And condensation and rarefaction are aggregation and disaggregation, in virtue of which substances are said to come to be and pass away" (*Ph.* VIII 7 260ᵇ7–12). Skin that is *manon* has large ducts or pores as opposed to narrow ones, and the hairs follow suit. See *GA* V 3 782ᵃ34–ᵇ2, also 783ᵃ37–ᵇ2.

Note 886
But both hairs and their analogue come not from the flesh but from the skin, when the liquid evaporates and is exhaled in these. That is why coarse hairs come from coarse skin, fine hairs from fine skin: Reading ἐξατμίζοντος καὶ ἀναθυνιωμένου ἐν αὐτοῖς τοῦ ὑγροῦ. διὸ παχεῖαι μὲν ἐκ τοῦ παχέος λεπταὶ δὲ ἐκ τοῦ λεπτοῦ δέρματος γίγνονται. with OCT, Louis-3, and Lefebvre; Platt, followed by Peck-3, secludes.

Note 887
What is oily does not easily get dry: "[What is oily] becomes coarse-grained, then, due to both [heat and cold], but it does not become dry due to either (for neither the sun nor cold dries it), not only because it is viscous but because it contains air. For the water does not get dried out or boiled off due to the fire, because, due to the viscosity, it does not evaporate" (*Mete.* IV 7 383ᵇ33–384ᵃ2).

Note 888
The ones with skin that is most coarse do not have hairs that are more coarse [than others with such skin], due to the causes just mentioned: Coarseness in hairs is a function of two variables: duct or pore size and quantity of earthy material. Thus once ducts are big enough for the hairs to be coarse rather than fine, making them bigger will not necessarily result in hairs that are yet coarser.

Note 889
The skin on [the head] is coarsest and lies over a very great quantity of liquid: Namely, the liquid in the brain. See II 6 432ᵇ32.

Note 890
The exhalation (*anathumiasin*) in the hairs: "There are, we say, two exhalations, one vaporous and one smoky" (*Mete.* III 6 378ᵃ18–19); "smoky exhalation . . . is a compound (*koinon*) of air and earth" (*Sens.* 5 443ᵃ27–28). See also *GA* V 4 784ᵇ8–13.

Note 891
Sarmatian sheep: The ancient Sarmatians were a large Iranian confederation, closely related to the Scythians, eventually inhabiting the greater part of western

Scythia, roughly corresponding to modern Ukraine, southern Russia, northeastern Balkans, and Moldova.

Note 892
Sea-urchins that are used to treat stranguries: The eggs of sea-urchins were used as diuretics to treat this condition, which is caused by irritation or blockage at the base of the bladder, resulting in severe pain, a desire to urinate, and difficulty in doing so.

Note 893
The liquid is evaporated due to both—intrinsically by the heat, coincidentally by the cold (for the liquid goes out along with the heat; for there is no liquid without heat): "For as a thing's proper heat leaves it, its in-accord-with-nature liquid evaporates" (*Mete.* IV 1 379ª23–24).

Note 894
Whereas cold not only hardens but condenses, heat makes more rarified: The reference is to external (dry) heat and cold. See IV 7 776ª1n on the different effects of boiling (wet external heat) and broiling (dry external heat). The effects of the internal natural heat involved in concoction and embryogenesis are, of course, quite different.

Note 895
Among the birds the hibernating ones shed their feathers: A mysterious statement, since in fact only the common poorwill (a relative of the nightjar) is known to hibernate. Moreover, far from losing their feathers during cold winters, many birds fluff them up to keep themselves warm.

Note 896
The cause of the affection is a deficiency of hot liquid, and the oily ones among the liquids are most of all of this sort: "Oily things are not liable to putrefy. The cause is that they contain air, and air in relation to the other [elements] is fire, and fire does not become putrid" (*Long.* 5 466ª23–25); "For just as in dry things that have been burnt (for example, ash) some fire remains behind in them, so it is too in wet ones that have been concocted. For some part of the heat that was operative is left behind in them. That is why what is oily is light and rises to surface in liquids" (*PA* III 9 672ª6–9). The hotness in oily liquids, then, is internal natural heat, not the acquired heat of, for example, boiling water. The idea that air is like fire to the other elements is best explored in connection with the parallel claim that in the series of the elements in terms of their proper places, with fire highest up, earth lowest down, and air and water in between, "the relation of each higher [elemental] body to the one falling below it is that of form to matter" (*Cael.* IV 3 310ᵇ14–15). For when up is associated with form and down with matter (312ª15–16), earth is least formed (and so is closer to matter), water more formed than earth (and so closer to fire and the upward place), air yet more formed, and fire most formed.

Note 897
The cause of this must be spoken about elsewhere: In the lost treatise on plants, also referred to at I 1 716^{a}1, 23 731^{a}29–30.

Note 898
When things are weak and in poor condition small causes shift the balance: "Though the brain is a very important organ in the opinion of A., yet its importance is negative rather than positive. Heat is the sovereign quality of life, and the brain exists mainly to cool the blood, and is itself the coldest part. It is because of this cold that it is described as 'weak and in poor condition'" (Platt, n5).

Note 899
It would seem quite reasonable for it to happen to those with much seed that they go bald around this time of life: Because, having much seed, they are more eager for sexual intercourse.

Note 900
The front part of the head alone goes bald . . . because the brain is there: Repeated at *HA* I 16 494^{b}25–495^{a}1 (this vol.) and at *PA* II 10 656^{b}13, on which Ogle comments: "An error . . . but very possibly deriving support from examination of the brains of cold-blooded animals. For in Fishes and Reptiles the brain is not large enough to fill the cranial cavity." See *HA* I 16 495^{b}22–24n (this vol.).

Note 901
Sterile (*agona*): Or, "nonproductive."

Note 902
White-sickness (*leukê*): Perhaps, albinism, since it can affect the hair as well as the skin, whereas leucodermia or vitiligo, a long-term skin condition in which patches of skin lose their pigmentation, does not. The condition Plato describes at *Ti.* 85a as "decking the body with white, leprous (*alphous*) spots" may be leucodermia, while that described at Herodotus I.138 is leprosy.

Note 903
The proper heat (*oikeia thermotês*) **present in each part:** Proper heat is natural, soul-involving, form-transmitting heat. See *Mete.* IV 2 379^{b}18–35 (Introduction, pp. lxii–lxxii).

Note 904
The treatise *On Growth and Nourishment*: No treatise with this title has survived.

Note 905
All putrefaction comes about due to heat, but not—as was said elsewhere—due to connate heat: "Putrefaction is the passing away of the proper and in-accord-

with-nature heat within a given wet thing due to alien heat, that is, heat from what encompasses it" (*Mete.* IV 1 379ª16–18). On the difference between these two sorts of heat, see *GC* II 2 330ª12–24.

Note 906
Putrefaction, though, occurs in the case of water, earth, and all bodies of this sort, which is why it also occurs in the case of earthy vapor (*atmidos*): "Vapor (*atmis*) is a disaggregation due to burning heat, from liquid into air and wind, capable of wetting things" (*Mete.* IV 9 387ª24–26). The vapor in hair is earthy because, as a smoky exhalation, is a compound of air and earth. See *GA* V 3 782ᵇ18–20n.

Note 907
All earthy vapor has the capacity of coarse-grained air: "We must understand that of what we call 'air' the part surrounding the earth is wet and hot because it is vaporous and contains exhalations from the earth" (*Mete.* I 3 340ᵇ24–26).

Note 908
The poets make a good metaphor when jestingly calling gray hairs mold of old age and hoar-frost. For the one is in genus (*genos*) **and the other in species** (*eidos*) **the same: hoar-frost in genus (for both are a vapor), mold in species (for both are a putrefaction):** "Metaphors should not be far-fetched, but rather should be transferred, in the form of names, from things that are of the same genus and same species" (*Rh.* III 2 1405ª35–36).

Note 909
The back of the head is empty of liquid because it does not have brain in it: See V 3 784ª2n.
Bregma: See II 6 744ª24n.

Note 910
"There . . . mortal": Homer, *Iliad* VIII.83–84 (slightly misquoted).

Note 911
All weak things age more quickly: See IV 6 775ª19–22.

Note 912
Cranes, though, are said to go darker as they get older: "This may refer to the heron, which would easily be confused with the crane. At least . . . [the darker back] is only found in the adult heron" (Platt, n6).

Note 913
The cause of this affection would be that the nature of their feathers is whiter by nature, and as they grow old there is more liquid in their feathers than is more easily putrefied: Reading λευκοτέραν ("whiter") with the mss.; OCT and Louis-3

read λεπτοτέραν ("thinner"); Peck-3 and Platt, ὑγροτέραν ("more liquid"). And reading εὔσηπτον with OCT, Peck-3, and Platt for mss. and Louis-3 εὐσηπτότερον ("more easily putrefied"). The idea is this. The feathers on the heron, that is, on the heron's head (since the topic is going gray—but perhaps whichever ones are said to darken), are naturally whiter (that is, whiter than the others). Thus a darkening of these is more visible, since they are lighter colored to begin with. The cause of their darkening is the greater quantity of non-concocted liquid that results in all animals from the cooling and drying effects of old age, which—simply because it is greater (V 4 785^{a}2)—is more resistant to the putrefaction that results in grayness.

Note 914

In the other animals, however, the skin, because of its coarseness, has the capacity of the region: That is, the capacity to influence the color of hair, which itself depends in part on diet and environment (see IV 2 767^{a}28–32). Because the skin is coarse, it is resistant, unlike fine human skin, to the subsequent effects of sun and wind.

Note 915

The [fish] called *thrattai*: Perhaps, shad, but the identity is uncertain. See *HA* IX 37 621^{b}16.

Note 916

The whole-colored, though, exhibit change (*metaballei de ta holochroa*) **much more than the single-colored:** Literally, "the whole colored change," the meaning, however, is not that parents whose bodies are a single color change color themselves, but rather that their offspring are of a different color than they are, so that the kind they belong to (which also does not change) exhibits more of this sort of change than does the kind whose members are single-colored.

Note 917

The ones that exhibit most change are those which, though by nature whole-colored, are in genus many-colored, due to the waters [they drink]: See IV 2 767^{a}28–32.

Note 918

The hot ones contain more pneuma than they do water, and the air shining through produces whiteness, as it also does in foam: "Pneuma is hot air" (II 2 736^{a}1). On foam, see II 2 735^{b}10–13.

Note 919

The cause is the one mentioned previously: At V 5 785^{b}2–6.

Note 920

It is most of all to [human beings] that nature has assigned this capacity, because they alone among the animals make us of rational speech (*logos*), **and the matter for rational speech is the voice** (*phônês*): "A voiced sound (*phônê*) is a sign of what is pleasant or painful, which is why it is also possessed by the other animals (for their nature goes this far: they not only perceive what is pleasant or painful but also signify them to each other). But a *logos* is for making clear what is beneficial or harmful, and hence also what is just or unjust" (*Pol.* I 2 1253ª10–15).

Note 921

What animals have a voice for the sake of, and what a voice is, and, in general, a sound, has been stated partly in *De Sensu*, partly in *De Anima*: "The perceptual capacities that operate through external media, such as smell, hearing, and sight, are characteristic of animals capable of movement. In all that have them they exist for the sake of preservation, in order that they may perceive their food before they pursue it, and avoid what is bad or destructive, while in those that also happen to have practical wisdom, they exist for the sake of doing well, since they make us aware of many differences, from which arises practical wisdom concerning both intelligible things and things doable in action. Of these, sight is intrinsically superior as regards the necessities of life, while hearing is coincidentally so as regards understanding. For the different qualities that the capacity of sight reports are many and multifarious because all bodies are colored, so that it is to the highest degree by this perceptual capacity that the common perceptibles are perceived (I mean, figure, magnitude, movement, and number), whereas hearing reports only differences in sound, and in a few cases differences in voice too. Coincidentally, however, it is hearing that plays the biggest part as regards practical wisdom. For speech (*logos*) is a cause of learning, not intrinsically, but coincidentally; for it consists of words, and each of the words is a symbol. Because of this, of those who have been deprived from birth of one or other of these perceptual capacities, the blind are more practically-wise than deaf mutes" (*Sens.* 1 436ᵇ18–437ª17); "Sound is the movement of something that can be moved in the way in which things bounce back from a smooth surface when someone strikes it. . . . But what is struck must be even, so that the air may as a single mass bounce back and vibrate" (*DA* II 8 420ª23–26); "Voiced sound (*phônê*) is a sort of sound, one belonging to something animate" (420ᵇ5–6); "the blow struck on the so-called windpipe by the air that is breathed in is voice" (420ᵇ27–29).

Note 922

Low-pitch in a voice lies in the movement being slow, and high-pitch in its being fast: The movement in question is a movement in air. See V 7 787ª29 and previous note.

Note 923

A low-pitched voice seems to be characteristic of a nobler nature: In part, no doubt, because it is characteristic of the acme of nobility, the great-souled man: "The movements characteristic of a great-souled person seem to be slow, his voice deep, and his speech steady. For a person who takes few things seriously is not the sort to hurry, nor is someone who thinks that nothing is all that great inclined to be tense. But shrillness of voice and hastiness come about because of these" (*NE* IV 4 1125ª12–16).

Nobler (*gennaioteras*): Here *gennaios* means "noble" or "high-born" rather than "true to its stock," as at III 1 749ᵇ30–31.

What is low-pitched is better than what is strained (*suntonôn*): As one must strain one's vocal cords (or tighten an instrument's strings) in order to reach high notes. That is why "it is not easy for people exhausted by age to sing harmonies that are strained; rather, nature suggests the relaxed harmonies at their stage of life" (*Pol.* VIII 7 1342ᵇ20–23).

Note 924

If what is moved exceeds the strength of what moves it, it is necessary for what is spatially moved to be spatially moved slowly; if it is exceeded, quickly: "If a capacity equal to A moves what is equal to B as much as D in a time equal to t, and half of D in half of t, then half its strength will move half of B the half of D in a time equal to t. For example, let E equal half the capacity of A and F equal half of B. Then the strength is similarly and proportionally related to the weight in each case, so A will move B and E will move F an equal distance in an equal time" (*Ph.* VII 5 250ª4–9).

Note 925

[1] Sometimes, then, the strong, moving much because of their strength, make the movement slowly, [2] other times, because of its superiority (*to kratein*)**, quickly:** In [1] the voice is both big and low-pitched; in [2] the voice is both big and high-pitched.

Note 926

Sometimes weak movers, moving what is for their capacity much, make the movement slowly, other times, moving little because of their weakness, quickly: In [1] the voice is small and low-pitched; in [2] small and high-pitched.

Note 927

The part by which they move [the air]: Namely, the windpipe. See V 7 786ᵇ25n.

Note 928

Heavy [or low]: The adjective *barus* means both "low" and "heavy."

Note 929

Whereas in the others it is easily regulated: See V 7 788ª28–34.

Note 930

What makes it clear that the heart of male oxen has this sort of nature is the fact that a bone actually occurs in some of them: "There is a genus of ox that has a bone in its heart, but not all have it. The heart of horses also has a bone in it" (*HA* II 15 506ª8–10); "In [horses and a certain genus of oxen], because of the heart's large size, a bone lies underneath for the sake of providing a sort of support, just as bones do for whole bodies" (*PA* III 4 666^{b}19–21). On the latter Ogle, n2, comments: "It is not uncommon to find in large mammalia, especially in Pachyderms and Ruminants, a cruciform ossification in the heart, below the origin of the aorta. In the ox this is a normal formation, as also in the stag. But in Pachyderms, or at any rate in the horse, it is only found in old individuals, and appears to be the result of pathological degeneration."

Note 931
Bones seek (*zētei*) the nature of sinews: *Zētein* means "seek," "inquire," but is no doubt used somewhat metaphorically here. See *PA* I 1 641^{b}12n. The basis for the metaphor is, presumably, that (1) "what is sinewy in nature . . . is just what holds together the parts of an animal" (II 3 737^{b}2–3); "bones are bound together by the sinews" (*PA* II 9 654^{b}19); "bones [provide support] for whole bodies" (III 4 666^{b}20–21). The idea is that the bones could not perform their function without sinews, and so could not in fact be *bones* (II 9 654^{b}4–5) without them. To be a bone, then, is to "seek" the nature of sinew.

Note 932
When castrated all animals change to the female condition, and because of the slackening of the sinewy strength in its starting-point emit a voiced-sound similar to that of the females: The female condition in voice may be high-pitched or, as in the case of oxen, low-pitched. However, the slackening of sinewy strength, as in a slack lyre string, seems to result only in a lower-pitched voice. Thus Aristotle's account, while it fits the case of castrated bulls, which he may have primarily in mind, does not seem to fit the case where, as in human castrati, the voice becomes higher as a result of castration.
[The voice's] starting-point: That is, the heart. See IV 8 776^{b}16–18.

Note 933
What some people call "bleating like a goat" results, when the voice is uneven: It is "breaking," we say.

Note 934
Those who use hotter pneuma, and emit it in the same way as people who are groaning, play at a lower pitch: "The phenomenon noted is probably that pitch is lowered if the player's mouth-cavity is made wider (as in yawning or groaning)" (Barker, p. 83 n61).

Note 935
When there is any wetness about the windpipe, or when it becomes rough due to some affection: Phlegm in the throat; hoarseness.

Note 936
Where the teeth are concerned, it has been stated previously that they are not for one purpose . . . : At *HA* II 1 501^{a}8–^{b}5, *PA* II 9 655^{b}8–11, III 1 661^{a}34–^{b}27.

Note 937

[Democritus] says that the shedding is due to the fact that the teeth are produced prematurely . . . while of their being produced prematurely suckling is the cause assigned: = DK A147 = TEGP 100.

Note 938

The pig also suckles but does not shed its teeth: The pig does in fact shed its teeth.

Note 939

Animals with saw-like teeth all suckle: "Some animals have teeth . . . for the purposes of nourishment alone. But those that have them also for protection and for strength, in some cases have tusks, as the pig does, and in other cases have sharp, interlocking teeth, from which they are called saw-toothed" (*PA* III 1 661^{b}16–19). See also *HA* II 1 501^{a}18–19.

But some of them do not shed any teeth except the canines—for example, lions: In fact, lions shed their milk teeth but not their canines.

Further Reading

Detailed and regularly updated bibliographies of works on Aristotle's natural philosophy (compiled by István Bodnár) and on his philosophy generally (compiled by Christopher Shields) are available online at:
https://plato.stanford.edu/entries/aristotle-natphil/
http://plato.stanford.edu/entries/aristotle/

Thesaurus Linguae Graeca (http://www.tlg.uci.edu) has excellent searchable Greek texts and English translations of Aristotle's writings, with linked dictionaries and grammars.

Editions of *Generation of Animals*, *History of Animals*, and *Parts of Animals*, and translations and commentaries on them are listed under Abbreviations at the beginning of the present volume.

Relevant Works of Mine

Substantial Knowledge: Aristotle's Metaphysics (Indianapolis, 2000).

Action, Contemplation, and Happiness: An Essay on Aristotle (Cambridge, Mass., 2012).

"Aristotle's Method of Philosophy." C. Shields (ed.), *The Oxford Handbook of Aristotle* (Oxford, 2012): 150–170.

Aristotle: Metaphysics (Indianapolis, 2016).

Aristotle: De Anima (Indianapolis, 2017).

Aristotle: Physics (Indianapolis, 2018).

Aristotle: De Caelo (Indianapolis, 2020).

Aristotle: On Coming to Be and Passing Away & Meteorology IV (Indianapolis, 2020).

Index

Note: References to *HA* and *PA* are in italics and begin in *HA* with *4* and in *PA* with *6*. References to *GA* are non-italic with the initial 7 omitted—for example, 715ᵃ = 15ᵃ. Line numbers are to the Greek text but are closely approximate in the translation. References are typically to key doctrines or discussions in the text and, when in bold, also in the associated notes.

Abdomen (*gastêr*), *493ᵃ17, 16ᵇ27, 17ᵇ17,*
  19ᵇ25, 75ᵇ29, 86ᵃ14
  lower- (*hêtron*), *493ᵃ19*
  upper- (*hupochondrion*), *493ᵃ20, 496ᵇ12*
Account (*logos*), **15ᵃ5**
  of substance, 15ᵃ5, 31ᵇ19
universal, *645ᵇ26*
Action (*praxis*), ***645ᵃ15***
  multipartite, *645ᵃ16*
Activity, active, activated, actively
  (*energeia*), 17ᵃ26, **26ᵇ17**
  distinct, 40ᵃ4
  movement, 30ᵇ21; in semen, 68ᵃ12
  possession of the capacity to move, 43ᵃ23
  vs. potentially existing universal seed-
    bed, 69ᵇ1
  vs. potential possession of fetal parts,
    37ᵃ24, 41ᵇ7
  vs. potential possession of nutritive soul,
    36ᵇ10, 37ᵃ18, 39ᵇ35; of perceptual soul,
    41ᵃ11
Actuality, actually (*entelecheia*), *642ᵃ1,* **26ᵇ17**
  what is potentially comes to be due to
    what is, 34ᵃ30
Affection (*pathos*), ***639ᵃ22***, 21ᵇ16
  s. capacity, *639ᵃ22,* 22ᵇ31
Air (*aer*)
  blend of the surrounding, and the
    condition of the body, 67ᵃ30; and
    longevity, 77ᵇ7

coarse-grained, 84ᵇ15
  vaporized, as a cause of whiteness in
    things, 86ᵃ13
Alcmaeon of Croton, *492ᵃ14,* 52ᵇ25
Analogous, analogue (*analogos*), *487ᵃ5*
  nature, 18ᵇ13
  of blood, *489ᵃ22, 645ᵃ9,* 26ᵇ2, 28ᵇ1,
    40ᵃ22, 65ᵇ34, 66ᵃ34
  of blood-vessel, *489ᵃ22*
  of bone, 45ᵃ8
  of element belonging to the stars, 36ᵇ37
  of feet, *489ᵃ29*
  of flesh, 43ᵃ10
  of hair, 82ᵃ17, 31
  of lungs, *645ᵃ7*
  of menses, 29ᵃ23
  of semen, 27ᵃ3
  of sinew, 37ᵇ4
  of sleep in plants, 79ᵃ3
  of teeth, 45ᵇ10
  of the heart, 35ᵃ24, 38ᵇ16, 41ᵇ15, 42ᵇ37,
    66ᵇ3, 81ᵃ23
  of the uterus, 489ᵃ14, 54ᵃ1
  of wings, *489ᵃ29*
  part, 21ᵃ21
  similarity vs. the more and the less,
    644ᵇ11
  See also proportion
Analogy, by (*kat' analogian*), **15ᵇ20**
  vs. the more and the less, *644ᵃ18, ᵇ11*